REGENERATION: BLACK CINEMA 1898–1971

Fayard (left) and Harold Nicholas in
Stormy Weather (1943), production still

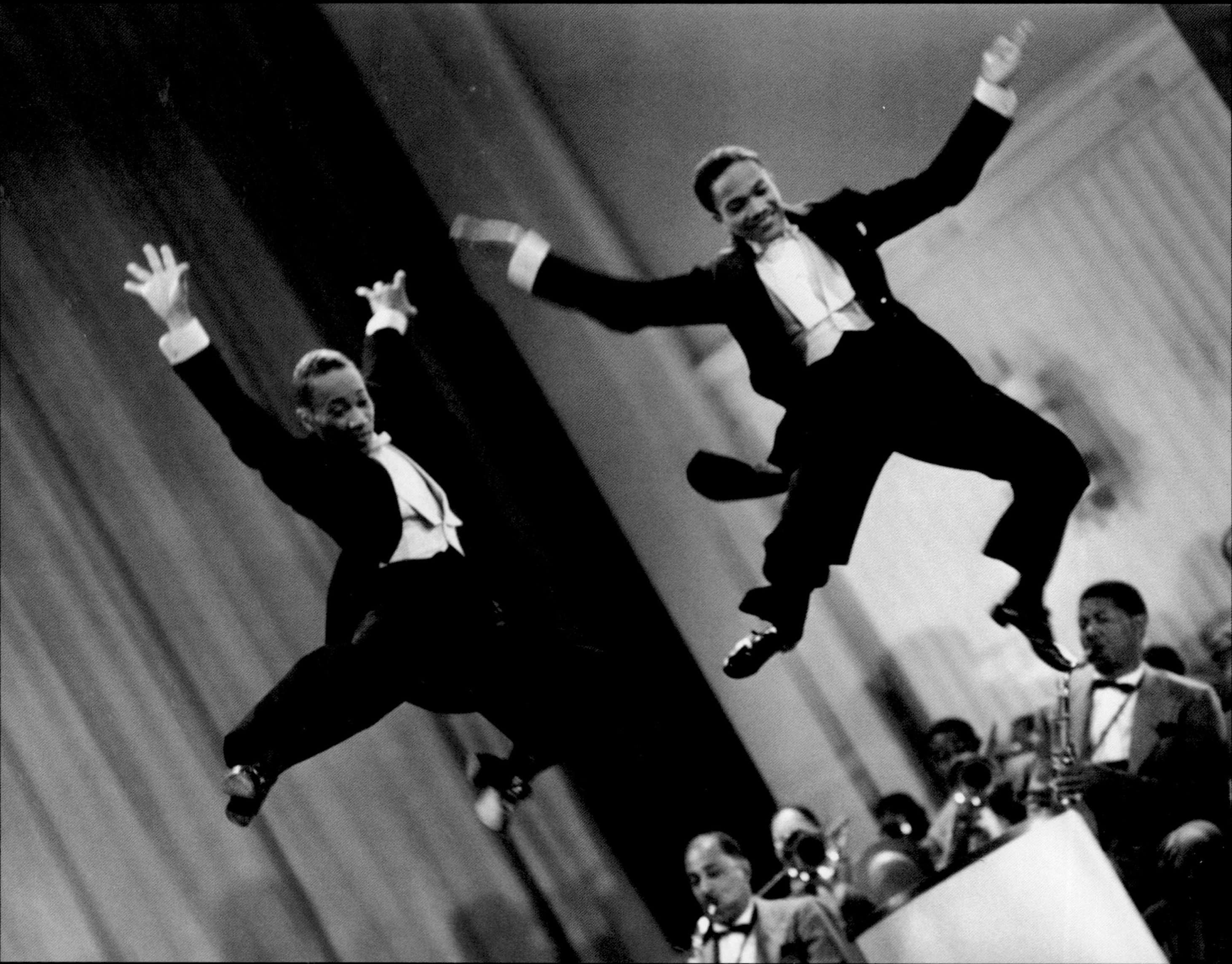

REGENERATION BLACK CINEMA 1898–1971

EDITED BY
Doris Berger
Rhea L. Combs

CONTRIBUTIONS BY
Donald Bogle
Cara Caddoo
Terri Simone Francis
Michael Boyce Gillespie
J. Raúl Guzmán
Shola Lynch
Ron Magliozzi
Ellen C. Scott
Jacqueline Stewart

FOREWORD BY
Whoopi Goldberg

Academy Museum
of Motion Pictures
Los Angeles

DelMonico Books • D.A.P.
New York

Director's Foreword

Regeneration: Black Cinema 1898–1971 represents a milestone for the Academy Museum of Motion Pictures. Thoughtful, engaging, and poetic, the exhibition is the culmination of a multiyear research-driven exploration of Black participation in cinema, in front of and behind the camera. In the early years of our cinematic history, intrepid Black film artists began using the moving image to create new forms of representation. They realized the transformative power of these images. It is fitting that the exhibition begins with the newly rediscovered film versions of *Something Good—Negro Kiss* (1898), one of the earliest films showing Black affection on-screen. These captivating frames are transforming our understanding of early Black performance, the complexity of which—including its integral role in popular culture around the turn of the twentieth century—has been underrecognized.

The creation of the Academy Museum has provided a needed platform for the Academy of Motion Picture Arts and Sciences to expand how it explores the full spectrum of moviemaking. Through our exhibition spaces, theaters, programs, and publications, we critically engage in the many ways that cinema has shaped and continues to influence our society—and to elevate and examine artists and works that have been unrecognized or undervalued. *Regeneration* represents such an approach.

The exhibition originated when the Academy Museum's curatorial team began looking into the collection of the late Edward C. Mapp, a beloved benefactor of the Academy's Margaret Herrick Library and a vital collector and scholar of Black cinema. The curatorial team then researched archives nationally and internationally, creating a powerful exhibition that explores the ways in which Black artists and entrepreneurs engaged with film as writers, producers, directors, distributors, critics, actors, musicians, and photographers. As the exhibition shows, the contributions of these artists and entrepreneurs deeply impacted the cinematic landscape, offering a broader variety of representations of Black identity at several junctures in American history.

I extend my profound gratitude to cocurators Doris Berger and Rhea L. Combs for their compelling and thoughtful curatorial vision and to assistant curator J. Raúl Guzmán and research assistants Emily Rauber Rodriguez and Manouchka Kelly Labouba for their vital contributions to the project. All curatorial, educational, publications, and programming efforts at the Academy Museum are overseen by Jacqueline Stewart, the museum's chief artistic and programming officer. I am deeply grateful to Jacqueline for her leadership and scholarship.

Other key exhibition partners at the Academy include Randy Haberkamp, senior vice president, preservation and foundation programs; Matt Severson, director of the Margaret Herrick Library; and Linda Harris Mehr, the library's former director. They and their teams have made invaluable contributions from the project's outset. It has been through their thoughtful efforts that the Academy has developed a significant collection of materials related to Black cinema.

In addition, Michael Pogorzelski, director of the Academy Film Archive, oversaw the restoration of *Harlem on the Prairie* (1937), starring the singing cowboy Herb Jeffries and highlighting the alluring voice that captured the hearts of a generation of fans, and *Reform School* (1939), featuring a magnetic and unforgettable performance by Louise Beavers. These works were donated to the Academy by Giancarlo Esposito and had been considered lost by many film scholars. I thank Michael and his expert archival team, Giancarlo, and the National Endowment for the Arts and Capital Group Companies Charitable Foundation for their support in restoring these films.

I extend my deepest appreciation to the catalogue's wonderful contributors—including Donald Bogle, Charles Burnett, Cara Caddoo, Julie Dash, Ava DuVernay, Terri Simone Francis, Michael Boyce Gillespie, Whoopi Goldberg, Barry Jenkins, Shola Lynch, Ron Magliozzi, Dawn Porter, Ellen C. Scott, and Jacqueline Stewart—for their inspiring thoughts on key aspects of Black cinema.

Many thanks to Lonnie G. Bunch III, secretary of the Smithsonian Institution, and Kim Sajet, director of the National Portrait Gallery, Washington, DC, who have been wonderful institutional partners, and to all of the lenders who made this exhibition possible. I am very pleased that the exhibition will be seen at the Detroit Institute of Arts, thanks to museum director Salvador Salort-Pons.

The development of an exhibition of this size and scale is made possible only through the assistance of many supporters, including Sotheby's, which awarded the exhibition the 2018 Sotheby's Prize for curatorial excellence; the National Endowment for the Humanities; the Los Angeles County Board of Supervisors through the Los Angeles County Department of Arts and Culture; Christie Technology; Campari; Lyndon J. Barrois Sr. and Janine Sherman Barrois; Max and Kahlia Konen; Emma Koss; Mary Parent and Javier Chapa; and Yeardley Smith.

As always, we owe so much to the members of the Academy Museum Board of Trustees, chaired by Ted Sarandos. Their governance, guidance, and support have made all that we do possible.

Regeneration has set the bar for how we present critical moments in film history. I hope this exhibition continues to spark dialogue and leads to additional discoveries and a deeper appreciation of the legacy of Black film artists and their importance to the cinematic canon.

Bill Kramer
Director and President
Academy Museum of
Motion Pictures

Acknowledgments

A project of this magnitude requires the support of many. We first want to acknowledge the groundbreaking work of those whose early scholarship on this topic helped make this project possible. The late Edward C. Mapp and his collection of nearly twelve hundred posters and other documents highlighting African American participation in film from the 1920s through the early 2000s, now held at the Academy's Margaret Herrick Library, ignited the flame for this project. The work of visionary collectors such as Pearl Bowser, John Kisch, and Phyllis Klotman, to name a few, has also been essential to its development.

Regeneration: Black Cinema 1898–1971 was many years in the making and would not have been possible without the early support of major funders, in particular the National Endowment for the Humanities for research and implementation grants under the guidance of acting deputy director Patricia Brooks. The exhibition was the recipient of the 2018 Sotheby's Prize, which offered crucial support at a key stage of its development. Our gratitude also goes to the National Endowment for the Arts and the Capital Group Companies Charitable Foundation for underwriting the restoration of *Harlem on the Prairie* (1937), *Reform School* (1939), and *Mr. Washington Goes to Town* (1940), as well as the trailers for *Boarding House Blues* (1948), *Harlem Follies of 1949* (1950), and *Carib Gold* (1956). We owe particular thanks to Joanne Lammers of the Capital Group. The National Film Preservation Foundation supported the restoration of *Black Chariot* (1971), which was undertaken by the Smithsonian National Museum of African American History and Culture. We must acknowledge Christie Technology as well for its invaluable technical support for the exhibition.

The bold leadership of Bill Kramer, the Academy Museum's director and president, has been critical to ensuring that this project made it to the finish line. As well, many thanks to the museum's senior leadership team, Brendan Connell, Jr., chief operating officer and general counsel and Jacqueline Stewart, chief artistic and programming officer, for their invaluable support. We would also like to acknowledge the early backing for this project from the Academy Museum's founding director, Kerry Brougher, and its former deputy director, Deborah Horowitz. In addition, we are indebted to Lonnie G. Bunch III, secretary of the Smithsonian Institution and founding director of the National Museum of African American History and Culture, and to Kim Sajet, director of the National Portrait Gallery.

From the inception of this project, assistant curator J. Raúl Guzmán has been a thoughtful partner in developing *Regeneration*. The diligence of research assistants Emily Rauber Rodriguez and Manouchka Kelly Labouba cannot be overestimated. We are enormously thankful to this core *Regeneration* team, whose commitment to the work has kept the passion for this project going for years.

We would like to express our deep gratitude to the *Regeneration* advisory committee: Charles Burnett, Ava DuVernay, Michael Boyce Gillespie, Shola Lynch, Ron Magliozzi, Ellen C. Scott, and Jacqueline Stewart. The dedication of this stalwart group has been critical to the project.

This catalogue was greatly enriched by the work of our contributors—Donald Bogle, Cara Caddoo, Terri Simone Francis, Michael Boyce Gillespie, Shola Lynch, Ron Magliozzi, Ellen C. Scott, and Jacqueline Stewart—and the powerful personal insights of Whoopi Goldberg. The filmmakers Charles Burnett, Julie Dash, Ava DuVernay, Barry Jenkins, and Dawn Porter also shared important perspectives with us in their interviews in this volume. Each of them has been working to expand the notion of Black cinema for many years, and we feel very fortunate to have been able to include their voices.

Stacey Allan, who heads the museum's publications department, has adeptly overseen the development of this catalogue. We thank our copublisher, DelMonico Books, especially Mary DelMonico and Karen Farquhar, for their additional guidance. The texts benefited from Karen Jacobson's refined editing skills and Dianne Woo's meticulous proofreading. We are grateful to Jane Friedman for compiling the index. And we offer our heartfelt thanks to the team at Pentagram—Eddie Opara with Brankica Harvey, Jack Collins, and Dana Reginiano—for developing a book design that reflects the historical content in contemporary ways.

From the beginning, *Regeneration* has benefited from the excellent grant-writing skills of Dawn Mori, whose commitment to this project has been critical. Her colleagues Ryan Koprek, Dan Faltz, and Sabira Parajuli supported these efforts. Current and former members of the advancement team—led by Matt Youngner and his predecessor, Katharine DeShaw, and including Omar Sharif Jr. and Christine Joyce Rodriguez—helped to secure important funds.

We thank Sonja Wong Leaon and her collections and conservation teams, in particular registrar Ross Auerbach, who never got tired of securing yet another loan for us, and Sophie Hunter, who carefully oversaw the conservation of objects and costumes, supported by Rio Lopez. Thanks are also due to Nathalie Morris, who helped us acquire critical objects for the Academy Museum collection.

Susan Jenkins has guided the various stakeholders with her project management support, and her exhibition planning team—Cindy Ha, Kate Weinberg, and Stephanie Willsey—helped us stay on track. The audiovisual production was overseen by Bert Thomas and his team, Corey Saldana and Levan Tkabladze. Special gratitude goes to Kim Hendrickson at the Criterion Collection, Livia Bloom at Icarus Channel, Loren Roberts, and Jeselle Hicks for their timely assistance with licensing—and to Gina Broze, who has been instrumental in licensing images.

It has been our pleasure to collaborate closely on exhibition design and production with Shraddha Aryal, along with her production team—Lance Bad Heart Bull, Jessie Closson, Phyllis Cottrell, Joe Gott, Ryan Lentini, Omar Madkour, Stephen Morrissey, Andrew Mueller, and Christopher Richmond—and designer Sherry Huang. The exhibition graphics were shaped by Peter Raphael Castro and Vanessa McKenzie, who worked with the exhibition design team to create the look of the show.

We also thank Gary Dauphin and Mike Schiro, who have worked to create the digital components for our exhibition, and Erwin Hines and Impossible Bureau, who created the *Regeneration* website. Our thanks to Martha Polk and Lindsey Westbrook for deftly editing the exhibition labels.

We are appreciative of the efforts of the marketing and communications team, led by Shawn Anderson, with particular thanks to Stephanie Sykes, Daniel Gomez, and Emma Jacobson-Sive. Thank you to the visitor experience staff, led by Jack Cummings and Atshumi Richards, and to their predecessor, Lauren Girard, as well as to Mariko Yoshimura-Rank and Marty Preciado for their community outreach. Thank you also to Mariah Gelhard and her retail team for initiating new collaborations and to the facilities and security teams, led by Akadeth Obphrachanh and Gerry Perez, respectively.

This project also lives beyond its gallery walls in public programs and with students and teachers. Our gratitude to Amy Homma and her team—Tuni Chatterji, Eduardo Sánchez, and Stephanie Samera—for their programming efforts, including curriculum, summit, and tours. Some of the films in the exhibition will be regenerated and finally shown again, thanks to the efforts of the film programming group, led by Bernardo Rondeau and his team, and guest programmer Maya Cade of the Black Film Archive.

We want to acknowledge current and past colleagues at the Smithsonian National Museum of African American History and Culture's Earl W. and Amanda Stafford Center for African American Media Arts, particularly Ina Archer, Walter Forsberg, Jon Goff, Blake McDowell, Loren Miller, and CK Ming, along with the museum's chief registrar, Drew Talley, and its director, Kevin Young.

So many colleagues at the Academy's Film Archive and Margaret Herrick Library were partners in the development of this project. Our deep gratitude to Randy Haberkamp, who oversees both. A special thank-you goes to Linda Harris Mehr, the library's former director, who brought the Mapp collection to the library. We are indebted to Matt Severson and his team of leaders—Russell Butner, Anne Coco, Howard Prouty, Warren Sherk, Lea Whittington, and Elizabeth Youle—and to Dawn Jaros for critical conservation work.

We are grateful to colleagues at the Academy Film Archive—Michael Pogorzelski, Joe Lindner, Cassie Blake, and Taylor Morales—for restoring films we discovered in the course of our research and making them accessible to a wider public in the future. Thank you also to Lynne Kirste for collecting home movies, to Teague Schneiter for heading the Visual History Archive, and to the leaders of the Film Archive's Cultural Equity and Inclusion Project—Jess DePrest, Kate Dollenmayer, and Angie Villafañe—for sharing their research. These were all exceptionally valuable resources. We are also grateful to May Hong HaDuong, formerly of the Film Archive and an early supporter of our project, who helped with film research.

Additional thanks go to collector Pauline Brooks, who has entrusted us with a part of her collection; to Mark Cantor, who advised us on Soundies; to Miriam Posner, who gave us insights into the UCLA Digital Humanities project about race films; to David Norman and Barbara Wingo, who offered us additional access to Norman Film Company materials; to Susan Robeson for enlightening conversations about Paul Robeson; to Lebert Sandy Bethune for insights on Malcolm X; to Allyson Nadia Field for sharing recent discoveries on early cinema; and to Angélique de Saint-Exupéry for a deeper understanding of Josephine Baker's legacy in the region of Périgord. We also thank collector Hubert Cavaniol and Martine Vignot and her team at La Cinémathèque Française in Paris; Uta Klawitter at the German Federal Archive as well as Peter Mänz and his staff at the Deutsche Kinemathek in Berlin; Terri Simone Francis, formerly at Indiana University's Black Film Center & Archive, and the entire team at the archive; Ron Magliozzi and his colleagues at the Museum of Modern Art; and Joy L. Bivins and the staff at New York Public Library's Schomburg Center for Research in Black Culture for allowing us access to their collections.

The generosity of the institutions and individuals who lent objects to the exhibition has been essential to this show; their names are listed on page 286. In addition, we owe special thanks to the pioneering filmmakers who inspired this project along with the artists whose work allowed us to highlight critical dialogues between past and present. Glenn Ligon permitted us to make an exhibition copy of *Double America 2* (2014), and Regen Projects in Los Angeles worked with the artist and us to make this possible. We are profoundly grateful to Theaster Gates, Gary Simmons and Hauser & Wirth, Kara Walker and Sikkema Jenkins & Co., and Carrie Mae Weems and Jack Shainman Gallery. A sincere thank-you also to Isaac Julien for his openness to working with us.

Last but not least, we must extend heartfelt gratitude to our families, particularly Kojo Boateng, Selah Brown, and Steven Steinman. Throughout this process they have been sounding boards, continually offering support, patience, and understanding—all of which have been invaluable in making this project feel possible.

Doris Berger and Rhea L. Combs
Cocurators

Foreword

Whoopi Goldberg

I have loved movies all my life. They have called to me ever since I was a kid, when I'd watch the *Million Dollar Movie* every night on Channel 9 in New York City. Back then we also had *The Early Show*, *The Late Show*, and *The Late Late Show* broadcasting movies around the clock, with stars like Bette Davis and Claudette Colbert and scores of others. I saw Black actors in many of these films too—talents like Butterfly McQueen, Rex Ingram, Juanita Moore—and wrongly assumed we had a place at the table. But understand that back then, without these early and late shows, I wouldn't have had access to the fact that Black folks *existed* in Hollywood outside of the Tarzan movies. Tarzan apparently spoke every dialect in the African jungle; even as a little kid, I found it hard to believe that he only had to do *that* yell and all the Black folks would lose their minds and "behave." (Perhaps what Tarzan said in that cry was, "All right, N***rs, get your act together! And you there, elephants, tigers, and lions, you get in line too!")

Today, when I watch these films that were shot in the early half of the twentieth century, I immediately see how many places I am not: I'm not in beach blanket movies, not in WWI or WWII stories, not in romantic comedies, musicals, or science-fiction films, not in any kind of superhero movie—it's almost like not being anywhere. This may not seem relevant to some of you, but it is very much so to others. However, once you begin to see the spaces where you are not, you begin to wonder: Where *are* all the people of color? And where are the Black folks in particular? Where are the singing cowboys, the bull riders, the stories of the Black GIs and officers, the love stories?

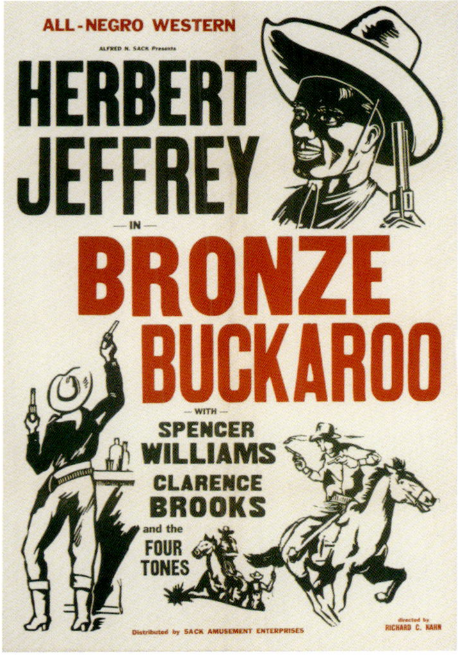

The Bronze Buckaroo (1938), theatrical release poster

Where are the screenwriters, producers, and costume designers? How can it be that we are just not there?

Sure, there were some actors of color on-screen. We might make a brief appearance in the lives and stories of others, as someone's maid or in someone's kitchen or somebody's jungle—in other words, the places where people thought we belonged. Our own stories were never shown in Hollywood movies, despite them happening out in the world, every day, in real time. For more than a hundred years, people thought we were only maids and butlers who had no real place in this industry except as, well, "color."

In reality, however, we helped *build* this industry. Take a look and you will find a whole lot of the Black Hollywood that Johnny Weissmuller's Tarzan eclipsed. Take Oscar Micheaux, for one. He was producing, writing, and directing independent films in the early 1910s. With his movies, he placed Black people at the center of the narrative, as human beings and as Americans. When you look back at his films, there we are, with the same hopes, dreams, mistakes, and dastardly behavior as any other characters you'd find in the mainstream movies of the time. This was merely a glimmer of everything to come.

I also think, of course, of Hattie McDaniel. In 1940 she was nominated for an Academy Award for Best Supporting Actress, for her role in *Gone with the Wind* (1939). She was the first Black nominee, seated at a segregated table at the awards ceremony instead of with her costars, and she actually won! After that, it took almost twenty-five years for the next Black performer to win in the acting categories—that was Mr. Sidney Poitier, Best Actor for *Lilies of the Field* (1963)—and more than fifty years before the next Black woman would win. That was my Best Supporting Actress Oscar for *Ghost* (1990). I guess what I'm saying is maybe Hattie McDaniel—and her award-winning performance—was perceived as a bit of a threat; maybe folks felt challenged by this woman and other people who were determined to keep fighting for their place in the sun.

So many have been part of that fight. McDaniel paved the way for later nominees, including Ethel Waters and Dorothy Dandridge; the latter became the first Black woman nominated for a leading role with *Carmen Jones* (1954). There was Herb Jeffries, the Black singing cowboy, who was so fair-skinned he could have passed for white but chose not to, as the story goes. Others include Paul Robeson, Harry Belafonte, Cicely Tyson, Louis Gossett Jr., Diana Ross, Denzel Washington, and those whose names are less well known: Louise Beavers, Spencer Williams Jr., Nina Mae McKinney, Canada Lee, Juano Hernandez, Fredi Washington, Ethel Moses, Roscoe Lee Browne, Pearl Bailey. The list goes on and on, and their incredible stories are worth exploring.

This landmark exhibition, and the wonderful accompanying catalogue you hold in your hands, examines seven decades of Black participation in filmmaking. Black folks have been loving the movies for so long, just like I did as a kid. We have been adding so much to this industry all along the way. It is an honor to introduce this book, which is devoted to the many individuals who made movies about Black people and for Black people, and for anyone interested in what is known as "the Black experience." Don't get me wrong; there are other groups missing from this landscape as well. I can't speak for them, but somebody will. Black folks are far from the only ones left wondering, "Where am *I*? Where are *our* stories?" These questions are finally beginning to shine a light on the amazing artists, directors, actors, writers, and musicians who have been there all along, in the spaces and shadows where history often doesn't look. There are so many who have persevered and found ways to tell their stories—our stories—despite tremendous obstacles. So, please read on; we have so much to share with you.

Introduction

Doris Berger

and Rhea L. Combs

Regeneration: Black Cinema 1898–1971 is the first large-scale exhibition of its kind to examine the compellingly rich history of Black participation in American cinema, both within and outside the Hollywood studio system. In its exploration of a history that is still largely unknown to a wider public, *Regeneration* builds on the efforts of filmmakers, archivists, and scholars to present a more expansive view of the development of American cinema and how it has been shaped by African American creative expression. This project recognizes the efforts of many who have dedicated their professional lives to researching and bringing attention to the perspectives and contributions of African American artists and practitioners. Although not comprehensive, the bibliography at the back of this volume provides an overview of the long-standing, robust work in this area.

Regeneration focuses primarily on material culture that showcases Black representation in cinema over the course of more than seven decades. Representation matters, to be sure, but this project also explores the various meanings of representation. Central to the exhibition is the question of how African American points of view impacted cinematic storytelling, reaching far beyond narrative tropes and stereotypes of Black people as perpetuated by a largely white entertainment industry. Moreover, it recognizes the fortitude and resilience of pioneering artists who chose to break ground on treacherous terrain. By incorporating a selection of works by contemporary Black visual artists, *Regeneration* also aims to show the interdisciplinary and transhistorical parallels between art and film history. In this regard it follows recent exhibitions such

15

Cake Walk (1897), film still

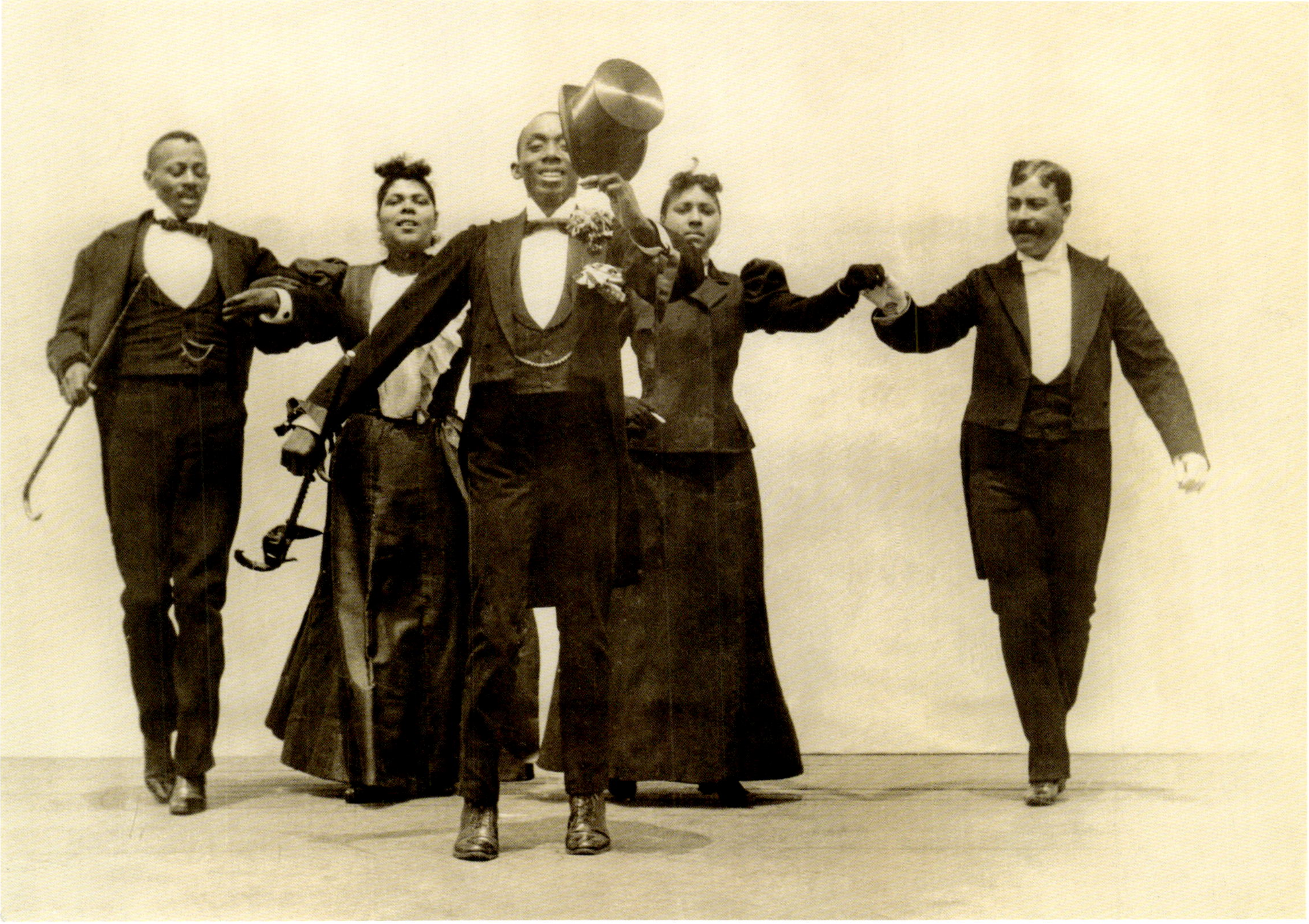

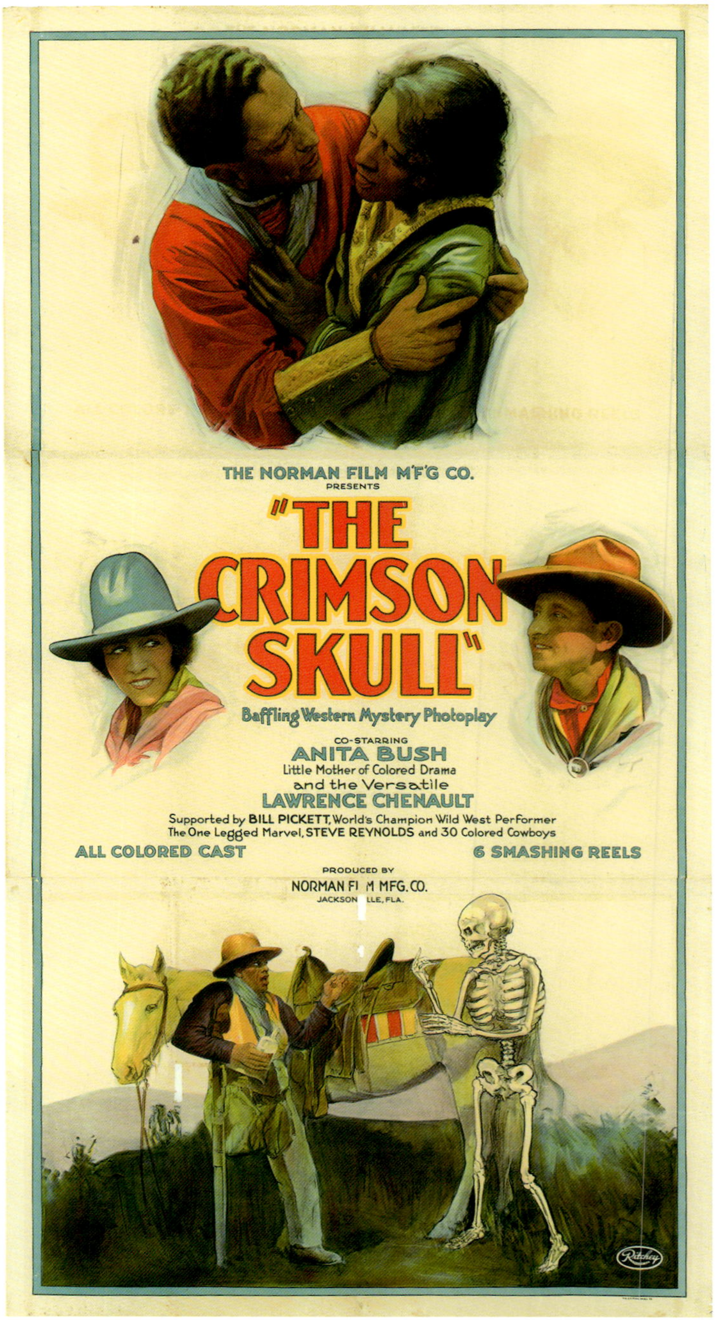

The Crimson Skull (1922), theatrical release poster

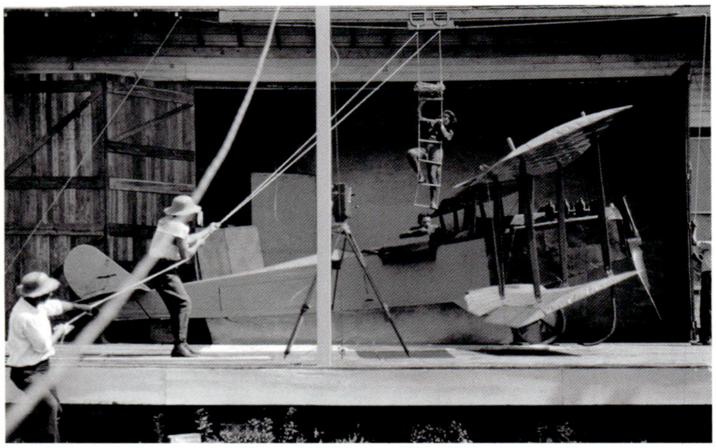

Kathryn Boyd (on ladder) in *The Flying Ace* (1926), production still

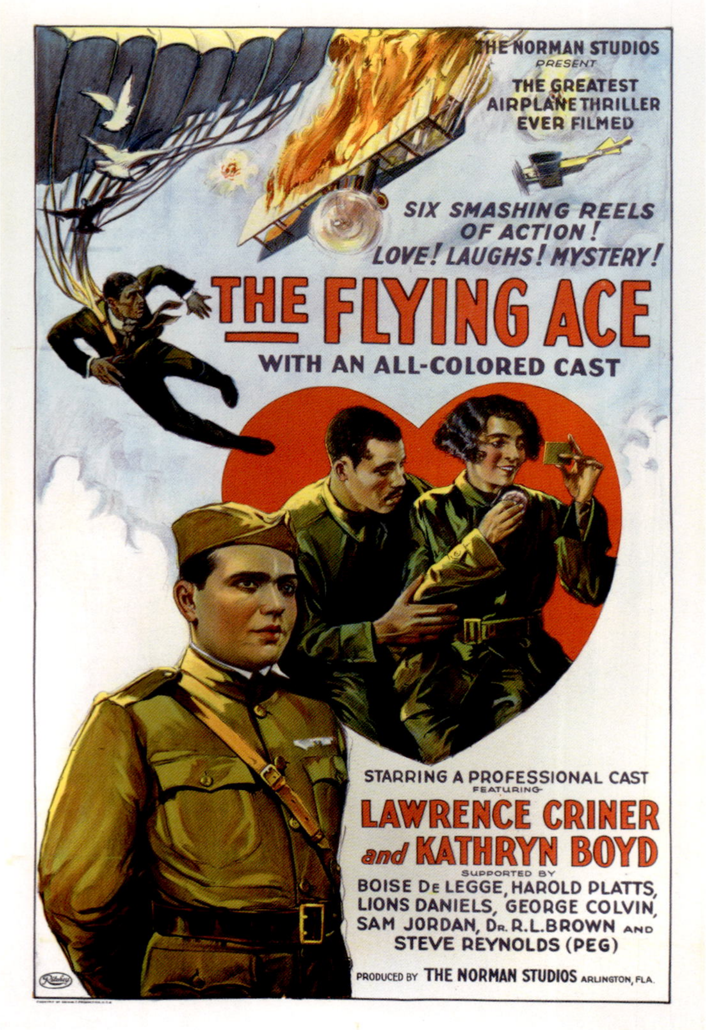

The Flying Ace (1926), theatrical release poster

as *Soul of a Nation: Art in the Age of Black Power* (2017–20), *We Wanted a Revolution: Black Radical Women, 1965–85* (2017–18), *Le modèle noir: De Géricault à Matisse* (2019), and *The Dirty South: Contemporary Art, Material Culture, and the Sonic Impulse* (2021–22), to name a few, that have responded to an increased interest in cross-disciplinary discussions within art history.[1]

Regeneration is generative in its desire to dismantle disciplinary barriers. In other words, we hope that presenting historical films and related materials in conjunction with contemporary art can create a visual dialogue and reveal social, cultural, and historical urgencies that have persisted over decades. As James Baldwin wrote, "The isolation that menaces all American artists is multiplied a thousand times, and becomes absolutely crucial and dangerous, for all black artists."[2] In showcasing work by contemporary Black artists alongside this largely unknown film history, we shed a brighter light on some of the issues that have faced African American visual artists and filmmakers for generations.

This project had its genesis nearly five years ago, when Doris Berger was conducting research in the Academy's Margaret Herrick Library in Beverly Hills and came across posters and lobby cards for Black-cast movies such as *The Crimson Skull* (1922), *The Flying Ace* (1926), and *Gang Smashers* (1938) that are part of the library's vast Edward Mapp Collection.[3] Having studied art and film history in Europe with a focus on gender and cultural studies, she was unfamiliar with the history of race films—that is, films produced for African American audiences between the 1910s and the 1940s. Convinced that an exhibition on the topic would be of interest to visitors to the Academy Museum, Berger sought a partner with expertise in this field, ideally one who could also bring an African American perspective to the project. Rhea L. Combs has been studying the history of Black cinema for more than twenty-five years. Questions of race and representation have informed her academic and professional career.

We teamed up and developed this project as cocurators. Over the course of our research, we recognized that there is a dearth of information about many of these films, which are unknown not only to the general public but also to some scholars of film history. Researchers face challenges in their efforts to uncover these "hidden histories" because many race films and related materials, primarily from Black-owned production studios, are filed away in archives and libraries or, worse yet, are uncataloged or presumed lost.

An important aspect of race films is that many of them are not known to have survived. In that sense, the title of our exhibition and publication is multifaceted and aspirational, as it was inspired by the race film *Regeneration* (*A Romance of the South Seas*) (1923), which survives only in fragments and through lobby cards and production stills.[4] As part of our project, we also looked to find and restore lost and forgotten films and "regenerate" them for contemporary audiences. While conducting research for the exhibition, we identified three race films in the Toddy Pictures Company Collection at the Academy Film Archive that were previously believed to be lost.[5] Through grants from the National Endowment for the Arts and the Capital Group Companies Charitable Foundation, *Harlem on the Prairie* (1937), with "the Sepia Singing Cowboy," Herb Jeffries; the social drama *Reform School* (1939), with Louise Beavers in a powerful leading role; and the comedy *Mr. Washington Goes to Town* (1940), starring the famed Mantan Moreland, were all restored. And critical funding from the National Film Preservation Foundation aided the National Museum of African American History and Culture in the restoration of *Black Chariot* (1971), a precursor to the highly lucrative blaxploitation-era films that was also considered lost and that will premiere in its restored state in this exhibition. As part of the public programming associated with this project, many of the films mentioned in this catalogue will be screened at the Academy Museum and made widely available: regeneration in action.[6] We hope the exhibition prompts even more discoveries and restorations in the future.

It is of the utmost importance that a black child see on that screen *someone who looks like him*. Our children have been suffering from the lack of identifiable images for as long as our children have been born.

—James Baldwin (1968)[7]

Regeneration opens with two recently discovered film versions of *Something Good—Negro Kiss* (1898), which are presented alongside a contemporary artwork, the neon sculpture *Double America 2* (2014) by Glenn Ligon. The film is the first moving image known to date that shows affection between African American performers on-screen. The actors Saint Suttle and Gertie Brown are well dressed and not wearing minstrel makeup, which was de rigueur for Black performers at the time. The powerful pairing of their large-scale projected image with Ligon's work, in which the word "America" and its upside-down version alternately blink in black and white, conjures the scholar and activist W. E. B. Du Bois's notion of "double consciousness," referring to Black Americans' constant awareness of how their self-images coexist with the ways in which they are viewed by others. At the same time, however, it alludes to the moments of agency and determination that counter that stark reality. This constellation sets up the ideas that animate the entire exhibition: a dialogue between Black representation, Black thought, various social and historical parameters in the United States, and new film discoveries.

While the exhibition is structured chronologically, it also examines topics thematically. The work in the first gallery is grounded by the influence of four important Black intellectuals who recognized the power of indexical representation: Frederick Douglass, Sojourner Truth, W. E. B. Du Bois, and Booker T. Washington. Douglass and Truth lived before the era of cinema, but each of these individuals saw photography (and moving pictures as well, in the case of Du Bois and Washington) as a strategic and necessary tool for asserting the humanity of Black people. As Douglass explained, "This picture-making and picture-appreciating power . . . is a power of great dignity and is closely allied to, if not identical with, the poetic and religious element of man's nature."[8] Curatorially, it was important that we establish the sociohistorical context in which Black performers and artists operated in order to offer a nuanced presentation of their work and professional choices.

Beginning with early cinema, roughly from 1898 to 1915, the exhibition contextualizes the pernicious depictions of African Americans that were pervasive during that era and seeped into nearly every form of popular culture. Many early moving images were shaped by the traditions of minstrelsy and vaudeville, forms of popular entertainment that perpetuated racial stereotypes through blackface performances. Stereotypical figures such as the mammy, the faithful servant, and the shiftless character were further popularized by stage and screen adaptations of Harriet Beecher Stowe's paternalistic novel, *Uncle Tom's Cabin* (1852), which Kara Walker's silhouette installation *The End of Uncle Tom and the Grand Allegorical Tableau of Eva in Heaven* (1995) brilliantly interrogates. And while D. W. Griffith's *Birth of a Nation* (1915), with its derogatory performances by white actors in blackface and its reimagined account of the Civil War shaped by white supremacist values, was being lauded by a US president, the Black vaudeville entertainer Bert Williams was offering brilliant satirical comedy onstage and playing resourceful and independent characters in films.[9] This early section of the exhibition reminds us that despite hardships and social upheaval, there remained a through line of resilience and self-determination, particularly reflected in works like *Lime Kiln Club Field Day* (1913), which features Williams and a cadre of Black performers. Although the film includes some stereotypes—they were pervasive—

the overall takeaway is a demonstration of dignity through the efforts of a robust creative community that provides a counternarrative to established film history. As discussed in Ron Magliozzi's essay in this volume, the film was never completed and exists as an "archival assembly" of footage that was preserved and edited by the Museum of Modern Art, New York. It is considered the earliest surviving feature-length film with an all-Black cast.

Audiences have always been a crucial part of the filmmaking process. The popularity of Black-cast independent films in all genres from the 1910s to the 1940s demonstrates their significance. More than 150 race films were made during this period, offering tremendous opportunities for Black actors and intrepid entrepreneurs like the Lincoln Motion Picture Company, William D. Foster, and Oscar Micheaux. White-owned film and distribution companies like the Norman Film Manufacturing Company and Toddy Pictures also capitalized on this largely untapped audience. Overall, race film producers and directors offered opportunities to African American writers and actors that were not afforded them in Hollywood studio releases.

The casts and crews of these all-Black movies often worked with limited budgets and demonstrated ingenuity and audacity in devising innovative ways to make films. During a period of segregation and extreme racial tensions, there was an ecosystem of creative artists committed to the art of visual storytelling. Writers for Black-owned newspapers were some of the earliest film critics; many acting and musical careers were established and fostered during this period, and filmmakers were able to discuss social topics of the day through the art of film. Moving pictures were very popular at the time, even though many theaters in the South barred Black viewers from orchestra seats and required them to use separate entrances that in some cases involved climbing a stairway in a dark alley.[10] Gary Simmons's large-scale sculpture *Balcony Seating Only* (2017) serves as a reminder of the separate spaces Blacks had to inhabit, both as viewers and as cultural producers. The word "colored," rendered in lettering smudged by the artist yet still legible, reminds us of the delicate tension between past and present.

**I once told you, dear,
America is not for me.**

—Josephine Baker (1934)[11]

Regeneration also considers the international aspect of Black film history. Expanding the definition of African American cinema to include contributions by expatriate Americans brings complexity to the discussion. Artists such as Josephine Baker and Paul Robeson, as well as numerous writers and musicians, left the United States in order to remove themselves from the discrimination and racial tension they experienced in their home country. While there was no legal segregation in Europe and many artists enjoyed expanded opportunities during their time abroad, they often had to contend with colonialist attitudes and being regarded as the exotic other.

From the burgeoning years of sound film in the late 1920s and well into the 1940s, Black talent was scouted in nightclubs, and Hollywood hired Black musicians, dancers, and singers. Americans were hungry to see and hear great musical performances on-screen. For some performers, the technological development of synchronized sound facilitated their transition from stage to screen. It had a negative impact, however, on Black-owned production companies, which found it difficult to finance the transition to sound and in some cases went out of business.

As interest in musicals blossomed in the sound film era, African American performers were offered more opportunities in Hollywood, in movies with all-Black casts as well as in interracial productions. In some instances the Black talent was confined to specific scenes that could easily be edited out when the movies were shown in theaters in the Jim Crow South.[12] Between 1940 and 1947 a new cinematic genre flourished, the three-minute musical shorts known as Soundies.

I Am Somebody (dir. Madeline Anderson, 1970), film still

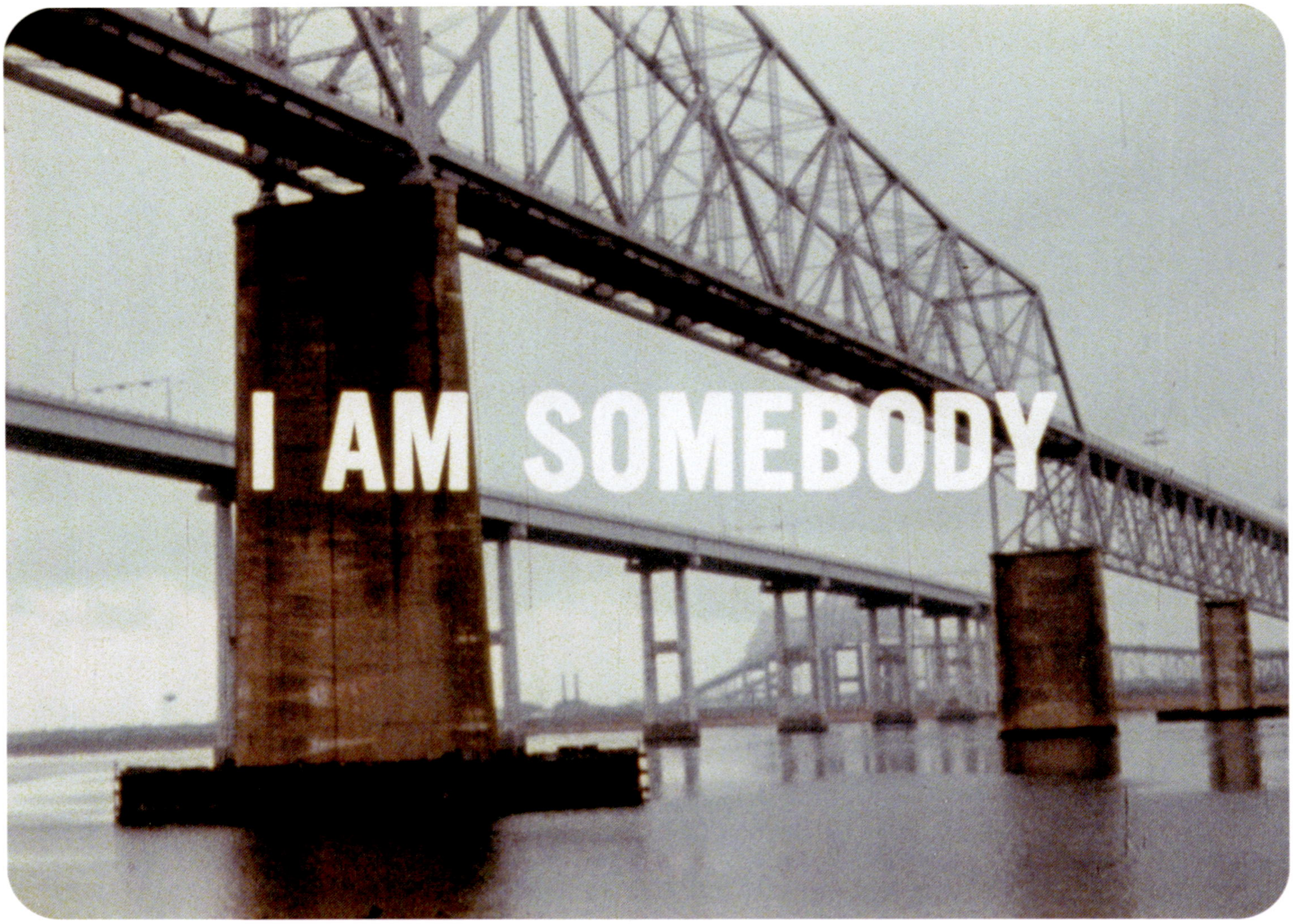

These productions featured jazz and swing numbers and were shown in freestanding projection cabinets, similar to jukeboxes, in bars. This platform also provided new opportunities for Black musicians and vocalists.

> I sincerely hope I shall always be a credit to my race and to the motion picture industry. My heart is too full to tell you just how I feel.
>
> —Hattie McDaniel (1940)[13]

Black actors working in Hollywood experienced opportunities as well as barriers. Between the 1920s and the 1950s, talented Black artists were often overlooked, uncredited, or typecast based on their complexion and stature. This exhibition examines how individuals who are now regarded as iconic figures—such as Lena Horne, Hattie McDaniel, and Lincoln Perry (a.k.a. Stepin Fetchit)—coped with such harsh realities. A large grouping of glamour photographs brings together iconic figures and lesser-known Black stars, while Carrie Mae Weems's seventeen-piece photo installation *Slow Fade to Black II* (2010) prompts us to consider what it means when an industry keeps some of its brightest stars in the shadows and their accomplishments fade from collective memory.

The civil rights movement unfolded during a time of change in the United States. Activists, religious leaders, and artists were all speaking out against war, discrimination against people of color, and sexism. The frustrations had reached fever pitch. The films produced during this period, documentaries and narrative features alike, were not immune to the times. Hollywood films began to offer more varied roles for Black actors. Sidney Poitier made his screen debut in 1950 in the film *No Way Out*, playing a doctor who must deal with the blatant racism of a patient. Black actors understood their position within the context of a larger social cultural conversation, and many of them used their influence to advocate for social justice and equality. Theaster Gates's artwork *Some Remember Sock Hops, Others Remember Riots* (2020) incorporates strips of decommissioned fire hoses, which reference the high-pressure water jets that were used by police to attack people, including children, during nonviolent protests against segregation in the 1950s and 1960s. In conversation with the work of film artists including Harry Belafonte, Ossie Davis, Ruby Dee, Sidney Poitier, and Paul Robeson, who supported and contributed to civil rights efforts in various ways, Gates's work calls attention to the dual realities that Black and white citizens experienced and the sacrifices that many endured to bend the arc of history toward justice.

The emergence in the late 1960s and 1970s of the Black Power movement—which rejected the civil rights movement's push for integration and accommodation with white society and instead called for self-determination and self-reliance—had a profound influence on Black artists in all mediums. During this period, self-financed feature films that candidly addressed issues specific to the Black community resonated greatly with audiences. The history of Black cinema is one that ebbs and flows. There are moments of flourishing and periods of frustration. Throughout, Black artists have found ways to persevere. Sometimes this requires working within the Hollywood system and delivering stellar performances despite the limitations of the script. At other times a complete rupture with the system is necessary to ensure that the message is not co-opted. Traversing this landscape has involved tremendous sacrifice and has given rise to extraordinary creativity.

The approaches taken by the directors William Greaves (*Symbiopsychotaxiplasm: Take One*, 1968), Robert L. Goodwin (*Black Chariot*), and Melvin Van Peebles (*Sweet Sweetback's Baadasssss Song*, 1971) in terms of the financing, production, and directing of their films were similar to how filmmakers worked during the first half of the twentieth century. The need for and reliance on community-based resources were at the heart of their practices, just as they were for their predecessors. Even Gordon Parks (*The Learning Tree*, 1969), who was the first Black filmmaker to direct a studio release, and Madeline Anderson (*I Am Somebody*, 1970), an independent producer/director and one of the first women union editors, hired and worked with people of color in front of and behind the camera.

This book complements the exhibition in encouraging a more open approach to history. Just as the contemporary artworks in the exhibition engage in dialogue with the historical film materials, the interviews with contemporary filmmakers echo themes addressed by film historians and curators in this volume. The interviews with Charles Burnett, Julie Dash, Ava DuVernay, Barry Jenkins, and Dawn Porter connect the conditions faced by earlier Black filmmakers with those of the present. Many themes addressed in the early twentieth century—for example, the need for fuller representation of Black life on-screen—remain relevant today. We asked the contemporary filmmakers to respond to a statement made by the Black producer and director William D. Foster in 1913: "Nothing has done so much to awaken the race consciousness of the colored man in the United States as the motion picture."[14] Most of the filmmakers had never heard of Foster, whose films are not known to have survived, apart from some shorts from 1929.[15] His movies are documented primarily through writings in the Black press, which also reiterates the important need to consider whose stories are being told, collected, and preserved. Each contemporary filmmaker had a strong reaction to Foster's words, however. While not all agreed with him, they all related to the critical notion of the moving image influencing how individuals see themselves.

Regeneration highlights the challenges faced by African American film artists on-screen and behind the camera and unpacks issues of representation, inequality, and discrimination that resonate in the film industry and in society at large today. In exploring this complex history, with its many vicissitudes, we have been struck by the resilience, dedication, and creative ingenuity displayed by the African American film artists who have helped to push the ideals on which this nation was founded closer to realization. We hope that this project serves to regenerate awareness of their efforts and that visitors to *Regeneration* and readers of this volume come to share the admiration we feel for this work and the joy that it inspires.

> **Because it is a long journey to this moment, I am naturally indebted to countless numbers of people.**
>
> —Sidney Poitier (1964)[16]

Notes

1 A pioneering multidisciplinary exhibition in this field was *Black Male: Representations of Masculinity in Contemporary American Art* (1995), curated by Thelma Golden for the Whitney Museum of American Art.

2 James Baldwin, "Sidney Poitier," in *The Cross of Redemption: Uncollected Writings*, ed. Randall Kenan (New York: Vintage, 2010), 223; originally published in *Look*, July 23, 1968, 50–58.

3 The Edward Mapp Collection includes materials dating from 1921 to 2001 that document race films and Hollywood studio productions featuring African American performers. See also Torene Svitil, ed., *Close Up in Black: African American Film Posters from the Academy of Motion Picture Arts and Sciences* (Beverly Hills: Academy of Motion Picture Arts and Sciences, 2002). Berger conducted this research with J. Raúl Guzmán, who has been part of the *Regeneration* team as assistant curator from its inception.

4 See the Richard E. Norman and Race Filmmaking Collection, 1912–1997, Black Film Center & Archive, Indiana University, as well as http://normanstudios.org/ and the private collection of David Norman.

5 For *Reform School* and *Mr. Washington Goes to Town*, see Jan-Christopher Horak, "Preserving Race Films," in *Early Race Filmmaking in America*, ed. Barbara Tepa Lupack (New York: Routledge, 2016), 222. For *Harlem on the Prairie*, see Michael K. Johnson, *Hoo-Doo Cowboys and Bronze Buckaroos: Conceptions of the African American West* (Jackson: University Press of Mississippi, 2014), 110.

6 We are indebted to the groundbreaking work of the Pioneers of African-American Cinema project, which reintroduced numerous race films to a wider public through a large-scale film preservation project. *Pioneers of African-American Cinema*, curated by Charles Musser and Jacqueline Najuma Stewart (New York: Kino Lorber, 2016), DVD and Blu-ray. See also "Kino Lorber Releases Pioneers of African-American Cinema in 5-Disc Blu-ray and DVD Set," June 6, 2016, https://www.kinolorber.com/news/article/id/31.

7 Baldwin, "Sidney Poitier," 225.

8 Frederick Douglass, "Age of Pictures," in *Picturing Frederick Douglass: An Illustrated Biography of the Nineteenth Century's Most Photographed American*, by John Stauffer, Zoe Trodd, and Celeste-Marie Bernier, rev. ed. (New York: Liveright, 2018), 144.

9 See Ann Charters, *Nobody: The Story of Bert Williams* (London: Macmillan, 1970), 11. Also see Mel Watkins, *On the Real Side: Laughing, Lying, and Signifying—the Underground Tradition of African-American Humor That Transformed American Culture, from Slavery to Richard Pryor* (New York: Simon & Schuster, 1994), 13, as quoted in Richard J. Powell, *Going There: Black Visual Satire* (New Haven, CT: Yale University Press, 2020), 117.

10 Pearl Bowser and Louise Spence, *Writing Himself into History: Oscar Micheaux, His Silent Films, and His Audiences* (New Brunswick, NJ: Rutgers University Press, 2000), 60–61.

11 Josephine Baker to Miki Sawada, July 5, 1934, Josephine Baker Collection, Sc MG 778, Schomburg Center for Research in Black Culture, Manuscripts, Archives and Rare Books Division, New York Public Library.

12 See Makenzie "Taylor" Perry, "Complex Ramifications: Musical Short Films of the 1930s–1940s and African-American Jazz Musicians," *Classic Journal*, November 4, 2016, https://theclassicjournal.uga.edu/index.php/2016/11/04/complex-ramifications-musical-short-films-of-the-1930s-1940s-african-american-jazz-musicians/. Also see Susan Delson, *Soundies and the Changing Image of Black Americans on Screen: One Dime at a Time* (Bloomington: Indiana University Press, 2021), 192.

13 "Hattie McDaniel winning Best Supporting Actress," YouTube video, 1:40, posted by "Oscars," September 27, 2011, https://www.youtube.com/watch?v=e7t4pTNZshA.

14 William D. Foster [Juli Jones Jr., pseud.], "News of the Moving Picture," *Indianapolis Freeman*, December 20, 1913.

15 Allyson Nadia Field, "The Ambitions of William Foster: Entrepreneurial Filmmaking at the Limits of Uplift Cinema," in Lupack, *Early Race Filmmaking*, 66–67.

16 Sidney Poitier, in his acceptance speech for the 1964 Academy Award for Best Actor for his performance in *Lilies of the Field* (1963), quoted in Wil Haygood, *Colorization: One Hundred Years of Black Films in a White World* (New York: Knopf, 2021), 178.

A Spectrum of

Black Cinema

Doris Berger
and Rhea L. Combs

History is not the past.
It is the present.
We carry our history with us.
We are our history.

James Baldwin (1980)

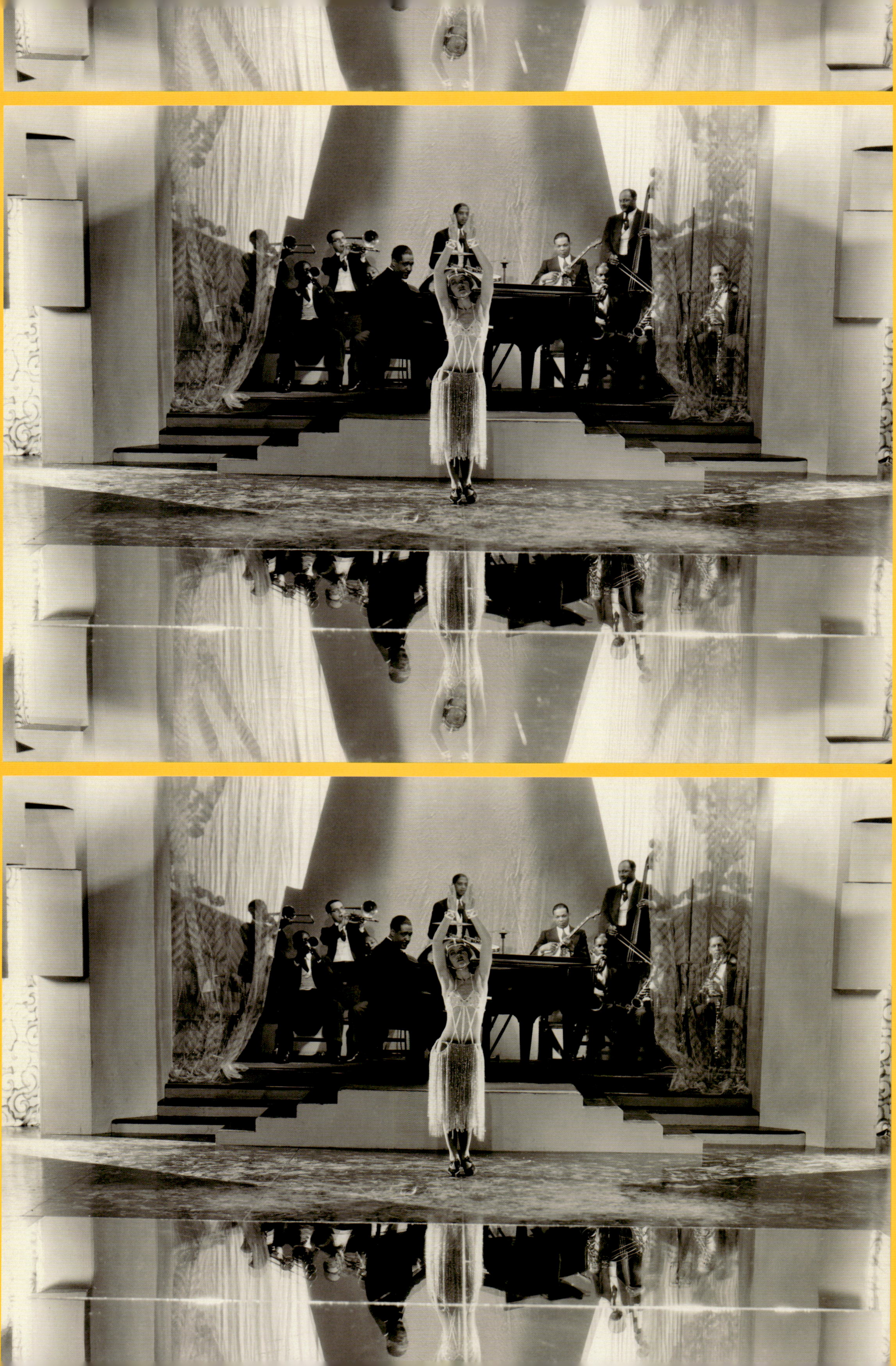

Fredi Washington (center) performing with Duke Ellington (at piano) and his band in *Black and Tan* (1929), production still

WHAT IS BLACK CINEMA?

In an interview that appears in this volume, the director Charles Burnett recalls having heated debates about the question of what constitutes a Black film while studying at UCLA in the 1970s: "We didn't come to a conclusion, but it was easier to say what was *not* a Black film." As the film historian Michael Boyce Gillespie has observed, "The idea of Black film is always a question and never an answer."[1] *Regeneration: Black Cinema 1898–1971* also does not attempt to provide a definitive answer, although the question drives this project, which accepts the premise that Black cinema is not a genre, nor is it tied to any specific era. It assumes some form of Black authorship through participation by Black directors, screenwriters, or casts. It also recognizes the critical importance of narrative and the role Black performers play within the story. Reactions to the work are also key, as is the reception of a film by Black audiences. Black authorship of films and film criticism can be traced to the early years of the medium. *Regeneration* demonstrates that despite incredible social, cultural, and economic hurdles, there has always been a Black creative class committed to producing work that examines social concerns, offers hope, and dares to dream. Moreover, this exhibition recognizes cinema as an art form and presents historical works by and about African Americans alongside selected works by contemporary Black artists to demonstrate the persistence of certain themes and ideas in different eras and mediums.

The desire to see oneself in images and stories, aspirational or imagined, is a human impulse that long predates movies.

Nothing has done so much to awaken the race consciousness of the colored man in the United States as the motion picture. It has made him hungry to see himself as he has come to be.

—William D. Foster (1913)

This could be challenging for early Black filmgoers, however, because the dominant images seen in film created and perpetuated stereotypical notions of Black people. The history of African Americans in cinema reflects the structural inequities and injustices within American society. Until at least the 1980s Black representation in American cinema was heavily informed by racist tropes and minstrel performance practices in various ways.[2] And pre–World War II cinematic narratives, often derived from the blackface tradition, made strong claims to truth and reality and thus were effective in reinscribing white supremacist beliefs. Segregation excluded Black filmmakers from equal participation and enforced a separate moviegoing experience for Black audiences. Nevertheless, as the film historian Jacqueline Stewart has argued, "Black urban populations and the cinematic institution exercised greater influence over each other during these formative years than has been previously acknowledged."[3] The Chicago-based entrepreneur William D. Foster, for example, widely considered one of the first Black film producers, recognized the power of the moving image early on, writing in 1913, "Nothing has done so much to awaken the race consciousness of the colored man in the United States as the motion picture. It has made him hungry to see himself as he has come to be."[4] Perhaps this was a bit hyperbolic, but Foster understood the economic and creative possibilities of cinema, particularly for African Americans. He formed the first Black-owned film production business, the Foster Photoplay Company, in 1910, shooting his first movie, the one-reel comedy *The Railroad Porter* (1912), with an all-Black cast and going on to work on a number of others between 1913 and 1918.[5]

When tracing the history of African Americans and cinema, it is useful to consider technological advancements that predate the development of moving images. The invention of early photographic processes such as the daguerreotype, which was widely used in the 1840s and 1850s, prompted greater visual documentation of social conditions. Photographic images could convey a variety of messages, both negative and positive. For example, the biologist Louis Agassiz commissioned the photographer Joseph T. Zealy to make daguerreotypes of enslaved South Carolinians in order to promote notions of Black inferiority,[6] whereas the statesman and abolitionist Frederick Douglass regarded photography as "a great democratic art."[7] The antislavery activist Sojourner Truth, who, like Douglass, understood that photography could serve a larger strategic purpose, often captioned her photographic portraits with the statement "I Sell the Shadow to Support the Substance."[8] Douglass and Truth believed that photographs—unlike paintings, which were often singular commissioned works produced for and by an elite class of landowning gentry—offered people from different social strata a chance to present themselves, on a mass scale, honestly and more humanely.

With the introduction of moving-image technology, African Americans recognized its potential and used it to showcase their humanity, just as Douglass and Truth had used photography in earlier decades. According to Stewart, "African Americans migrated to the movies—as producers and consumers—as part of their individual and collective efforts to challenge static, Old Negro stereotypes and to try on the roles of modern New Negroes entering urban modernity and seeking full American citizenship."[9] *Regeneration* explores the myriad ways in which Black artists, filmmakers, and critics navigated an often prejudiced and segregated system over seven decades, either finding ways to work within dominant industry structures or choosing to develop their own dynamic, creative communities.

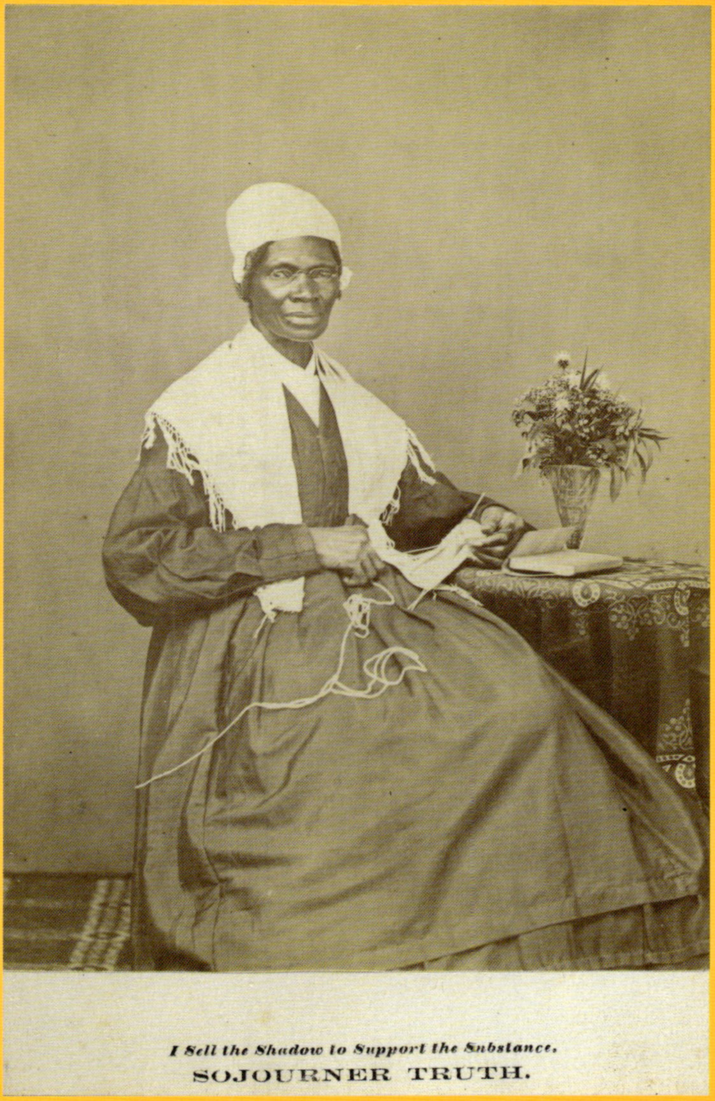

Cabinet card of Sojourner Truth, 1864, albumen and silver on photographic paper on cardboard, 6 ½ × 4 ¼ in. (16.5 × 10.8 cm)

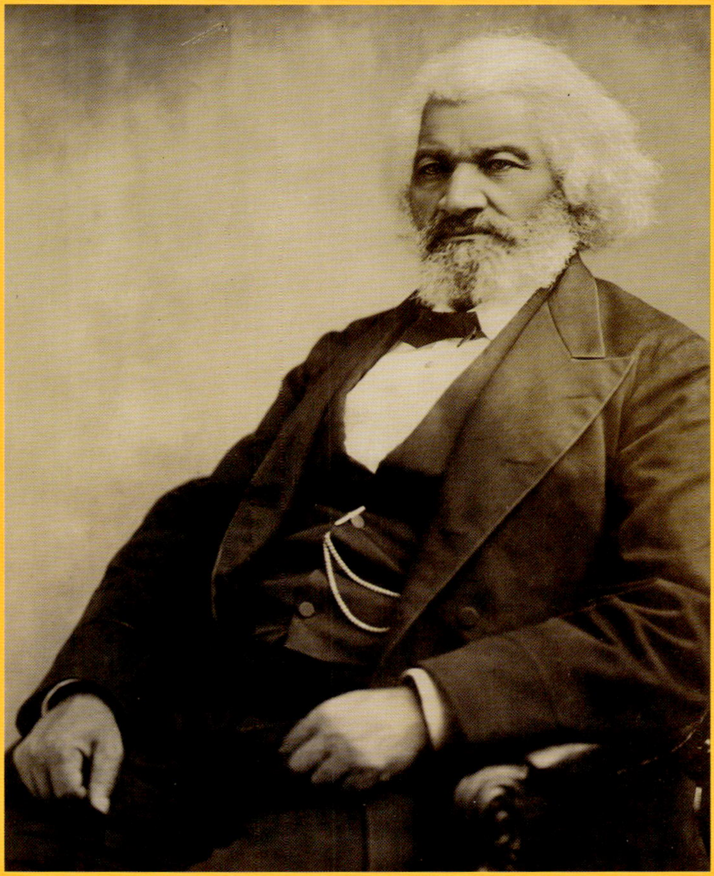

C. M. Battey (American, 1873–1927), *Frederick Douglass*, ca. 1895, gelatin silver print, 12 1/16 × 10 ¼ in. (30.6 × 26 cm)

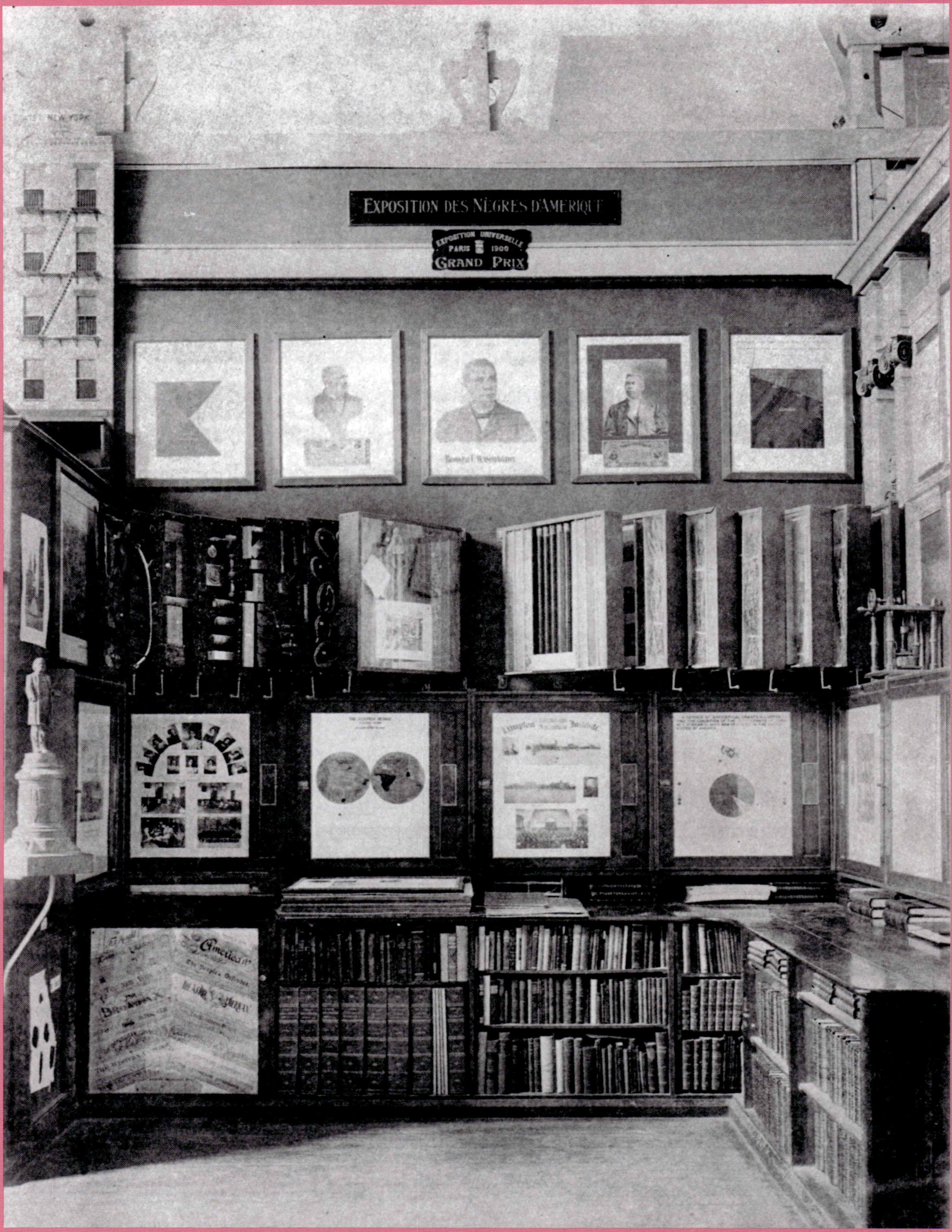
EXPOSITION DES NÈGRES D'AMERIQUE
EXPOSITION UNIVERSELLE
PARIS 1900
GRAND PRIX

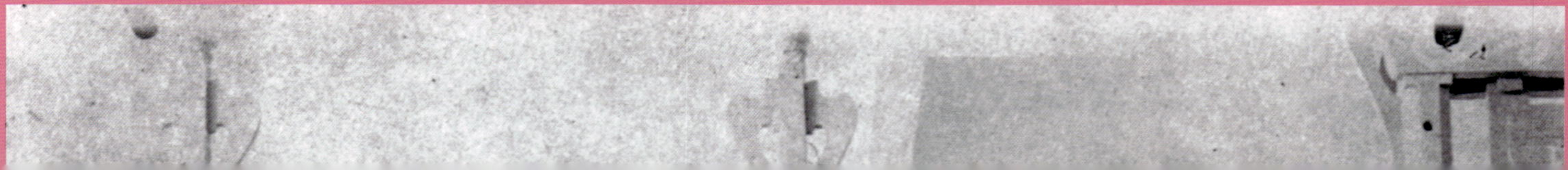

Installation view of the Exhibition of American Negroes at the Exposition Universelle in Paris, 1900

UPLIFT AND VISUAL EDUCATION

One of the most ambitious efforts to counteract misrepresentation during the early years of moving pictures was a noncinematic project undertaken by the Black sociologist and activist W. E. B. Du Bois when he was asked by a friend and former classmate, the attorney Thomas J. Calloway, to curate the Exhibition of American Negroes for the 1900 Exposition Universelle in Paris. Du Bois created a display of the "small nation of people" through a series of books, 363 photographs of African Americans, and colorful hand-drawn illustrations showing "Negro progress" in a variety of areas, including education, agriculture, and business.[10] The award-winning efforts of Du Bois and his team of university students were an exemplar of Black modernity that presented a "narrative of Black agency."[11] Their approach reflected the attitudes of many African Americans who were deeply invested in offering the world a respectable view of Black progress and self-reliance.

The principal of Tuskegee Normal and Industrial Institute (now Tuskegee University), Booker T. Washington, was less vocal than Du Bois in publicly condemning racism. He believed that hard work, self-determination, and a vocational education were sufficient counters to white supremacy. He did not necessarily

W. E. B. Du Bois, diagram from
The Georgia Negro: A Social Study, 1900

The diagram illustrates African slave trade routes, with the state of Georgia starred.

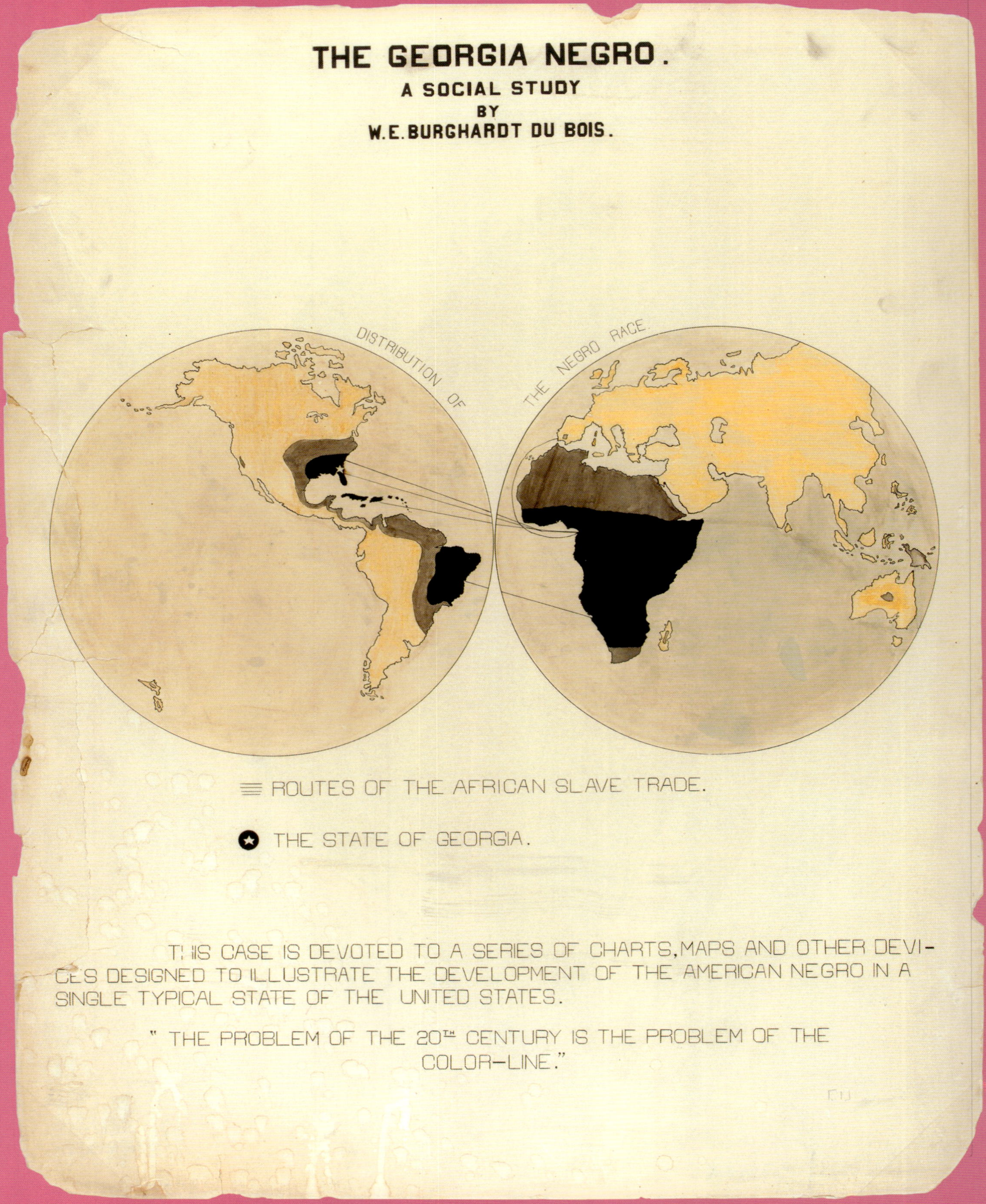

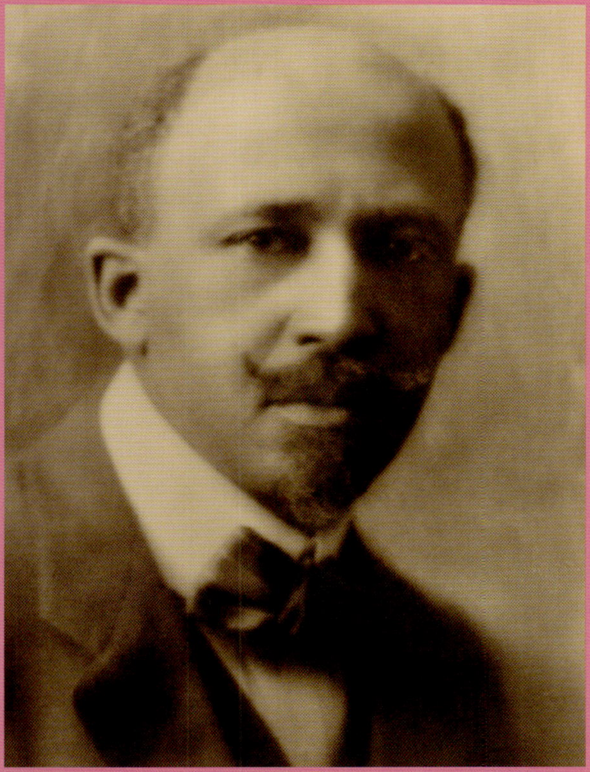

C. M. Battey (American, 1873–1927), *W. E. B. Du Bois*, 1918, silver and photographic gelatin on photographic paper, 13 ⅝ × 10 ⁵⁄₁₆ in. (34.6 × 26.2 cm)

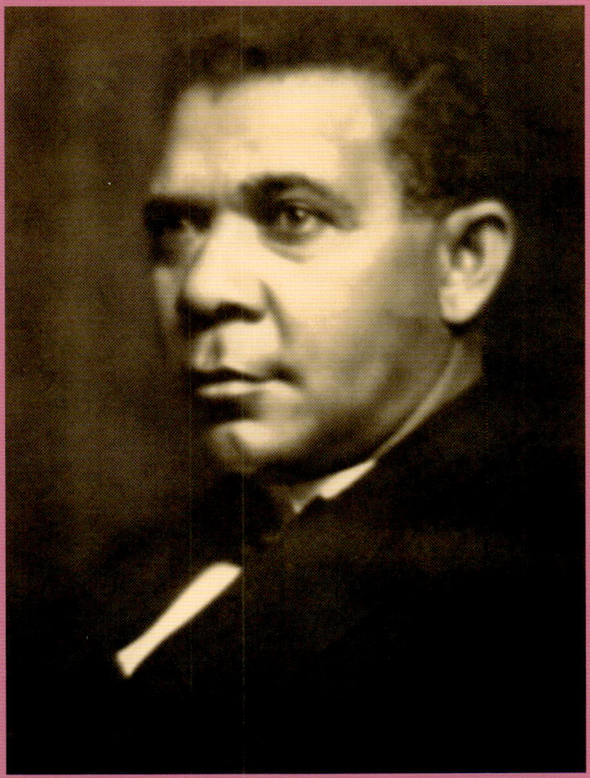

C. M. Battey (American, 1873–1927), *Booker T. Washington*, ca. 1908, gelatin silver print, 9 ¼ × 6 ¾ in. (23.5 × 17.1 cm)

challenge racist notions of the social order of things, but he did wield significant influence, particularly as a founding member of the National Negro Business League. As a successful fundraiser, he also had access to many powerful white philanthropists such as the Carnegies, the Rockefellers, and Julius Rosenwald, the philanthropist who supported the development of schools in the South dedicated to teaching Black students. Washington used these affiliations to help raise money for small schools throughout the South. It was no surprise, then, that Calloway asked Washington to support the showcase of American Negroes at the Paris Exposition.[12] Washington believed that this project would help change minds about the role and legacy of African Americans. While it did receive significant international recognition, unfortunately it did not shift attitudes in the United States.

Historians have long recognized the different approaches of Du Bois and Washington, but there were times, early in their respective careers—and later, during the Paris Exposition—when the pair were aligned in efforts to further African American progress. At the very least, one thing they had in common was a dedication to that cause and a recognition of the important role that the new technologies of photography and moving pictures played in these efforts.[13]

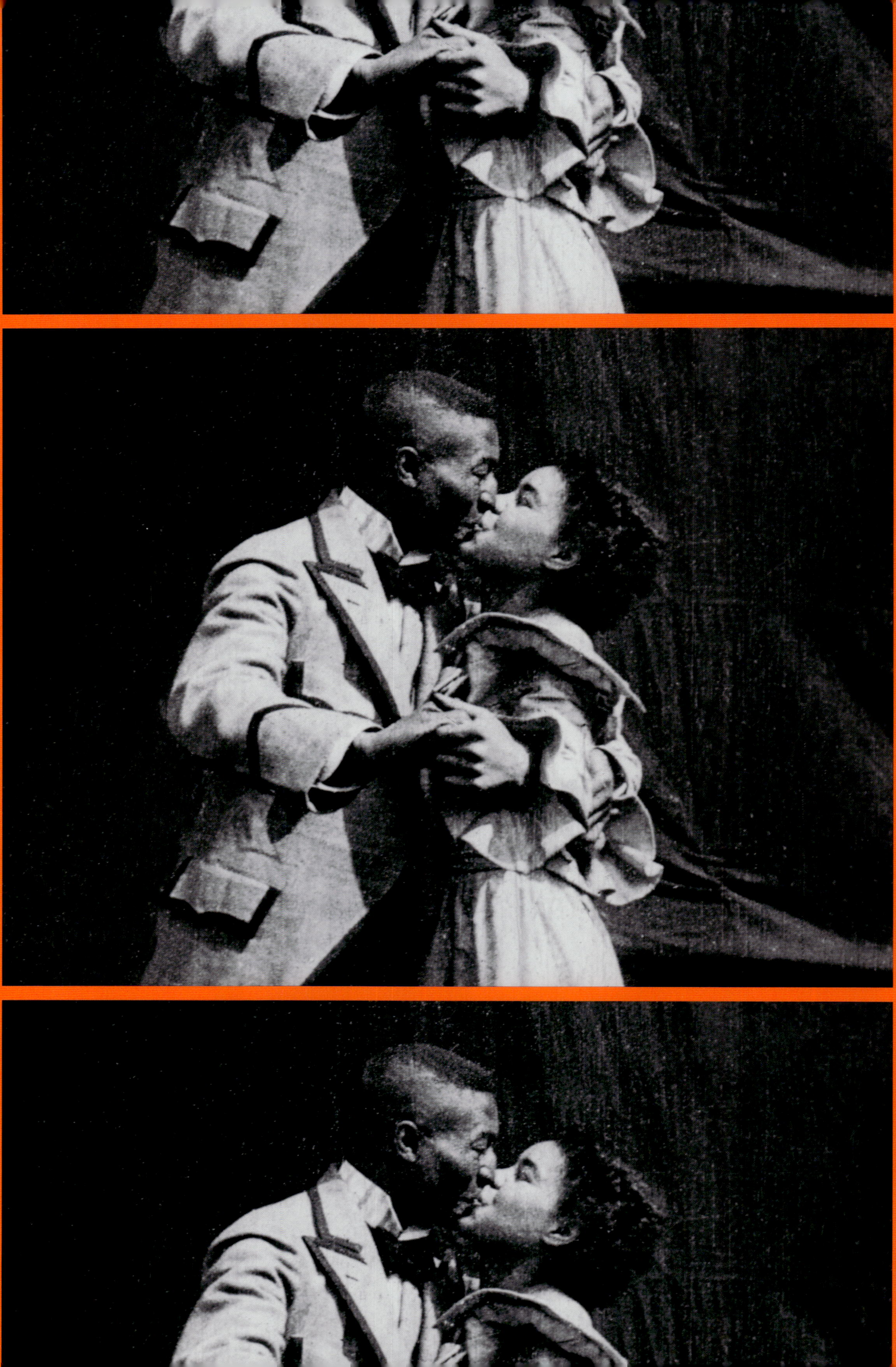

Something Good—Negro Kiss (prod. William N. Selig, 1898), film still (version restored by the University of Southern California)

COUNTERIMAGES AND COUNTERNARRATIVES

In the 1890s African Americans made up one-eighth of the US population, or almost eight million people.[14] Most Black families resided in the American South, while others moved north during the post-Reconstruction period (after 1877). The progress that occurred during Reconstruction—including redistribution of land, the establishment of state-funded public school systems, and a guaranteed right to vote for African American men—was stripped away during the period that followed. Poll taxes and campaigns of intimidation suppressed the Black vote. Black people could be lynched for the slightest of (presumed) offenses, and angry white mobs terrorized neighborhoods. On November 10, 1898, for example, white supremacists staged an insurrection in the town of Wilmington, North Carolina, deposing its lawfully elected integrated government and installing their own all-white council of aldermen. Black businesses were looted and burned, and as many as three hundred people were murdered.

It was against the backdrop of such events that *Something Good—Negro Kiss* (1898), the film that opens this exhibition, was produced. It captures the smartly dressed vaudeville performers Gertie Brown and Saint Suttle as they embrace, kiss, and dance with each other. Scholars and archivists believe that the twenty-nine-second film by the Selig Polyscope Company "may represent the earliest example of African-American intimacy on-screen."[15] *Something Good—Negro Kiss* was discovered by the archivist Dino Everett and the film scholar Allyson Nadia Field in 2017 and added to the National Film Registry in 2018. A similar version featuring the same performers was found in

Glenn Ligon (American, b. 1960), *Double America 2*, 2014, neon and paint, 48 × 145 × 3 in. (121.9 × 368.3 × 7.6 cm)

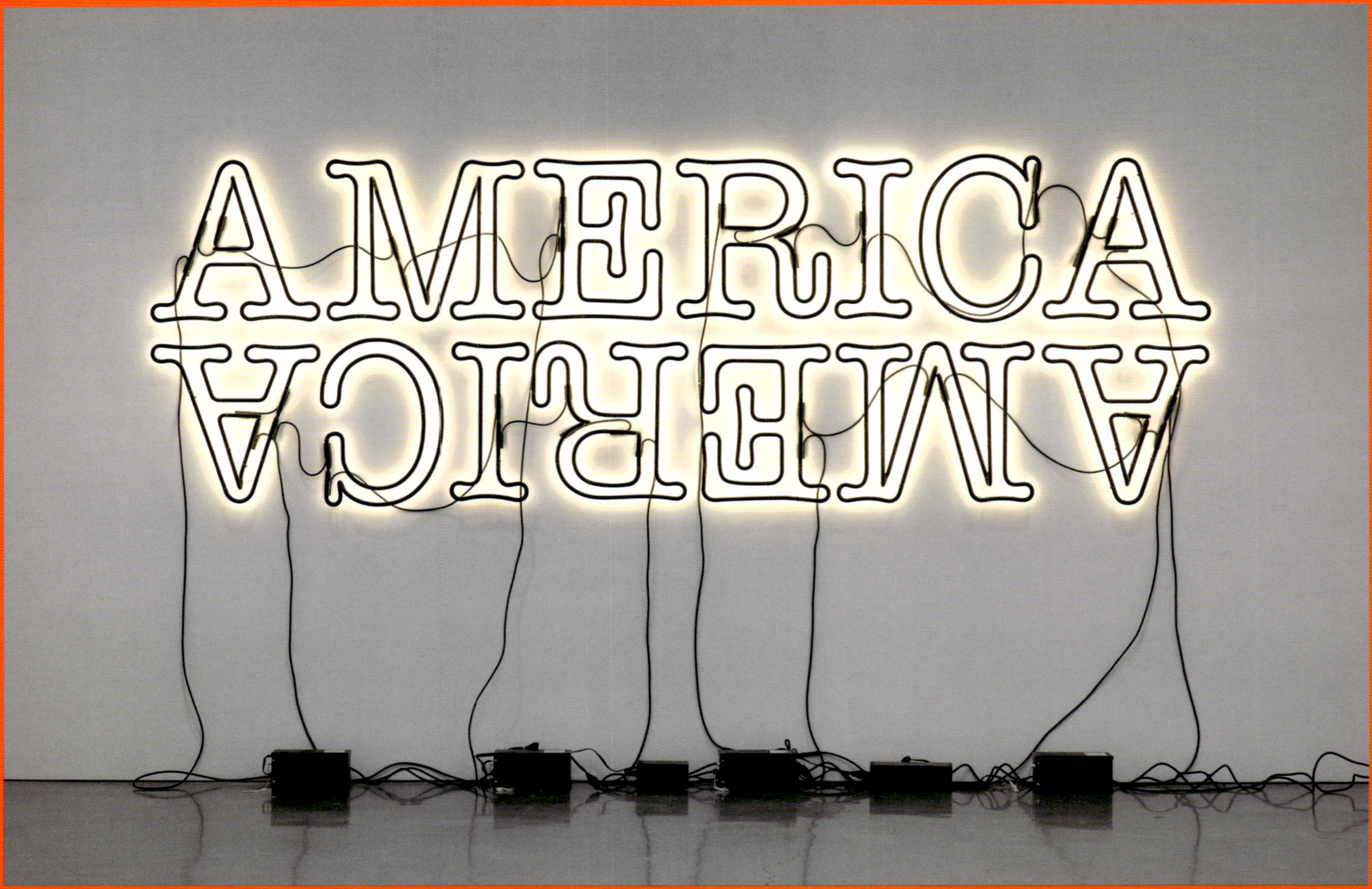

2019 at the National Library of Norway.[16] Field describes Brown and Suttle's performance as a "significant counter to the racist portrayal of African Americans otherwise seen in the cinema of its time."[17] This previously unknown work was purportedly produced for Thomas Edison as a parody of *The Kiss* (1896), a twenty-second film featuring the white actors May Irwin and John Rice reenacting the final scene of the 1895 stage production of *The Widow Jones*. No matter its brevity, *The Kiss* was considered provocative at the time because films were no longer viewed in individual nickelodeons but were projected on a big screen. While some critics denounced the performance of on-screen tenderness as vulgar, the film also garnered tremendous attention from audiences and was soon showing in theaters at the end of every film.[18] The success of *The Kiss* prompted many spin-offs, and *Something Good—Negro Kiss* was one of them. Given how *The Kiss* was exhibited in theaters, is it possible that *Something Good—Negro Kiss* was presented together with other films?

In the present exhibition, *Something Good—Negro Kiss* is paired with Glenn Ligon's *Double America 2* (2014). In Ligon's work, two neon signs spelling out the word "America" are mounted together, one right side up and the other upside down. One set of neon letters is outlined in black and the other in white, and the two words flash on and off in a random rhythm. *Double America 2* evokes the notion that there are often two Americas—one for those who are Black and one for those who are white, one for those who are considered to be on top and one for those who are at the bottom. For some it may also recall W. E. B. Du Bois's notion of double-consciousness, which he described in 1903 as central to the Black experience: "It is a peculiar sensation, this double-consciousness, this sense of always looking at oneself through the eyes of others, of measuring one's soul by the tape of a world that looks on in amused contempt and pity. One ever feels his two-ness, an American, a Negro; two souls, two thoughts, two unreconciled strivings; two warring ideals in one dark body, whose dogged strength alone keeps it from being torn asunder."[19] Du Bois's ideas, seen within the context of *Regeneration*, offer possible insights into some of the ways in which Black people responded to this harsh fact: they created spaces free from the burdens of the white gaze and produced, directed, and exhibited their own films.

American visual culture of this period provides ample evidence of just how burdensome that gaze would have been. Henry Louis Gates Jr. has observed that between roughly 1890 and 1910 racist imagery flooded the American market, "with tens of thousands of the most heinous representations of black people, on children's games, portable saving banks, trade cards, postcards, calendars, . . . cooking and eating utensils—in short just about anywhere and everywhere a middle- or working-class person might peer in the course of a day."[20] The images popularized in consumer products and also seen in early cinema were aimed at demeaning Black people rather than offering the variety of role models afforded to a white moviegoing audience. The first Black-cast films were generally short films shown in nickelodeons across the United States until about 1907 and usually featured Black performers dancing or performing a task. They include *The Pickaninny Dance* (1894), *Darkey Cake Walk* (1897), *Dancing Darkies* (1904), and *A Nigger in the Woodpile* (1904), all produced by American Mutoscope and Biograph Company in New York. The titles offer insight into the ideological framing of these moving images, which often mythologized the antebellum South and symbolically established a social and racialized other. It is unknown whether these films were willingly seen by Black audiences.

The cinematic adaptations of Harriet Beecher Stowe's hugely popular abolitionist novel, *Uncle Tom's Cabin* (1852), offer testimony to the pervasive power of negative narrative tropes. Although Stowe's intention was to expose the evils of slavery, her book was not free of racial stereotypes. The novel sold a record-breaking three hundred thousand copies in the year after its publication and was immediately adapted into a stage play. Even after the end of the Civil War in 1865, more than two hundred touring shows crisscrossed the country.[21] Many of these "Tom shows," especially those performed for southern audiences, were actually pro-slavery, and they likely contributed to the hardening of stereotypes of Black characters by the 1870s. In the silent era there were numerous adaptations of *Uncle Tom's Cabin*, from a short in 1903 to a feature-length film from 1927, released as the industry was transitioning to sound.[22] Uncle Tom was the "good Negro"—who was enslaved, kept in fear, and insulted—whereas the girl Topsy fit the pickaninny stereotype, wild and unkempt in look and demeanor. It is telling that these were the first Black characters in the history of American narrative film. Additionally, most actors who appeared in the 1903 film, as well as in ensuing adaptations, were white actors performing in blackface, propelling the minstrel show tradition from the stage to the screen. The first Black man cast as Tom in the United States was the celebrated stage actor Sam Lucas, who played the role onstage in 1878 and on-screen in 1914, toward the end of his life. The other Black actor cast as Tom was James B. Lowe in the 1927 adaptation.

As Donald Bogle has written, Black character types included not only the submissive Uncle Tom figure but also "a variety of black presences bearing the fanciful names of the coon, the tragic mulatto, the mammy, and the brutal black buck." All had existed since slavery and were used "to entertain by stressing Negro inferiority. Fun was poked at the American Negro by presenting him as either a nitwit or a childlike lackey."[23] The Uncle Tom stereotype, in particular, has inspired various works by contemporary Black artists. Ligon's 16mm short film *Death of Tom* (2008) blurs Tom's visibility and adds an interpretation of a vaudeville song by Jason Moran. Kara Walker's stark silhouette installation *The End of Uncle Tom and the Grand Allegorical Tableau of Eva in Heaven* (1995) exposes the violence implicit in the characterizations in *Uncle Tom's Cabin* and further perpetuated in material and popular culture. Walker's work presents an imagined visual history from an African American woman's perspective. Between the 1750s and the 1850s cut-paper silhouettes were a popular form of portraiture, as they offered a less expensive alternative to painting. While the most common use was for portraits in profile, silhouettes were also created as conversation pieces depicting genre scenes, historical events, and landscapes.[24] Darby English describes Walker's works, including this one, as "imaginative reprojection of disagreeable images and themes drawn from the American South during the antebellum period." For English, "Walker's work gives figurative and conceptual representation to the pursuit of history, pleasure, humanity, and value by a black American woman provoked by numerous forces to work against formations in which she *is seen* but never *sees for herself*."[25] The inclusion in *Regeneration* of Walker's artistic interpretation, with its racial and gendered perspective, represents an important counternarrative to the film adaptations of *Uncle Tom's Cabin*.

The work that looms largest in this early film history, however, is undoubtedly D. W. Griffith's epic *The Birth of a Nation* (1915), which became the first American blockbuster. Based on Thomas Dixon Jr.'s book *The Clansman* (1905), the movie promoted white supremacy. President Woodrow Wilson screened the film at the White House, thereby sanctioning its message of fear and racial intolerance. *Birth of a Nation* also had devastating effects in real life. Although the film is likely only one of several factors that contributed to the revival of the Ku Klux Klan, it disseminated and normalized the organization's racist ideology and was used as a tool to recruit new members. Scenes involving the burning of crosses, ostensibly employed in the film for dramatic cinematic effect, led the Klan to take up the practice as a means of intimidating Black people.[26] Film historians have long regarded the movie as a cinematic masterpiece that introduced new filmmaking and editing techniques. Its canonization has often overshadowed the realities of its messaging, and only in the last few decades have scholars begun to analyze the interrelationship between its technical virtuosity and its blatant racism.[27] From the film's release in February 1915 to this day, however, African Americans have been outspoken in their opposition. The National Association for the Advancement of Colored People (NAACP) organized protests against it, and Black filmmakers continue to create cinematic responses—from Oscar Micheaux's *Within Our Gates* (1920) to Spike Lee's *The Answer* (1980) and *BlacKkKlansman* (2018).[28]

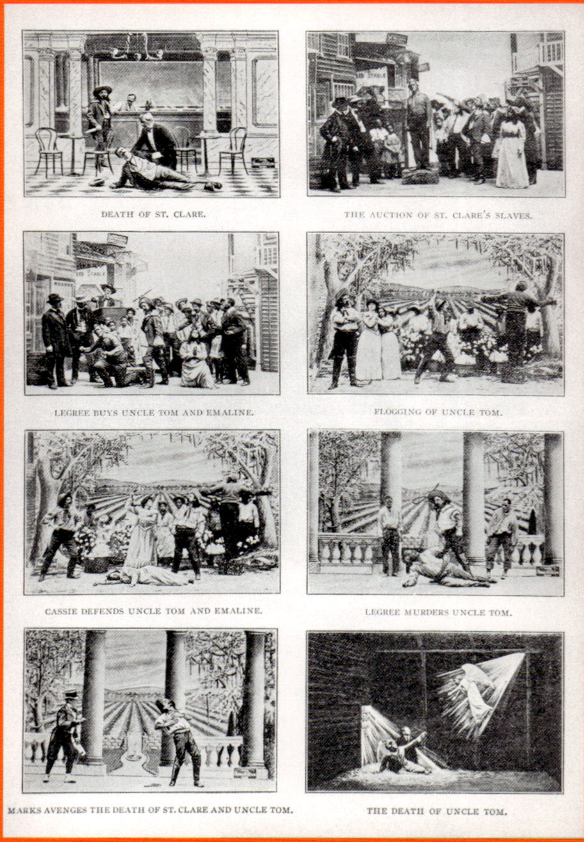

Page from Edison-Porter film catalogue with scenes from *Uncle Tom's Cabin, or, Slavery Days* (1903).

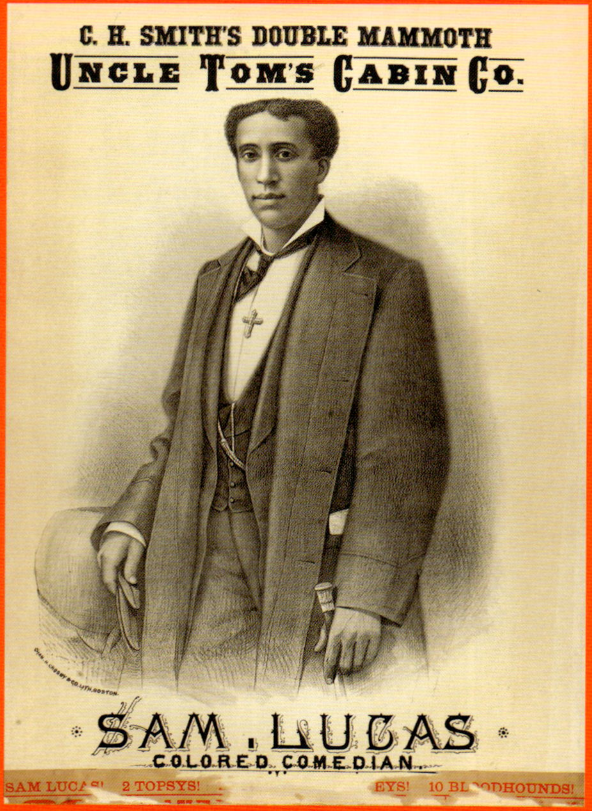

Sam Lucas in advertisement for C. H. Smith's Double Mammoth Uncle Tom's Cabin Co., ca. 1870s, poster

Kara Walker (American, b. 1969), *The End of Uncle Tom and the Grand Allegorical Tableau of Eva in Heaven*, 1995, cut paper and adhesive on wall, 13 × 35 ft. (4.0 × 10.7 m)

Installation view, *Kara Walker: My Complement, My Enemy, My Oppressor, My Love*, Walker Art Center, 2007

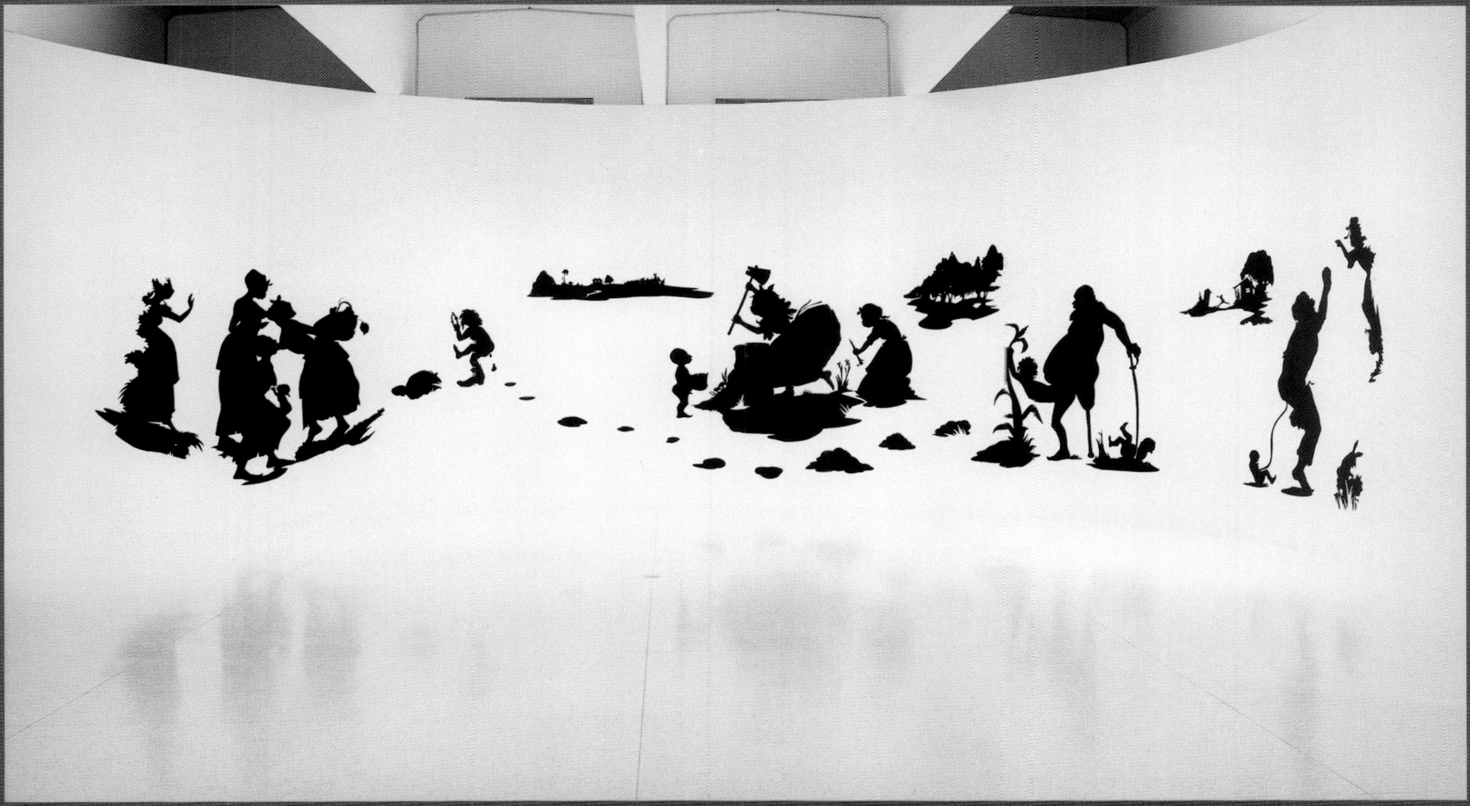

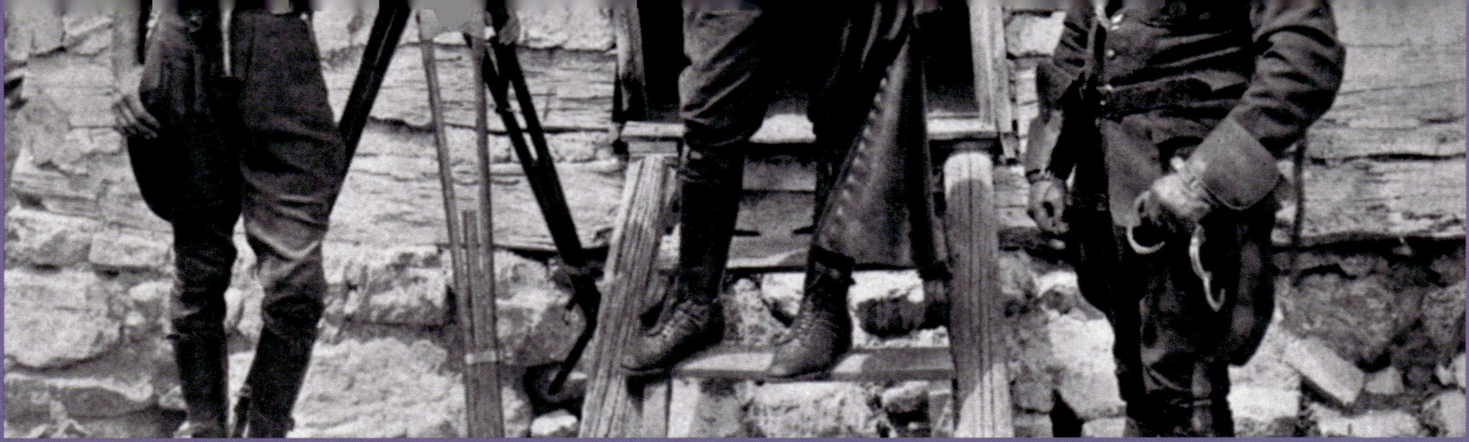
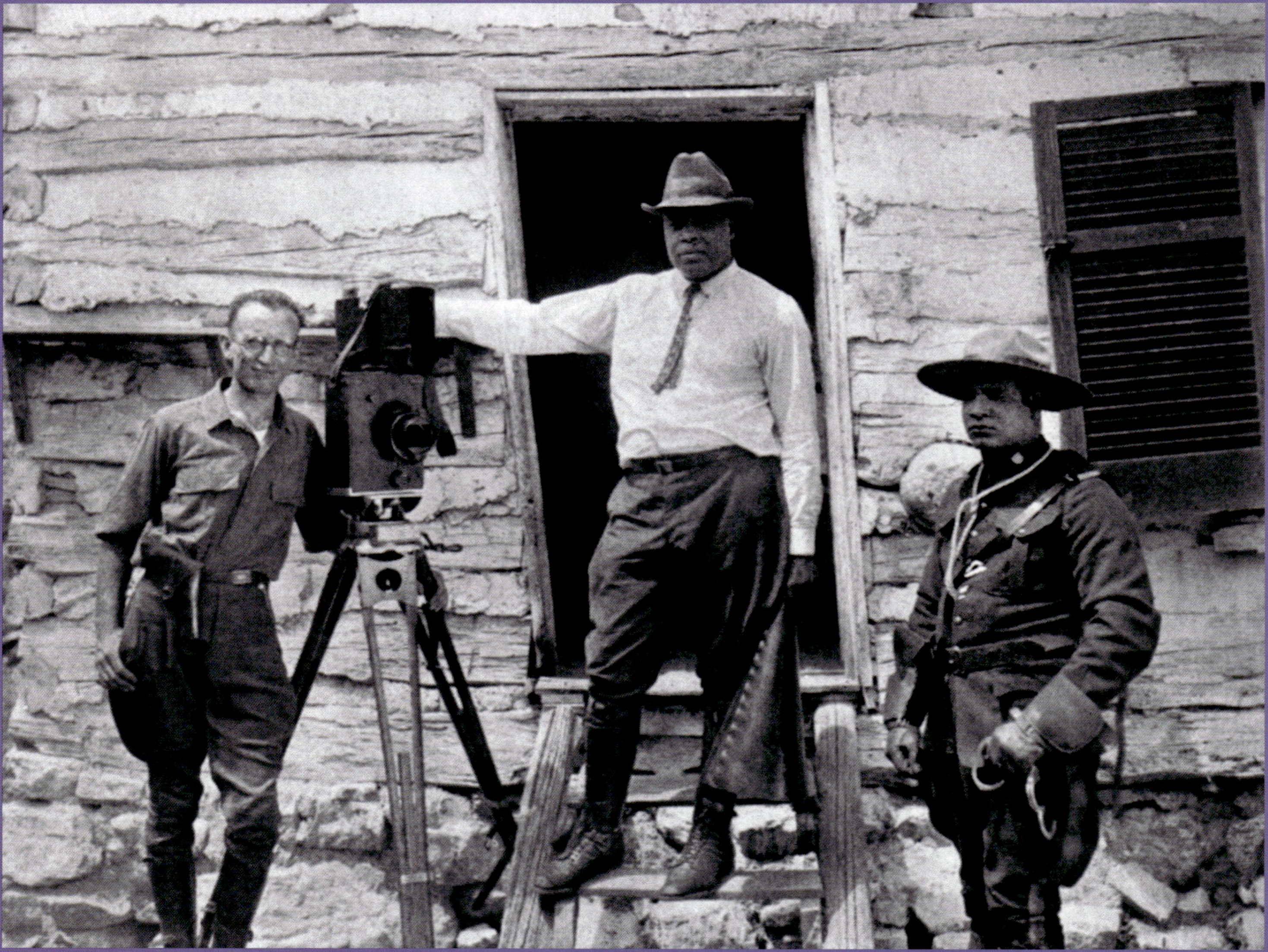
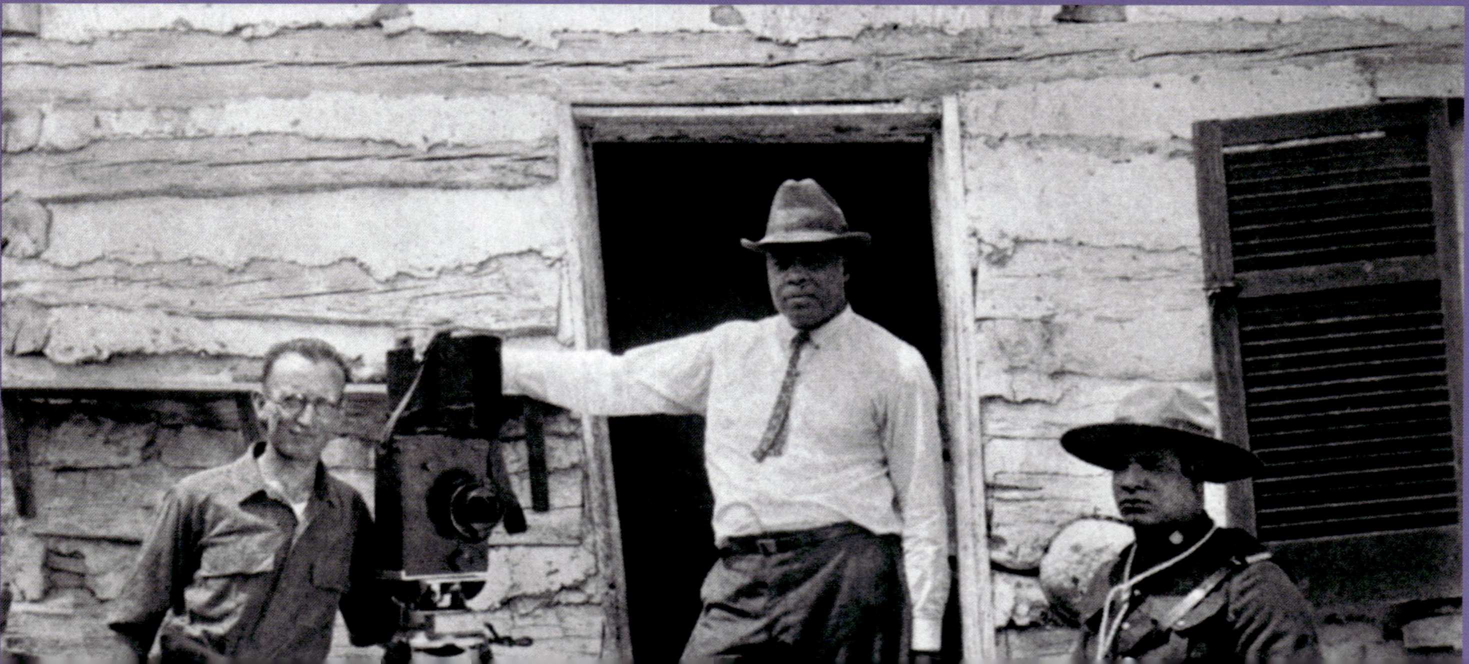

Oscar Micheaux (center) with crew on set, ca. 1923, advertisement

ESTABLISHING SHOTS: NEW IMAGES

Describing the situation faced by an African American filmmaker in 1914, a year before the release of *Birth of a Nation*, Allyson Nadia Field writes, "Although moving pictures were a contested site of racist depictions that perpetuated stereotypes and further maligned a marginalized people, more recently the capability of motion pictures to counteract prejudicial representation had provided hope for the possibilities of the medium."[29] African American intellectuals, activists, and artists—who had long understood the power of telling their own stories—responded to Griffith's film through protests as well as independent productions. As W. E. B. Du Bois wrote in *The Crisis:* "the [Negro] race must learn to use its money for films, poetry, music and its own history."[30]

Several intrepid entrepreneurs appeared to heed this call to action. One of them was William D. Foster, and a member of the Black press chronicling his activities wrote: "The cry from Race people is for better pictures of their race on the screen. White corporations defiantly say 'If you want better pictures of your race make them yourself,' and the reply of the Foster Photo Play company is, 'We will!'"[31] In addition to making films, Foster was

The cry from Race people is for better pictures of their race on the screen. White corporations defiantly say "If you want better pictures of your race make them yourself," and the reply of the Foster Photo Play company is, "We will!"

—*Chicago Defender* (November 23, 1929)

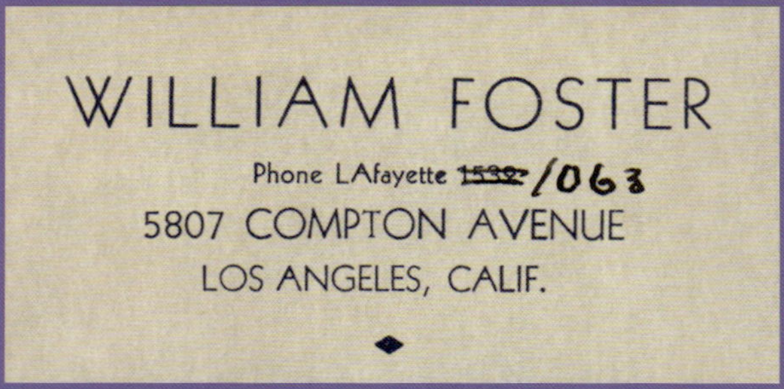
WILLIAM FOSTER
Phone LAfayette ~~1532~~ /063
5807 COMPTON AVENUE
LOS ANGELES, CALIF.

William Foster letterhead, n.d.

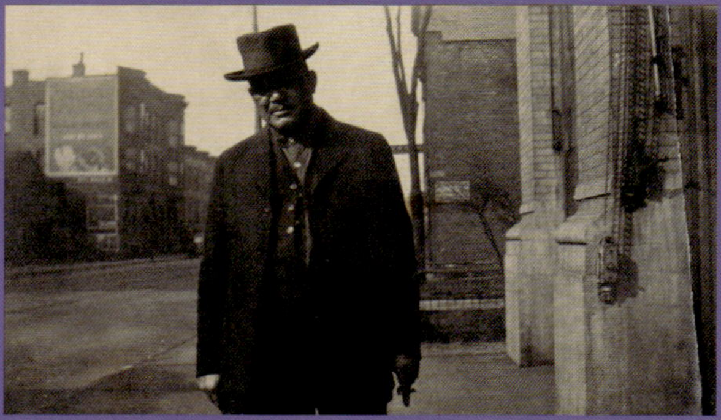

William Foster in Chicago, n.d.

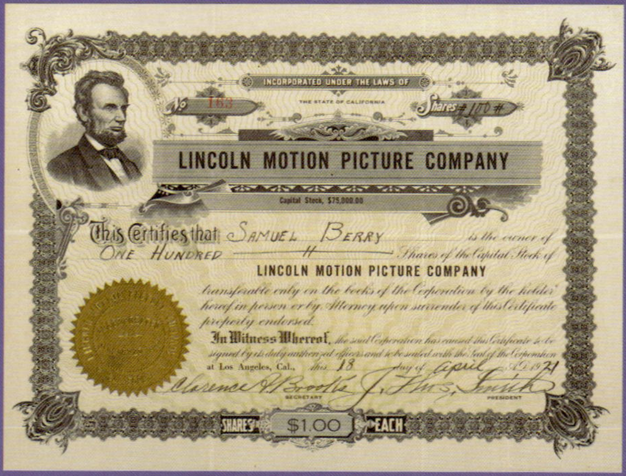
INCORPORATED UNDER THE LAWS OF THE STATE OF CALIFORNIA

No 163 Shares #100#

LINCOLN MOTION PICTURE COMPANY

Capital Stock, $75,000.00

This Certifies that Samuel Berry is the owner of One Hundred ---- Shares of the Capital Stock of LINCOLN MOTION PICTURE COMPANY transferable only on the books of the Corporation by the holder hereof in person or by Attorney upon surrender of this Certificate properly endorsed.

In Witness Whereof, the said Corporation has caused this Certificate to be signed by its duly authorized officers and to be sealed with the Seal of the Corporation at Los Angeles, Cal., this 18 day of April A.D. 1921

Clarence A. Brooks, Secretary — J. Thos. Smith, President

SHARES $1.00 EACH

Lincoln Motion Picture Company stock certificate, 1921

a publicist who wrote theater criticism in Black newspapers under the pen name Juli Jones Jr. and worked as a theater manager for vaudeville acts and musicals, including Bob Cole and Billy Johnson's *A Trip to Coontown* (1897) and *In Dahomey* (1903), starring George Walker and Bert Williams. As a booking agent, Foster was keenly aware of the tremendous talent pool of Black performers—and the limited roles available to them.[32] Foster often showed *The Railroad Porter* alongside parade footage in community-based theaters, thus also pioneering Black-produced newsreels.[33]

Although the *The Railroad Porter* and many of the early silent film–era moving image works are not known to have survived, archival research and primary sources such as the Black press (see Cara Caddoo's essay in this volume) show that African Americans were invested in using the new technology of moving images to showcase progress. Another key example is the documentary *A Trip to Tuskegee* (1909) by the Boston-based African American entrepreneur George Broome, who produced it as part of a fundraising effort for the Tuskegee Institute. The film *A Day at Tuskegee* (1913) was developed in conjunction with Booker T. Washington by the Chicago-based entrepreneur and attorney Louis B. Anderson. William F. Watkins, a dentist in Montgomery, Alabama, established the Anderson-Watkins Film Company with the intention of filming African American institutions across the country.[34] African Americans recognized the power and potential of this modern technology and used it to showcase their humanity, just as Douglass and Truth had used photography years prior.

Members of the Lincoln Motion Picture Company, Los Angeles, ca. 1917. From left: Clarence Ahart Brooks, Beulah Hall, Noble M. Johnson, Dudley Alfonzo Brooks, Dr. James Thomas Smith

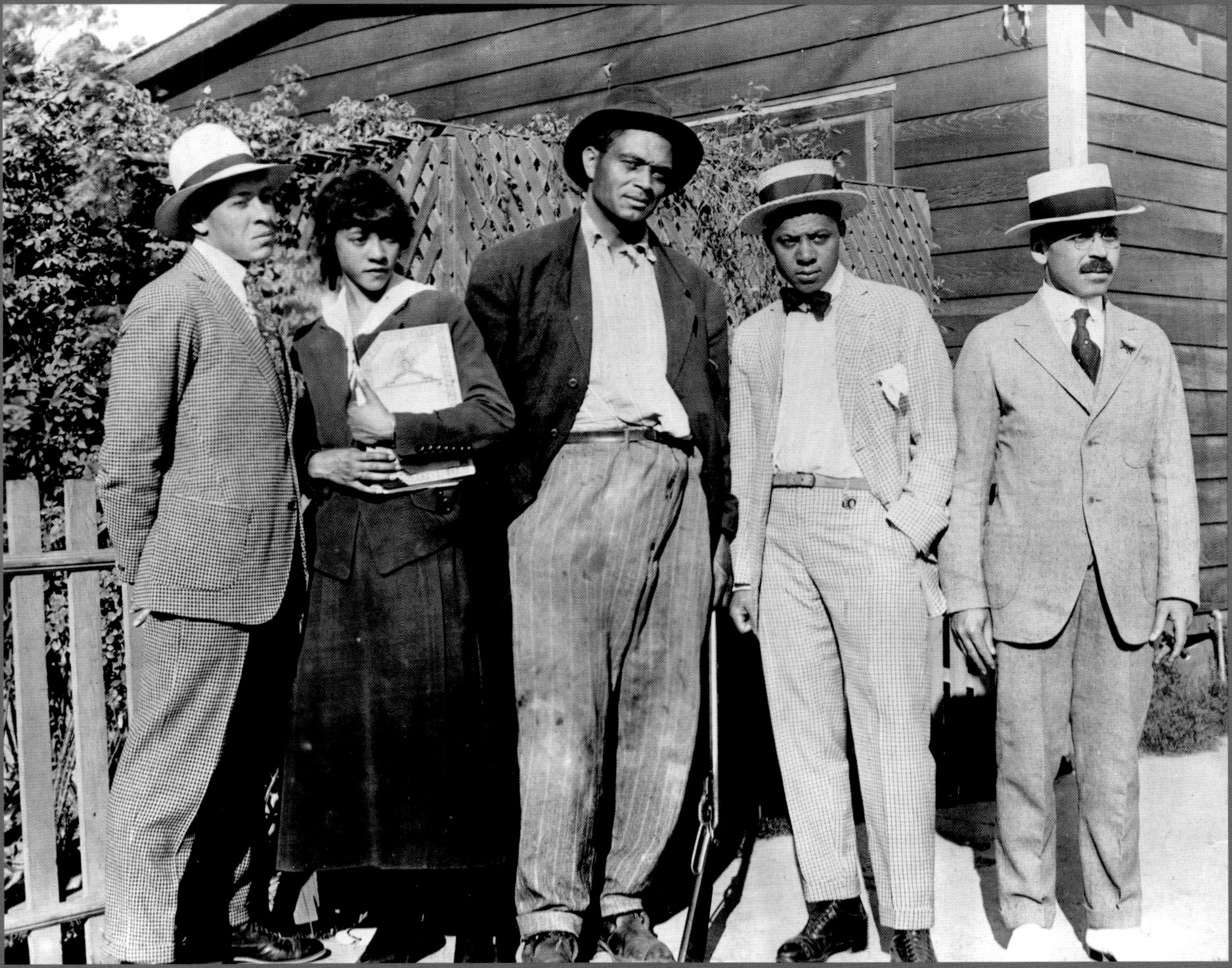

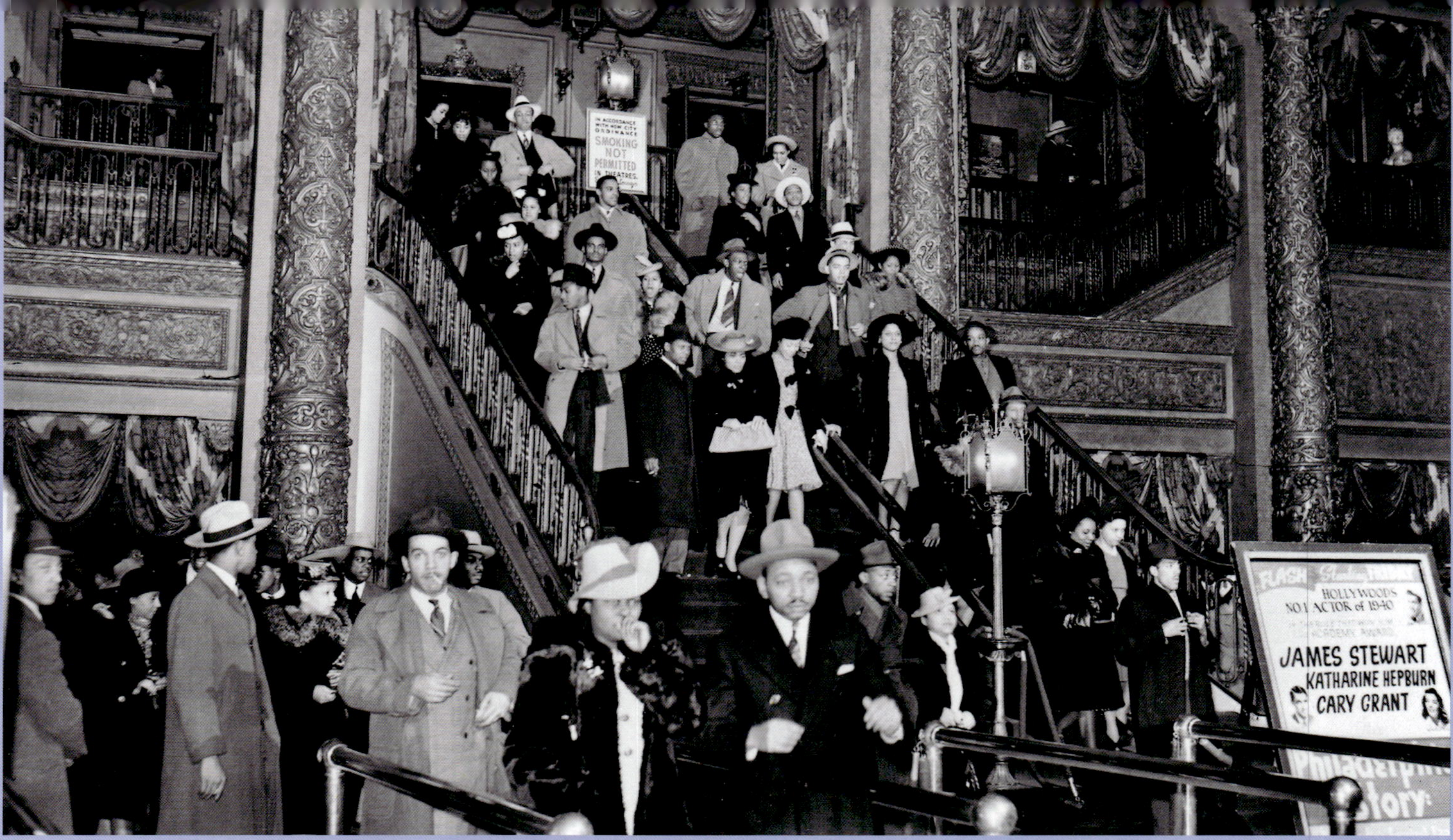
SMOKING NOT PERMITTED
HOLLYWOODS
NO.1 ACTOR of 1940
JAMES STEWART
KATHARINE HEPBURN
CARY GRANT

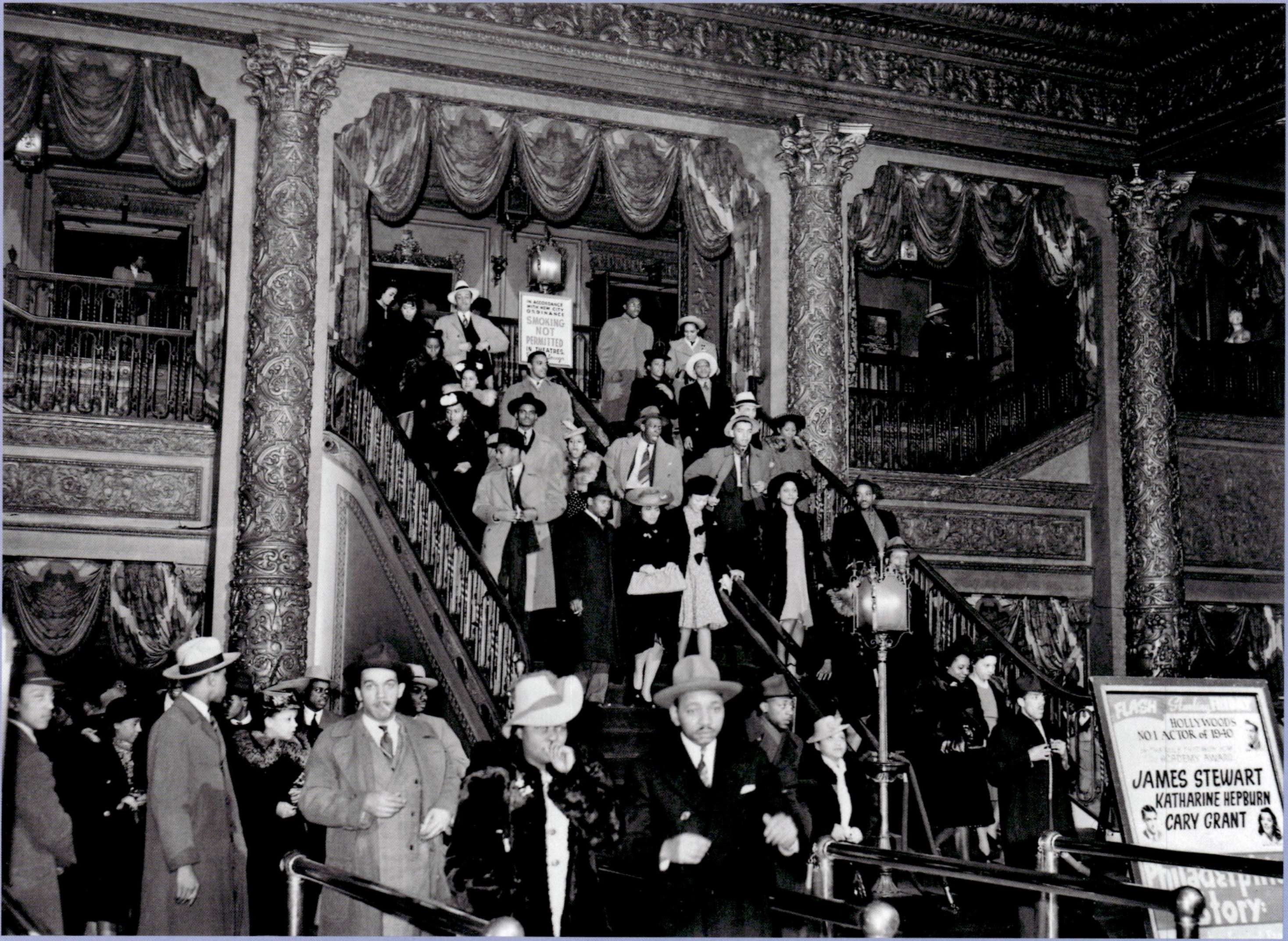
SMOKING NOT PERMITTED
HOLLYWOODS
NO.1 ACTOR of 1940
JAMES STEWART
KATHARINE HEPBURN
CARY GRANT

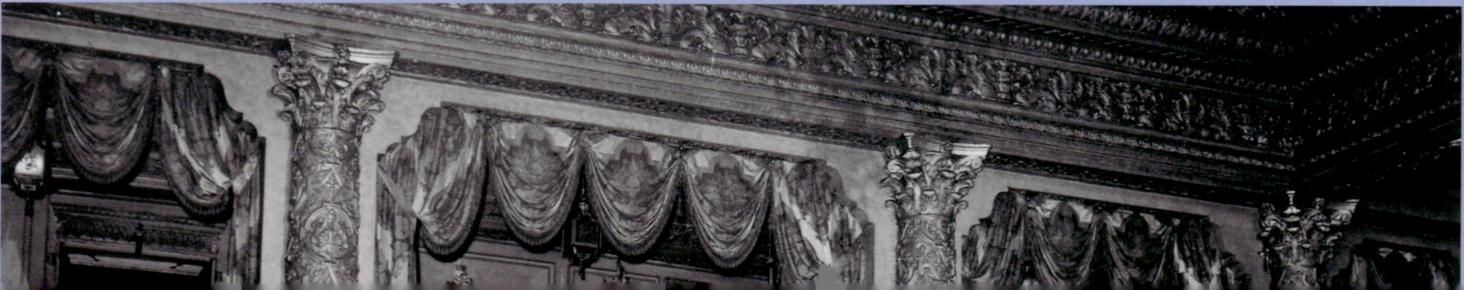

Interior lobby, Regal Theater, Chicago, 1941

The three-thousand-seat theater, located in the historically African American Bronzeville neighborhood, presented motion pictures and stage shows featuring entertainers such as Cab Calloway, Duke Ellington, and Ella Fitzgerald.

CULTIVATING BLACK AUDIENCES

Between 1909 and 1948 more than 150 independent companies attempted to produce, create, and distribute Black-cast films, or race movies. Many Black filmmakers endeavored to generate work that would provide a counternarrative to the more stereotypical presentations of African Americans, a movement that Field has identified as "uplift cinema."[35] Brothers Noble M. and George P. Johnson established the Lincoln Motion Picture Company in Los Angeles in 1915.[36] The following year they expanded, opening a facility in Omaha. George P. Johnson stated: "[Instead of] a lot of slapstick, chicken-eating, watermelon Negro pictures like they had been making . . . we made something that had never been made before. . . . We were pioneers."[37] The creative efforts of these visionary entrepreneurs were not completely devoid of stereotypical aspects, but they did offer an array of cinematic experiences and genres directed primarily toward Black audiences while also providing opportunities for actors who might otherwise have been strictly relegated to racist character types—or excluded completely. By presenting a variety of cinematic expressions, these movies, at the very least, challenged the more pervasive attitudes of white filmmakers.

Although the trailblazing efforts of Foster and the Johnsons were cut short for a variety of reasons, primarily a lack of funding, Oscar Micheaux—born the same year as Foster, 1884—managed to produce, write, and direct more than forty films examining some of the most pressing issues of the time. Often developing his stories from current headlines, Micheaux, along with many other Black pioneering filmmakers, used the art form of film to challenge some of the cultural and social mores within the African American community. Micheaux's directorial approach was daring and nuanced, complicated by its use of a type of Black visual satire that the art historian Richard J. Powell associates with African American creators whose critiques not only target racism but are also "frequently directed at the black community itself."[38] As with Foster and the Johnsons, Micheaux also gave young actors and actresses opportunities. For instance, Paul Robeson's first role was in Micheaux's film *Body and Soul* (1925), which centers on a corrupt preacher and his relationship with his gullible churchgoers. Robeson would go on to star in a total of twelve films, roles he might not have received without getting his first break in a film produced, directed, and written by a Black filmmaker.

Men were not the only individuals creating films during this period. In many instances, wives were uncredited producing partners and codirectors. Recent film scholarship has uncovered at least eight Black women who made films during the silent era. Jennie Louise Touissant Welcome (also known as Madame E. Touissant Welcome), sister of the Harlem-based photographer James Van der Zee, worked with her husband to produce a documentary on Black soldiers serving in World War I called *Doing Their Bit* (1918). Tressie Souders is credited with directing *A Woman's Error* (1922), the first feature known to have been made by an African American woman, and contracting for its distribution.[39] *Motherhood: Life's Greatest Miracle* (1925) by Lita Lawrence is another early feature directed by an African American woman.[40] Maria P. Williams published her own newspaper, the *Woman's Voice*, and was a public speaker and social activist before turning to filmmaking. Along with her husband, she owned Western Film Producing Company and is credited with writing, producing, and acting in *The Flames of Wrath* (1923). During this time the lines of producing and directing were porous, however, and some suggest that her responsibilities were more extensive.[41] Another underrecognized film artist is Alice B. Russell, Micheaux's second wife. She started out as an actor and was credited as a producer on three of her husband's films. She, too, is believed to have had an even more substantial role in his film productions.[42]

There were also white entrepreneurs who recognized that there was an underrepresented segment of society interested in seeing themselves on-screen. *Lime Kiln Club Field Day* (1913), discussed in Ron Magliozzi's essay in this volume, was never completed but stands as an early example of a Black-cast film with an interracial crew. Richard E. Norman Jr. was a white producer who dedicated several years of his career to making race films.[43] He started out during the 1910s as a producer of white-cast "home talent" pictures, traveling throughout the Midwest. The producers of these films recruited and nurtured local actors, writers, and directors to make movies primarily for rural audiences. Norman eventually returned to his native Florida, which was a thriving place for movie production at the time, and shifted his focus to developing films for the underserved and often overlooked African American audience. It is likely that during his years producing home talent films, he traveled through

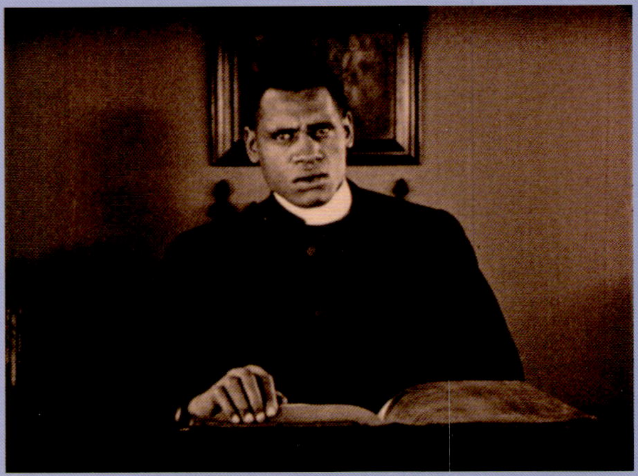

Paul Robeson in *Body and Soul* (dir. Oscar Micheaux, 1925), film still

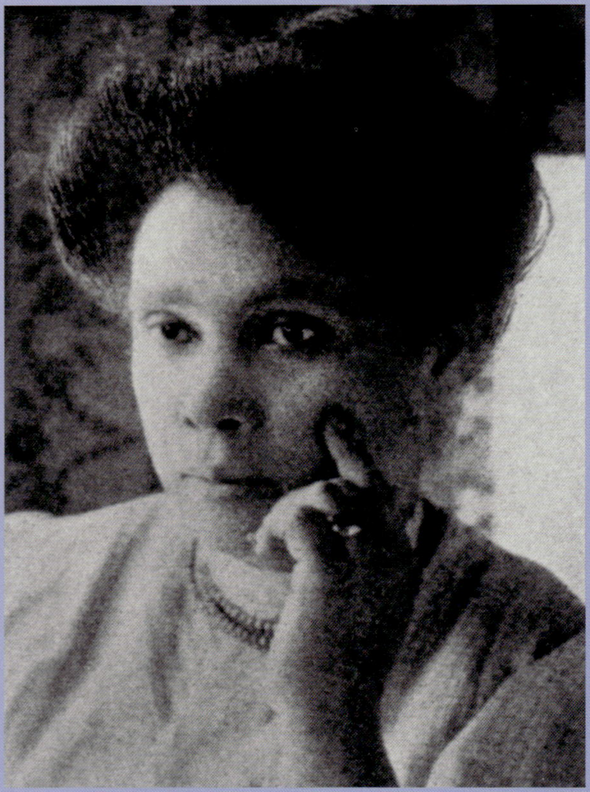

Maria P. Williams, 1916

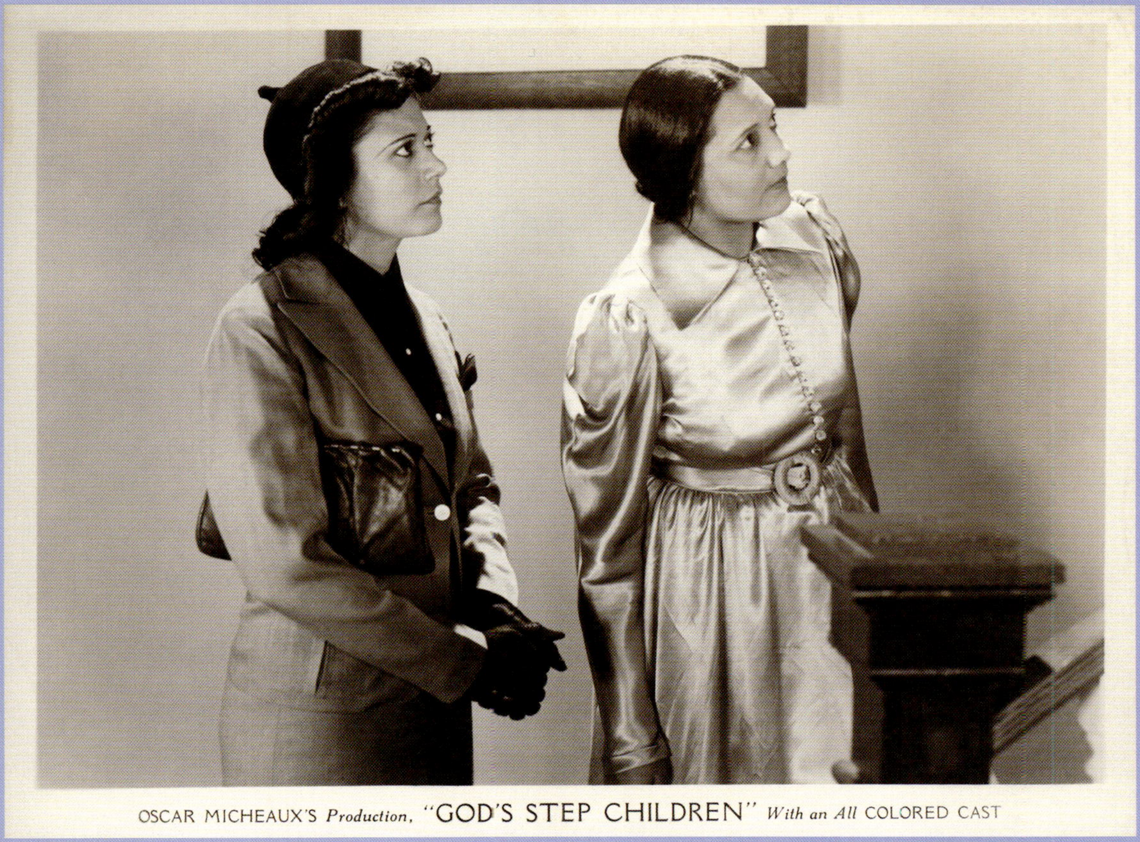

Ethel Moses (left) and Alice B. Russell in
God's Stepchildren (1938), production still

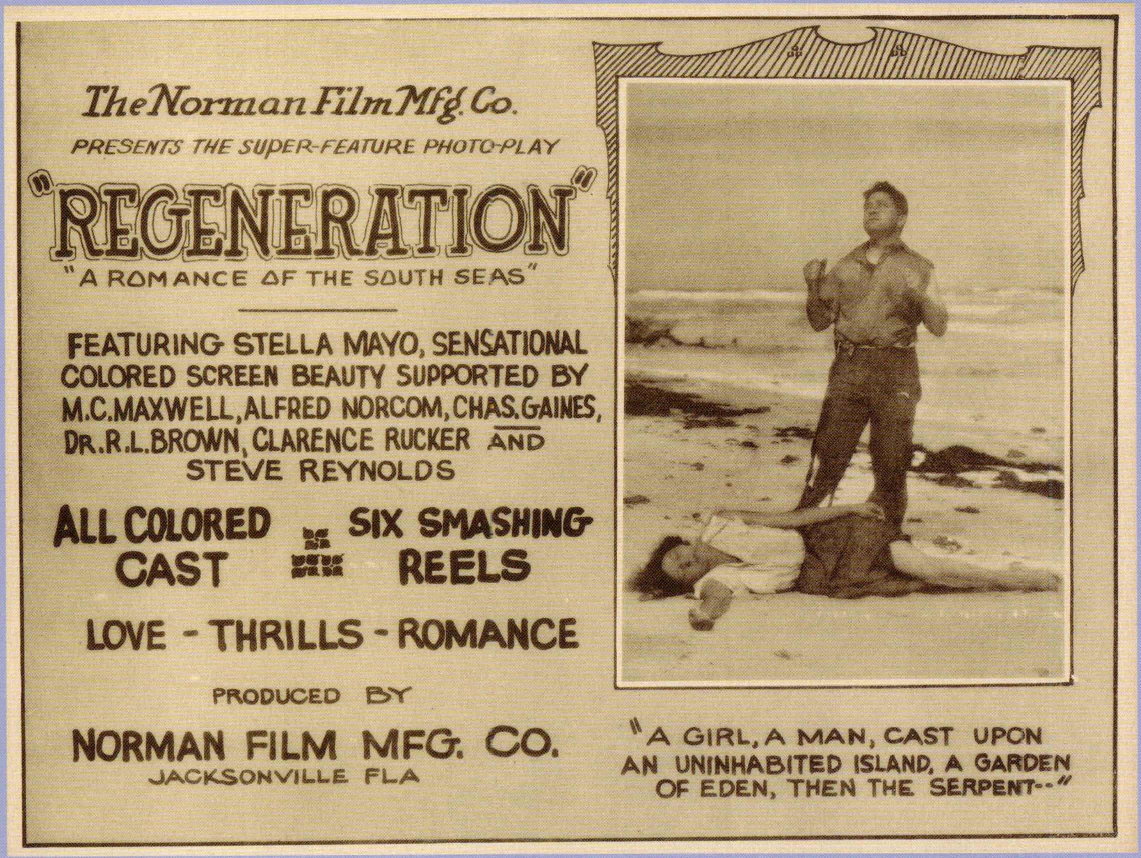

Regeneration (1923),
lobby card

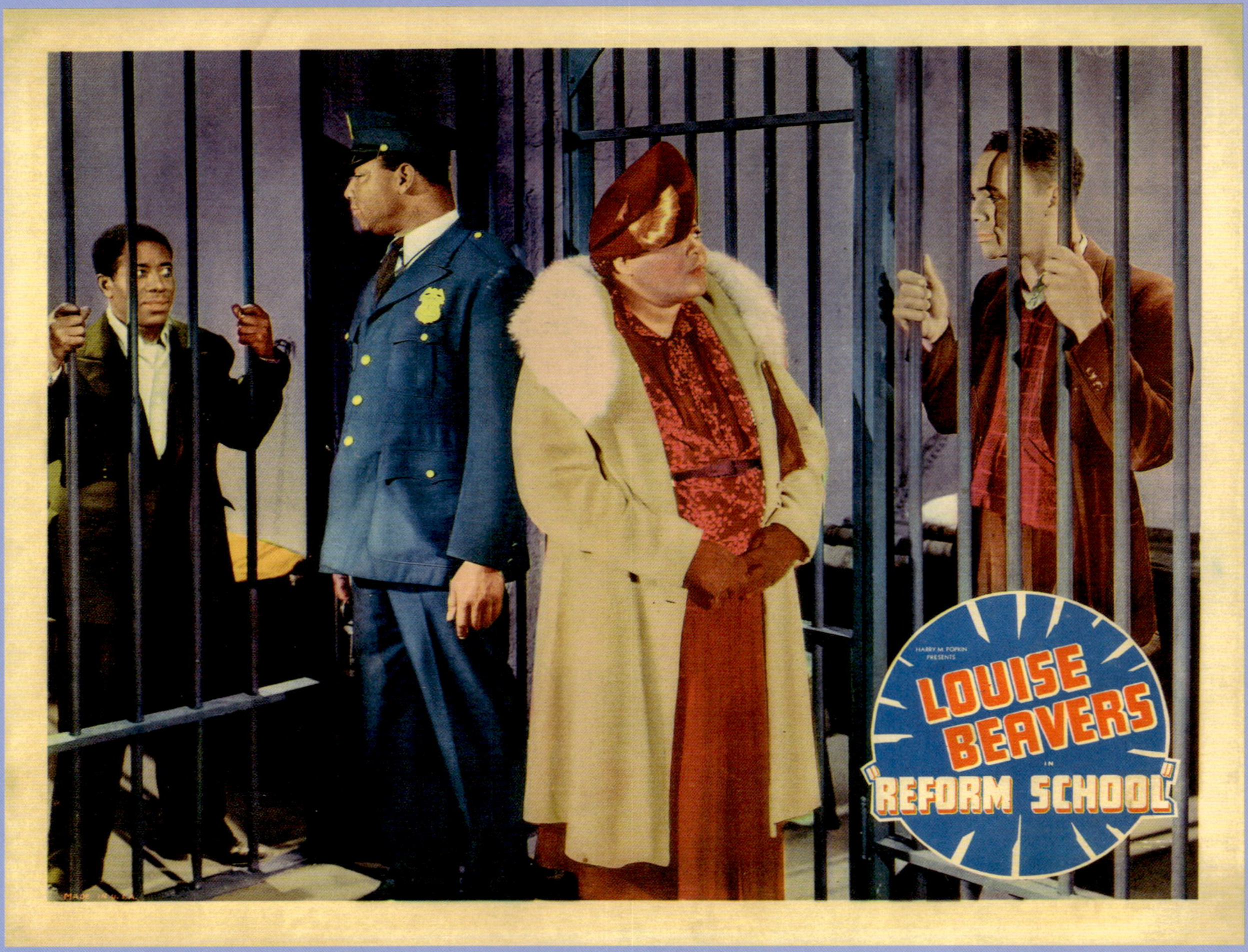
LOUISE
BEAVERS
"REFORM SCHOOL"

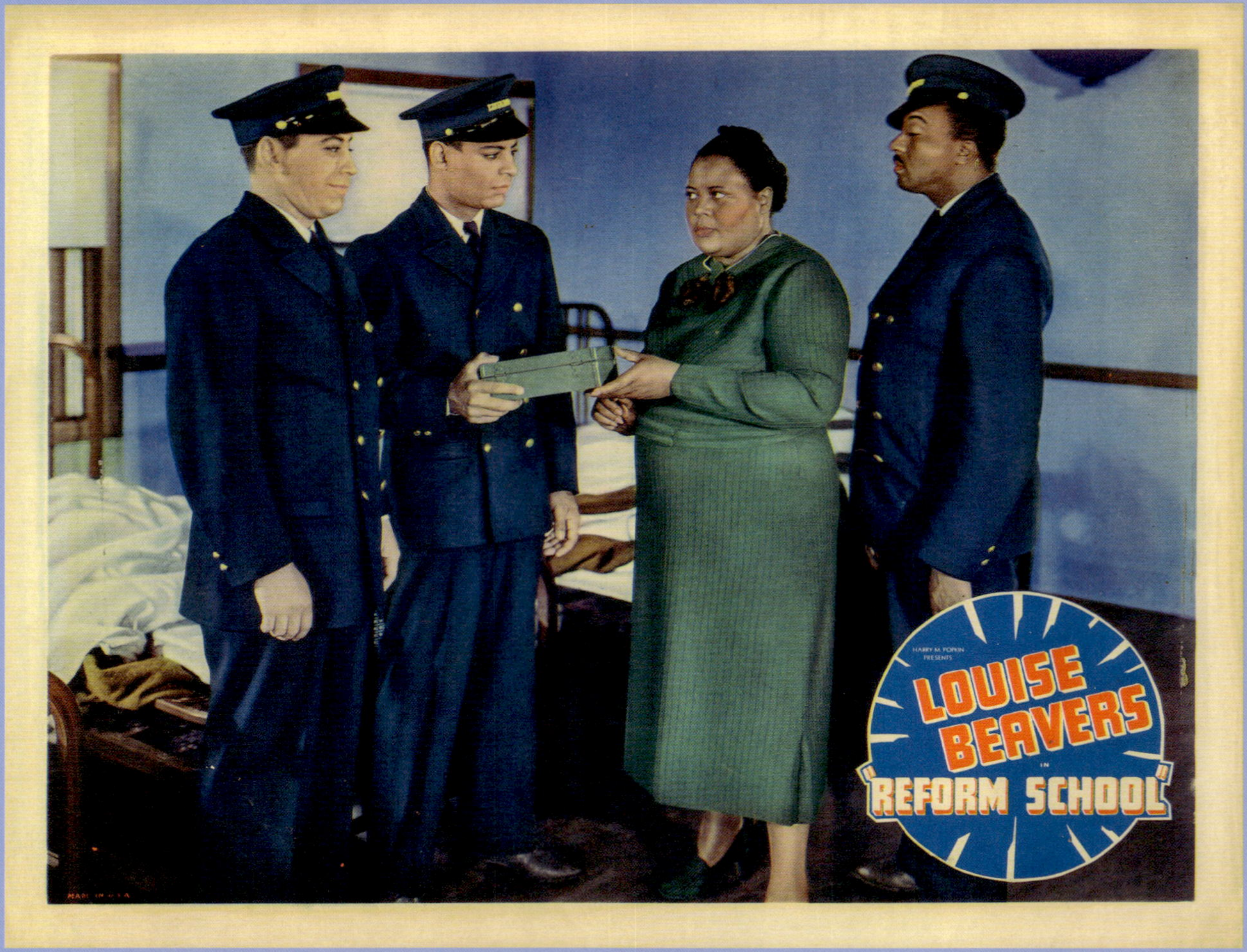
LOUISE
BEAVERS
"REFORM SCHOOL"

rural towns that had large African American communities and perceived this demographic as an untapped film market. When he returned to Florida, he produced and distributed seven popular films with the Norman Film Manufacturing Company before the development of sound productions curtailed his ability to make movies. His works revolved around people and topics important to the Black community. He featured the African American rodeo champion Bill Pickett in *The Bull-Dogger* (1921) and made the mystery and adventure film *The Flying Ace* (1926), loosely based on the inspirational life of Bessie Coleman, the first African American woman pilot with an international pilot's license. His film *Regeneration* (1923)—pitched as a "romance of the south seas" with an "all-colored cast," including Stella Mayo as lead—was extremely popular with both Black and white audiences, who lined up for blocks to see it.[44] Only portions of this film currently survive, a fate shared by many independent race films. The existing footage offers a glimpse into this lesser-known history as well as insights into how African American artists and integrated production crews worked to bring ambitious projects to fruition during some of the most racially stratified periods in American history. These films are reminders that even under such conditions, people found a way to live, work, and create art together.

From Jacksonville to Chicago to parts of Oklahoma to San Antonio and westward to Los Angeles, films in all genres featuring all-Black casts that told nuanced stories with complex characters were being produced. The production of race movies continued well into the 1940s, providing opportunities for enterprising directors who were masterful at creating films informed by an insider's knowledge of the cultural mores of the African American community, among them Spencer Williams Jr.[45] Popular movies including *The Duke Is Tops* (1938), which featured the multitalented Ralph Cooper and the film debut of Lena Horne, and *Reform School* (1939), starring Louise Beavers, provided good, steady work for African American actors in roles distinct from those offered by Hollywood productions.

Consistent with laws and social norms, however, movie sets as well as theaters were often segregated. And for many moviegoers, the all-Black spaces likely felt safer than sitting in a cramped balcony or a separate section of the theater. Churches, community centers, open-air pop-up theaters, and "all-Black" nights provided opportunities for entrepreneurial filmmakers to market and promote their films. Attendees could watch films and laugh at race-specific inside jokes, which reflect the complicated relationship many African American performers and moviegoers experienced while simultaneously navigating the restrictions of segregation. Gary Simmons's large-scale sculpture *Balcony Seating Only* (2017)—inspired by a historical photograph of the exterior of a segregated theater in Anniston, Alabama, depicting signage that indicates a separate entrance for people of color—elicits a visceral reaction.

Balcony Seating Only is part of a body of work dating to the 1990s that, in the words of the curator Thelma Golden, "min[es] the iconography of oppression and hate. Symbols of domination, segregation, and the Ku Klux Klan appear in drawings and sculptures."[46] By employing his "erasure drawing" technique in a sculpture of a life-size staircase, Simmons rendered the word *colored* as a ghostlike memory of the past. When the work is seen next to the historical photograph, however, the smudging of the letters makes the effects on a segregated moviegoing audience painfully present. "The physical act of Simmons's erasure of problematic images further underscores its transformative power," as the late Maurice Berger observed. "Simmons's work both transgresses and reiterates the power of these offensive icons, blurring them while at the same time underscoring their persistence and inevitability."[47]

Gary Simmons (American, b. 1964), *Balcony Seating Only*, 2017, oil paint on aluminum, steel, 156 × 192 × 30 in. (396.2 × 487.7 × 76.2 cm)

Installation view, Regen Projects, 2017

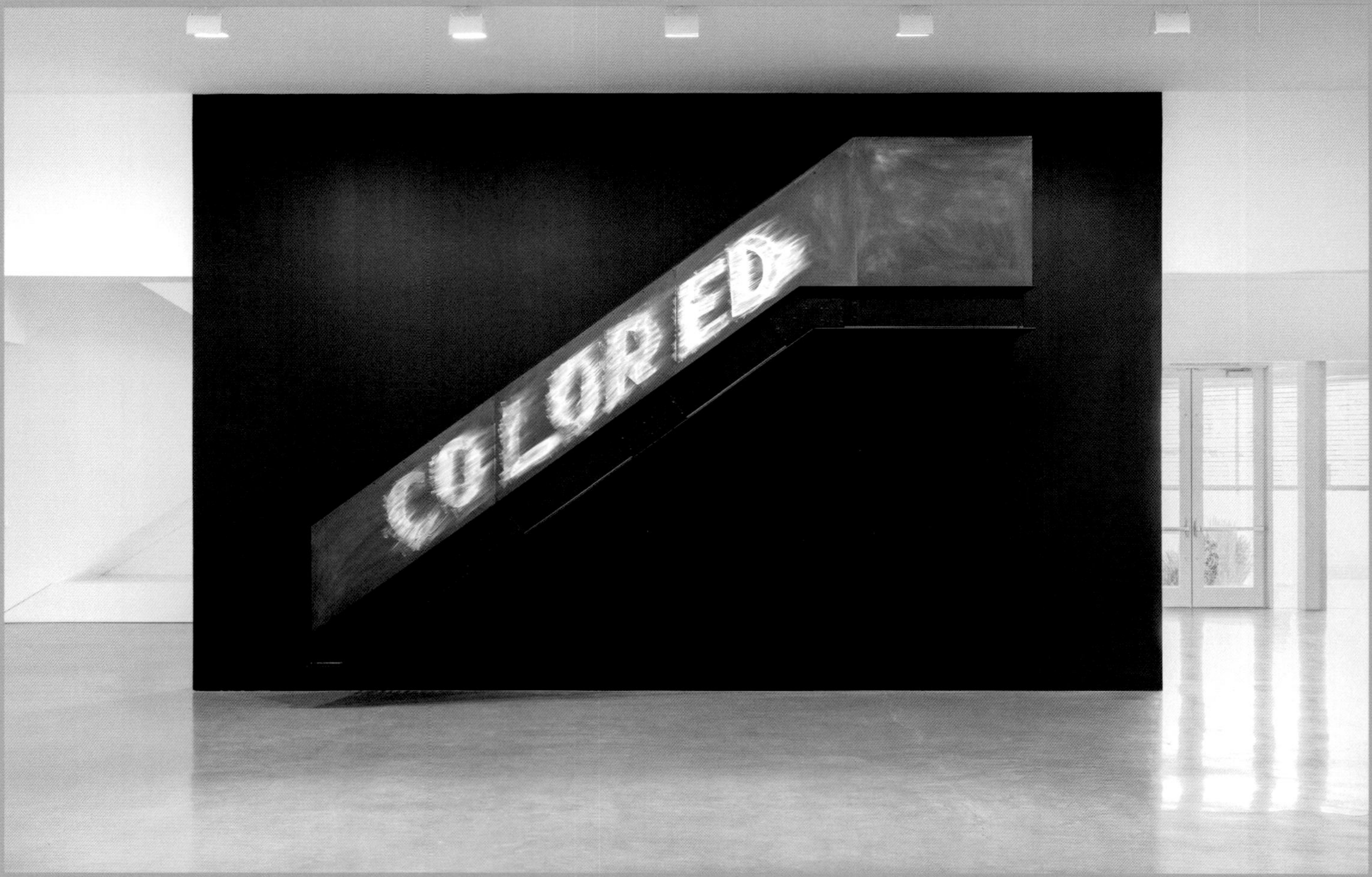

Peter Sekaer (Danish, 1901–1950), *Anniston, Alabama*, 1936, gelatin silver print, 7 ¼ × 9 ½ in. (18.4 × 24.1 cm)

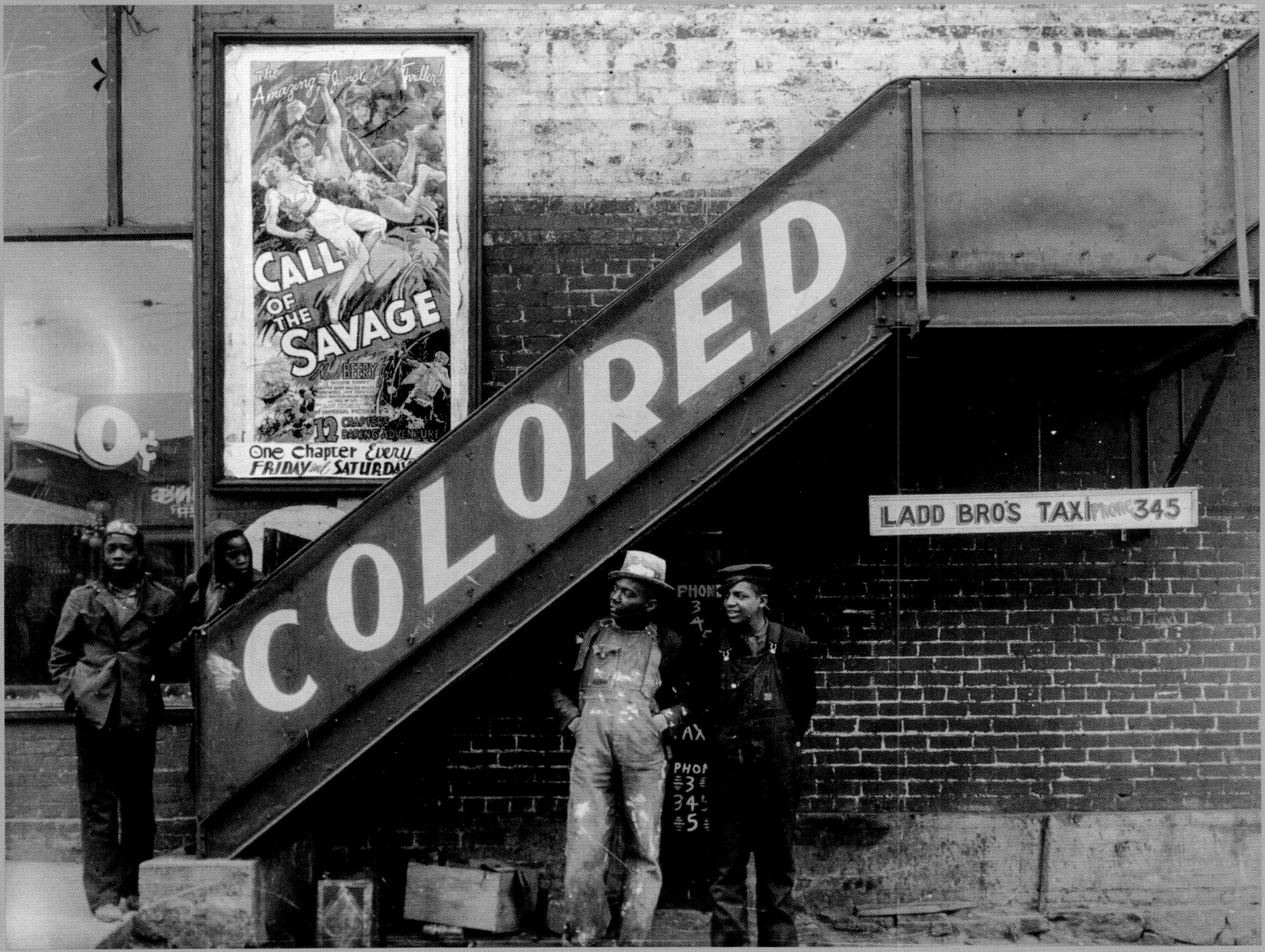

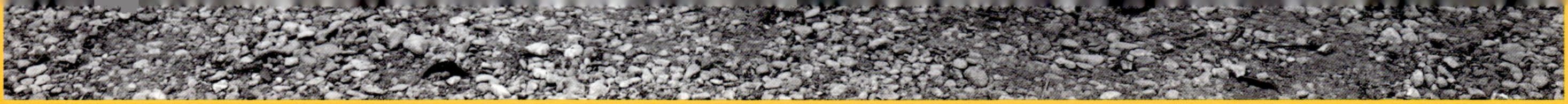

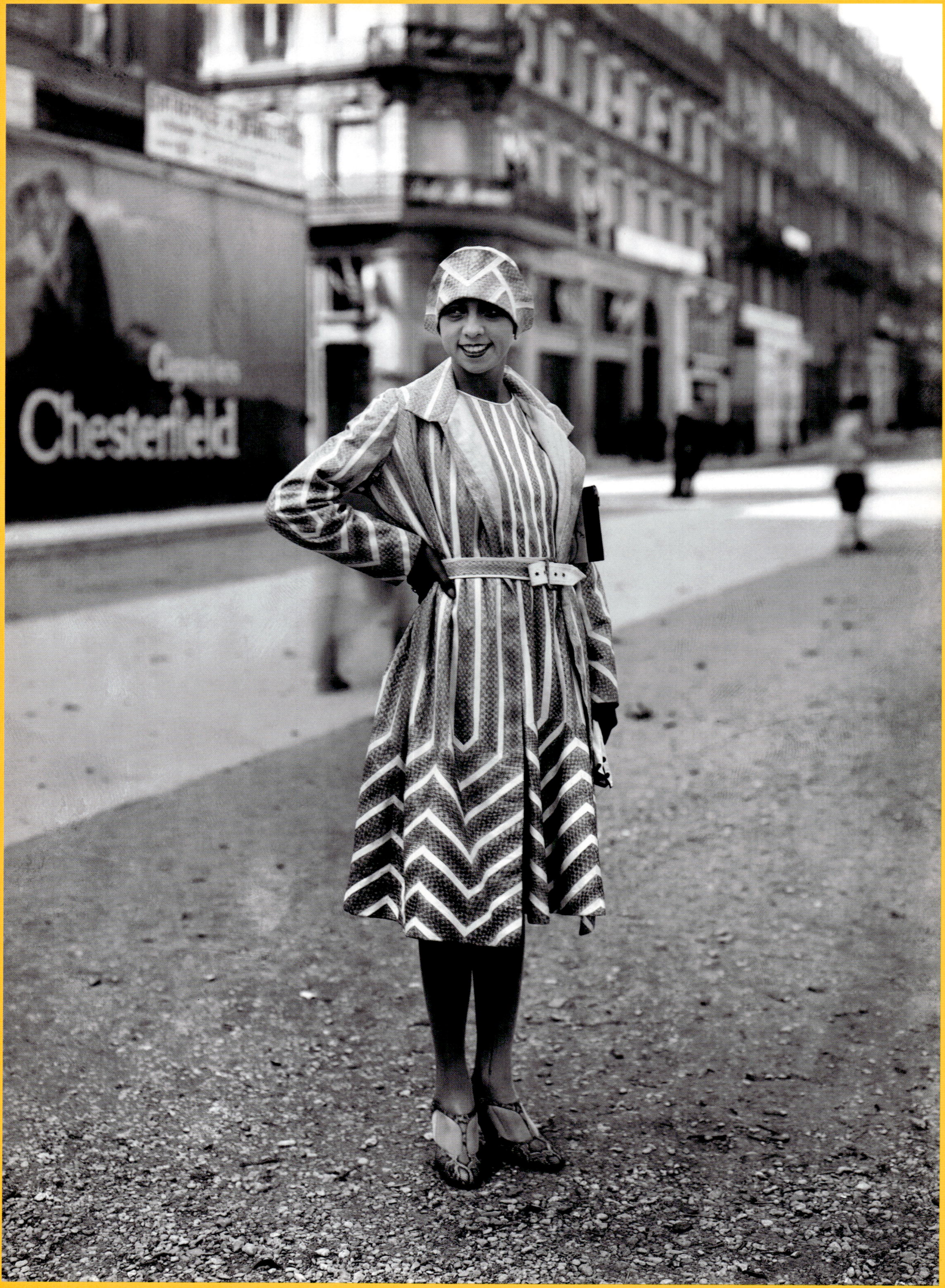
Chesterfield

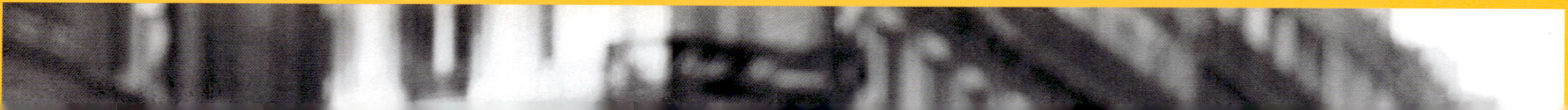

INTERLUDE: BLACK EUROPE

During the 1920s and 1930s, a few Black performers left the United States and found more fulfilling careers in Europe. Paris, London, and Berlin (pre-1933) were entertainment hubs that offered spaces for cultural production that welcomed African American artists, entertainers, and intellectuals, and some of them became major stars. While Europe was not without racism and was entangled with colonialist power dynamics, there was no legal segregation, and Black entertainers were offered a wider spectrum of opportunities, even though they often had to navigate being exoticized and were performing for mostly white audiences. When looking back at the 1920s and 1930s in particular, the situation was even more complicated, as Carole Sweeney has observed: "Most striking of all perhaps is the fact that a popular cultural negrophilia existed alongside a gradual resurgence of aggressively xenophobic nationalism in France."[48]

Despite fraught circumstances, entertainers such as Josephine Baker and Nina Mae McKinney, the writers Richard Wright and James Baldwin, and jazz musicians including Arthur Briggs and Sidney Bechet found opportunities, especially in Paris, that they wouldn't have had in the United States during that time. The presence of African Americans in Paris has often been understood as "a commentary on race," as Tyler Stovall writes: "Some blacks left the United States expressly to escape the burdens of discrimination and came to Paris as self-conscious refugees from racism. . . . The myth of color-blind France is complex and flawed. Nevertheless it has exercised a

I thought I could do something for the Negro race in the films: show the truth about them—about other people, too.

—Paul Robeson (1937)

powerful attraction upon both black Americans and the French themselves."[49]

Josephine Baker became a star in Paris and remains an icon.[50] Born in Saint Louis, Missouri, in 1906, she began her career as a dancer in New York and was invited to come to Paris to perform in *La revue nègre* at the Théâtre des Champs-Elysées in 1925. She quickly became the main attraction. Her fame was built on fantasies of non-Western cultures, and she created an exoticized image of herself through her sexualized dance moves, costumes, and characters. Baker played the lead role in four feature films made in France between 1927 and 1945. While the entertainer would never appear in an American film, Terri Simone Francis, who discusses Baker's career trajectory and influence in this volume, argues that including her films in the discourse on Black film and modernity offers a new perspective.[51]

Baker was repeatedly on the cover of the most popular movie magazines in France and was at one point the richest Black woman in the world.[52] During World War II she fought against the Nazis in the French Resistance, for which she was awarded a medal of honor by General Charles de Gaulle. After the war she bought the castle Les Milandes in the Dordogne region of France, where she built a new life and purpose around multiculturalism. She adopted twelve children from different ethnic, cultural, and religious backgrounds and countries, referring to them as "the rainbow tribe,"[53] and planned to build a theme park on the grounds of her castle.[54] Baker also leveraged her fame to advocate for political and social causes, promoting humanity, equality, and multiculturalism around the world.

Another important star who had an international career was Paul Robeson. Born in 1898 in Princeton, New Jersey, Robeson was an athlete at Rutgers University and went to law school at Columbia, graduating with high honors. Following his film debut in Micheaux's *Body and Soul*, he went on to have a substantial singing and acting career in theater and films in the United States and Europe, most notably in England and Wales (see Ellen C. Scott's essay on Robeson in this volume). The movies he made in Europe had a different focus from that of his American films; many were social dramas with critical undertones, which he preferred. He ended his film career in 1942 but was already

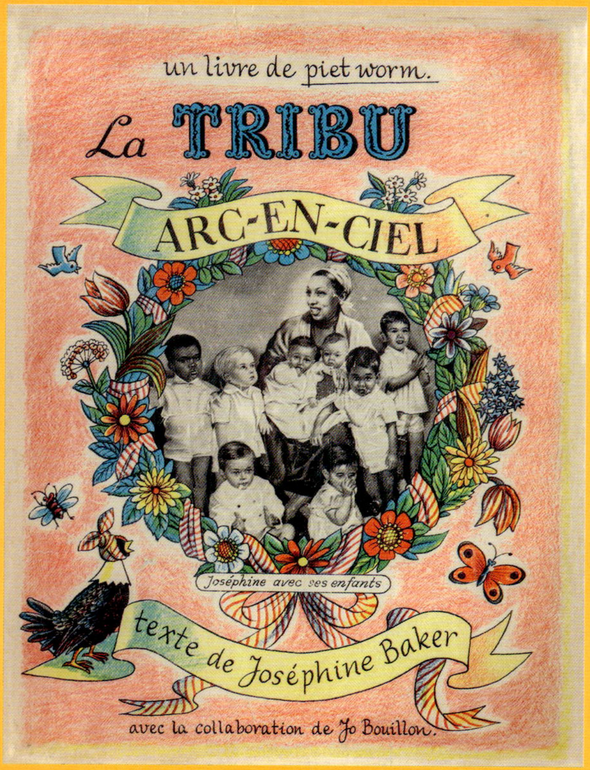

La tribu arc-en-ciel (The rainbow tribe), written by Josephine Baker with Jo Bouillon, illustrated by Piet Worm (Amsterdam: Mulder & Zoon, 1957)

ESSAY
CASE STUDIES
PORTRAITS
FILMOGRAPHY
CHRONOLOGY
INTERVIEWS

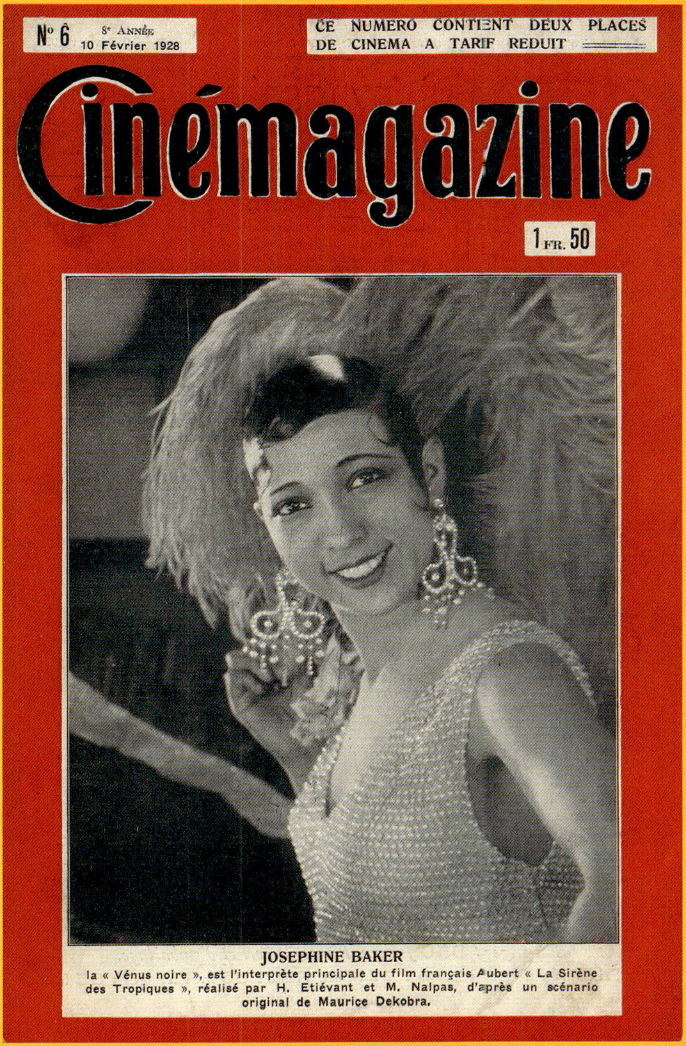

Cinémagazine, no. 6
(February 10, 1928)

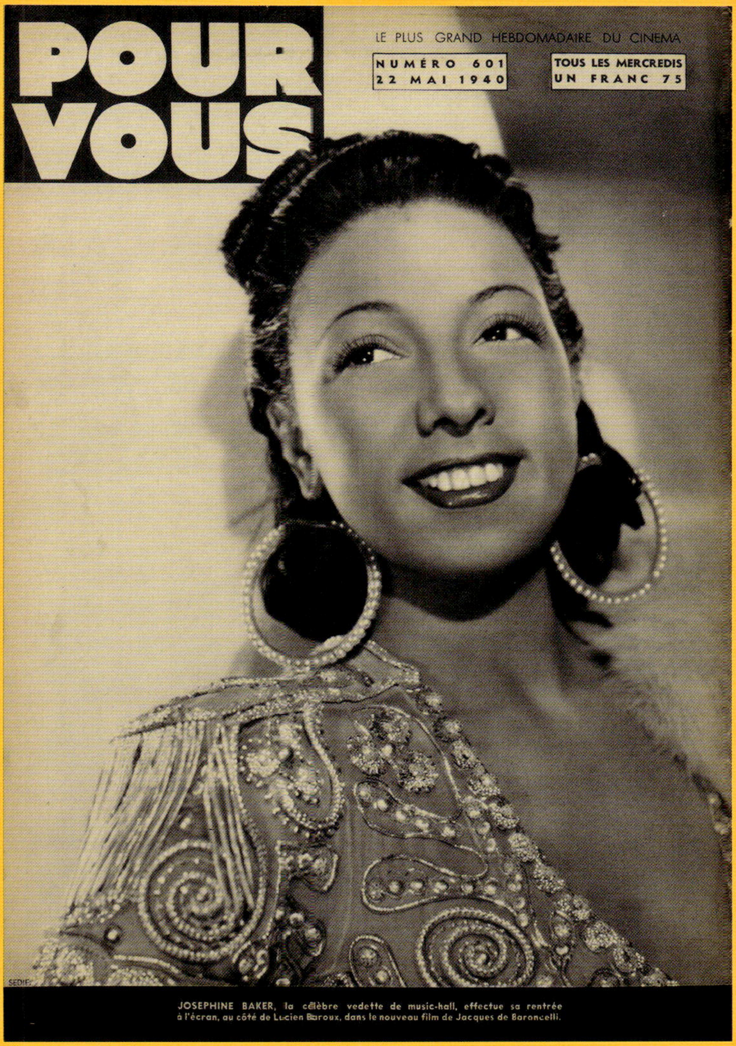

Pour Vous, no. 601
(May 22, 1940)

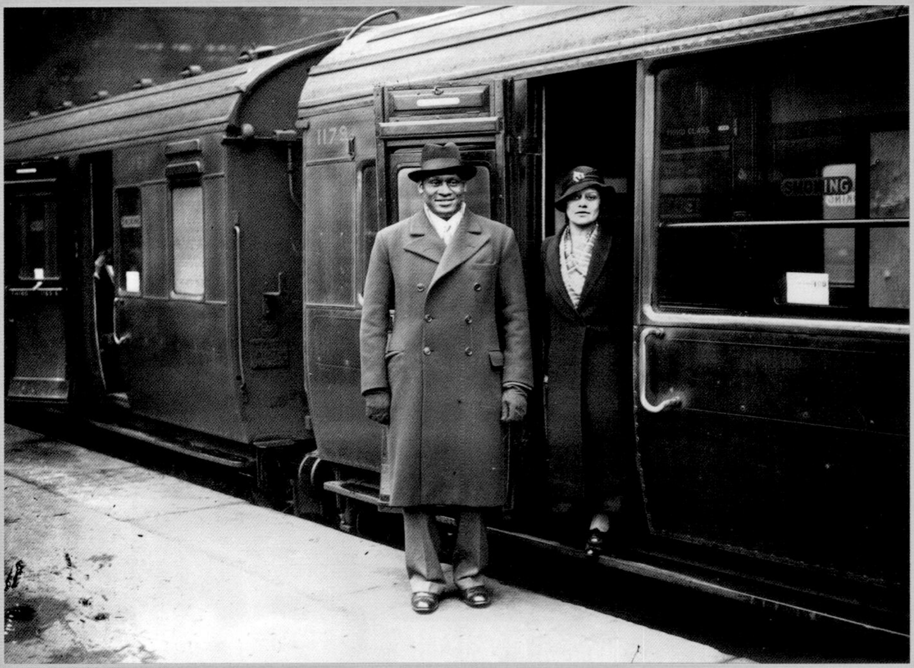

Paul and Eslanda Goode Robeson at Waterloo Station, London, 1933

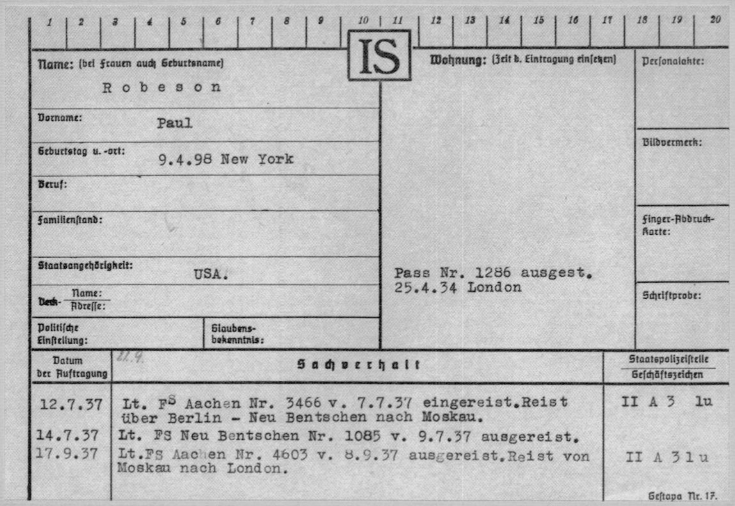

1 2 3 4 5 6 7 8 9 10 11 12 13 14 15 16 17 18 19 20

IS

Name: (bei Frauen auch Geburtsname) R o b e s o n

Vorname: Paul

Geburtstag u. -ort: 9.4.98 New York

Beruf:

Familienstand:

Staatsangehörigkeit: USA.

Verh.- Name: / Adresse:

Politische Einstellung:

Glaubensbekenntnis:

Wohnung: (Zeit d. Eintragung einsetzen)

Pass Nr. 1286 ausgest.
25.4.34 London

Personalakte:

Bildvermerk:

Finger-Abdruck-Karte:

Schriftprobe:

Datum der Auftragung	Sachverhalt	Staatspolizeistelle Geschäftszeichen
12.7.37	Lt. FS Aachen Nr. 3466 v. 7.7.37 eingereist.Reist über Berlin - Neu Bentschen nach Moskau.	II A 3 lu
14.7.37	Lt. FS Neu Bentschen Nr. 1085 v. 9.7.37 ausgereist.	
17.9.37	Lt.FS Aachen Nr. 4603 v. 8.9.37 ausgereist.Reist von Moskau nach London.	II A 3 1 u

Gestapo Nr. 17.

Gestapo surveillance card of Paul Robeson, 1937

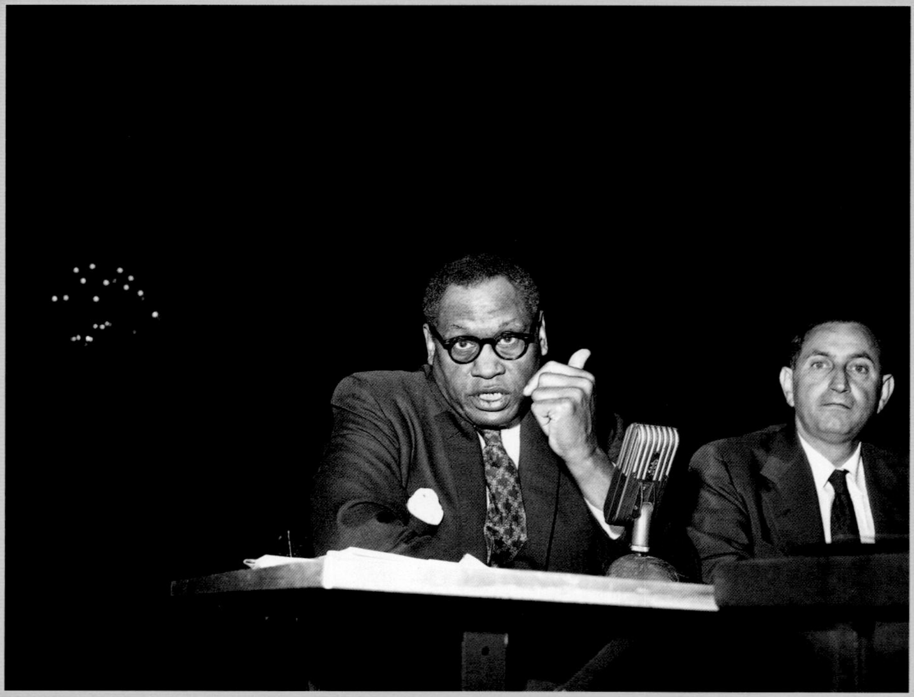

Paul Robeson testifying before the House Un-American Activities Committee, June 13, 1956

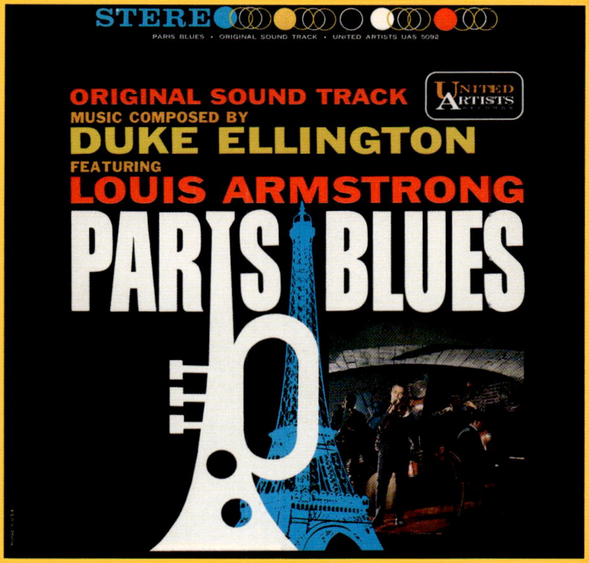

Paris Blues (1961), composed by Duke Ellington, soundtrack album

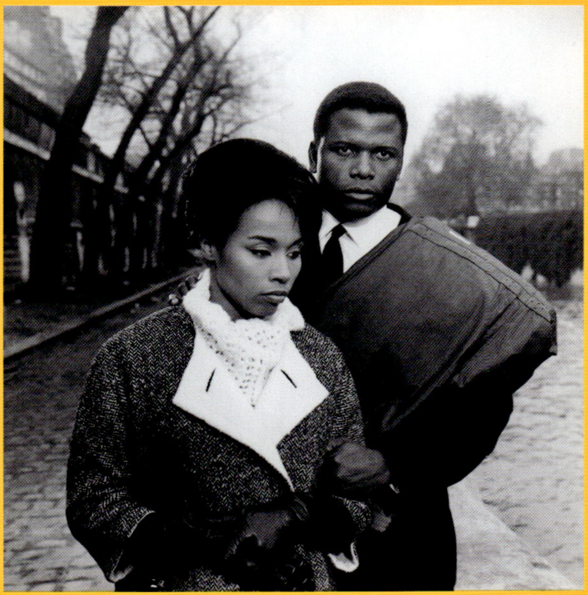

Diahann Carroll and Sidney Poitier in *Paris Blues* (1961), production still

expressing disillusionment with the movie industry in 1937: "I thought I could do something for the Negro race in the films: show the truth about them—about other people, too. . . . One man can't face the film companies. They represent about the biggest aggregate of finance capital in the world: That's why they make their films that way. So no more films for me."[55]

Robeson was also an outspoken activist, calling attention to the injustices Black people had to endure. Long before he was persecuted and blacklisted in the United States for being a communist in the McCarthy era, the Nazis had him on a watchlist in Germany and surveilled him.[56] Robeson's US passport was revoked in 1951, which significantly curtailed his international career and livelihood. Despite not being able to travel abroad for many years, he never gave up fighting for justice and equal rights through his speeches and writings. After he regained his passport in 1958, he picked up his career as a singer and activist in countries of the so-called Eastern Bloc. The German Democratic Republic, for example, not only welcomed him with open arms but also afforded him state honors in 1961, which probably served propaganda purposes as it allowed the communist government to criticize the United States.[57]

The popular notion of Europe, and especially Paris, as a refuge for Black artists and intellectuals retained its allure throughout the twentieth century. Hollywood took up this subject in the feature film *Paris Blues* (1961), which starred Sidney Poitier, Diahann Carroll, Paul Newman, and Joanne Woodward, with a score by Duke Ellington.[58] Louis Armstrong and Aaron Bridgers perform in the film, a nod to the importance of Black musicians to the Paris jazz scene. The film revolves around two expatriate jazz musicians—one Black, one white—who meet two American tourists—one Black, one white. During a stroll through Paris, Poitier and Carroll have a conversation in which they address being Black in France, which meant facing less discrimination than in the United States. Eddie (Poitier) says to Connie (Carroll): "Look, here nobody says Eddie Cook, Negro musician. They say Eddie Cook, musician, period. And that's all I wanna be." This sparks a dialogue about race relations in France and the United States. Such explicitly racialized moments are rare, however, and most of the film misses out on any deeper engagement with race in France or the jazz scene. The script loosely follows Harold Flender's 1957 novel of the same title, which was more nuanced than the movie in its treatment of race relations. In the book the Black character Eddie, not the white character Ram, was the main protagonist. It also included an interracial couple and episodes of racial injustice in France.[59] Andy Fry observes that to downplay the "race problem" in France is typical "not only of fictional approaches to African Americans in Paris but also of many historical ones."[60]

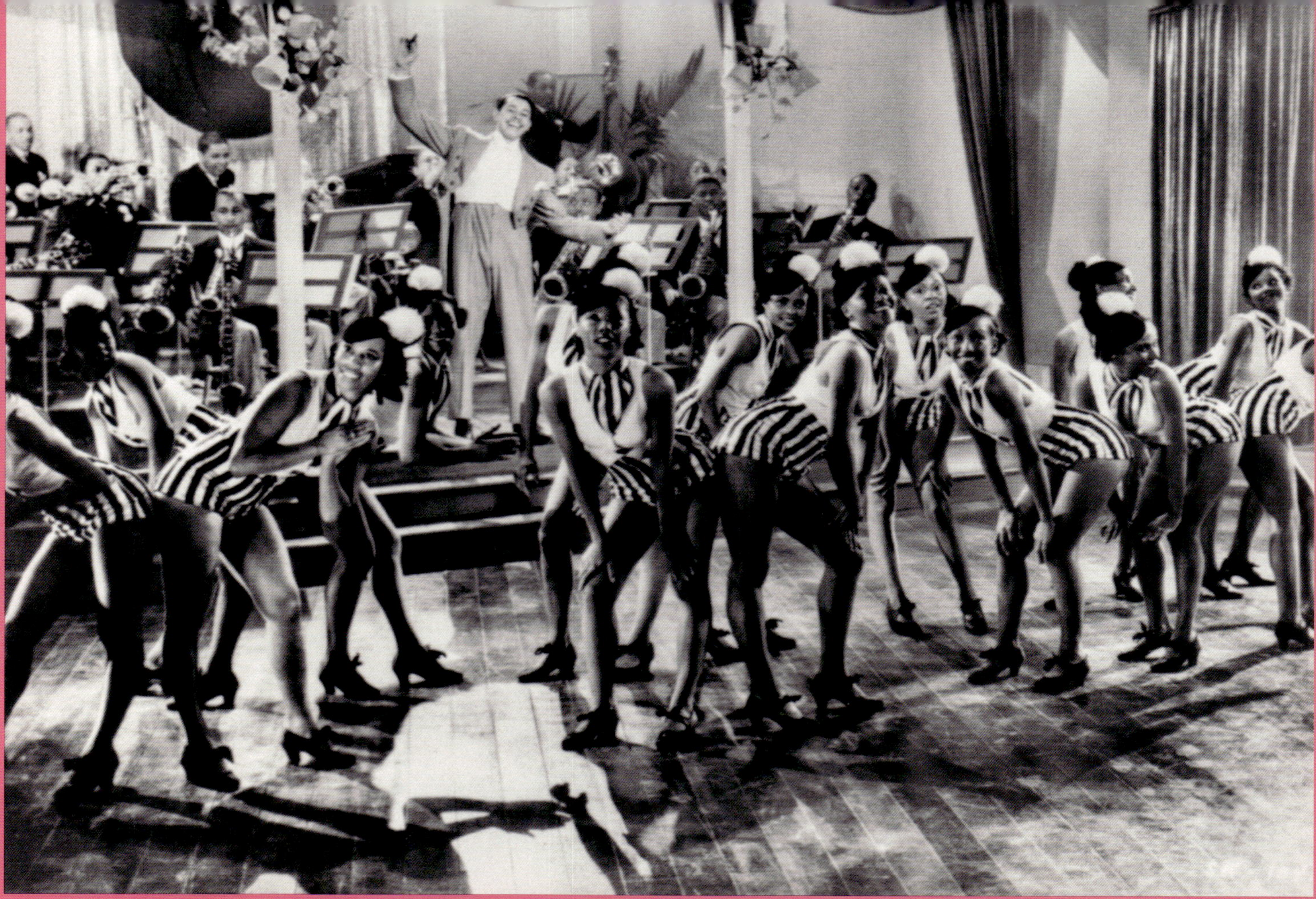

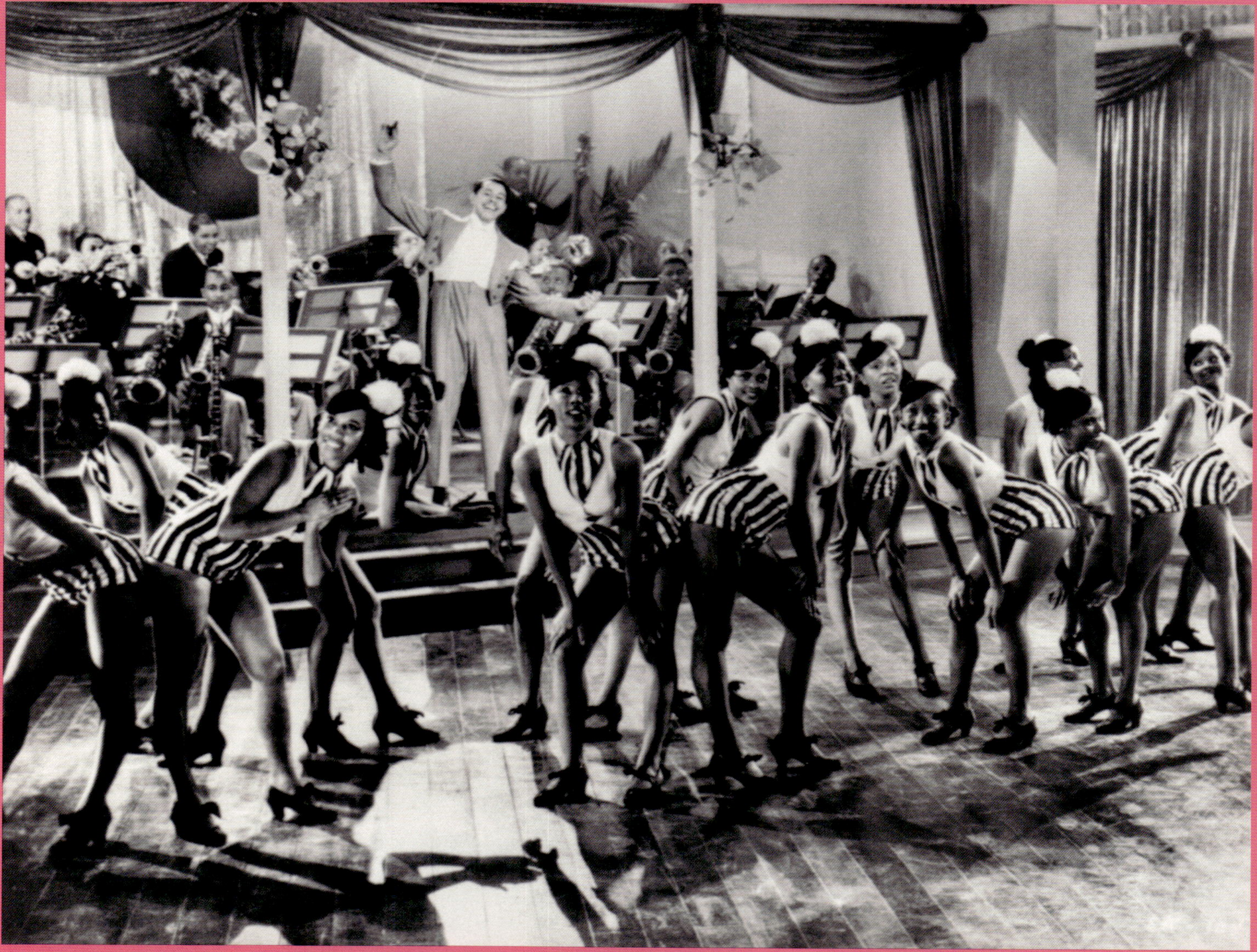

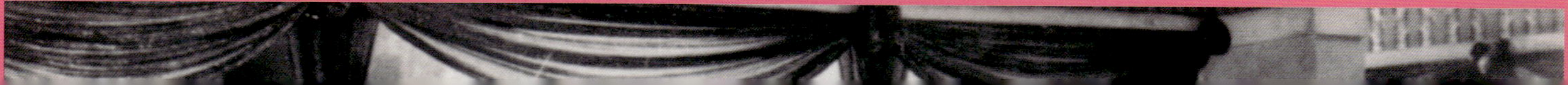

Cab Calloway (onstage, standing), his band, and dancers at the Cotton Club, 1937

BLACK HOLLYWOOD

The period from 1910 through the 1940s in the United States was marked by world wars, race riots, and lynchings, but there were also periods of creativity and opportunity. In the entertainment business of the 1920s and 1930s, despite racial tensions and a depressed economy, many Black writers, musicians, and entertainers thrived even as they relied on white patronage for support or had to cater to all-white audiences in venues like the Cotton Club in Harlem.[61] With advances in moviemaking technology, particularly the introduction of "talkies," the landscape of filmmaking shifted, and Black-cast movies grew in popularity. With the exception of Oscar Micheaux, many of the pioneering African American filmmakers were outpaced by the major studios in terms of budgets, especially as Hollywood started producing sound films that included entertainers and musicians like Duke Ellington, Cab Calloway, Louis Armstrong, and Lena Horne. Some of their appearances were designed strictly as musical interludes that had little to do with the film's narrative arc, making it easier to remove them if needed to accede to the wishes (primarily in the South) of censorship boards.

The years between roughly 1940 and 1947 also saw the emergence and popularization of a new cinematic genre that offered an additional platform for Black talent. Soundies, the precursors of music videos, are three-minute films featuring a song, dance, or musical number.[62] Numerous Black performers—including Ellington, Armstrong, and the singers and musicians Dorothy Dandridge, Nat "King" Cole, Count Basie, and Fats Waller; big bands such as the Cab Calloway Orchestra; and all-female ensembles such as the V's and the International Sweethearts of Rhythm; and dancers like Bill "Bojangles" Robinson—appeared in Soundies. These shorts were shot on 16mm film and projected in Panoram machines made by Mills Novelty Company and installed in bars and other public places. Often designed in elegant art deco style, with a screen at eye level, the machines functioned much like jukeboxes. For one dime, one could not only listen to songs but also watch great performances. Every week a new reel with eight Soundies spliced together was shipped out to Panoram owners, offering an array of musical styles, including many classic jazz and swing numbers. Three production studios—in New York, Chicago, and Hollywood—were recording the reels week by week, producing more than eighteen hundred Soundies during those years. Performances with heightened sex appeal, generally targeted toward the male heterosexual gaze, were a successful recipe for entertainment. When the United States entered the war at the end of 1941, producers of Soundies experienced production difficulties. Nevertheless, the short films reached their peak popularity during the war since they were an affordable form of entertainment offering escapism for troops overseas as well as Americans at home. Once the Office of War Information realized their popularity, the government agency started to produce Soundies with propagandistic content. Another effect of the war was more visibility for women musicians. While men were overseas, women stepped in, and this gave more prominence to female big bands, which had often faced prior discrimination.[63]

Despite the outstanding Black performers who appeared in Soundies, racism and racial segregation were as much a part of Soundie productions as they were of US society in general. Blackface performances, watermelon stage sets, and shoeshine and exoticized jungle themes were among the racist tropes commonly employed. Almost all Soundie productions were segregated, with either all-Black or all-white performers, and when the reels of eight Soundies were distributed, those featuring Black performers were placed at the end.[64] *Regeneration* includes a Panoram machine with a reel of eight exceptional performances featuring exclusively Black musicians. Arguably, Soundies were more of a precursor of television, but they offered another platform, next to the stages of Harlem nightclubs, for Black performers to be discovered by Hollywood's talent scouts.

World War II was a watershed for African Americans. The Double V campaign, which called for victory over enemies abroad and enemies at home, specifically those who were curtailing the freedoms of African Americans, would help lay the groundwork for the civil rights campaigns of the postwar period. The embrace of race films in all genres reflected this

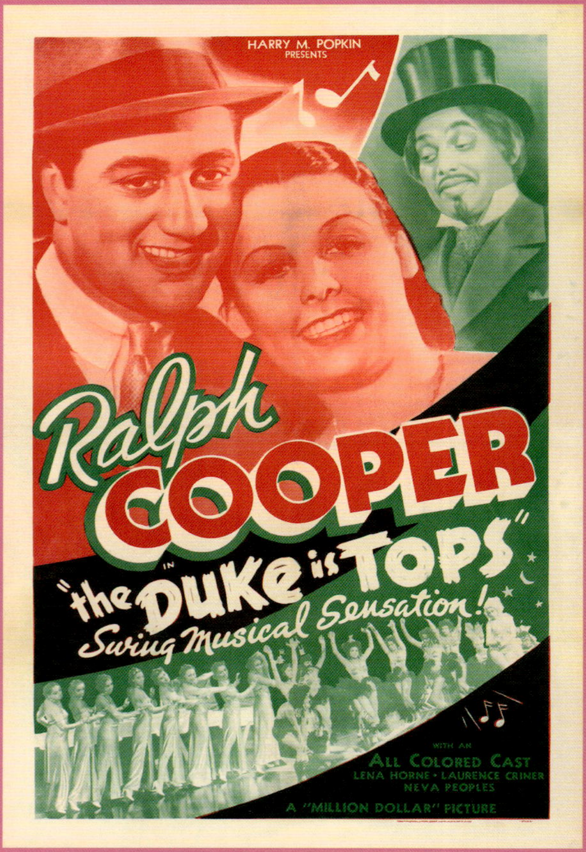

The Duke Is Tops (1938), theatrical release poster

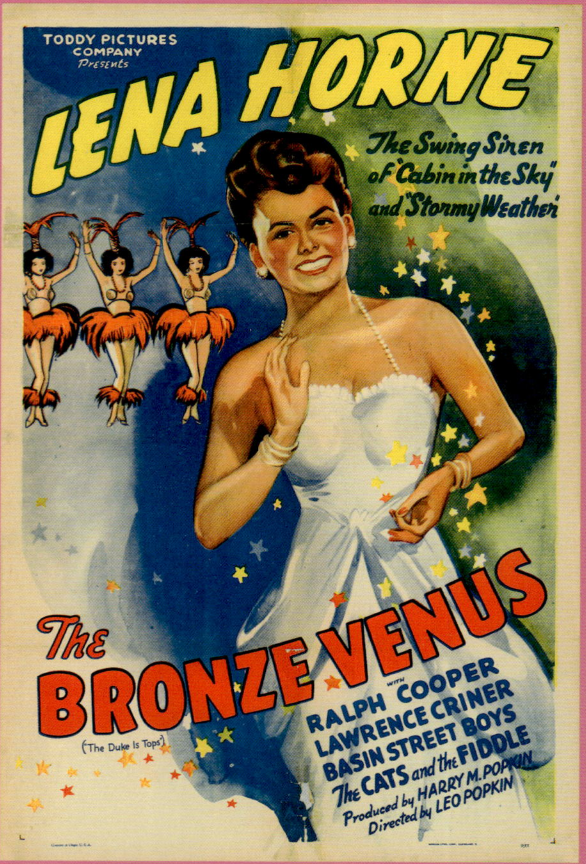

The Bronze Venus (1943), theatrical rerelease poster

E. Simms Campbell's "A Night-Club Map of Harlem," 1932, published in *Manhattan: A Weekly for Wakeful New Yorkers*, January 18, 1933

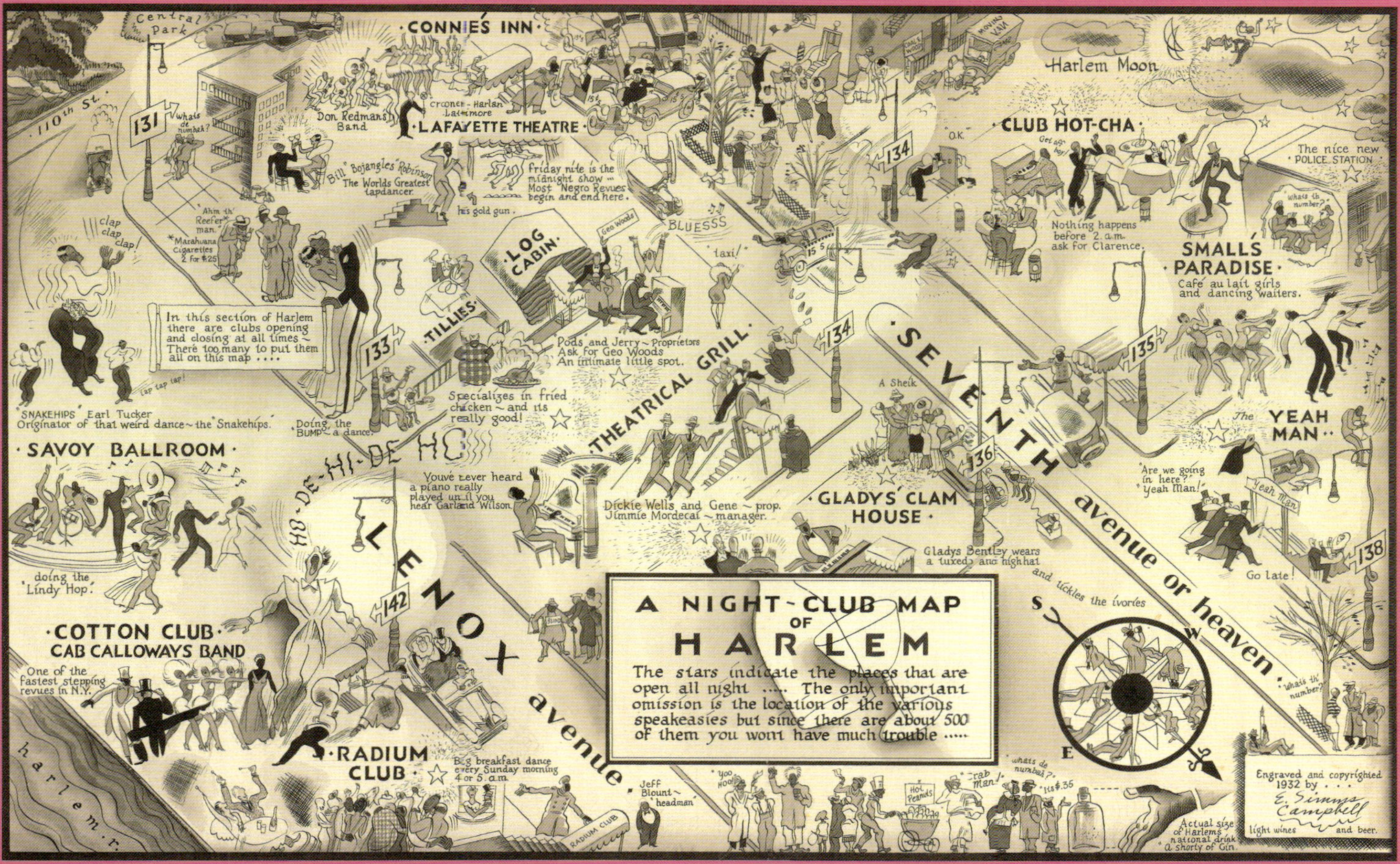

Mills Panoram, ca. 1939

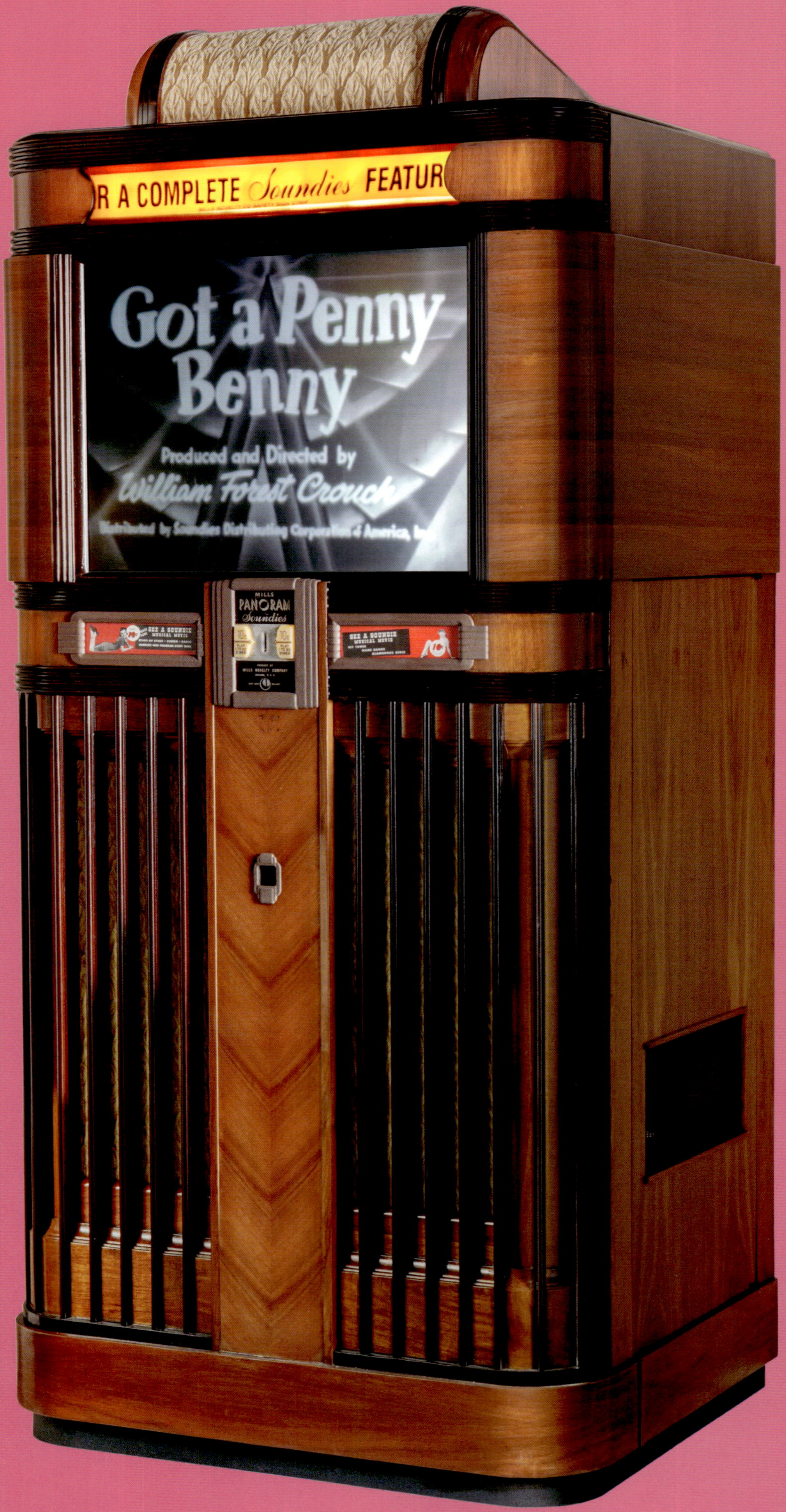

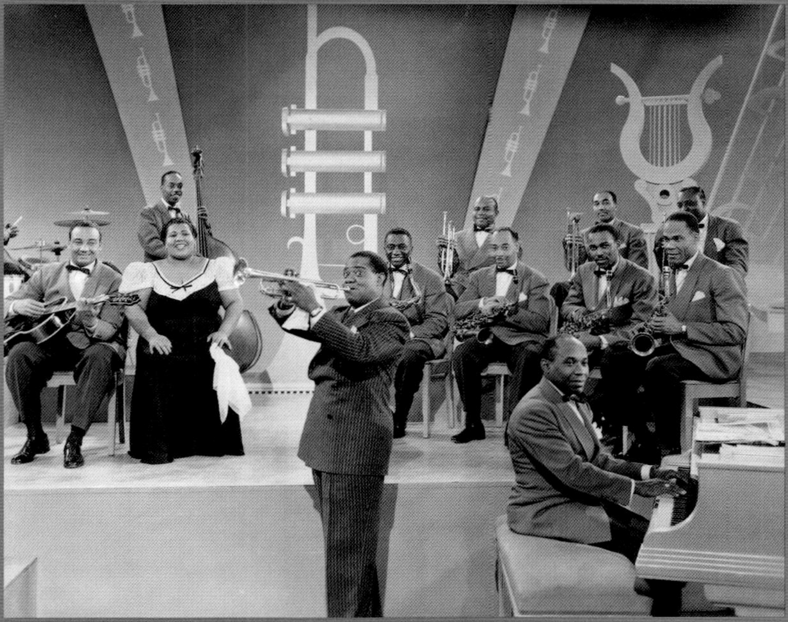

Velma Middleton (left) and Luis Russell (right, at piano) with Louis Armstrong (center) and his orchestra in *Swingin' on Nothin'* (1942), production still

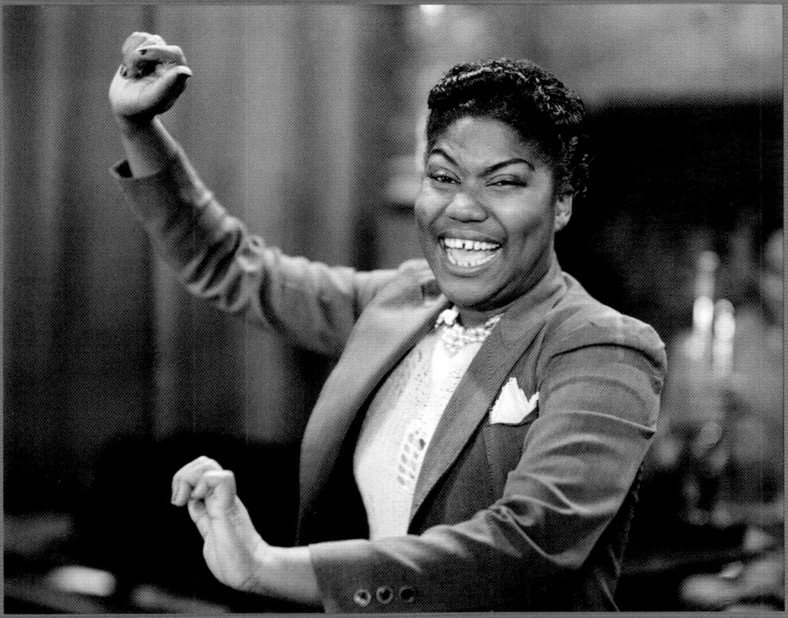

Sister Rosetta Tharpe in *The Lonesome Road* (1941), production still

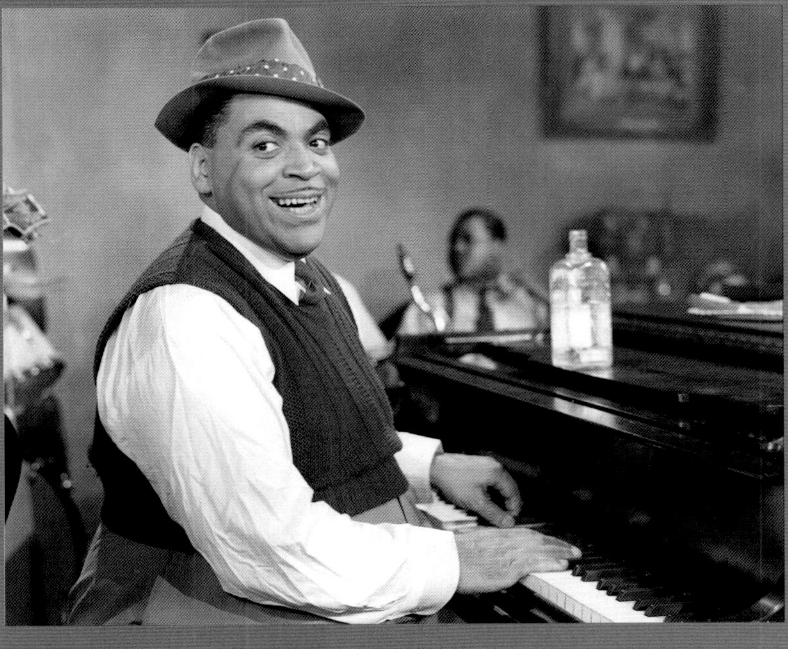

Fats Waller in *The Joint Is Jumpin'* (1941), procuction still

The Negro Soldier (1944), theatrical release poster

sense of promise, as did a gradual opening up of opportunities in Hollywood. This progress was predicated on the support and advocacy of organizations including the NAACP, which worked directly with the major Hollywood studios to create opportunities for Black actors beyond serving as foils for white mainstream actors. Among the more notable films directed at African American audiences during this period was the race film *Marching On!* (1943), directed by Spencer Williams Jr., which offered a fictionalized story from the perspective of a Black soldier. The thought-provoking documentary *The Negro Soldier* (1944)—written by Carlton Moss, directed by Stuart Heisler, and produced by Frank Capra and the US Department of War—was used as a recruitment tool to encourage Black men to enlist in the military despite the fact that Black people were living with rampant racism and discrimination on American soil.

The Negro Soldier is important in many ways. It serves as a reminder that the African American story is inextricably connected with the broader American story, but it also expands the definition of African American cinema. Nonfiction works were opportunities to tell important stories that would otherwise be overlooked. Another key example is the work of William Alexander (discussed in Shola Lynch's essay in this volume), who began to produce nonfiction narratives during the war as a way to ensure that African American stories would not be overshadowed and would also be presented to white audiences. In many respects the work of filmmakers like Alexander harks back to the insights of Frederick Douglass or the cinematic work of Madame E. Touissant Welcome, who understood the importance not only of images but also of the contribution that African Americans could make to telling a complete and honest story of the United States.

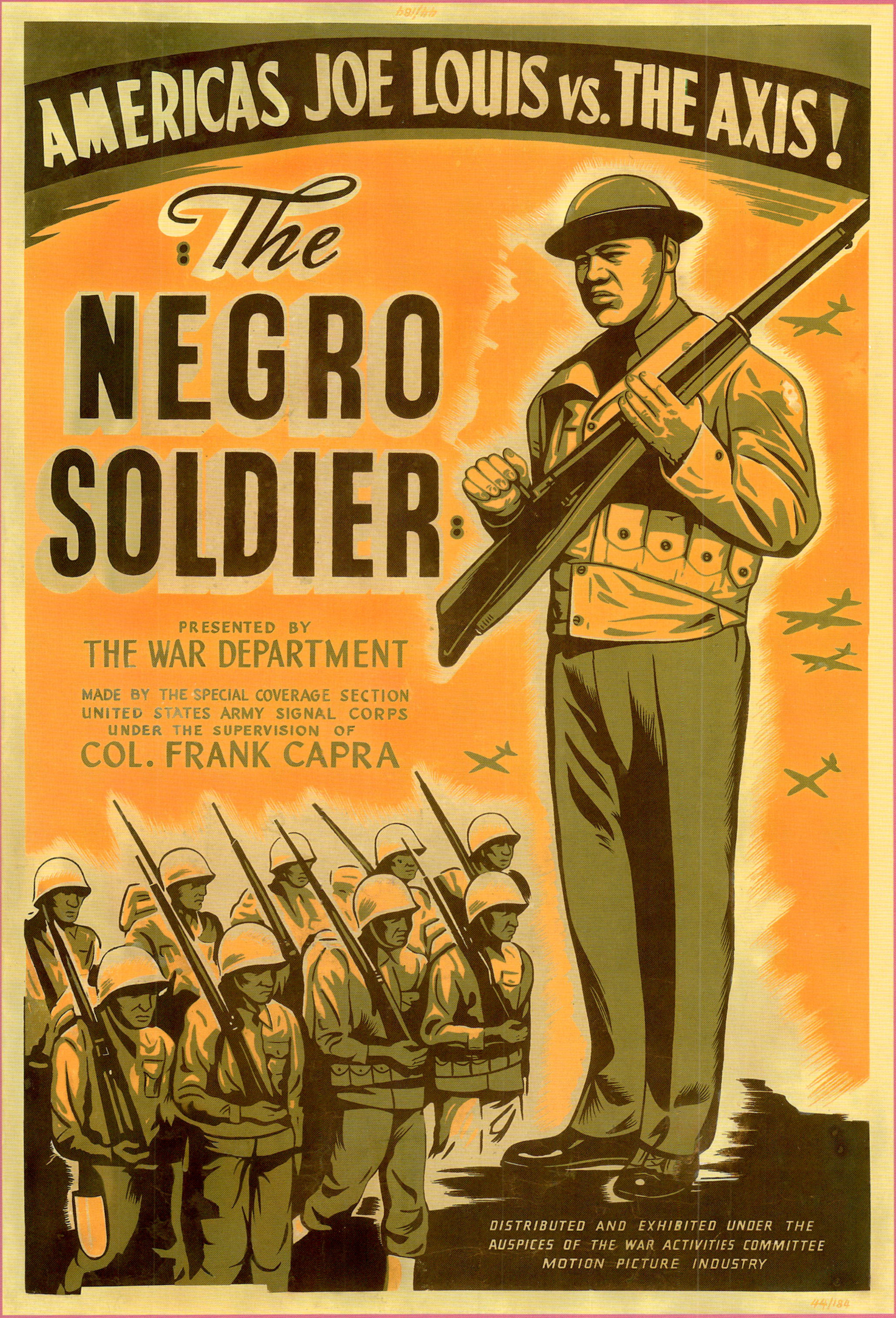
AMERICAS JOE LOUIS vs. THE AXIS!
The
NEGRO
SOLDIER
PRESENTED BY
THE WAR DEPARTMENT
MADE BY THE SPECIAL COVERAGE SECTION
UNITED STATES ARMY SIGNAL CORPS
UNDER THE SUPERVISION OF
COL. FRANK CAPRA
DISTRIBUTED AND EXHIBITED UNDER THE
AUSPICES OF THE WAR ACTIVITIES COMMITTEE
MOTION PICTURE INDUSTRY

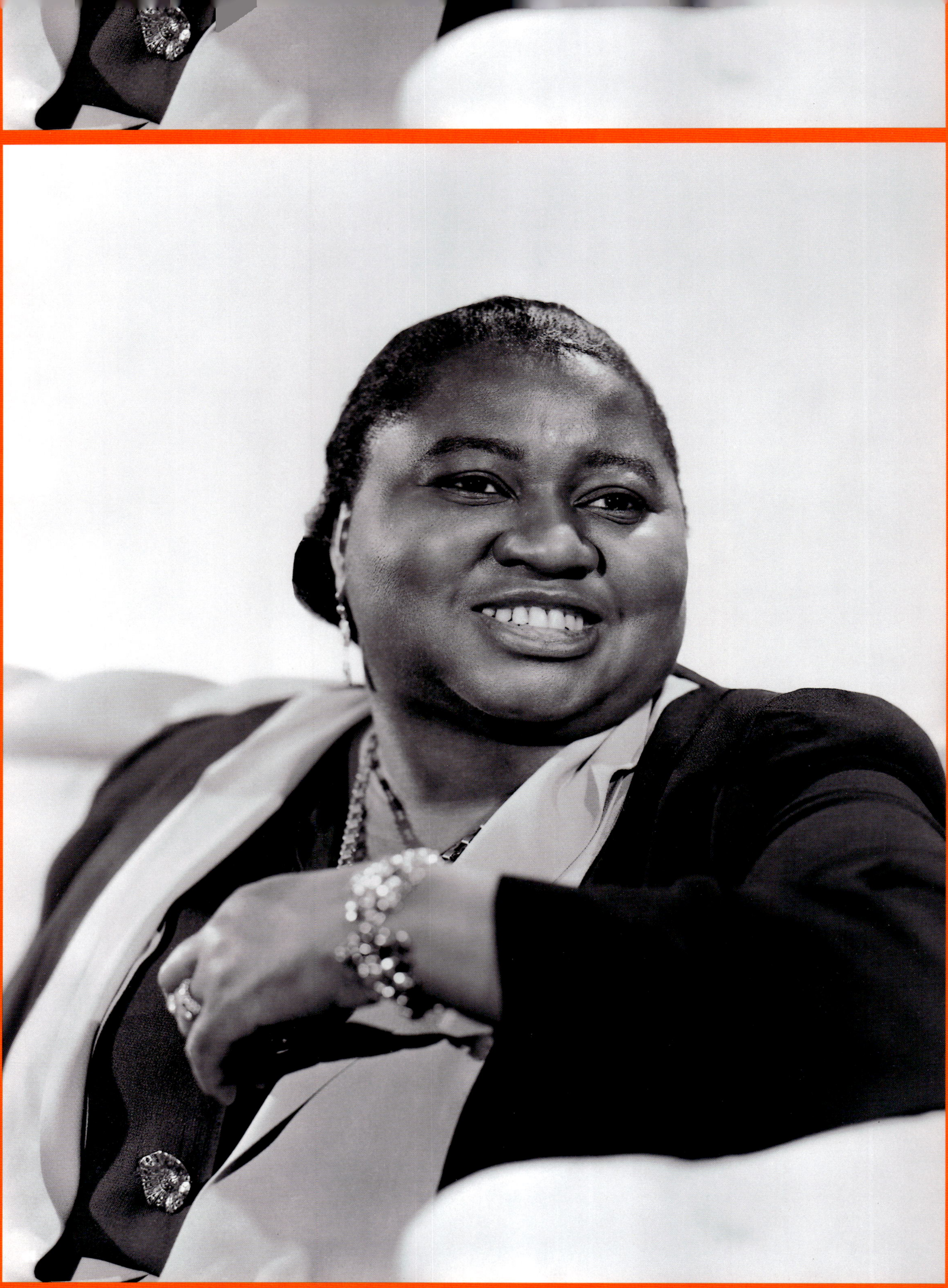

Hattie McDaniel, ca. 1940

BLACK STARS AND ICONS

In 1940 Hattie McDaniel became the first African American actor to win an Academy Award. She was named Best Supporting Actress for her role as a mammy character, called Mammy, in *Gone with the Wind* (1939), a movie that romanticized the antebellum South and the Confederacy. McDaniel gave a stellar performance in one of the very limited and stereotypical roles afforded to Black actors at the time. But as Donald Bogle notes in his essay on McDaniel in this volume, she was faced with unequal treatment even after the film was finished: along with other Black actors in the film, such as Butterfly McQueen and Oscar Polk, she was barred from attending the film premiere in Atlanta, in the Jim Crow South. And even in Hollywood, segregation was in force: at the Academy Awards ceremony at the Ambassador Hotel's Cocoanut Grove, McDaniel and her guest, Ferdinand Yober, were seated separately from the cast of the film, at the rear of the room. The response to McDaniel's win in the Black press was ambivalent. While she was celebrated for her success in mainstream Hollywood, she was also criticized for playing roles that perpetuated stereotypes.[65]

There was another injustice at play: as a darker-skinned woman of substantial physique, she wasn't offered the same opportunities as Black actors with lighter skin and slimmer builds. Compared to McDaniel, the slender, lighter-skinned Lena Horne was able to choose from a wider portfolio of roles in Hollywood, and she refused to play stereotypical ones. She was able to do so in part because of the efforts of the

Carrie Mae Weems (American, b. 1953),
Slow Fade to Black II, 2010, 17 inkjet prints,
13 × 10 ¹⁄₁₆ × 1 ½ in. (33 × 25.6 × 3.8 cm)
each (framed)

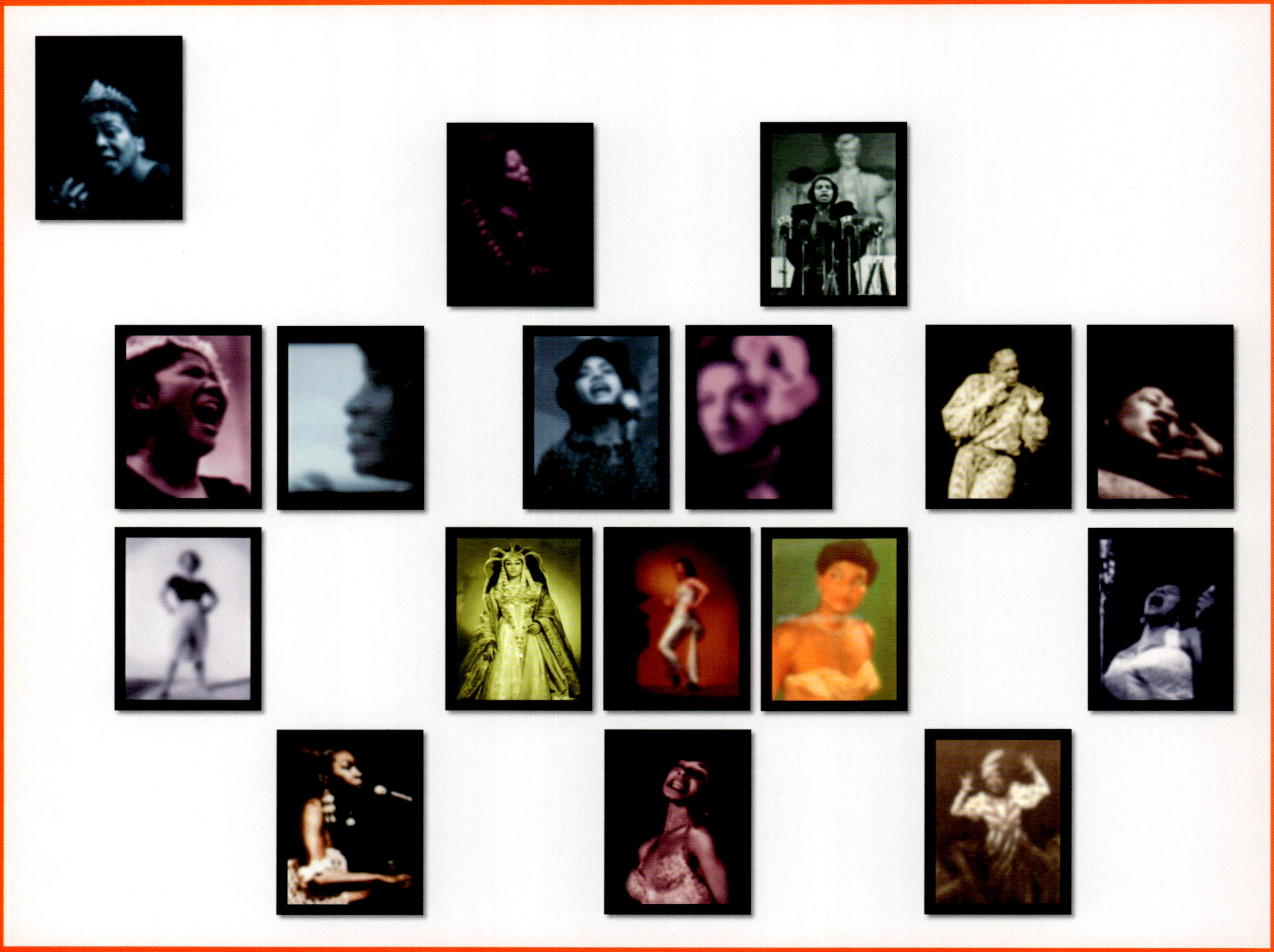

NAACP's executive secretary at the time, Walter White. White worked with the Office of War Information to increase the opportunities for African American actors in Hollywood. The NAACP executive urged Hollywood studio bosses, as Bogle has written, to "use more courage and imagination in the handling of roles of dark-skinned minorities." White "wanted to see Negro extras in scenes depicting everyday American life—blacks on city streets or in restaurants or train stations," giving visibility to the "diverse fabric of American life" on-screen.[66] According to Horne, White wanted "to bend the color line in movies."[67]

While White's demand for more opportunities for Black actors was important, he criticized stereotypical roles and hence implicitly McDaniel's success. She reportedly was "so offended that she refused to dine with or even appear in the same church with Walter White."[68] McDaniel and Horne also received different coverage in the Black press. While McDaniel appeared on the cover of *The Crisis*, the NAACP magazine, shortly after her Oscar win in April 1940 with a documentary photograph, Horne adorned the cover of *The Crisis* twice (February 1941 and January 1943) with glamour shots. According to Megan Williams, she was presented as a "sophisticated songstress and Hollywood actress with ties to the black bourgeoisie and fame among white Americans." Williams notes that the NAACP magazine preferred "headshots of well-dressed, light-skinned African American women who were college-educated ladies, beauty-contest winners, soldiers' wives, or celebrated entertainers, over photographs of dark-skinned women engaged in war-production work."[69]

White thought that Horne was the right actress to possibly change the image of Black women on-screen.[70] Horne signed a seven-year contract with Metro-Goldwyn-Mayer, which gave her roles in the Black-cast Hollywood musicals *Cabin in the Sky* and *Stormy Weather* (both 1943) and in mixed-race movies. Even though she enjoyed star treatment from the studio, she experienced racial discrimination through Hollywood's hair and makeup practices. For example, Max Factor created a special makeup color called Light Egyptian for her, which ended up being too dark on Horne and was used on white actresses playing biracial characters. This had the devastating effect that she lost roles that she wanted to play to white actresses in brownface makeup.[71] Horne also experienced discrimination when she appeared in movies with mixed-race casts. She was often relegated to singing roles and not fully embedded in the story line so that censors could cut out her scenes when the movies were shown in the South.

Both McDaniel and Horne were also activists. They used their platforms to engage in the war effort during World War II: McDaniel sold war bonds, while Horne entertained the troops. McDaniel was instrumental in desegregating housing in Los Angeles.[72] Horne remained active during the height of the civil rights movement of the 1960s.[73] McDaniel and Horne are just two of numerous Black stars and icons featured in *Regeneration* who had to work within a system of discriminatory practices in the American entertainment business. Resilience and self-determination were essential to the successful careers of Black actors and musicians of this era. To recognize their achievements, *Regeneration* presents an installation of glamour photographs of more than fifty Black performers working in Hollywood between the 1920s and the 1950s.

Alongside the glamour shots is the artist Carrie Mae Weems's seventeen-piece series *Slow Fade to Black II* (2010), which presents soft-focus images of mid-twentieth-century Black women stars, including Dorothy Dandridge and Eartha Kitt. As Maurice Berger writes, "The photographs, on the verge of dissolution, serve as metaphors of past struggles to remain visible and relevant in a culture that, at best, relegated many of these women to the sidelines. Viewed in this historical context, it is difficult to separate what we know about their subjugation—the stereotypical roles, the lack of financial reward, isolation—from their extraordinary and trailblazing work."[74]

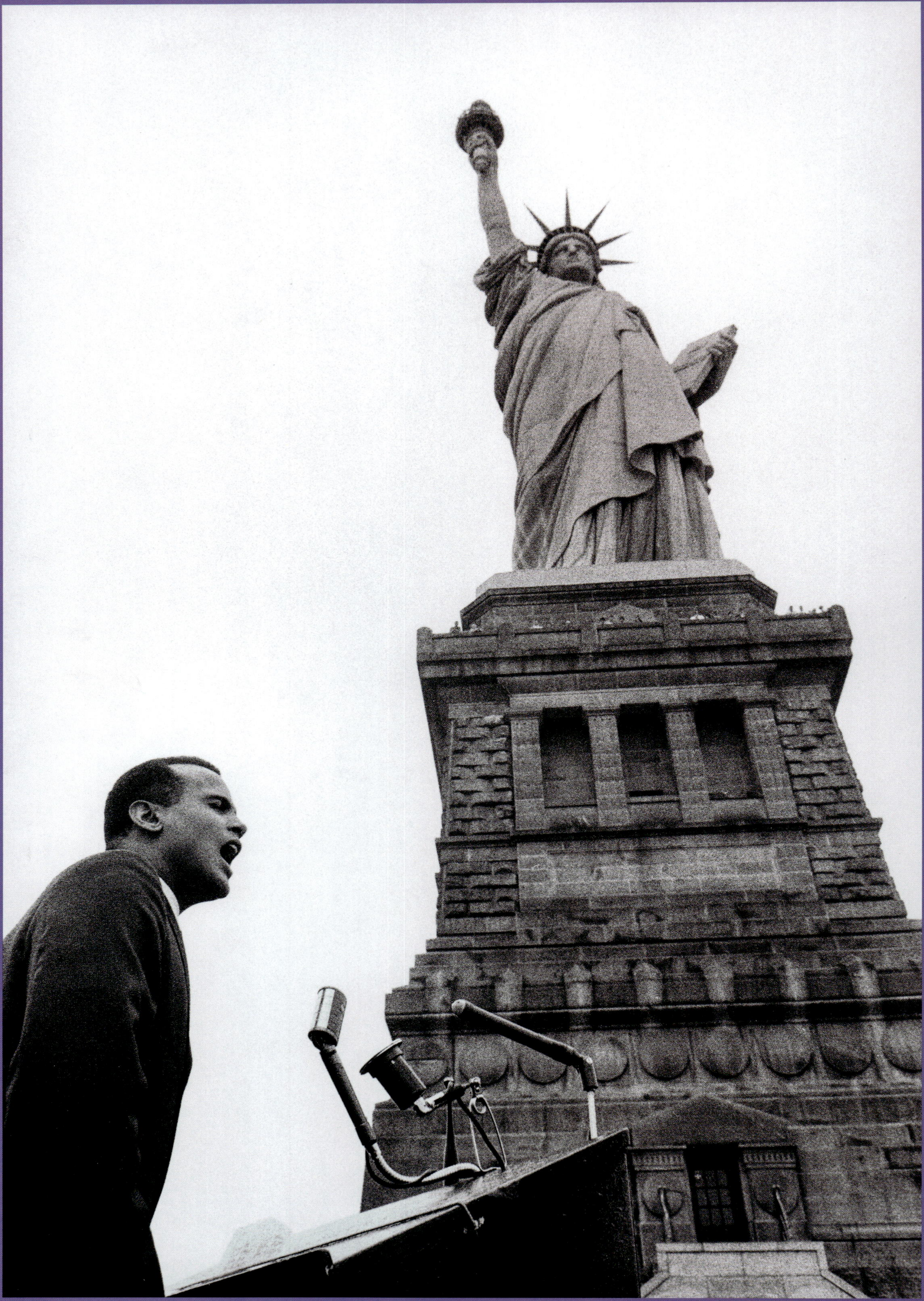

Albert Fenn (photographer),
Harry Belafonte speaks at a civil rights rally at the Statue of Liberty, 1960

FREEDOM MOVEMENTS

The 1950s and 1960s were fraught decades in the United States for a variety of reasons. Landmark Supreme Court decisions including *Brown v. Board of Education of Topeka* (1954), which deemed segregation in public schools unconstitutional, and legislative milestones such as the Civil Rights Act of 1964—which barred discrimination based on race, color, religion, sex, and national origin—marked tremendous progress toward a more just society but also, in the eyes of some citizens, threatened the social order and provoked a backlash. In 1955 Rosa Parks was arrested for refusing to give up her seat on a bus to a white patron, sparking a yearlong boycott against the public transit system in Montgomery, Alabama, that would become a foundational event for the civil rights movement. Between 1950 and 1953 the United States was involved in the Korean War and again asked Black men to fight on behalf of the United States, a country unwilling to fight for their human and civil rights. Ministers and activists like Martin Luther King Jr. and Malcolm X were gaining notoriety by speaking out against the social injustices impacting Black Americans.

This was also a time that saw the emergence of more Black film stars in Hollywood. The stage served as a training ground and repository for talent, particularly the Harlem-based American Negro Theater, a community group that launched a training program for actors in 1942. Its graduates included Harry Belafonte, Ossie Davis, Ruby Dee, and Sidney Poitier, all of whom would eventually parlay their theater training to the screen. These stars are but a few of the individuals who toiled in the performing arts, however, many without receiving much recognition.

Hollywood's attempt at examining this fraught moment in postwar American history required a conscious evaluation of race relations, but film studios struggled to create stories that did not feel reductive or off-putting. The year 1949 saw the release of four social dramas—*Home of the Brave*, *Lost Boundaries*, *Intruder in the Dust*, and *Pinky*—with stories that centered on race relations and racial injustice. These "Negro Problem Pictures," as Donald Bogle called them, "placed black/white conflict front and center, . . . arriving just at the dawn of the civil rights movement."[75] However well intentioned their makers may have been in acknowledging racial tensions in different societal settings, those films, as Bogle asserts, also showcased an "idealized theme of racial reconciliation and unity between black and white—when, in reality, off-screen racial tensions would soon build and escalate."[76] Films like these paved the way for studio executives to realize that Black actors could successfully play main characters and that stories about racial injustice were a viable business. As a result, more of these so-called social problem films were produced in the 1950s and 1960s, giving Poitier, Belafonte, Dorothy Dandridge, and other actors opportunities for stardom. Nevertheless, these films, which were usually told from a white perspective, came with their own set of challenges.

Poitier, in particular, "projected a new image for African Americans in the movies" as an "intelligent, disciplined, dignified young black man," as Bogle notes.[77] The actor had his first screen role in *No Way Out* (1950), in which he played a doctor with incredible composure who has to treat a racist white man in a hospital. Similarly, in *Pressure Point* (1962), Poitier played a prison psychiatrist who has a racist Nazi sympathizer as a patient, and in *Lilies of the Field* (1963), he starred as a charismatic handyman who helps white nuns build a chapel. As Michael Schulman wrote in a commentary following Poitier's death: "This was a vast improvement on the Mammy and Stepin Fetchit roles that preceded Poitier—and he had the megawatt charisma to pull it off—but it became another kind of trap. His characters were rarely able to show sexuality or anger."[78] One of the few exceptions during that time was *A Raisin in the Sun* (1961), based on the stage play by Lorraine Hansberry. Poitier had already successfully played the role of Walter Lee Younger on Broadway in 1959. In the film adaptation he clearly shows a Black man's frustration at not being able to provide for his family because of racial injustice.

Poitier achieved much success during this period and received an Oscar for *Lilies of the Field*, which made him the first African American to win the Academy Award for Best Actor.[79] He offered a realistic assessment of this honor in his autobiography: "I knew we hadn't 'overcome,' because I was still the only one. My career was unique in all of Hollywood. I know that I was a one-man show, and it simply shouldn't be that way."[80] *Lilies of the Field* was a small production, and Poitier would go on to appear in numerous blockbuster films. In 1967 alone, he starred in three movies, and in 1968 he grossed more than $9 million.[81] He offered film executives an actor who could help fulfill Hollywood's desire to be inclusive. He also reminded African American audiences that acting was a viable career—even in Hollywood. His success was complicated, however, and many critics within the Black press saw his roles as embodying a new stereotype, the "ebony saint," since he often played characters who either saved white characters or helped them feel more comfortable.

In writing on Poitier's career, James Baldwin, whose incisive reflections on cinema are discussed in Michael Boyce Gillespie's essay in this volume, explained: "The industry is compelled, given the way it is built, to present to the American people a self-perpetuating fantasy of American life. . . . *And the black face, truthfully reflected, is not only no part of this dream, it is antithetical to it.* And thus puts the black performer in a rather grim bind." In other words, Black performers were often faced with a dilemma. There was still very little opportunity outside presenting a fantastical notion of Black life to white America, but at the same time performers did find a way to, in Baldwin's words, "smuggle in a reality that [they know] is not in the script."[82] This idea had been personified many decades earlier in the vaudevillian Bert Williams, a man of extreme talent who had to reconcile white patrons' nostalgic Lost Cause fantasies about the antebellum South with his desire to work. Hattie McDaniel also wrestled with this in her career in Hollywood. One can observe within the performances of all these actors not only their superb talent but also a self-awareness that comes with the complexities of taking on certain roles and the cultural significance and responsibility of this privileged position within such a fraught and contested space.

And like Williams or McDaniel in earlier years, Poitier was not alone. Belafonte, Dandridge, Davis, Dee, and others were finding commercial success in Hollywood.[83] One difference, however, between them and earlier Black stars was how vocal they were in speaking out against racial and social injustices. The March on Washington for Jobs and Freedom on August 28, 1963, brought together more than 250,000 people, including a number of Hollywood celebrities, and ended with King's famous "I Have a Dream" speech. The charter flight list for the march, along with numerous photographs published in various media outlets, shows that Black celebrities and intellectuals such as Baldwin, Baker, Belafonte, Davis, Dee, Hansberry, Horne, and Poitier joined with white stars including Marlon Brando, Tony Curtis, Charlton Heston, Paul Newman, Gregory Peck, and Joanne Woodward, to name just a few, in support of the highly publicized event. Belafonte, Dee, and Davis also spoke at the march. Belafonte, a close friend of King's, was involved in many civil rights causes, and Davis eulogized Malcolm X at his funeral. These artists understood the responsibility associated with their status and delicately walked the line between their commitment to the art of acting and their activism.

The movies being produced in Hollywood were also challenged by the emergence of the Black Arts Movement around 1965 and its resistance to traditional Western aesthetics and influences. The Black Arts Movement was aligned with the Black Power movement, which advocated for self-reliance

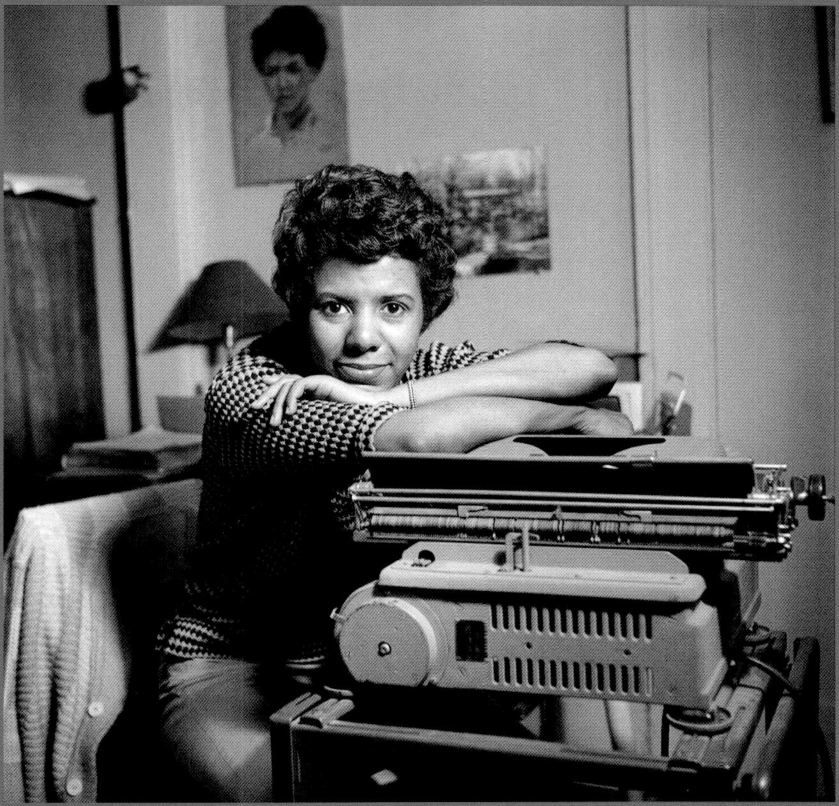

David Attie (photographer), Lorraine Hansberry in her New York City apartment, 1959

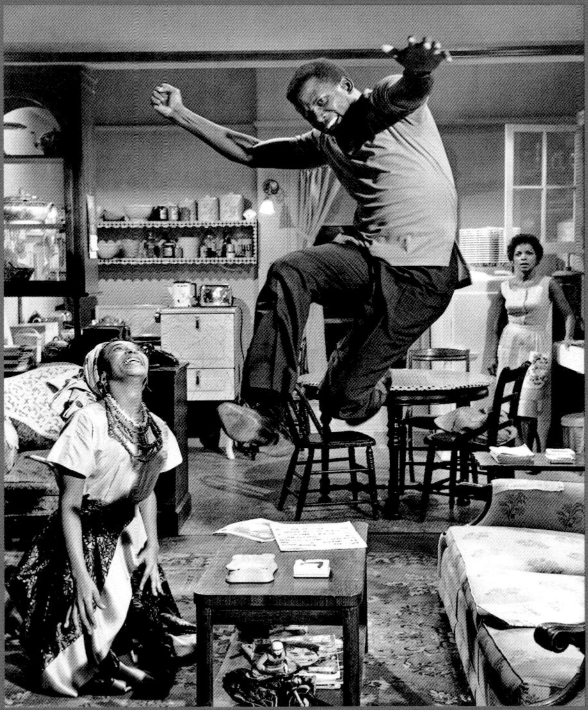

From left: Diana Sands, Sidney Poitier, and Ruby Dee in *A Raisin in the Sun* (1961), production still

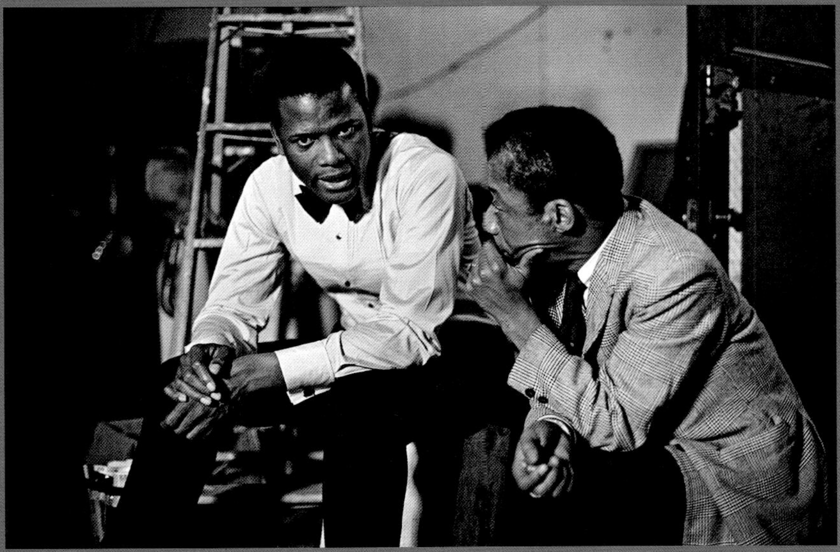

Bob Adelman (photographer), Sidney Poitier and James Baldwin on the set of *For Love of Ivy* (1968)

Charles Del Vecchio (photographer),
Ruby Dee addressing the crowd at
the March on Washington, 1963

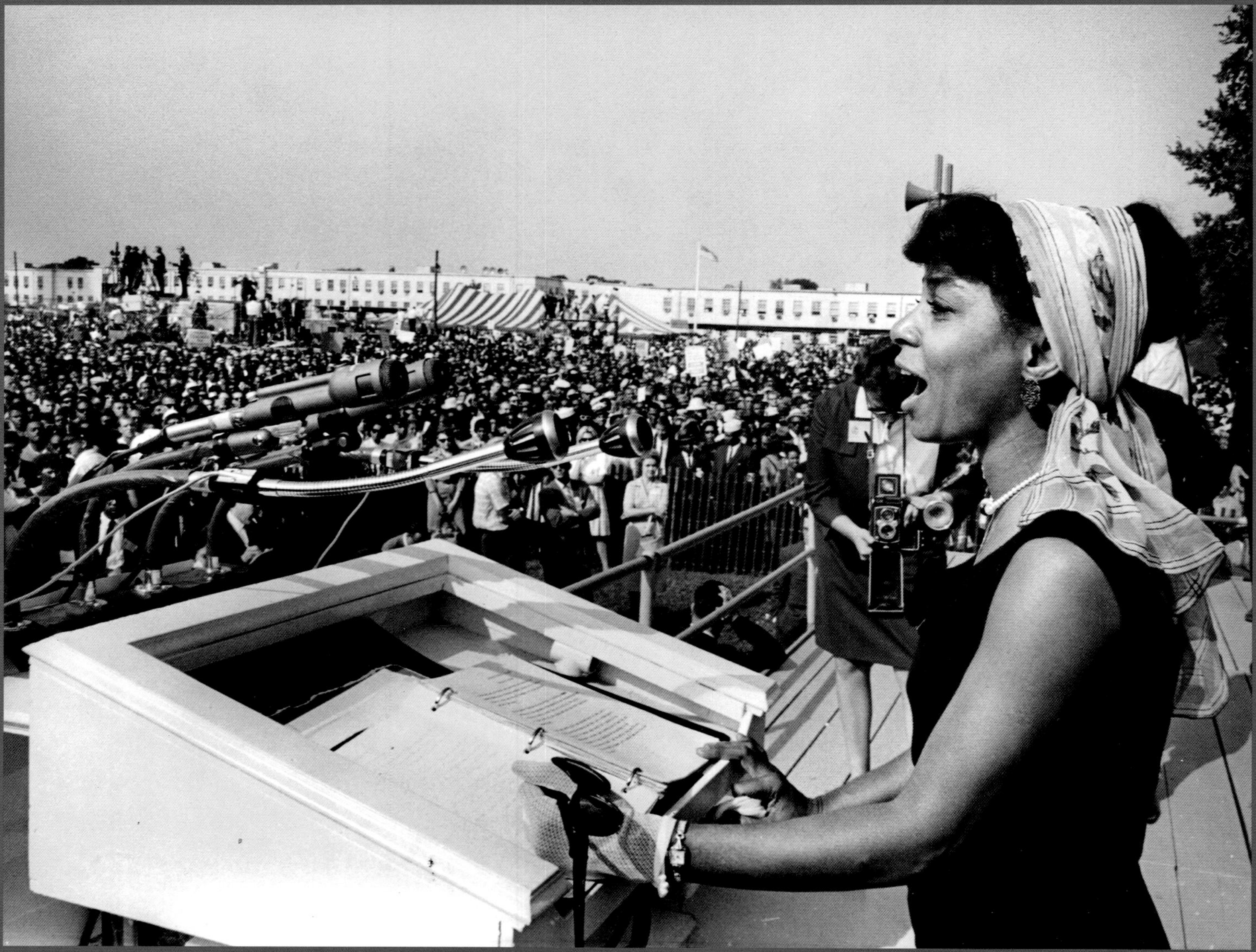

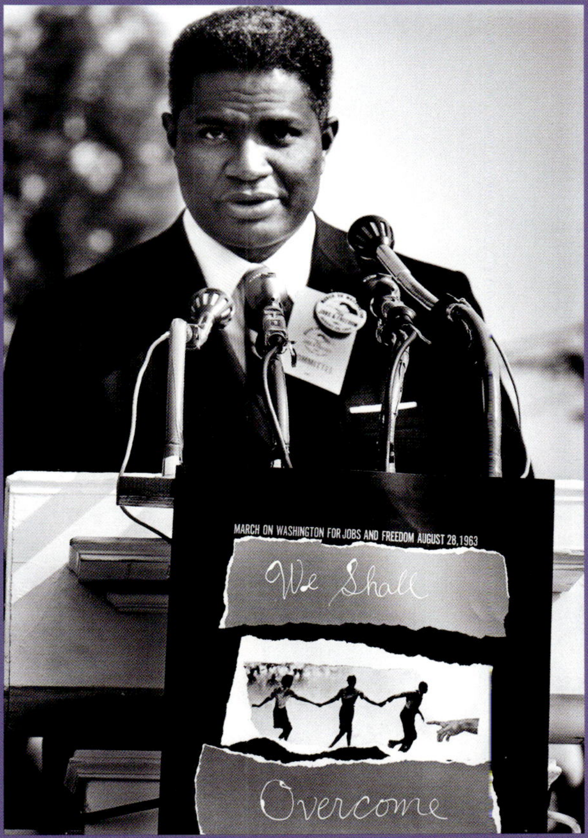

Rowland Scherman (photographer), Ossie Davis at the March on Washington, 1963

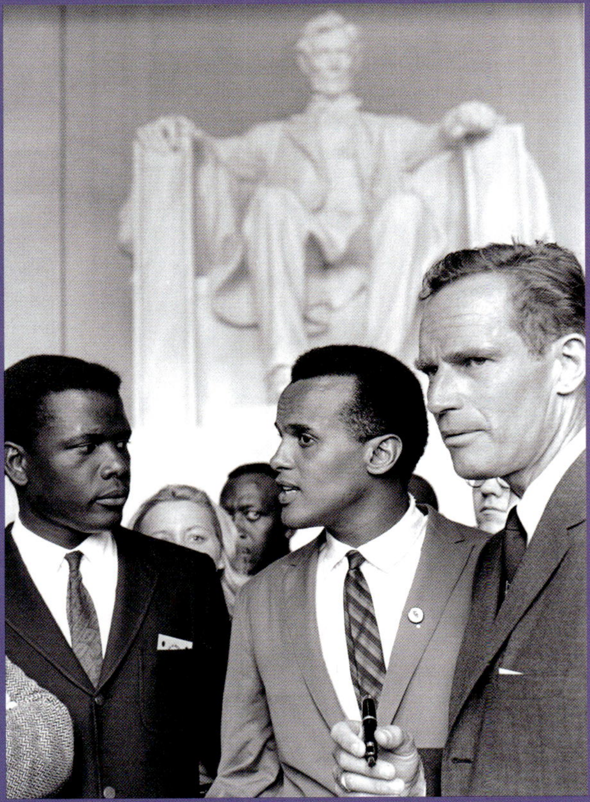

From left: Sidney Poitier, Harry Belafonte, and Charlton Heston at the Lincoln Memorial during the March on Washington, 1963

and separation from so-called white power structures. After the assassinations of Malcolm X and King in 1965 and 1968, respectively, many young Black people grew disaffected by society and more interested in creating systems and principles that transcended a dependence on whiteness, including its ideals, values, and aesthetics.

The slogan "We want Black Power!" was initially coined by Stokely Carmichael (Kwame Ture), a student activist and member of the Student Nonviolent Coordinating Committee (SNCC), following a series of assaults, including the shooting of the civil rights activist James Meredith in 1962 during a lone march through the South to encourage African American voter registration. Ture continued the march started by Meredith, and during a rally he shouted the phrase, which was inspired by *Black Power* (1954), a nonfiction book by the expatriate African American writer Richard Wright. This public declaration stood in contrast to the civil rights movement's emphasis on demanding freedom. The Black Power movement challenged the more assimilationist attitudes of civil rights leaders. The affiliated Black Arts Movement ignited all sectors of the arts—literature, music, visual art, and film—and gave rise to groups such as Afri-Cobra, Spiral, and Kamoinge Workshop, which examined the role of visual artists within the community. As Baldwin wrote, reflecting on popular culture, "white Americans appear to be under the compulsion to dream, whereas black Americans are under the compulsion to awaken."[84]

Baldwin's perceptive understanding of the different ways in which people experienced life in the United States is reflected in the title of Theaster Gates's artwork *Some Remember Sock Hops, Others Remember Riots* (2020). Sock hops were typically school-sponsored dances held in gymnasiums. Attendees removed their shoes to avoid scuffing the wood floors. Collective memories of this late 1950s phenomenon often involve girls in poodle skirts and boys in cardigans leading a seemingly carefree existence, whereas other young people had a different experience of the late 1950s and 1960s. Gates's incorporation of wood, denim, and decommissioned fire hoses highlights the complexities. Denim was the uniform for many young people involved in the SNCC, and high-power water hoses were often used on those fighting for social justice and equal rights. The work's irreverent title highlights the dichotomy and challenges of the period. This era of awakening also led artists to create their own film projects. Ruby Dee, for instance, cowrote the 1968 film *Uptight*, an adaption of John Ford's 1935 film *The Informer*. The Irish tale is revisited through the lens of an all-Black cast and Black liberation. The original version of the film was not overtly political, but true to her work as an activist, Dee added scenes that address the politics of the moment. In part she was responding to her experience of being typecast, often in supporting roles as the perfect wife or girlfriend. Cowriting a screenplay offered the actress the opportunity to develop another aspect of her talent by drawing on her lived experiences as both an artist and a Black woman.

The period also saw the emergence of independent filmmakers who offered alternatives to the roles and story lines typical of Hollywood films that featured Black actors. Among

White Americans appear to be under the compulsion to dream, whereas black Americans are under the compulsion to awaken.

—James Baldwin (1968)

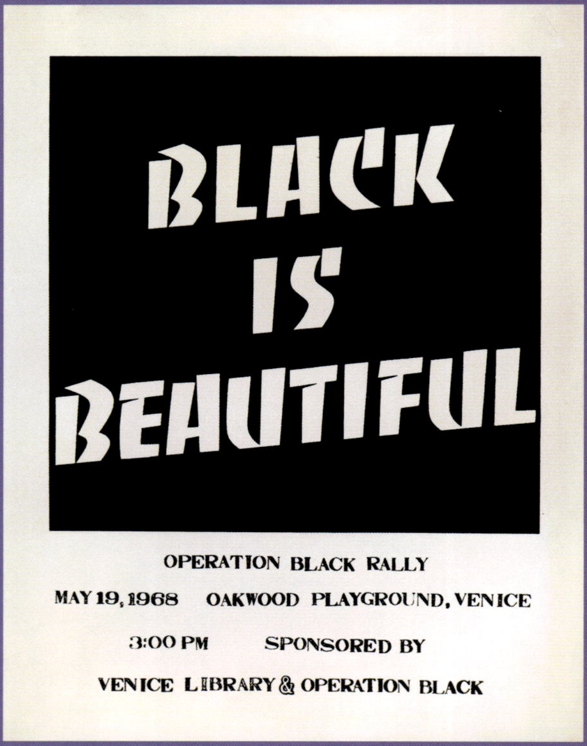

Poster made for the Operation Black rally held on May 19, 1968, at Oakwood Playground, Venice, California.

them was Robert L. Goodwin, who is less well known than his contemporaries Gordon Parks and Melvin Van Peebles. Goodwin, a California native, was the son of Ruby Berkley Goodwin, personal secretary to Hattie McDaniel and later to Ethel Waters.[85] In 1948 Robert Goodwin began writing and producing stage plays, and in the late 1950s he took on small acting roles in Hollywood features like *Watusi* (1959) and television shows such as *Laredo* (1966), as well as some uncredited roles, including that of a Nigerian delegate in the original *Batman* theatrical release (1966). During this time Goodwin was one of the few Black television writers creating material for major networks. In 1968 and 1969 he wrote episodes for *Julia*, which featured Diahann Carroll; he also wrote for *Bonanza* in 1965–66.[86] And he self-produced and directed a religious-themed TV play that aired for a limited time, *The Upper Chamber* (1961), which starred two stalwarts from the Hollywood studio era, Lew Ayres and Reed Hadley, alongside Goodwin. Winning acclaim for the writing and production of *The Upper Chamber* from critics and viewers, Goodwin became the first Black man to break the color barrier in episodic television as a writer and producer of a dramatic special.

Despite this success, his feature film, *Black Chariot* (1971), has not received the acclaim garnered by other pioneering films that served as precursors to the so-called blaxploitation genre.[87] Goodwin's financing for *Black Chariot*, like that of his predecessors in the race movie era, was crowdsourced. He ran ads in the Black newspaper the *Los Angeles Sentinel* seeking backers for his project: "I have formed a limited partnership and have begun to solicit investors in the black community. Any brother or sister can buy a four-share interest in my 'Black Chariot.' If a brother is low on bread, he can use his stamp books, and we will redeem them for their cash value."[88]

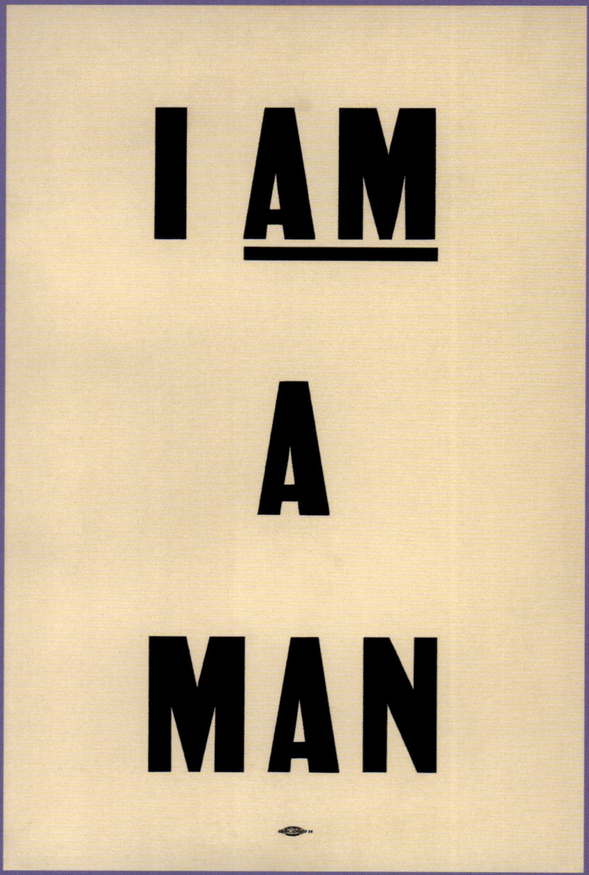

Placard produced by the Allied Printing Trades Council, 1968

These placards were carried by marchers during the Memphis sanitation workers' strike in 1968.

Theaster Gates (American, b. 1973), *Some Remember Sock Hops, Others Remember Riots*, 2020, wood, denim, and decommissioned fire hose, 84 × 84 × 3 ½ in. (213.4 × 213.4 × 8.9 cm)

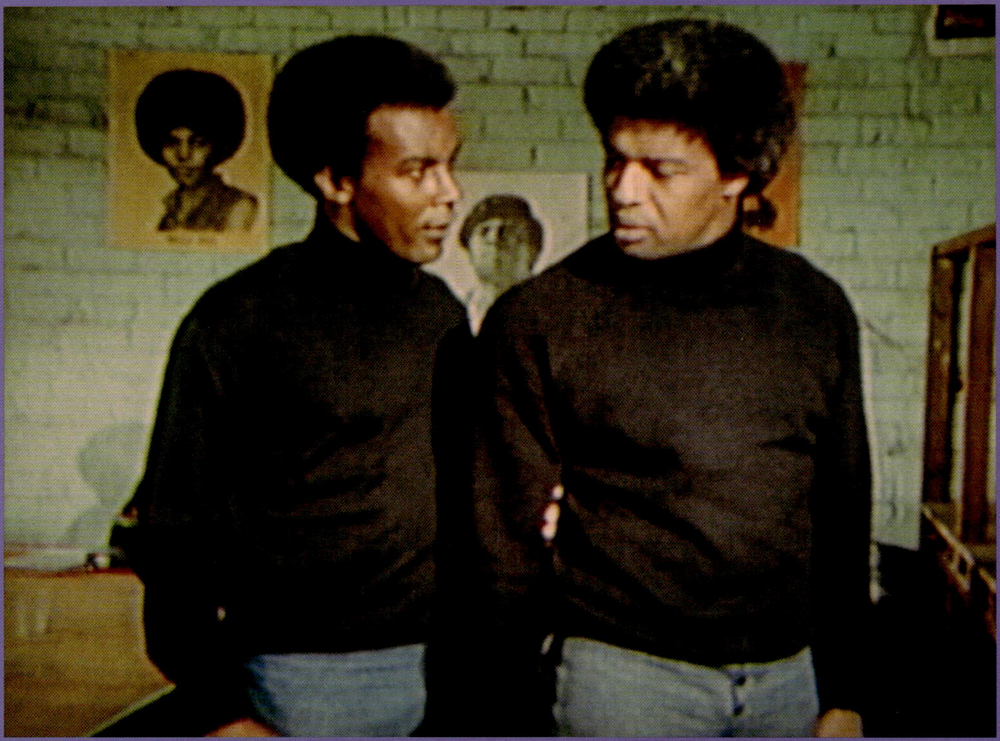

Richard Elkins (left) and Bernie Casey in *Black Chariot* (dir. Robert L. Goodwin, 1971), film still

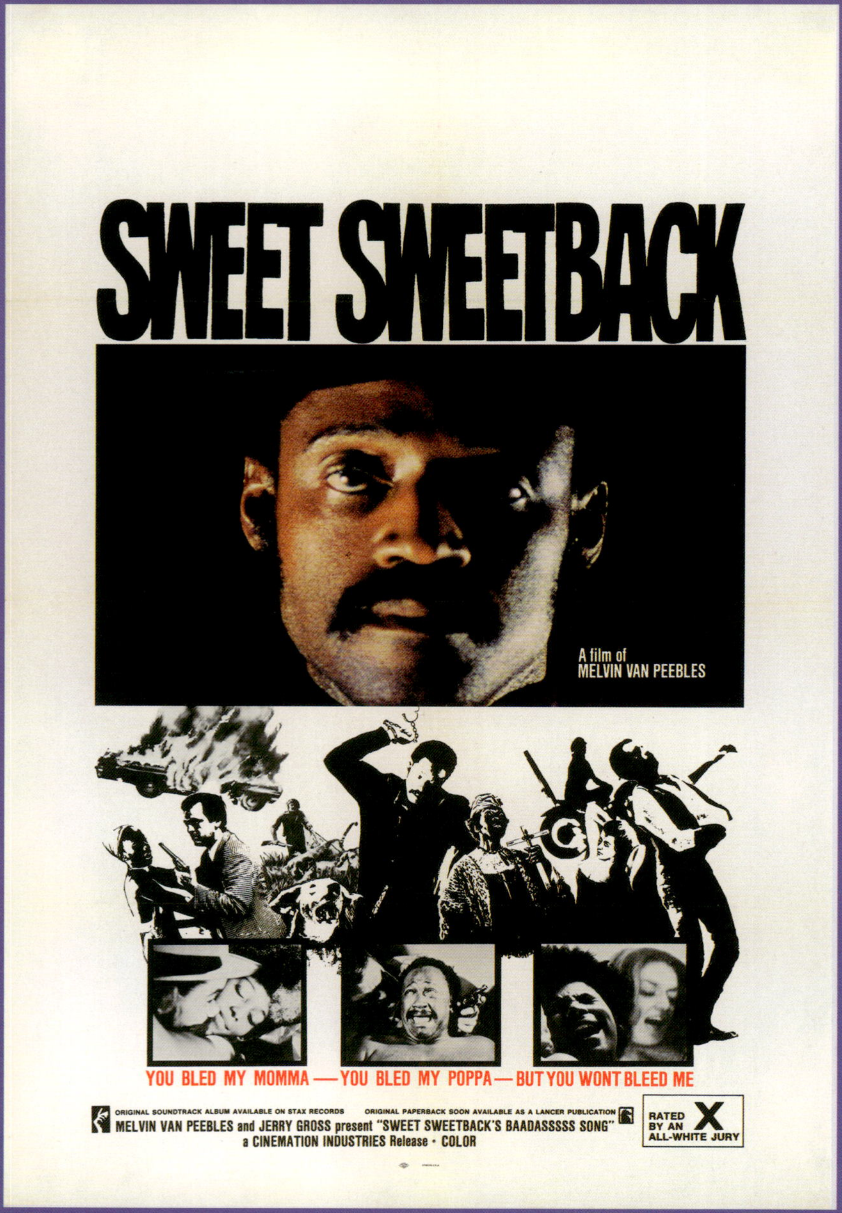

Sweet Sweetback's Baadasssss Song (1971), theatrical release poster

As a Black artist and independent producer of motion pictures, I refuse to submit this film, made from Black perspective for Blacks, to the Motion Picture Code and Administration for rating that would be applicable to the Black community.

—Melvin Van Peebles (1971)

Black Chariot is situated at the intersection of Goodwin's writing and entrepreneurial acumen, his commitment to the Black community, and his desire to produce something culturally relevant. In what Nikki Wine, writing for the *Los Angeles Times* in December 1970, called a "new concept," the production of *Black Chariot* was a "dramatic attempt to break the traditional cycle of having a white writer, backed by a white studio, produce an explanation of the black man aimed at the white public—Robert L. Goodwin is producing a black explanation of a black situation aimed primarily at black people—and, most significantly, produced and financed with black capital."[89] Produced at a reported cost of between $42,000 and $125,000, *Black Chariot* is the story of a young militant (Bernie Casey) who attempts to find the right way to become involved in the Black liberation struggle by joining "the Organization," a Black Panther–like group.[90] Goodwin described *Black Chariot* as a movie that "truly says black is beautiful in a number of forms, it also says, 'We're this way because of these factors.' And the explanation is more to blacks than whites."[91] Critical reaction to the film was lukewarm, and following its premiere on July 2, 1971, at the Santa Monica Civic Auditorium, it was screened only a few times and was considered lost until it was recently located, preserved, and restored.[92] It was similar to Van Peebles's *Sweet Sweetback's Baadasssss Song* (1971) in both its community financing and its challenge to the status quo.

After serving in the army in the 1950s, Van Peebles wrote his first novel in 1957 and tried without success to find a job in Hollywood. He moved to Europe and in the 1960s lived in France, where he published novels and short stories in French before making his first feature, *La permission* (*The Story of a Three-Day Pass*, 1967), which premiered at the San Francisco Film Festival. Shot and produced in France in a Nouvelle Vague (French New Wave) style yet featuring an interracial love story and commentary on French racial politics, it was unique during its time. Van Peebles moved back to the United States and made his first American film, the satire *Watermelon Man* (1970), produced by Columbia Pictures. Disputes over the ending of the film made him decide to produce his next movie, *Sweet Sweetback's Baadasssss Song* (1971), independently. It received an X rating and had only a limited release due to its sexually explicit content but nevertheless achieved great success at the box office and is credited with helping to "usher in a golden era of independent film" and with heralding the blaxploitation era.[93] Van Peebles defied the Motion Picture Association of America (MPAA) rating system by reading the following statement at a press conference in Los Angeles: "As a black artist and independent producer of motion pictures, I refuse to submit this film, made from Black perspective for Blacks, to the Motion Picture Code and Administration for rating that would be applicable to the Black community."[94] He then launched a marketing campaign using T-shirts and the film's poster with the slogan "Rated X by an all white jury," yet another reminder that even when a film is produced independently, the distribution system follows established power structures and structural inequities.[95] His son Mario Van Peebles, who had his film debut as a child in a controversial sex scene in *Sweet Sweetback's Baadasssss Song*, made his own film, titled *Baadasssss!* (2003), which is part recollection and part homage to the movie's place in Black film culture. Another homage to Melvin Van Peebles's legacy as a filmmaker is *Baltimore* (2003), the three-screen video installation by the contemporary British artist Isaac Julien, in which Van Peebles encounters his likeness next to those of other Black luminaries in the Great Blacks in Wax Museum in Baltimore in a subplot that combines blaxploitation with Afrofuturism.[96]

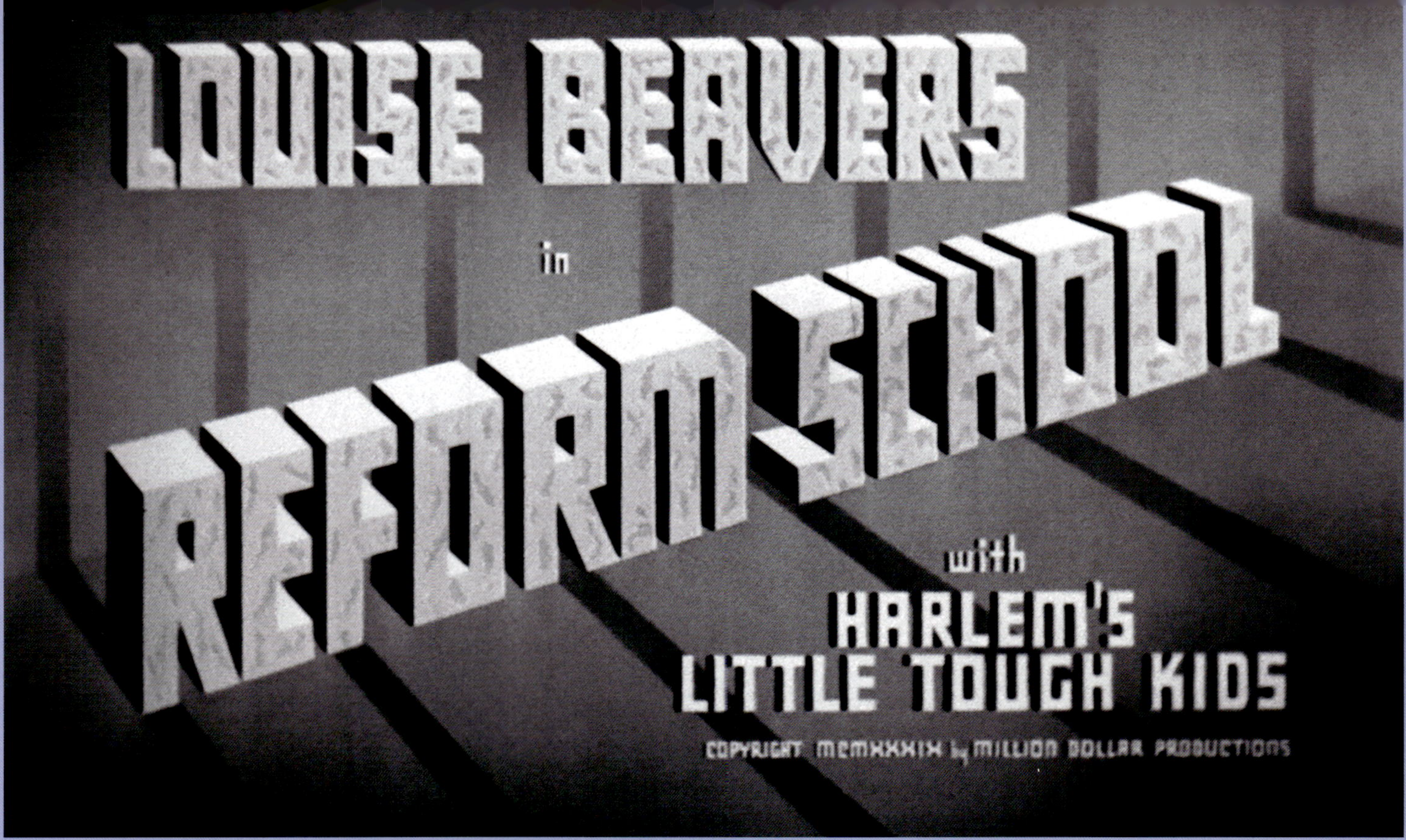
LOUISE BEAVERS
in
REFORM SCHOOL
with
HARLEM'S
LITTLE TOUGH KIDS
COPYRIGHT MCMXXXIX by MILLION DOLLAR PRODUCTIONS

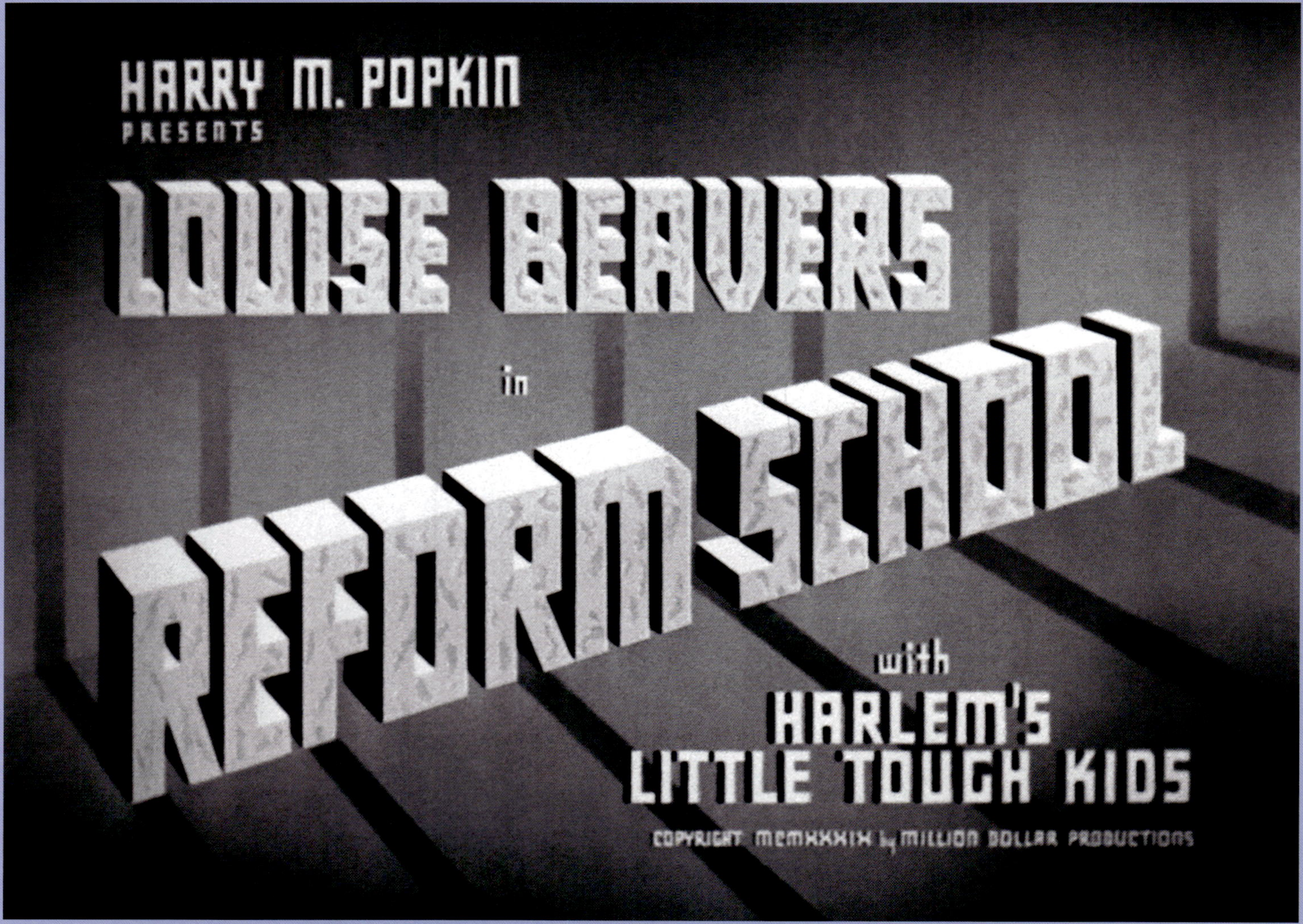
HARRY M. POPKIN
PRESENTS
LOUISE BEAVERS
in
REFORM SCHOOL
with
HARLEM'S
LITTLE TOUGH KIDS
COPYRIGHT MCMXXXIX by MILLION DOLLAR PRODUCTIONS

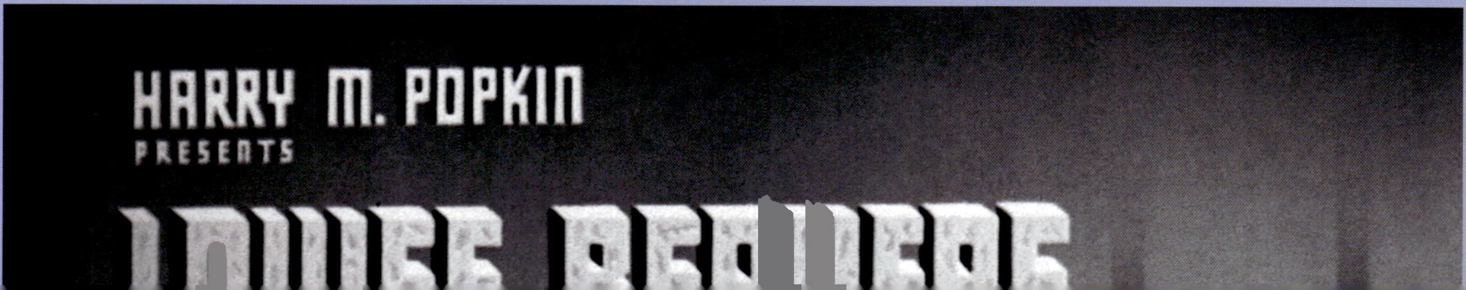
HARRY M. POPKIN
PRESENTS

Reform School (dir. Leo C. Popkin, 1939), film still of title card

REGENERATING BLACK CINEMA

Regeneration recognizes the audacity of many Black film pioneers and their rejection of the status quo. An objective in organizing this exhibition was to shed light on filmmakers and performers whose work is lesser known, in addition to recognizing the achievements and challenges of Black stars in Hollywood. Black films and filmmakers have often been overshadowed and banished to the margins, and many Black films no longer exist or may be mislabeled and languishing in archives or private storage units around the world. This project builds on the groundbreaking scholarly work of the Pioneers of African-American Cinema collection, which brought numerous race films to a wider audience, and we hope that our project inspires more discovery of lost or forgotten films.[97] Among the films that were "regenerated" during the span of our work are three race films in the Toddy Pictures Company collection at the Academy Film Archive that were previously considered lost. The Academy Film Archive has restored the western *Harlem on the Prairie* (1937), which stars the famous "singing cowboy" Herb Jeffries; the social drama *Reform School* (1939), featuring Louise Beavers in a powerful leading role

Connie Harris and Herb Jeffries in *Harlem on the Prairie* (dir. Sam Newfield, 1937), film still

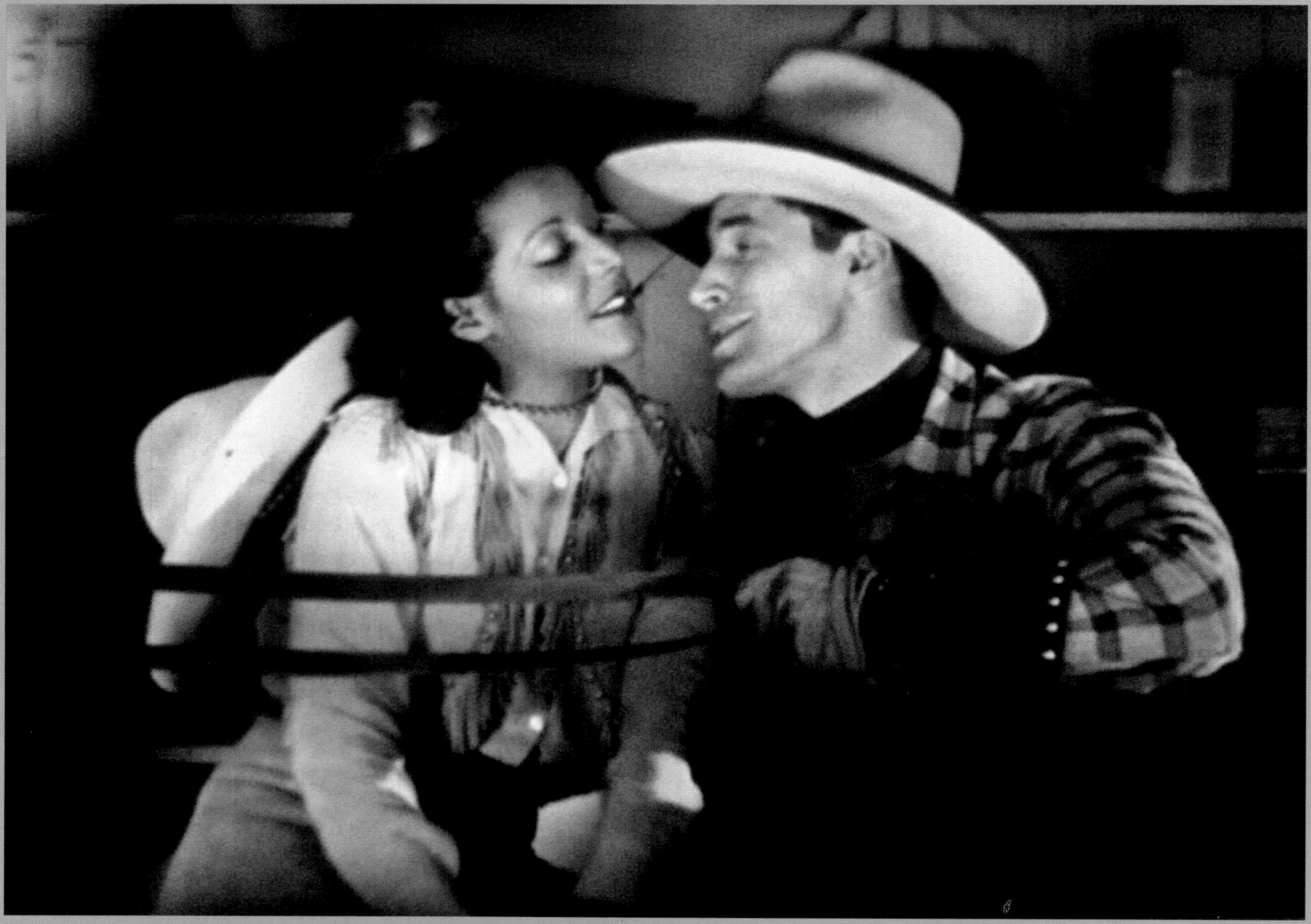

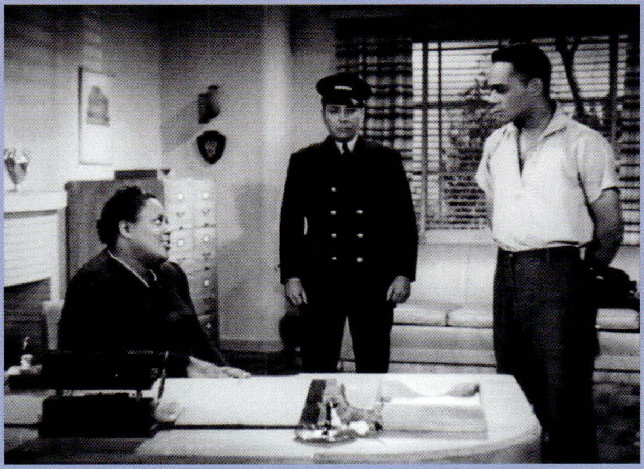

Louise Beavers with Reginald Fenderson (right) in *Reform School* (dir. Leo C. Popkin, 1939), film still

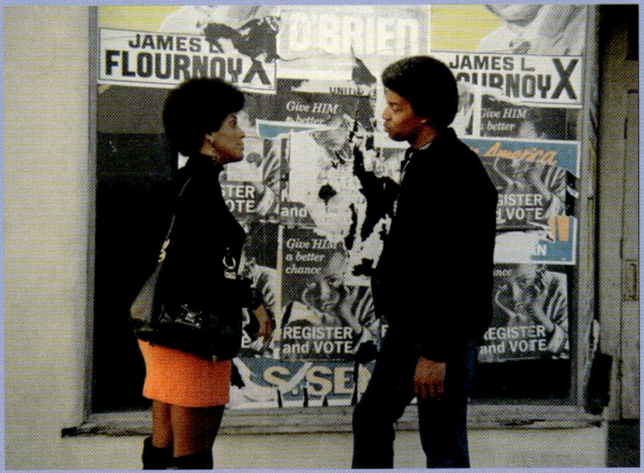

Barbara O. Jones and Bernie Casey in *Black Chariot* (dir. Robert L. Goodwin, 1971), film still

(discussed by Ellen C. Scott in her essay in this volume); and the comedy *Mr. Washington Goes to Town* (1940), starring Mantan Moreland, as well as trailers for *Boarding House Blues* (1948), *Harlem Follies of 1949* (1950), and *Carib Gold* (1956).[98] And the National Museum of African American History and Culture has preserved Goodwin's *Black Chariot*, which had also been considered lost. Preserving such films is significant because it calls into question preconceived notions about their social and cultural value and allows for a revitalization of the film canon, offering cinephiles and scholars of film and visual culture an opportunity to deepen their understanding of the period. Furthermore, it highlights the work of talented performers who have been overlooked, discounted, or erased.

Scouring archives and discovering lesser-known films by or starring African American filmmakers or performers and preserving these works opens conversations around cinematic storytelling, aesthetics, and history. *Regeneration* is a reminder that "Black film" is not only nuanced but also expansive. Works by non-Black filmmakers that feature stories that are culturally or socially relevant have been generative to notions of Black cinema, as have been nontheatrical films such as African American home movies (see the essay by Rhea L. Combs and Jacqueline Stewart in this volume), which highlight the significance and power of self-representation. Without proposing a definition of what Black cinema is or should be, *Regeneration* aims instead to encourage ongoing discussions about African American film history and its many reverberations in contemporary art, visual culture, and social movements. *Regeneration* also hopes to be an inspiration for archivists, scholars, programmers, and curators to find more Black films and to create various platforms to bring them to wider audiences in the future.

Notes

Epigraph
James Baldwin, "Black English: A Dishonest Argument," in *The Cross of Redemption: Uncollected Writings*, ed. Randall Kenan (New York: Vintage, 2010), 125.

1 Michael Boyce Gillespie, *Film Blackness: American Cinema and the Idea of Black Film* (Durham, NC: Duke University Press, 2016), 16.

2 Richard J. Powell, *Going There: Black Visual Satire* (New Haven, CT: Yale University Press, 2020), 104. See also Anna Everett, *Returning the Gaze: A Genealogy of Black Film Criticism, 1909–1949* (Durham, NC: Duke University Press, 2001), 13.

3 Jacqueline Najuma Stewart, *Migrating to the Movies: Cinema and Black Urban Modernity* (Berkeley: University of California Press, 2005), 5.

4 William D. Foster [Juli Jones Jr., pseud.], "News of the Moving Picture," *Indianapolis Freeman*, December 20, 1913.

5 None of Foster's narrative films are known to have survived, but he produced and directed, in addition to *The Railroad Porter*, *The Butler* (1913), *The Grafter and the Girl* (1913), *The Fall Guy* (1913), *The Barber* (1916), and *Mother* (1917). Three more film projects are not confirmed to have been completed: *Birth Mark*, *Fool and Fire*, and *Brother*. Later, in 1933, Foster published the vampire drama *Fool and Fire* as a serial in the Los Angeles African American newspaper the *California Eagle*, where he worked as a journalist. See Allyson Nadia Field, *Uplift Cinema: The Emergence of African American Film and the Possibility of Black Modernity* (Durham, NC: Duke University Press, 2015), 12, 195, 198, 204–5, 242.

6 Ilisa Barbash, Molly Rogers, and Deborah Willis, eds., *To Make Their Own Way in the World: The Enduring Legacy of the Zealy Daguerreotypes* (Cambridge, MA: Peabody Museum Press; New York: Aperture, 2020).

7 John Stauffer, Zoe Trodd, and Celeste-Marie Bernier, introduction to *Picturing Frederick Douglass: An Illustrated Biography of the Nineteenth Century's Most Photographed American*, rev. ed. (New York: Liveright, 2018), xii.

8 See Darcy Grimaldo Grigsby, *Enduring Truths: Sojourner's Shadows and Substance* (Chicago: University of Chicago Press, 2015).

9 Stewart, *Migrating to the Movies*, 7.

10 Du Bois called the project "an honest, straightforward exhibit of a small nation of people, picturing their life and development without apology or gloss, and above all made by themselves." Quoted in David Levering Lewis and Deborah Willis, introduction to *A Small Nation of People: W. E. B. Du Bois and African American Portraits of Progress* (New York: Amistad, 2003), 18.

11 Aldon Morris, "American Negro at Paris, 1900," in *W. E. B. Du Bois's Data Portraits: Visualizing Black America; The Color Line at the Turn of the Twentieth Century*, ed. Whitney Battle-Baptiste and Britt Rusert (Amherst: W. E. B. Du Bois Center, University of Massachusetts; New York: Princeton Architectural Press, 2018), 27.

12 Lewis and Willis, introduction to *Small Nation of People*, 16.

13 While Washington did not choose to combat white supremacy through agitation and protest, he did understand the power of representation. Prior to his death in 1915, he was seeking funding to turn his 1901 memoir *Up from Slavery* into a film. Washington's protégé Emmett Scott pushed on with the film *Birth of a Race* in 1918, which, despite being distorted by its investors, was an attempt to challenge the imagery brought forward by D. W. Griffith in *The Birth of a Nation* (1915). Henry Louis Gates Jr., foreword to *Separate Cinema: The First 100 Years of Black Poster Art*, ed. John Duke Kisch (London: Rare Art Press, 2014), 12. See also Thomas Cripps, "The Birth of a Race Company: An Early Stride toward a Black Cinema," *Journal of Negro History* 59, no. 1 (1974): 28–37.

14 Julian Rothstein, *Black Lives 1900* (London: Redstone, 2019), 41.

15 National Film Preservation Board, Library of Congress, "Brief Descriptions and Expanded Essays of National Film Registry Titles," https://www.loc.gov/programs/national-film-preservation-board/film-registry/descriptions-and-essays/.

16 Allyson Nadia Field, "Archival Rediscovery and the Production of History: Solving the Mystery of *Something Good–Negro Kiss* (1898)," *Film History: An International Journal* 33, no.2 (2021): 1–33. See also Ben Kenigsberg, "It Started with a Kiss. Then Film Scholars Found More," *New York Times*, January 12, 2022, https://www.nytimes.com/2022/01/12/movies/moma-black-cinema.html, and "A Piece of American Film History in Norway," *A.Frame: The*

Academy's Guide to Movies, February 25, 2021, https://aframe.oscars.org/news/post/something-good-negro-kiss.

17 Allyson Nadia Field, quoted in National Film Preservation Board, "Brief Descriptions."

18 National Film Preservation Board, "Brief Descriptions," and Daniel Eagan, *America's Film Legacy: The Authoritative Guide to the Landmark Movies in the National Film Registry* (New York: Continuum, 2010), 5.

19 W. E. B. Du Bois, *The Souls of Black Folk* (New Haven, CT: Yale University Press, 2015), 5.

20 Henry Louis Gates Jr., preface to *Black Male: Representations of Masculinity in Contemporary American Art*, by Thelma Golden (New York: Whitney Museum of American Art and Abrams, 1994), 11–12.

21 Grigsby, *Enduring Truths*, 37.

22 Silent film adaptations: 1903 (Edwin S. Porter, Thomas A. Edison Company); 1903 (Siegmund Lubin, Lubin Manufacturing Company); 1910 (J. Stuart Blackton, Vitagraph Company of America); 1910 (Barry O'Neil, Thanhouser Company); 1913 (Otis Turner, Imperial Company), 1913 (Sidney Olcott, Kalem Company); 1914 (William Robert Daly, World Producing Corporation, with Black actor Sam Lucas); 1918 (J. Searle Dawley, Famous Players–Lasky/Paramount), and 1927 (Harry A. Pollard, Universal Pictures Corporation, with Black actors James B. Lowe and an uncredited Louise Beavers and Madame Sul-Te-Wan). The Universal film was rereleased as a talkie with an added Movietone soundtrack in 1928.

23 Donald Bogle, *Toms, Coons, Mulattoes, Mammies, and Bucks: An Interpretive History of Blacks in American Film*, 5th ed. (New York: Bloomsbury, 2016), 1.

24 Ian Chilvers, *The Oxford Dictionary of Art*, 3rd ed. (Oxford: Oxford University Press, 2004), 652.

25 Darby English, "This Is Not about the Past: Silhouettes in the Work of Kara Walker," in *Kara Walker: Narratives of a Negress*, ed. Ian Berry et al. (Saratoga Springs, NY: Frances Young Tang Teaching Museum and Art Gallery, Skidmore College; Williamstown, MA: Williams College Museum of Art; Cambridge, MA: MIT Press, 2003), 142.

26 See the documentary *Birth of a Movement*, directed by Susan Gray and Bestor Cram (PBS, 2017). Also useful is John Hope Franklin, "'Birth of a Nation': Propaganda as History," *Massachusetts Review* 20, no. 3 (1979): 417–34.

27 See Melvyn Stokes, *D. W. Griffith's "The Birth of a Nation": A History of "the Most Controversial Motion Picture of All Time"* (Oxford: Oxford University Press, 2007), 11–12.

28 During growing protests against *The Birth of a Nation*, Griffith asked Booker T. Washington if Tuskegee could be part of a prologue film accompanying the blockbuster. Ever the shrewd strategist, Washington refused, but he supposedly advised another historically Black college, Hampton Institute (his alma mater), to participate.

29 Field, *Uplift Cinema*, 186.

30 "The Slanderous Film," *The Crisis*, December 1915, 76–77.

31 Quoted in Field, *Uplift Cinema*, 241. See also "Race Movie Co. Given Charter to Make Films," *Chicago Defender*, November 23, 1929.

32 Ron Magliozzi discusses the "sizable" talent pool of Black entertainers working in New York, for example, in his essay in this volume.

33 See Rhea L. Combs and Jacqueline Stewart's essay on home movies in this volume, which discusses community screenings and the work of Solomon Sir Jones, whose travel footage often showcased parades while documenting Black life, predominantly in the West, during the 1920s.

34 Field, *Uplift Cinema*, 104. See also "Col. John B. Marshal, and His Trip through the South," *Broad Ax*, January 15, 1913.

35 See Field, *Uplift Cinema*. Field defines "uplift cinema" as films dedicated to notions of self-sufficiency, education, and respectability. An uplift approach to filmmaking also placed an emphasis on portraying African Americans in a positive and progressive light.

36 Noble M. Johnson also had an impressive acting career in Hollywood movies from 1916 to 1950. The roles he was offered in the studio system, however, were never as refined as those in the films he produced with his brother for the Lincoln Motion Picture Company. Aside from playing Black supporting characters, he was exoticized and cast as Native American, Latin, and Arab characters.

37 George P. Johnson, quoted in Barbara Tepa Lupack, *Richard E. Norman and Race Filmmaking* (Bloomington: Indiana University Press, 2014), 9.

38 Powell, *Going There*, 24; see also viii, 25.

39 Aimee Dixon Anthony, "Early African-American Female Filmmakers," in *Silent Women: Pioneers of Cinema*, ed. Melody Bridges and Cheryl Robson (Twickenham, UK: Supernova, 2016), 38.

40 On its restoration, see "Kino Lorber to Restore *Motherhood: Life's Greatest Miracle*," November 16, 2016, https://www.kinolorber.com/news/article/id/43.

41 Emily Kubincanek, "'Flames of Wrath' and the Pioneering African-American Women of the Silent Cinema," *Film School Rejects* (blog), February 28, 2021, https://filmschoolrejects.com/flames-of-wrath/.

42 See "Profile: Alice B. Russell," Women Film Pioneers Project, https://web.archive.org/web/20190803012456/https://wfpp.cdrs.columbia.edu/pioneer/alice-b-russell-2/.

43 See Lupack, *Richard E. Norman*.

44 "Regeneration," Norman Studios, http://normanstudios.org/films-stars/norman-films/regeneration/.

45 In many respects the work of Williams, with its spotlight on religion and its culturally specific resonances within the Black community, serves as a harbinger of later films like those of Tyler Perry, whose work also engages with religion and notions of good and evil.

46 Thelma Golden, "Sonic Boom," in *Gary Simmons* (Chicago: Museum of Contemporary Art; New York: Studio Museum in Harlem, 2002), 13.

47 Maurice Berger, "The Image under Erasure," in *Gary Simmons*, 24–25.

48 Carole Sweeney, *From Fetish to Subject: Race, Modernism, and Primitivism, 1919–1935* (Westport, CT: Praeger, 2004), 3.

49 Tyler Stovall, *Paris Noir: African Americans in the City of Light* (Boston: Houghton Mifflin, 1996), xiii.

50 Baker's image and legacy are omnipresent in Paris, including on murals in the restaurant La Coupole and on street signs for Place Joséphine Baker. When Baker died in 1975, she became the first Black woman to receive a state funeral in Paris. In 2021 she became the first Black woman to be honored at the Panthéon in Paris along with other luminaries of French culture. See Roger Cohen, "Josephine Baker Becomes First Black Woman Inducted into France's Tomb of Heroes," *New York Times*, November 30, 2021, https://www.nytimes.com/2021/11/30/world/europe/josephine-baker-buried-pantheon.html.

51 See also Terri Simone Francis, *Josephine Baker's Cinematic Prism* (Bloomington: Indiana University Press, 2021).

52 See, for example, *Cinemagazine*, no. 1 (January 6, 1928); *Cine-miroir*, no. 144 (January 6, 1928); *Pour Vous*, no. 101 (October 23, 1930); *Cine-miroir*, no. 506 (December 14, 1934); *Pour Vous*, no. 323 (January 24, 1935), and *Pour Vous*, no. 601 (May 22, 1940).

53 Baker also wrote the children's book *La tribu arc-en-ciel* (Amsterdam: Mulder & Zoon, 1957).

54 While the remnants of the never-completed theme park are no longer extant, the current owner, Angélique de Saint-Exupéry, is restoring the castle and opened it to the public as a tourist site that celebrates Baker's legacy through installations with costumes, photographs, and personal memorabilia. https://www.milandes.com/en/josephine-baker/.

55 Paul Robeson, interview in the *Daily Worker* (London), November 24, 1937, reprinted in *Paul Robeson Speaks: Writings, Speeches, Interviews, 1918–1974*, ed. Philip S. Foner (New York: Brunner/Mazel, 1978), 120.

56 The surveillance card issued by the Gestapo indicates that Robeson's movements were monitored between Aachen, Berlin, Neu Bentschen, Moscow, and London from July to September 1937. Bestand R 58/9692 Reichssicherheitshauptamt, Deutsches Bundesarchiv (file of persecuted people, dossier R 58/9692, Reich Security Main Office, German Federal Archive).

57 An East German documentary records a state reception at the DEFA Stiftung, "Paul Robeson bei uns" (East Germany, 1961). In 1983 the GDR issued a postal stamp in his honor with the legend "For Peace against Racism. Paul Robeson 1898–1976."

58 The director of *Paris Blues*, Martin Ritt, is known for socially conscious films. He made *Edge of the City* (1957), with Sidney Poitier and John Cassavetes, as well as the acclaimed *Sounder* (1972), with Cicely Tyson and Paul Winfield.

59 Early plans for the film still involved interracial couples, according to producer Sam Shaw, but the studio insisted that this be changed. See Andy Fry, *Paris Blues: African American Music and French Popular Culture, 1920–1960* (Chicago: University of Chicago Press, 2014), 2n4.

60 Fry, *Paris Blues*, 5.

61 The Cotton Club was originally called Cafe Deluxe and owned by the heavyweight champion Jack Johnson. When Johnson suffered economic hardship, he sold the club to the gangster Owney Madden, who reopened it in 1923 with a new name. The club thrived during Prohibition, and weekly broadcasts of its performances made it one of the most popular venues of the 1920s for its nearly all-white patrons. Its decor created a plantation-like atmosphere, with the mostly Black staff often presented as plantation residents, and the high-energy musical acts at times perpetuated stereotypical notions of African Americans. The Cotton Club nevertheless showcased some of the most widely known artists of the day, including Duke Ellington, Cab Calloway, the Nicholas Brothers, and Ethel Waters. A dance club that was not segregated and had a thriving Black clientele was the Savoy Ballroom on Lenox Avenue in Harlem.

62 For an in-depth exploration of Soundies, see Susan Delson, *Soundies and the Changing Image of Black Americans on Screen: One Dime at a Time* (Bloomington: Indiana University Press, 2021).

63 See the documentary *Soundies: A Musical History* (2007), directed by Chris Lamson.

64 The authors wish to thank Soundies collector Mark Cantor, who provided valuable insights into this history. To explore some of his collection, see his project, the Celluloid Improvisations Music Film Archive: https://www.jazz-on-film.com.

65 See Charlene Regester, *African American Actresses: The Struggle for Visibility, 1900–1960* (Bloomington: Indiana University Press, 2010), 139–45.

66 Donald Bogle, *Bright Boulevards, Bold Dreams: The Story of Black Hollywood* (New York: One World, 2006), 212.

67 Lena Horne and Richard Schickel, *Lena* (Garden City, NY: Doubleday, 1965), 121.

68 Thomas Cripps, "'Walter's Thing': The NAACP's Hollywood Bureau of 1946—a Cautionary Tale," *Journal of Popular Film and Television* 33, no. 2 (July 2005): 116.

69 Megan E. Williams, "The *Crisis* Cover Girl: Lena Horne, the NAACP, and Representation of African American Femininity, 1941–1945," *American Periodicals* 16, no. 2 (2006): 210, 204.

70 Bogle, *Bright Boulevards*, 214.

71 Bogle, 219.

72 Victoria M. Massie, "The First Black Oscar Winner Fought Segregated Housing in LA—and Won," *Vox*, February 24, 2016, https://www.vox.com/2016/2/24/11105204/hattie-mcdaniel-housing-oscars.

73 Horne is honored in the National Park Service's International Civil Rights Walk of Fame; see https://www.nps.gov/features/malu/feat0002/wof/lena_horne.htm.

74 Maurice Berger, "Black Performers, Fading from Frame, and Memory," *Lens* (blog), *New York Times*, January 22, 2014, https://lens.blogs.nytimes.com/2014/01/22/black-performers-fading-from-frame-and-memory/.

75 Donald Bogle, *Hollywood Black: The Stars, the Films, the Filmmakers* (Philadelphia: Running Press, 2018), 86.

76 Bogle, *Hollywood Black*, 89.

77 Bogle, 93.

78 Michael Schulman, "The Meaning of Sidney Poitier's Historic 1964 Oscar," *New Yorker*, January 12, 2022, https://www.newyorker.com/culture/cultural-comment/the-meaning-of-sidney-poitiers-historic-1964-oscar.

79 He was also only the second Black person to win an Oscar in an acting category, after Hattie McDaniel in 1940.

80 Sidney Poitier, *The Measure of a Man: A Spiritual Autobiography* (New York: Harper Collins, 2000), 107.

81 Ed Guerrero, *Framing Blackness: The African American Image in Film* (Philadelphia: Temple University Press, 1993), 75.

82 James Baldwin, "Sidney Poitier," in Kenan, *Cross of Redemption*, 183–84; originally published in *Look*, July 23, 1968, 50–58.

83 Poitier recalled, "Ossie, Ruby, and I knew we represented a slight departure from the norm. Black actors earning as much as a middle-class living amounted to less than one percent of all black actors in the profession." Poitier, *Measure of a Man*, 101.

84 Baldwin, "Sidney Poitier," 183.

85 For more on Ruby Berkley Goodwin, see her autobiography, *It's Good to Be Black* (Garden City, NY: Doubleday, 1953).

86 "Robert Goodwin, Dramatist; an Early Black Writer for TV," *New York Times*, February 18, 1983.

87 Blaxploitation includes films made primarily in the 1970s, largely for Black urban audiences, that featured strong, self-possessed Black characters and took on themes such as crime, drugs, vigilante justice, racial tensions, and youth culture. Their generally modest budgets made these productions extremely lucrative.

88 The advertisements appeared in the *Los Angeles Sentinel* on July 30, 1970, and December 17, 1970.

89 Nikki Wine, "'Black Chariot' Is a First for Filmdom," *Los Angeles Times*, December 13, 1970.

90 *Black Chariot* was completed on a budget of $44,000, according to Josiah Howard, *Blaxploitation Cinema: The Essential Reference Guide* (Godalming, Surrey: FAB Press, 2008), 93. Interviews conducted by Rhea L. Combs in 2018 and 2019 in Santa Monica, California, with Goodwin family members, and receipts and ledgers in the unprocessed Goodwin Family Archive, located at the Smithsonian's National Museum of African American History and Culture in Washington, DC, offer a range of $42,000 to $125,000 for funds raised. Prior to Combs's discovery of this film, it was considered lost. Special thanks to media archivist and conservator Blake McDowell, who has been instrumental in overseeing the restoration and preservation of this work, with the support of the National Film Preservation Foundation.

91 Kevin Thomas, "Casey at the Reins in 'Black Chariot,'" *Los Angeles Times*, December 18, 1971.

92 Howard, *Blaxploitation Cinema*, 93.

93 Ann Hornaday, "'Baadasssss!': Sweet, Mario," *Washington Post*, June 11, 2004, https://www.washingtonpost.com/archive/lifestyle/2004/06/11/baadasssss-sweet-mario/68746988-7513-44d7-9510-14008dba309d/. For more on Van Peebles's life and career, see Douglas Martin, "Melvin Van Peebles, Champion of New Black Cinema, Dies at 89," *New York Times*, September 22, 2021, https://www.nytimes.com/2021/09/22/movies/melvin-van-peebles-champion-of-new-black-cinema-dies-at-89.html.

94 Letter from Melvin Van Peebles to Jack Valenti of the MPAA, read by the former at the movie's press conference in Los Angeles on March 22, 1971; quoted in Melvin Van Peebles, *Sweet Sweetback's Baadasssss Song: A Guerilla Filmmaking Manifesto*, 3rd ed. (New York: Thunder's Mouth, 2004), loc. 1675 of 1707, Kindle.

95 Mario Van Peebles, introduction to *Guerilla Filmmaking Manifesto*, loc. 351 of 1707, Kindle.

96 This artwork is being shown during the run of *Regeneration* in an adjacent gallery at the Academy Museum. See also the description of the work on the artist's website, https://www.isaacjulien.com/projects/baltimore/.

97 *Pioneers of African-American Cinema*, curated by Charles Musser and Jacqueline N. Stewart (New York: Kino Lorber, 2016), DVD and Blu-ray.

98 For the previously lost status of *Reform School* and *Mr. Washington Goes to Town*, see Jan-Christopher Horak, "Preserving Race Films," in *Early Race Filmmaking in America*, ed. Barbara Tepa Lupack (New York: Routledge, 2016), 222. For *Harlem on the Prairie*, see Michael K. Johnson, *Hoo-Doo Cowboys and Bronze Buckaroos: Conceptions of the African American West* (Jackson: University Press of Mississippi, 2014), 110.

CASE STUDIES

BERT WILLIAMS AND BLACK PERFORMANCE CULTURE

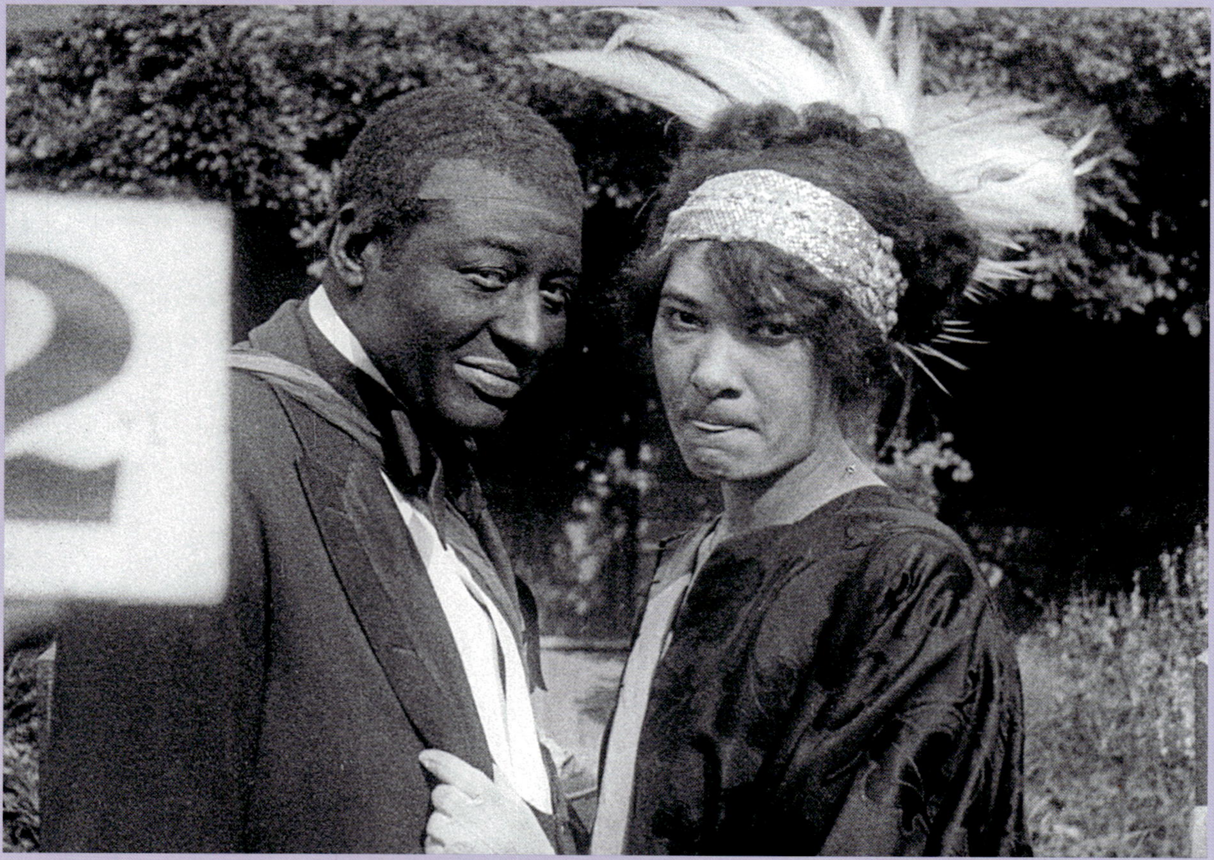

RON MAGLIOZZI

This page and opposite
Bert Williams and Odessa Warren Grey in *Lime Kiln Club Field Day* (dir. Edwin Middleton, T. Hays Hunter, 1913), film stills

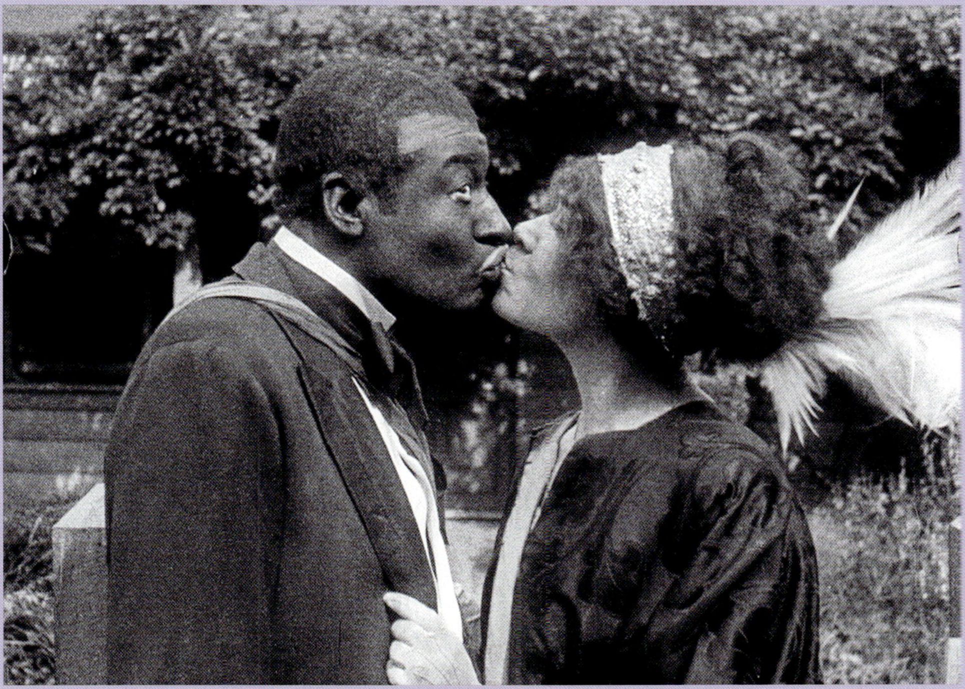

And we want our folks to like us. Not for the sake of the box office, but because over and behind all the money and prestige which move Williams and Walker, is a love for the race. Because we feel that, in a degree, we represent the race and every hair's breath of achievement we make is to its credit. For first, last and all the time, we are Negroes. . . . Now, do you see us in the light of a race institution?
—George W. Walker (1908)

The proper place to begin a history of Black performance on-screen is well before the invention of motion pictures, on the live theater stages of the United States and Europe. When the Bahamian-born Bert Williams (1874–1922) and his African American partner, George W. Walker, began their entertainment careers together in 1896, it was a remarkably rich period of employment opportunity and creativity for Black artists in the United States; it was also a racially conflicted period.

In the three decades that followed the Civil War, African Americans had begun a process of reshaping entertainment culture in the fields of music, dance, and theater. It was a time of genuine accomplishment and compromise, scarred by violent political and social backlash. Faced with white audiences' affection for demeaning minstrel stereotypes of racial inferiority rooted in nostalgic fantasies of prewar slave culture, a progressive-minded faction of the Black entertainment community struggled to raise consciousness. These entertainers' desire to represent themselves authentically and to control the performance of race onstage led to the production of a once-lost film, known since its rediscovery in 2014 as *Lime Kiln Club Field Day*, which now stands as a testament to their determination.

In the first two decades of commercial film production, beginning in 1896, the pool of professional and semiprofessional Black stage craftspeople and performers available to filmmakers was large. Well over two hundred African American performers and composers were celebrated enough from their work onstage to have their photographs appear on postcards and sheet music that white consumers started purchasing in the 1870s.[1] By 1903, when they began producing the first full-length, all-Black shows to appear on Broadway, Williams and Walker were employing upward of sixty to seventy individuals.[2] During these years of achievement in theater, major US film producers released more than one hundred race-themed short films, often using uncredited Black performers. But rather than picture the contemporary lives of African Americans, these films consistently fed white audiences' taste for tableaux of plantation life, exhibitions of eccentric dancing, lessons of complicit servitude, and comedies of compulsive behavior involving petty theft and punishment. Titles such as *A Watermelon Feast* (1896), *Dancing Darkey Boy* (1897), *On the Old Plantation* (1901), *Uncle Tom's Cabin, or, Slavery Days* (1903), and *The Chicken Thief* (1904) sum up their messages.[3] Reviewing a Williams short released in 1916, a critic for the African American weekly *Chicago Defender* complained, "Moving picture directors know very little about what to do with the 'brother' on celluloid."[4]

The annual *Ziegfeld Follies*, in which Williams appeared for all but two years between 1910 and 1919, was the most lavish and prestigious theatrical revue of its time. Commenting on Williams's debut in the 1910 *Follies*, a white critic for the *Chicago Examiner* remarked, "He was the needed artist in this great assemblage of good-looking nobodies. . . . Here was a human-being, whose veins ran blood, rather than champagne or beer; whose black countenance was—I say it modestly—as unbeautiful as Lincoln's. . . . Bert Williams—again I say it modestly—is the Mark Twain of his color."[5] After three years of press like this, the white-owned theatrical production giant Klaw & Erlanger

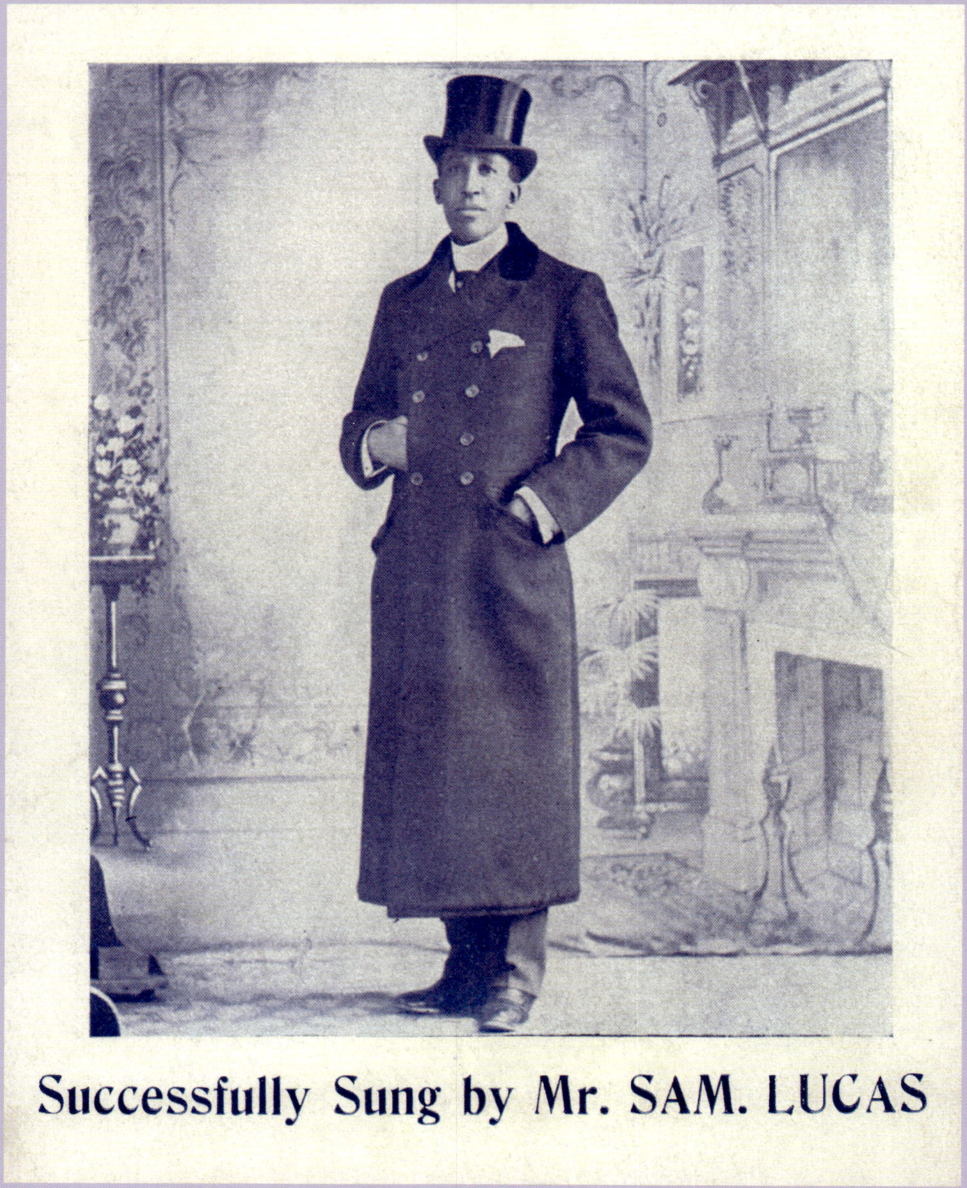

Sam Lucas, 1901, sheet music cover

was encouraged to gamble on his celebrity, announcing an alliance with the Biograph Company for the production of a Black-cast feature intended for interracial audiences.[6] Thus Williams found himself with the opportunity to appear in front of a camera and bring a sizable company of African American performers with him.

As a solo act and the only Black performer with the *Ziegfeld Follies* in the years leading up to the filming of *Lime Kiln*, Williams was occasionally criticized in the Black press for performing before segregated audiences and abandoning the "half a hundred of bright colored artists who need the opportunity" of employment that working in a Williams and Walker show had previously provided. "The colored people would prefer to see Mr. Williams as the head of a first-class combination of Negro performers for many good reasons."[7] Although his career choices as the first Black superstar were inevitably controversial, his fame and accomplishments benefited a community of friends and professional colleagues who were eager and exceptionally talented.[8]

The cast of Black performers who came to Biograph's Bronx film studio in the fall of 1913 represented two generations of stage experience playing before multiracial audiences. Joining Williams were Abbie Mitchell, who would later sing in the premiere of George Gershwin's *Porgy and Bess* (1935), and featured performers Henry Troy, John Wesley Jenkins, Julius "Happy" Glenn, and Walker Thompson, the last of whom later appeared in Oscar Micheaux's *The Symbol of the Unconquered* (1920). Extras included the stage producer J. Leubrie Hill, whose musical *Darktown Follies* supplied a dance chorus for the film; Sam Corker Jr., who also served as the film's assistant director; and sixty-five-year-old Sam Lucas, the pioneering "grand old man of the Negro Stage," whose four-decade-long career ended a year later, after he made history as the first Black man to play the lead in *Uncle Tom's Cabin* on film.[9] Sharing the most screen time with Williams was his leading lady, Odessa Warren Grey (known as Odessa Warren), who had performed in the chorus and designed costumes for Williams and Walker before retiring to become a leading Harlem businesswoman and philanthropist. Although it would be one hundred years before *Lime Kiln* was seen, her role makes her the first Black female film star.

Judging from the scale of the production mounted by the *Lime Kiln* producers, their commitment to a Black-cast feature was genuine. A romantic comedy that centers on three suitors competing for the affections of the town's prettiest girl, the film includes an innovative courtship scene aboard a moving merry-go-round and an ambitiously choreographed cakewalk production number. Although *Lime Kiln* does not completely break from period stereotypes of Black social life, the actors supporting Williams behave maturely, comport themselves naturally, and dress in modern style. For African American entertainers, fashion had been a means of expressing professionalism and uplift as far back as the Fisk University Jubilee Singers, who toured in evening wear before 1900. Odessa Warren designed the exceptionally stylish clothing she wears, and her costumes contribute to the impression that her character's interest in Williams is adult and significant. His eccentric outfits and makeup are derived from his stage persona, but his character and performance on-screen contradict his typical portrayal of the mournful, resigned "Jonah Man."[10] After his death Williams was compared to Charles Chaplin, whose film career began in 1914, just as Williams's was effectively ending.[11] Both practiced a contemplative style of comic pantomime that served well for expressing pathos and were known as intellectuals in their private lives. Just so, appearing before the camera in *Lime Kiln*, Williams is a thoughtful, self-motivated, and resourceful Black man who achieves the thing of most value in a romantic film: the loved one. The lingering close-up kiss between Williams and Warren that ends the footage shot for the film in a slow fade would have been among the boldest expressions of racial progress in popular entertainment at the time—had it been seen.

What market there might have been for the benevolent depiction of African American life in *Lime Kiln Club Field Day* evaporated with the devastating impact of *The Birth of a Nation* when the latter was released in February 1915. D. W. Griffith's phenomenally successful epic film demonized African Americans and reinvigorated racist sentiment to such a degree that Williams's lawyer reported, "The Southern territory would resent and would not exhibit the pictures of a Negro star."[12] And so the unedited *Lime Kiln* footage went into dead storage in the Biograph studio vaults.[13] The coincident rise of motion pictures reduced opportunities for Black stage performers, further marginalizing the pioneering community of creative artists who made the film. It was a setback for the cause of unbiased representation on-screen that would take generations to put right. Late in his career, Williams wrote, "Humiliations and persecutions . . . have to be faced by every person of colored blood, no matter his brain, education, or the integrity of his conduct. . . . Each time I come back to America this thing they call race prejudice follows me everywhere I go."[14]

Bert Williams (bottom) and George Walker in a publicity photograph promoting *In Dahomey*, ca. 1903

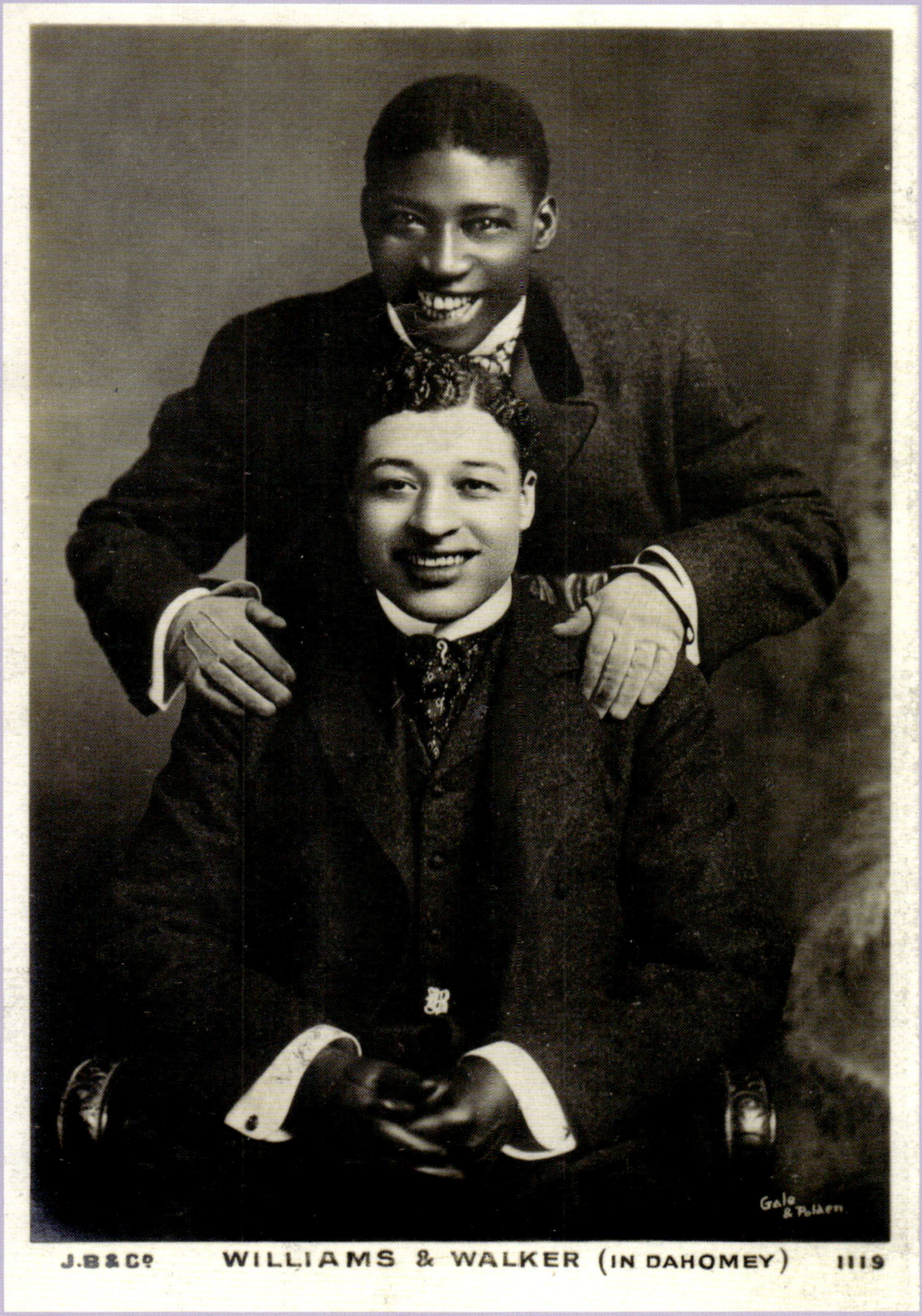

Notes

Epigraph
George W. Walker, "Bert Williams and Me and Them," *New York Age*, December 24, 1908, 4.

1 Sandra Jean Graham, "Composing in Black and White: Code-Switching in the Songs of Sam Lucas," in *The Oxford Handbook of Music Censorship* (New York: Oxford University Press, 2018), 570.

2 Three of these shows were *In Dahomey* (1903), *Abyssinia* (1906), *Bandanna Land* (1908), and *Mr. Lode of Koal* (1909).

3 The pool of Black talent in the New York area alone was sizable. The outdoor spectacle *Black America*—staged in Brooklyn, Boston, and Philadelphia in 1895—reportedly employed five hundred men, women, and children. Black vaudeville performers pioneering on-screen included Tom Fletcher, Al Bailey, Bertha Regustus, and James Grundy for Edison; Gertie Brown and Saint Suttle for Selig; Belle Davis, Louis Douglas, Fernandez Jones, and Irving Williams for Pathé; Ruth and Frederick Walker for Lumière; and Lottie Grady and Jerry Mills for the Foster Photoplay Company.

4 "The Gambler," *Chicago Defender*, August 5, 1916.

5 "Bert Williams—Ziegfeld's Follies of 1910," *Indianapolis Freeman*, September 17, 1910, cited in Henry T. Sampson, *Blacks in Blackface: A Sourcebook on Early Black Musical Shows* (Lanham, NJ: Scarecrow, 2014), 711–12.

6 In fact, it was the rising popularity of filmgoing that triggered Klaw & Erlanger's announcement of their partnership with the Biograph Company for a series of 104 motion pictures exploiting stage plays and performers under contract to them, including Williams. Trade advertisement in *Moving Picture News*, June 21, 1913, reprinted in Kemp R. Niver, *Klaw & Erlanger Present Famous Plays* (Los Angeles: Locare Research Group, 1976), 36–37.

7 R. W. Thompson, "Bert Williams Performing in Segregated Theatres," *Indianapolis Freeman*, January 14, 1911, cited in Sampson, *Blacks in Blackface*, 228.

8 Also shot with members of the same cast during the production of *Lime Kiln Club Field Day* in 1913 were *A Natural Born Gambler* and *Fish*, based on Williams's stage routines. Unlike *Lime Kiln*, both were eventually released in 1916 to profit from his continuing popularity in the *Follies* but failed to find favor with white or Black audiences.

9 James Weldon Johnson, *Black Manhattan* (1930; New York: Da Capo, 1991), 90.

10 Reviewing his debut in the 1910 edition of the *Ziegfeld Follies*, a white critic for the *Chicago Examiner* wrote, "the three vital qualities for Williams' peculiar stage personality: humor, mournful tunefulness and utter resignation." Cited in Sampson, *Blacks in Blackface*, 712. The songs "I'm a Jonah Man" (1903) and his signature number, "Nobody" (1906), which he recorded multiple times, are commonly referenced in descriptions of Williams.

11 Among the first to compare them was the famed music publisher Edward B. Marks, in *They All Sang: From Tony Pastor to Rudy Vallee* (New York: Viking, 1935), 94.

12 Mabel Rowland, ed., *Bert Williams: Son of Laughter* (New York: English Crafters, 1923), 150.

13 The unlabeled cans of camera negative were acquired by New York's Museum of Modern Art Film Library in 1938 and preserved in the late 1970s. After a decade-long identification process, an "archival assembly" of the footage premiered at the museum in November 2014.

14 Bert Williams, "The Comic Side of Trouble," *American Magazine*, December 1917, 33–34, 58.

SPECTATORSHIP AND THE BLACK PRESS

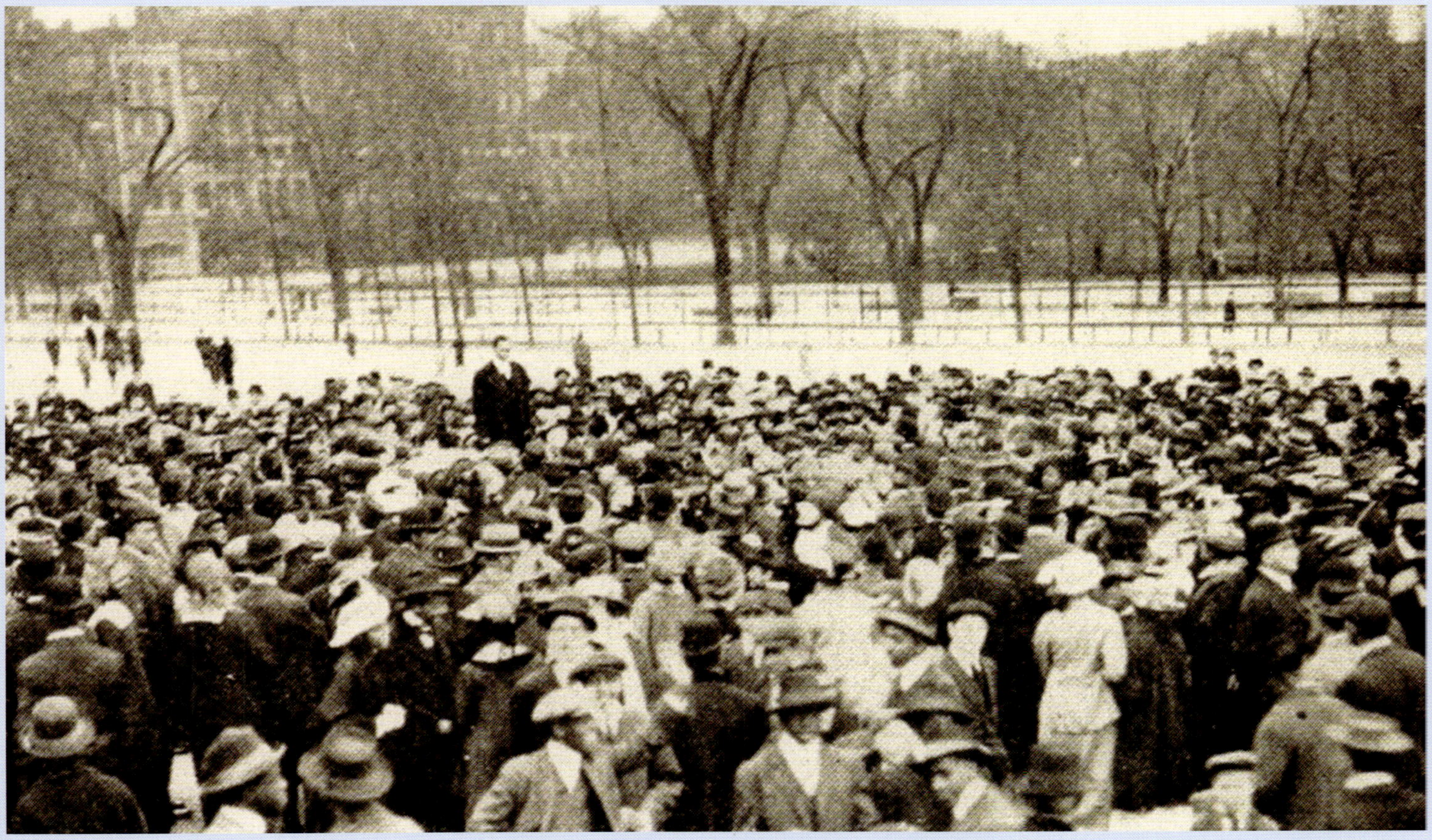

CARA CADDOO

Previous page
Protest against *The Birth of a Nation* on Boston Common, 1915, published in *The Crisis*, June 1915

The interconnected history of the Black press and African American film spectatorship vividly illustrates the creative means by which Black Americans pursued their dream of racial progress during the first half of the twentieth century. Not only did the Black press critique the racism of mainstream white cinema and publicize the activities of Black actors and filmmakers, but it also figured in an entire constellation of ideas, places, and practices that informed how African American filmgoers understood their shared investment in cinema and their relationships with one another.

After the Civil War, Black print culture experienced a period of tremendous growth.[1] A wide array of media—including magazines, newspapers, and broadsides—collectively known as the Black press provided African Americans with alternative forums for spreading information and exchanging ideas. Increasing literacy rates, migration from the rural South, and the expansion of the railroad system further broadened circulation and Black readership. Hundreds of Black newspapers, from T. Thomas Fortune's widely circulated *New York Age* to Ida B. Wells's short-lived *Memphis Free Speech*, were founded in response to the rising tide of Jim Crow segregation. As African Americans directed their hopes for the future inward, addressing their own communities and institutions, these publications served as tools for and evidence of racial uplift—the belief that the advancement of the race depended on the collective efforts of Black Americans.

The Black press established markets and systems of distribution that enabled the emergence of African American cinema. First, traveling film exhibitors and, later, "colored theatres" relied on Black newspapers to reach their audiences. The Black press offered one of the few channels through which motion pictures could be promoted and advertised to the African American public. In particular, newspaper announcements and advertisements figured prominently in what scholars refer to as the public dimensions of cinema spectatorship.[2] The Black press promoted the practice of screening films in Black churches, schools, and lodges. These sites frequently doubled as motion picture theaters because white-owned venues excluded Black patrons altogether or relegated them to the least desirable seats in the house (known as the buzzard's roost). Advertisements for Black motion picture shows underscored their "uplifting" themes and contributions to collective Black progress. Of course, the very notion of what counted as progressive was often a matter of debate. For example, the itinerant preacher and showman H. Charles Pope's advertisements for *The Devil's Cook Kitchen* promised to teach Black youth about the contributions of African Americans to the nation's history and the "26 ways in which there is harm in dancing."[3]

As moving pictures grew increasingly popular, the Black press imbued the cinema with deeper cultural and political significance. "A Negro theatrical enterprise is like a Negro business," wrote Vere E. Johns in the *New York Age*, "as long as the goods are worthwhile it becomes a duty as well as a necessity for us to go ahead and support it."[4] For Earl J. Morris, drama critic for the *Pittsburgh Courier*, Black-produced motion pictures afforded "employment to our ambitious young boys and girls with movie aspirations."[5] Demands for fair and authentic representation could erupt into boycotts, petitions, and picket lines. Editors such as Beatrice Morrow Cannady of the *Portland Advocate*, Robert Sengstacke Abbott of the *Chicago Defender*, and William Monroe Trotter of the *Boston Guardian* published scathing critiques of racial discrimination on the screen and in the theater. When D. W. Griffith released *The Birth of a Nation* (1915), their publications played a pivotal role in transforming local campaigns against the film into the first mass Black protest movement of the twentieth century.[6]

Film critics contributed to the rise of Black popular culture by publicly invoking the now commonplace idea of the Black spectator with particular aesthetic sensibilities, practices, and consumer interests.[7] As critics for the Black press, Juli Jones Jr. (the nom de plume of the Black filmmaker William D. Foster), the "Harlem Hostess" and radio personality Geraldyn Dismond (later known as Gerri Major), and the actor Clarence Muse wrote extensively of the assumed tastes and sensibilities of this imagined Black filmgoing public. The work of Black critics was often inflected with class and gender biases common to race newspapers, an enterprise largely overseen by the middle class. In particular, the politics of respectability informed Black critics' preoccupation with supposedly "negative" and "positive" depictions of Blackness on-screen. These debates, which continue today, demonstrate not only a diversity of

Advertisement promoting H. Charles Pope's *The Devil's Cook Kitchen* (1905) in the *Indianapolis Freeman*, 1905

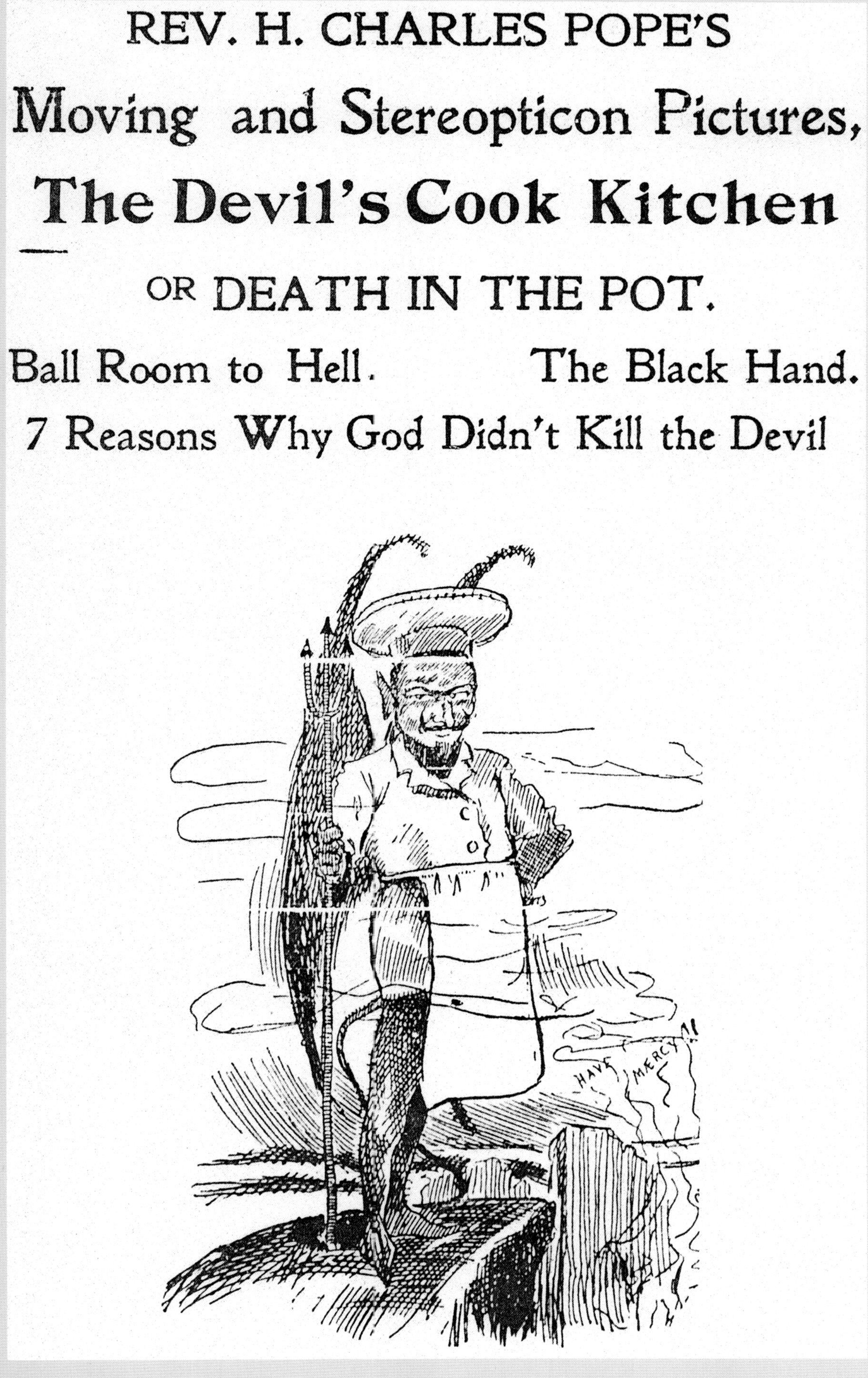

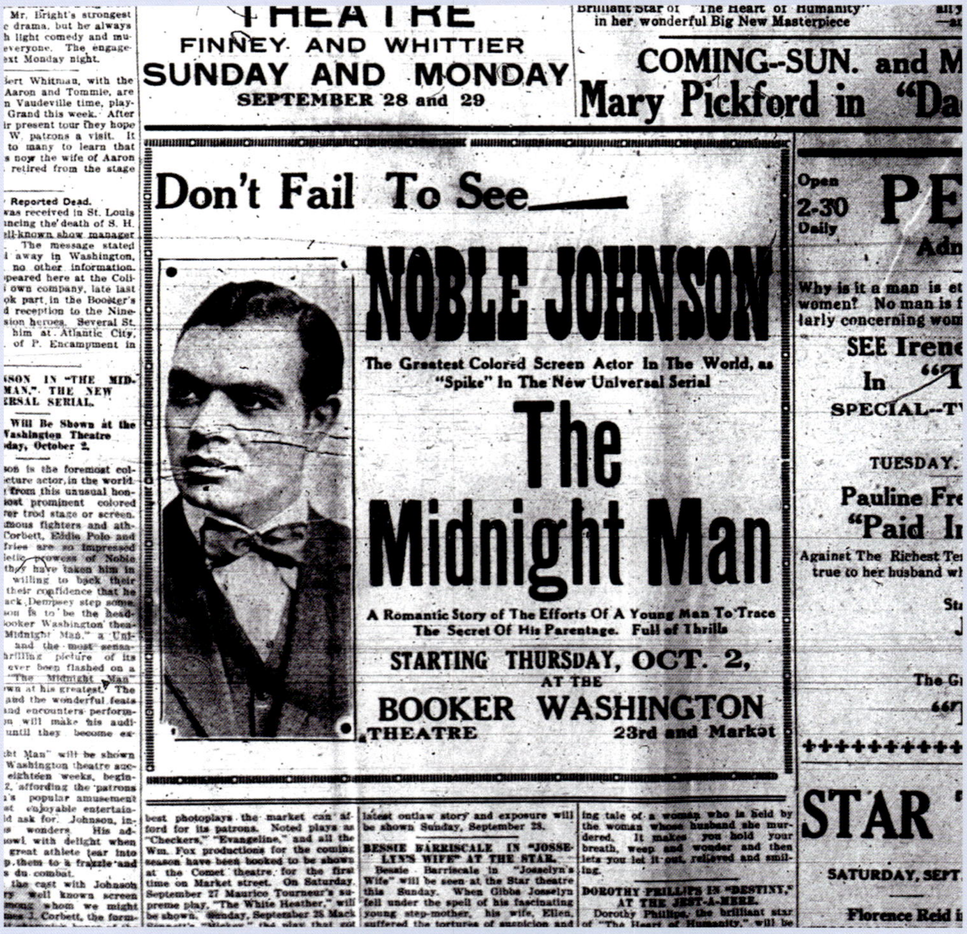

Advertisement for the film serial *The Midnight Man* (1919), featuring Noble Johnson, in the *St. Louis Argus*, 1919

The serial played at the 506-seat Booker T. Washington Theatre in Saint Louis.

interpretations regarding Blackness and how Black people should be portrayed in films but also the widespread investment in racial representation on-screen.

The rise of Black movie stars owes much to race publications and their coverage of the personal lives and on-screen performances of Black actors. By shifting attention away from white leads and focusing on Black actors, even when the latter were cast in minor roles, the Black press contributed to the type of extracinematic discourse that enabled Black actors' performances to outshine those of their white counterparts.[8] An advertisement in the *St. Louis Argus* for an exhibition at the Booker T. Washington Theatre of the film serial *The Midnight Man* (1919), for instance, featured an image of the actor Noble Johnson with his name in large, bold type and the words "the Greatest Colored Screen Actor In the World." Nowhere is it acknowledged that Johnson played a supporting role to the white star and former champion boxer James J. Corbett, who neither appears nor is mentioned in the advertisement.[9]

The race film industry, which produced motion pictures for Black and mixed-race audiences, reflected a recognition of the economic and social significance of the Black spectator. Race film producers and journalists developed symbiotic relationships intended to increase their profits. For instance, both the filmmaker Oscar Micheaux and the Lincoln Motion Picture Company hired journalists from Black newspapers to serve as their companies' salesmen and representatives. Tony Langston, the theatrical editor for the *Chicago Defender*, received a cut for renting Lincoln films to Chicago theaters, an endeavor that he supported with glowing reviews of the films in his newspaper.[10]

Black cinema culture also transformed the content, circulation, and financial stakes of the Black press. By the 1920s motion picture advertisements constituted an essential source of revenue for race newspapers and magazines, a fact that reflects how these spheres of Black public life continued to develop. The demands for celebrity gossip, film reviews, and other cinema-related news led race newspapers to debut special columns or entire entertainment sections with titles such as The Screen, Camera Eye, and Movie Snapshots.[11] Hollywood studios, realizing the influence of the Black press, cultivated relationships with Black journalists. "I am sending you an exclusive story to be released to your services on the Negro players who are lately taking part in Metro-Goldwyn-Mayer's pictures," the MGM publicist Joseph Polonsky wrote George P. Johnson of the Pacific Coast News Bureau in 1927.[12] When Cecil B. DeMille planned to produce a film version of *Porgy and Bess* with the actor Paul Robeson, DeMille's studio supervisor and writer Bertram Millhauser reached out to

Johnson for advice. The project was ultimately scrapped, but Millhauser's correspondence and promises to "have our publicity department communicate with you for publicity purposes all of the data in relation to the production" demonstrates Hollywood producers' recognition of the power and influence of the Black press.[13]

"The moving pictures today, more than any agency, except perhaps the newspaper, is responsible for building up or breaking down the recognized status of any racial group," Helen James, a reader of the *New York Age*, wrote to the newspaper's editors in September 1940.[14] James's assessment of the power of the press and the moving pictures, which remains relevant, was informed by a longer history. As African Americans pursued goals of racial progress across ideological and geographic differences, they not only generated their own print and cinema cultures but also gave public meaning and recognition to a collective understanding of what it meant to be Black and to be free.

Notes

1 For example, I. Garland Penn identified approximately 10 Black newspapers in print in 1870; by 1890 he knew of 154 being published in the United States. I. Garland Penn, *The Afro-American Press and Its Editors* (Springfield, MA: Willey & Co., 1891), 112. See also Cara Caddoo, "Black Newspapers, Real Property, and Mobility in Memphis after Emancipation," *Journal of African American History* 102 (Fall 2017): 468–91.

2 Miriam Hansen, *Babel and Babylon: Spectatorship in American Silent Film* (Cambridge, MA: Harvard University Press, 1991), 1–20, and Jacqueline Najuma Stewart, *Migrating to the Movies: Cinema and Black Urban Modernity* (Berkeley: University of California Press, 2005), 1–19.

3 "The Devil's Cook Kitchen," *Indianapolis Freeman*, October 21, 1905, 5.

4 Vere E. Johns, "Radio Drama," *New York Age*, August 20, 1932, 6.

5 Earl J. Morris, "George Randol to Feature 'Shorts,'" *Pittsburgh Courier*, July 23, 1938, 21.

6 Cara Caddoo, *Envisioning Freedom: Cinema and the Building of Modern Black Life* (Cambridge, MA: Harvard University Press, 2014), 139–70.

7 Anna Everett, *Returning the Gaze: A Genealogy of Black Film Criticism* (Durham, NC: Duke University Press, 2001), and Charlene Regester, "The African-American Press and Race Movies, 1919–1929," in *Oscar Micheaux and His Circle*, ed. Pearl Bowser, Jane Gaines, and Charles Musser (Bloomington: Indiana University Press, 2001), 34–49.

8 Miriam J. Petty, *Stealing the Show: African American Performers and Audiences in 1930s Hollywood* (Oakland: University of California Press, 2016).

9 Advertisement, *St. Louis Argus*, September 26, 1919, 4.

10 Tony Langston to George P. Johnson, November 24, 1916, George P. Johnson Negro Film Collection, 1916–1977 (LSC 1042), reel 7, Library Special Collections, University of California, Los Angeles.

11 Everett, *Returning the Gaze*, 10.

12 George P. Johnson, interviewed by Elizabeth Dixon and Adelaide Tusler, July 21, 1967, oral history transcript (1970), Oral History Program, University of California, Los Angeles, 84.

13 Jos. [Joseph] Pelonsky to Mr. [George P.] Johnson, Pacific Coast News Bureau, October 31, 1927, Johnson Negro Film Collection, reel 6.

14 Helen James, letter to the editor, *New York Age*, September 14, 1940, 2.

PAUL ROBESON

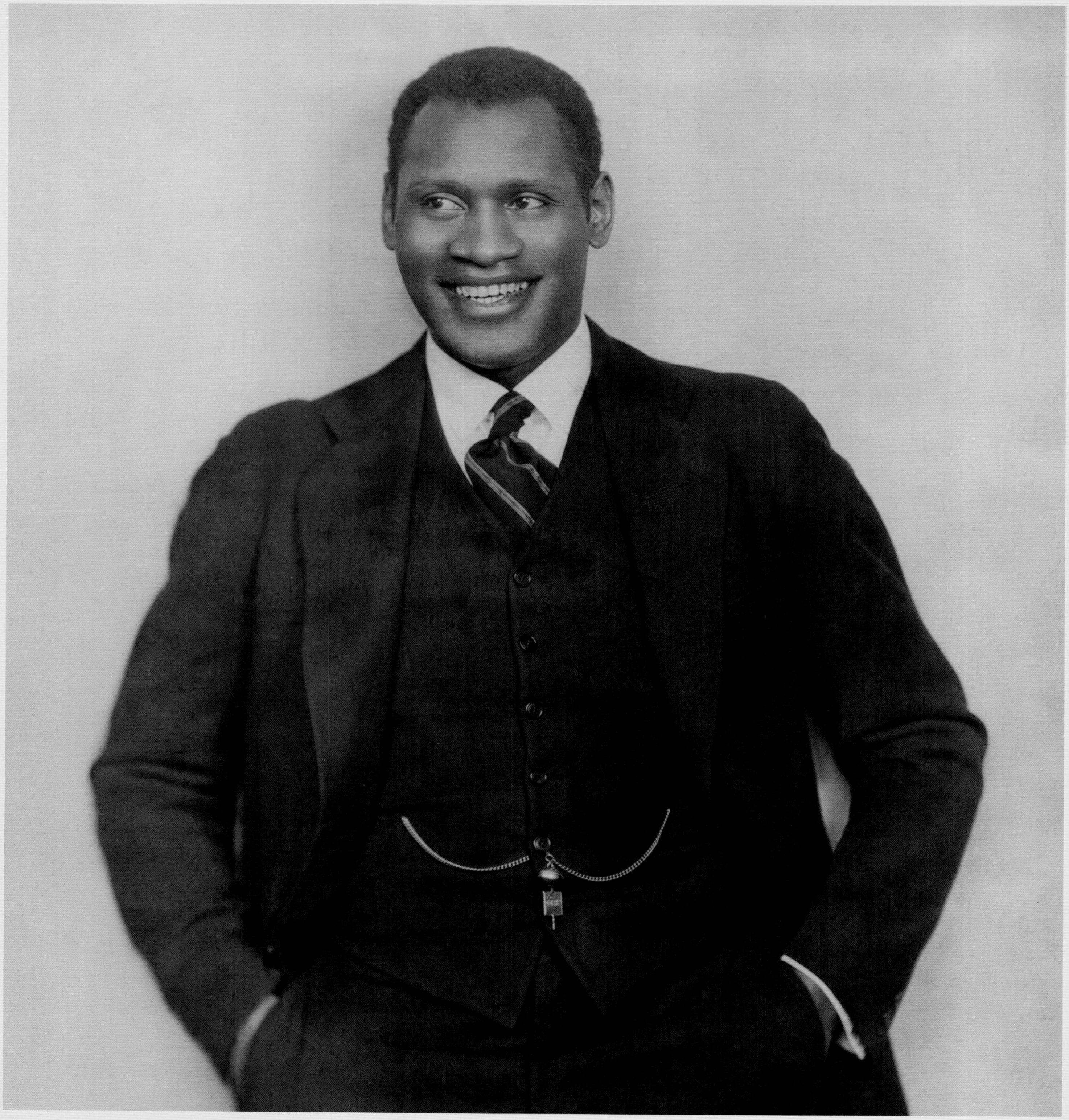

ELLEN C. SCOTT

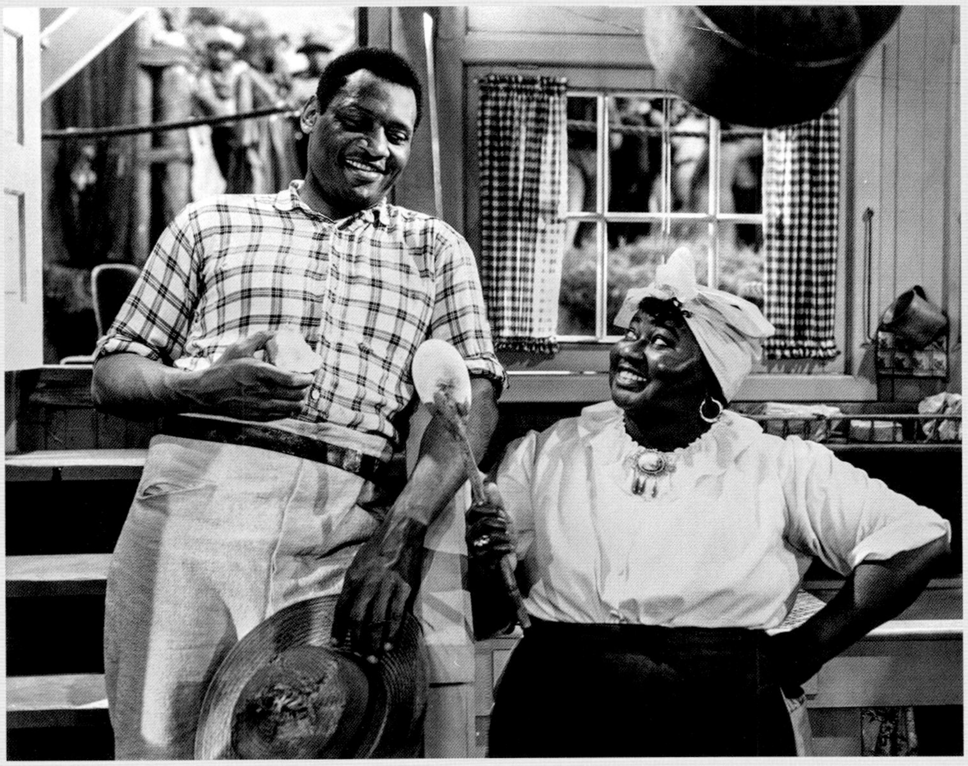

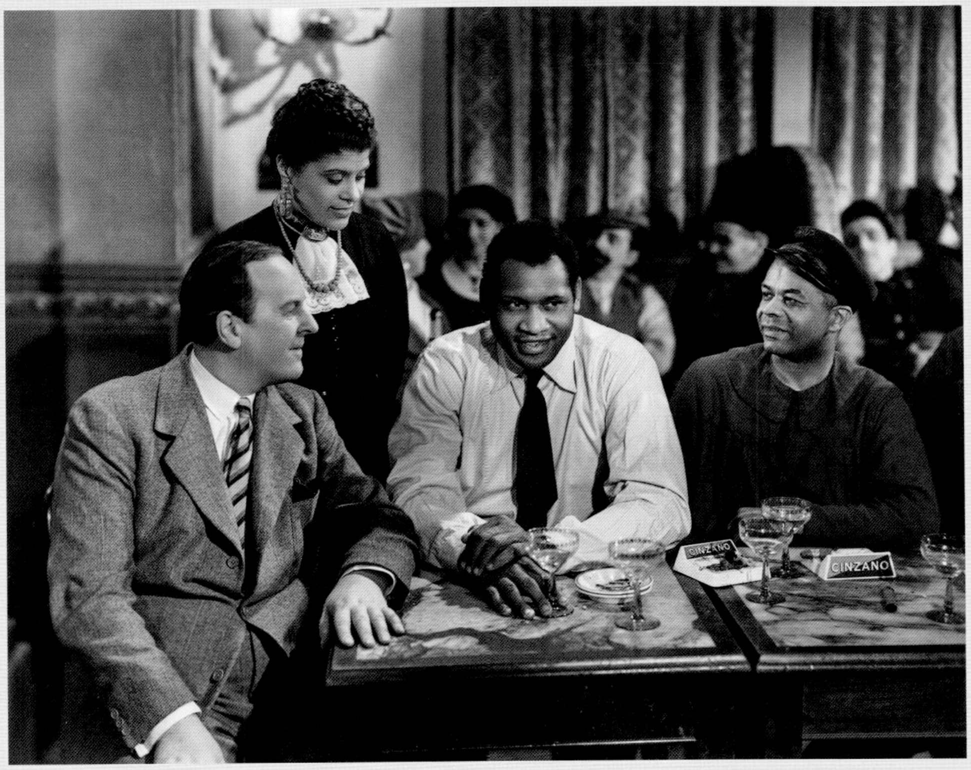

Opposite
Paul Robeson, ca. 1930s

Top
Paul Robeson and Hattie McDaniel in *Show Boat* (1936), production still

Bottom
Eslanda Goode Robeson (standing), Paul Robeson (center), and Lawrence Brown (right) in *Big Fella* (Great Britain, 1938), production still

Perhaps no individual embodies the promise and failure of Black actors in the American cinema more fully than Paul Robeson (1898–1976). As Shana Redmond has argued, Robeson powerfully marshaled his own image in his performances, especially in song, often altering the lyrics of white-authored tunes to sharpen their racial critique and elide their racist caricatures.[1] Controlling one's cinematic representation was a far more slippery proposition, however. Robeson appeared in only twelve films throughout his long career as a public figure and entertainer, a fact that reflects the difficulties he encountered in establishing control over images that others directed and that speaks more generally of the challenges of presenting a fluid and nonexploitative image of African American manhood on the American screen.[2]

Robeson began his film career in Oscar Micheaux's *Body and Soul* (1925), in which he played both an evil preacher and his brother, a hardworking inventor, a portrayal that caused consternation in the Black press.[3] In contrast with Micheaux's auteurist project, Robeson's second set of films represents more collective experiments with the medium, again outside the Hollywood context but working in collaboration with global intellectuals and artists. In 1926 he appeared as Alexandre Dumas in an amateur film by Ralph Barton, a cartoonist and graphic artist, alongside such prominent figures as Sinclair Lewis, Theodore Dreiser, and Clarence Darrow. Barton's decision to use the clearly Black Robeson to render the biracial Dumas, whom many Americans did not realize had African ancestry, represents a provocative choice, albeit for a limited audience. Robeson's next film role was in *Borderline* (1930), an interracial avant-garde production that featured both Robeson and his marital partner and business manager, Eslanda Goode Robeson, a "ubiquitous figure in international arts circles" whose commitment to Black internationalism was as significant as her husband's.[4]

In 1933 Robeson made his first Hollywood film, *The Emperor Jones*, in which he attempted to bring complexity and dignity to the role that Charles Gilpin made famous on the stage. As press photographs indicate, however, the image the camera captured was often one that rendered him unserious. The film nevertheless raised important issues about Black imprisonment and the prospect of Black self-rule in a world in which white colonialism dominated. In 1936 he appeared in *Show Boat* as Joe, a role he had made famous on the stage. Here Robeson offered his famous rendition of "Ol' Man River" in an expressionistic sequence. The prominent cotton bale, combined with the darkened images of field-workers in a row, offered a rare Hollywood image dramatizing the

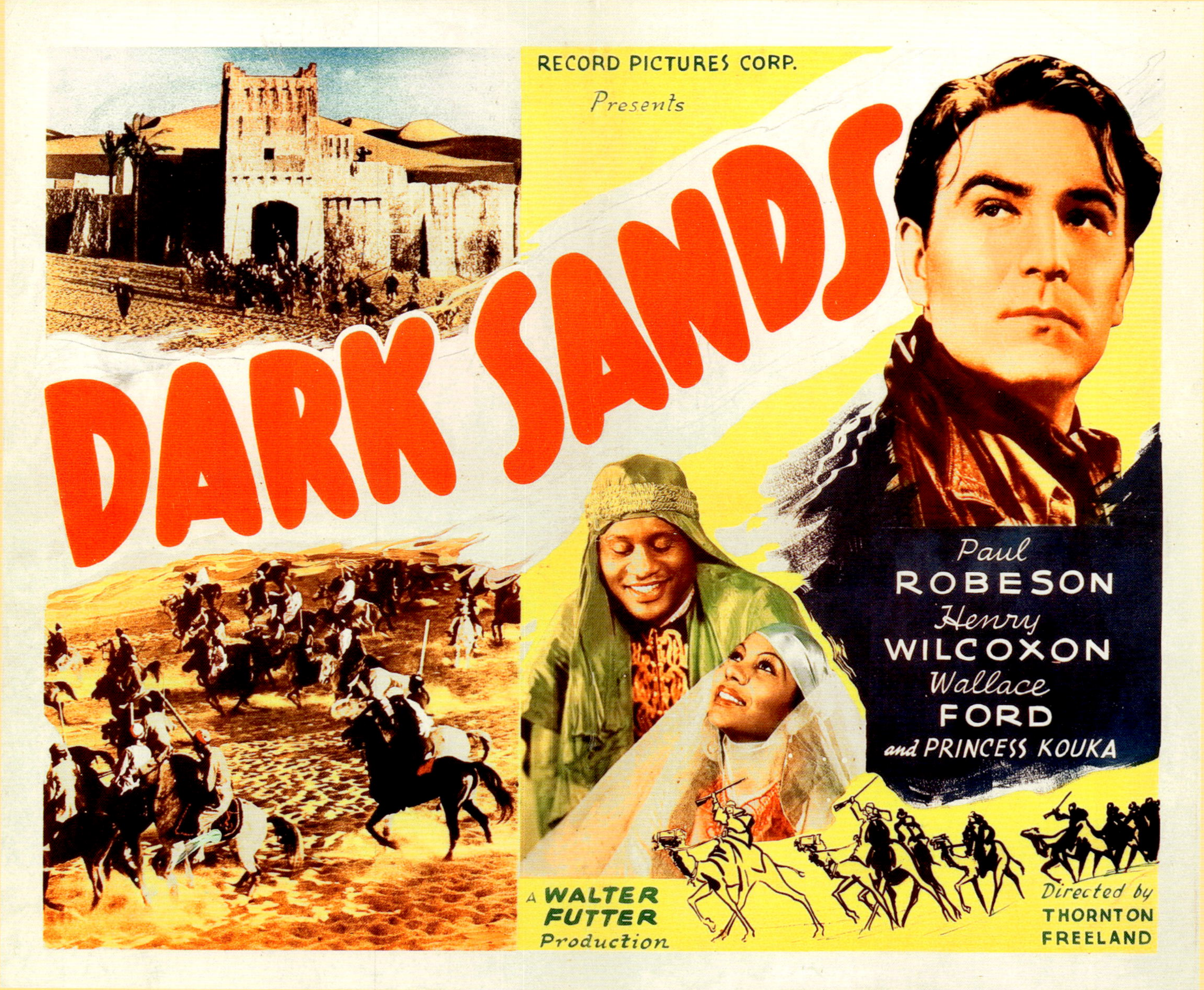

Dark Sands **(Great Britain, 1937), theatrical release poster**

magnitude of Black labor both during and after slavery. Despite stereotypical lyrics, Robeson's performance showed grit, power, and earnestness.

Robeson's British films (six in total) compose an important chapter in his film career and are underappreciated for his contributions in representing the Black international on-screen. *Sanders of the River* (1935) was perhaps the worst of these in that, as critics in the Black press noted, Robeson plays a chief who is a loyal servant of the empire.[5] It is easy to see, however, why he initially saw some promise in the film and his role in it. The opening credits employ Robeson's booming baritone voice in a song that links Africa to African America. The use of international musical exchange as a way of bridging cultures and positing identity must have appealed to Robeson. That his character hails from Liberia, an African country populated in 1821 by formerly enslaved Americans and the only African state never subject to colonial rule, also sets it apart from most American films of its time.

Robeson's character, Bosambo, first appears barely clothed in an approximation of African Indigenous garb. But his rap sheet, complemented with a suave photo shown minutes later, raises doubt about both his identity and his loyalties, suggesting he is neither naive nor pliant. He is, he later admits in the film, actually a "Liberian Negro, convicted for habitual petty larceny—escaped from St. Thome prison," a revelation that completes his image as a master of disguise. Robeson likely regarded *Sanders of the River* as more forward-looking than American films in that his character becomes a leader involved in government affairs. Very rarely in 1930s Hollywood films were Black people shown in such roles. Further, the film allowed Black spectators to see African Indigenous leaders as a form of royalty.

Perhaps even more important is the vision of Black romance in Robeson's British films. Kris Jones has noted that in the United States, "at the nascence of sound film, Hollywood self-regulators . . . worked to curtail public disdain from particular interest groups, as well as loss of profits from censorship bans" by restricting the Black kiss on-screen.[6] By contrast, *Sanders of the River* shows a natural, uncaricatured, and smoldering romance between Robeson's Bosambo and Nina Mae McKinney's Lolongo. And the procreative, happy nuclear family so often denied Black spectators is present in both *Sanders* and *Dark Sands* (1937). Indeed, in both films Robeson's character's family is the only nuclear family depicted, and the song sequences between Robeson and his son in both films draw attention to the Black father-son relationship, which was almost never explored in American cinema. Further, in *Sanders*, *Song of Freedom* (1936), and *Big Fella* (1937), Black American actors play the love interests, a boon for Black American audiences denied these images. What is more, in *Sanders* the camera's treatment of McKinney and Robeson—especially McKinney, whose glamorous hair and makeup render her cinematically beautiful—refuses to subsume Nigeria, where the film is set, in the past or to revile rural, Black ethnic, non-Western folkways, adornment, or styles of dress as "primitive" or passé. As Lolongo and Bosambo quip, they are not from the "interior" but are two cosmopolitan Black people whose ability to play to and against white expectations is an outgrowth of their modern sophistication. In *Big Fella*, Elisabeth Welch plays the cool, composed Mae West–like singer with whom Robeson's character has a subtle but unmistakable romantic relationship. Indeed, the film closes with the two of them standing on the dock and then leaving for her apartment to have breakfast. When he asks what she's got, she responds with the film's closing line—"You just wait and see"—a sexual innuendo that would never have made it into a Hollywood production with Black leads.

While the filmmakers often used Robeson's costuming and the white men that he played against to other him and estrange his performances, making them awkward, on the page Robeson's characters read as much meatier and more culturally significant than the servant roles Hollywood offered. They may even have seemed subversive in that they allowed Black spectators Pan-African identification, an image of Black leadership (though never over whites), and Black romance. He played the Black British descendant of an enslaved king from a fictional island off the west coast of Africa who eventually goes back to lead the people from which he came (*Song of Freedom*); a wily Liberian who is a self-made chief in Nigeria (*Sanders*); a compassionate London dockworker who cares for a lost child (*Big Fella*); an American sailor who joins with white miners in a labor struggle (*The Proud Valley*, 1940); an Indigenous guide who talks back to the whites he leads and eventually takes his rightful throne as king (*King Solomon's Mines*, 1937); and a talented and rebellious medical student who becomes a soldier (*Dark Sands*). A repeated theme in these films is the return to and reconciliation with Africa as place, identity, and construct and the braiding together of African and African American cultures. Increasing the verisimilitude of these Black male characters is the persistent theme of fugitivity: each is at some point wrongly hunted by white or colonial forces. Another feature of Robeson's British films is their insistent interracialism, evident in the interracial ensembles in each of these films.

Dark Sands was perhaps the best of these films, though it still contained stereotypes of Black soldiers gambling at dice and white commanders saying without rebuke that the Black soldiers are "like children." Here, however, Robeson finally played a role with the stature he had long strived for. His character, Jericho, is a medical student turned World War I officer. He is wrongly held responsible by an angry white military leader for punching a superior officer, even though his action saved many men. He flees punishment by a plainly racist white military, employing his talents at going undercover and using his knowledge of culture and language to evade capture. He partners with a white American who provides comic relief.

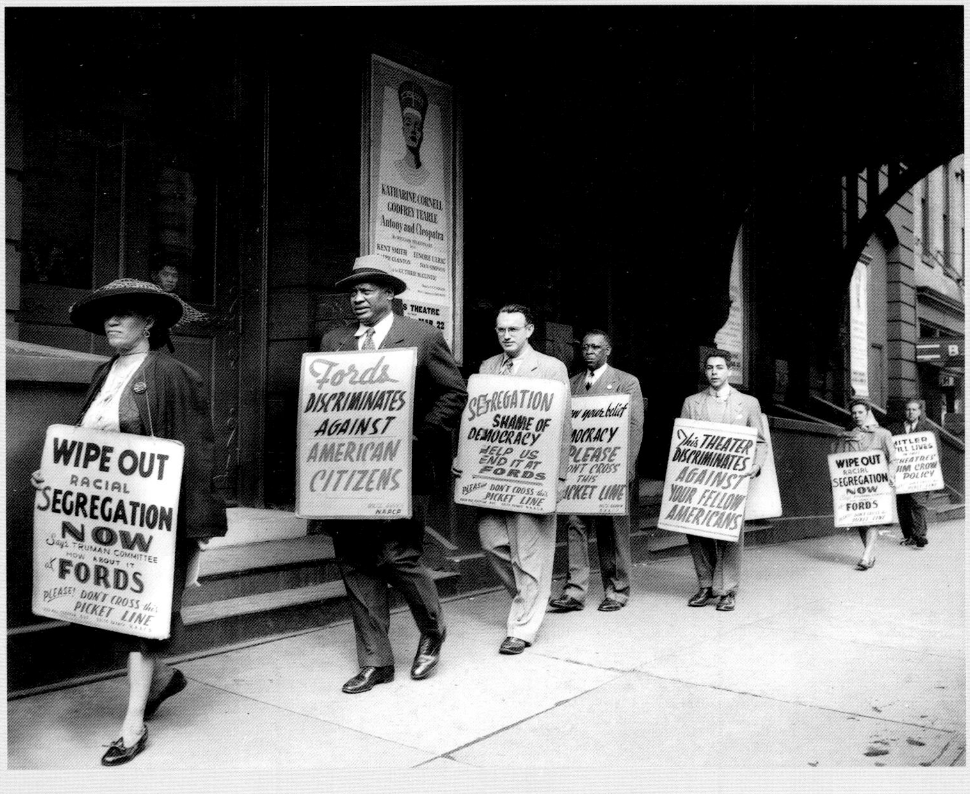

Paul S. Henderson (photographer), Paul Robeson (second from left) and members of the Baltimore chapter of the NAACP protest the racial segregation of Ford's Theatre, 1948

Jericho not only builds a life for himself in exile in Africa but also becomes a leader. In this film—as a soldier, doctor, leader, and handsome desert warrior—Robeson came the closest to depicting the renaissance man that he was in real life. His portrayal of a fugitive from the law who dedicates himself to doing good and saving lives was an important counterpart to the American cinema's Black characters—especially the criminalized. In the original script, Jericho goes back to clear the name of the commanding officer who defended him at his court-martial and was subsequently held responsible for his escape. In a win for nomadism, exile, freedom, and Black self-determination, however, Robeson convinced the filmmakers to end the film with Jericho continuing to evade authorities.

In 1942 Robeson starred in his last Hollywood film. His friend Boris Morros, a Hollywood leftist and the film's musical director, had assured him that *Tales of Manhattan* (1942) would be a solid project exploring the power of collective organizing and communal ownership. Some African Americans were so offended by the film, however, which situated Black people not in Manhattan but in a rural outpost, that they threatened to picket. An embarrassed Robeson, again foiled by editing and the larger narrative arc into which his image was enlisted, said he would join the picket lines if they formed in New York. By 1943 he had essentially retired from film acting.

Although he last appeared in a Hollywood film in 1942, Robeson's ghost haunts the American cinema. As the film historian Charles Musser has indicated, Robeson continued to both work on and appear in documentary films after his Hollywood career ended.[7] Little scholarly exploration has met his important collaborations with the leftist filmmaker Leo Hurwitz, whose postwar films showed the apocalyptic lining of American prosperity and World War II victory. The two collaborated on the important documentary *Native Land* in 1942. But later they also sought to bring to the screen Howard Fast's international best seller *Freedom Road* (1944), the story of a former slave who, having served in the Union army, becomes a member of the South Carolina Constitutional Convention and later a congressman in Washington during Radical Reconstruction. Robeson was to star. *Freedom Road* represented a chance—perhaps his last—to finally appear in a film he could be proud of. And it seems that he initially poured himself into the project, serving as president of the Freedom Road Production Company. The cast was to be made up almost entirely of committed leftists or fellow travelers. The film fell victim to the blacklist, however, as many of its key players were called before the House Un-American Activities Committee. Though the project was never realized, it represents, perhaps more than any of the films Robeson made, the realization of his principles and a firm rejection of the oligarchic, capitalist model of Hollywood production.

Notes

1 Shana Redmond, *Anthem: Social Movements and the Sound of Solidarity* (New York: New York University Press, 2013), 102.

2 For more on Robeson's career and activism, see Shana Redmond, *Everything Man: The Form and Function of Paul Robeson* (Durham, NC: Duke University Press, 2020), and Martin Duberman, *Paul Robeson: A Biography* (New York: Open Road Media, 2014).

3 See Maybelle Chew, "Along the White Way," *Baltimore Afro-American*, September 11, 1926. Charlene Regester also discusses the trouble that New York censors, Black and white, had with the film's depiction of the minister played by Robeson. Charlene Regester, "Black Films, White Censor," in *Movie Censorship and American Culture*, ed. Francis Couvares (Washington, DC: Smithsonian Institution Press, 1996), 180–81.

4 Barbara Ransby, *Eslanda: The Large and Unconventional Life of Mrs. Paul Robeson* (New Haven, CT: Yale University Press, 2013), 4.

5 "Africans Believe Paul Robeson Was Tricked in British Film," *Chicago Defender*, October 5, 1935, 24.

6 Kris Jones, "More Than Just a Kiss: Finding the Black Romantic Image in Classical Hollywood Film, 1929–1954" (dissertation prospectus, University of California, Los Angeles, May 24, 2019).

7 Charles Musser, "Paul Robeson and the End of His 'Movie' Career," *Cinémas: Revue d'études cinématographiques* 19, no. 1 (2008): 147–79.

JOSEPHINE BAKER: BLACK FILM'S FRENCH STAR

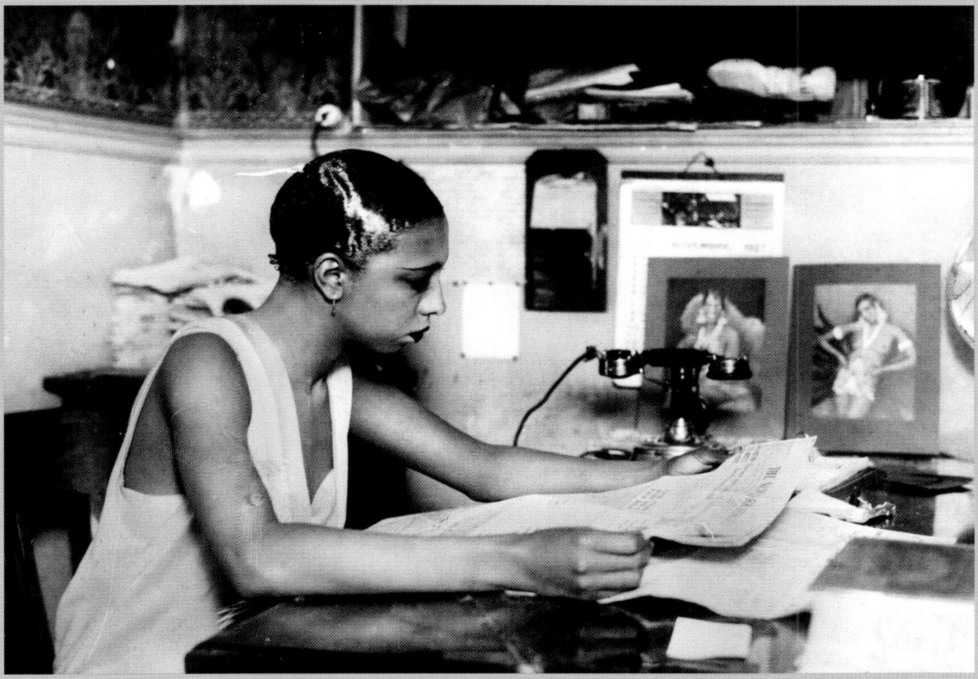

TERRI SIMONE FRANCIS

Previous page
Josephine Baker at Chez Joséphine, her cabaret in Paris, 1928

Stanislaus Julian Walery (Polish, 1863–1935), *Josephine Baker Performing at the Folies Bergère*, 1926, gelatin silver print, 11 13⁄16 × 8 5⁄16 in. (30 × 21.1 cm)

It may be surprising to see Josephine Baker (1906–1975) in an account of Black American cinema, given her fifty-year international career as a live entertainer and her few film appearances: Baker had top-billed roles in only four French feature films.[1] Her outsider status, however, makes her belong more profoundly because of all that she illuminates. Born Freda Josephine McDonald in Saint Louis, Baker left home at a young age for the vaudeville circuit run by the Theatre Owners Booking Association (TOBA, an acronym that some said stood for "tough on Black asses"). She performed with the Dixie Steppers, traveled as a dresser for the blues singer Clara Smith, and toured with the groundbreaking musical *Shuffle Along* in the early 1920s. Baker became known as "the lightning of jazz" for a comedic dance role she created. She would delight audiences by playing the chorus girl who danced out of sync, breaking the line, making funny faces, rubber-legging, and goofing around. In New York the socialite and producer Caroline Dudley invited her to perform in Paris as part of the cast of *La revue nègre*, a musical showcasing Black American talent. In 1925 Baker relocated to Paris, a city where she knew no one but her castmates and did not yet speak the language. Baker did understand beauty and hard work, however, and her fluency in both brought her international celebrity as a dancer, singer, and film star.

Baker discounted her formative years in the United States, telling *The Guardian* in 1974, "No, I didn't get my first break on Broadway. I was only in the chorus in 'Shuffle Along' and 'Chocolate Dandies.' . . . I became famous first in France in the twenties. I just couldn't stand America and I was one of the first coloured Americans to move to Paris."[2] Yet her dance repertoire in Paris drew heavily on Black American dances such as the Charleston and the Black Bottom, mixed with her unique choreography. What's more, Baker's rise coincided with—and fueled—the trend of *le tumulte noir* (literally, "the Black craze"), the fascination with Black American jazz, dance, and popular culture in general among the Parisian cultural elite. Her significance in France drew largely on her capacity, as an American of African descent, to appeal to both the French fascination with the United States and French ideas about Blackness.

Baker made her film debut just two years after her arrival in Paris, in *La sirène des tropiques / Siren of the Tropics* (1927). The film, which was well received in Europe, had its American premiere at the Lafayette Theater in New York on September 22, 1929. The American distribution of *Siren* and press coverage of the film in the *Afro-American* and the *Chicago Defender* firmly connect Baker to the American race movie circuit and to Black-cast mainstream films such as *Hallelujah* and *Hearts in Dixie* (both 1929).[3] Black American cinephiles hoped that Baker's success in Europe would create additional opportunities for other Black actors, especially in light of the breakthrough success of *Hallelujah*, which starred Nina Mae McKinney, who is said to have earned a five-year contract with Metro-Goldwyn-Mayer on the strength of her performance in the film.[4] Leading up to *Siren*'s US premiere, the September 4, 1929, issue of the *New York Amsterdam News* reported that filmmakers "have been looking with intense interest to the Harlem performers in hopes of finding someone with 'IT' to portray the rapidly mounting scripts that await but the arrival of the proper character to depict the roles. . . . From across the sea comes an ominous rumble of thunder. The dark cloud of hope on the horizon is Josephine Baker."[5]

But would this hope materialize? Although *Siren* had the novelty of Baker, several factors worked against its success. It was a silent film released after the premiere in October 1927 of *The Jazz Singer*, the first feature film presented as a talkie. *Siren* thus depended on Baker's fame and its positive reception in the United States as well as the degree to which the film satisfied the critical frameworks of the Black press and fulfilled the ideal of dignified cinematic African American representation.

How might engaging Baker's films today change or reinvigorate our understanding of "Black film"? Defining Black film is ever an adventure in parsing authorship, subject matter, production, and performance. With Baker's work, however, it's more a question of where her film career belongs, given the current conventions of film study, which consider genre, nation, authorship, temporality, and stardom. Baker touches on all these areas, and she makes the question of place in particular more complex. *Siren of the Tropics*, like her other films, is situated within and between two national cinemas in that it was a French production that starred an American actress. Although Baker's films drew heavily on her stage persona and a colonialist mindset in which the Black body represented an exotic foreign body, I would argue that *Siren* is specifically a Black film, encompassing France, the United States, and the amorphous category of Black film. The film's circulation in the United States among independently produced race films and Black-cast Hollywood films offers a potential basis for a redefinition of what constitutes a Black film in the United States. In particular, *Siren*'s American exhibition sheds light on the complexities inherent to the categories of African American cinema and French cinema. Does the term *Black cinema* instead offer a rubric capacious enough to encompass independently produced race films, Black-cast Hollywood films, and Baker's French films in a meaningful way?

Baker was an unlikely muse for race films or any other type of African American films. In 1926 and 1927, when she filmed *la danse des bananes* and other brief excerpts of her performances at the Folies Bergère, "she had not enjoyed those brief flings, the lights had burned her eyes, she had looked at the cameraman when she should have looked elsewhere, but she wanted to learn the new medium, 'because my greatest wish is to act in a great film, beautiful and true.'"[6] *Siren of the Tropics* was nevertheless a frustrating experience for her, and her account of the filmmaking process includes a few barbed comments: "I played the part of a West Indian girl named Papitou, who longed to come to Paris and was astonished when she couldn't pay her boat fare with beads. A real featherbrain. A 'native village' hastily constructed in the studio served as our set. Its freshly built straw huts absolutely glistened. 'We could use some manure around here,' I remarked to the designer. Film-making involves hours of waiting."[7]

In the films starring Baker that followed *Siren of the Tropics*, *Zouzou* (1934) and *Princesse Tam-Tam* (1935), her dialogue is entirely in French. As with *Siren*, the filming of *Zouzou* took place in France, while *Princesse Tam-Tam* was shot partly on location in North Africa. Baker introduced a cinematic

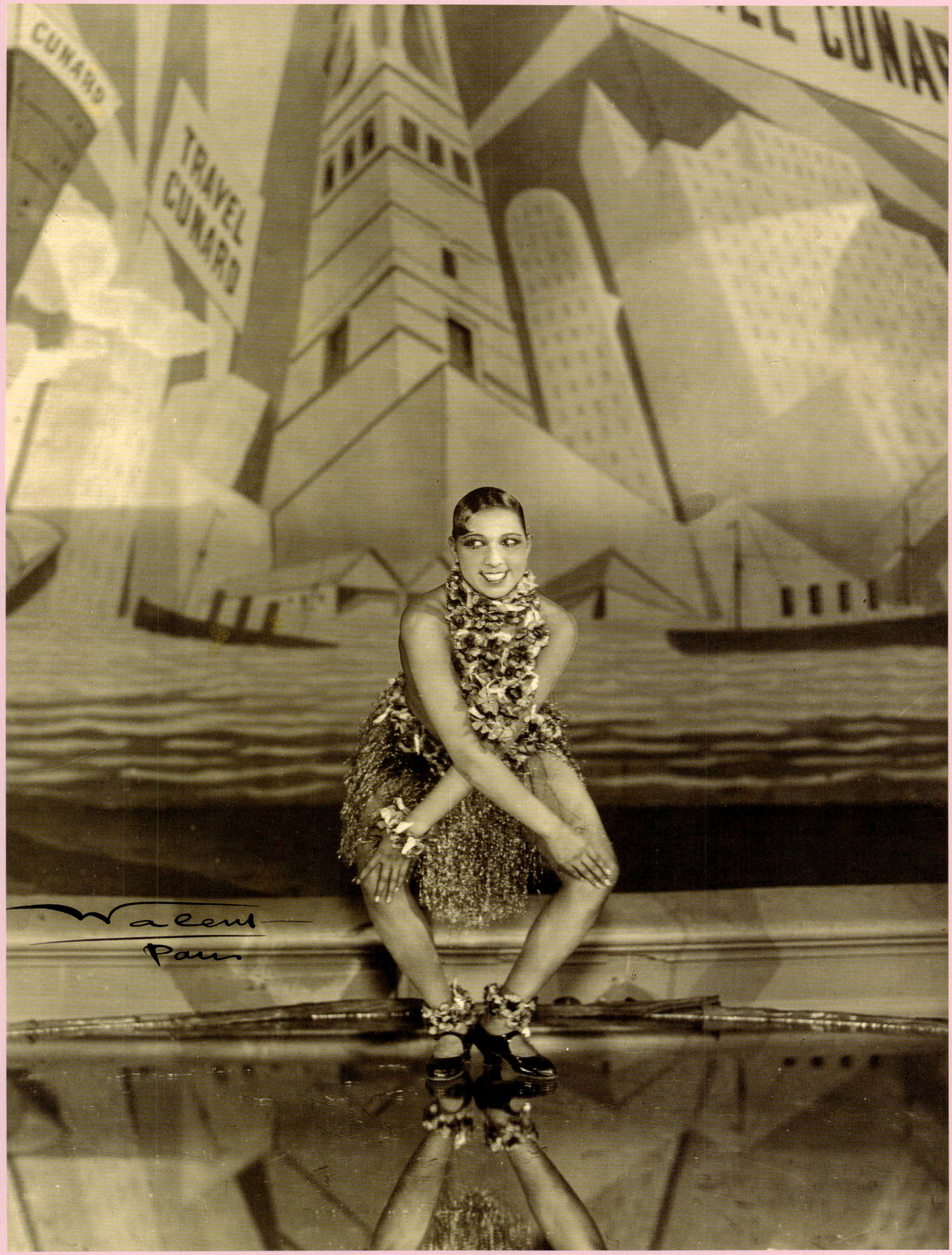
CUNARD
TRAVEL
CUNARD

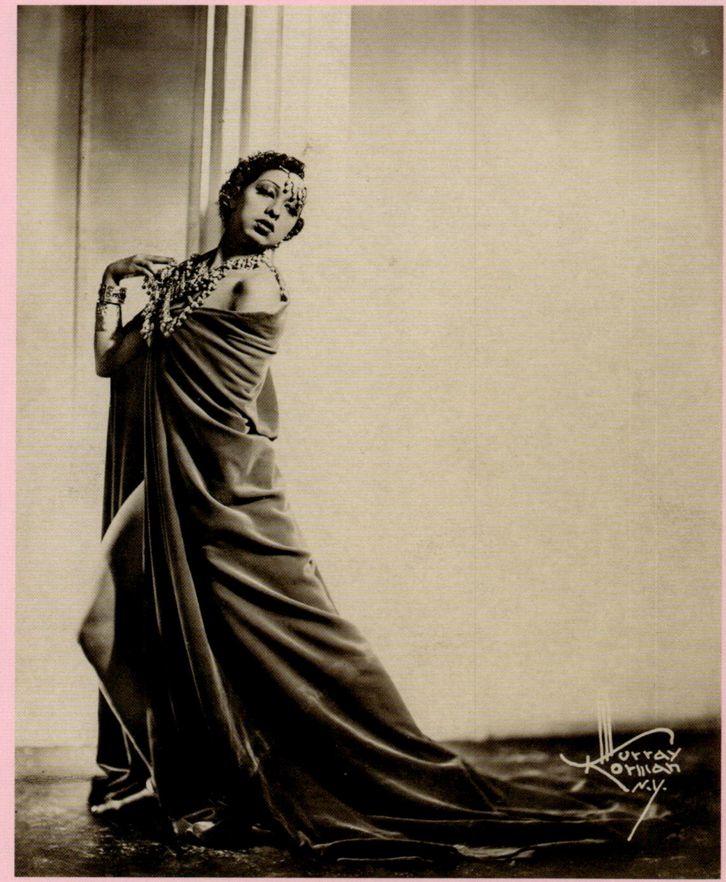

Murray Korman (American, 1902–1961), *Josephine Baker*, 1937, gelatin silver print, 9 × 7 in. (22.9 × 17.8 cm)

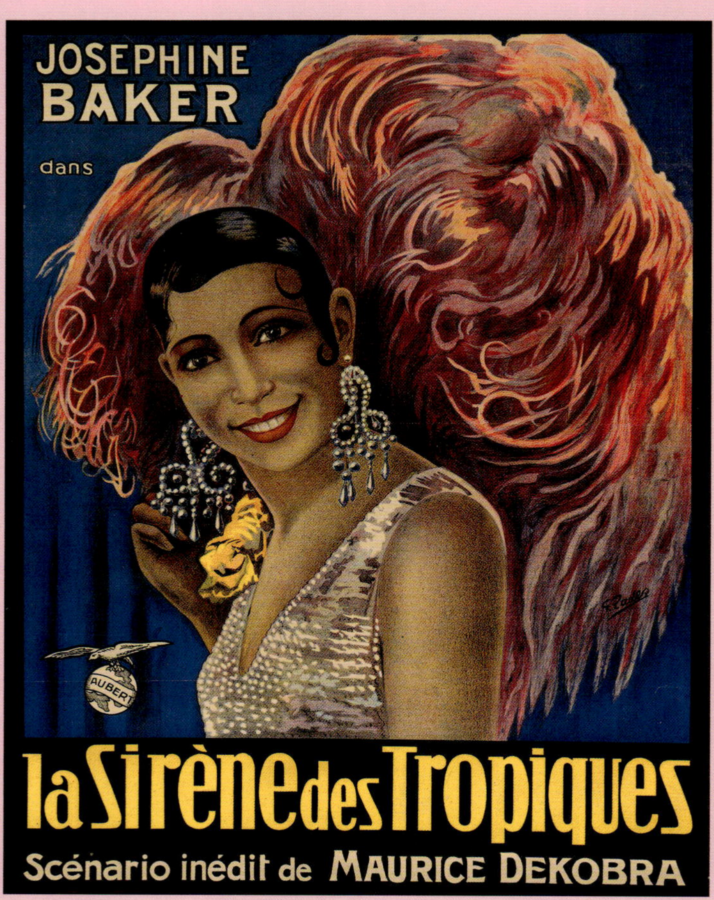

Siren of the Tropics (France, 1927), French theatrical release poster

voice into global Black film that was French with an American accent and mediated through her partnerships with journalists, her management, and screenwriters. *Siren of the Tropics*, *Zouzou*, and *Princesse Tam-Tam* were collaborative projects. The novelist Maurice Dekobra penned the screenplay for *Siren*. Baker's manager, Giuseppe "Pepito" Abatino, wrote the novel on which *Zouzou* was based and is credited with the screenplay. Yves Mirande composed the dialogue for *Princesse Tam-Tam*. Michel Duran wrote her fourth and last feature, *Fausse alerte* (*The French Way*, 1945).

Josephine Baker's expatriate status, as well as her films' international settings in France, the Caribbean, and Tunisia, destabilizes the US focus of early African American film narratives and brings in a colonial and European context. Including her story in the history of Black film opens an aperture in which we can more clearly view the history of race films and Hollywood in a transatlantic context. The Black in Black film is global. Despite her impatience with some aspects of being in the movies, Baker's film presence made her a goddess of the emerging African American cinema of the early twentieth century. Many conventional timelines of Black film do not consider Baker because they do not consider her films to be American. But precisely because this French-speaking African American entertainer worked exclusively with a white film company, white costars, white writers, and white directors in French productions, she profoundly expanded the physical, cultural, and thematic geography of African American cinema. African American cinema includes Europe. The very fact that Baker as a Black American played French-speaking African and Caribbean roles places her performances in a transnational context; the films crossed genres too, as musical romantic comedies that offered meditations on race and identity with a touch of the burlesque. As film products and as discursive scenes, Baker's films proposed new and alternative futures for African American creativity in the cinema, beyond Harlem and the United States in general and on the leading edge of Black popular culture in Paris, however nascent and ambivalent it might have been.

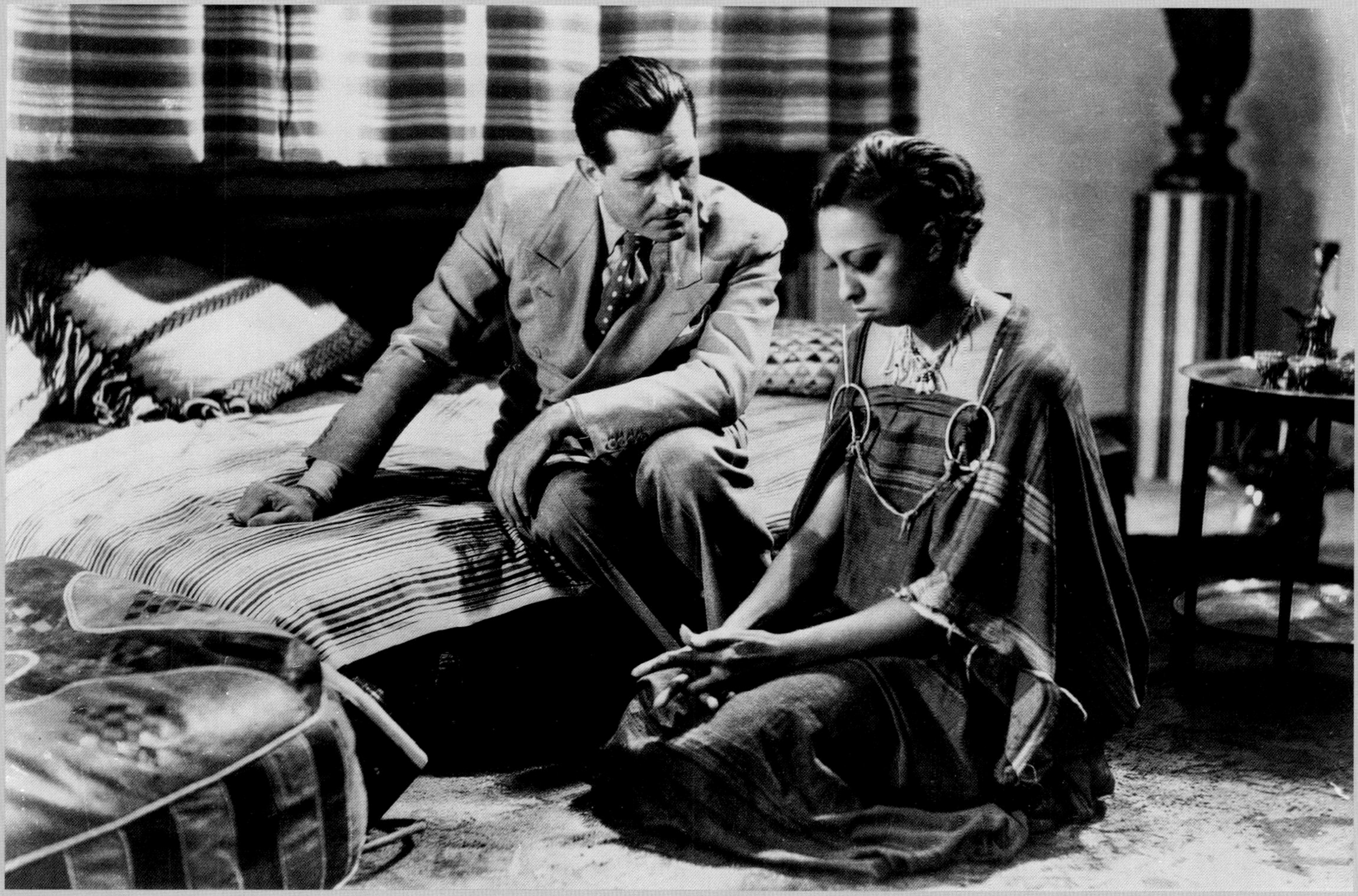

Albert Préjean and Josephine Baker in *Princesse Tam-Tam* (France, 1935), production still

Notes

1 Portions of this essay expand on research that I presented in "Josephine Baker's French African-American Films," *In Media Res*, August 28, 2014, http://mediacommons.org/imr/2014/08/06/josephine-baker-s-french-african-american-films, and that was later elaborated in my book *Josephine Baker's Cinematic Prism* (Bloomington: Indiana University Press, 2021).

2 Tim Murari, "An Interview with Josephine Baker," *The Guardian*, August 26, 1974, https://www.theguardian.com/stage/2015/aug/26/josephine-baker-interview-1974.

3 On the press coverage, see Terri Simone Francis, "Shouting at Shadows: The Black American Press, French Colonial Culture, and *La sirène des tropiques*," in *Josephine Baker's Cinematic Prism*, 64–98.

4 Manohla Dargis writes, "MGM may have put McKinney under contract; the record remains sketchy." Manohla Dargis, "The Glory of Nina Mae McKinney, an Early Black Star in White Hollywood," *New York Times*, November 10, 2021, https://www.nytimes.com/2021/11/10/movies/nina-mae-mckinney.html.

5 "Baker Picture Now Looms," *New York Amsterdam News*, September 4, 1929, 8.

6 "Baker Picture Now Looms," 8.

7 Josephine Baker and Jo Bouillon, *Josephine*, trans. Mariana Fitzpatrick (New York: Marlowe & Co., 1988), 72.

HATTIE McDANIEL: TALENT, DRIVE, AUDACITY, AGENCY

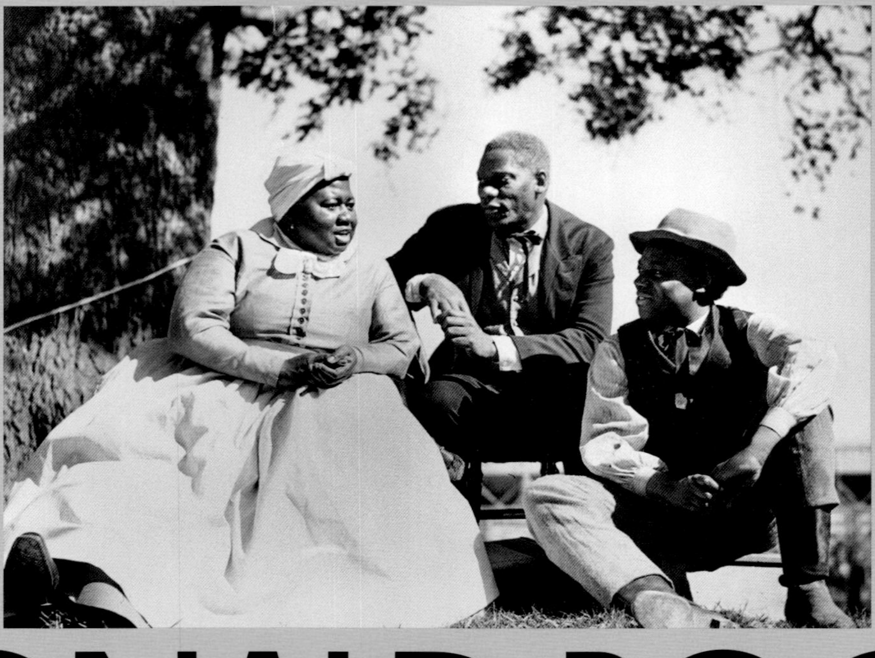

DONALD BOGLE

Opposite
From left: Hattie McDaniel, Oscar Polk, and Ben Carter during the filming of *Gone with the Wind* (1939), production still

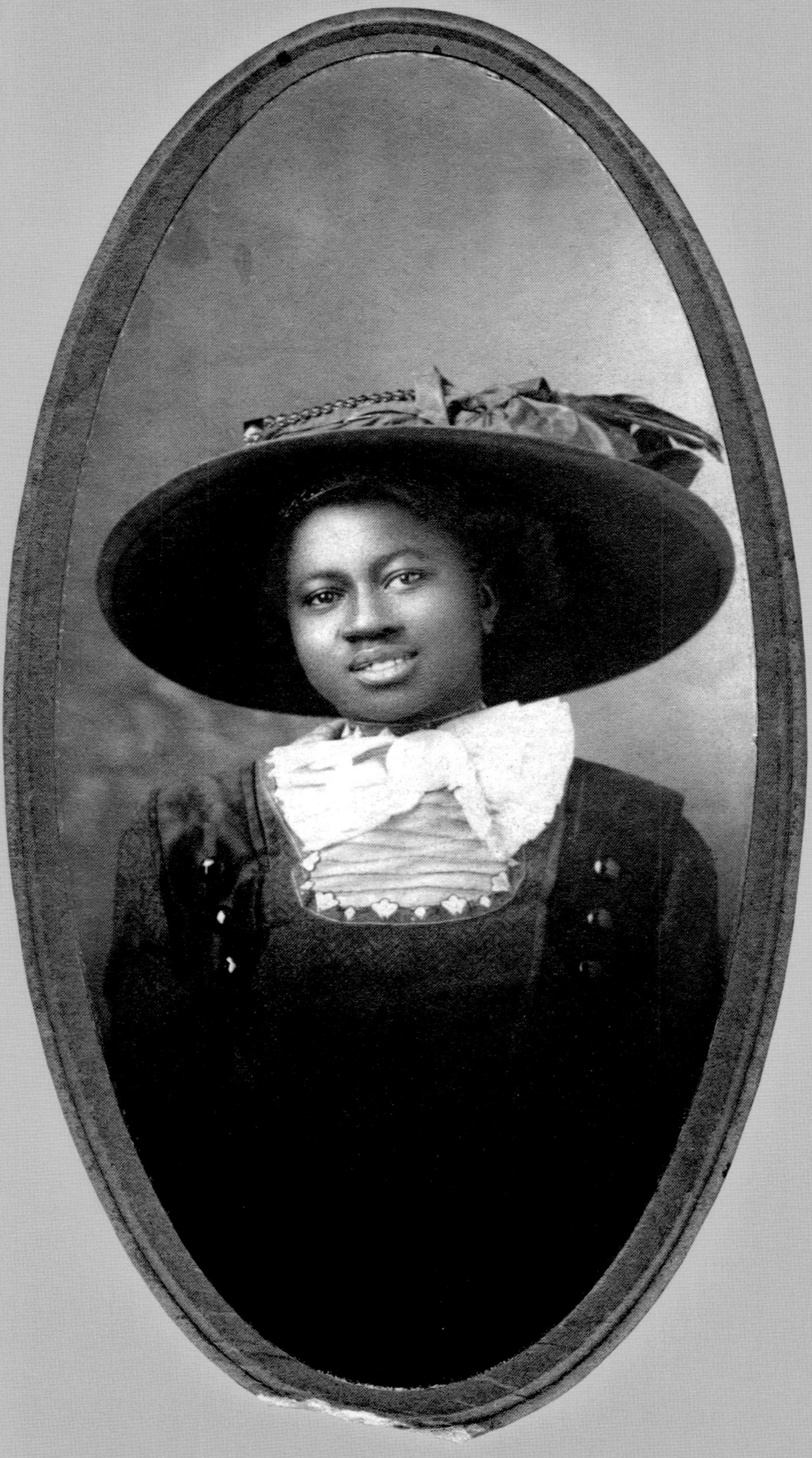

Hattie McDaniel at age eighteen, ca. 1911

By the time Hattie McDaniel (1893–1952) appeared in *Gone with the Wind* (1939), she had worked in films for seven years and had an entertainment career that stretched back decades. Even after that film's success—and her Academy Award—she would find herself still struggling for challenging roles within the confines of the studio system. In the end, with well over a hundred films to her credit, her career would encapsulate the complexities and complications faced by Black actors working in Hollywood in the first half of the twentieth century. Ultimately hers was a career defined by her relentless drive, her fierce audacity and authority, and her triumphant talent.

Born in Wichita, Kansas, the youngest of thirteen children, Hattie McDaniel grew up in Denver—the daughter of Henry McDaniel, a veteran of the Union army, and Susan Holbert McDaniel, a domestic worker. Like many other Black entertainers of the early twentieth century, McDaniel received her professional training in minstrel shows, carnivals, and the grueling, rough-and-tumble world of vaudeville, which infused popular culture with African American cultural markers, references, and signposts. Though her mother had taught McDaniel the skills required of a maid to prepare her to support herself—and though she indeed worked at times as a domestic—the young McDaniel was determined to make a career in entertainment. Hattie's brother Otis staged his own productions and formed what he referred to as a "carnival company," an entertainment troupe in which she participated.[1] Working with her sister Etta, Hattie herself formed in 1914 a company of female minstrels known as the McDaniel Sisters Company.[2]

Early on, McDaniel was drawn to such new twentieth-century media as the phonograph record, radio, and eventually motion pictures. In the 1920s—when blues goddesses Ma Rainey, Bessie Smith, and Ethel Waters performed provocative songs that reached large Black audiences—McDaniel honed her underappreciated talents as a singer, appeared on radio, and made recordings in Chicago on the Okeh and Paramount labels.[3] But her career needed more direction and stability—and a jolt that would provide her steady employment.

That jolt came in 1927 with the success of Al Jolson in *The Jazz Singer*, in which moviegoers heard him speak briefly but also perform in song—in blackface, no less. In 1929 those grand titans of the recording world—Smith, Waters, and Duke Ellington—brought their innovative musical sounds to cinema. That same year the Hollywood studios Fox and Metro-Goldwyn-Mayer released two Black-cast features: *Hearts in Dixie* and *Hallelujah*. The critic Robert Benchley enthusiastically wrote, "The future of the talking-movie has taken on a rosier

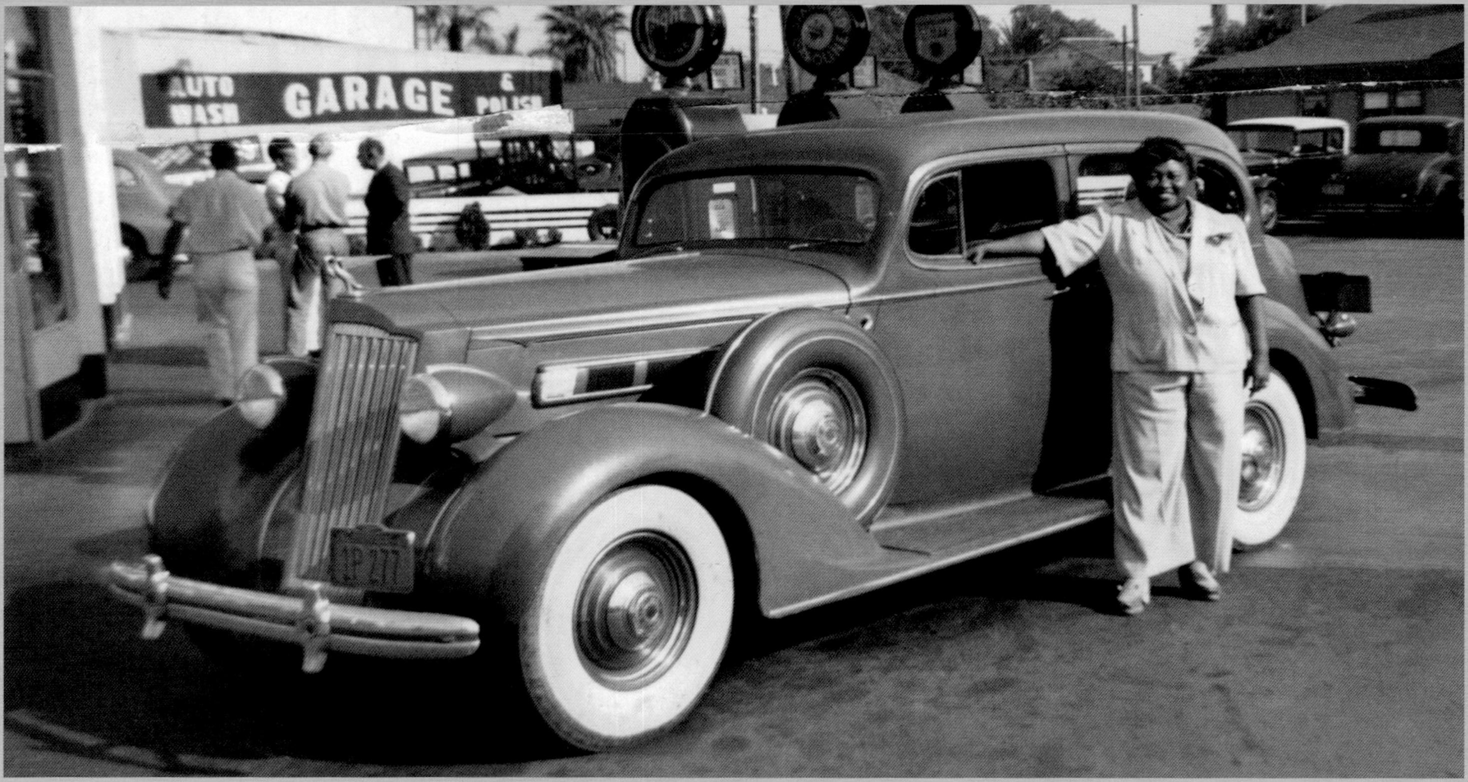

Hattie McDaniel with her green Packard Twelve, ca. 1940

hue. Voices *can* be found which will register perfectly. Personalities *can* be found which are ideal for this medium. It may be that the talking-movies must be participated in exclusively by Negroes, but, if so, then so be it. In the Negro the sound-picture has found its ideal protagonist."[4] Among those Black performers who would soon find employment in motion pictures were Lincoln Perry (aka Stepin Fetchit), Louise Beavers, Willie Best, Bill "Bojangles" Robinson, Paul Robeson, and Theresa Harris.

By the late 1920s Hattie's brother Sam had migrated west to Hollywood and found some success on radio's *Optimistic Do-Nut Hour* and in films (in fact, he appeared in *Hallelujah*), usually playing unbilled servant roles.[5] Other members of the McDaniel family also settled in Los Angeles. Etta McDaniel acted in movies, and Orlena McDaniel ran a boardinghouse. Hattie arrived in 1931. With the help of Sam, she performed on radio and found work in movies such as *Crooner* (1932), *The Golden West* (1932), and *Hypnotized* (1932). In these films she had no billing and nothing that resembled a fully developed character. Instead she found herself immersed in a world of rigid stereotypes and demeaning hack tropes of African Americans.

McDaniel most often played characters that conformed to the mammy stereotype: larger, often darker Black women who were desexed and deglamorized. As giddy, eager-to-please mother surrogates, her characters were often trusted confidantes who were there to comfort, aid, assist, and reassure troubled, vexed, or confused white characters. In an early speaking role in *Blonde Venus* (1932), she befriended Marlene Dietrich, whose character was on the run from the law, and alerted her when a detective was on the prowl. In *I'm No Angel* (1933), McDaniel was one of the Black maids tending to the needs of vamping blonde star Mae West. In *The Little Colonel* (1935), she played Shirley Temple's loyal servant Mom Beck, with Robinson playing another faithful servant.

McDaniel climbed her way to showy roles in *Judge Priest* (1934), *Alice Adams* (1935), *Show Boat* (1936), and *The Mad Miss Manton* (1938). Working under such filmmakers as John Ford, Josef von Sternberg, George Stevens, Victor Fleming, and James Whale, she frequently seemed to be directing herself as she acted side by side with major stars, among them Jean Harlow, Clark Gable, Barbara Stanwyck, Henry Fonda, Katharine Hepburn, and even Paul Robeson (in *Show Boat*). Facing them eye-to-eye, neither threatened nor intimidated, she was always an undeniably strong screen presence, sometimes charming audiences, other times ruffling their feathers.

Yet, in film after film, little was known about the lives of *her* characters: *their* families, *their* other relationships, *their* perspectives, *their* aspirations, *their* true feelings about those they served so devotedly. Rarely did films venture into quarters where servants might "dish the dirt" on those they worked for—or where they might openly reveal discontent or dissent. If another perspective were to be shown, it had to be done covertly, by getting inside or under the dialogue to create a knowing subtext. For Hattie McDaniel, a key signal to such a subtext was, foremost, her *attitude*. There was also her powerful, thundering *voice*. Once you heard her speak, you knew she was born to give orders, not take them. Her voice and attitude were hallmarks of her screen persona, revealing her confidence, resilience, and assertiveness and providing a way to subvert the content of a script or a written characterization.

McDaniel's voice and attitude enabled her to retain her power and personal identity. Her character in *Alice Adams* seems to feel she's slumming by working as a maid for the poor family of Katharine Hepburn. As the maid Hilda in *The Mad Miss Manton*, she fusses and fumes with the socialite friends of her on-screen employer, played by Stanwyck. "Hilda," says Stanwyck, "Miss Beverly is our guest." "I didn't ask her up," snaps McDaniel as Hilda. McDaniel used clever dialogue to establish herself as the power broker, the social arbiter, the woman who sets the standards and calls the shots, making key decisions and declarations that overturn traditional social/racial roles while seemingly observing them. In the shipboard drama *China Seas* (1935), she was teamed with Harlow but with a twist. In her first important scene, she casually lounges—as if such leisure were her right and privilege—while flipping through a magazine in the stateroom she shares with her costar. When an insecure Harlow questions her about the manner in which she (Harlow) has been gossiped about, McDaniel shrewdly plays on Harlow's doubts yet proves herself someone Harlow should trust. Her attitude works perfectly to the point that Harlow gives McDaniel one of her dresses. McDaniel grasped the fact that the role was written in an unusual way; the character was less a maid and more a traveling companion. And her scenes do not seem organic to the story; they are closer to energetic comic inserts written expressly for McDaniel.

Then came *Gone with the Wind*, the epic saga centered on Scarlett O'Hara and Rhett Butler against the backdrop of the Civil War. Hoping to avoid the controversy that had enveloped D. W. Griffith's racist *Birth of a Nation* (1915), producer David O. Selznick—after communicating with Walter White of the National Association for the Advancement of Colored People (NAACP)—dropped the N-word from the script. White also suggested that the film's production crew read W. E. B. Du Bois's *Black Reconstruction in America* (1935).[6] In the end Selznick chose to focus on the fall of a "pretty world" that wants only to be "graceful and beautiful."[7] The fact that this idealized world was built on the backs of brutalized slave labor was not addressed. Selznick chose to avoid the issue of slavery altogether.

Thus evasions and distortions run throughout *Gone with the Wind*. The enslaved characters—Prissy, Pork, Uncle Peter, Big Sam, and McDaniel's Mammy—are fundamentally content. About all one knows about Mammy, who has no other name in the film, is that she takes pride in having served the family for generations. Never does the audience see where she goes when she leaves Scarlett O'Hara's side. Does she retire to slave quarters at the end of the day? Does she have a room in the big house? Missing was a significant

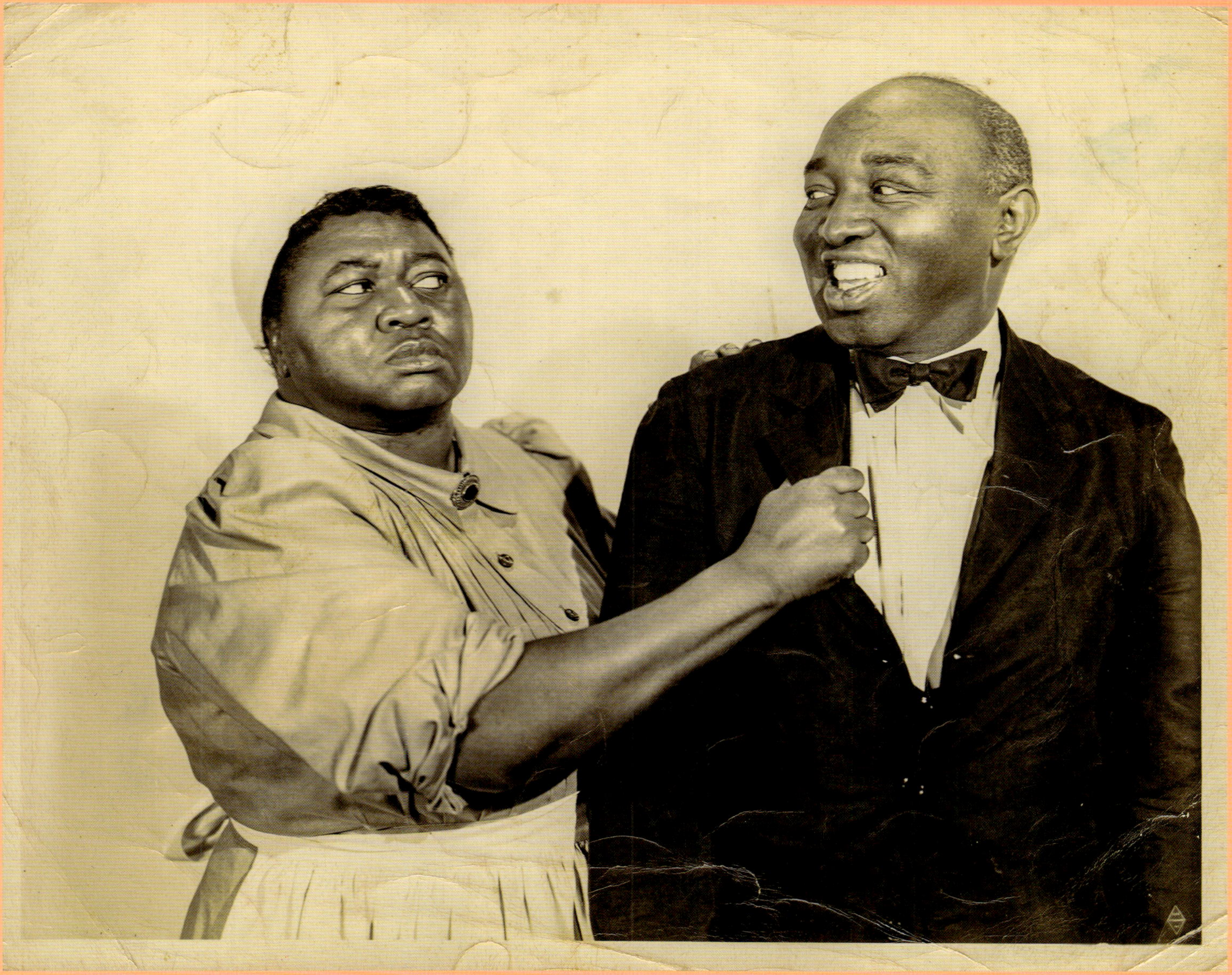

Hattie McDaniel and her brother Sam in *The Great Lie* (1941), publicity still

backstory that would have taken moviegoers into Mammy's psyche and possibly clarified and illuminated the effects of slavery on her psyche as well as those of the other Black characters.

Despite the narrow and distorted perspective of the script, however, McDaniel was able to inject covert messages as she had in previous films. From her first full scene with Scarlett, she is in command as she insists that the young woman abide by the dictates of proper Old South ladylike behavior and eat at home before attending the Wilkes barbecue. When Scarlett refuses to eat, McDaniel reveals that she knows of Scarlett's secret passion for Ashley Wilkes. "I ain't notice Mr. Ashley askin' for to marry you," she says. It is a threat, made all the more evident when the camera focuses on McDaniel, who slyly smiles. Scarlett eats.

Though her character supports the values of the dominant culture, she repeatedly berates Scarlett and questions her motives, understanding her far better than Scarlett's mother, Ellen. McDaniel elevates her performance by way of that familiar underlying anger and resentment that come through when we hear her speak: again that full sonic boom is tough and in control. Through the force of her personality, she has an agency—seen in everything she does, from her posture to the way she moves—that the film cannot explain. Further, her character is free of the great burden enslavement had imposed on African Americans: she has no feelings of inferiority. McDaniel created something out of nothing, perhaps digging into her family history and stories she had heard growing up. Both her parents had been born into slavery. Significantly, as Ruby Dee once explained, McDaniel's performance was "coming from a real place."[8]

For her performance, Hattie McDaniel became the first African American to be accorded the film industry's greatest accolade, the Academy Award, here for Best Supporting Actress. In her acceptance speech she said she hoped she would always be a credit to her race and the motion picture industry. The speech was all the more poignant because at the Oscar ceremony McDaniel and her escort were not seated at Selznick's table with the other stars of the film. Nor had McDaniel been permitted to attend the film's premiere in Atlanta.

Following *Gone with the Wind*, McDaniel appeared in such films as *Maryland* (1940), *Affectionately Yours* (1941), *The Great Lie* (1941), and *Since You Went Away* (1944). No significant film turned up except for John Huston's 1942 *In This Our Life*, a heady melodrama in which Bette Davis portrayed a spoiled, reckless young woman who is the driver in a hit-and-run accident that leaves a little girl dead. Davis's character pins the accident on a forward-looking young Black man, played by Ernest Anderson, who works for her family. Despite his hope of becoming a lawyer, he is aware of the racial atmosphere in which he lives. His mother, Minerva, played by McDaniel, is the maid for Davis's family and has cautioned him (so we assume) about dreaming too big; as her son explains, she "is afraid for a colored boy to have too much ambition." Without saying it, she understands how easily Black folks' hopes can be overturned.

McDaniel toned down her extroverted style for this role. Cast in only a few scenes, she makes the most of each minute of screen time to etch a character. She moves more slowly. The powerful voice and attitude are subdued. In a telling scene with Olivia de Havilland, she poignantly states: "Child, this seems hard to say, but what Miss Stanley [Davis] told the police about my poor boy, there ain't a word of truth, so help me." Her son tries "to tell them [of his innocence]. But they don't listen to no colored boy." Here she delineates a character who is aware of injustices and feels discarded and betrayed, fearful of the lie of a white woman. McDaniel is convincing and compelling in a beautifully delivered performance.

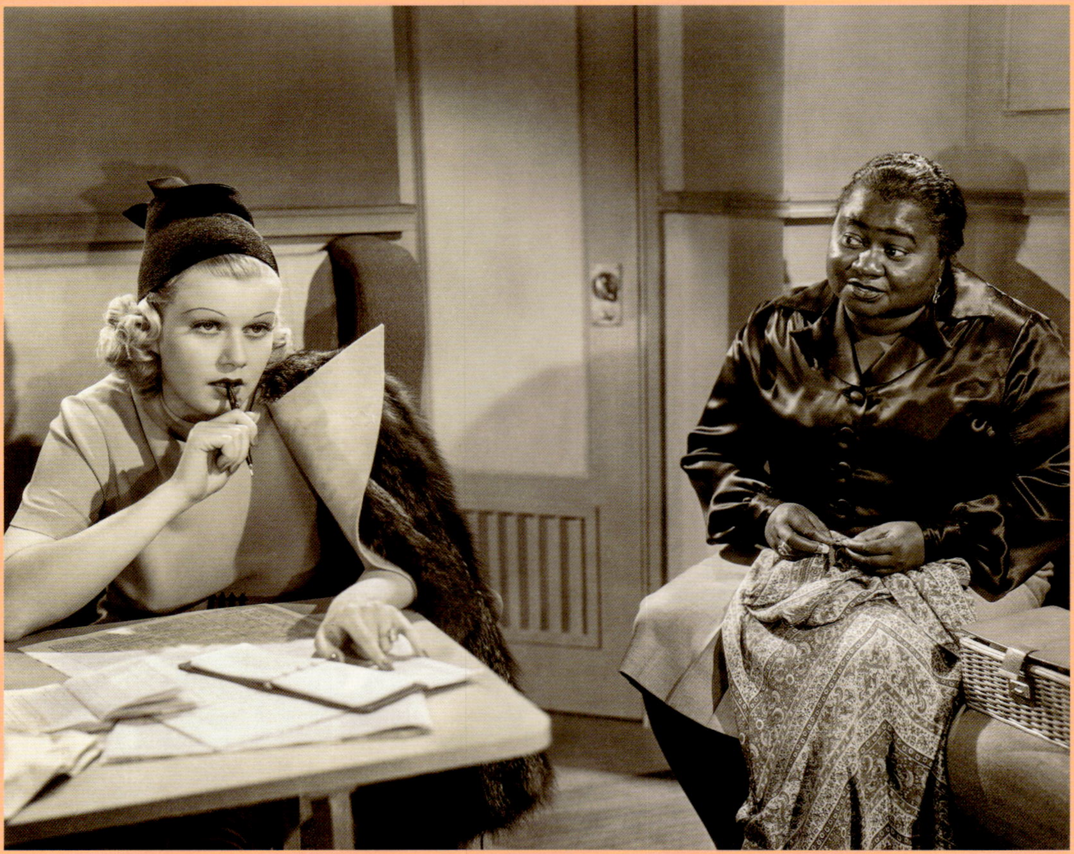

Jean Harlow and Hattie McDaniel in *Saratoga* (1937), production still

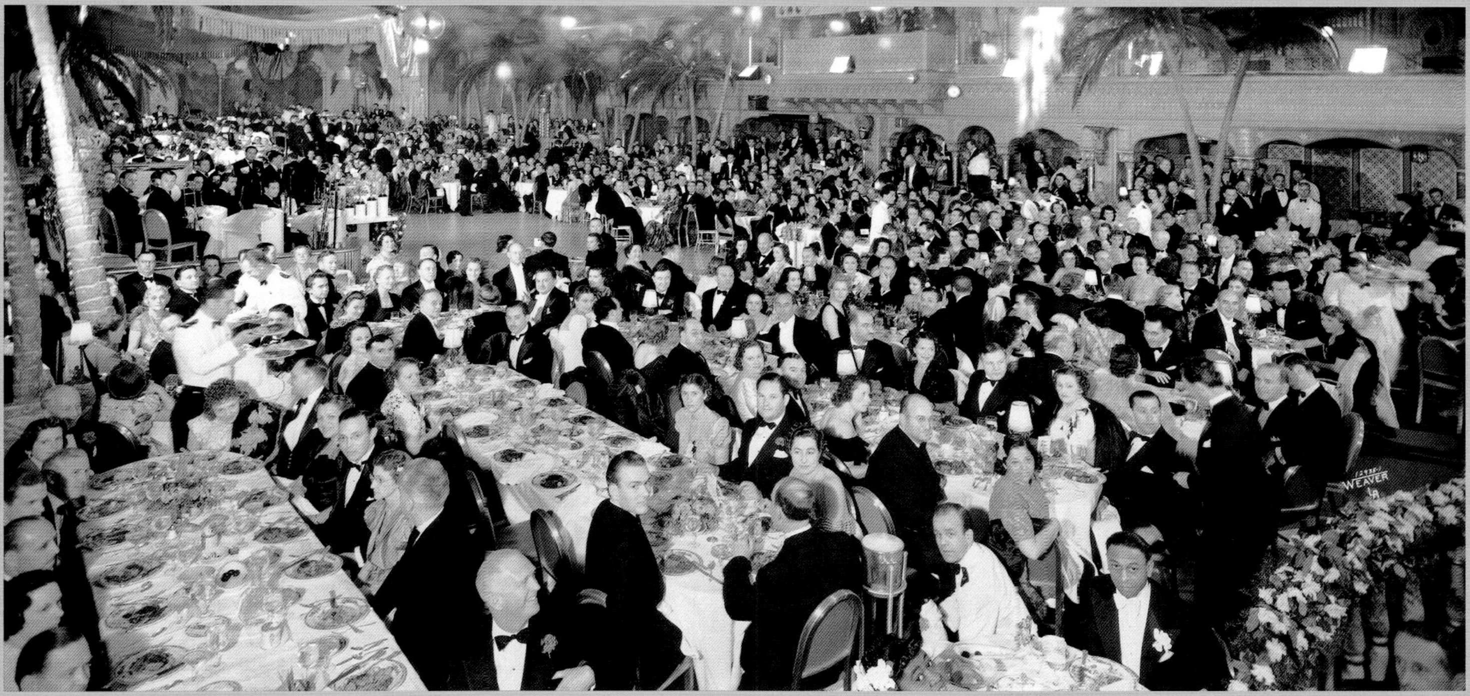

Hattie McDaniel (partially visible at lower edge) and Ferdinand Yober, at the banquet for the 12th Academy Awards, Cocoanut Grove, Ambassador Hotel, 1940

Away from the studios, she revealed that her mammy characters were simply that: characters. Hardly an asexual maternal figure, McDaniel had four husbands. Recognized as Black Hollywood's queen, she entertained lavishly in her home in the West Adams neighborhood of Los Angeles. She also fought against housing segregation in the area—and won. Lena Horne described her gratitude for the friendship that McDaniel offered when Horne arrived in Hollywood in the early 1940s. The younger actress was sometimes viewed with suspicion by other Blacks at the time, but McDaniel invited her to her home—which Horne described as exquisite—and encouraged her to move forward with her career.[9]

After World War II, the roles began to dry up. She appeared in the controversial Disney film *Song of the South* (1946) at age fifty-three, looking dispirited and tired. Turning her sights to radio, she played the title role in the sitcom *Beulah* (aka *The Beulah Show*, 1947–52), the story of a Black maid working contentedly for a white family. When a television version of the show premiered concurrently in 1950, Ethel Waters played the character but left the series after a year. McDaniel then was signed to take over the role. But after filming several episodes, she had to drop out. She was ill. As much as other Black actors then working in Hollywood, Hattie McDaniel was no doubt ready for a change. She died at the age of fifty-nine in 1952.

Notes

1 Jill Watts, *Hattie McDaniel: Black Ambition, White Hollywood* (New York: Amistad, 2005), 34.

2 Watts, *Hattie McDaniel*, 38.

3 Carlton Jackson, *Hattie: The Life of Hattie McDaniel* (Lanham, MD: Madison, 1990), 15.

4 Robert Benchley, "Hearts in Dixie (The First Real Talking Picture)," *Opportunity: A Journal of Negro Life* 7 (April 1929): 122.

5 *Dance, Fools, Dance* (1931), *The Public Enemy* (1931), *Guilty Hands* (1931), *The Great American Broadcast* (1941), and *Ice Palace* (1960) are but a few of the films in which Sam McDaniel made uncredited appearances during his five-decade-long film career. https://www.imdb.com/name/nm0567434/.

6 Jackson, *Hattie*, 41–42.

7 Dialogue spoken by the character Melanie Wilkes, describing life in the Old South, in *Gone with the Wind*.

8 Ruby Dee, conversation with the author, 1989 (also ca. 2003).

9 Lena Horne, interviewed by Dick Cavett, *The Dick Cavett Show*, November 5, 1981.

REFORM SCHOOL

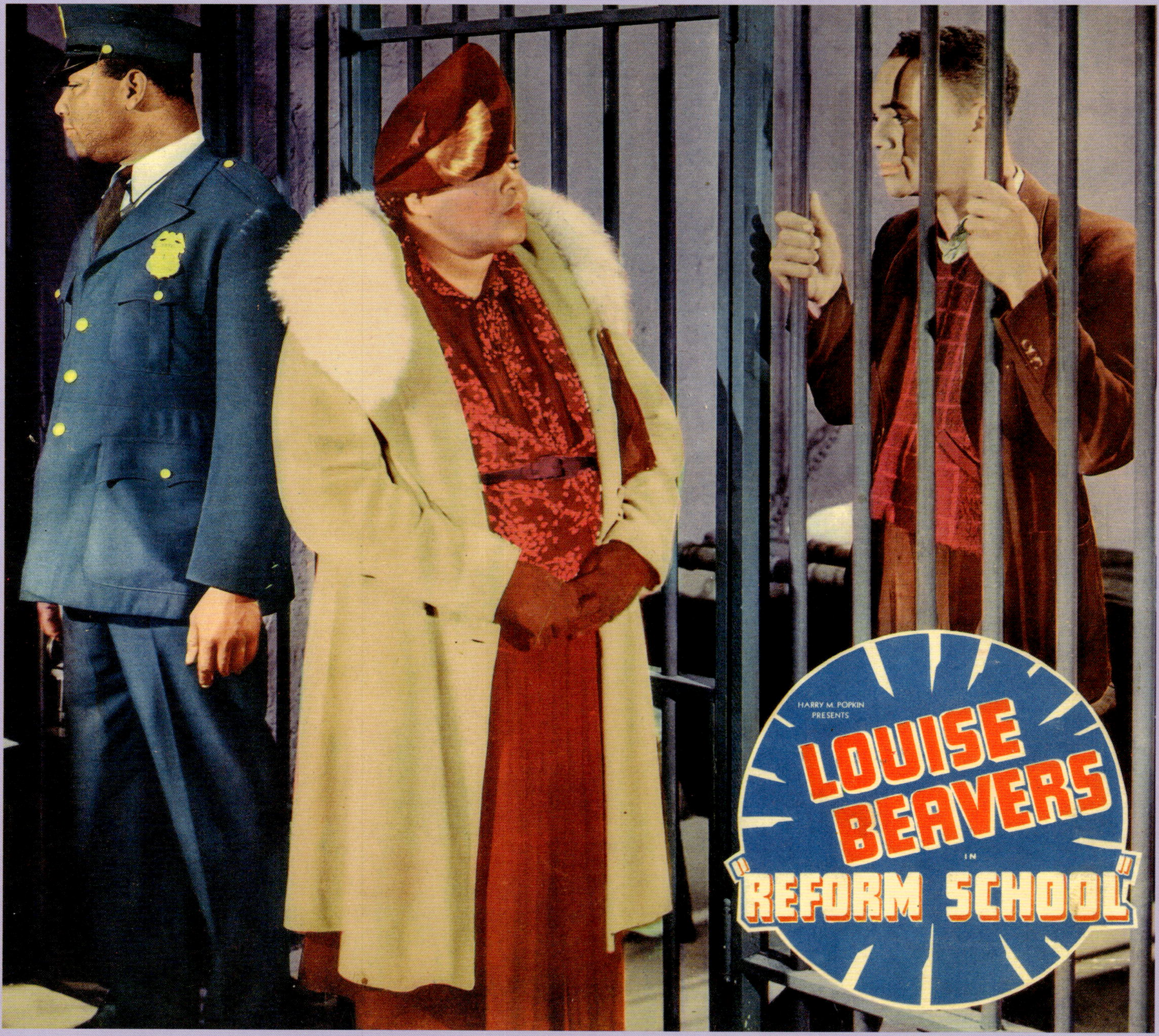

ELLEN C. SCOTT

ESSAY
CASE STUDIES
PORTRAITS
FILMOGRAPHY
CHRONOLOGY
INTERVIEWS

Opposite
Reform School (1939), lobby card

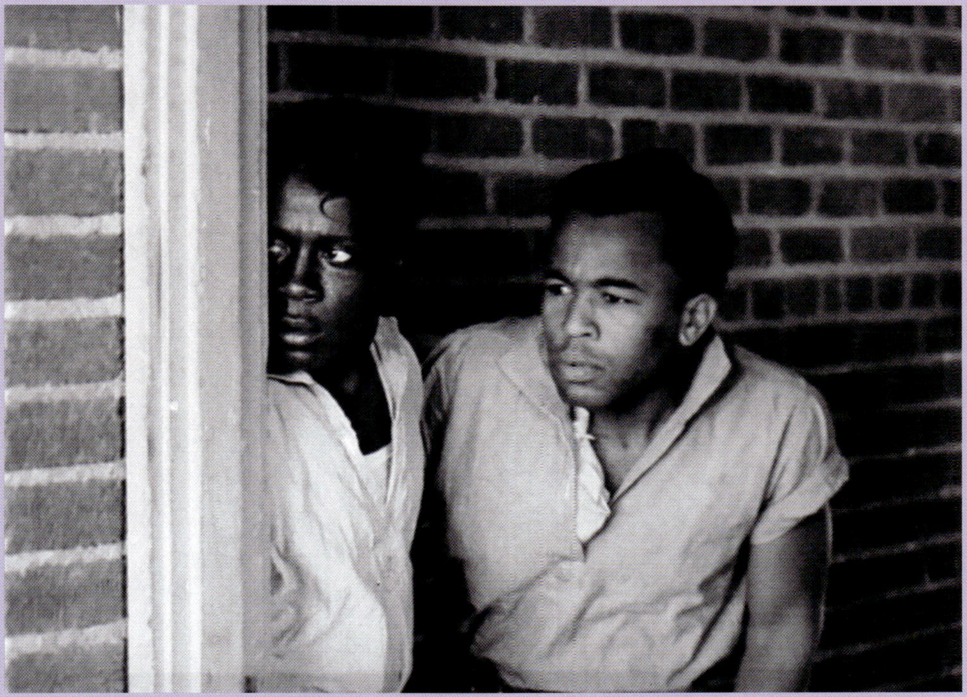

The Harlem Tuff Kids in *Reform School* (dir. Leo C. Popkin, 1939), film still

In the silent cinema era, race filmmaking was an established and prolific mode of production, with a number of Black- and white-owned outfits dotting the field.[1] Often these films had an epic scope and a real, if uneven, complexity in their depiction of Black life: they portrayed aspirational narratives of Black success while also revealing, if sometimes inadvertently, the realities of racial injustice and poverty.

With the arrival of sound in the late 1920s, many of the makers of race films could not afford the technology to continue producing films. But *Reform School* (1939), made by white producers who could secure the capital to finance it, carried on the tradition of what the film historian Jacqueline Stewart has spoken of as "interracial film production."[2] It also continued the race film's unique mode of engagement with the complexities of the Black community.

Reform School tells the story of Freddie Barton (Reginald Fenderson), a Black teenager convicted of a petty offense who consequently cannot find work and falls back into a life of crime. After he is caught by police and confined to reform school under a cruel superintendent named Stone (Edward Thompson), his criminal tendencies are reinforced. Mother Barton (Louise Beavers), an understanding and tough probation officer, witnesses Freddie in agony, beaten and starved in solitary confinement, and works to have Stone removed. She takes over as superintendent, putting in place an honor system to teach the troubled youth to respect the law rather than fear it. Although the boys take advantage of her at first, eventually they grow to respect her, and it appears that her apprach is working. But Stone's deputy, Jackson (Monte Hawley), steals from the school safe and frames Freddie. Believing in Freddie's innocence, the boys pursue Jackson, who confesses and attempts to flee but is ultimately captured by the boys and turned over to police. So successful are Barton's policies that they are implemented statewide, and the boys secure good jobs upon leaving reform school.

Harry M. Popkin and Leo C. Popkin's Million Dollar Productions, the company that produced *Reform School*, is notable for having consistently worked closely with Black community members to make race films that reflected social issues such as criminalization, justice denied, fugitivity, and Black-on-Black crime.[3] The Popkins broached racial oppression but did so without pessimism. While their main characters included college students, gangsters, middle-class professionals, and working-class laborers, their films maintained fluidity in defining Black success and avoided portraying the middle class as superior. The Popkins' association with the Apollo Theater emcee Ralph Cooper played a key part in the company's establishment of a cinematic voice that was more in tune with Black culture and community than many of the race films of

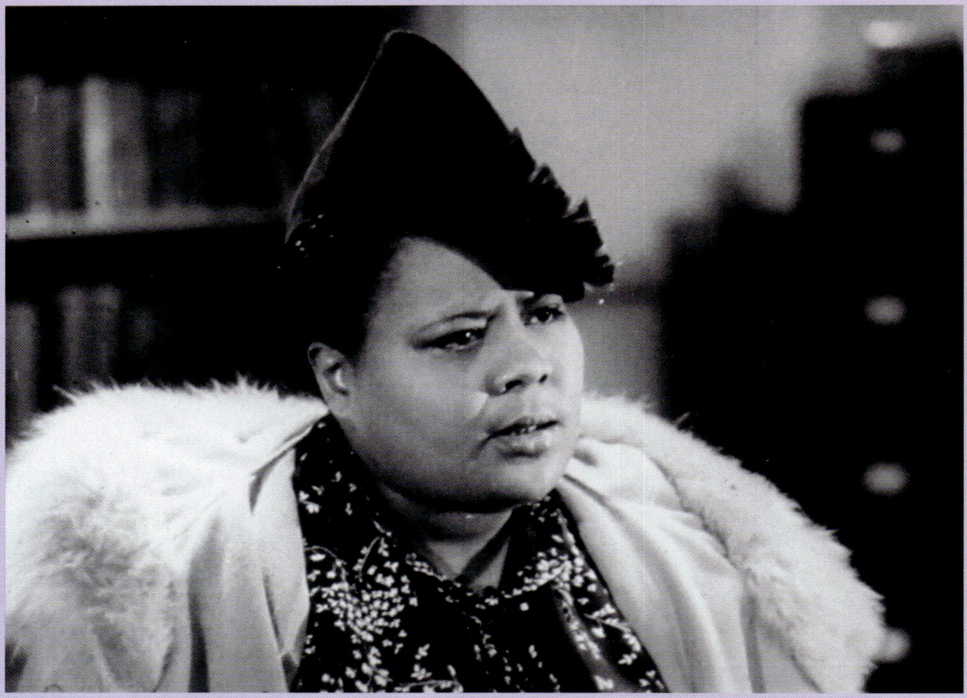

Louise Beavers in *Reform School* (dir. Leo C. Popkin, 1939), film still

the day.[4] They maintained good relations with the Black press and the white trade press, eliciting consistently positive reviews in *Variety* and regular coverage in the Black press. They also sold their films to both Black and white theaters.[5]

What the Popkins' scrappy outfit lacked in budget for props and sets it made up for with complex cinematography and editing. Diverging from the bare-bones, B-cinema visual style of race films, the cinematographer William Hyer, a veteran of Hollywood westerns, artfully filmed *Reform School* using a complex shot structure and stylized tracking shots. The editing was efficient and creative, as in the film's cross-cut opening chase scene, which builds drama and subverts Hollywood's ideology by leading the audience to root for the "criminal" to escape.

The concept for the film (and perhaps the justification that facilitated its financing) came from the Humphrey Bogart film *Crime School* (1938). Much changed, however, with the shift in the racial composition of the narrative and the protagonist's gender. Bogart's superintendent, Mark Braden, could identify with the boys in *Crime School* because he was once a rascally boy himself. Barton, who embodies the "lifting as we climb" ideals of the historical Black women's club movement, condemns the criminal justice system for the way that it imperils "her" boys.[6] Dressed in furs and high hats as matron of the reform school—a far cry from the mammies Beavers often played in white Hollywood films—Barton takes on all the dignity of middle-class Black uplift that we might expect from Mary Church Terrell.[7] Indeed, *Reform School* is remarkable in its depiction of Black female leadership.[8] Once she is appointed superintendent, Barton calls on the guards to leave their guns and clubs behind and become supervisors. She comments that the men may feel awkward because a woman is now in charge, but never does she cede authority. In transforming Barton into the upstanding "mother" to a community of Black boys, the film represents the important roles that Black women have historically played in their own communities, roles that Hollywood largely erased.

The film makes the racial politics of the criminal justice system visible and advocates for a more just and humane alternative. In her exchange with the authorities in charge of the reform system, Mother Barton points out the conditions of structural racism and unemployment: "You gentlemen will agree that boys from the reform school aren't trusted by the public when they are released.... They can't get jobs. Finally they become desperate and disillusioned. Their last resort is to turn to crime just to get enough food to put life in their body." The warden insists that the boys have committed crimes and must be punished. "But not by brutality!" she forcefully rejoins. Long before Angela Davis would write her provocative treatise on prison abolition,[9] Barton dreams of a progressive penal system in which the boys would be permitted to "talk, play games, sing, dance, have regular recreation hours." Her two-pronged approach would involve reforming the boys *and* educating the public, so that those who come out of reform school are truly able to take their places in society. After the wardens laugh this off as a "dream," Barton says, "It's a dream, yes, a dream that's going to come true."[10]

The mixing of social classes is the film's hallmark. The middle-class Barton establishes trusting relationships with the boys in her school, whom she humanizes across lines of class, generation, gender, and skin tone. After the boys escape from school, they stay at the home of one of their neighbors, who appears to be a university student, showing brotherhood across class lines and pointing to the few degrees of separation between criminal and college-bound Black men. In the film's hopeful perspective, reform—like racial uplift—opens the door to freedom and transcendence.

Reform School admits to the violence that haunts Black life but believes more wholeheartedly in the goodness of Black youth and the necessity of removing the punitive edge of reform than do many crime dramas today. The film's history opens a rare window into the unique filmmaking practices of one of the only production companies in Hollywood making race films, one that took its production techniques from the studios but its cues on racial representation from members of the Black community. The film allowed Black audiences not only to consider the wrongs of the criminal justice system but also to share Mother Barton's prescient dream (one not altogether different from that of Martin Luther King Jr.) of justice for Black youth who have been systematically maligned and impoverished.

Notes

1 A relatively complete list of these companies is captured in the George P. Johnson Negro Film Collection, 1916–1977 (LSC 1042), Library Special Collections, University of California, Los Angeles. Among these were the Norman Film Manufacturing Company (owned by the white filmmaker Richard Norman), the Lincoln Motion Picture Company (founded by the African American filmmakers George P. Johnson and Noble M. Johnson), the Haynes Photoplay Company (founded by the African American filmmaker Hunter C. Haynes in New York), REOL Productions (founded by the Jewish filmmaker Robert Levy), and the Ebony Motion Picture Company (a white-owned company that employed the Black producer Luther Pollard). For more on early Black film companies, see Jacqueline Najuma Stewart, *Migrating to the Movies: Cinema and Black Urban Modernity* (Berkeley: University of California Press, 2005), 189–219.

2 Jacqueline Najuma Stewart, quoted in Felicia R. Lee, "Coming Soon, a Century Late: A Black Film Gem," *New York Times*, September 21, 2014. In her comments for the article, Stewart explores the uniqueness of equal power relations in interracial film productions, claiming that *Lime Kiln Club Field Day* (1913) is "an interracial production, but not in the way scholars have talked about early film history in which black filmmakers had to rely on expertise and money of white filmmakers. Here we see a negotiation between performers and filmmakers."

3 *The Well* (1951)—a later film from the Popkins that treats race riots with a singular combination of force and racial delicacy—is a good example of this.

4 According to the *Norfolk Journal and Guide*, Cooper was the manager of Million Dollar Productions in the late 1930s. Faye Jackson, "All-Colored Films Offer Outlet to Professional Talent of Race, Says Star of New Gangster Pic," *Norfolk Journal and Guide*, August 28, 1937. Harry Popkin also credited Cooper with his decision to come to Hollywood to produce Black films. See Harry Levette, "Movieland Graces Premier of 'Bargain with Bullets,'" *Chicago Defender*, September 25, 1937, 5.

5 For more on their being marketed to white theaters, see "'Bargain with Bullets' Is Cinematic Bargain," *New York Age*, December 4, 1937. The author states that the film was shown to the Loew's theater chain.

6 See Deborah Gray White, *Too Heavy a Load: Black Women in Defense of Themselves, 1894–1994* (New York: Norton, 1999). The concept of "lifting as we climb" has been an ethos guiding Black feminist political activism for generations and was the motto of the National Association of Colored Women.

7 Mary Church Terrell (1863–1954) was an influential Black suffragist who devoted her life's work to the idea that Blacks could help diminish white racism by advancing themselves through work, education, and community organizing.

8 The credits in part reflect the femme focus of the drama: the film's associate producer (Sara Francis) and two of the three screenwriters (Hazel Jamieson and Zella Young) were white women, which was unusua for any Hollywood, independent, exploitation, or race film of the time.

9 Angela Davis, *Are Prisons Obsolete?* (New York: Seven Stories, 2003).

10 The color politics of most race films are reversed when the boys capture Jackson and turn him over to the police, putting working-class Black youth on the right side of the law.

WILLIAM D. ALEXANDER: ALL-AMERICAN

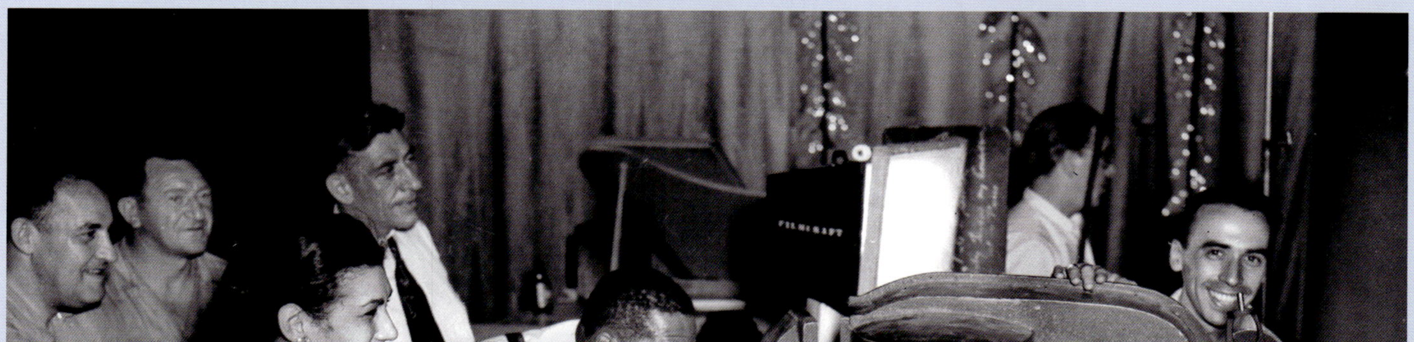

SHOLA LYNCH

Opposite
William Alexander (center, standing) on set with crew, Filmcraft Studios, Bronx, New York, ca. 1946

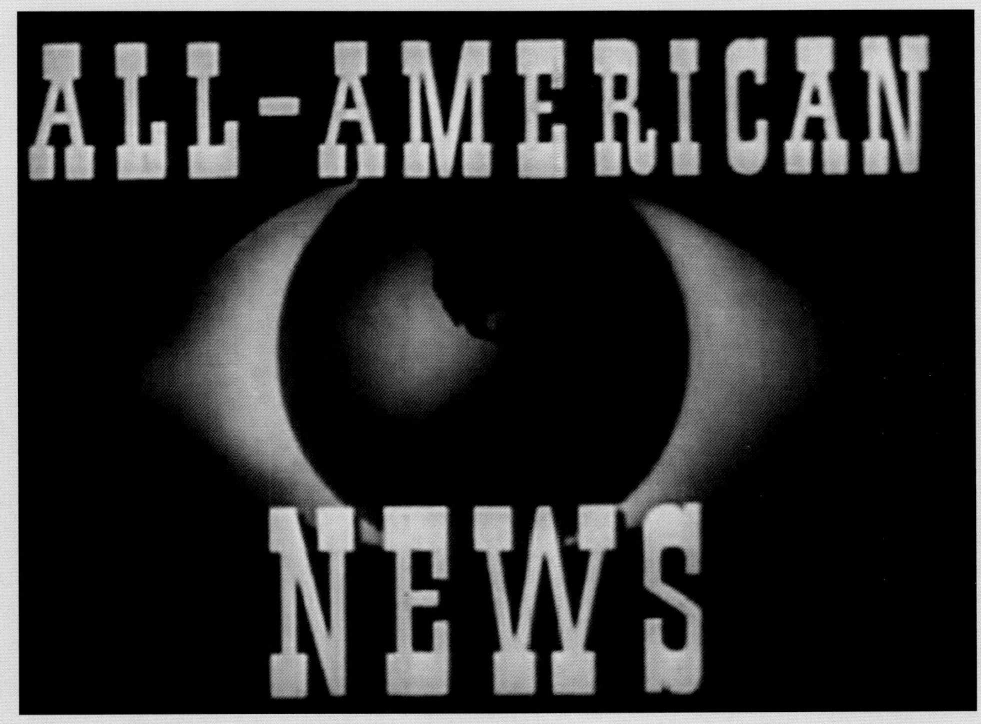

All-American News (1941–45), film still of title card

Described as a "consummate producer," William D. Alexander (1916–1991) made hundreds of newsreels, documentaries, and Soundies in addition to race films and feature films.[1] Whether Alexander had always wanted to be a filmmaker is unknown. His early career choices suggest a desire to chronicle Black stories overlooked by the mainstream media, and Alexander clearly possessed the creative and entrepreneurial spirit that a Black filmmaker of his generation needed in order to succeed. His entrée to the field came through his employment as a journalist. Just after the United States entered World War II, the recent college graduate began working in radio, interviewing Blacks in government and covering his community in segregated Washington, DC.

The Office of War Information (OWI), headed by the veteran newsman Elmer Davis, was formed to focus on marketing the war. Empowered by Executive Order 8802, which banned discriminatory hiring practices in federal agencies and in the nation's defense industry, Davis recruited journalists and filmmakers to boost Black morale on the home front. Alexander became part of a group sometimes known as the Black Brain Trust, mirroring President Franklin Delano Roosevelt's "Black Cabinet."[2] The group's goal was to distribute government press releases and photographs to Black newspapers across the country.

The United States found that the practice of racial segregation caused a public relations problem in the country's fight against fascism. As Thomas Cripps and David Culbert write, "By inducting 875,000 Negroes into a fighting force of some twelve million, the Army discovered that it was operating a social relations laboratory." The military needed to promote racial harmony for the war effort but was "officially committed to maintaining existing patterns of segregation."[3] Films like Frank Capra's *Negro Soldier* (1944) oriented Black troops as well as millions of white soldiers to an adjusted reality of racial cooperation. Additional pressure came from Black newspapers and organizations such as the National Association for the Advancement of Colored People (NAACP), which pointed out the hypocrisy of fighting fascism abroad while upholding racial segregation at home and supported a campaign for "Double Victory"—defeating fascism abroad and racism at home.

Alexander argued that the newsreels shown in segregated movie theaters at the time didn't speak to the African American audience and instead presented a "white man's war" devoid of Black participation or heroics. He proposed creating the first newsreels for a Black audience, the *All-American News*, which, like his radio work, would focus on Black achievement and the contributions of "our boys" abroad. Supported by the OWI and working with the journalist Claude Barnett, Alexander cowrote, produced, and sometimes narrated more than 250

His early career choices suggest a desire to chronicle Black stories overlooked by the mainstream media, and Alexander clearly possessed the creative and entrepreneurial spirit that a Black filmmaker of his generation needed in order to succeed.

segments for more than forty newsreels.[4] Distributed by the longtime Hollywood exhibitor Emmanuel Glucksman, *All-American News* reached Black moviegoers in more than nine hundred theaters across the country from 1942 until the end of the war in 1945. From war updates featuring footage of the all-Black Ninety-Second Infantry Division to sports, music, literature, and human-interest stories, the documentary shorts offered an alternative to the pervasive and denigrating stereotypes that served to justify, reinforce, and normalize race-based segregation. They have been described as "some of the best and first consciously produced, positive images of Black people other than the race movies."[5]

After the war Alexander established the Associated Film Producers of Negro Motion Pictures in New York.[6] His goal was to distribute documentaries "in non-Negro theaters in this country and in the foreign market."[7] He started with two short films about African Americans in the US Navy and the US Army titled, respectively, *The Call of Duty* and *The Highest Tradition* (both 1946). Alexander began broadening his reach into Soundies—the music videos of their day—which electrified audiences. From 1946 to 1948 he produced and sometimes directed more than twenty short musical films that resembled variety shows with interstitial acts and had catchy titles like *Rhythm in Riff*, *Jiving in Bebop*, and *Boogie Woogie Blues*. Drawing a through line from his radio days, his Soundies presented a variety of talent, from the handsome crooner Billy Eckstine and the all-female band International Sweethearts of Rhythm to the up-and-coming jazz trumpeter Dizzy Gillespie. Shown in theaters across the nation before the main feature, as well as in Soundie machines (video jukeboxes), these shorts introduced Black audiences to an array of top acts with glamour, laughter, and a toe-tapping good time and gave white audiences a peek into a Black world they often could not even imagine. Playing to both audiences, they sold easily to distributors and were popular with moviegoers.

In 1948 Alexander released his first feature film, *The Fight Never Ends*, which starred the heavyweight boxing champion Joe Louis and, in one of her earliest film roles, Ruby Dee. Alexander followed the effort with *Souls of Sin* (1949), written and directed by Powell Lindsay and starring a young actor who would later become a prolific documentary filmmaker, William Greaves. Alexander told the *Los Angeles Sentinel* in 1946 that his films would present "Negroes in an intelligent and dignified manner, thus setting the pace for Hollywood to follow."[8] But it proved harder to gain traction in the feature business with this concept. Black respectability was thought to appeal to a niche market—that is, to Black audiences only—and was not a concept that would be embraced by white audiences in a racially segregated country more comfortable with presenting Negroes in an undignified and stereotypical manner.

Rather than capitulate, the always practical and prolific Alexander returned to newsreels. From 1953 to 1956 he produced his second documentary-based series, *By-line*, also serving as the on-camera interviewer. He traveled all over the country profiling notable Black people, capturing many who contributed to the simmering flame of civil rights activism that would erupt in the 1960s. At a time when studio newsreels neglected the stories of Black Americans, Alexander centered them. As the historian G. William Jones writes, Alexander "captur[ed] on film an era of accomplishment and position for blacks which had not been seen since Reconstruction."[9]

In the late 1950s Alexander moved to London to establish Blue Nile Productions with the goal of making documentary films for the emerging independent nations of Africa. He became the official film producer for the Republic of Liberia and later for Ethiopia. He filmed many of the first conferences of the Organization of African States and produced a twelve-part series for the American ABC television network. His 1964 documentary *The Village of Hope*, about a Liberian leper colony, would win the Palme d'Or in the short film category at the Cannes International Film Festival. The Venice Film Festival honored his production *A Portrait of Ethiopia* in 1965. His documentary *Wealth in Wood* (1967) received the United Nations Award at the Madrid International Film Festival. Unfortunately, most of the films Alexander produced over eighteen years have been lost or are scattered in the archives of the more than twenty African countries that were the subject of his work.[10]

By the early 1970s Alexander had returned to the United States, having purchased the rights to *The Klansman* (1967), a novel by William Bradford Huie. Violent and dramatic, the story strove for a complicated view of race relations in a small Alabama town. Given the contentious political and cultural climate of the day, bringing together the counterculture, pulp, and Blaxploitation audiences may have been the calculation. Alexander partnered with the agent Bill Shiffrin to have a script written by Sam Fuller. He rallied Paramount Pictures to back the film and, with an assortment of additional financiers, raised $4.5 million. Richard Burton and Lee Marvin starred, with Lola Falana costarring as a hometown girl who returns with big-city ways and must be put in her place. The football star O. J. Simpson made his film debut as a sniper who carries out revenge killings of Klan members. Given the many partners and competing interests, script rewrites resulted in a story that was more melodrama than incendiary social commentary. Alexander and Shiffrin, as first-time Hollywood producers, could not mitigate the damage, and the film did not land with audiences or critics, as evidenced by the lackluster box office and one-star reviews. But Vincent Canby of the *New York Times* managed to capture what makes it worth revisiting when he opened his review by observing, "'The Klansman' is one of the rare films that are not as bad as they seem when you're watching them. That's a warning to be disregarded only by lunatics, but the point should be made that it's not an uninteresting film to think about afterward." Despite what Canby described as a "clumsy adaptation," the filmmakers' intentions are palpable, and central to the film is the question of white silence on matters of racial justice, which still resonates today.[11]

What should have opened more doors for Alexander, unfortunately, closed them instead. *The Klansman* would be his last known completed film and the final credit listed in his *New York Times* obituary.[12] But as the film historian Pearl Bowser notes, his "expansive filmmaking career" almost single-handedly

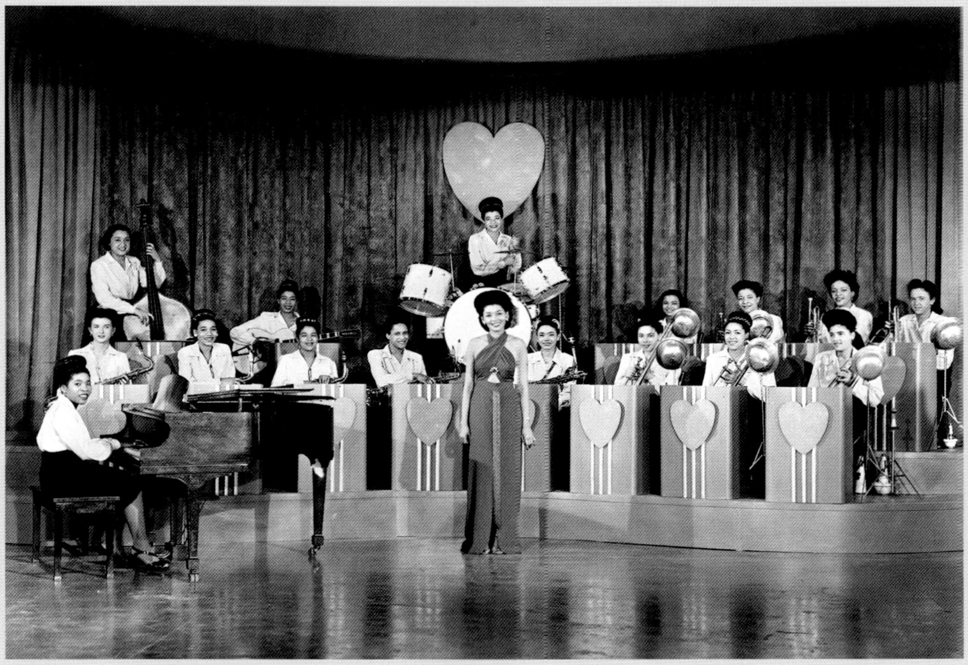

Anna Mae Winburn (center, standing) and the International Sweethearts of Rhythm in *International Sweethearts of Rhythm* (1947), production still

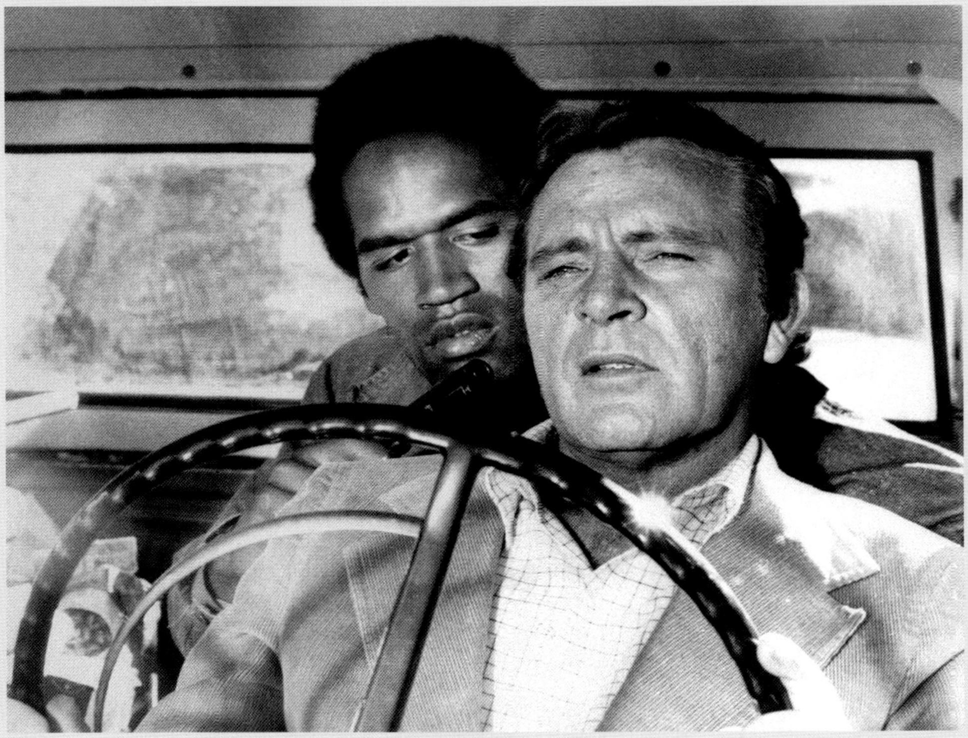

O. J. Simpson (left) and Richard Burton in *The Klansman* (1974), production still

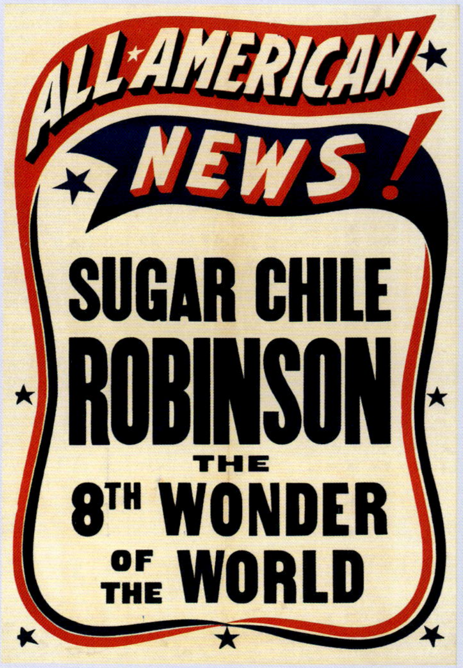

All-American News (1945), theatrical release poster

"bridged a gap" between the first generation of Black filmmakers and the independent voices that came of age in the 1960s and 1970s.[13] Greaves, one such filmmaker, in a 1990 interview, stated it more plainly: "Blacks simply weren't in the production end of the Hollywood industry. . . . Any notion that a black person could get into that aspect of the industry was considered ludicrous." What Greaves admired about Alexander was that he "was a wheeler-dealer and was unstoppable, not in any way intimidated by the notion that he was black and 'couldn't' make movies because of his blackness."[14]

For what he accomplished despite the obstacles presented by institutional racism, William Alexander should be remembered in film history as "a daring self-starter, full of original ideas, with the aggressiveness to set the domino theory in motion and effect its ultimate results," and as a filmmaker who forged a career "performing minor miracles in communication."[15] In that sense Alexander, like his early newsreel series, was all-American.

Notes

1 Paramount Pictures press biography (1973), quoted in Pearl Bowser, "Pioneers of Black Documentary Film," in *Struggles for Representation: African American Documentary Film and Video*, ed. Phyllis R. Klotman and Janet K. Cutler (Bloomington: Indiana University Press, 1999), 26.

2 Bowser, "Pioneers," 26.

3 Thomas Cripps and David Culbert, "*The Negro Soldier* (1944): Film Propaganda in Black and White," *American Quarterly* 31 (Winter 1979): 616.

4 Exactly how many newsreels were made has not been documented. The New York Public Library's Schomburg Center for Research in Black Culture has thirty-nine. The Library of Congress has thirty-five as well as some excerpts. See Amanda Jenkins, "All-American News: The First African American Newsreel," *Now See Hear! The National Audio-Visual Conservation Center Blog*, February 15, 2019, https://blogs.loc.gov/now-see-hear/2019/02/all-american-news-the-first-african-american-newsreel/.

5 Spencer Moon, *Reel Black Talk: A Sourcebook of 50 American Filmmakers* (Westport, CT: Greenwood, 1997), 3–4.

6 G. William Jones, "William Alexander," in *Black Cinema Treasures: Lost and Found* (Denton: University of North Texas Press, 1997), 36.

7 "Negro Film Group Asks U.S. Use Its Pictures," *Film World* 2 (April 1946): 149.

8 Jones, "William Alexander," 36.

9 Jones, 38.

10 Bowser, "Pioneers," 29. Bowser states that Alexander worked in "22 countries, including Liberia, Ethiopia, the Sudan, Morocco, the United Arab Republic, Zaire, Kenya, Senegal, Ghana, Algeria, Malagasy, Dahomey, Togo, Malawi, Sierra Leone, Tanzania, Zambia, French Congo, the Ivory Coast, Guinea, and the Central African Republic."

11 Vincent Canby, "'The Klansman,' a Deep South Melodrama," *New York Times*, November 21, 1974.

12 "William Alexander, Producer Featuring Blacks, Dies at 75," *New York Times*, December 6, 1991.

13 Bowser, "Pioneers," 29.

14 William Greaves, interviewed by James Hatch, in *Artist and Influence* 9 (1990): 60.

15 Paramount Pictures press biography, quoted in Bowser, "Pioneers," 26.

AFRICAN AMERICAN HOME MOVIES

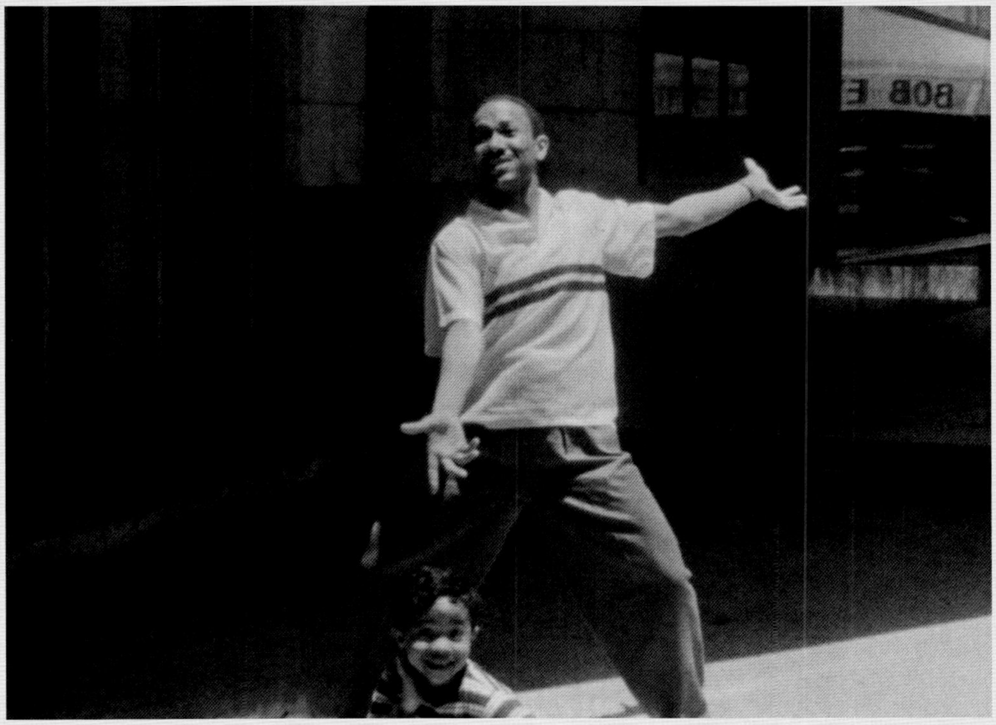

RHEA L. COMBS AND JACQUELINE STEWART

Previous page
Fayard Nicholas with his son Tony, home movie, ca. 1950, film still

Right
Solomon Sir Jones, home movie, ca. 1924–28, film still

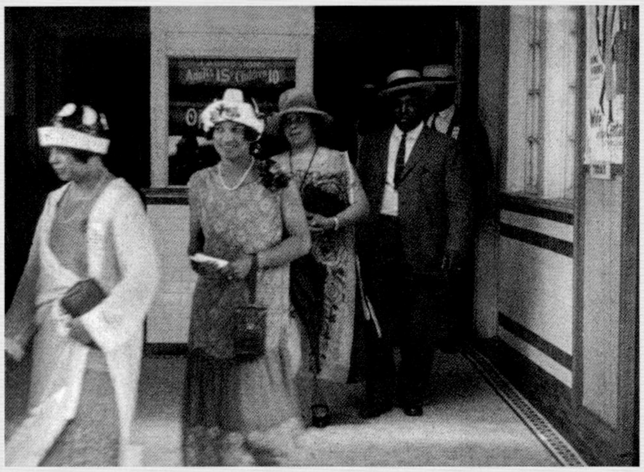

A little African American boy with a cherubic face, maybe five or six years old, dances with his uncle, landing a series of acrobatic splits. Next, he clowns around with his father, sliding comically between his dad's legs and then posing with a triumphant smile. Home movies are filled with scenes like these of families goofing around, showing off, and mugging for the camera. This particular film happens to capture a boy dancing with the legendary Nicholas Brothers, his uncle Harold and his father, Fayard, who made up one of the most celebrated dance teams in history.[1]

The Nicholas Brothers' home movies were added to the National Film Registry in 2011, joining a small group of amateur films identified by the Library of Congress as "culturally, historically or aesthetically significant" and deserving of preservation.[2] The nine reels of the brothers' home movies held at the Academy Film Archive date from 1934 through 1951 and document vacations to the Chicago World's Fair, Yosemite, and the California redwoods; special performances with artists including Bill "Bojangles" Robinson, Ethel Waters, and Duke Ellington; fictional stories created by the brothers, like "Mutiny on Sugar Hill"; mundane family clips showing Harold and Fayard palling around with their wives and children; and travels to Europe, Central America, and North Africa. The running times vary from three minutes to more than sixty minutes, with many of the longer ones made up of short clips and unrelated snippets.

Until recently African American home movies have not been included in histories of Black filmmaking, which, like the field of film studies as a whole, have tended to focus primarily on commercial narrative films, whether fiction or documentary. Fortunately the films people made casually, as nonprofessionals for private enjoyment, are now being preserved and studied more carefully as part of the vast bodies of films made for "nontheatrical" circulation (along with educational films, training films, student films, and sponsored films).[3] Home movies point to a crucial history of cinematic self-representation, one that we can trace forward to our contemporary selfie culture. In addition, they offer key insights into the ways in which African Americans and people from other historically marginalized groups have used film cameras to record, remember, and share details of their lives that were misrepresented, if not completely ignored, in the mainstream media.

When we examine the Nicholas Brothers' home movies, we can see that they are important "Black films," not simply because they were made by a family in the entertainment industry but also because they are Black-authored works presenting Black points of view.[4] The Nicholas family purchased a camera in the 1930s and over two decades captured aspects of their professional lives (marquees emblazoned with their names and footage shot from the wings in theaters across the United States and Europe), blended with their personal interactions with family, friends, and colleagues while they traveled and matured. Although Fayard and Harold were professional entertainers, they were amateur filmmakers, and their films are connected to a larger history of nontheatrical Black filmmaking. Like those of many middle-class Black families who experimented with making home movies, the Nicholas films affirmed Black lives during a period when most commercial productions treated Black subjects in a stereotypical and marginal fashion. In their home movies the Nicholas Brothers are not an isolated specialty act. Instead they are at the center of the places and relationships that shaped their lives, and more importantly, they play roles in front of and behind the camera.

We might go so far as to say that Black amateur and home movies are the most "independent" of Black films. Pioneering Black film writer-directors like Oscar Micheaux and Spencer Williams Jr. worked outside of Hollywood, making Black-cast race movies for African American audiences in an effort to provide alternatives to mainstream films. Their features such as *Within Our Gates* (1920) and *The Blood of Jesus* (1941) incorporated nuances of cultural expression (for example, inside jokes and intraracial commentaries on skin color, class, and gender roles) that appealed to Black viewers within the forced but sometimes more comfortable contexts of segregated theatrical exhibition.

Black home movies from this period open up even more intimate realms of Black cinematic representation and exhibition. They were shared with friends and family in the "safe space" of home or with community members at churches or social clubs. From the footage that the Black surgeon C. Allen Alexander shot in 1937 of the legendary scientist George Washington Carver crocheting at his home and working in his laboratory at Tuskegee Institute,[5] to the carefree scenes of Cab Calloway on tour in the Caribbean and South America and with his young family during the 1950s,[6] to the Alsup family's playful report from the 1979 ChicagoFest music festival,[7] Black amateur films and home movies have been made by and for Black families and communities without the involvement of the white funders, censors, or theater owners with whom Micheaux and Williams negotiated.

Given where they were shown and shot, Black home movies include a wealth of details of everyday life unfettered from the dictates of narrative and commercial filmmaking. They document, in both deliberate and incidental ways, details of fashion, hairstyling, home decor, foodways, architecture, social status, and so much more. Shots of Christmas mornings and birthday parties, graduations and family vacations, new cars and new babies capture in their foregrounds and backgrounds unparalleled evidence of Black home life and cultural practices.

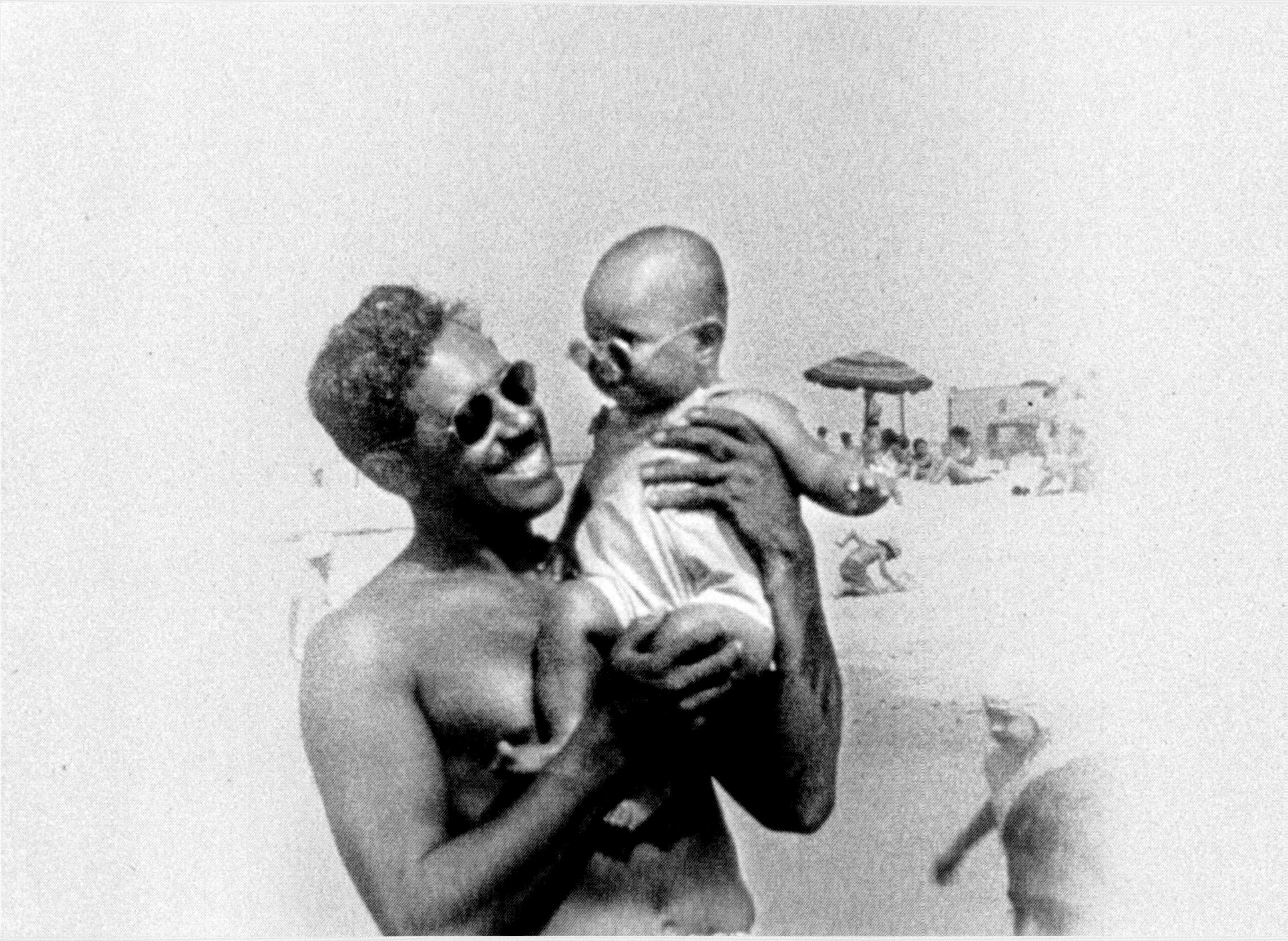

Cab Calloway and daughter, home movie, 1950s, film still

People also clearly perform in home movies, often "hamming it up" for the camera. And yet these and other gestures and expressions have an improvisational quality, showing how people interact with the camera, with one another, and with their environments (posing, dancing, setting the scene, or simply walking down the street) when they feel free to express themselves fully. These universal gestures occur regardless of a person's renown, making the connection to them more meaningful.

When we pay more careful attention to these movies, we see how avidly African Americans—those who could afford to—picked up cameras to create and share images for their own families and communities. These films offer a freedom of expression that is often erased or overshadowed when considering the history of Black people and filmmaking. As the archivist CK Ming explains, "The portrayal of everyday situations—picnics, bike rides, beach going—not only allows a marginalized group control of their own images, but corrects and subverts the traditional narrative of their lives."[8]

Home movies add to official narratives and expose hidden treasures. From the first amateurs shooting in the 1920s through the adoption of 8mm and Super 8mm technologies and later camcorders and mobile phones, Black home-movie makers have recorded the things they wanted to remember and show off. This impulse has special significance for socially devalued people. The films of Solomon Sir Jones (produced from 1924 to 1928) highlighted Black life in Oklahoma three years after the Tulsa race massacre of 1921, which decimated much of "Black Wall Street" and killed hundreds of people. His travelogue footage presents scenes from across the state of prominent landowners, vibrant school and church communities, bustling general and department stores, parades and social gatherings, entrepreneurs, and Black oil barons producing "thousands of barrels of oil daily."[9]

Looking at home movies of prosperous Black Oklahomans or well-known entertainers may produce a false narrative about race and representation, since these economically privileged groups would have access to film technology that was not available to other members of the Black community. But these films should call our attention to the importance of home movies by lesser-known African Americans as well. These films demonstrate that, as the archivist Ina Archer has written, "many of the cinematic archives and histories we thought we knew are not as white as we tend to think them to be."[10] Experiences that are shared by many can serve as a bridge connecting people from all walks of life to the human condition. At the same time, however, Black home movies reflect image making that is entirely in the hands of Black people, which is significantly different from our previous understandings of Black film history.

Given the fragile, ephemeral quality of amateur films, many have been lost because they are stored (if they are kept at all) in basements, garages, and attics—none of which provide optimal archival conditions. This makes preserving them, and reclaiming the unique stories they contain, even more crucial. There are several initiatives dedicated to collecting, preserving, and sharing African American home movies. The Smithsonian's National Museum of African American History and Culture's Great Migration Home Movie Project, the South Side Home Movie Project at the University of Chicago, and the African American Home Movie Archive allow people to view and relive these special memories that otherwise may deteriorate and become obsolete.[11]

Like all small-gauge home movies, those shot by Black filmmakers document people and places that may no longer be living or extant. In doing so, these records of midcentury life highlight the significance of racial segregation and, as we see in the Nicholas Brothers' home movies, mark the differences for Black people between living in the United States and traveling internationally. African American home movies also display and offer joy, presenting unique opportunities to reexamine the nexus of Black cultural life and film history.

Notes

1 Tony Nicholas and Luisa Ribeiro, "Nicholas Brothers' Family Home Movies," Center for Home Movies, https://www.centerforhomemovies.org/other-histories/essays/nicholas-brothers-family-home-movies-tony-nicholas-and-luisa-ribeiro/.

2 "Home Movies and Amateur Films on the National Film Registry," Center for Home Movies, https://www.centerforhomemovies.org/home-movies-on-the-national-film-registry/.

3 See Allyson Nadia Field and Marsha Gordon, eds., *Screening Race in American Nontheatrical Film* (Durham, NC: Duke University Press, 2019). *Private Lives Public Spaces*, the Museum of Modern Art's first gallery installation of home movies and amateur films from its collection, was on view from October 21, 2019, to May 23, 2021, and reflected the growing interest in studying casually made films. The presentation included examples of Black home movies.

4 For discussions of criteria for classifying a "Black film" over time, see Thomas Cripps, *Black Film as Genre* (Bloomington: Indiana University Press, 1979); Mark Reid, *Redefining Black Film* (Berkeley: University of California Press, 1993); and Michael Boyce Gillespie, *Film Blackness: American Cinema and the Idea of Black Film* (Durham, NC: Duke University Press, 2016).

5 "Moving Image Film Related to George Washington Carver," YouTube video, 12:20, posted by US National Archives, July 9, 2018, https://www.youtube.com/watch?v=5_yn6Qz81Y8, and Heidi Holstrom, "Now Showing: George Washington Carver on Kodachrome," *The Unwritten Record* (blog), National Archives, June 14, 2018, https://unwritten-record.blogs.archives.gov/2018/06/14/now-showing-george-washington-carver-on-kodachrome/.

6 Compilation reel of 16mm home movies filmed by Cab Calloway during a tour of South America, with both Kodachrome and black-and-white film edge codes indicating the years 1950 and 1955, National Museum of African American History and Culture, 2015.273.2.4.1a, https://nmaahc.si.edu/explore/initiatives/great-migration-home-movie-project.

7 Alsup Smith Collection, "Summerfest 1979," South Side Home Movie Project Digital Archive, https://sshmpportal.uchicago.edu/index.php/Detail/objects/1735.

8 CK Ming, "The South Side Home Movie Project: Re-Imagining Black Chicago," *Black Camera* 10, no. 1 (Fall 2018): 294.

9 Jones's films entered the Library of Congress National Film Registry in 2016 and are located at Yale University (https://beinecke.library.yale.edu/collections/highlights/solomon-sir-jones-films-1924-1928). Nine reels of films from 1924 to 1928 have been digitized and made available at the Smithsonian's National Museum of African American History and Culture.

10 Ina Archer, "Conspiracies and Caretakers: Making Homes for African American Home Movies," *World Records Journal* 3, no. 1 (2020): 3, https://vols.worldrecordsjournal.org/03/02.

11 The Great Migration Home Movie Project, National Museum of African American History and Culture, https://nmaahc.si.edu/explore/initiatives/great-migration-home-movie-project; South Side Home Movie Project Digital Archive, University of Chicago, https://sshmpportal.uchicago.edu/; and African American Home Movie Archive, https://www.aahma.org.

WILLIAM GREAVES: BRIDGING GENERATIONS

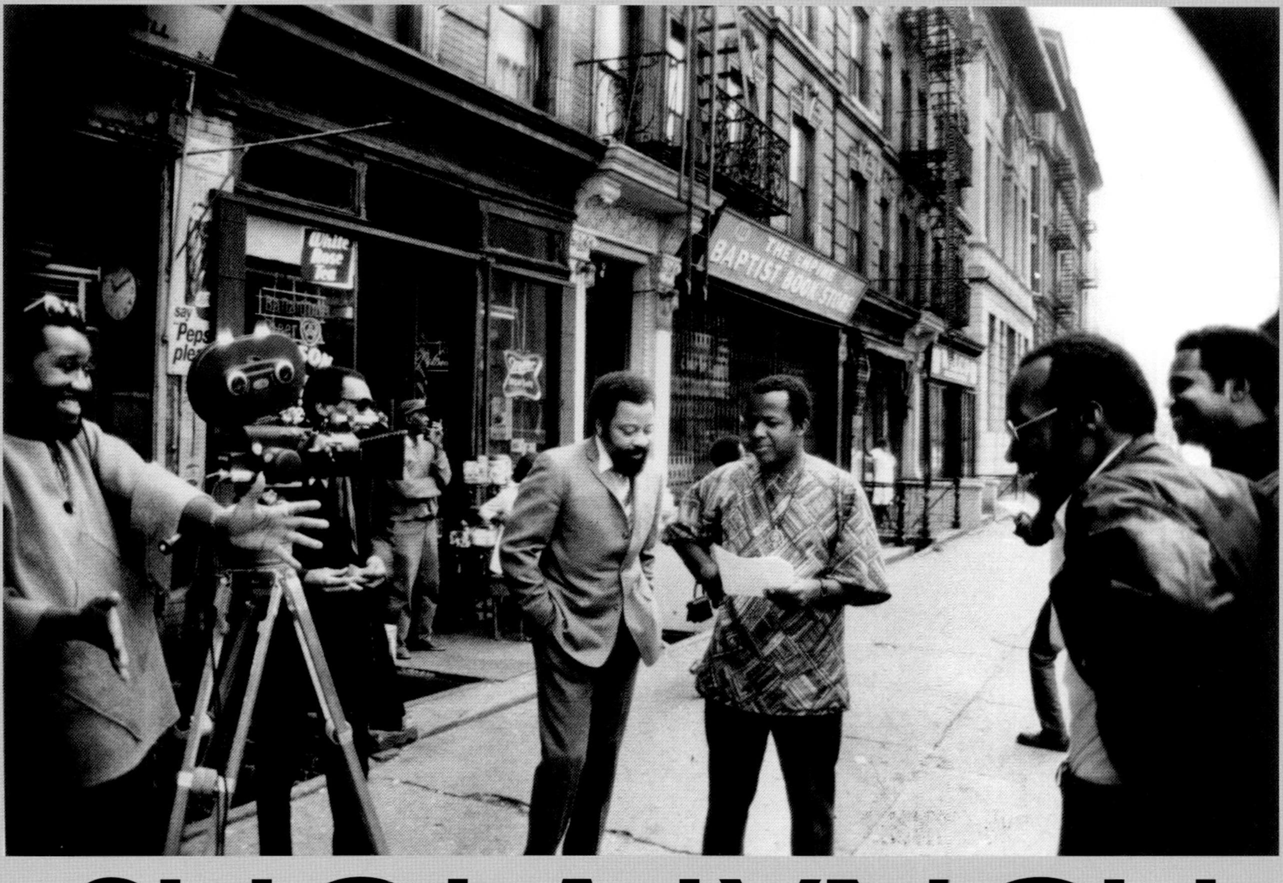

SHOLA LYNCH

Previous page
William Greaves (center, right) on location in Harlem for *Black Journal*, ca. 1970

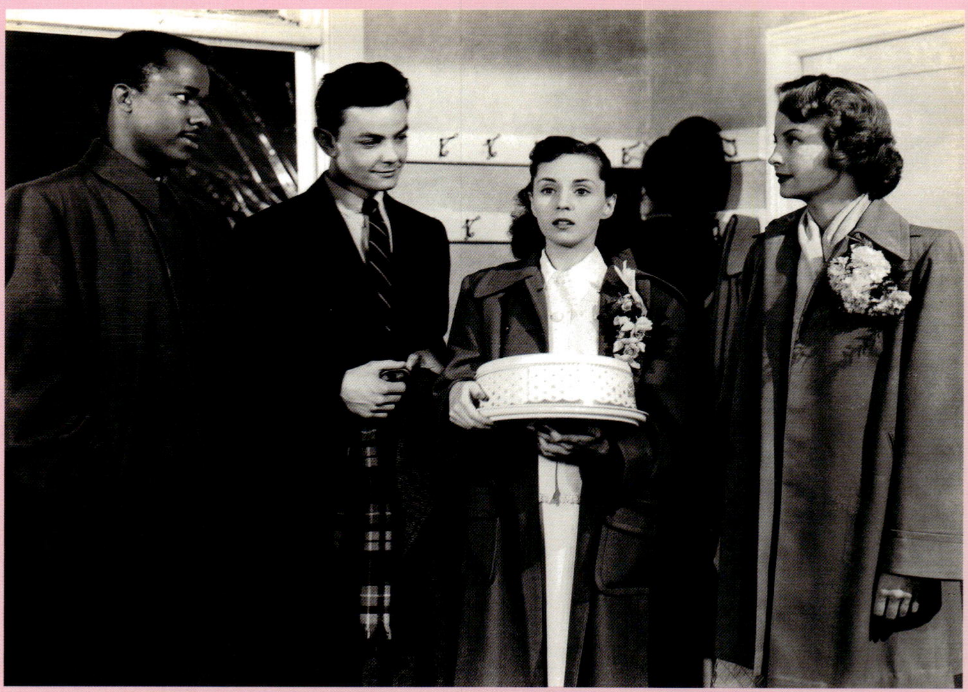

William Greaves (left) in *Lost Boundaries* (1949), production still

During his pioneering career William Greaves (1926–2014) worked on an immense body of documentary films as a producer, director, writer, editor, or cameraman, including some experimental hybrid narrative films.[1] Despite having lived through the Great Depression and World War II, Greaves forged new ground in a craft that drew him regardless of its impractical nature in a segregated America. He had a talent for being in the right place at the right time—and with the right credentials. Throughout his career he cultivated a distinct voice as a filmmaker, proceeding as if his only choice was to be independent or not to make films at all.

Born in Harlem, he considered himself "drenched in the afterglow of the Harlem Renaissance," imbued with the spirit of the "New Negroes" asserting themselves at the dawn of a new era.[2] History was not an abstract concept for the young Greaves. He grew up down the street from the Harlem branch of the New York Public Library, which became a nexus for Black thought with the purchase of the bibliophile Arturo Schomburg's ten-thousand-item collection of books, photographs, and artworks in 1926. Black history also lived and breathed through the people Greaves encountered in his neighborhood, including the filmmaker Oscar Micheaux, the poet Langston Hughes, the historian Leo Hansberry (uncle to the playwright Lorraine Hansberry), the songwriter Eubie Blake, and the actors Canada Lee, Ruby Dee, and Ossie Davis. The library became a refuge and an inspiration for Greaves while he was attending Stuyvesant High School, a magnet school known for its accelerated math and science curriculum.

The library also housed the American Negro Theater, where the young student made his acting debut in 1944. Greaves remembered getting "terrible reviews" but began to study and worked on various productions. He appeared in the musical race film *Sepia Cinderella* (1947), in which Sidney Poitier also appeared as an uncredited extra. By 1948 Greaves had earned a membership in Lee Strasberg's Actors Studio and a reasonable level of success. He went on to named roles in *Miracle in Harlem* (1948) and the William Alexander productions *The Fight Never Ends* (1948) and *Souls of Sin* (1949). (The latter is generally considered the last race film made by a Black producer.)[3] In 1949 Greaves also appeared in *Lost Boundaries*, and behind the scenes he apprenticed with the film's producer, Louis Rochemont.

Greaves found himself frustrated by the limited and often stereotypical character types available to Black actors, as he recalled in 2001: "I was studying Africa and African American history. . . . Acting in a stereotypical way really disturbed me." He gravitated toward working behind the camera "to

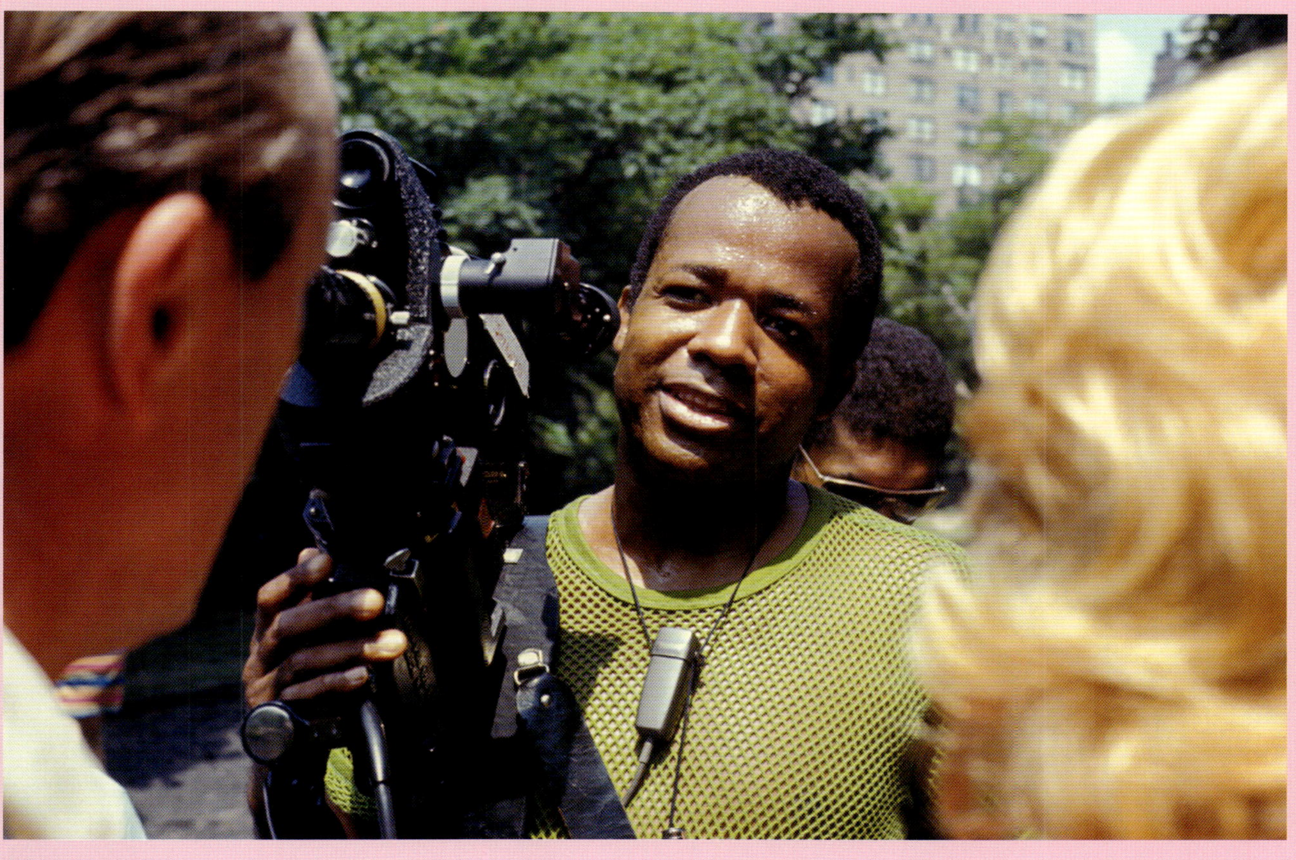

William Greaves in *Symbiopsychotaxiplasm: Take One* (dir. William Greaves, 1968), film still

produce films that in one way or another paid either homage to the African American experience or to Africa and that variously would attack the outrageous vilification campaign that had been launched against Black people ever since the end of slavery." By this he meant the lie of assumed race-based Black inferiority because the dominant white culture "needed to try and find some sort of philosophical basis for oppressing us." Embarking on what would become his lifelong mission, he resolved to "try and make films that would balance the scale somewhat."

While attending City College of New York, Greaves shifted from mechanical engineering to film studies, which quickly became his sole focus. He also studied production at the New Film Institute. After he left school, there were few job prospects for Black men in the film or television industries in the United States, so he moved to Canada in 1952, eventually landing a job at the National Canadian Film Board. There he honed his craft for the next eleven years, working on approximately eighty films for the Canadian government, including the now classic *Emergency Ward* (1959).[4] While the film board was a critical training ground, as he climbed up the production ladder from assistant editor to assistant director, sound effects editor, film editor, chief editor, and later producer and director, Greaves was troubled by the fact that "none of those films dealt with the Black experience." As civil rights activists began to challenge the distinctly undemocratic realities faced by Black Americans, Greaves felt compelled to return to the United States. In 1963, when the opportunity arose to make films for the United Nations, he finally went back to New York and formed William Greaves Productions.

The United States Information Agency became one of Greaves's main clients after "learn[ing] of [his] expertise in film production," in part through a strong recommendation from the independent filmmaker Shirley Clarke, who had seen *Emergency Ward*. Among the documentaries he directed, produced, and wrote for the agency were *Wealth of a Nation* (1964), which "explores how freedom of speech is afforded to all Americans, showing freedom of expression in art, music, dance, architecture, and science," and *The First World Festival of Negro Arts* (1966), the official documentary of the festival held in Dakar, Senegal, in 1966.[5]

But it was not until 1968, with the tragic assassination of Martin Luther King Jr. and the summer of rage and uprisings that followed, that mission met opportunity. Compelled by social and federal pressure, broadcasters looked for Black filmmakers. Uniquely qualified and already a seasoned director, Greaves became involved with a new public affairs program aptly titled *Black Journal*, which broadcast from National Educational Television's New York affiliate. He produced and cohosted the show, under white supervision and direction, until what he described as "a palace revolt of sorts" by the Black staff members catapulted him to the role of executive producer. When he took the creative reins, Greaves recognized the opportunity given that "America was a heavily apartheid nation, and nothing was more apartheid than the motion picture industry." Under his leadership the show would actually live up to its tagline, "By, for, and about black Americans." *Black Journal* unmuted the views of Black Americans, who for years had felt silenced and ignored. Despite fears to the contrary, the show found a national audience and won accolades (including an Emmy Award in 1969 for excellence in public affairs programming).[6] Greaves's policy of shedding light on topics ranging from Black Power and prisons to Black theater and soul music in ways that would resonate as much in the barbershops of his Harlem youth as with his college-educated colleagues contributed to its success.[7] Greaves also made a point of hiring young Black talent. *Black Journal* became a training ground for the next generation of Black filmmakers, including Madeline Anderson, St. Clair Bourne, Julie Dash, Henry Hampton, and Stan Lathan.[8]

Despite his success at *Black Journal*, Greaves missed running his own company, and in 1970 he returned to his independent filmmaking roots. In some sense, this marked a new beginning. He fully reconnected with his passion for both filmmaking and Black culture, one that shaped the rest of his long and productive career, in which he expanded the documentary genre. Through the stories Greaves dedicated himself to telling, the volume of award-winning work he created, and the attention to craft that he practiced but also inspired, he marked his place in the pantheon of independent filmmakers. Without bitterness, he carved out space for his work in a hostile and often dismissive environment that limited the heights that he could reach yet never curtailed his vision. Greaves's 1968 experimental fiction-documentary hybrid, *Symbiopsychotaxiplasm: Take One,* a metatextual film, for instance, would be rediscovered in 1992, distributed in 2005, and added to the Library of Congress's National Film Registry in 2015.[9] The rest of his life's work remains to be fully explored.[10]

Greaves created films connecting generations and spanning contemporary Black history. As he stated, "When one makes a good film, whether dramatic or documentary, one is performing a major surgery on the psyches of the audience." His dedication to craft and storytelling lives on through his timeless films, which continue to inform and reshape our psychic and cultural landscapes.

Notes

1 Spencer Moon, *Reel Black Talk: A Sourcebook of 50 American Filmmakers* (Westport, CT: Greenwood, 1997), 126. For Greaves's filmography, see http://www.williamgreaves.com/william-greaves-biography-filmography/.

2 William Greaves, video oral history interview conducted by James Briggs Murray, curator, Moving Image & Recorded Sound Division, Schomburg Center for Research in Black Culture, New York Public Library, 2001. Unless otherwise noted, all quotations from Greaves and biographical details are from this interview.

3 John Kisch and Edward Mapp, *A Separate Cinema: Fifty Years of Black-Cast Posters* (New York: Noonday, 1992), 145. Greaves stated in an interview, "I have the honor of being featured in the last two black-cast films of that era, *Souls of Sin* [1949] and *Miracle in Harlem* [1948]." Scott MacDonald, "William Greaves," in *Critical Cinema 3: Interviews with Independent Filmmakers* (Berkeley: University of California Press, 1998), 43–44.

4 William Greaves, interviewed by James Hatch, in *Artist and Influence* 9 (1990): 64.

5 Criss Kovac, "Wealth Comes in Many Forms: William Greaves' USIA Films," *The Unwritten Record* (blog), National Archives, https://unwritten-record.blogs.archives.gov/2015/07/14/wealth-comes-in-many-forms-william-greaves-usia-films/.

6 Elizabeth Amelia Hadley, "*Eyes on the Prize*: Reclaiming Black Images, Culture, and History," in *Struggles for Representation: African American Documentary Film and Video*, ed. Phyllis R. Klotman and Janet K. Cutler (Bloomington: Indiana University Press, 1999), 109.

7 For more, see the American Archive of Public Broadcasting's *Black Journal* Collection, https://americanarchive.org/special_collections/black-journal.

8 Pearl Bowser, "Pioneers of Black Documentary Film," in Klotman and Cutler, *Struggles for Representation*, 30.

9 Richard Brody, "The Daring, Original, and Overlooked *Symbiopsychotaxiplasm: Take One*," *New Yorker*, February 5, 2015, https://www.newyorker.com/culture/richard-brody/daring-original-overlooked-symbiopsychotaxiplasm-take-one.

10 The William Greaves Archive is held by the Schomburg Center for Research in Black Culture. On the discovery of this rich repository, see Shola Lynch, "Revealing Greaves: Unhiding His Archive," in *William Greaves: Filmmaking as Mission*, ed. Scott MacDonald and Jacqueline Najuma Stewart (New York: Columbia University Press, 2021), 413.

JAMES BALDWIN: WHAT HE SAW

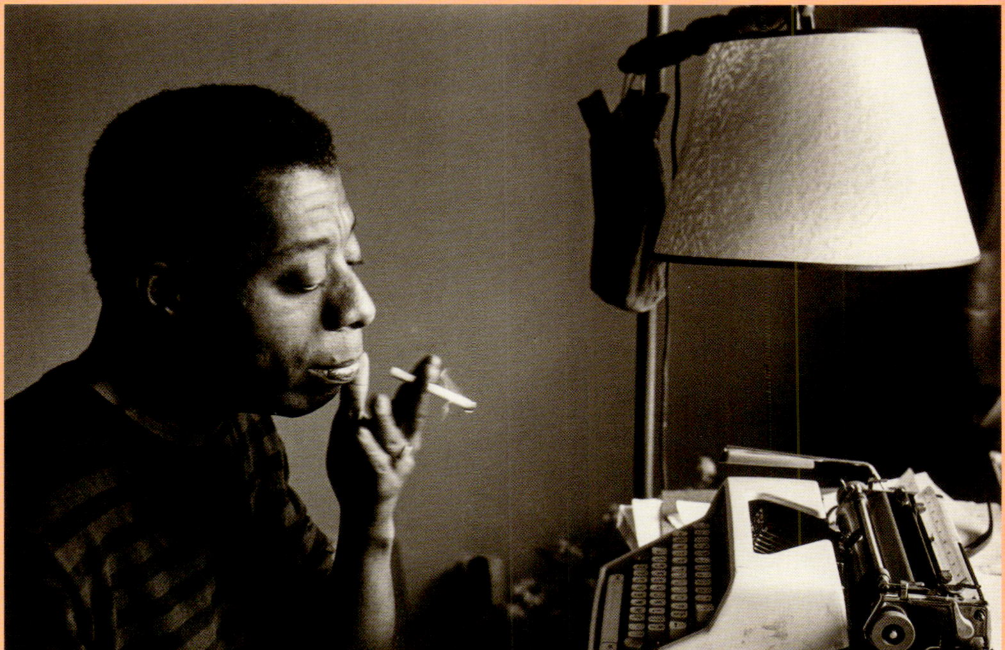

MICHAEL BOYCE GILLESPIE

Previous page
Sedat Pakay (Turkish, 1945–2016), *James Baldwin by His Typewriter, Istanbul, 1966*, 1966, gelatin silver print, 10 15⁄16 × 13 15⁄16 in. (27.8 × 35.4 cm)

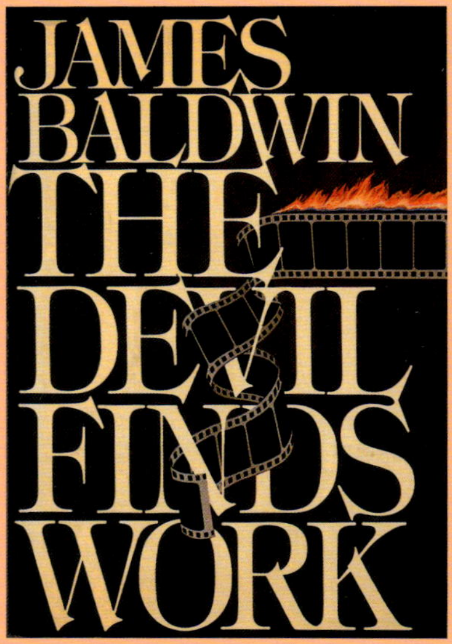

James Baldwin, *The Devil Finds Work: An Essay* (New York: Dial, 1976), first edition

To encounter oneself is to encounter the other: and this is love. If I know that my soul trembles, I know that yours does, too: and, if I can respect this, both of us can live. Neither of us, truly, can live without the other: a statement which would not sound so banal if one were not endlessly compelled to repeat it, and, further, believe it, and act on that belief.
—James Baldwin,
The Devil Finds Work (1976)

James Baldwin's work as an essayist, novelist, and playwright, coupled with his activism as a public intellectual and witness to twentieth-century America, continues to inform our understanding of this country as an unfinished project riddled with horrors, generative possibilities, cowardice, and love. Baldwin's writings were particularly focused on Black life and questions of class, desire, whiteness, anti-blackness, and the ideal of democracy. Throughout, they offered stunning displays of aesthetic craft and critical commentary. By the end of the 1960s many of his heroes and comrades of the civil rights era were dead, and his status as an expatriate elder dimmed across the decade leading up to the publication of *The Devil Finds Work* in 1976.[1] A book-length essay that began as an article on black film for *Esquire*, the text is in truth not a departure but a culmination of his long-standing deliberation on blackness, America, and the arts.

Richly hybrid in form, *The Devil Finds Work* is at once a history of American film, an autobiography, film criticism, and a treatise on the politics of popular culture. Baldwin, Francey Russell writes, "presents cinema not just as a popular art form but also as a shared, public site of collective instruction."[2] Poignantly, this measure of instruction is mediated by rich reflections on Baldwin's own experience as a film spectator. His engagement with cinema shines as part of the legacy of black film criticism, which is not a monolithic discourse but a canon of varied approaches and investments in art and culture. Baldwin's distinct contribution to the field is a detailing of the stakes of identity with regard to how one processes cinema and, by extension, the world. He understood, and sometimes adored, cinema as an art practice, but he remained equally attuned to its capacity to abide as ideology. As Jacqueline Stewart crucially notes, "Spectatorship is typically characterized as an activity fraught with social, psychological, and political contradictions for black viewers who are subjected to films that privilege white (racist, hegemonic) values and perspectives."[3] Through a prosaic mapping of his own fraught spectatorship, Baldwin deprivileged the authority of whiteness through a sustained refusal of the totalizing fantasy of cinema's innocuousness.

The book begins with microportraits of Baldwin's early film experiences, including his nascent ideas of beauty by way of Joan Crawford, the cowboy hat and white horse semiotics of Tom Mix westerns, the lazily paced cowardice evident in the adaptation of George B. Seitz's *Last of the Mohicans* (1936), and a meditation on Bette Davis and the trait of frog-eyedness he shared with her. His analytic fusing of questions of celebrity, desire, and self is a critical maneuver that José Esteban Muñoz described as an act of disidentification whereby Baldwin "simultaneously position[s] himself within and outside the image of the movie star."[4] As a Black queer subject, Baldwin tacitly writes throughout *The Devil Finds Work* of his own disidentification, his own history of identification with cinema as a logic of refusal and resistance. Significantly, in this section of the book he mentions Orilla "Bill" Miller—"a young white schoolteacher, a beautiful woman, very important to me"—who took Baldwin to film screenings and theater performances.[5] This early exposure triggered what became a serious preoccupation for him throughout his life: the critical consequences generated by the distance between Black life and the rendering of Black life on the screen and stage. This informed his sense of the function of stereotypes: "It is not entirely true that no one from the world I knew had yet made an appearance on the American screen: there were, for example, Stepin Fetchit and Willie Best and Manton Moreland, all of whom, rightly or wrongly, I loathed. It seemed to me that they lied about the world I knew, and debased it, and certainly I did not know anybody like them—as far as I could tell; for it is also possible that their comic, bug-eyed terror contained the truth concerning a terror by which I hoped never to be engulfed."[6] Baldwin's noting of the debasement and deception of stereotypicality centers the question of whom these images serve and for what purposes. As Lauren Berlant remarks, "For Baldwin, the pleasure of the stereotype and the narratives of dominant and revolutionary violence waged on its behalf

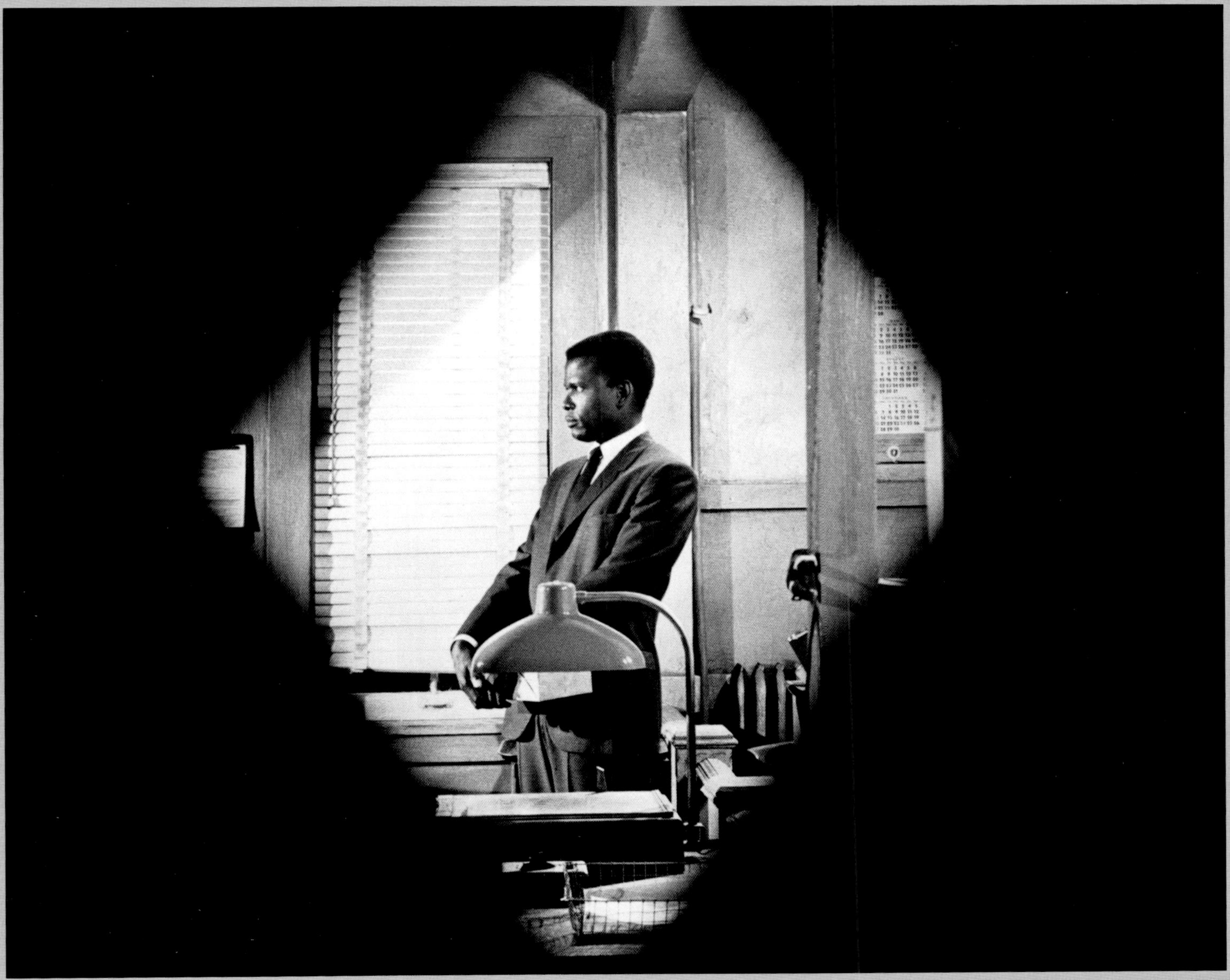

Sidney Poitier in *In the Heat of the Night* (1967), production still

constituted his fundamental experience of white privilege."[7] He pivots through and from "comic, bug-eyed terror" to a question of its utility in the service of *terror* or white supremacy. In this way, Baldwin avoids those staid approaches that focus on fantasies of the redemptive quality of images and questions of positive/negative representation.

Baldwin describes his earliest comprehension of the tension in black performance when Miller took him to see his first play, Orson Welles's 1936 production of *Macbeth*: "The first time I ever really saw black actors at work was on the stage: and it is important to emphasize that the people I was watching were black, like me. Nothing that I had seen before had prepared me for this—which is a melancholy comment indeed, but I cannot be blamed for an ignorance which an entire republic had deliberately inculcated."[8] A profound reckoning with performativity and the art of blackness, Baldwin's recollection of the theater and seeing Black performers on the stage impacted his determination of cinema's shortcomings: "For the tension in the theater is a very different, and very particular tension: this tension between the real and the imagined is the theater, and this is why the theater will always remain a necessity. One is not in the presence of shadows, but responding to one's flesh and blood: in the theater, we are re-creating each other."[9] Here Baldwin juxtaposes the animacy of the theater with the elusive and illusory shadows of the movie house as a demand for a more tangible spectatorial experience. Thus, as Jane Gaines notes, "Baldwin's quarrel with the cinema is not just that it fails to return his own image to him. The motion picture creates the illusion of intimacy but holds the viewer at a distance. In his hierarchy, flesh-and-blood-theater is *over* shadowy film, the 'like me' of theater over the 'not like me' of film."[10]

Fundamentally Baldwin's point about the "flesh and blood" ways of his theater spectatorship marks the limits of his thoughts on cinema. He does not quibble in the unproductive and fantastical terms of cinema's capacity to embody truth. Instead his thoughts on cinema bear out a demand for a more generative sense of spectatorship as an irreconcilable blend of incitement and refutation.[11]

Baldwin's brutal precision in identifying the ideological resonances of race and the cinematic mechanisms of disavowal and fantasy continues in the second chapter. It opens with a focus on a French film, Michel Gast's *I Spit on Your Grave* (1959), an adaptation of Boris Vian's 1946 novel, which prompts him to think about how literary stories are rendered cinematically. He does not fixate on fidelity or equivalence but instead examines the perception of the film as pornographic through an account of the source work. For Baldwin, Vian demonstrates an impressive attention to African American cultural life, whereas the film adaptation is marred by European moralism and a preoccupation with sex that misses the point of "a truth which has nothing to do with Europe."[12] This sets up Baldwin's address of D. W. Griffith's *Birth of a Nation* (1915). He rightfully does not linger on its canonical status, choosing instead to read Griffith's much-lauded and epic account of American history, justice, and heroism as nothing more than a genocidal epic, "an elaborate justification of mass murder."[13] He refutes the hagiography surrounding a film he sees as driven by miscegenation anxieties acutely manifested in the mixed-race figure of the "mulatto," dismissing it as a dangerous enabling and validation of white supremacist revisionism.

Baldwin does not move on to celebrate the progress of American cinema. Rather, he discusses protest cinema of the 1960s in terms that echo his previous contentions about protest literature. As he wrote almost three decades earlier in "Everybody's Protest Novel" (1949), "The failure of the protest novel lies in its rejection of life, the human being, the denial of his beauty, dread, power, in its insistence that it is his categorization alone which is real and which cannot be transcended."[14] He comments similarly in his assessment of Norman Jewison's *In the Heat of the Night* (1967): "The film helplessly conveys—without confronting—the anguish of people trapped in a legend. They cannot live within this legend; neither can they step out of it."[15] American "social problem" films tend to address racial intolerance in colorblind humanist terms rather than through an acknowledgment of white supremacy and anti-blackness as systemic. The films Baldwin considers and indicts in this section—Mark Robson's *Home of the Brave* (1949) and Stanley Kramer's *The Defiant Ones* (1958) and *Guess Who's Coming to Dinner* (1967)—all offer the disavowing impression that racism is accidental and never a premeditated intent of American democracy. These films tacitly thrive on a sense of exceptionalism whereby merely watching the films is presumed to produce a "self-congratulatory sense of moral accomplishment."[16]

The third and final chapter begins with Baldwin's recollection of his experience working in Hollywood on the screenplay for the film adaptation of *The Autobiography of Malcolm X* (1965). Eventually disenchanted, he describes a "strangling" process wherein his writing was consistently met with studio oversight that seemingly translated it into clichéd cinematic tropes.[17] This story serves as a prelude to his deeper concentration on the Hollywood tendency toward the hackneyed and depthless regarding black representation, as evidenced by *Lady Sings the Blues* (1972). Baldwin takes issue with the depiction of Billie Holiday as a predictable victim, a Black woman gifted yet weak. His reckoning with the distance between Holiday's accounts of her own life and her life as rendered on the screen speaks to the always diminished returns of cinema as truth. His insistence on examining the ideological textures of cinema is strikingly evident in the book's concluding comments on William Friedkin's *The Exorcist* (1973). He refuses to believe that American audiences would be as untutored in matters of evil and fiendishness as the sensational responses to *The Exorcist* would suggest: "The Americans should certainly know more about evil than that; if they pretend otherwise, they are lying,

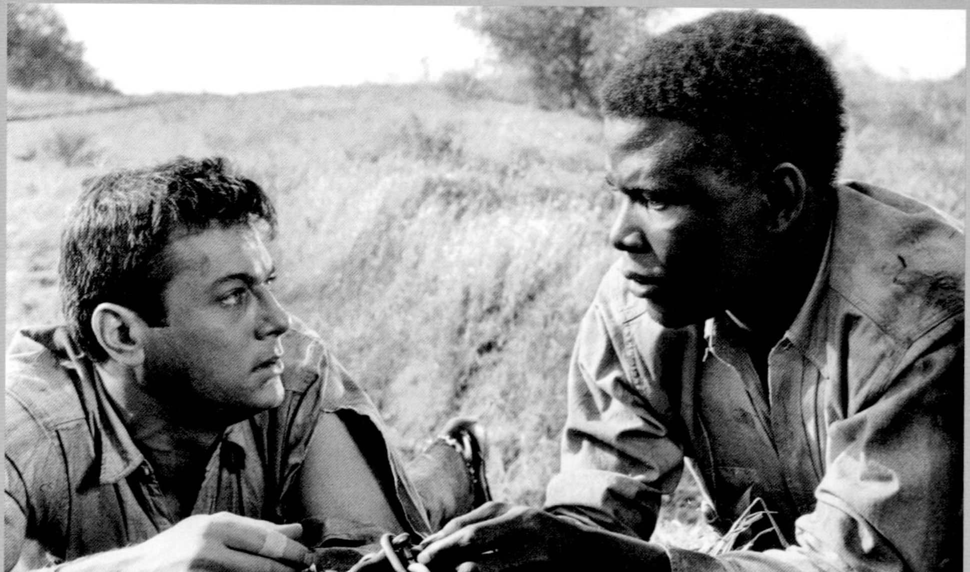

Tony Curtis and Sidney Poitier in *The Defiant Ones* (1958), production still

and any black man, and not only blacks—many, many others, including white children—can call them on this lie; he who has been treated as the devil recognizes the devil when they meet." Baldwin remains unmoved by the film's speculation of a supernatural and fantastical evil in the world: "For, I have seen the devil, by day and by night, and have seen him in you and in me. . . . This devil has no need of any dogma—though he can use them all—nor does he need any historical justification, history being so largely his invention. He does not levitate beds, or fool around with little girls: we do."[18] Baldwin pointedly determines that this is a kind of scapegoating of the satanic as the ultimate evil in such a way that people may absolve themselves of their own immoral and nefarious actions.

The Devil Finds Work remains a vital text because Baldwin's multimodal scripting across the personal and the analytic continues to stir as a perpetual query of the relationship between blackness and cinema as it "lays bare the rhetorical and imagistic sleight of hand that enables the fiction and terror of race in American life to persist with such a renewed and deadly power."[19] For Baldwin, the question was always one of *how* representation operates and *why* it bears such critical and cultural consequences. In the absence of the totalizing fantasy of suspension of disbelief, he models how pleasure, history, and culture impact the spectatorial process and the idea of the nation. His ideas can continue to inform new and emergent channels of cinephilia attentive to cultural and historical contexts that push for more substantial forms of critical engagement. *The Devil Finds Work* insists on attention to film's indelible and irrefutable resonances of history and culture as popular culture, and as a compelling vessel of ideological consequence.

Notes

In this essay *black* is capitalized only when it refers to the social category or with reference to lived experience. It is not capitalized when referring to objects or ideas. In this way, *blackness* is not capitalized as it always refers to a cultural and aesthetic concept and not a definitive notion.

Epigraph
James Baldwin, *The Devil Finds Work*, in *Collected Essays* (New York: Library of America, 1988), 571.

1 Baldwin's unfinished manuscript "Remember This House" is a profound accounting of the loss of three of his friends and comrades across the 1960s: Medgar Evers, Malcolm X, and Martin Luther King Jr. This manuscript consequentially structures Raoul Peck's meditation on Baldwin in the film *I Am Not Your Negro* (2016). See Warren Crichlow, "Baldwin's Rendezvous with the Twenty-First Century: *I Am Not Your Negro*," *Film Quarterly* 70, no. 4 (June 2017): 9–22.

2 Francey Russell, "'How Shall We Put Ourselves in Touch with Reality?': On Baldwin, Film, and Acknowledgment," *Social Research: An International Quarterly* 87, no. 4 (Winter 2020): 999.

3 Jacqueline Najuma Stewart, *Migrating to the Movies: Cinema and Black Urban Modernity* (Berkeley: University of California Press, 2005), 95.

4 See José Esteban Muñoz, *Disidentifications: Queers of Color and the Performance of Politics* (Minneapolis: University of Minnesota Press, 1999), 18.

5 Baldwin, *Devil Finds Work*, 480.

6 Baldwin, 492.

7 Lauren Berlant, *The Female Complaint: The Unfinished Business of Sentimentality in American Culture* (Durham, NC: Duke University Press, 2008), 58.

8 Baldwin, *Devil Finds Work*, 500.

9 Baldwin, 501.

10 Jane Gaines, *Fire and Desire: Mixed-Race Movies in the Silent Era* (Chicago: University of Chicago Press, 2001), 49.

11 See Amber Jamilla Musser, "Bette Davis's Eyes and Minoritarian Survival: Camp, Melodrama, and Spectatorship," in *Affect and Literature*, ed. Alex Houen (Cambridge: Cambridge University Press, 2020), 289.

12 Baldwin, *Devil Finds Work*, 510.

13 Baldwin, 511.

14 James Baldwin, "Everybody's Protest Novel," in *Notes of a Native Son* (Boston: Beacon, 2012), 23.

15 Baldwin, *Devil Finds Work*, 520.

16 Russell, "On Baldwin," 1000.

17 Baldwin's screenplay was published as *One Day When I Was Lost: A Scenario Based on "The Autobiography of Malcolm X"* (1972; New York: Vintage, 2007).

18 Baldwin, *Devil Finds Work*, 571.

19 Rich Blint, "'You're the Nigger, Baby': James Baldwin on Film," *Brooklyn Rail*, February 2017, https://brooklynrail.org/2017/02/film/James-Baldwin-on-Film. Blint's comments are in the context of a piece on *I Am Not Your Negro*, a film deeply informed by *The Devil Finds Work*.

Black actors and musicians working in Hollywood experienced both barriers and opportunities. These studio portraits shine a spotlight on the diversity of African American performers working in Hollywood between the 1920s and the 1950s.

While not comprehensive, this selection of images—some more familiar than others—showcases the legacy of Black stars and icons in American cinema.

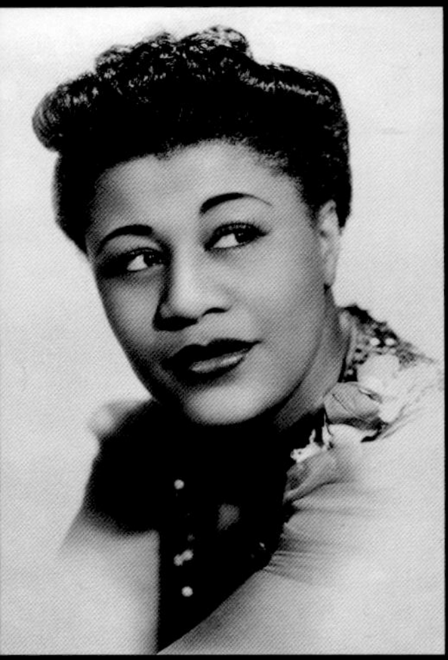
Ella Fitzgerald

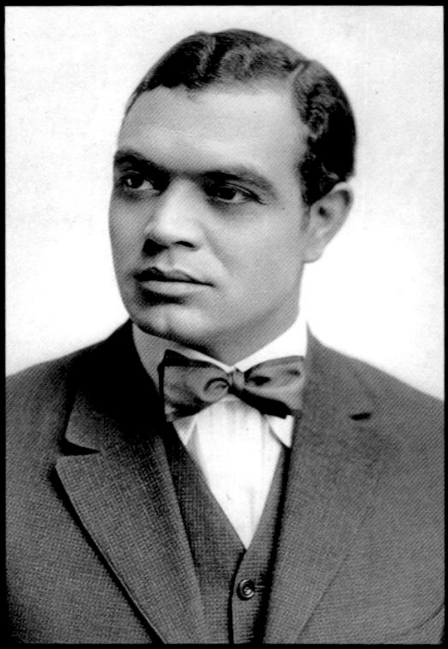
Noble M. Johnson

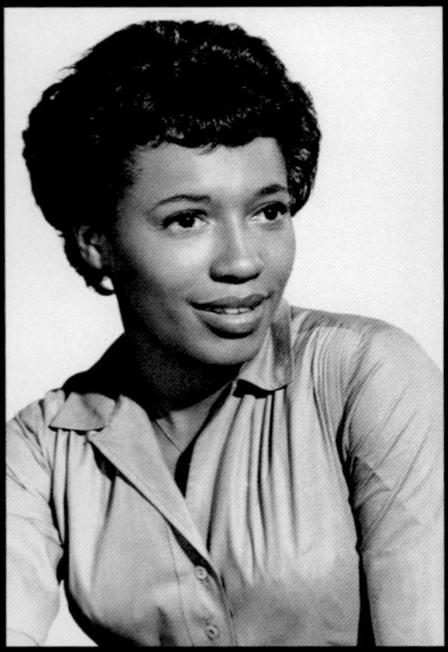
Diana Sands

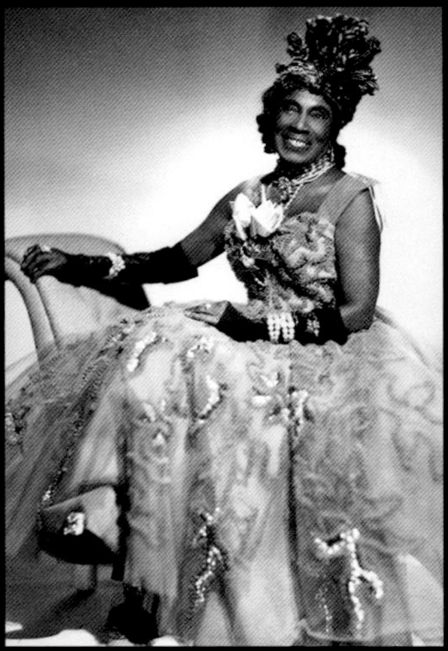
Madame Sul-Te-Wan

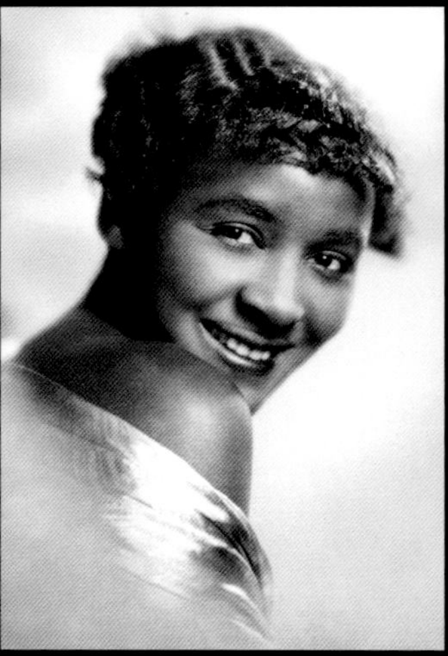
Victoria Spivey

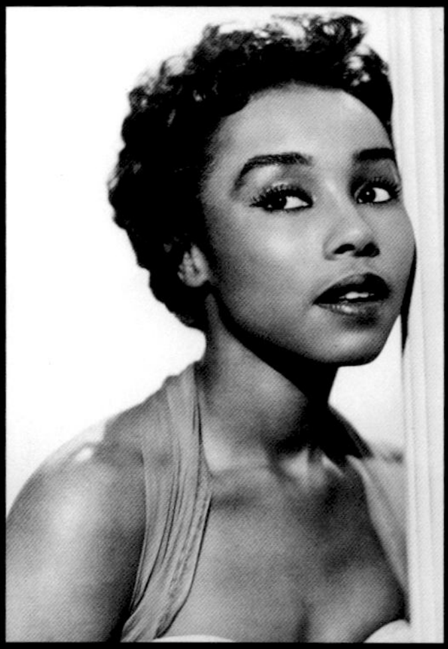
Diahann Carroll

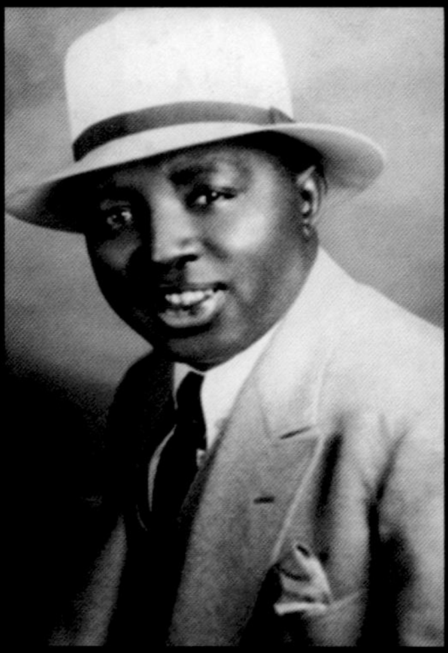
Sam McDaniel

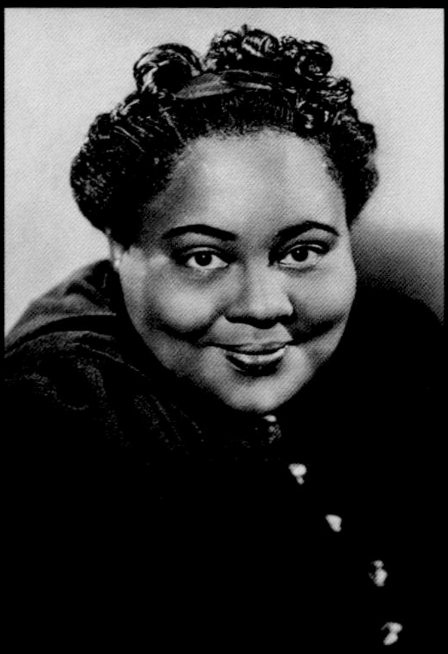
Louise Beavers

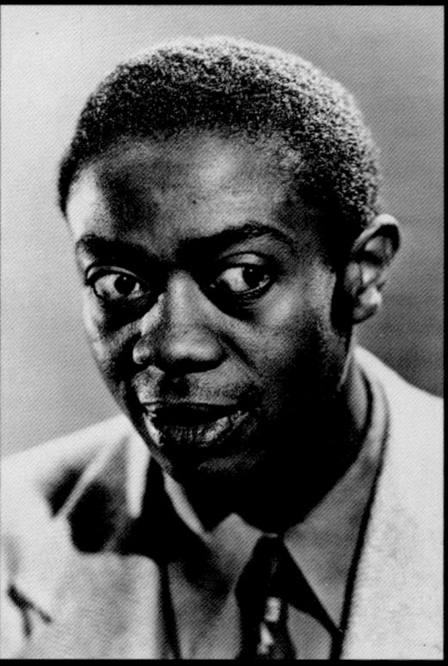
Willie Best

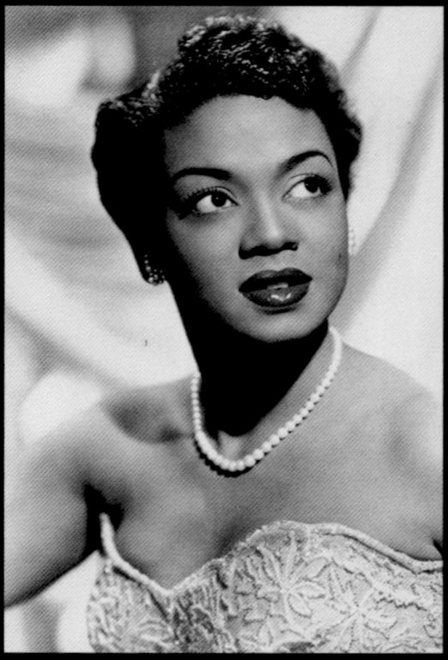
Hazel Scott

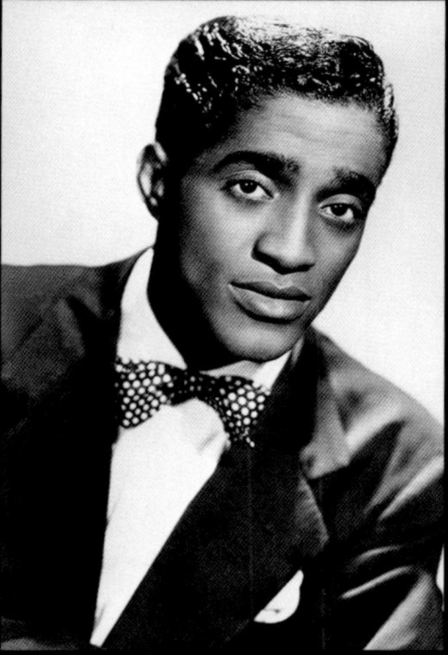
Sammy Davis Jr.

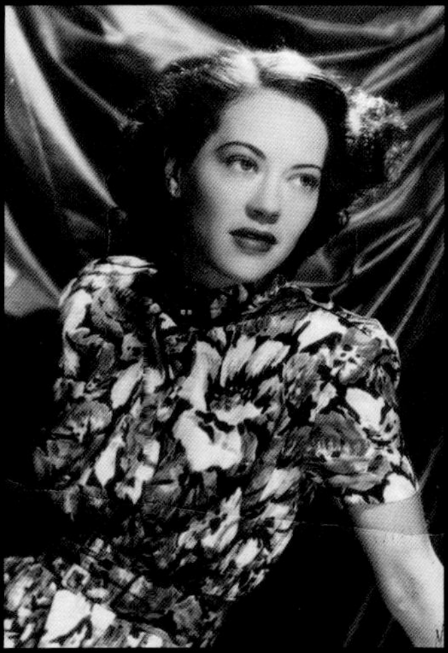
Fredi Washington

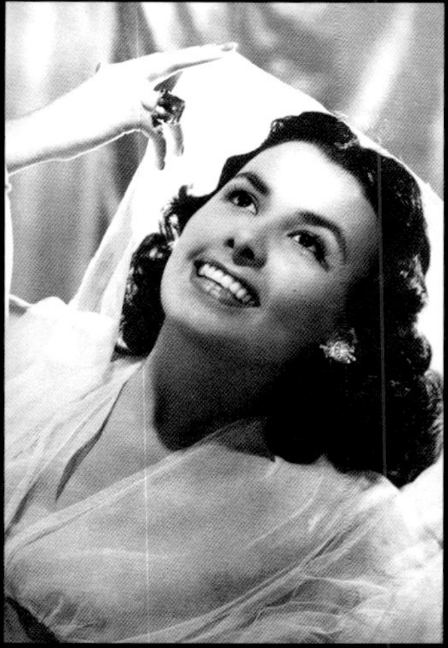
Lena Horne

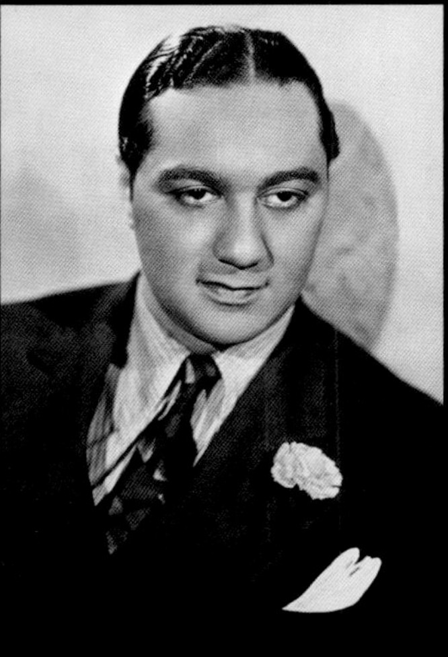
Ralph Cooper

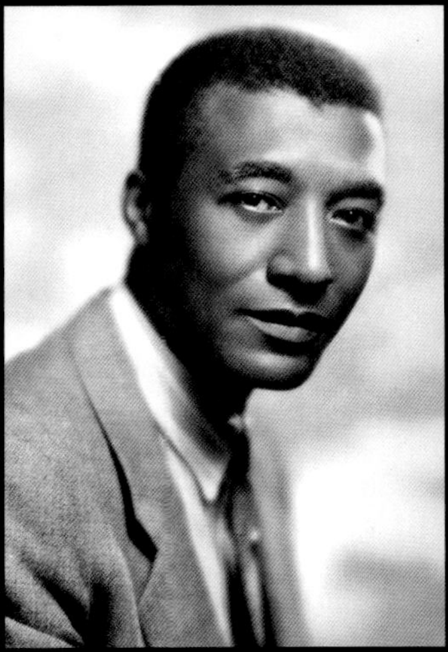
Daniel Haynes

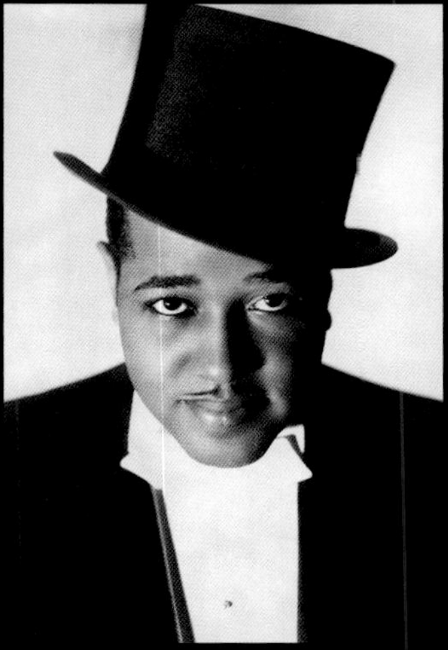
Duke Ellington

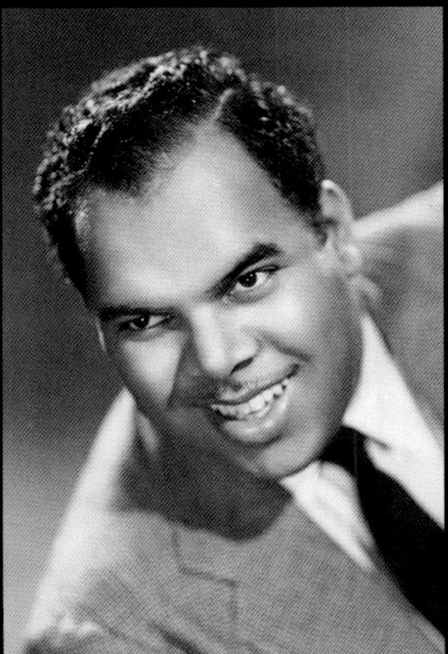
Phil Moore

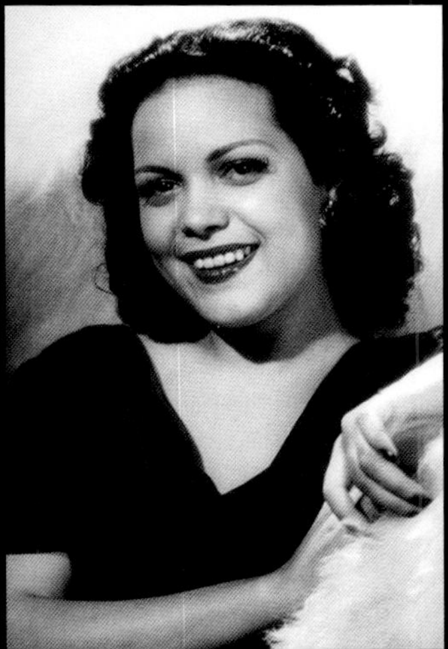
Hilda Simms

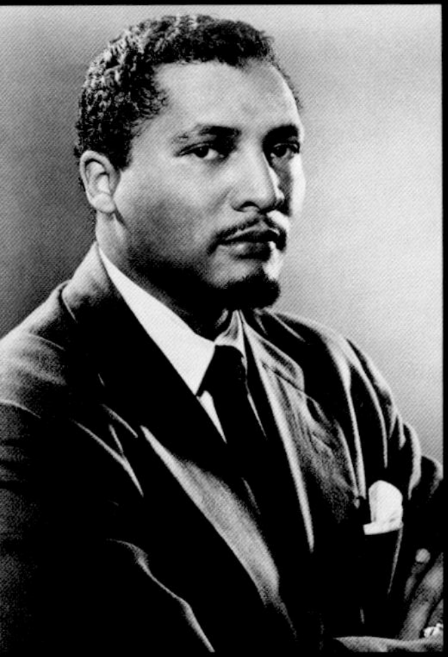
William Marshall

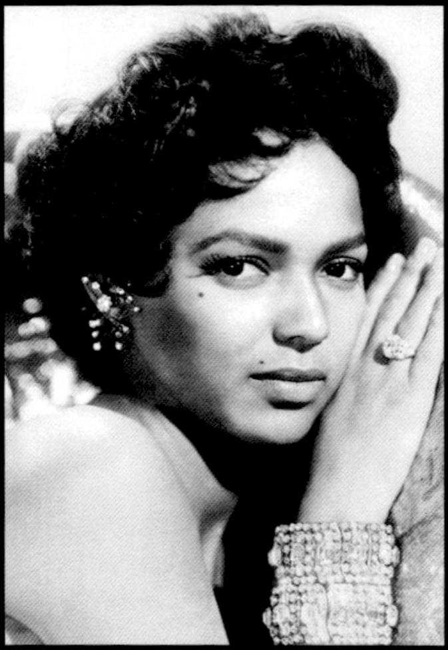
Dorothy Dandridge

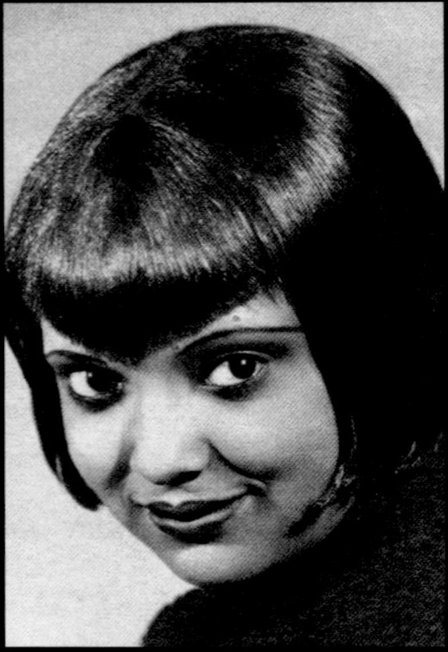
Nina Mae McKinney

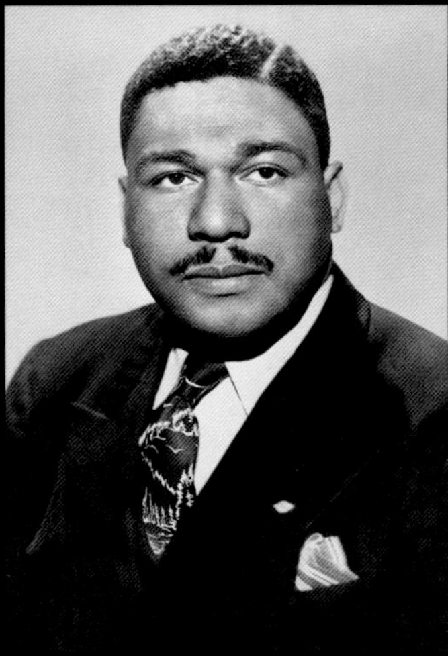
Frederick O' Neal

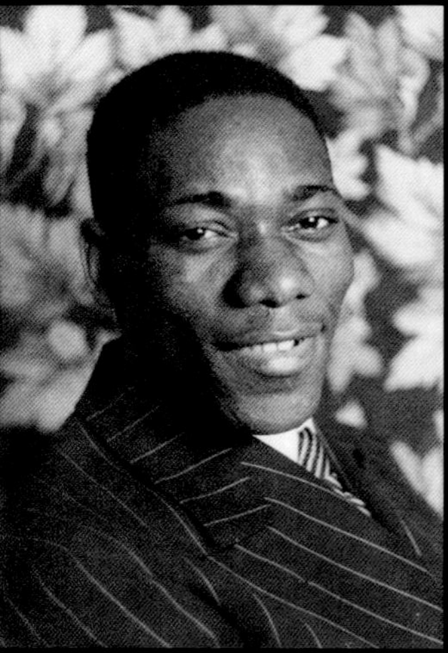
Oscar Polk

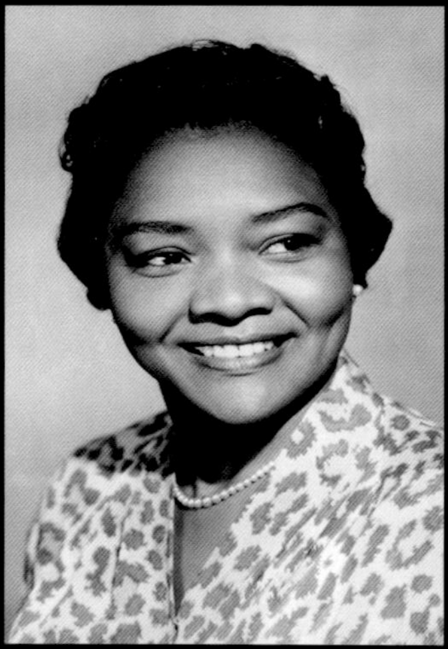
Juanita Moore

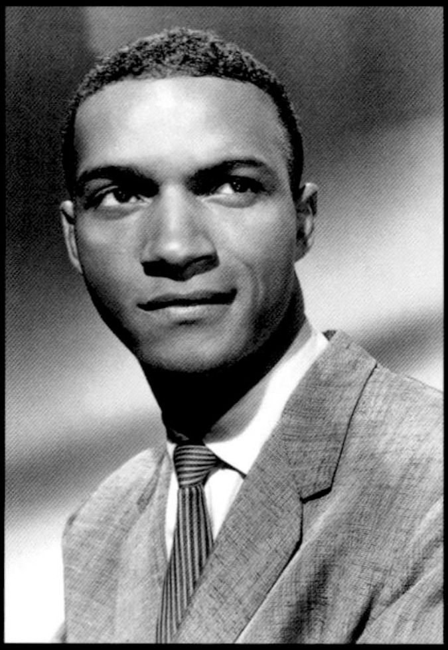
James Edwards

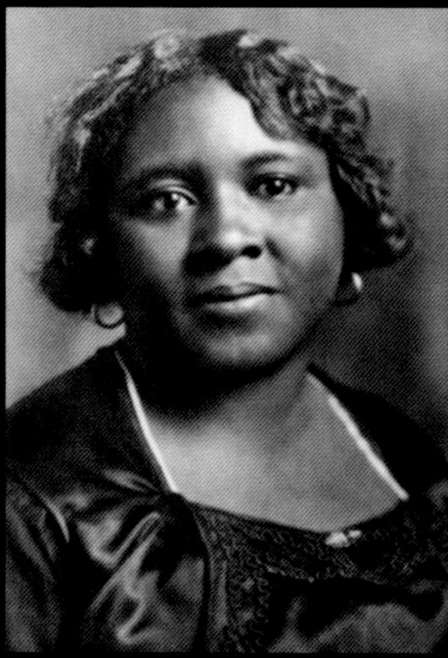
Etta McDaniel

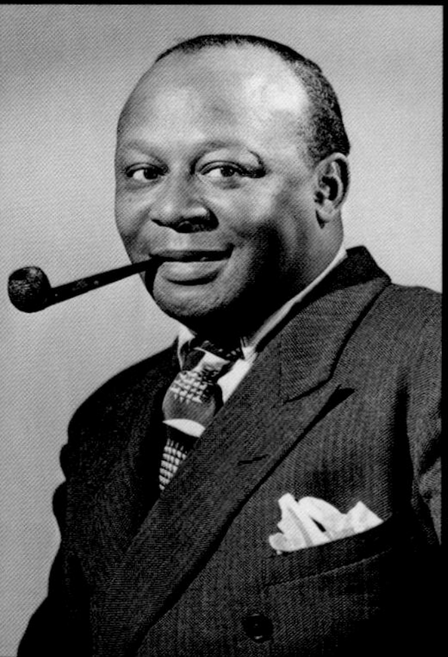
Mantan Moreland

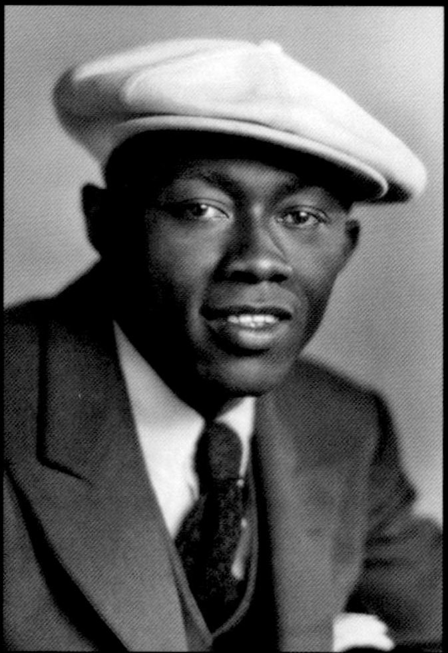
Lincoln "Stepin Fetchit" Perry

Josephine Baker

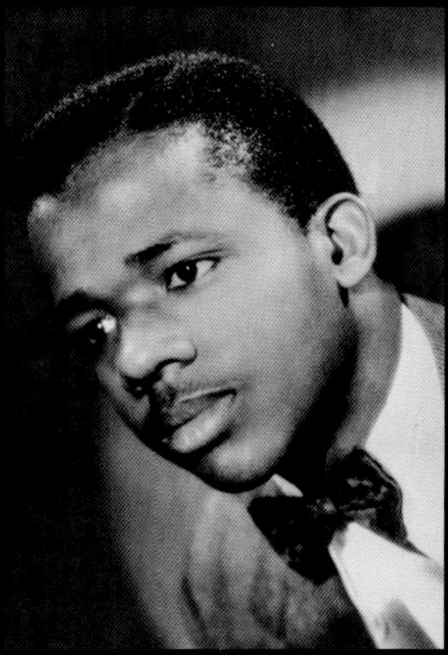

William Greaves

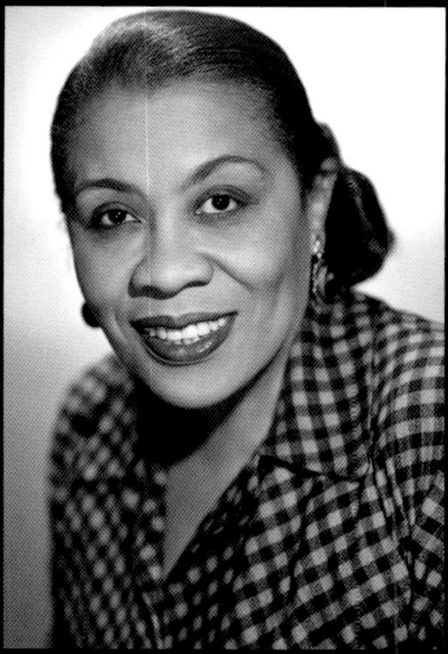

Lillian Randolph

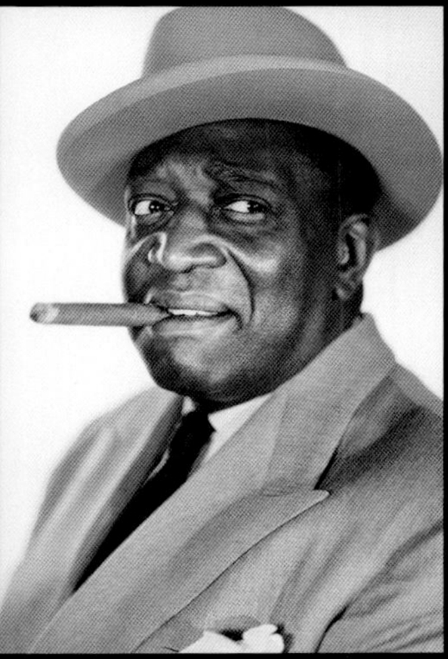

Ernest Whitman

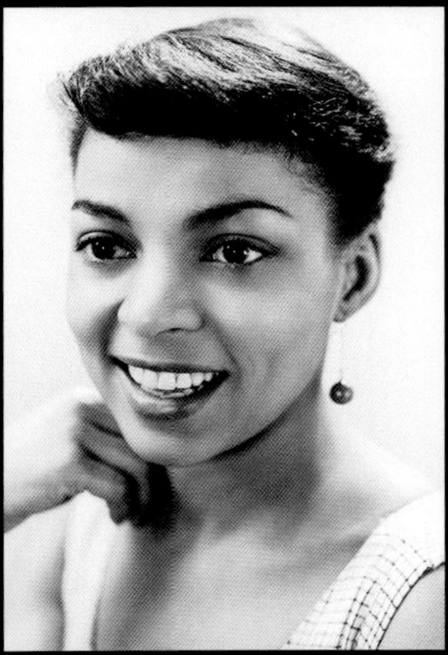

Ruby Dee

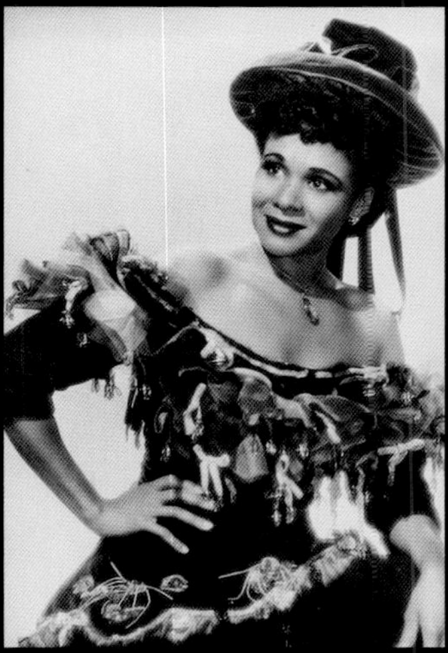

Katherine Dunham

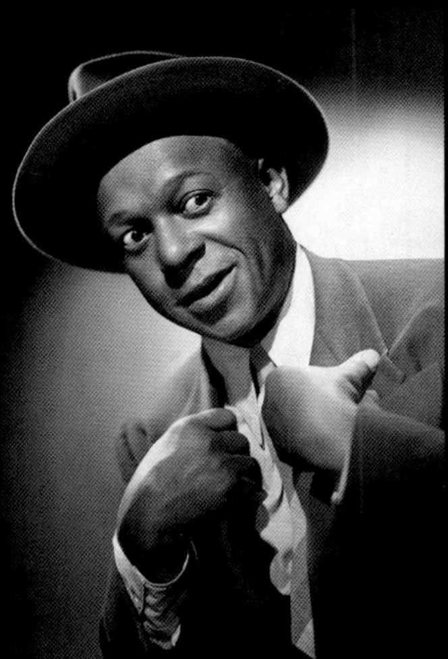

Eddie “Rochester” Anderson

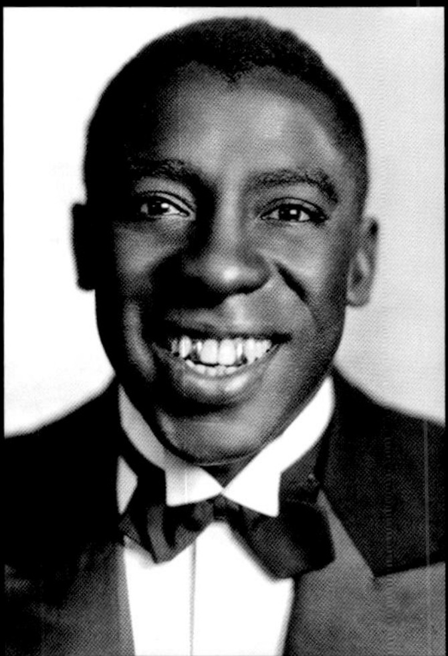

Clarence Muse

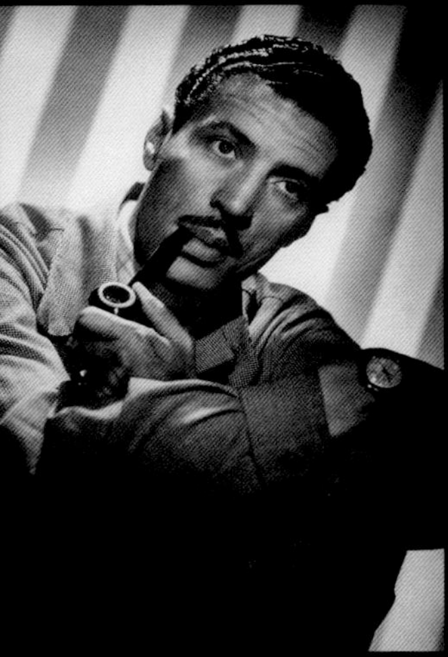

Herb Jeffries

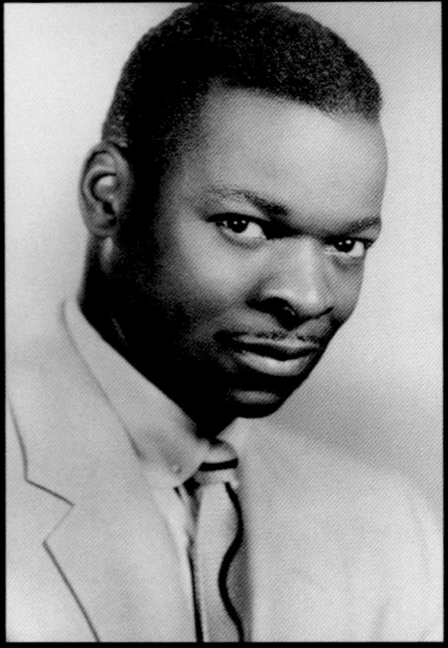

Brock Peters

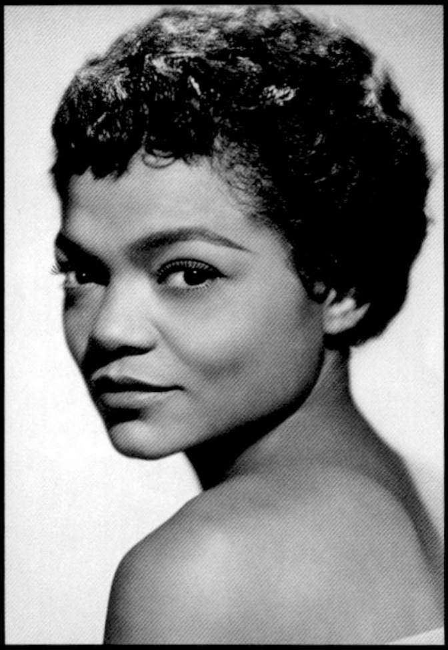

Eartha Kitt

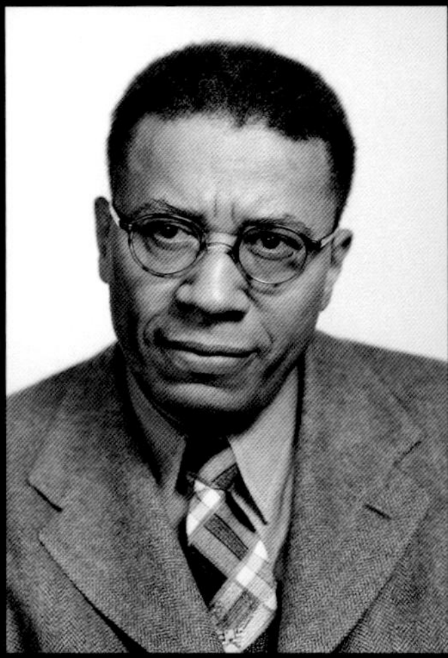

Hall Johnson

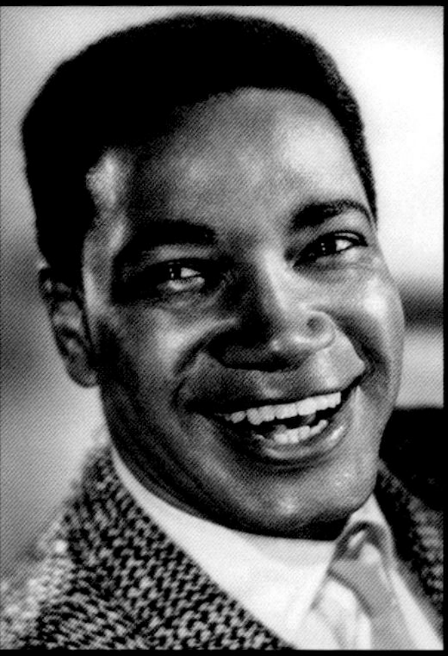

Kenneth Spencer

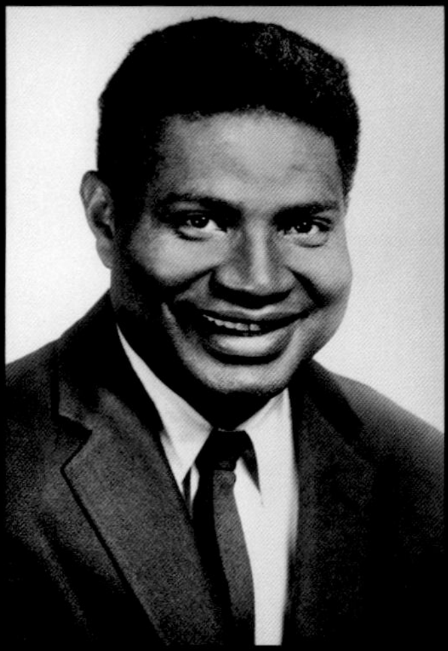

Ossie Davis

Theresa Harris

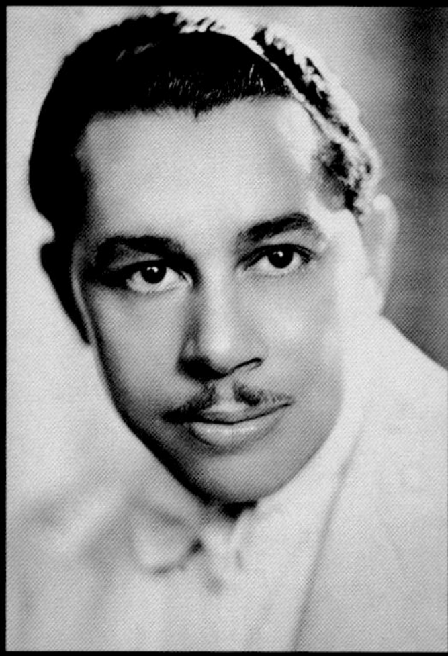

Cab Calloway

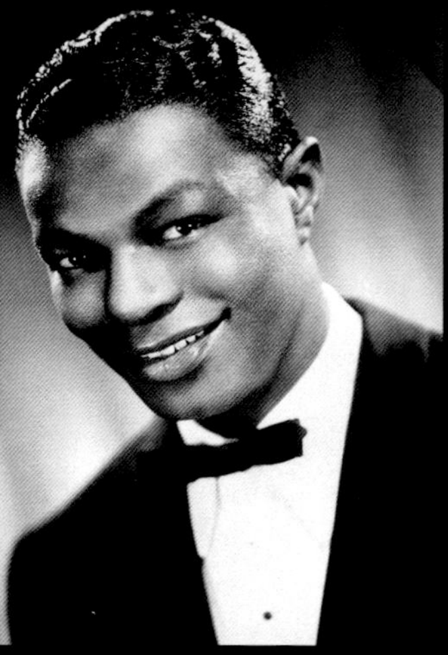

Nat King Cole

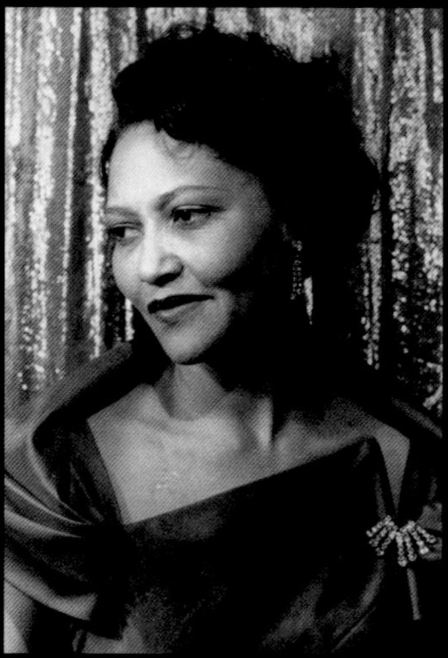

Maidie Norman

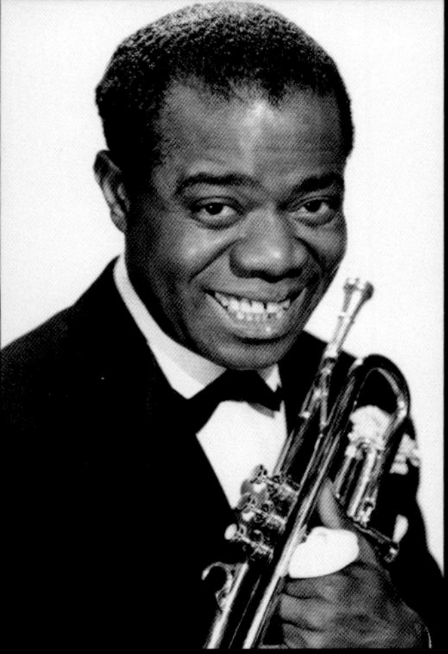

Louis Armstrong

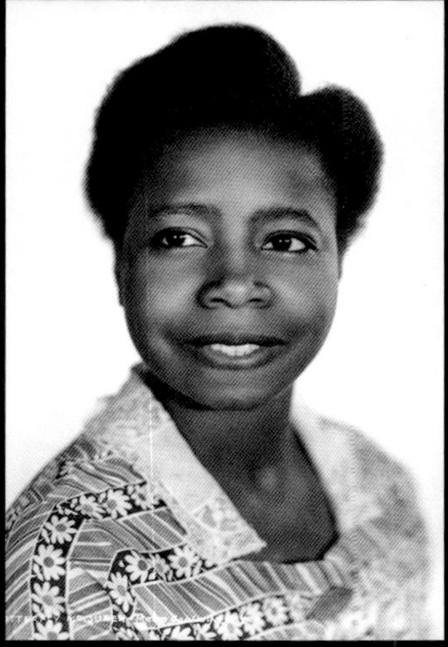

Butterfly McQueen

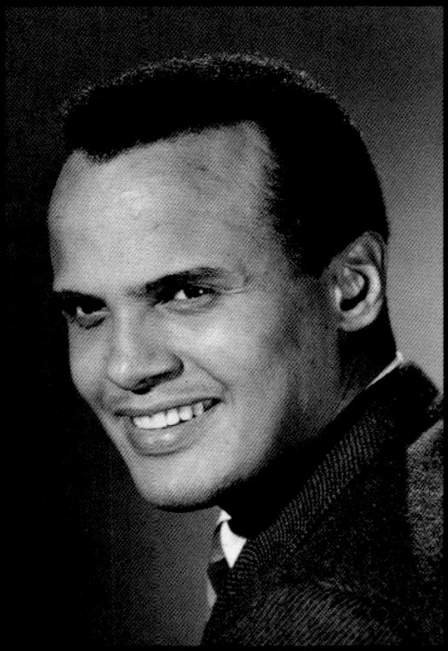

Harry Belafonte

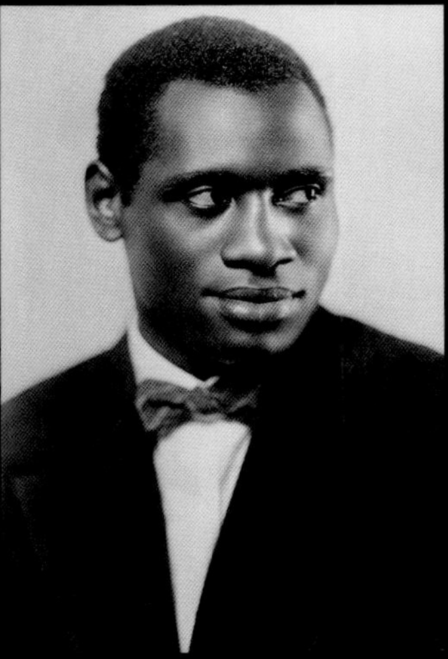

Paul Robeson

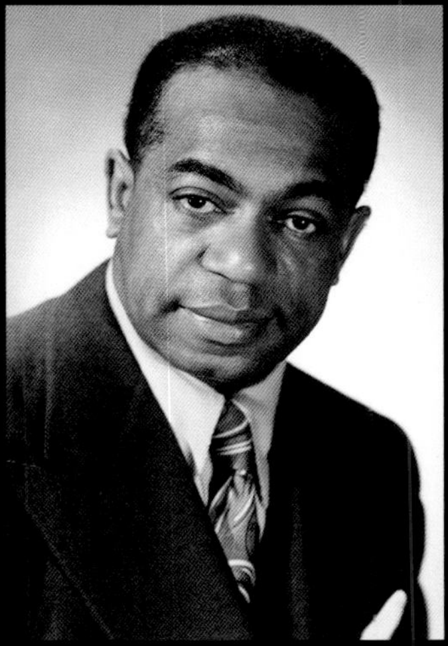

Dooley Wilson

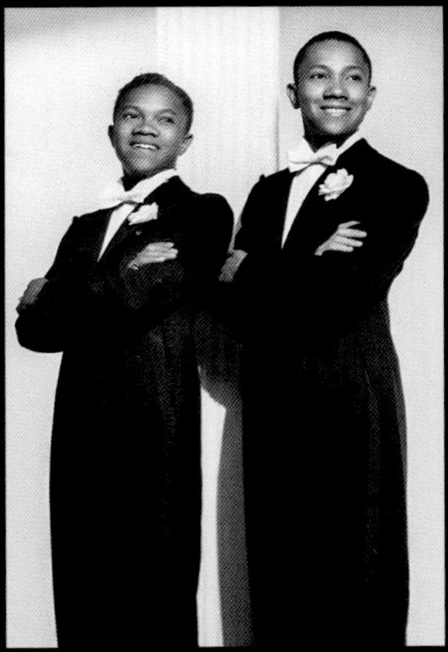

Harold and Fayard Nicholas

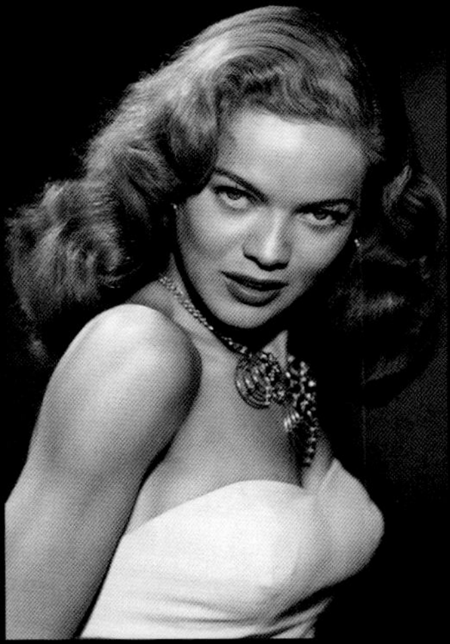

Dona Drake

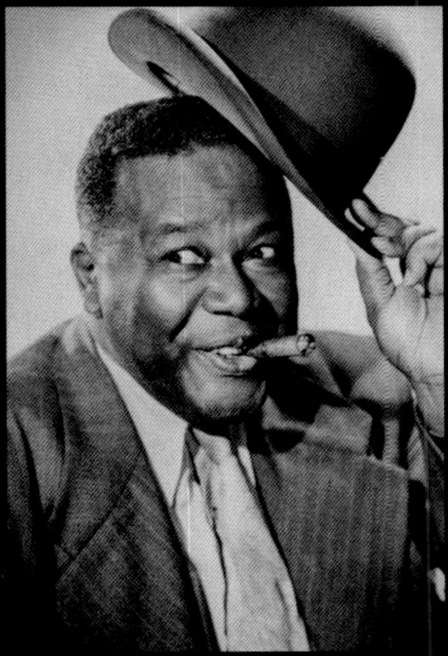

Spencer Williams Jr.

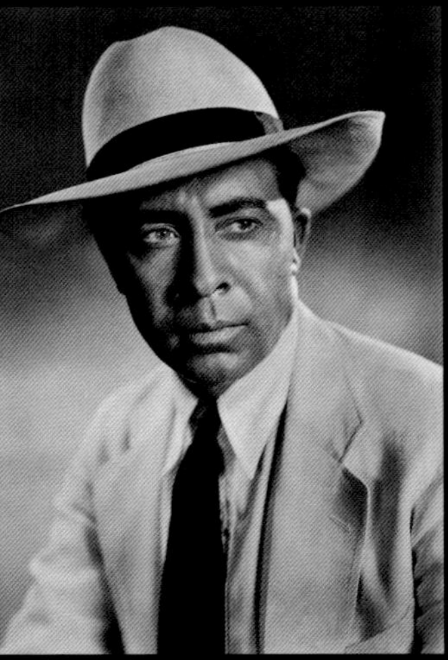
Clarence Brooks

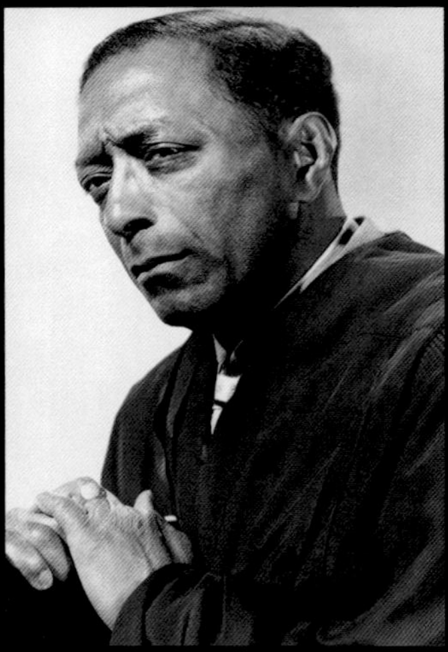
Juano Hernandez

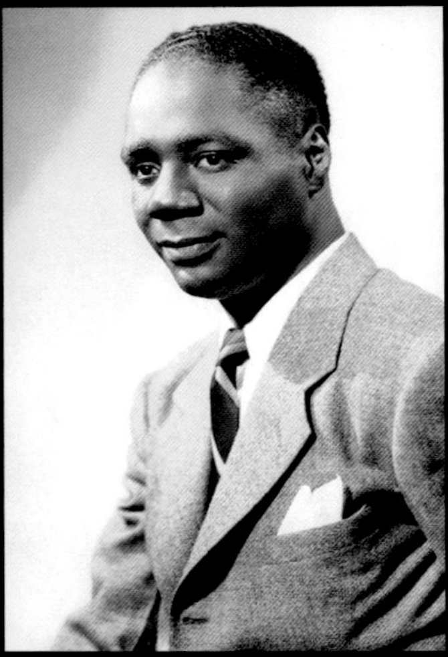
Canada Lee

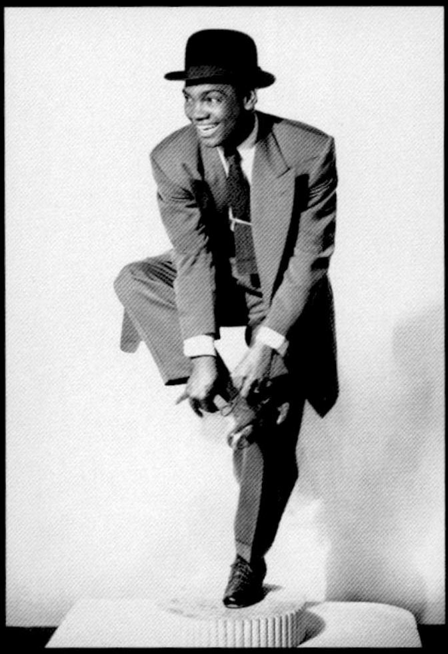
Bill Bailey

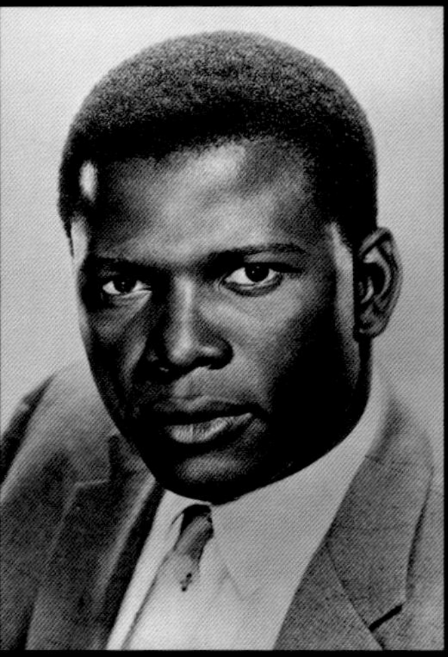
Sidney Poitier

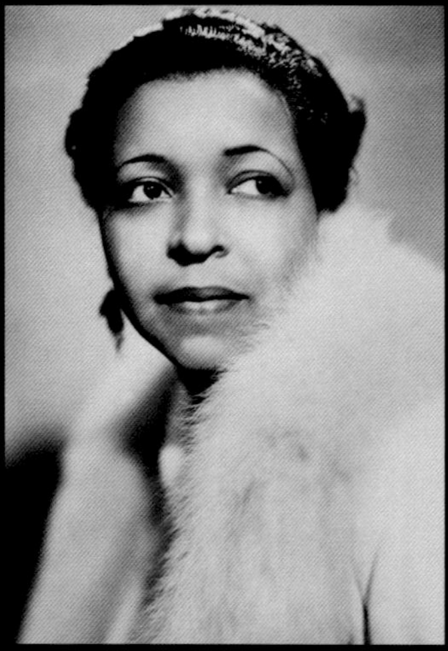
Ethel Waters

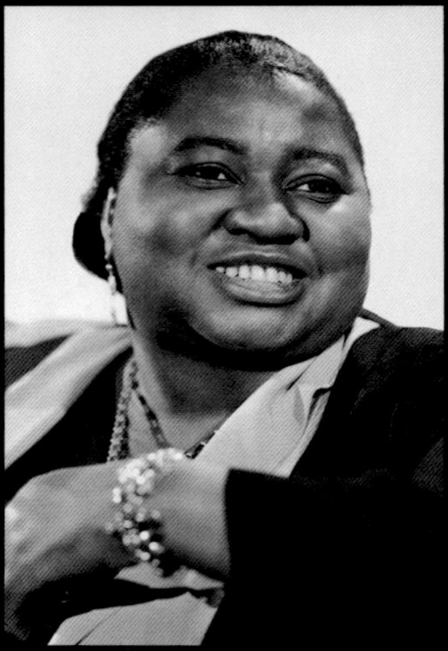
Hattie McDaniel

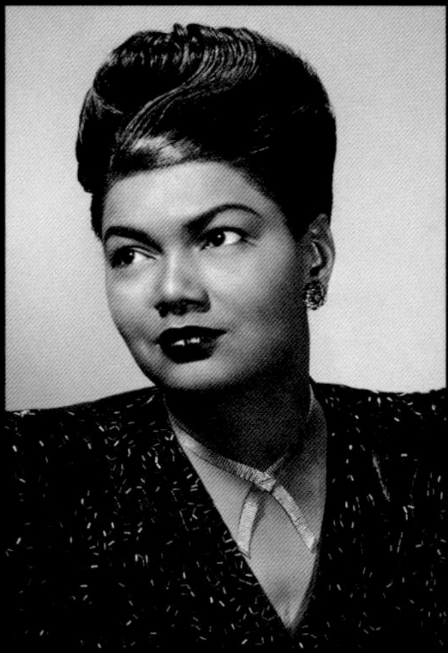
Pearl Bailey

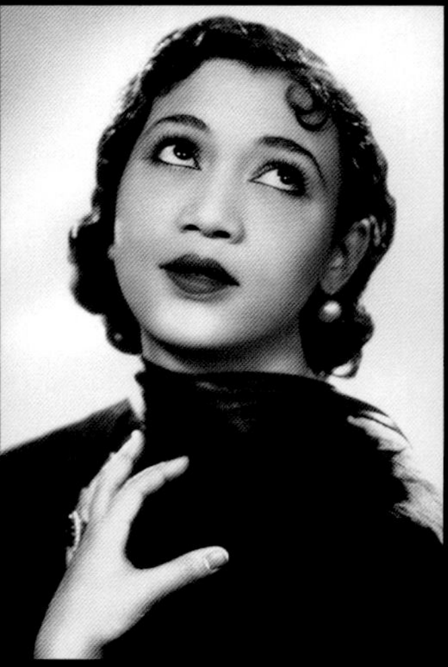
Elisabeth Welch

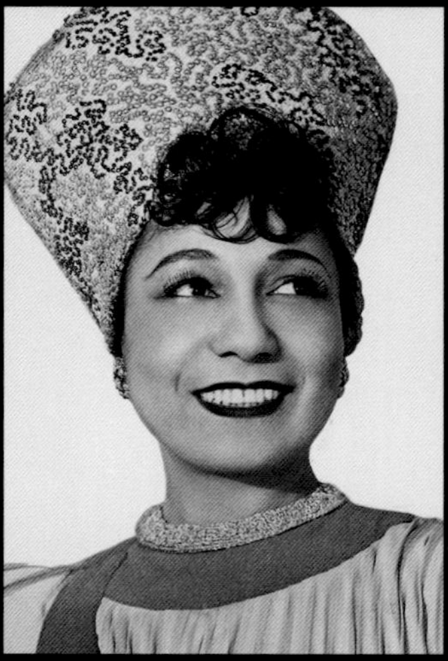
Etta Moten Barnett

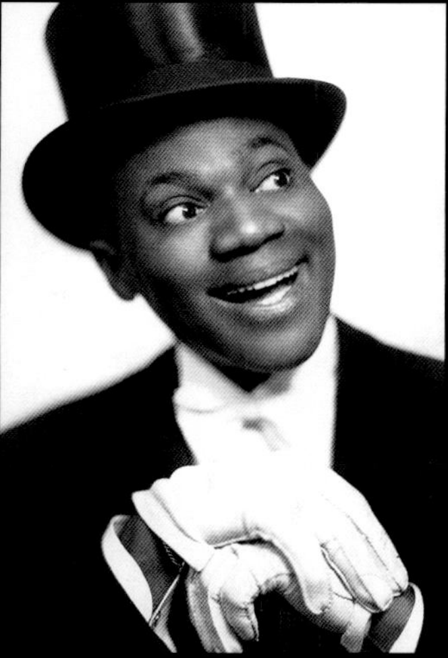

Bill “Bojangles” Robinson

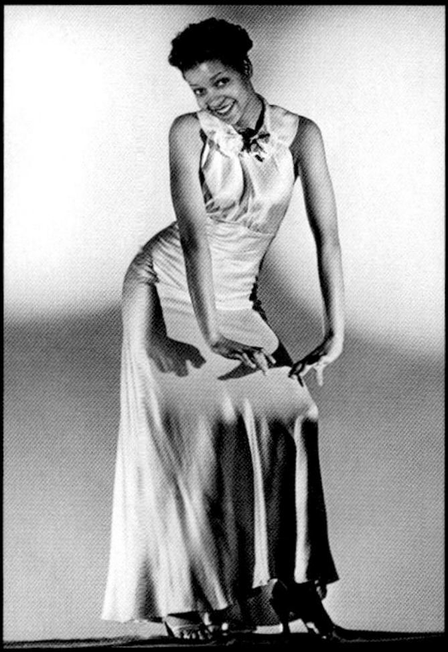

Jeni LeGon

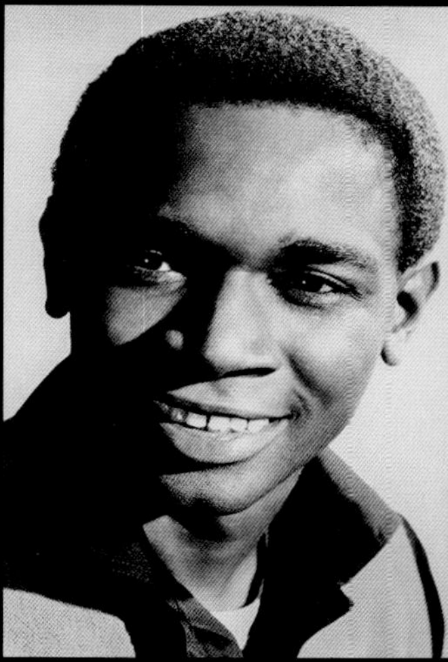

Ivan Dixon

Olga James

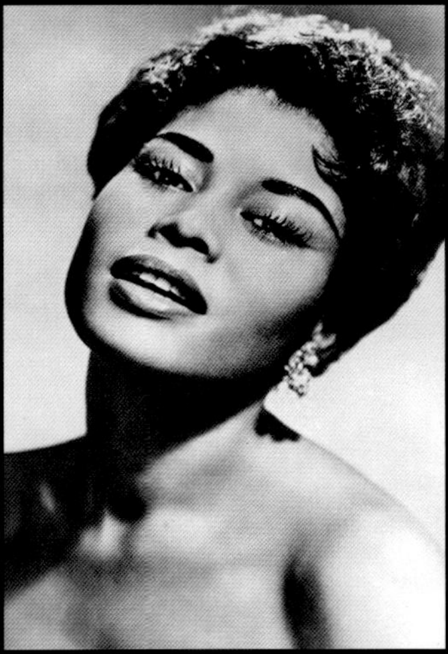

Abbey Lincoln

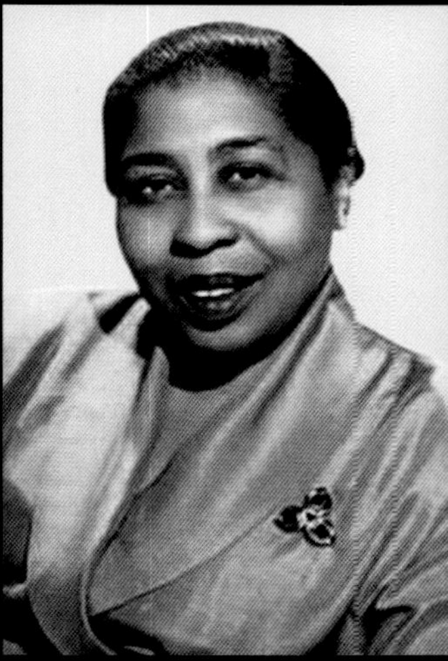

Amanda Randolph

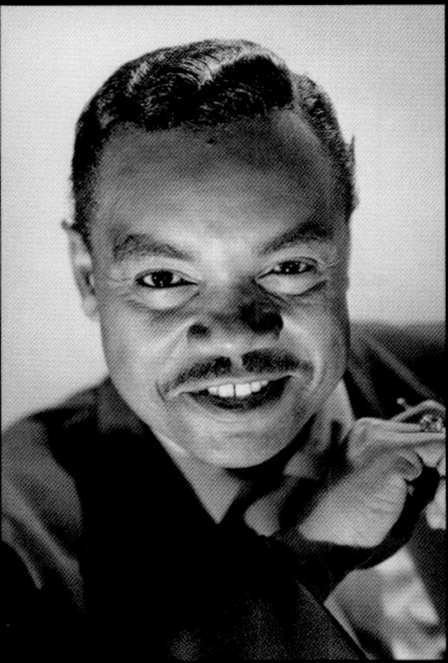

Roy Glenn

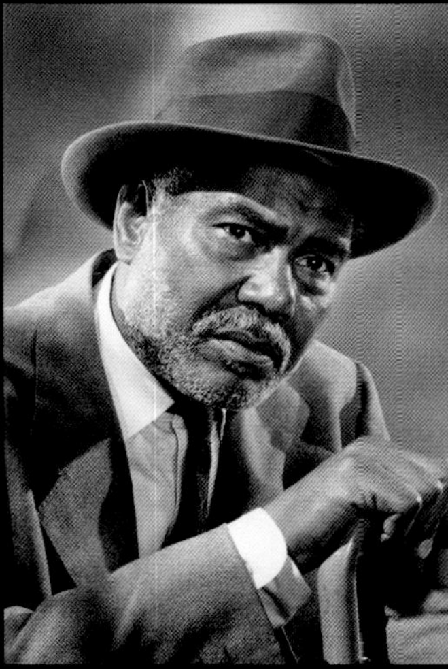

Rex Ingram

FILMOGRAPHY

The selected filmography for the years 1897–1971 includes works featured in the exhibition and others that are considered historically, socially, or politically relevant. It is followed by a selection of US and international theatrical release posters.

Hollywood productions are generally excluded; the focus is instead on independent films, particularly the works of Black filmmakers. Black Academy Award nominees and winners are noted.

This filmography was compiled using the AFI Catalog of Feature Films and various filmographies, including those by Klotman, Richards, and Hyatt. Primary production materials and contemporaneous film reviews were also consulted. Complete credits for many of the films are unavailable. All films are US productions unless otherwise noted, and distribution credits refer to the original distributors.

1890s

Short

1897
Cake Walk

Alternative Titles: **Coon Cake Walk, Darkey Cake Walk**

27 sec. • Silent • Black and white • 1.33:1
Five dancers in formal attire perform the popular cakewalk.

Production
American Mutoscope and Biograph Company

Distribution
American Mutoscope and Biograph Company

Documentary

1898
Colored Troops Disembarking

Alternative Title: **Colored Troops Disembarking (24th U.S. Infantry)**

1 min. 25 sec. • Silent • Black and white • 1.33:1
Black troops from the Twenty-Fourth Infantry Regiment disembark from the steamer *Mascotte* in Tampa, Florida, returning from fighting in the Spanish-American War.

Producer
William Daly Paley

Production
Edison Manufacturing Company

Distribution
Edison Manufacturing Company

Short

1898
Something Good–Negro Kiss

29 sec. and 49 sec. • Silent • Black and white • 1.33:1
A couple exchange several kisses in an emulation of Thomas Edison's *The Kiss* (1896). Two known versions survive, one at the University of Southern California's HMH Moving Image Archive and the other at the National Library of Norway.

Cast
Gertie Brown, Saint Suttle

Producer
William N. Selig

Production
Selig Polyscope Company

Distribution
Selig Polyscope Company

1900s

Documentary

1909
A Trip to Tuskegee

25 min. • Silent • Black and white • 1.33:1
This promotional film focuses on the positive influence of the Tuskegee Institute in Alabama. A second promotional film, *A Day at Tuskegee*, was released in 1913.

Director
George W. Broome

Production
George W. Broome Exhibition Company

Distribution
George W. Broome Exhibition Company

1910s

Documentary

1910
Jeffries-Johnson World's Championship Boxing Contest

Alternative Titles: **Jack Johnson vs. James J. Jeffries, The Johnson–Jeffries Fight**

100 min. • Silent • Black and white • 1.33:1
This film depicts the heavyweight championship "battle of the century" match between James J. Jeffries and Jack Johnson in Reno, Nevada.

Cast
James J. Jeffries,
Jack Johnson

Producer
J. Stuart Blackton

Distribution
J&J Company

Comedy

1912
A Fool and His Money

10 min. • Silent • Black and white • 1.33:1
One of the earliest surviving Black-cast films features an impoverished jilted man who finds money only to lose it gambling.

Director
Alice Guy-Blaché

Cast
James Russell

Producer
Alice Guy-Blaché

Production
Solax Film Company

Distribution
Film Supply Company

Comedy

1912
The Railroad Porter

Alternative Title: **The Pullman Porter**

2 reels • Silent • Black and white • 1.33:1
A wife, thinking her husband has left her, invites a man over for dinner. When her husband returns, a comedic chase ensues.

Cast
Lottie Grady, Jerry Mills,
Edgar Litterson, Cassie Burch
Slaughter, Bell Coles

Producer
William D. Foster

Production
Foster Photoplay Company

Distribution
Foster Photoplay Company

Comedy

1913
Lime Kiln Club Field Day

7 reels (unfinished) • Silent • Black and white • 1.33:1
Williams's character competes to win the heart of a local beauty. The film remained unfinished, although an "archival assembly" was screened by the Museum of Modern Art, New York, in 2014.

Directors
Edwin Middleton,
T. Hayes Hunter

Screenplay
Charles Bertrand Lewis

Cast
Bert Williams, Odessa
Warren Grey, Sam Lucas,
Sam Corker Jr., Abbie Mitchell

Producer
Klaw & Erlanger

Production
Biograph Company

Comedy

1914
Darktown Jubilee

1 reel • Silent • Black and white • 1.33:1

This film reportedly caused a race riot in Brooklyn since Williams appears in a top hat and zoot suit without blackface makeup.

Director
Bert Williams

Cast
Bert Williams

Production
Biograph

Distribution
General Film Company

Drama

1914
Uncle Tom's Cabin

5 reels • Silent • Black and white • 1.33:1

Lucas plays Uncle Tom in the first film adaptation of Harriet Beecher Stowe's antebellum story starring a Black actor.

Director
William R. Daly

Photography
Irvin Willat

Cast
Sam Lucas, Irving Cummings, Marie Eline, Hattie Delaro, Master Abernathy, Teresa Michelena, Paul Scardon, Garfield Thompson, Roy Applegate

Producer
J. V. Ritchey

Production
World Producing Corporation

Distribution
World Film Company

Comedy

1915
Two Nights of Vaudeville

11 min. • Silent • Black and white • 1.33:1

A slapstick comedy in which two men enter a vaudeville theater and try to perform, with disastrous results.

Cast
Frank Montgomery, Florence McClain, Vet Murphy, Jimmy Marshall

Producer
Luther Pollard

Production
Ebony Films Corporation

Distribution
Ebony Films Corporation

Comedy

1916
A Natural Born Gambler

22 min. • Silent • Black and white • 1.33:1

Police raid a poker game, jailing all the participants. While incarcerated, Williams performs his famous routine of playing poker by himself.

Director
Bert Williams

Screenplay
Bert Williams

Photography
G. W. Bitzer

Cast
Bert Williams, Wes Jenkins

Producer
Bert Williams

Production
Biograph Company

Distribution
General Film Company

Drama

1916
The Realization of a Negro's Ambition

2 reels • Silent • Black and white • 1.33:1
A recent engineering graduate from Tuskegee sets out for the West and rescues a woman, the daughter of an oil tycoon, earning a chance to succeed in the oil business.

Director
Harry A. Gant

Photography
Harry A. Gant

Cast
Bessie Baker, Lottie Boles, Clarence Brooks, A. Burns, Gertrude Christmas, Noble Johnson, Beulah Hall, Webb King, Bessie Mathews, George Reed

Producer
Noble Johnson

Production
Lincoln Motion Picture Company

Distribution
Lincoln Motion Picture Company

Western

1917
The Trooper of Troop K

Alternative Title: **Trooper of Company K**

3 reels • Silent • Black and white • 1.33:1
Joe, a shiftless man, enlists in the army. His heroic deeds win him recognition and the love of Clara, his childhood sweetheart.

Director
Harry A. Gant

Photography
Harry A. Gant

Cast
Noble Johnson, Beulah Hall, Jimmie Smith

Production
Lincoln Motion Picture Company

Distribution
Lincoln Motion Picture Company

Drama

1918
The Birth of a Race

Alternative Title: **Lincoln's Dream**

10 reels • Silent • Black and white • 1.33:1
The film was an early attempt to counteract the racist film *Birth of a Nation* (1915) by highlighting Black achievements starting with the Garden of Eden.

Director
John W. Noble

Screenplay
George F. Wheeler, Rudolph De Cordova, John W. Noble, Anthony Paul Kelly, Tom Bret

Music
Joseph Carl Breil

Photography
Herbert O. Carleton

Cast
Louis Dean, Harry Dumont, Carter B. Harkness, Doris Doscher, Charles Graham, Ben Hendricks, Alice Gale, John Reinhardt, Gertrude Braun, Stephen Grattan

Producer
John W. Noble

Production
Birth of a Race Photoplay Corporation, Frohman Amusement Corporation

Distribution
States' rights

Documentary

1918
Our Colored Fighters

2 reels • Silent • Black and white • 1.33:1
This documentary chronicles the activities of the Fifteenth Infantry Regiment during World War I, including the enlistment and training of Black troops.

Production
Division of Films, US Department of War, Downing Film Company

Distribution
Downing Film Company

Action

1919
The Green-Eyed Monster

8 reels • Silent • Black and white • 1.33:1

In this action film, two railroad tycoons fall in love with the same woman. A train race between the rivals determines their fate.

Director
Richard E. Norman

Cast
Jack Austin, Louise Dunbar, Steve Reynolds

Production
Norman Film Manufacturing Company

Distribution
Norman Film Manufacturing Company

Drama

1919
The Homesteader

8 reels • Silent • Black and white • 1.33:1

Oscar Micheaux's directorial debut, adapted from his own novel, features a homesteader who falls in love with a woman he believes is white. Because of anti-miscegenation laws, their relationship is doomed until he learns she is Black.

Director
Oscar Micheaux

Screenplay
Oscar Micheaux

Cast
Charles D. Lucas, Evelyn Preer, Iris Hall, Inez Smith, Vernon S. Duncan, Charles S. Moore, Trevy Woods, William George

Producer
Oscar Micheaux

Production
Micheaux Book & Film Company, Inc.

Distribution
Micheaux Book & Film Company, Inc.

Drama

1919
A Man's Duty

5 reels • Silent • Black and white • 1.33:1

This melodrama, in which two men spar for the love of a woman, is notable for its portrayal of the Black middle class.

Directors
Harry Gant, D. Ireland Thomas

Screenplay
Clarence Brooks

Photography
Harry Gant

Cast
Clarence Brooks, Webb King, Tasmania Darden, Ethel Gray, Eva Johnson, Anita Thompson, W. H. Sanders, Mrs. Connors, Frank White, Janette Criner

Producer
George P. Johnson

Production
Lincoln Motion Picture Company

Distribution
Lincoln Motion Picture Company

1920s

Drama

1920
The Symbol of the Unconquered

Alternative Title: **The Wilderness Trail**

8 reels • Silent • Black and white • 1.33:1

Micheaux depicts the reemergence of the Ku Klux Klan, called the Kings of the Black Cross in the film, who use racial violence to attempt to steal valuable land.

Director
Oscar Micheaux

Screenplay
Oscar Micheaux

Cast
Iris Hall, Walker Thompson, Lawrence Chenault, Jimmy Burress, Mattie Wilkes, E. G. Tatum, Leigh Whipper, James Burrough, George Catlin, Edward Elkas, Louis Dean

Producer
Oscar Micheaux

Production
Micheaux Film Corporation

Distribution
Micheaux Film Corporation

Drama

1920 Within Our Gates

8 reels • Silent • Black and white • 1.33:1

Preer stars as an educator at a school for Black youth in Micheaux's unflinching portrayal of racial violence and lynching in the South.

Director
Oscar Micheaux

Screenplay
Oscar Micheaux

Cast
Evelyn Preer, Flo Clements, James D. Ruffin, Jack Chenault, William Smith, Charles D. Lucas, Bernice Ladd, Mrs. Evelyn, William Starks, Ralph Johnson

Producer
Oscar Micheaux

Production
Micheaux Film Corporation, Micheaux Book & Film Company, Inc.

Distribution
Micheaux Film Corporation, Quality Amusement Corporation

Drama

1921 By Right of Birth

6 reels • Silent • Black and white • 1.33:1

An unscrupulous stockbroker steals oil-rich land from a woman who is later reunited with her birth mother and regains her fortune.

Director
Harry A. Gant

Screenplay
Dora Mitchell, George P. Johnson

Music
John C. Spikes

Photography
Harry A. Gant

Cast
Clarence Brooks, Anita Thompson, Webb King, Beatrice George, Lester Bates, Lew Meehan, Minnie Provost, Baby Ruth Kimbrough, Grace Ellenwood, Chief John Big Tree

Production
Lincoln Motion Picture Company

Distribution
Lincoln Motion Picture Company

Drama

1921 The Sport of the Gods

6 reels • Sound • Black and white • 1.33:1

After an innocent man is wrongly jailed, his family moves to New York City to avoid humiliation but encounters the hardships of urban life. Upon his release he reunites with them. Based on a novel by Paul Laurence Dunbar.

Director
Henry Vernot

Cast
Elizabeth Boyer, Edward R. Abrams, George Edward Brown, Leon Williams, Lucile Brown, Lindsay J. Hall, Jean Armour, Stanley Walpole, Walter Thomas, Lawrence Chenault

Producer
Robert Levy

Production
REOL Productions

Distribution
Cumming & Paul Distributing Company

Adventure

1923 Regeneration

6 reels • Silent • Black and white • 1.33:1

Violet, an orphan, is left a treasure map. She and her friend Jack seek the treasure, fighting off a villain and landing on the treasure island, called Regeneration.

Director
Richard E. Norman

Cast
Stella Mayo, M. C. Maxwell, Alfred Norcom, Charlie Gaines, Clarence Rucker, Dr. R. L. Brown, Steve Reynolds

Production
Norman Film Manufacturing Company

Distribution
Norman Film Manufacturing Company

Drama

1924
Smiling Hate

6 reels • Silent • Black and white • 1.33:1

A mine owner seeks out a thief who is stealing ore, only to discover that his daughter's fiancé is the culprit.

Director
Roy Calnek

Screenplay
Roy Calnek

Cast
Harry Henderson, Josephine Tally, Howard Augusta, George Graham, Gus Dail, Ethel Smith, Ann Kennedy, William Milton, Peggy Vance, William Smith

Producer
Roy Calnek

Production
Superior Art Motion Pictures, Inc.

Home Movies

1924-28
Rev. S. S. Jones Home Movies

9 reels • Silent • Black and white • 1.37:1

Reels showcasing the vibrant lives of African Americans several years after the 1921 Tulsa race massacre. They are archived at the Smithsonian National Museum of African American History and Culture and Beinecke Rare Book & Manuscript Library, Yale University.

Director
Rev. Solomon Sir Jones

Themes
Religion, daily life, business, farming, children, education, parades

Drama

1925
Body and Soul

102 min. • Silent • Tinted • 1.33:1

Robeson, in his screen debut, plays the dual role of a corrupt preacher and his brother, a righteous man, in a parable about the sins of urban life.

Director
Oscar Micheaux

Screenplay
Oscar Micheaux

Cast
Paul Robeson, Marshall Rodgers, Lawrence Chenault, Chester A. Alexander, Walter W. Conick, Lillian Johnson, Madame Robinson, Julia Theresa Russell, Tom Fletcher, Mercedes Gilbert

Producer
Oscar Micheaux

Production
Micheaux Film Corporation

Distribution
Micheaux Film Corporation

Action

1926
The Flying Ace

65 min. • Silent • Black and white • 1.33:1

A returning World War I veteran must recover a stolen satchel containing a railroad company's payroll, culminating in a daring plane chase.

Director
Richard E. Norman

Screenplay
Richard E. Norman

Photography
Dal Clawson

Cast
Laurence Criner, Kathryn Boyd, Boise De Legge, George Calvin, Sam Jordan, Lyons Daniels, Steve Reynolds

Producer
Richard E. Norman

Production
Norman Film Manufacturing Company

Distribution
Norman Film Manufacturing Company

Drama

1928
Absent

6 reels • Silent • Black and white • 1.33:1

A shell-shocked veteran returns from war to work in a mine and begin a new life.

Director
Harry A. Gant

Photography
Harry A. Gant

Cast
Clarence Brooks, George Reed, Virgil Owens, Rose Lee Lincoln, Floyd Shackelford, Clarence Williams

Producer
Harry A. Gant

Production
Rosebud Film Corporation

Distribution
Ira McGowan, D. I. Thomas

Drama

1929
The Scar of Shame

86 min. • Sound • Black and white • 1.33:1

A composer marries a woman from a lower social class, but he is unable to overcome his family's prejudice.

Director
Frank Perugini

Screenplay
David Starkman

Photography
Al Ligouri

Cast
Harry Henderson, Norman Johnstone, Ann Kennedy, Lucia Lynn Moses, William E. Pettus, Lawrence Chenault, Pearl McCormack

Production
Colored Players Film Corporation

Distribution
States' rights

1930s

Drama

1930
Georgia Rose

7 reels • Sound • Black and white • 1.33:1

A minister's daughter is tempted by her boyfriend's brother but changes her mind just in time.

Director
Harry A. Gant

Screenplay
Harry A. Gant

Photography
Harry A. Gant

Cast
Clarence Brooks, Irene Wilson, Evelyn Preer, Roberta Hyson, Allegretti Anderson, Edward Thompson, Webb King, Spencer Williams Jr., Dora Dean Johnson, E. C. Dyer

Production
Aristo Film Corporation

Distribution
Aristo Film Corporation

Drama

ca. 1930
Hell-Bound Train

50 min. • Silent • Black and white • 1.33:1

In this surreal allegory about the sins of modern life, each railroad car features a sin of the Jazz Age.

Directors
James Gist, Eloyce Gist

Screenplay
James Gist, Eloyce Gist

Distribution
James Gist, Eloyce Gist

Drama

1931
The Exile

93 min. • Sound • Black and white • 1.33:1

A young man leaves his fiancée after she inherits a brothel. He sets out for South Dakota, where he falls in love with a woman he assumes is white.

Director
Oscar Micheaux

Screenplay
Oscar Micheaux

Music
Donald Heywood

Photography
Lester Lang, Walter Strenge

Cast
Eunice Brooks, Stanley Morrell, Celeste Cole, Katherine Noisette, Charles Moore, Nora Newsome, George Randol, A. B. Comathiere, Carl Mahon, Lou Vernon, Louise Cook, Roland Holder

Producer
Frank Schiffman

Production
Micheaux Film Corporation

Distribution
Micheaux Film Corporation

Drama

1932
The Girl from Chicago

61 min. • Sound • Black and white • 1.33:1

A woman is framed for murder and sentenced to die in the electric chair until her love interest solves the crime.

Director
Oscar Micheaux

Screenplay
Oscar Micheaux

Photography
Sam Orleans

Cast
Carl Mahon, Star Calloway, Alice B. Russell, Eunice Brooks, Minta Cato, John Everett, Frank Wilson, Cherokee Thornton, Grace Smith, Erwin Gary, Juano Hernandez

Producer
Burton Russell

Production
Micheaux Pictures Corporation

Distribution
Micheaux Pictures Corporation

Musical

1932
Harlem Is Heaven

Alternative Title: **Harlem Rhapsody**

69 min. • Sound • Black and white • 1.33:1

Robinson stars in this musical as a theater director who helps two lovers unite despite his feelings for one of them, an actress in the troupe.

Director
Irwin R. Franklyn

Screenplay
Irwin R. Franklyn

Music
Porter Grainger, Joe Jordan, Shelton Brooks, Edgar Dorwell

Photography
Charles Levine

Editing
Elmer J. McGovern

Cast
Bill "Bojangles" Robinson, John Mason, Putney Dandridge, Jimmy Baskett, Anise Boyer, Henri Wessell, Alma Smith, Bob Sawyer, Eubie Blake and His Orchestra, Ferdie Lewis

Producers
Irving Yates, Tishman and O'Neal

Production
Lincoln Pictures, Inc.

Distribution
Lincoln Pictures, Inc.

Drama

1933
The Emperor Jones

80 min. • Sound • Black and white • 1.33:1

Robeson plays Brutus Jones, a Pullman porter who becomes the ruler of a Caribbean island. Based on the play by Eugene O'Neill.

Director
Dudley Murphy

Screenplay
Du Bose Heyward

Music
Rosamond Johnson, Frank Tours

Photography
Ernest Haller

Editing
Grant Whytock

Cast
Paul Robeson, Dudley Digges, Frank H. Wilson, Fredi Washington, Ruby Elzy

Producer
Gifford Cochran

Production
John Krimsky, Gifford Cochran Inc.

Distribution
United Artists Corporation

Home Movies

1934–51 Nicholas Brothers Home Movies

13 reels • Silent • Black and white • 1.37:1

These reels feature the Nicholas Brothers during their travels, with appearences by Dorothy Dandridge, Etta James, Dorothy Nicholas, Tony Nicholas, and Lupe Velez. They are held at the Academy Film Archive.

Directors
Harold Nicholas, Fayard Nicholas

Themes
Film premieres, dance, recreation, travel, Italy, Mexico, Brazil

Drama

1935 Murder in Harlem

Alternative Titles: **Lem Hawkins' Confession, The Brand of Cain**

98 min. • Sound • Black and white • 1.33:1

Micheaux's remake of his own *Gunsaulus Mystery* (1921), based on an actual incident in which a Black night watchman becomes the primary suspect after he discovers a white woman's body.

Director
Oscar Micheaux

Screenplay
Oscar Micheaux

Music
Clarence Williams

Photography
Shas Levine

Cast
Clarence Brooks, Dorothy Van Engle, Andrew Bishop, Alec Lovejoy, Laura Bowman, Bee Freeman, Lionel Monagas, Alice B. Russell, Sandy Burns, Lea Morris

Producers
Oscar Micheaux, Alice B. Russell

Production
Micheaux Pictures Corporation

Distribution
Micheaux Pictures Corporation

Drama | France

1935 Princesse Tam-Tam

Alternative Title: **Princess Tam Tam**

77 min. • Sound • Black and white • 1.33:1

A young novelist becomes infatuated with a Tunisian woman and passes her off as royalty when they return to Paris.

Director
Edmond T. Greville

Screenplay
Pepito Abatino, Yves Mirande

Music
Dallin, Grenet, Goehr, Al Romans

Photography
G. Benoit

Editing
J. Feyte

Cast
Josephine Baker, Max Montagu, Albert Préjean, Germaine Aussey, Viviane Romance

Producer
Arys Nissotti

Production
Arys Production

Distribution
DI CI MO

Western

1937 Harlem on the Prairie

Alternative Title: **Bad Man of Harlem**

61 min. • Sound • Black and white • 1.37:1

This musical western features Herb Jeffries as a singing cowboy who tries to return stolen gold to its rightful owners.

Director
Sam Newfield

Screenplay
Fred Myton, Flournoy E. Miller

Music
Lew Porter

Photography
William Hyer

Editing
Robert Jahns

Cast
Herbert Jeffries, Flournoy E. Miller, Mantan Moreland, Connie Harris, Maceo B. Sheffield, Spencer Williams Jr., George Randol, Nathan Curry, James Davis, Edward Brandon

Producer
Jed Buell

Production
Associated Features, Inc.

Distribution
Associated Features, Inc.

Drama

1938
The Duke Is Tops

Alternative Title: **The Bronze Venus** (1943 rerelease)

80 min. • Sound • Black and white • 1.37:1
Cooper and Horne star as an entertainment duo who split up after she becomes more popular. When her career begins to decline, they reunite.

Director
William L. Nolte

Screenplay
Phil Dunham, Ralph Cooper

Music
Lou Frohman, Ben Ellison, Harvey Brooks, Phil Moore

Photography
J. Henry Kruse, Robert Cline

Editing
Alice Greenwood

Cast
Ralph Cooper, Lena Horne, Laurence Criner, Monte Hawley, Neva Peoples, Vernon McCalla, Edward Thompson, Johnny Taylor, Roy Martin, Guernsey Morrow

Producer
Harry M. Popkin

Production
Million Dollar Productions, Inc.

Distribution
Million Dollar Productions, Inc.

Noir

1938
Gang Smashers

Alternative Title: **Gun Moll** (1944 rerelease)

65 min. • Sound • Black and white • 1.37:1
McKinney stars as an undercover detective who infiltrates the Dalton mob, which is extorting local businesses.

Director
Leo C. Popkin

Screenplay
Phil Dunham, Hazel Barnes Jamieson

Music
Phil Moore

Photography
Robert Cline

Editing
Bart Rauw

Cast
Nina Mae McKinney, Mantan Moreland, Laurence Criner, Monte Hawley

Producer
Harry M. Popkin

Production
Million Dollar Productions, Inc.

Distribution
Million Dollar Productions, Inc.

Drama

1939
Reform School

Alternative Title: **Prison Bait** (1944 rerelease)

82 min. • Sound • Black and white • 1.37:1
Beavers stars as a reform-minded probation officer who institutes drastic changes in a juvenile prison, in a sharp critique of the prison-industrial complex and its effects on Black youth. Based on a story by Joseph O'Donnell and Hazel Barnes Jamieson.

Director
Leo C. Popkin

Screenplay
Zella Young

Music
Lou Frohman

Photography
William Hyer

Editing
Bart Rauw

Cast
Louise Beavers, Reginald Fenderson, Monte Hawley, Eugene Jackson, Freddie Jackson, Eddie Lynn, DeForrest Covan, Bobby Simmons, Maceo B. Sheffield, Edward Thompson

Producer
Harry M. Popkin

Production
Million Dollar Productions

Distribution
Million Dollar Productions

1940s

Noir

1940
Am I Guilty?

Alternative Titles: **Free Clinic, Racket Doctor** (1945 rerelease)

70 min. • Sound • Black and white • 1.37:1
Dr. Dunbar establishes a clinic in his underserved neighborhood. The Bennet gang, in need of a mob doctor, starts bringing him along during their crime sprees, until the gang is captured.

Director
Sam Newfield

Screenplay
Sherman Lowe, Milton Raison, Earle Snell

Photography
Robert Cline

Editing
S. Roy Luby

Cast
Ralph Cooper, Sybil Lewis, Sam McDaniel, Laurence Criner, Marcella Moreland, Arthur Ray, Reginald Fenderson, Monte Hawley, Matthew Jones, "Pigmeat" Markham

Producer
A. W. Hackel

Production
Supreme Pictures Corporation

Distribution
Supreme Pictures Corporation

Comedy

1940
Mr. Washington Goes to Town

Alternative Title: **Mr. Jones Goes to Town**

65 min. • Sound • Black and white • 1.37:1
In this horror comedy, an incarcerated Moreland falls asleep and dreams he has inherited a hotel occupied by a number of strange guests.

Director
Jed Buell

Screenplay
Walter Weems, Lex Neal

Music
Harvey Brooks

Photography
Jack Greenhalgh

Editing
William J. Faris

Cast
F. E. Miller, Mantan Moreland, Maceo B. Sheffield, Arthur Ray, Margaret Whitten, Clarence Morehouse, Monte Hawley, Zerita Steptean, Florence O'Brien, Vernon McCalla

Producers
Jed Buell, James K. Friedrich

Production
Dixie National Pictures, Inc.

Distribution
Dixie National Pictures, Inc.; Consolidated National Film Exchanges

Drama

1941
The Blood of Jesus

Alternative Title: **Glory Road**

68 min. • Sound • Black and white • 1.37:1
A woman is accidentally shot. While on her deathbed she visits the crossroads between heaven and hell, where she is tempted by Satan's emissary until a vision of Jesus Christ leads her to embrace religion.

Director
Spencer Williams Jr.

Screenplay
Spencer Williams Jr.

Photography
Jack Whitman

Cast
Cathryn Caviness, Spencer Williams Jr., Juanita Riley, Rather Hardeman, Rogenia Goldthwaite, Jas B. Jones, Frank H. McClennan, Eddie DeBuse, Alva Fuller, Rev. R. L. Robertson

Producers
Spencer Williams Jr., Alfred N. Sack

Production
Amegro Films

Distribution
Sack Amusement Enterprises

Drama

1942
Brother Martin: Servant of Jesus

60 min. • Sound • Black and white • 1.37:1
This biographical drama focuses on Martin de Porres, a Dominican priest beatified in 1837.

Director
Spencer Williams Jr.

Screenplay
Spencer Williams Jr.

Cast
Spencer Williams Jr.

Production
Jenkins and Bourgeois

Distribution
Sack Amusement Enterprises

Drama

1943
Marching On!

Alternative Title: **Where's My Man To-Nite**

70 min. • Sound • Black and white • 1.37:1
In this film, set against the backdrop of World War II, a soldier deserts, only to encounter a drifter who happens to be his father, a World War I veteran long considered dead. The AWOL soldier then sees the error of his ways.

Director
Spencer Williams Jr.

Screenplay
Spencer Williams Jr.

Photography
Clark Ramsey

Cast
Emmet Jackson, George T. Sutton, L. K. Smith

Producer
H. W. Kier

Production
Sack Amusement Enterprises

Distribution
Astor Pictures Corporation

Documentary

1944
We've Come a Long, Long Way

70 min. • Sound • Black and white • 1.37:1

This documentary chronicles the contributions of Black soldiers during the war effort.

Director
Jack Goldberg

Cast
Elder Lightfoot Solomon Michaux (narration), Mary McLeod Bethune (additional narration), Major Wright (additional narration), George Washington Carver, Lena Horne, Joe Louis, Bill Robinson, Paul Robeson

Producers
Jack Goldberg, Elder Michaux

Production
Negro Marches On, Inc.

Distribution
States' rights

Drama

1946
Beale Street Mama

63 min. • Sound • Black and white • 1.37:1

A pair of street cleaners find stolen money, using it to give themselves a better life until they are discovered.

Director
Spencer Williams Jr.

Screenplay
Sam Elljay

Photography
H. Arthur Smith

Cast
July Jones, Spencer Williams Jr., Rosalie Larrimore, Howard Galloway, J. W. Hemmings, Motyne McCormick, Mary Louise Stevens, George T. Sutton, Allen and Allen, Joyce McElrath

Production
Sack Attractions

Distribution
Sack Amusement Enterprises

Drama

1946
Dirty Gertie from Harlem U.S.A.

60 min. • Sound • Black and white • 1.37:1

Nightclub performer Gertie leaves her boyfriend and sets out for Trinidad with her troupe. Things end tragically when her jilted lover finds her.

Director
Spencer Williams Jr.

Screenplay
True T. Thompson

Photography
John L. Herman

Cast
Francine Everett, Don Wilson, Katharine Moore, Alfred Hawkins, David Boykin, L. E. Lewis, Inez Newell, Piano Frank, John King, Shelly Ross

Producer
Bert Goldberg

Production
Sack Amusement Enterprises

Distribution
States' rights

Drama

1948
The Betrayal

183 min. • Sound • Black and white • 1.37:1

Micheaux's last film borrows elements from *The Homesteader* (1919). A farmer falls for a woman he believes to be white but instead marries someone else, ultimately divorcing and reuniting with his true love, who in fact is biracial.

Director
Oscar Micheaux

Screenplay
Oscar Micheaux

Photography
N. Spoor

Cast
Lou Vernon, Edward Fraction, Leroy Collins, Jessie Johnson, William Byrd, Myra Stanton, Frances De Young, Arthur McCoo, Vernetties Moore, Barbara Lee

Producer
Oscar Micheaux

Production
Astor Pictures Corporation

Distribution
Astor Pictures Corporation

Drama

1948
Miracle in Harlem

72 min. • Sound • Black and white • 1.37:1

A wealthy tycoon swindles Aunt Hattie and her niece out of a small candy store she operates in Harlem. When he ends up dead, the women become the primary suspects.

Director
Jack Kemp

Screenplay
Vincent Valenti

Music
John Gluskin

Photography
Don Malkames

Editing
Don Druke

Cast
Hilda Offley, Sheila Guyse, Kenneth Freeman, William Greaves, Sybil Lewis, Creighton Thompson, Laurence Criner, Jack Carter, Milton Williams, Monte Hawley

Producer
Jack Goldberg

Production
Herald Pictures, Inc.

Distribution
Screen Guild Productions Inc.

1950s

Drama

1950
The Jackie Robinson Story

76 min. • Sound • Black and white • 1.37:1

In this semiautobiographical drama, Jackie Robinson plays the first Black baseball player in the major leagues.

Director
Alfred E. Green

Screenplay
Lawrence Edmund Taylor, Arthur Mann

Music
Herschel Burke Gilbert

Photography
Ernest Laszlo

Editing
Arthur H. Nadel

Cast
Jackie Robinson, Ruby Dee, Minor Watson, Louise Beavers, Richard Lane, Harry Shannon, Ben Lessy, Bill Spaulding Billy Wayne, Joel Fluellen

Producer
Mort Briskin

Production
Jewel Pictures Corporation

Distribution
Eagle-Lion Films, Inc.

Drama

1950
No Way Out

106 min. • Sound • Black and white • 1.37:1

Dr. Brooks treats two brothers at a local hospital. When one dies, the other accuses Brooks of murder and tries to turn the community against him.

Director
Joseph L. Mankiewicz

Screenplay
Joseph L. Mankiewicz

Music
Alfred Newman

Photography
Milton Krasner

Editing
Barbara McLean

Cast
Sidney Poitier, Richard Widmark, Linda Darnell, Stephen McNally, Mildred Joanne, Harry Bellaver, Stanley Ridges, Dots Johnson, Amanda Randolph, Bill Walker

Producer
Darryl F. Zanuck

Production
Twentieth Century-Fox Film Corporation

Distribution
Twentieth Century-Fox Film Corporation

Home Movies

1951
Cab Calloway Home Movie, Haiti

1 reel • Silent • Color • 1.37:1

This home movie was shot by Cab Calloway during his 1951 tour in Haiti. It features footage of Calloway, his family, popular tourist attractions, and his band performing on an outdoor stage. The reel is archived at the Smithsonian National Museum of African American History and Culture.

Director
Cab Calloway

Themes
Performance, family, weddings, travel, Haiti, musicians

Drama

1951
The Harlem Globetrotters

80 min. • Sound • Black and white • 1.37:1

In this sports drama about the famous all-Black basketball team, a recruit drops out of college and becomes the star of the Globetrotters.

Directors
Phil Brown, Will Jason

Screenplay
Alfred Palca

Music
Arthur Morton

Photography
Philip Tannura

Editing
James Sweeney

Cast
Thomas Gomez, Dorothy Dandridge, Bill Walker, Angela Clarke, Peter Thompson, Billy Brown, Roscoe Cumberland, William "Pop" Gates, Marques Haynes, Louis "Babe" Pressley, Ermer Robinson

Producer
Buddy Adler

Production
Columbia Pictures Corporation, Sidney Buchman Enterprises

Distribution
Columbia Pictures Corporation

Drama

1953
The Joe Louis Story

88 min. • Sound • Black and white • 1.37:1

This biopic about the heavyweight champion boxer covers his rise from poverty to fame.

Director
Robert Gordon

Screenplay
Robert Sylvester

Music
George Bassman

Photography
Joseph Brun

Editing
David Kummins

Cast
Joe Louis, Coley Wallace, Paul Stewart, Hilda Simms, James Edwards, John Marley, Dots Johnson, Evelyn Ellis, Carl Rocky Latimer, John Marriott, Isaac Jones

Producer
Stirling Silliphant

Production
Federated Films, Inc.

Distribution
United Artists Corporation

Musical | Academy Award Nominee

1954
Carmen Jones

105 min. • Sound • Color • 2.55:1

Carmen seduces Joe, a soldier who is already engaged to Cindy Lou, in this tragic love story. The film received two Academy Award nominations.

Director
Otto Preminger

Screenplay
Harry Kleiner

Music
Georges Bizet

Photography
Sam Leavitt

Editing
Louis Loeffler

Cast
Dorothy Dandridge, Harry Belafonte, Pearl Bailey, Olga James, Joe Adams, Brock Peters, Roy Glenn Sr., Nicodemus Stewart, Diahann Carroll

Producer
Otto Preminger

Production
Carlyle Productions, Inc.; Twentieth Century–Fox Film Corporation

Distribution
Twentieth Century–Fox Film Corporation

Nominee
Best Actress
Dorothy Dandridge

Drama

1958
Anna Lucasta

97 min • Sound • Black and white • 1.37:1

After Anna is kicked out of her home, she must resort to sex work. Her plans to begin a new life with a suitor are thwarted by her vengeful father.

Director
Arnold Laven

Screenplay
Phillip Yordan

Music
Elmer Bernstein

Photography
Lucien Ballard

Editing
Richard C. Meyer, Robert Lawrence

Cast
Eartha Kitt, Frederick O'Neal, Henry Scott, Rex Ingram, James Edwards, Isabelle Cooley, Rosetta Le Noire, Georgia Burke, Claire Leyba, Alvin Childress, Sammy Davis Jr.

Producer
Sidney Harmon

Production
Longridge Enterprises

Distribution
United Artists Corporation

Drama | Academy Award Nominee

1958
The Defiant Ones

98 min. • Sound • Black and white • 1.85:1

Two chain-gang prisoners shackled together, one white and one black, must work together as they attempt to flee. The film received nine Academy Award nominations.

Director
Stanley Kramer

Screenplay
Nedrick Young,
Harold Jacob Smith

Music
Ernest Gold

Photography
Sam Leavitt

Editing
Frederic Knudtson

Cast
Tony Curtis, Sidney Poitier, Theodore Bikel, Charles McGraw, Lon Chaney Jr., King Donovan, Claude Akins, Larry Bobkin, Whit Bissell, Carl "Alfalfa" Switzer

Producer
Stanley Kramer

Production
Lomitas Productions Inc.,
Curleigh Productions Inc.

Distribution
United Artists Corporation

Nominee
Best Actor
Sidney Poitier

Drama

1959
Odds Against Tomorrow

95 min. • Sound • Black and white • 1.85:1

A former police officer recruits two men to pull off a bank heist and must address their racial animosity.

Director
Robert Wise

Screenplay
John O. Killens,
Nelson Gidding

Music
John Lewis

Photography
Joseph Brun

Editing
Dede Allen

Cast
Harry Belafonte, Robert Ryan, Shelley Winters, Ed Begley, Gloria Grahame, Will Kuluva, Kim Hamilton, Mae Barnes, Richard Bright, Carmen De Lavallade

Producer
Robert Wise

Production
HarBel Productions Inc.

Distribution
United Artists Corporation

Science Fiction

1959
The World, the Flesh, and the Devil

95 min. • Sound • Black and white • 2.35:1

Ralph emerges from a collapsed mine to find that humanity has been wiped out by nuclear war. He sets out for New York City and finds another survivor, Sarah, a twenty-year-old white woman. Despite their mutual attraction, they must confront their internalized racial prejudices.

Director
Ranald MacDougall

Screenplay
Ranald MacDougall

Music
Miklós Rózsa

Photography
Harold J. Marzorati

Editing
Harold F. Kress

Cast
Harry Belafonte, Inger Stevens, Mel Ferrer

Producer
George Englund

Production
Sol C. Siegel Productions Inc.,
Harbel Productions Inc.,
Metro-Goldwyn-Mayer Corporation

Distribution
Lowe's Inc.

1960s

Documentary

1960
Integration Report 1

24 min. • Sound • Black and white • 1.37:1

The focus of this documentary is on the struggle for racial equality in Alabama, in Brooklyn, New York, and in Washington, DC.

Director
Madeline Anderson

Screenplay
Loften Mitchell

Photography
Alfonso Burney, Richard Cressy, John Fletcher, Richard Leacock, Albert Maysles, Robert Puello

Editing
Zina Voynow

Cast
Robert Graham Brown (narration), Martin Luther King Jr., Bayard Rustin, Andrew Young

Producer
Madeline Anderson

Drama

1961
A Raisin in the Sun

128 min. • Sound • Black and white • 1.33:1
After the death of their patriarch, a Black family in Chicago must decide what to do with the insurance payout and negotiate clashing views of their future. Based on the play by Lorraine Hansberry.

Director
Daniel Petrie

Screenplay
Lorraine Hansberry

Music
Laurence Rosenthal

Photography
Charles "Bud" Lawton

Editing
William Lyon, Paul Weatherwax

Cast
Sidney Poitier, Claudia McNeil, Ruby Dee, Diana Sands, Ivan Dixon, John Fiedler, Lou Gossett, Stephen Perry, Joel Fluellen, Roy Glenn Sr.

Producers
David Susskind, Philip Rose

Production
Paman-Doris Productions

Distribution
Columbia Pictures

Drama

1963
Gone Are the Days

Alternative Titles: **The Man Called C.O.T.T.O.N., Purlie Victorious**

100 min. • Sound • Black and white • 1.33:1
A minister returns to his hometown with the hope of building an integrated church. Based on the popular Broadway play *Purlie Victorious*.

Director
Nicholas Webster

Screenplay
Ossie Davis

Music
Henry Cowen

Photography
Boris Kaufman

Editing
Ralph Rosenblum

Cast
Ruby Dee, Ossie Davis, Sorrell Booke, Godfrey Cambridge, Hilda Haynes, Alan Alda, Beah Richard, Charles Welch, Ralph Roberts

Producer
Nicholas Webster

Production
Hammer Film Corporation

Distribution
Hammer Brothers, Trans-Lux Corporation, Futurama Entertainment Corporation

Drama

1964
Nothing but a Man

92 min. • Sound • Black and white • 1.37:1
A recently married railroad worker and schoolteacher face racism and discrimination in their small Alabama town in this neorealist-style drama.

Director
Michael Roemer

Screenplay
Michael Roemer, Robert M. Young

Photography
Robert M. Young

Editing
Luke Bennett, Robert Machover

Cast
Ivan Dixon, Abbey Lincoln, Gloria Foster, Julius Harris, Martin Priest, Leonard Parker, Yaphet Kotto, Stanley Greene, Helen Lounck, Helene Arridell

Producers
Robert M. Young, Michael Roemer, Robert Rubin

Production
Duart Film Laboratories

Distribution
Cinema V Distributing, Inc.

Documentary

1967
Behind Every Good Man

8 min. • Sound • Black and white • 1.33:1
This UCLA student film offers an empathetic look at an unidentified trans woman as she navigates daily life.

Director
Nikolai Ursin

Screenplay
Nikolai Ursin

Producer
Nikolai Ursin

Documentary

1967
Portrait of Jason

105 min. • Sound • Black and white • 1.33:1

This cinema verité documentary zeroes in on Jason Holliday, a gay hustler, as he recounts aspects of his life over the course of a night.

Director
Shirley Clarke

Photography
Jeri Sapanen

Editing
Shirley Clarke

Cast
Jason Holliday, Shirley Clarke (narration), Carl Lee (narration)

Producer
Shirley Clarke

Production
Filmmakers' Distribution Center

Distribution
Filmmakers' Distribution Center

Documentary | France/USA

1968
Black Panthers

28 min. • Sound • Color • 1.37:1

Varda follows the Black Panther Party as they fight to release cofounder Huey P. Newton.

Director
Agnès Varda

Screenplay
Agnès Varda

Photography
David Meyers, Agnès Varda

Editing
Paddy Monk

Cast
Bill Brent, H. Rap Brown, Stokely Carmichael, Eldridge Cleaver, Kathleen Cleaver, Ron Dellums, James Forman, Huey P. Newton, Bobby Seale

Producer
Agnès Varda

Production
Ciné-Tamaris

Drama | France

1968
La permission (The Story of a Three-Day Pass)

87 min. • Sound • Black and white • 1.66:1

A Black American soldier on a three-day leave falls for a French woman in a Paris nightclub. Their interracial love results in penalization by the army.

Director
Melvin Van Peebles

Screenplay
Melvin Van Peebles

Music
Mickey Baker, Melvin Van Peebles

Photography
Michel Kelber

Editing
Liliane Korb

Cast
Harry Baird, Nicole Berger, Christian Marin, Pierre Doris, Hal Brav, Tria French

Producer
Guy Belford

Production
O.P.E.R.A.

Distribution
Sigma III Corporation

Experimental

1968
Symbiopsychotaxiplasm: Take One

75 min. • Sound • Color • 1.33:1

Greaves's experimental documentary-fiction hybrid features members of a film crew in Central Park who must figure out the type of movie they are making.

Director
William Greaves

Screenplay
William Greaves

Music
Miles Davis

Photography
Stevan Larner, Terence Macartney-Filgate

Editing
William Greaves

Cast
Patricia Ree Gilbert, Don Fellows, Jonathan Gordon, Bob Roses, William Greaves

Producers
William Greaves, Manuel Melamed

Production
Take One Productions

Drama

1968 Uptight

Alternative Title: **Betrayal**

104 min. • Sound • Color • 1.85:1
A group of Black militants begins to stockpile weapons but is betrayed by one of its members.

Director
Jules Dassin

Screenplay
Jules Dassin, Ruby Dee, Julian Mayfield

Music
Booker T. Jones

Photography
Boris Kaufman

Editing
Robert Lawrence, Stewart Linder

Cast
Raymond St. Jacques, Ruby Dee, Frank Silvera, Roscoe Lee Browne, Julian Mayfield, Janet MacLachlan, Ji-Tu Cumbuka, Max Julien, John Wesley Rodgers, Richard Anthony Williams

Producer
Jules Dassin

Production
Marlukin Productions

Distribution
Paramount Pictures

Drama

1969 The Learning Tree

107 min. • Sound • Color • 2.35:1
Parks adapted this coming-of-age tale from his own novel, in which a teenager navigates adulthood in the rural South.

Director
Gordon Parks

Screenplay
Gordon Parks, Genevieve Young

Music
Gordon Parks

Photography
Burnett Guffey

Editing
George Rohrs

Cast
Kyle Johnson, Alex Clarke, Estelle Evans, Dana Elcar, Mira Waters, Joel Fluellen, Malcolm Atterbury, Richard Ward, Russell Thorson, Peggy Rea

Producer
Gordon Parks

Production
Winger Enterprises

Distribution
Warner Bros., Seven Arts Inc.

1970s

Drama

1970 Cotton Comes to Harlem

97 min. • Sound • Color • 1.85:1
Two detectives, investigating Reverend O'Malley's use of church donations to buy parcels of land in Africa, chase after the money, which is stashed in a bale of hay.

Director
Ossie Davis

Screenplay
Arnold Perl, Ossie Davis

Music
Galt MacDermot

Photography
Gerald Hirschfeld

Editing
Robert Q. Lovett, John Carter

Cast
Godfrey Cambridge, Raymond St. Jacques, Calvin Lockhart, Judy Pace, Redd Foxx, John Anderson, Emily Yancy, J. D. Cannon, Mabel Robinson, Dick Sabol

Producer
Samuel Goldwyn Jr.

Production
Formosa Productions, Inc.

Distribution
United Artists Corporation

Documentary

1970 I Am Somebody

30 min. • Sound • Color • 1.37:1
Anderson chronicles the plight of four hundred hospital workers in South Carolina on strike and seeking union recognition.

Director
Madeline Anderson

Screenplay
Madeline Anderson

Photography
Don Hunstein, Roland Mitchell

Editing
Madeline Anderson

Cast
Coretta Scott King, Ralph Abernathy, Leon Davis, Andrew Young

Producer
Madeline Anderson

Production
American Foundation of Non-Violence

Documentary | Academy Award Nominee

1970
King: A Filmed Record... Montgomery to Memphis

185 min. • Sound • Black and White • 1.33:1

This documentary traces key events in Martin Luther King Jr.'s quest for racial equality, beginning with the Montgomery Bus Boycott.

Directors
Sidney Lumet, Joseph L. Mankiewicz

Screenplay
Ely Landau, Mitchell Grayson

Music
Coleridge-Taylor Perkinson

Editing
Lora Hays, John Carter

Cast
Paul Newman (narration), Joanne Woodward, Ruby Dee, James Earl Jones, Clarence Williams III, Burt Lancaster, Ben Gazzara, Charlton Heston, Harry Belafonte, Sidney Poitier

Producer
Ely Landau

Production
Commonwealth United Corp., Martin Luther King Film Project

Distribution
Commonwealth United Entertainment, Inc.; Maron Films, Ltd.

Nominee
Best Documentary (Feature)

Drama

1971
Black Chariot

90 min. • Sound • Color • 1.33:1

A drifter joins a militant organization and falls in love with a fellow member. The police kill a member of the organization, leading the drifter to rethink his desire for vengeance. The movie was shot on film and video.

Director
Robert L. Goodwin

Screenplay
Robert L. Goodwin

Cast
Bernie Casey, Barbara O. Jones, Richard Elkins, Pauline Myers, Gene Dynarski, Mike Warren, Dennis Pryor

Producer
Robert L. Goodwin

Production
Robert L. Goodwin Productions

Distribution
Third World Distributors

Action | Academy Award Winner

1971
Shaft

98 min. • Sound • Color • 1.85:1

Detective John Shaft is caught in the middle of a mob war when he is hired by a Harlem mobster to rescue his daughter, who has been abducted by the rival Italian mob.

Director
Gordon Parks

Screenplay
Ernest Tidyman, John D. F. Black

Music
Isaac Hayes

Photography
Urs Furrer

Editing
Hugh A. Robertson

Cast
Richard Roundtree, Moses Gunn, Charles Cioffi, Christopher St. John, Gwenn Mitchell, Lawrence Pressman, Victor Arnold, Sherri Brewer, Rex Robbins, Camille Yarbrough

Producers
Joel Freeman, Roger Lewis

Production
Shaft Productions Ltd., Metro-Goldwyn-Mayer Inc.

Distribution
Metro-Goldwyn-Mayer Inc.

Winner
Original Song
Isaac Hayes

Nominee
Original Dramatic Score
Isaac Hayes

Drama

1971
Sweet Sweetback's Baadasssss Song

97 min. • Sound • Color • 1.85:1

Sweet Sweetback, an orphan working in a Los Angeles brothel, is framed for murder by the police. An epic manhunt ensues, and with support from the Black community, Sweetback flees from the police.

Director
Melvin Van Peebles

Screenplay
Melvin Van Peebles

Music
Melvin Van Peebles

Photography
Bob Maxwell

Editing
Melvin Van Peebles

Cast
The Black community, Melvin Van Peebles, Bruce Adams, Michael Agustus, John H. Allen, John Amos, Mike Angel, Vincent Barbi, Maggie Bemlery, Bill Cade

Producers
Melvin Van Peebles, Jerry Gross

Production
Yeah Inc.

Distribution
Cinemation Industries Inc.

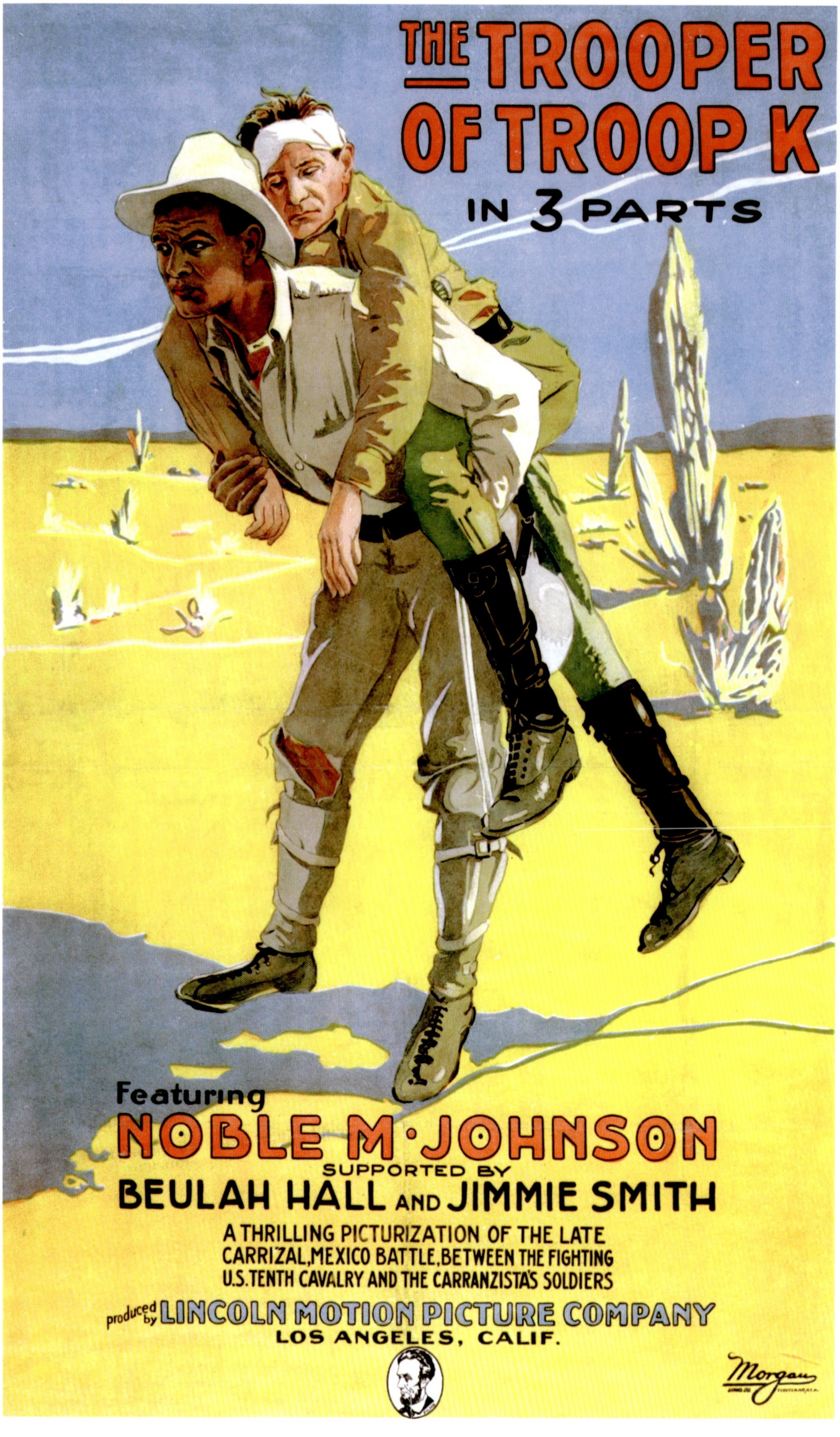
THE TROOPER OF TROOP K
IN 3 PARTS
Featuring
NOBLE M. JOHNSON
SUPPORTED BY
BEULAH HALL AND JIMMIE SMITH
A THRILLING PICTURIZATION OF THE LATE CARRIZAL, MEXICO BATTLE, BETWEEN THE FIGHTING U.S. TENTH CAVALRY AND THE CARRANZISTA'S SOLDIERS
produced by LINCOLN MOTION PICTURE COMPANY
LOS ANGELES, CALIF.
Morgan

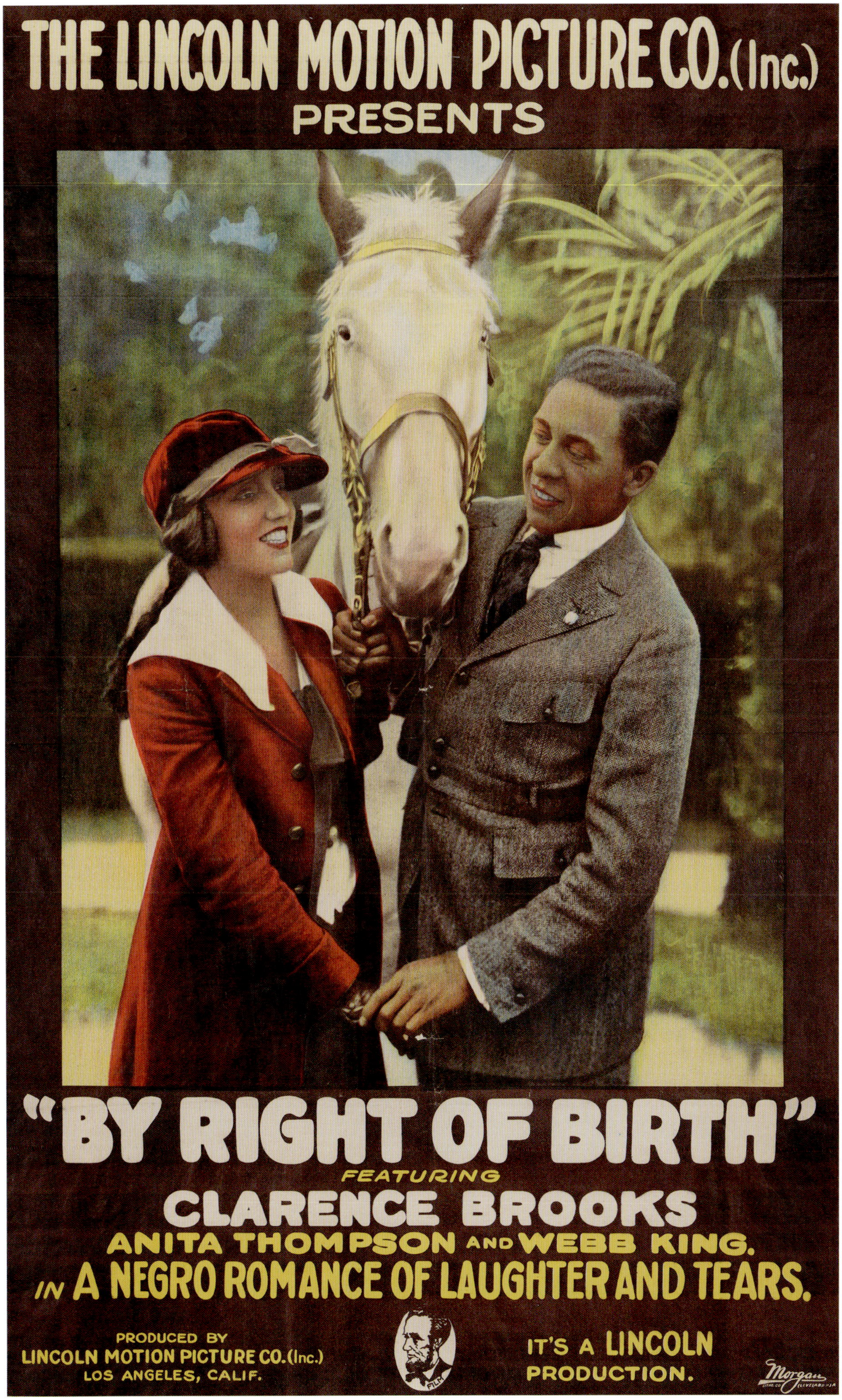
THE LINCOLN MOTION PICTURE CO. (Inc.)
PRESENTS
"BY RIGHT OF BIRTH"
FEATURING
CLARENCE BROOKS
ANITA THOMPSON AND WEBB KING.
IN A NEGRO ROMANCE OF LAUGHTER AND TEARS.
PRODUCED BY
LINCOLN MOTION PICTURE CO. (Inc.)
LOS ANGELES, CALIF.
IT'S A LINCOLN
PRODUCTION.
Morgan

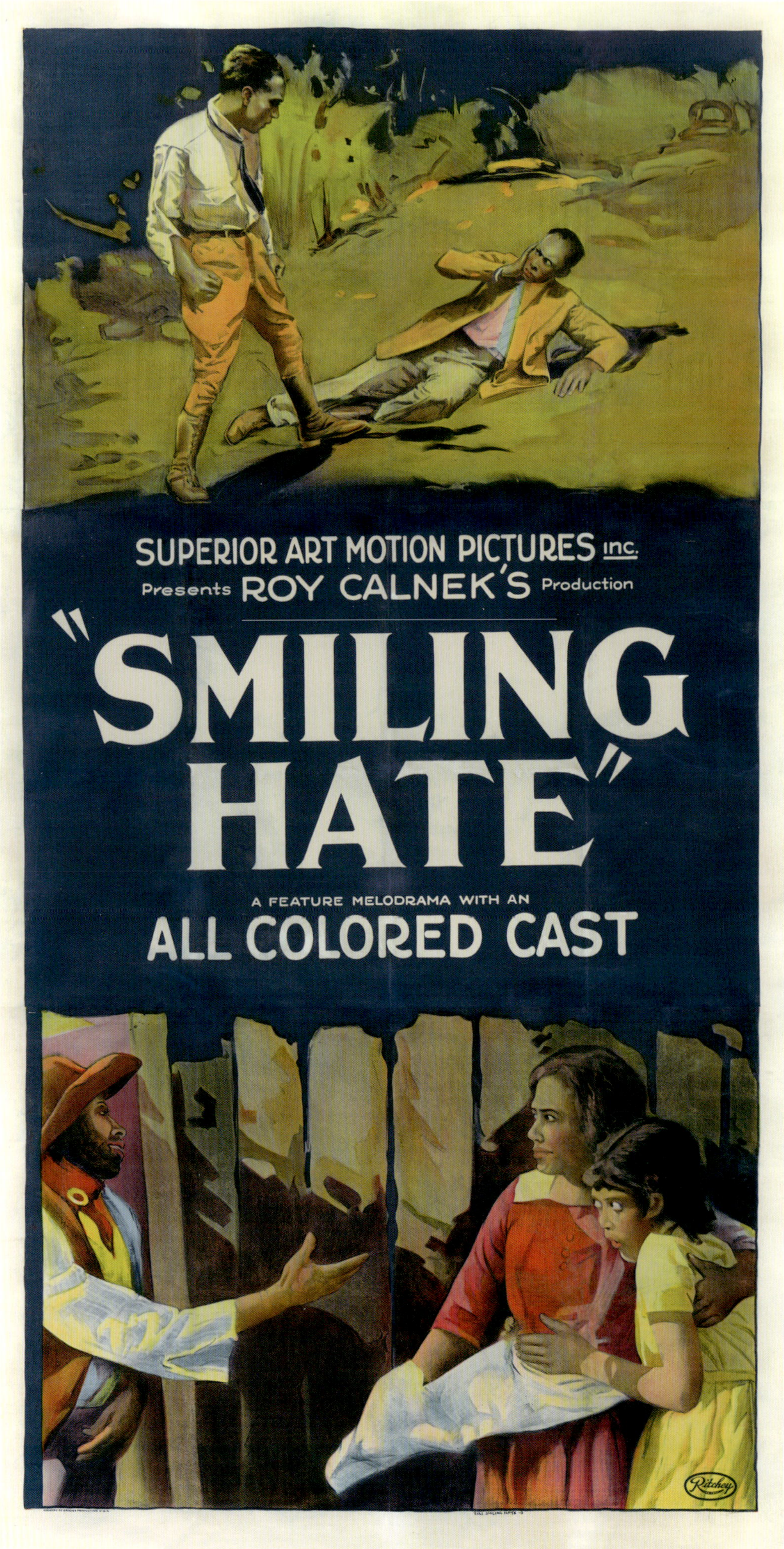
SUPERIOR ART MOTION PICTURES INC.
Presents ROY CALNEK'S Production
"SMILING HATE"
A FEATURE MELODRAMA WITH AN
ALL COLORED CAST
Ritchey

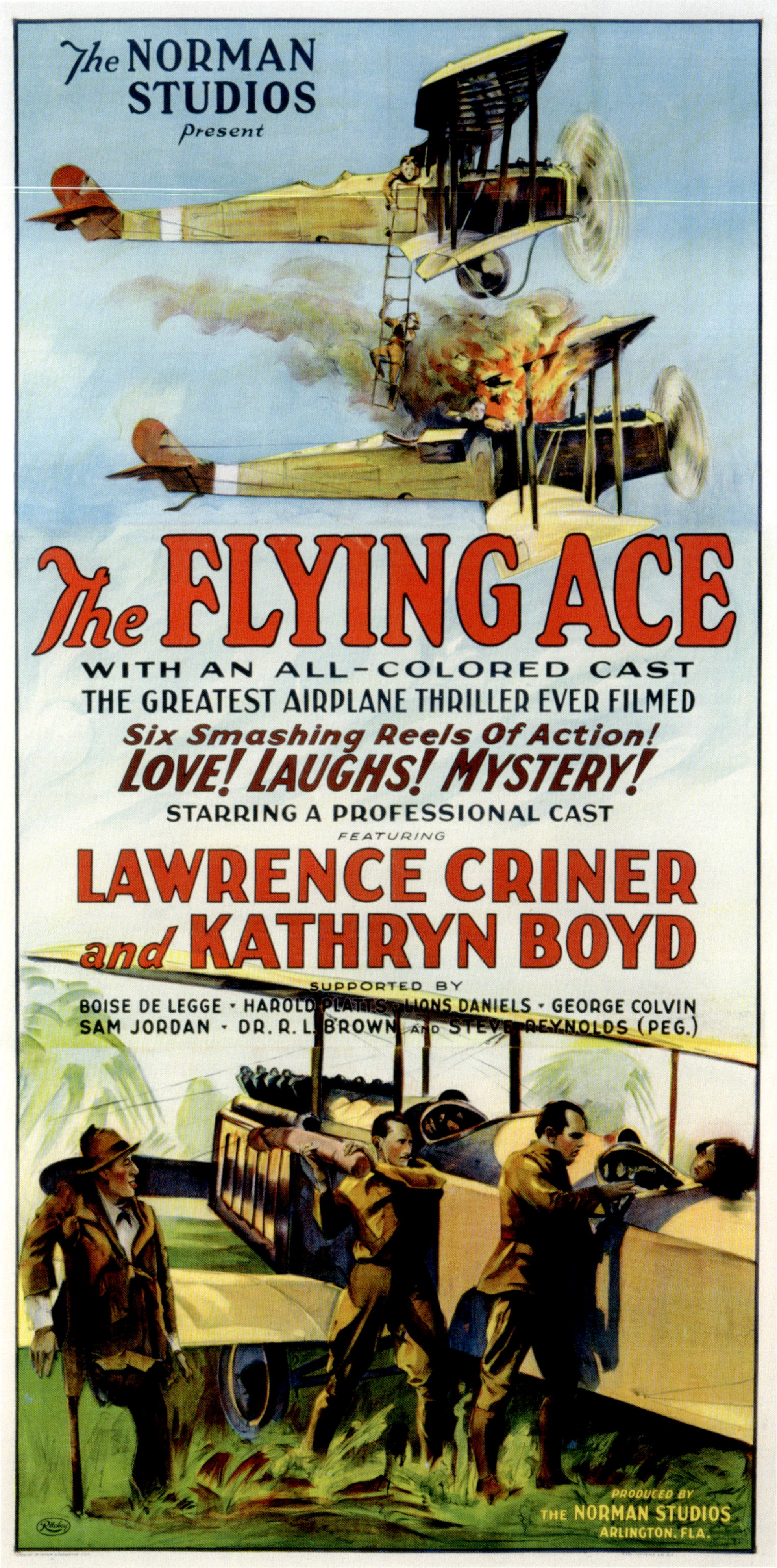
The NORMAN STUDIOS
present
The FLYING ACE
WITH AN ALL-COLORED CAST
THE GREATEST AIRPLANE THRILLER EVER FILMED
Six Smashing Reels Of Action!
LOVE! LAUGHS! MYSTERY!
STARRING A PROFESSIONAL CAST
FEATURING
LAWRENCE CRINER
and KATHRYN BOYD
SUPPORTED BY
BOISE DE LEGGE · HAROLD PLATTS · LIONS DANIELS · GEORGE COLVIN
SAM JORDAN · DR. R. L. BROWN AND STEVE REYNOLDS (PEG.)
PRODUCED BY
THE NORMAN STUDIOS
ARLINGTON, FLA.

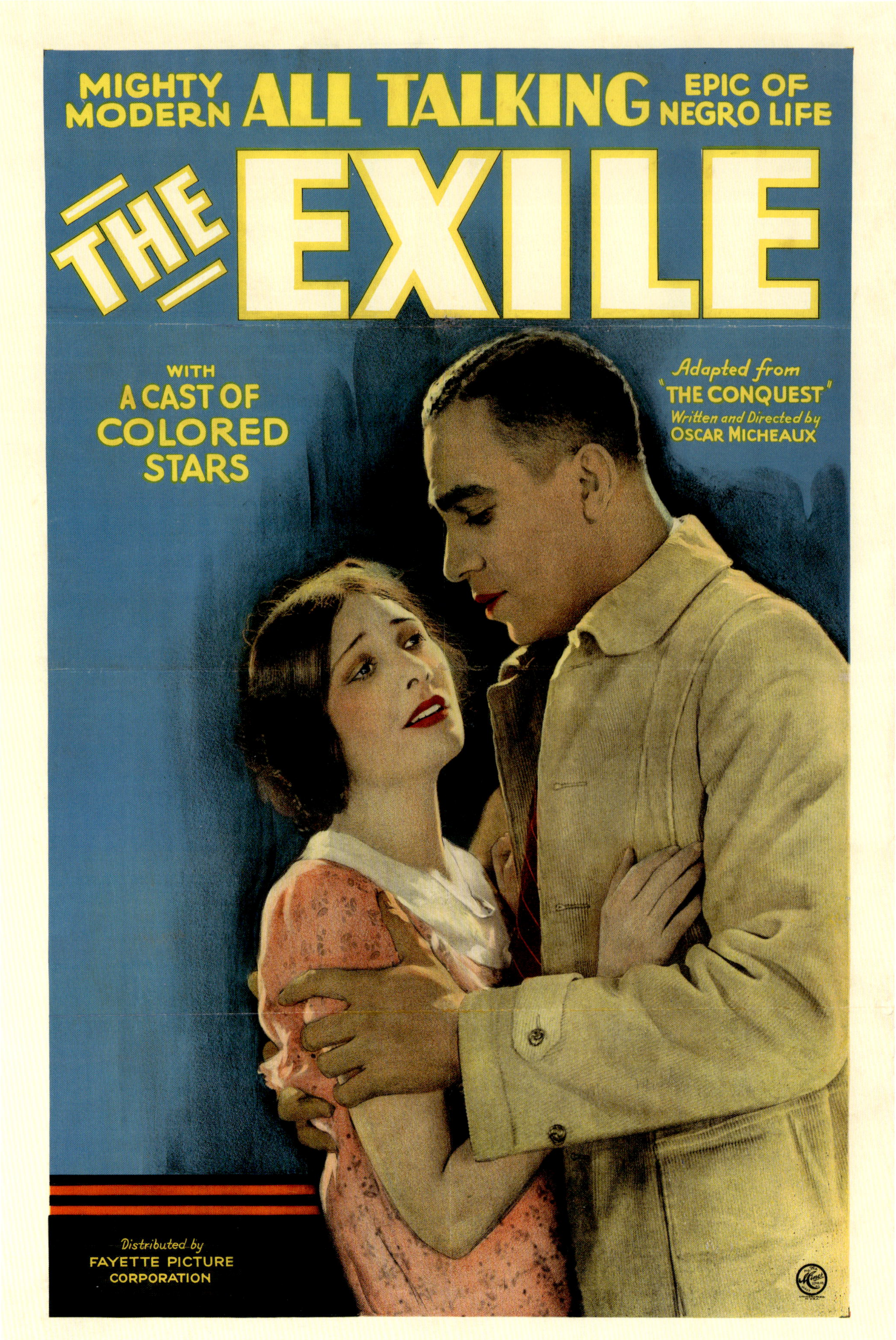
MIGHTY MODERN
ALL TALKING
EPIC OF NEGRO LIFE
THE EXILE
WITH
A CAST OF
COLORED
STARS
Adapted from
"THE CONQUEST"
Written and Directed by
OSCAR MICHEAUX
Distributed by
FAYETTE PICTURE
CORPORATION

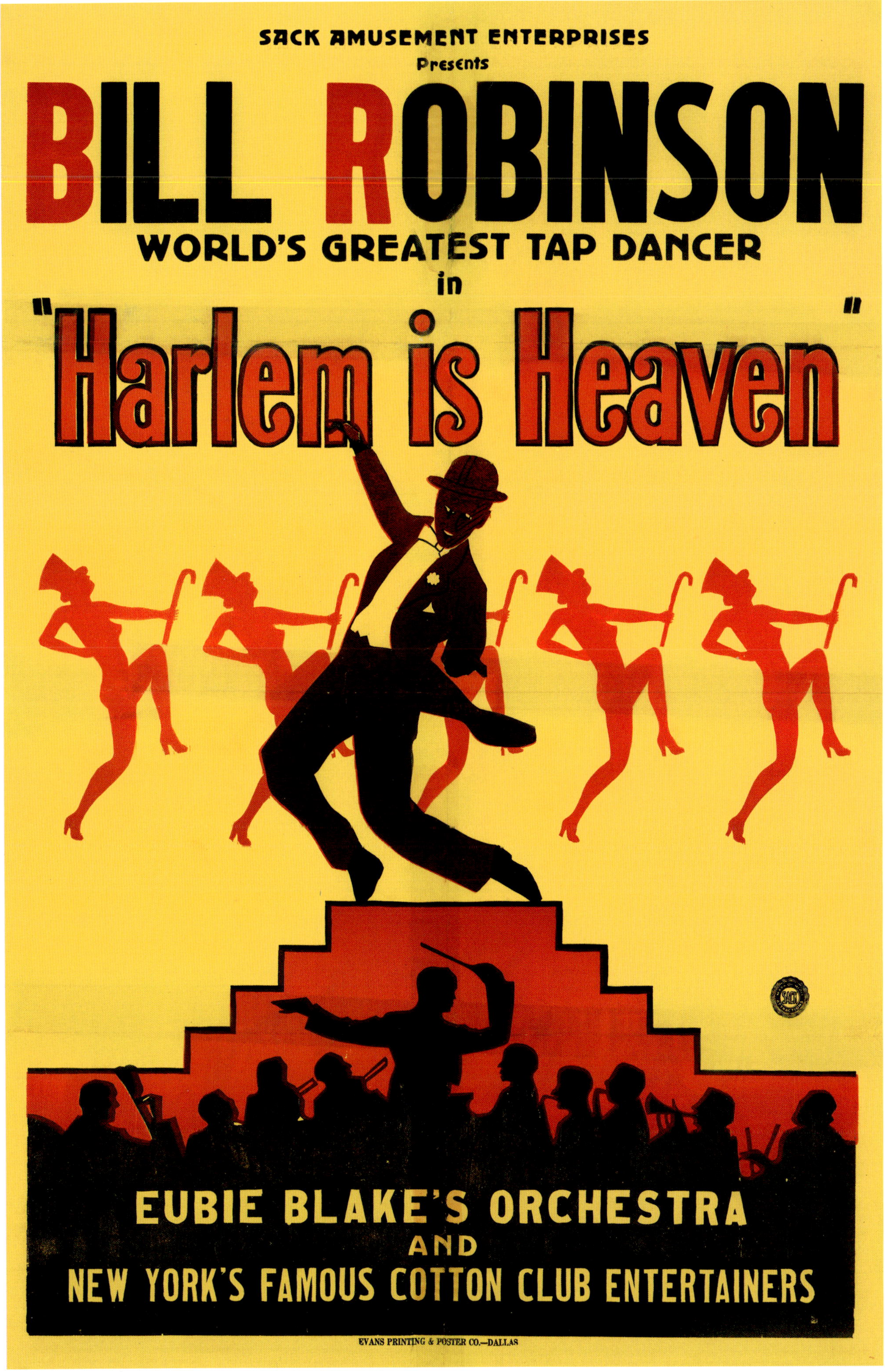
SACK AMUSEMENT ENTERPRISES
Presents
BILL ROBINSON
WORLD'S GREATEST TAP DANCER
in
"Harlem is Heaven"
EUBIE BLAKE'S ORCHESTRA
AND
NEW YORK'S FAMOUS COTTON CLUB ENTERTAINERS
EVANS PRINTING & POSTER CO.—DALLAS

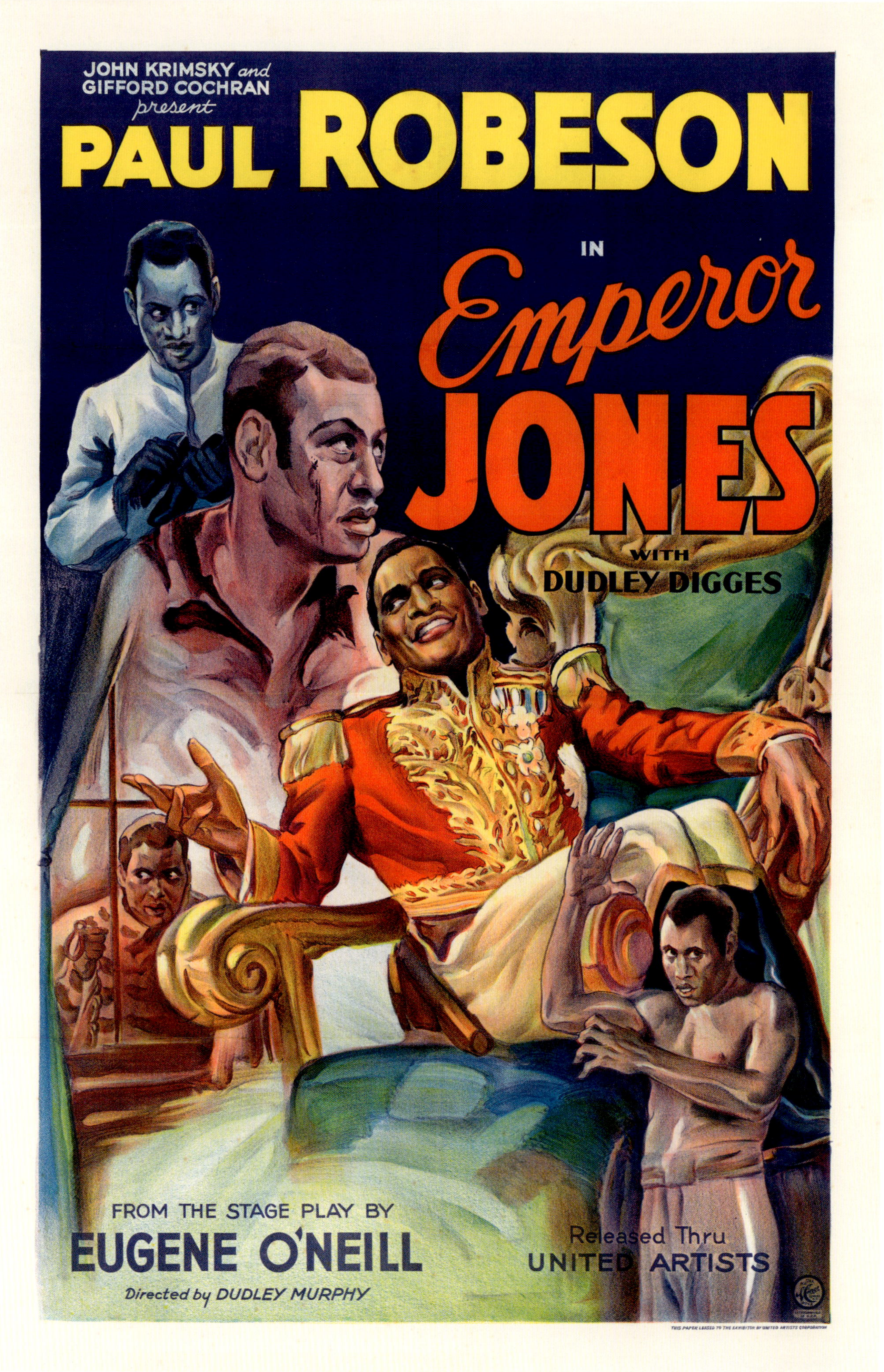
JOHN KRIMSKY and
GIFFORD COCHRAN
present
PAUL ROBESON
IN
Emperor
JONES
WITH
DUDLEY DIGGES
FROM THE STAGE PLAY BY
EUGENE O'NEILL
Directed by DUDLEY MURPHY
Released Thru
UNITED ARTISTS

1935 (Danish theatrical poster)
Princesse Tam-Tam

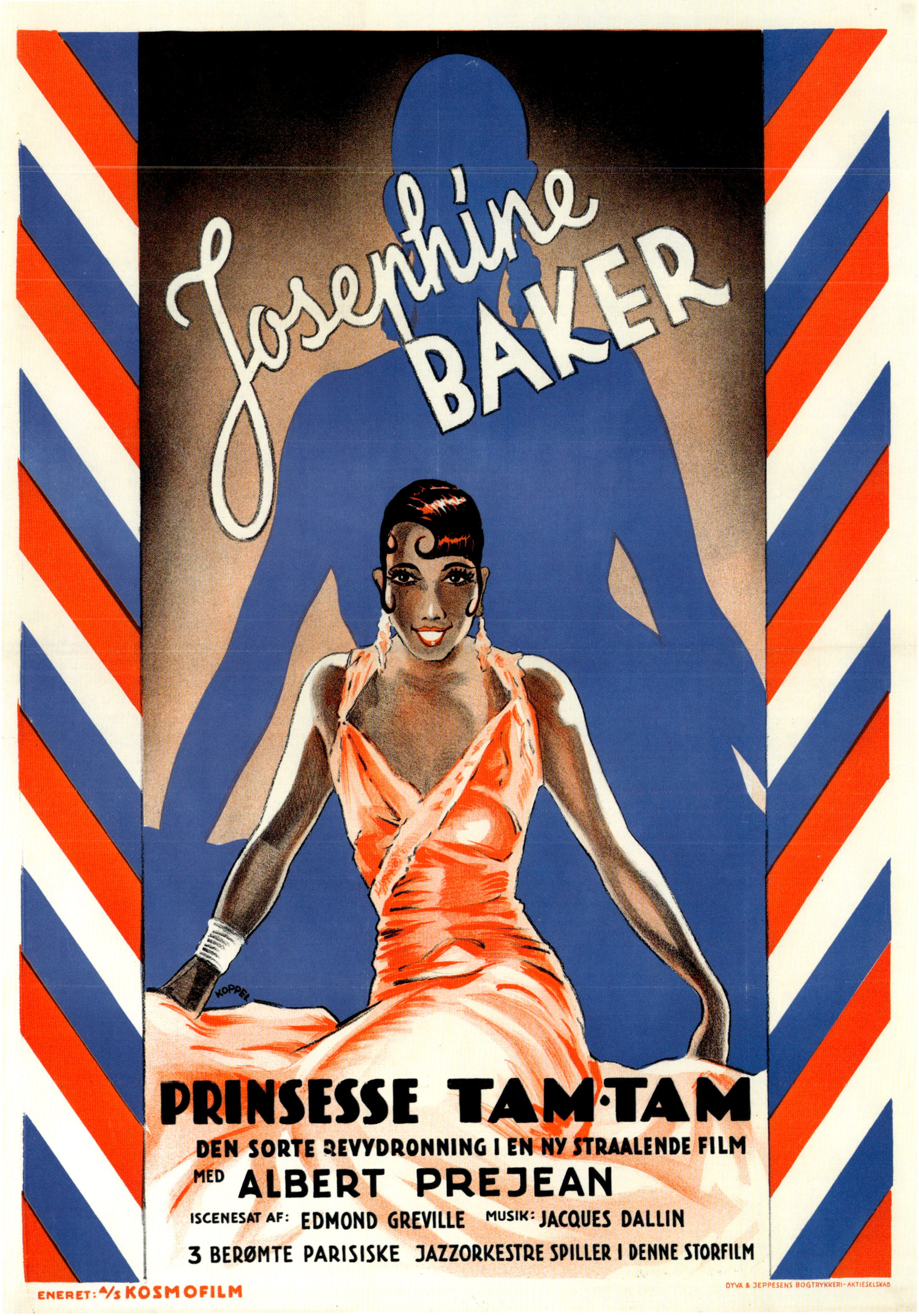

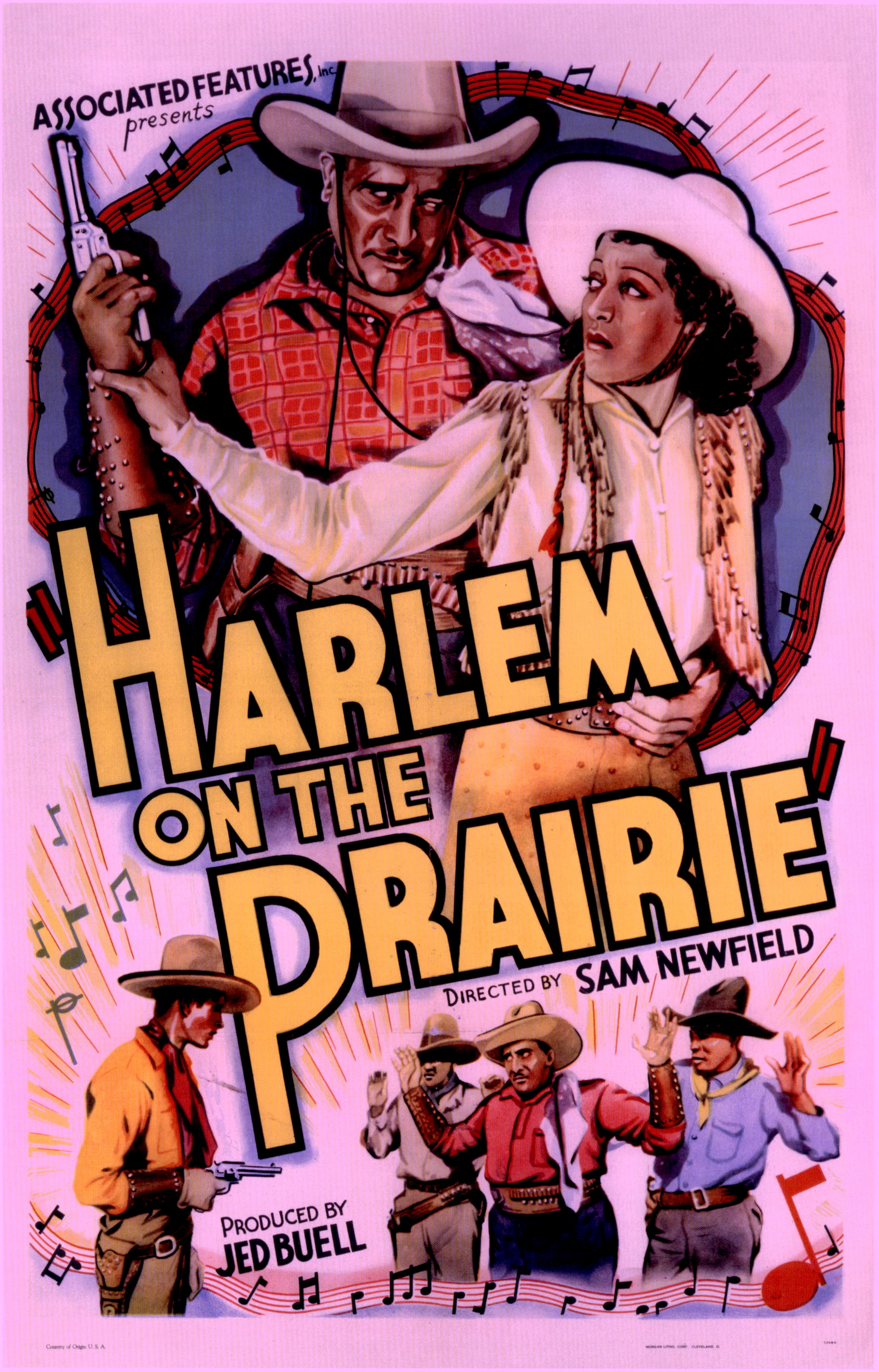
ASSOCIATED FEATURES, Inc.
presents
"HARLEM ON THE PRAIRIE"
DIRECTED BY SAM NEWFIELD
PRODUCED BY JED BUELL
Country of Origin U. S. A.
MORGAN LITHO. CORP. CLEVELAND, O.

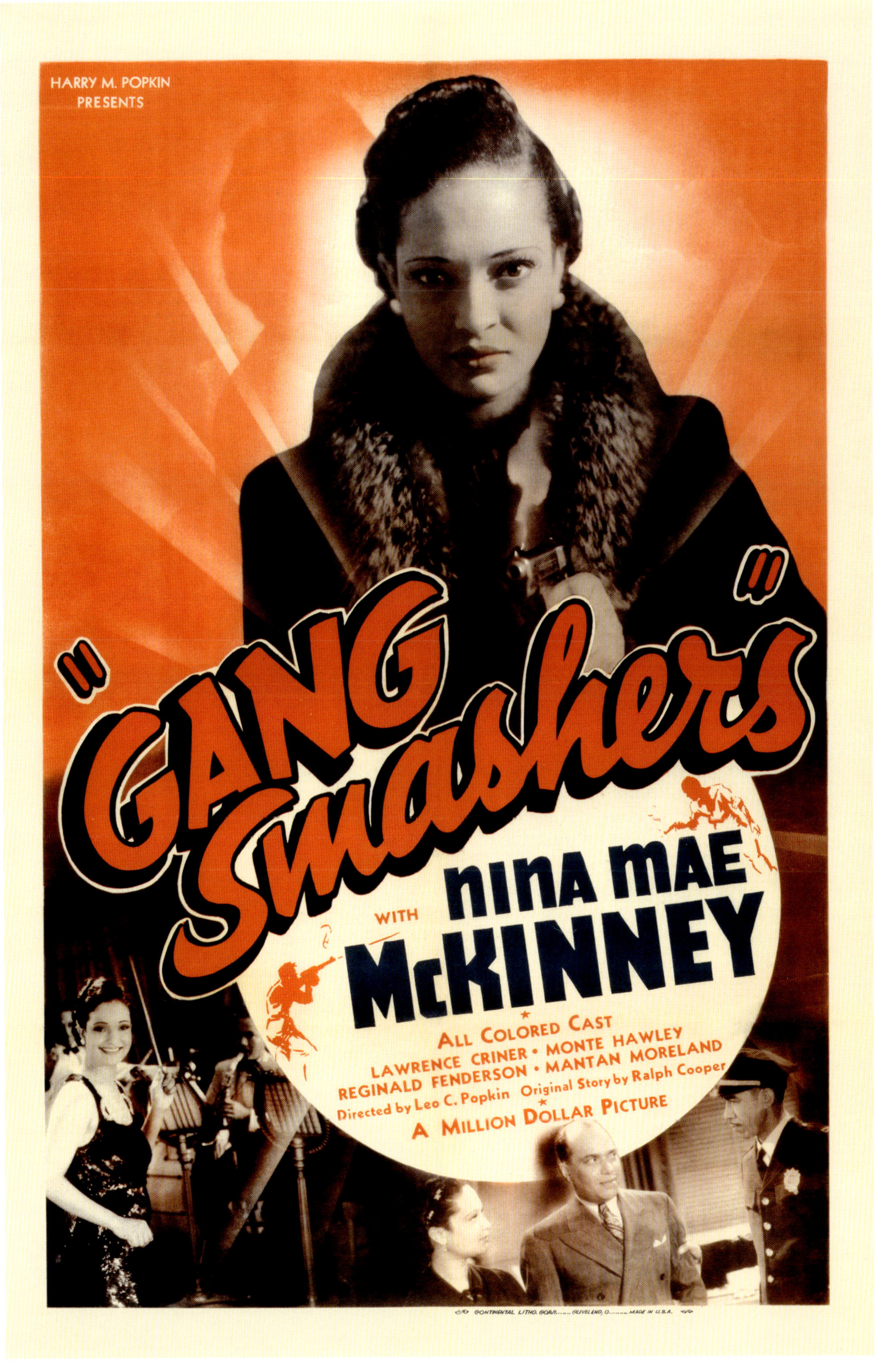
HARRY M. POPKIN
PRESENTS
"GANG Smashers"
WITH
NINA MAE
McKINNEY
ALL COLORED CAST
LAWRENCE CRINER • MONTE HAWLEY
REGINALD FENDERSON • MANTAN MORELAND
Directed by Leo C. Popkin Original Story by Ralph Cooper
A MILLION DOLLAR PICTURE

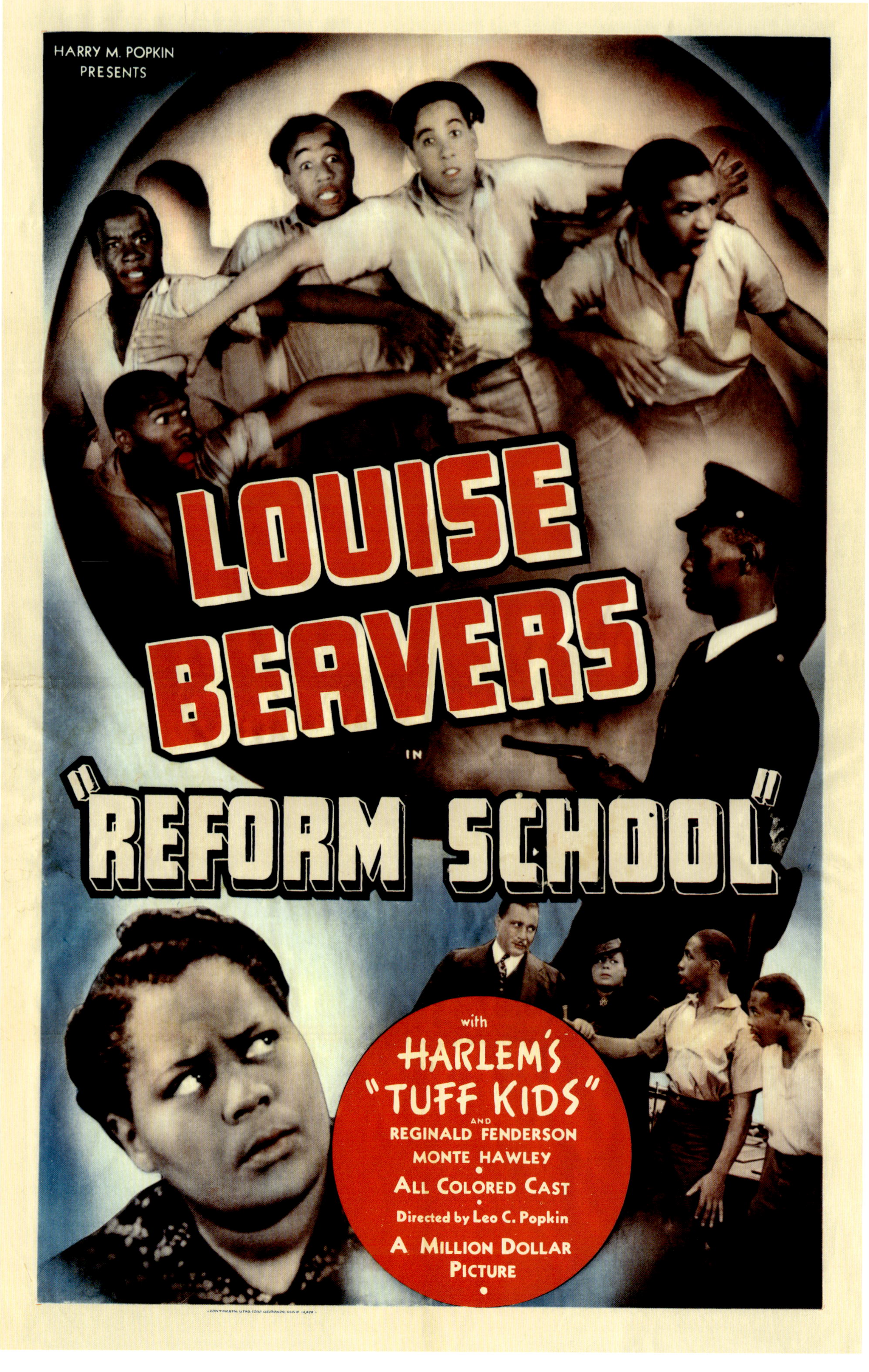
HARRY M. POPKIN
PRESENTS
LOUISE
BEAVERS
IN
"REFORM SCHOOL"
with
HARLEM'S
"TUFF KIDS"
AND
REGINALD FENDERSON
MONTE HAWLEY
ALL COLORED CAST
Directed by Leo C. Popkin
A MILLION DOLLAR
PICTURE

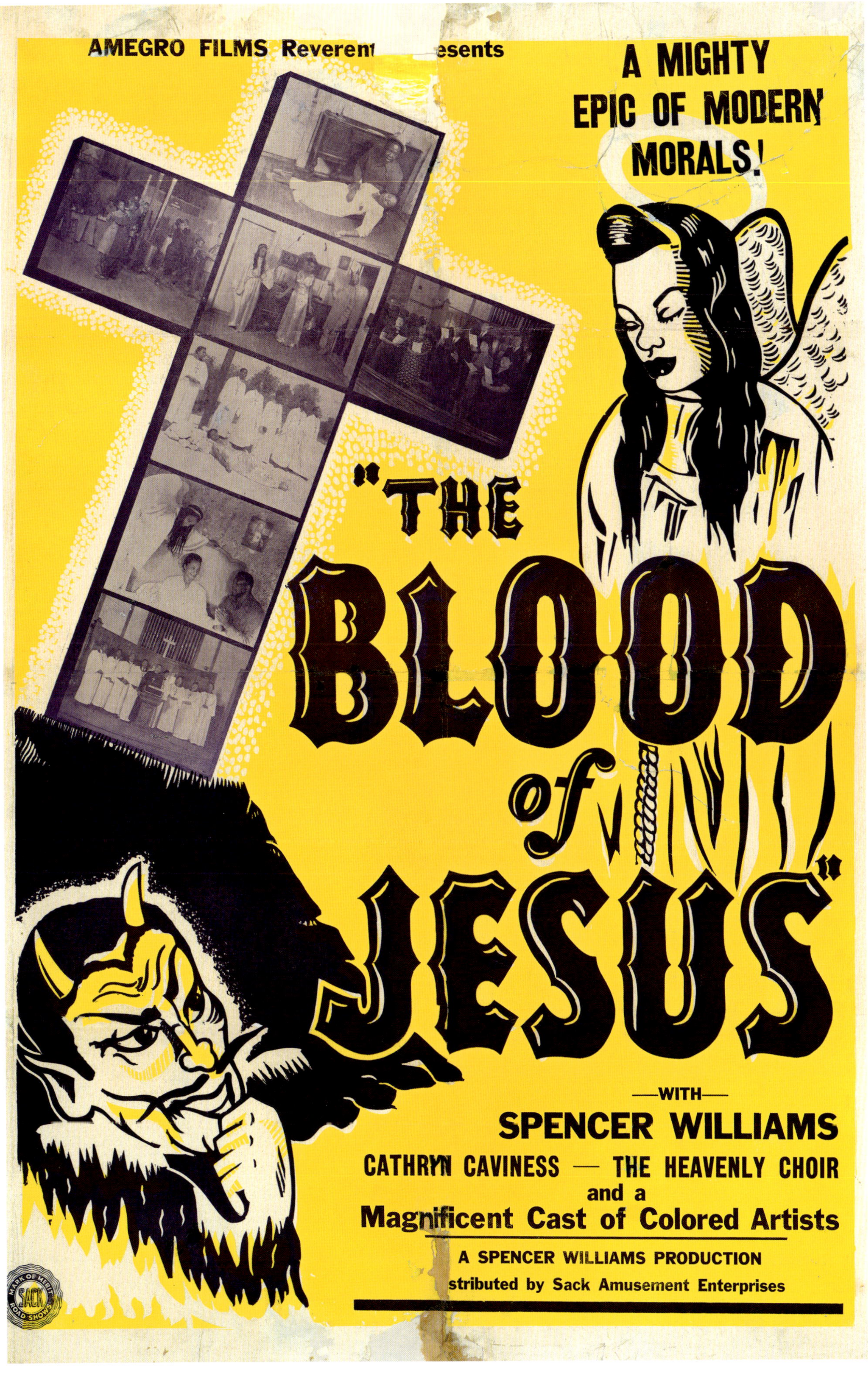
AMEGRO FILMS Reverent esents
A MIGHTY
EPIC OF MODERN
MORALS!
"THE
BLOOD
of
JESUS"
—WITH—
SPENCER WILLIAMS
CATHRYN CAVINESS — THE HEAVENLY CHOIR
and a
Magnificent Cast of Colored Artists
A SPENCER WILLIAMS PRODUCTION
stributed by Sack Amusement Enterprises
MARK OF MERIT
SACK
ROAD SHOWS

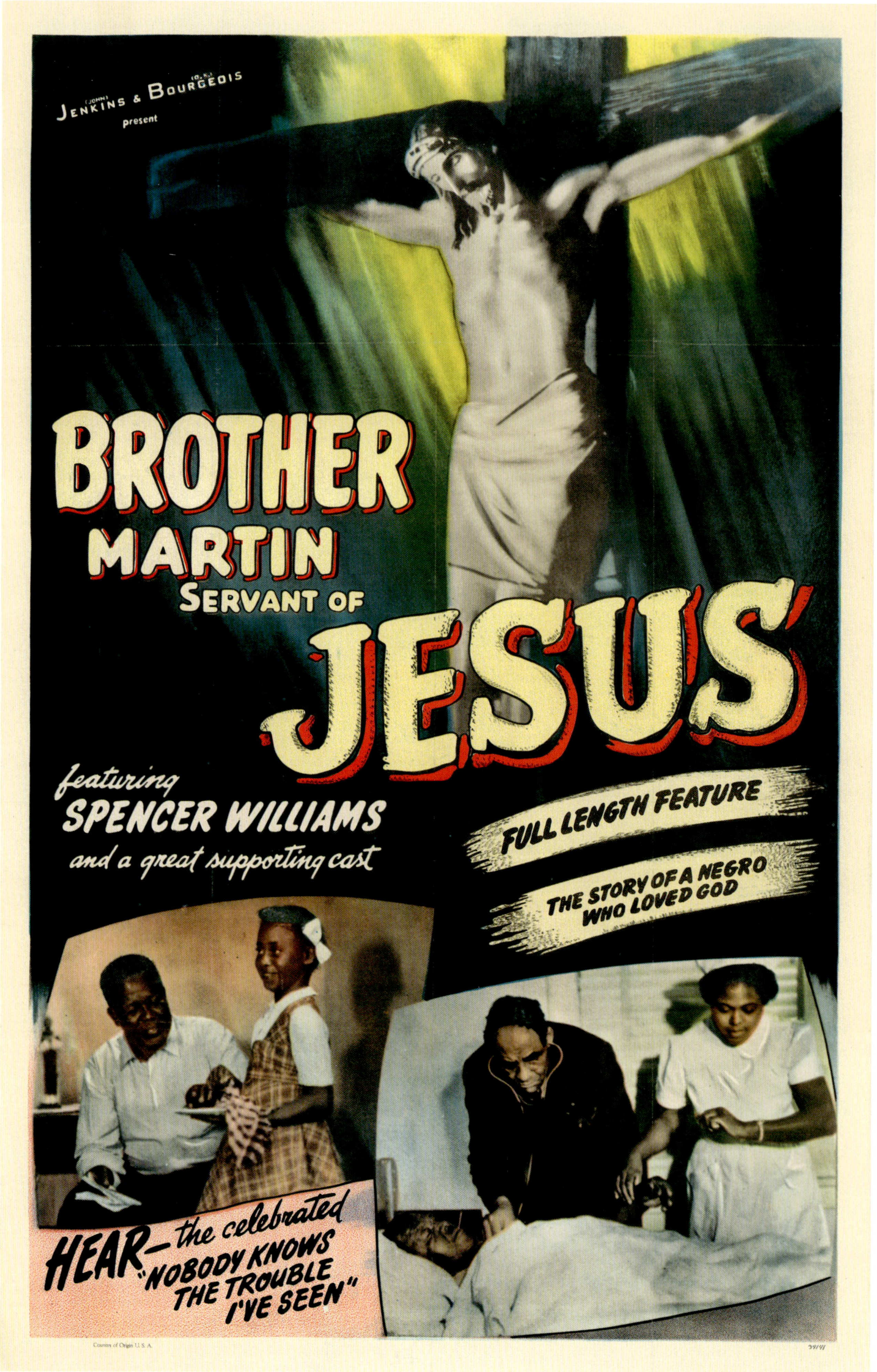
(JOHN) JENKINS & (O.K.) BOURGEOIS
present
BROTHER MARTIN
SERVANT OF
JESUS
featuring
SPENCER WILLIAMS
and a great supporting cast
FULL LENGTH FEATURE
THE STORY OF A NEGRO WHO LOVED GOD
HEAR—the celebrated
"NOBODY KNOWS THE TROUBLE I'VE SEEN"
Country of Origin U.S.A.

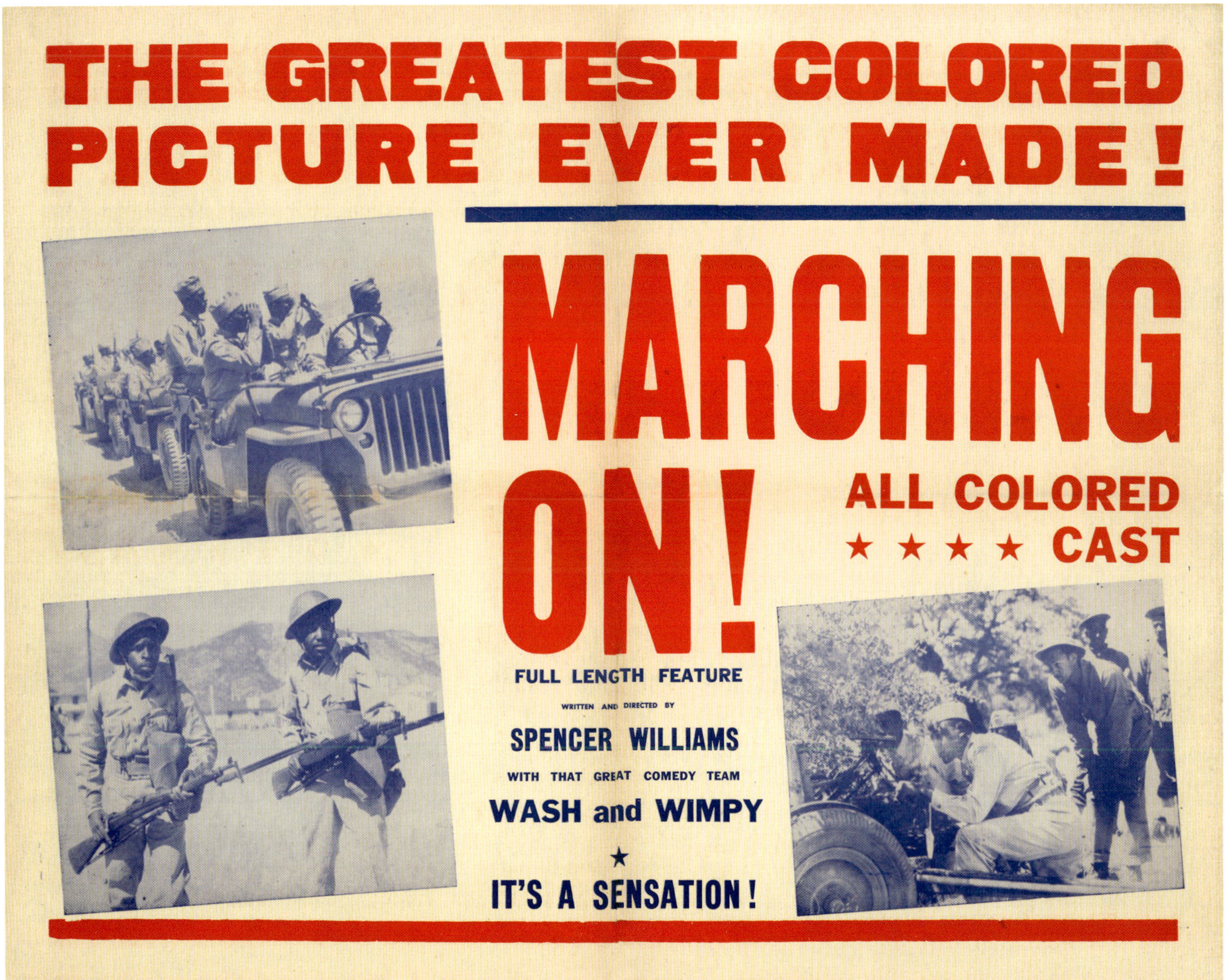
THE GREATEST COLORED PICTURE EVER MADE!
MARCHING ON!
ALL COLORED ★ ★ ★ ★ CAST
FULL LENGTH FEATURE
WRITTEN AND DIRECTED BY
SPENCER WILLIAMS
WITH THAT GREAT COMEDY TEAM
WASH and WIMPY
IT'S A SENSATION!

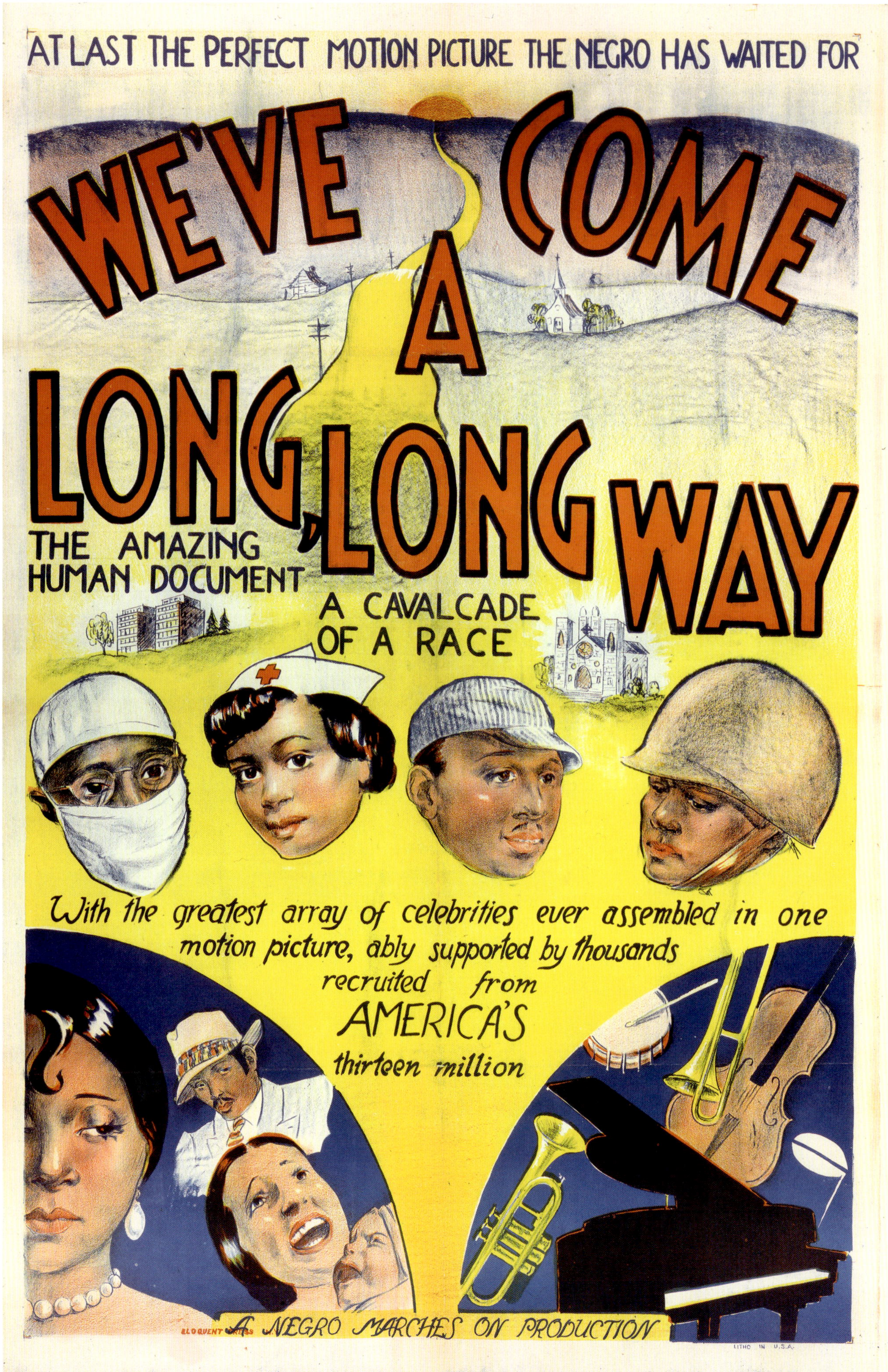
AT LAST THE PERFECT MOTION PICTURE THE NEGRO HAS WAITED FOR
WE'VE COME A LONG, LONG WAY
THE AMAZING HUMAN DOCUMENT
A CAVALCADE OF A RACE
With the greatest array of celebrities ever assembled in one motion picture, ably supported by thousands recruited from AMERICA'S thirteen million
A NEGRO MARCHES ON PRODUCTION
LITHO IN U.S.A.

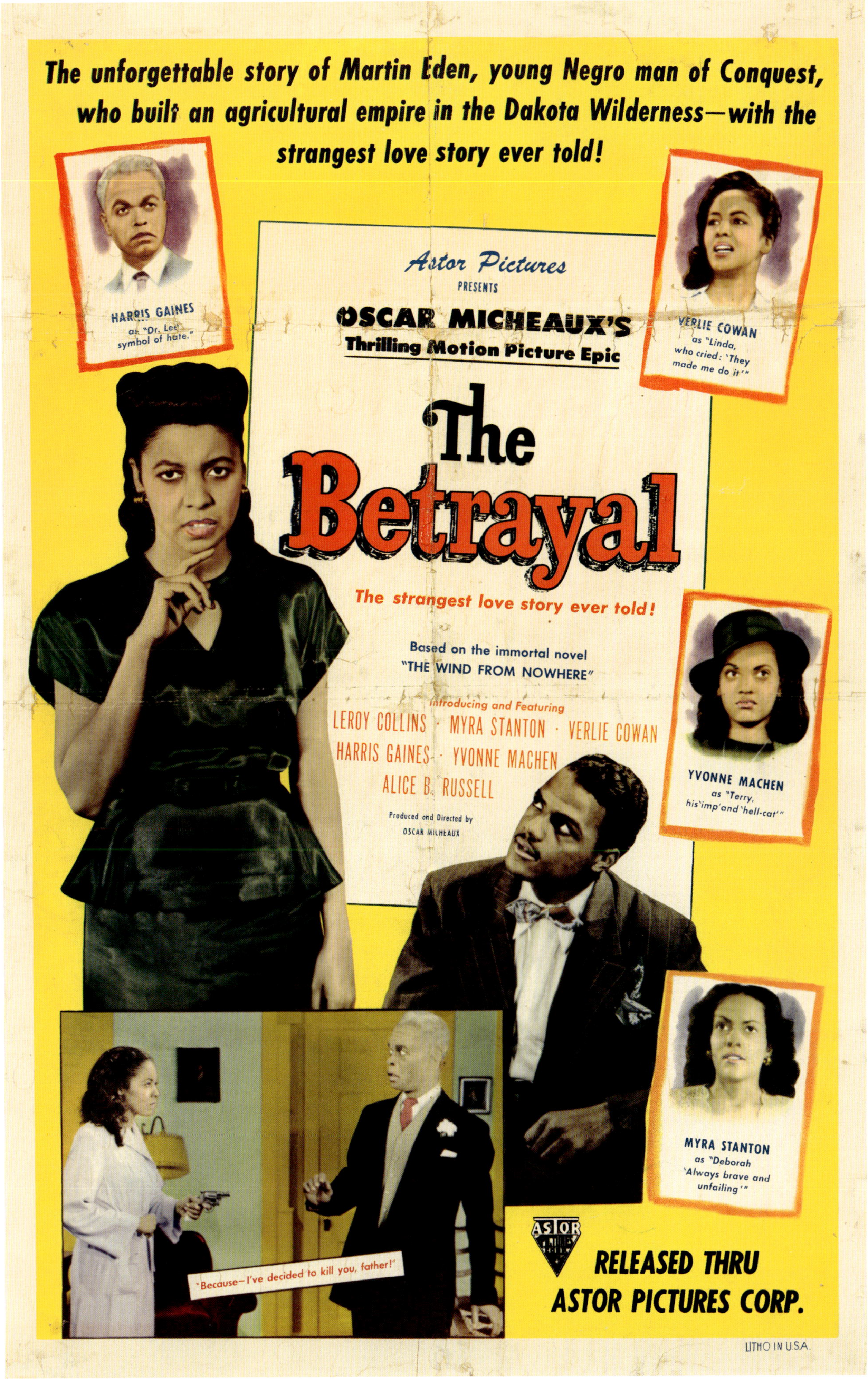
The unforgettable story of Martin Eden, young Negro man of Conquest, who built an agricultural empire in the Dakota Wilderness—with the strangest love story ever told!
HARRIS GAINES
symbol of hate."
Astor Pictures
PRESENTS
OSCAR MICHEAUX'S
Thrilling Motion Picture Epic
VERLIE COWAN
as "Linda,
who cried: 'They
made me do it'"
The Betrayal
The strangest love story ever told!
Based on the immortal novel
"THE WIND FROM NOWHERE"
Introducing and Featuring
LEROY COLLINS · MYRA STANTON · VERLIE COWAN
HARRIS GAINES · YVONNE MACHEN
ALICE B. RUSSELL
Produced and Directed by
OSCAR MICHEAUX
YVONNE MACHEN
as "Terry,
his 'imp' and 'hell-cat'"
MYRA STANTON
as "Deborah
'Always brave and
unfailing'"
"Because—I've decided to kill you, father!"
ASTOR
RELEASED THRU
ASTOR PICTURES CORP.
LITHO IN U.S.A.

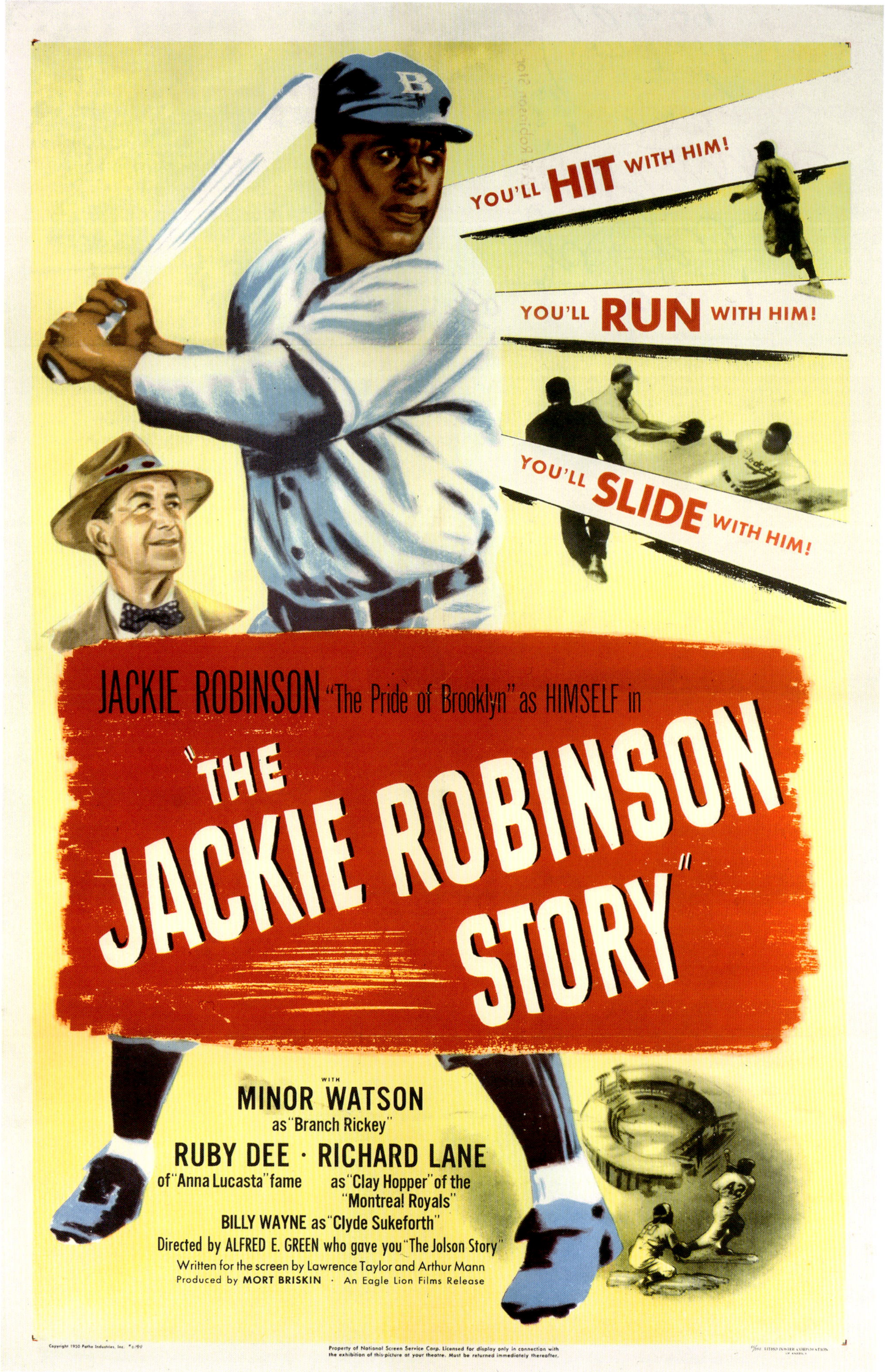
YOU'LL HIT WITH HIM!
YOU'LL RUN WITH HIM!
YOU'LL SLIDE WITH HIM!
JACKIE ROBINSON "The Pride of Brooklyn" as HIMSELF in
"THE JACKIE ROBINSON STORY"
WITH
MINOR WATSON
as "Branch Rickey"
RUBY DEE · RICHARD LANE
of "Anna Lucasta" fame
as "Clay Hopper" of the "Montreal Royals"
BILLY WAYNE as "Clyde Sukeforth"
Directed by ALFRED E. GREEN who gave you "The Jolson Story"
Written for the screen by Lawrence Taylor and Arthur Mann
Produced by MORT BRISKIN · An Eagle Lion Films Release

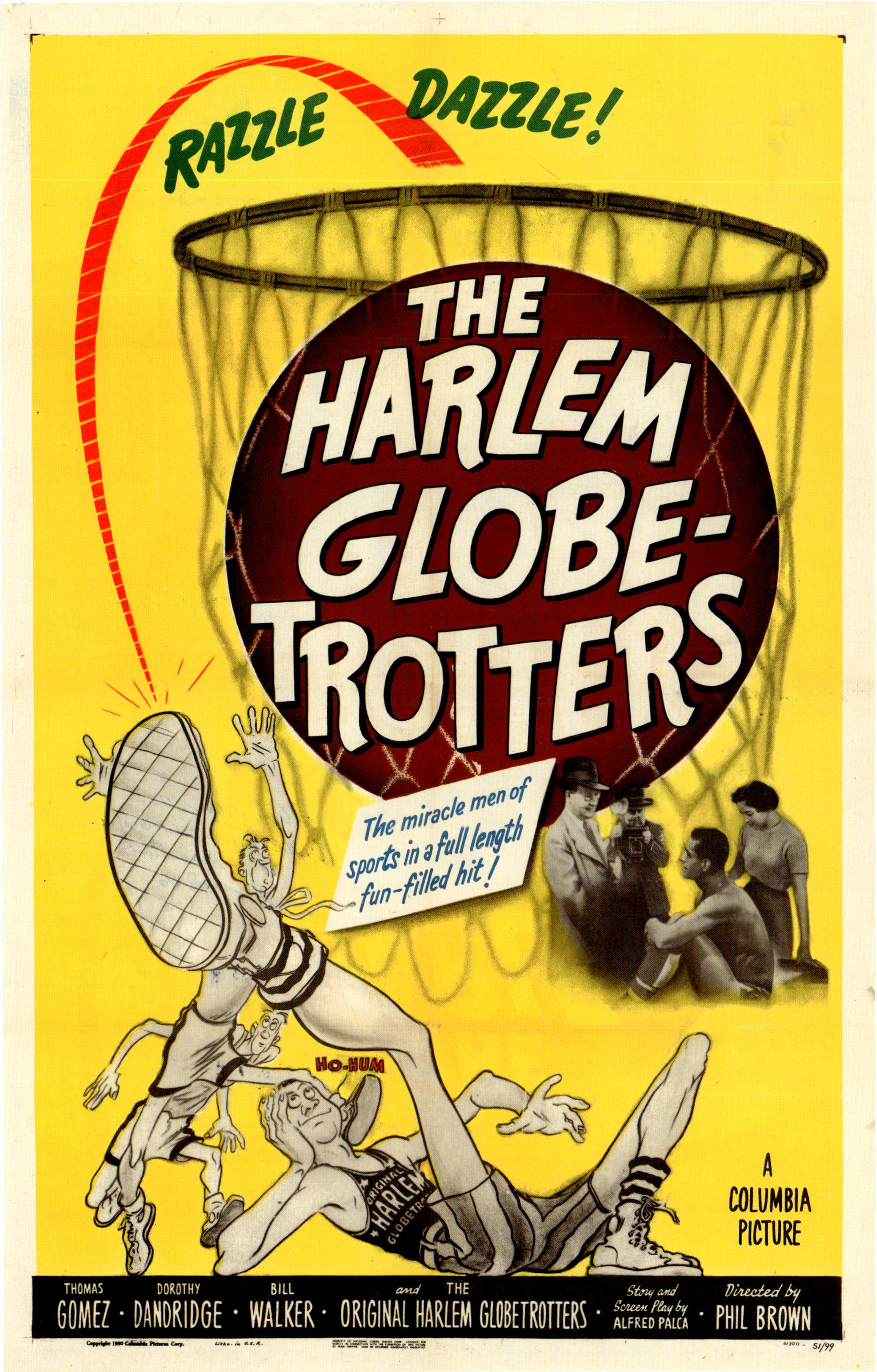
RAZZLE DAZZLE!
THE HARLEM GLOBE-TROTTERS
The miracle men of sports in a full length fun-filled hit!
HO-HUM
ORIGINAL HARLEM GLOBETROTTERS
A COLUMBIA PICTURE
THOMAS GOMEZ · DOROTHY DANDRIDGE · BILL WALKER · and THE ORIGINAL HARLEM GLOBETROTTERS · Story and Screen Play by ALFRED PALCA · Directed by PHIL BROWN

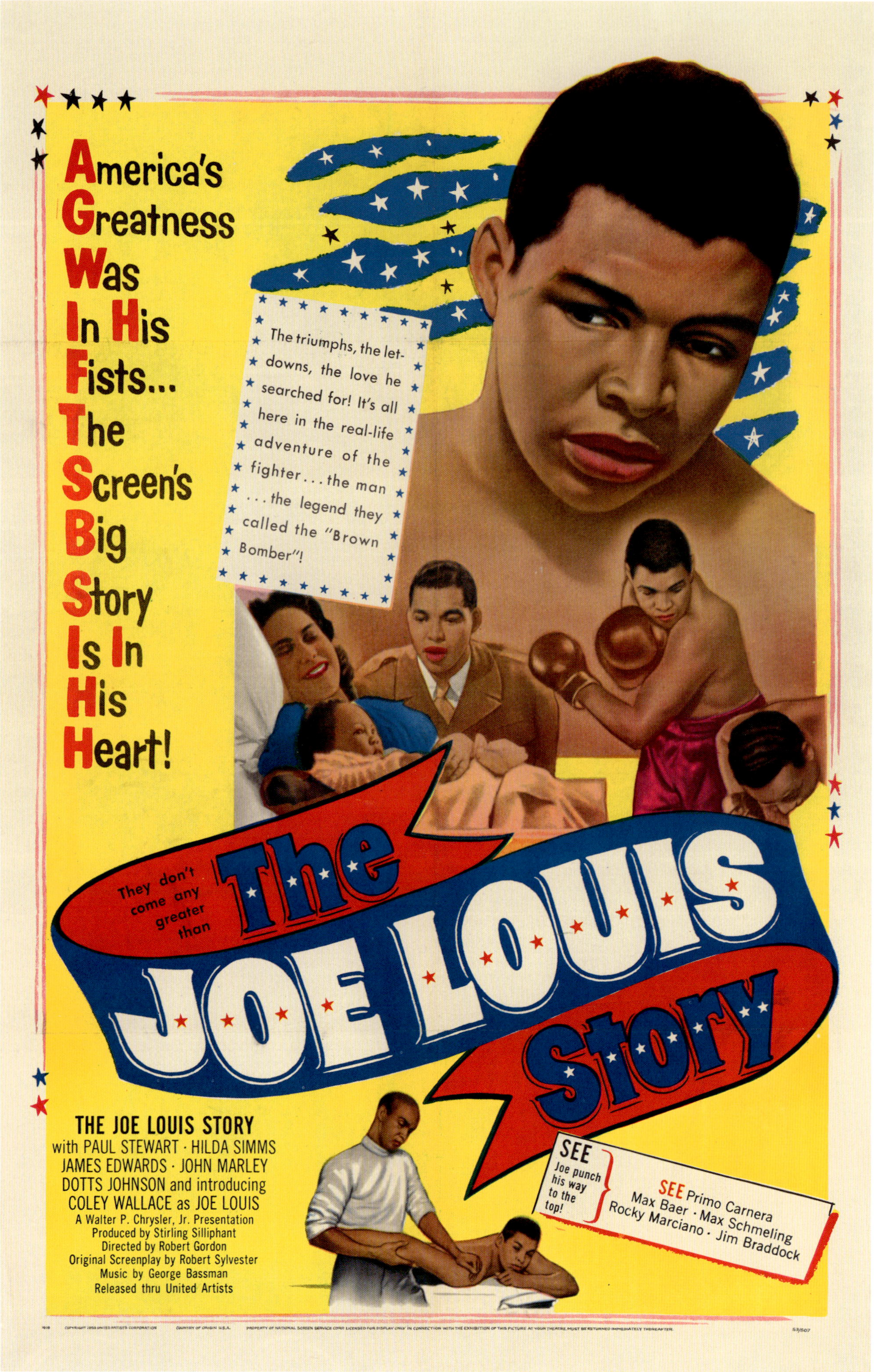
America's Greatness Was In His Fists... The Screen's Big Story Is In His Heart!
The triumphs, the let-downs, the love he searched for! It's all here in the real-life adventure of the fighter... the man ... the legend they called the "Brown Bomber"!
They don't come any greater than
The JOE LOUIS Story
SEE Joe punch his way to the top!
SEE Primo Carnera Max Baer · Max Schmeling Rocky Marciano · Jim Braddock
THE JOE LOUIS STORY
with PAUL STEWART · HILDA SIMMS
JAMES EDWARDS · JOHN MARLEY
DOTTS JOHNSON and introducing
COLEY WALLACE as JOE LOUIS
A Walter P. Chrysler, Jr. Presentation
Produced by Stirling Silliphant
Directed by Robert Gordon
Original Screenplay by Robert Sylvester
Music by George Bassman
Released thru United Artists
COPYRIGHT 1953 UNITED ARTISTS CORPORATION
COUNTRY OF ORIGIN U.S.A.
PROPERTY OF NATIONAL SCREEN SERVICE CORP. LICENSED FOR DISPLAY ONLY IN CONNECTION WITH THE EXHIBITION OF THIS PICTURE AT YOUR THEATRE. MUST BE RETURNED IMMEDIATELY THEREAFTER.
53/507

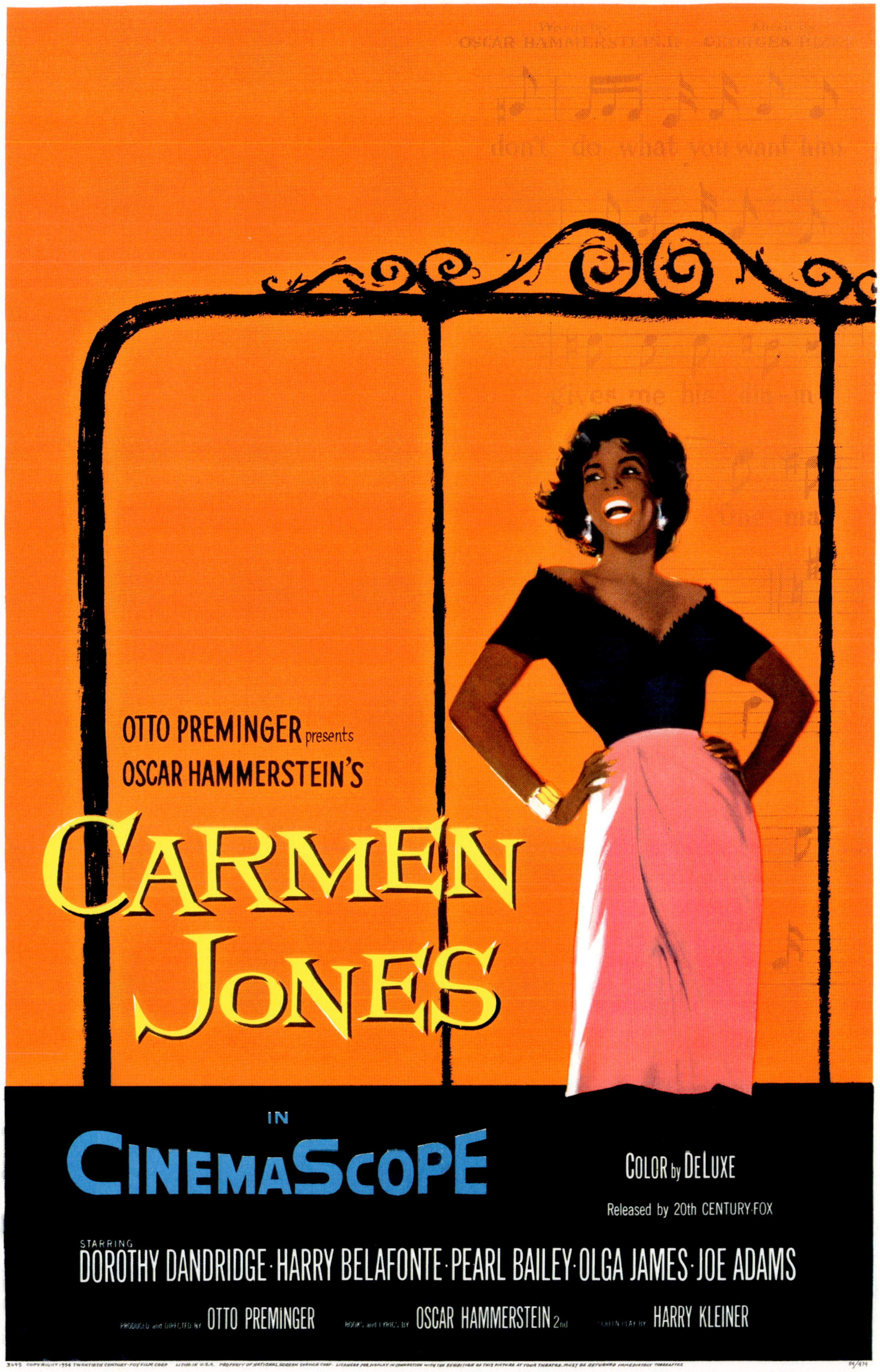
OTTO PREMINGER presents
OSCAR HAMMERSTEIN'S
CARMEN JONES
IN
CINEMASCOPE
COLOR by DELUXE
Released by 20th CENTURY-FOX
STARRING
DOROTHY DANDRIDGE · HARRY BELAFONTE · PEARL BAILEY · OLGA JAMES · JOE ADAMS
OTTO PREMINGER
OSCAR HAMMERSTEIN 2nd
HARRY KLEINER

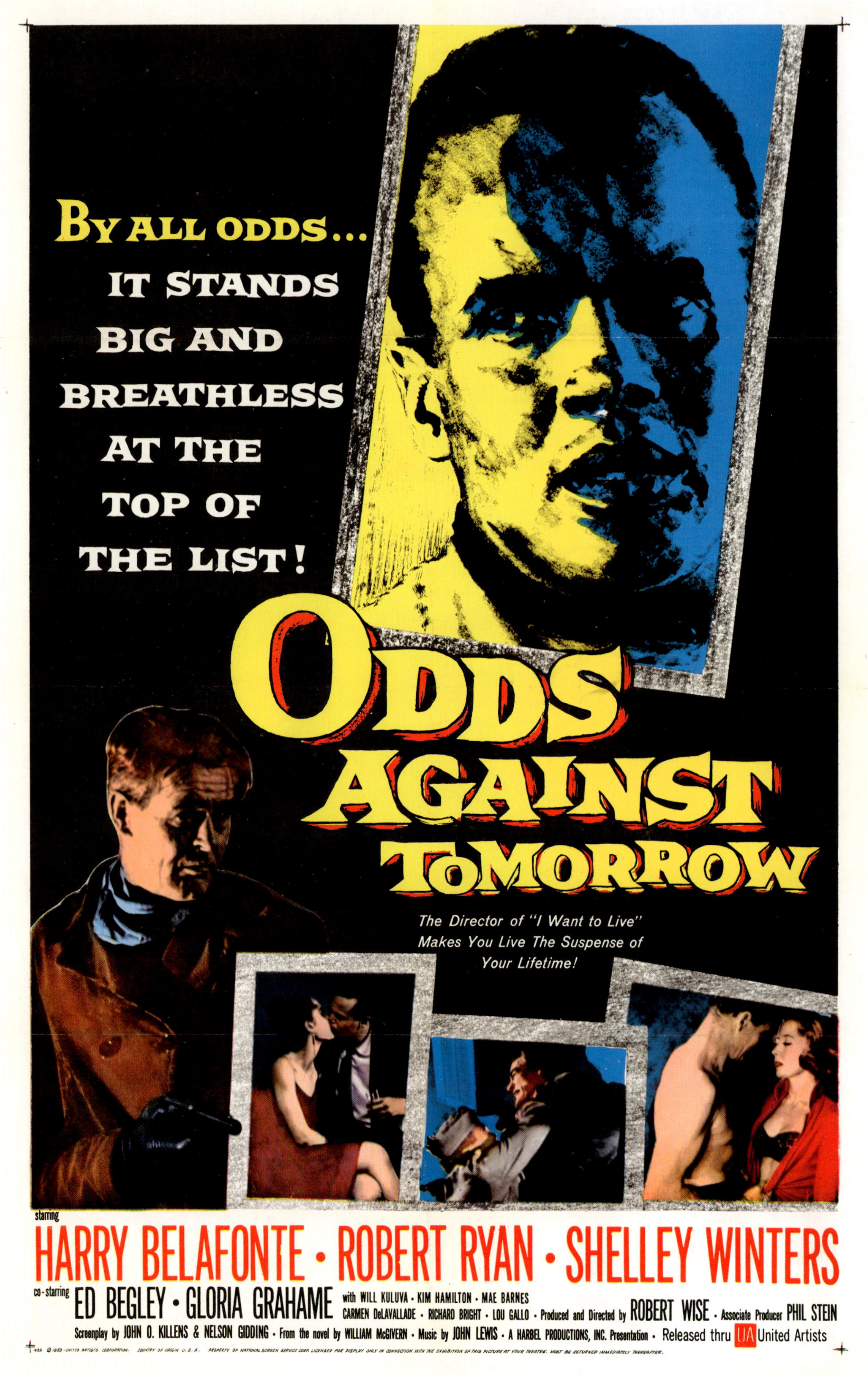
BY ALL ODDS...
IT STANDS
BIG AND
BREATHLESS
AT THE
TOP OF
THE LIST!
ODDS
AGAINST
TOMORROW
The Director of "I Want to Live"
Makes You Live The Suspense of
Your Lifetime!
starring
HARRY BELAFONTE · ROBERT RYAN · SHELLEY WINTERS
co-starring ED BEGLEY · GLORIA GRAHAME with WILL KULUVA · KIM HAMILTON · MAE BARNES
CARMEN DeLAVALLADE · RICHARD BRIGHT · LOU GALLO · Produced and Directed by ROBERT WISE · Associate Producer PHIL STEIN
Screenplay by JOHN O. KILLENS & NELSON GIDDING · From the novel by WILLIAM McGIVERN · Music by JOHN LEWIS · A HARBEL PRODUCTIONS, INC. Presentation · Released thru UA United Artists
409 © 1959 - UNITED ARTISTS CORPORATION. COUNTRY OF ORIGIN U.S.A. PROPERTY OF NATIONAL SCREEN SERVICE CORP. LICENSED FOR DISPLAY ONLY IN CONNECTION WITH THE EXHIBITION OF THIS PICTURE AT YOUR THEATRE. MUST BE RETURNED IMMEDIATELY THEREAFTER.

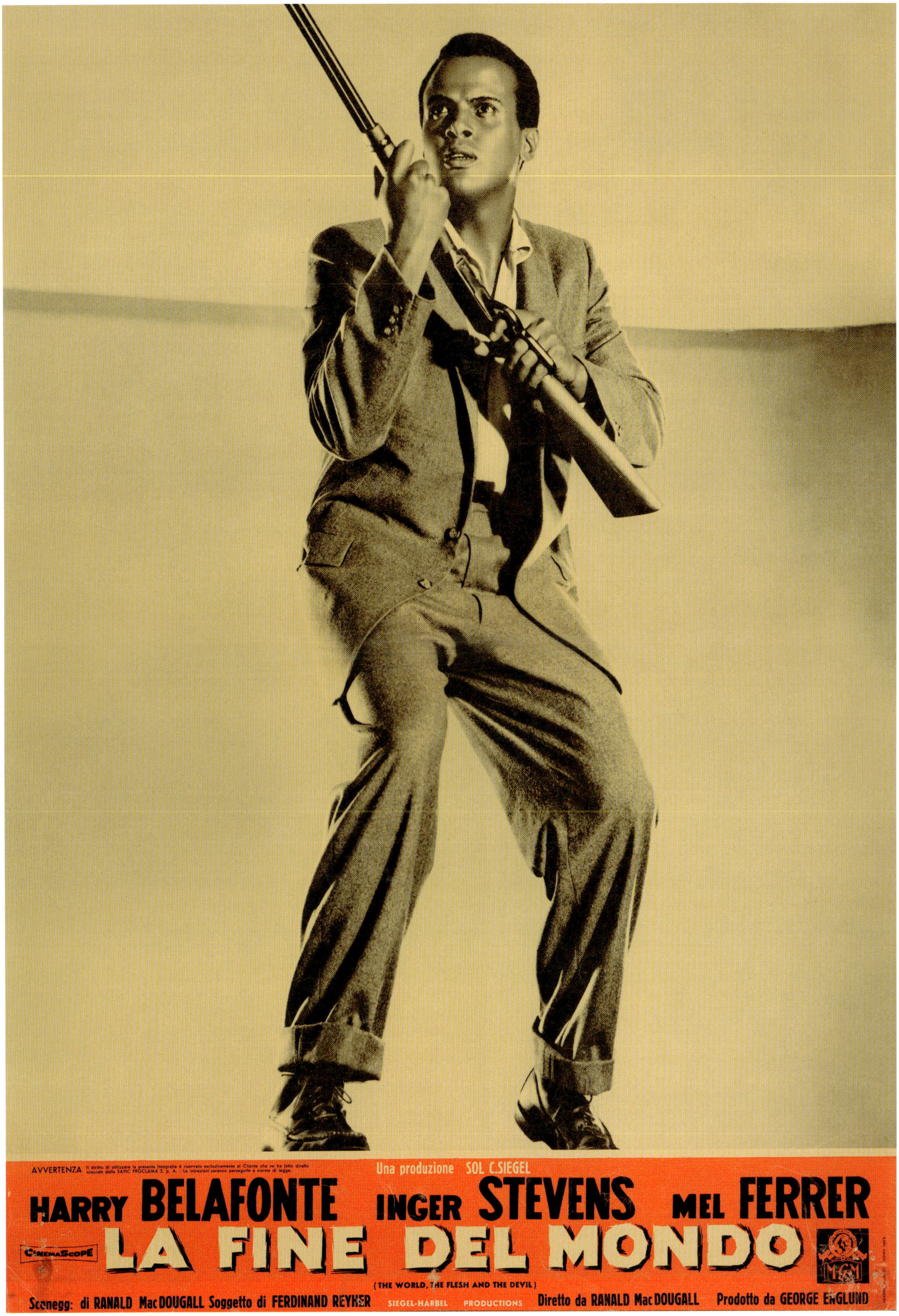
AVVERTENZA Il diritto di utilizzare la presente fotografia è riservato esclusivamente al Cliente che ne ha fatto diretto acquisto dalla SAPIC PROCLAMA S. p. A. - Le infrazioni saranno perseguite a norma di legge.
Una produzione SOL C.SIEGEL
HARRY BELAFONTE INGER STEVENS MEL FERRER
CINEMASCOPE
LA FINE DEL MONDO
MGM
(THE WORLD, THE FLESH AND THE DEVIL)
Scenegg: di RANALD MacDOUGALL Soggetto di FERDINAND REYHER
SIEGEL-HARBEL PRODUCTIONS
Diretto da RANALD MacDOUGALL Prodotto da GEORGE ENGLUND

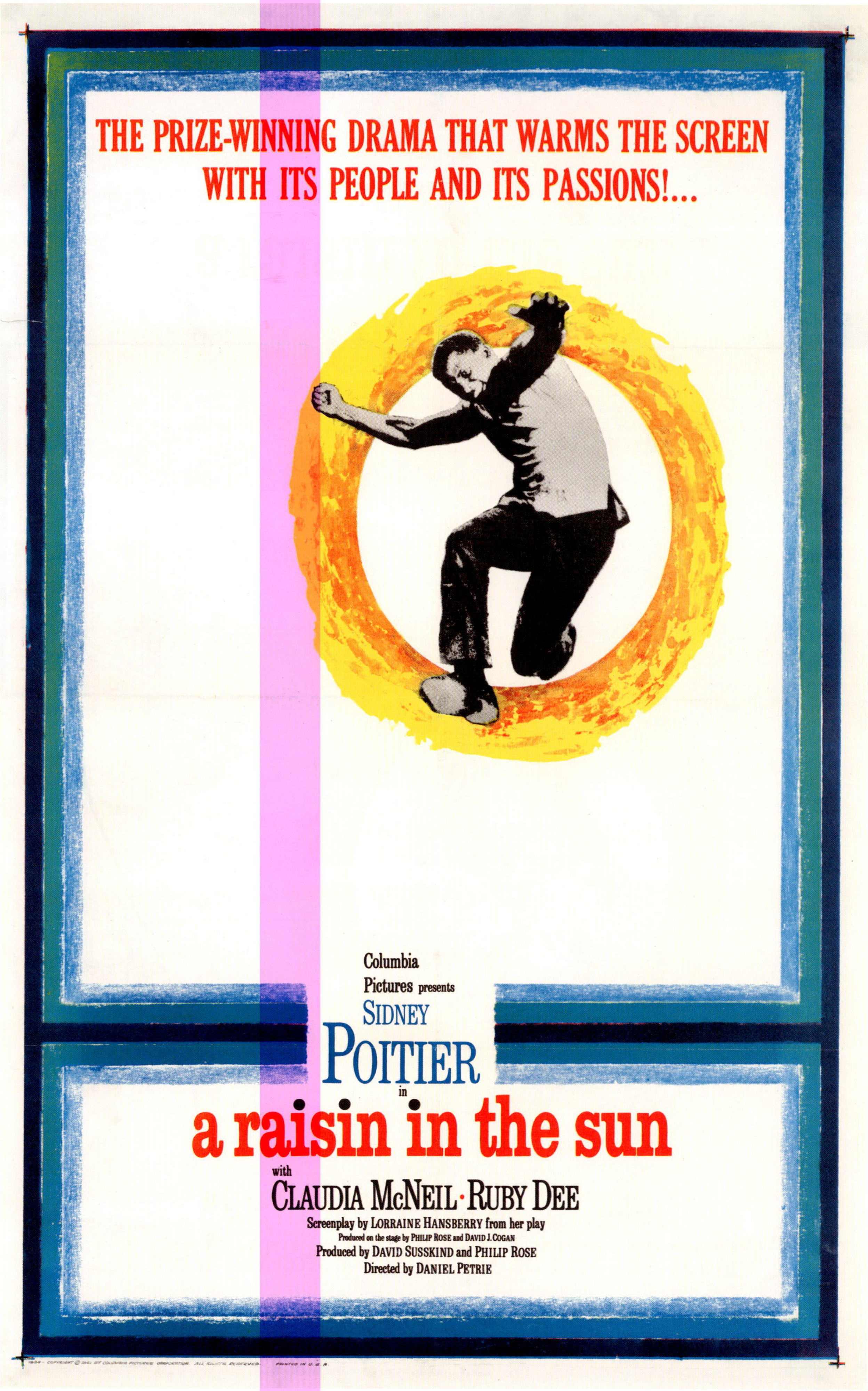
THE PRIZE-WINNING DRAMA THAT WARMS THE SCREEN
WITH ITS PEOPLE AND ITS PASSIONS!...
Columbia
Pictures presents
SIDNEY
POITIER
in
a raisin in the sun
with
CLAUDIA McNEIL · RUBY DEE
Screenplay by LORRAINE HANSBERRY from her play
Produced on the stage by PHILIP ROSE and DAVID J. COGAN
Produced by DAVID SUSSKIND and PHILIP ROSE
Directed by DANIEL PETRIE
COPYRIGHT © 1961 BY COLUMBIA PICTURES CORPORATION. ALL RIGHTS RESERVED.
PRINTED IN U.S.A.

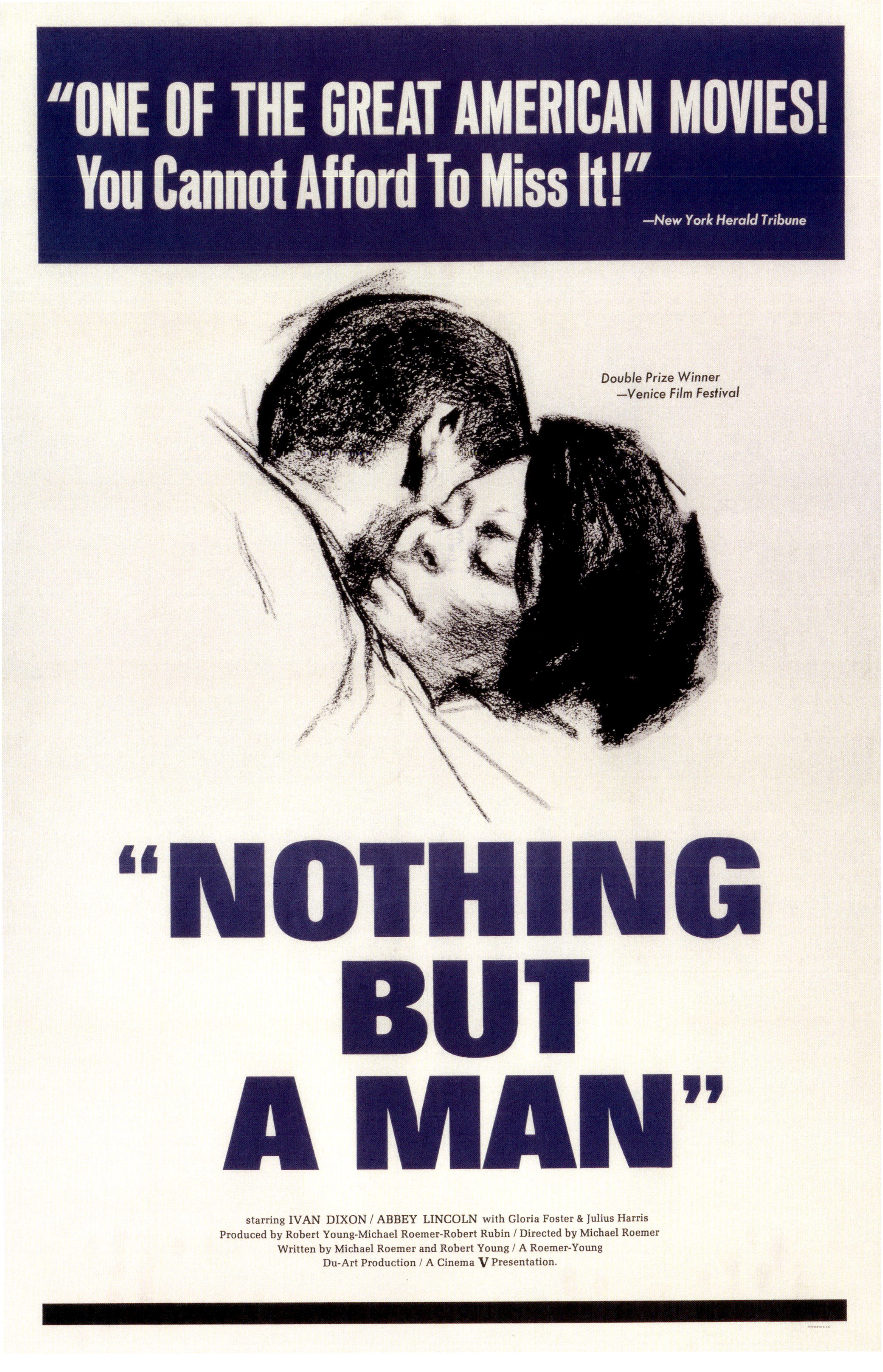
"ONE OF THE GREAT AMERICAN MOVIES!
You Cannot Afford To Miss It!"
—New York Herald Tribune
Double Prize Winner
—Venice Film Festival
"NOTHING
BUT
A MAN"
starring IVAN DIXON / ABBEY LINCOLN with Gloria Foster & Julius Harris
Produced by Robert Young-Michael Roemer-Robert Rubin / Directed by Michael Roemer
Written by Michael Roemer and Robert Young / A Roemer-Young
Du-Art Production / A Cinema V Presentation.

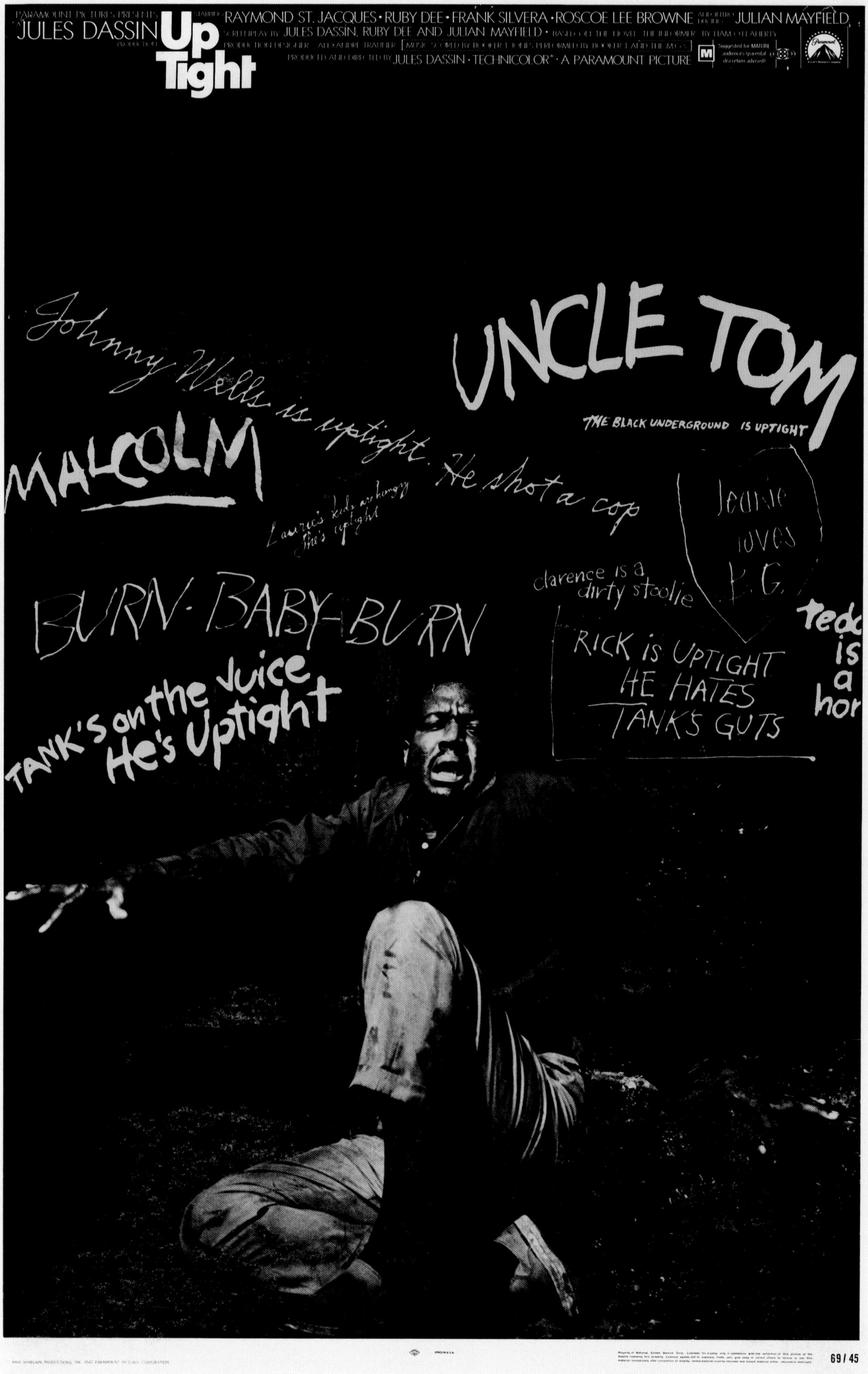
PARAMOUNT PICTURES PRESENTS
A JULES DASSIN PRODUCTION
Up Tight
STARRING RAYMOND ST. JACQUES • RUBY DEE • FRANK SILVERA • ROSCOE LEE BROWNE AND INTRODUCING JULIAN MAYFIELD
SCREENPLAY BY JULES DASSIN, RUBY DEE AND JULIAN MAYFIELD • BASED ON THE NOVEL "THE INFORMER" BY LIAM O'FLAHERTY
PRODUCTION DESIGNER ALEXANDRE TRAUNER
MUSIC SCORED BY BOOKER T. JONES PERFORMED BY BOOKER T. AND THE M.G.'S
PRODUCED AND DIRECTED BY JULES DASSIN • TECHNICOLOR® • A PARAMOUNT PICTURE
M
Suggested for MATURE audiences (parental discretion advised)
Paramount
Johnny Wells is uptight. He shot a cop
UNCLE TOM
THE BLACK UNDERGROUND IS UPTIGHT
MALCOLM
Laurie's kids are hungry She's uptight
Jeanie loves B.G.
clarence is a dirty stoolie
BURN-BABY-BURN
tedd is a hor
RICK is UPTIGHT HE HATES TANKS GUTS
TANK'S on the Juice He's Uptight
69/45

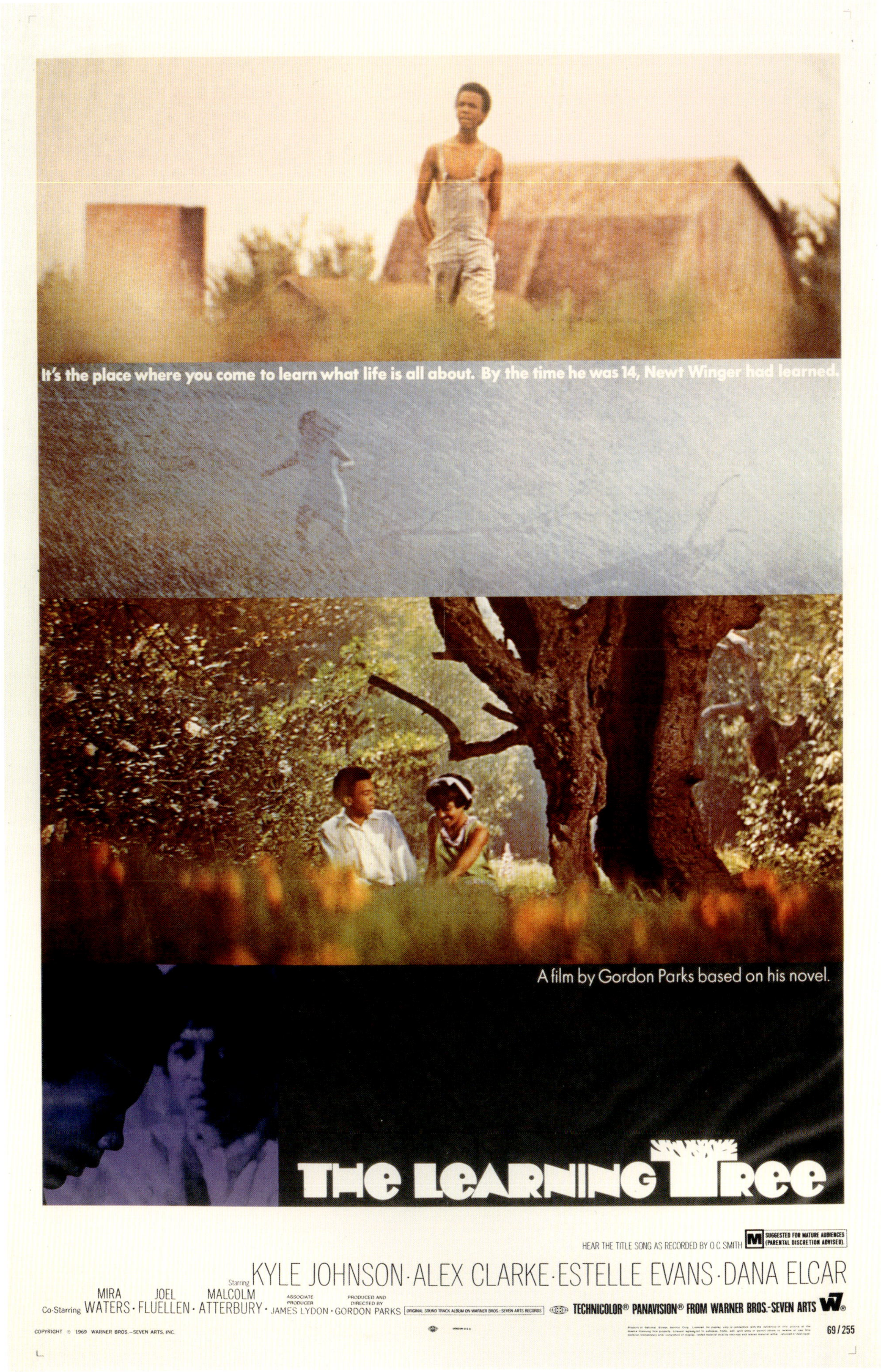
It's the place where you come to learn what life is all about. By the time he was 14, Newt Winger had learned.
A film by Gordon Parks based on his novel.
THE LEARNING TREE
HEAR THE TITLE SONG AS RECORDED BY O.C SMITH
M SUGGESTED FOR MATURE AUDIENCES (PARENTAL DISCRETION ADVISED).
Starring KYLE JOHNSON · ALEX CLARKE · ESTELLE EVANS · DANA ELCAR
Co-Starring MIRA WATERS · JOEL FLUELLEN · MALCOLM ATTERBURY · ASSOCIATE PRODUCER JAMES LYDON · PRODUCED AND DIRECTED BY GORDON PARKS
ORIGINAL SOUND TRACK ALBUM ON WARNER BROS.-SEVEN ARTS RECORDS
TECHNICOLOR® PANAVISION® FROM WARNER BROS.-SEVEN ARTS
COPYRIGHT © 1969 WARNER BROS.—SEVEN ARTS, INC.
69/255

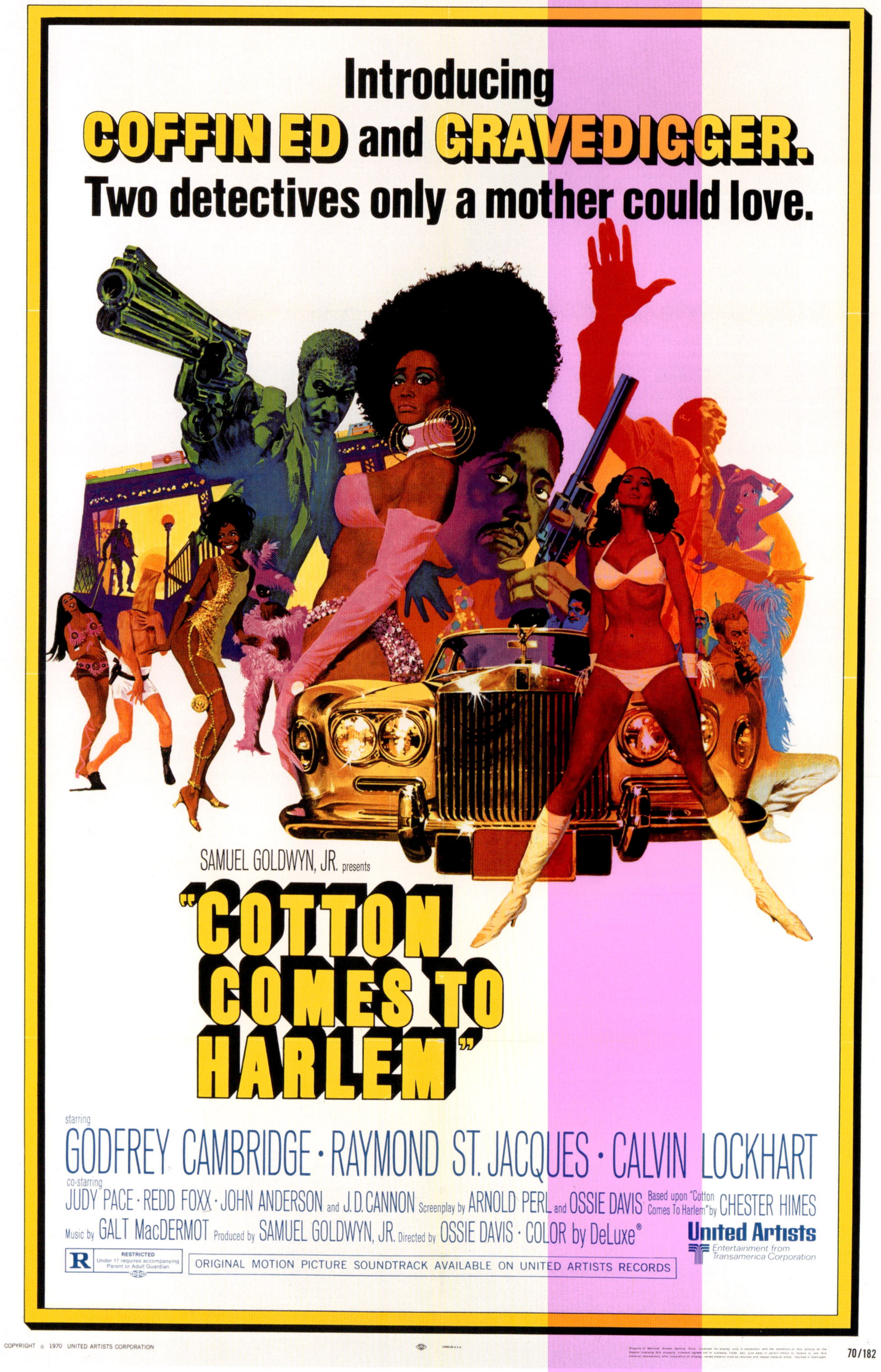
Introducing
COFFIN ED and GRAVEDIGGER.
Two detectives only a mother could love.
SAMUEL GOLDWYN, JR. presents
"COTTON COMES TO HARLEM"
starring
GODFREY CAMBRIDGE · RAYMOND ST. JACQUES · CALVIN LOCKHART
co-starring
JUDY PACE · REDD FOXX · JOHN ANDERSON and J.D. CANNON Screenplay by ARNOLD PERL and OSSIE DAVIS Based upon "Cotton Comes To Harlem" by CHESTER HIMES
Music by GALT MacDERMOT Produced by SAMUEL GOLDWYN, JR. Directed by OSSIE DAVIS · COLOR by DeLuxe®
United Artists
Entertainment from Transamerica Corporation
R
RESTRICTED
Under 17 requires accompanying Parent or Adult Guardian
ORIGINAL MOTION PICTURE SOUNDTRACK AVAILABLE ON UNITED ARTISTS RECORDS
COPYRIGHT © 1970 UNITED ARTISTS CORPORATION
70/182

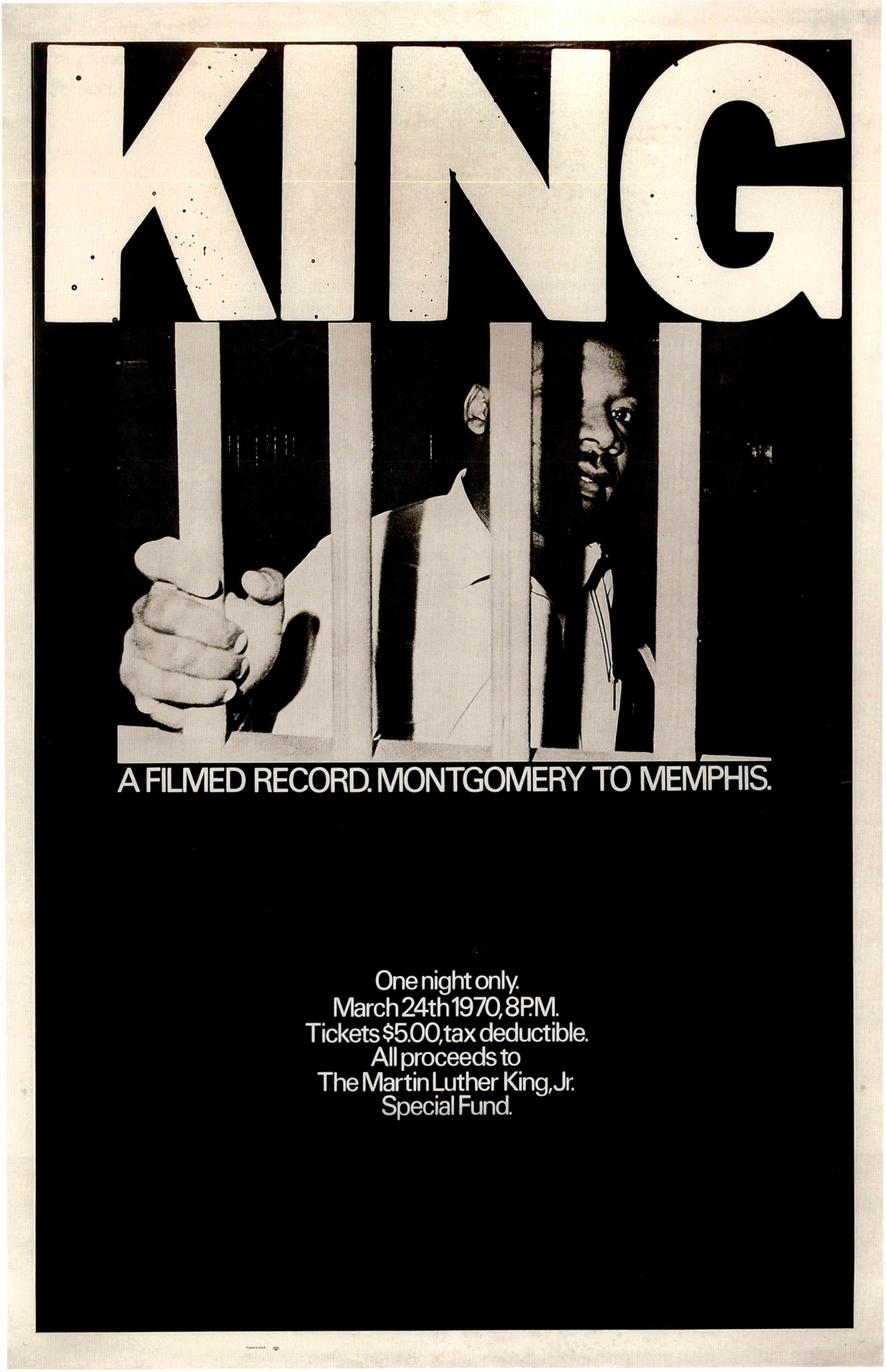
KING
A FILMED RECORD. MONTGOMERY TO MEMPHIS.
One night only.
March 24th 1970, 8P.M.
Tickets $5.00, tax deductible.
All proceeds to
The Martin Luther King, Jr.
Special Fund.

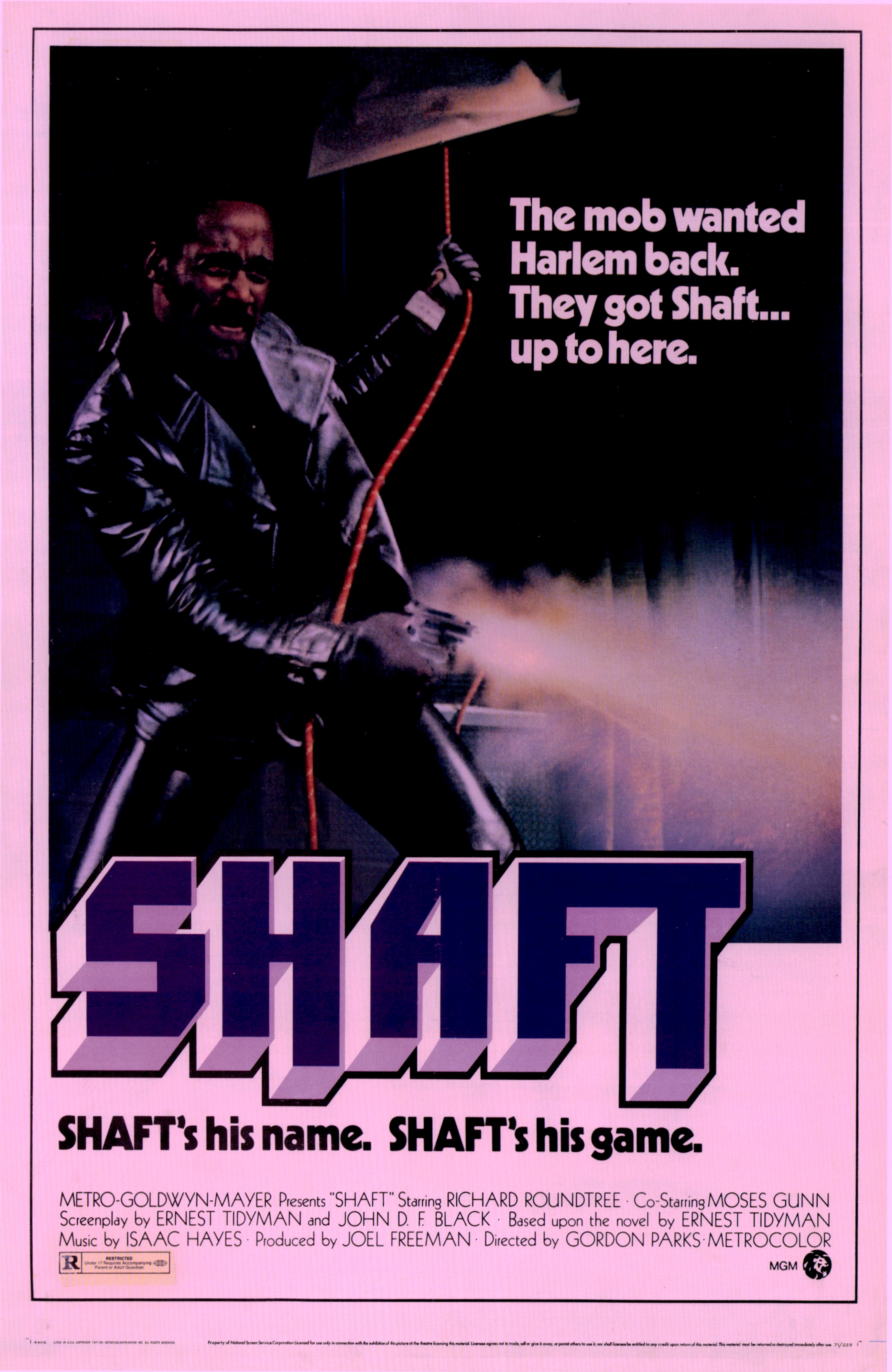
The mob wanted Harlem back. They got Shaft... up to here.
SHAFT
SHAFT's his name. SHAFT's his game.
METRO-GOLDWYN-MAYER Presents "SHAFT" Starring RICHARD ROUNDTREE · Co-Starring MOSES GUNN
Screenplay by ERNEST TIDYMAN and JOHN D. F. BLACK · Based upon the novel by ERNEST TIDYMAN
Music by ISAAC HAYES · Produced by JOEL FREEMAN · Directed by GORDON PARKS · METROCOLOR
R RESTRICTED Under 17 Requires Accompanying Parent or Adult Guardian
MGM

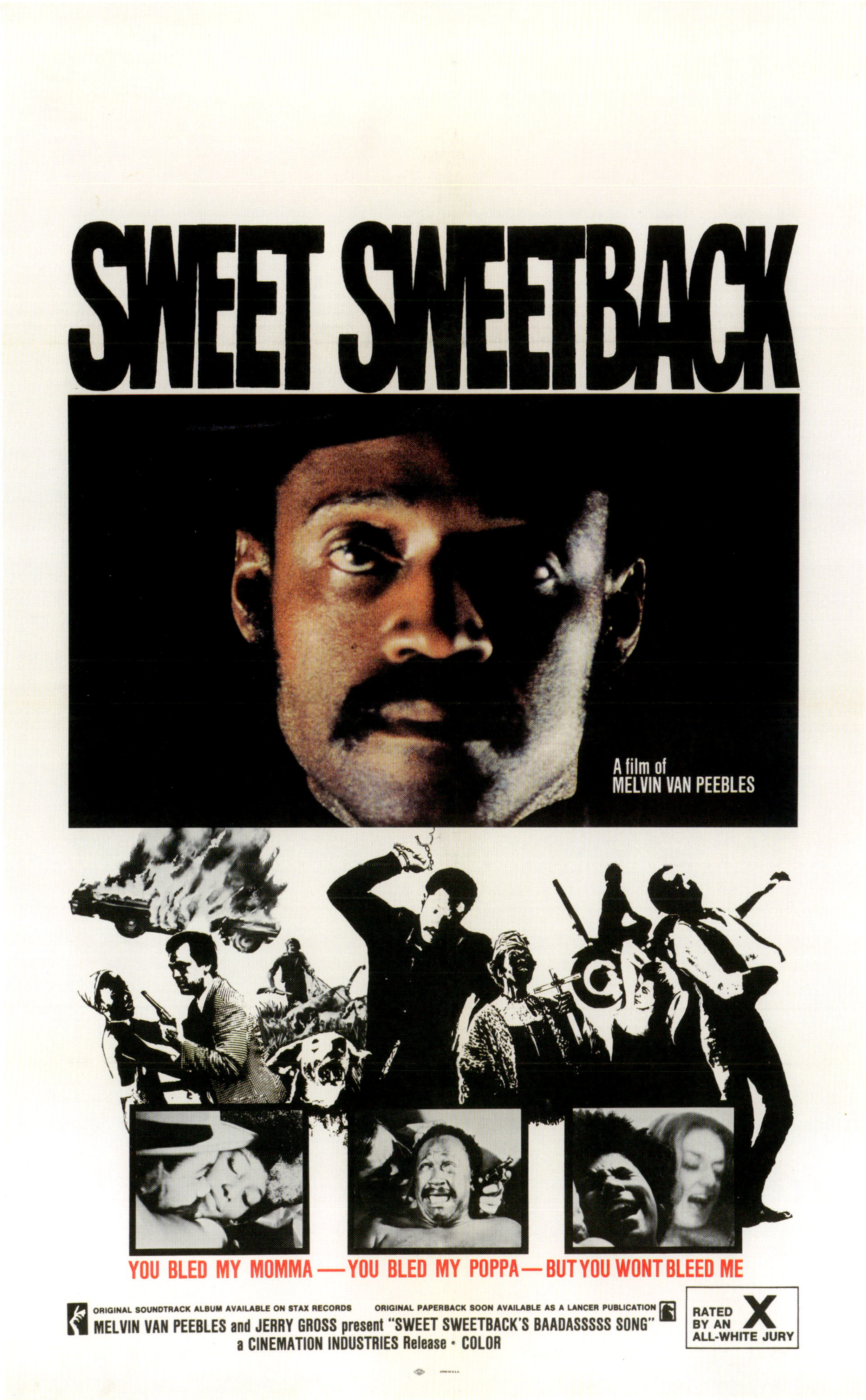
SWEET SWEETBACK
A film of
MELVIN VAN PEEBLES
YOU BLED MY MOMMA — YOU BLED MY POPPA — BUT YOU WONT BLEED ME
ORIGINAL SOUNDTRACK ALBUM AVAILABLE ON STAX RECORDS
ORIGINAL PAPERBACK SOON AVAILABLE AS A LANCER PUBLICATION
MELVIN VAN PEEBLES and JERRY GROSS present "SWEET SWEETBACK'S BAADASSSSS SONG"
a CINEMATION INDUSTRIES Release • COLOR
RATED X BY AN ALL-WHITE JURY

CHRONOLOGY

Covering the approximate time span of the exhibition, this illustrated chronology includes important moments in cinema history alongside contemporaneous social, political, and cultural events, demonstrating the interplay between the moving image and society.

It includes important milestones in the careers of Black film artists and highlights their activism and social engagement to show how they have influenced and been influenced by historical events.

This compilation of events was developed primarily by using exhibition catalogues, film history texts, newspaper articles, anthologies, and archival documents in order to provide a broad framework and understanding of the film activity of the period.

1895

CINEMATIC HISTORY

On December 28, Auguste and Louis Lumière hold the first commercial film screening at the Grand Café in Paris.

Vaudeville performers Bert Williams and George Walker begin their creative collaboration, later becoming one of the most successful comedic duos.

SOCIAL & POLITICAL HISTORY

The statesman and orator Frederick Douglass, a leader of the abolitionist movement and the most photographed man of the nineteenth century, dies on February 20.

The educator Booker T. Washington delivers the "Atlanta Compromise" speech on September 18, urging a focus on vocational training as a means to achieve economic self-determination for African Americans instead of prioritizing resistance to systemic discrimination and racial segregation.

The journalist and civil rights activist Ida B. Wells publishes the first set of lynching statistics in her book *The Red Record.*

1897

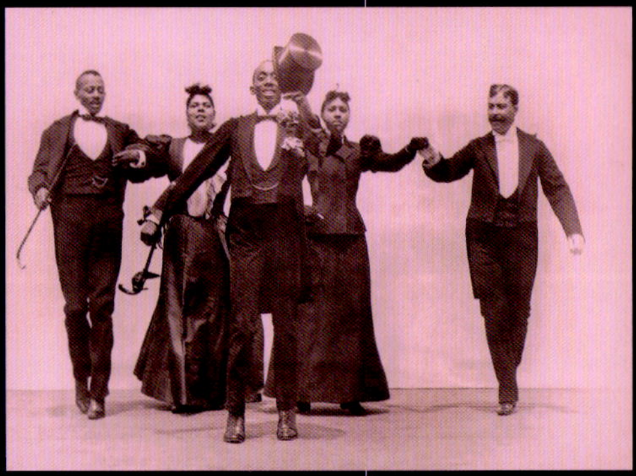

Cake Walk (1897), production still

American Mutoscope and Biograph Company films five Black performers dancing the popular cakewalk.

Plessy v. Ferguson establishes the "separate but equal" doctrine for upholding the constitutionality of laws requiring racial segregation. This permits public accommodations, including theaters, to be segregated by race.

1898

The Edison Manufacturing Company captures the return of soldiers of the Twenty-Fourth Infantry Regiment from the Spanish-American War in *Colored Troops Disembarking*.

The producer William Selig films the vaudeville performers Gertie Brown and Saint Suttle in *Something Good—Negro Kiss*.

1900

The sociologist and civil rights activist W. E. B. Du Bois organizes the Exhibition of American Negroes for the Exposition Universelle in Paris, featuring hundreds of photographs of African Americans.

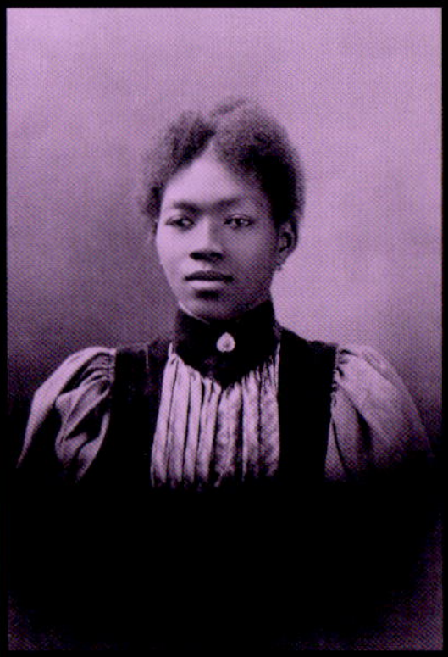

Portrait of an African American woman, 1900

1901

Bert Williams and George Walker record an album with Victor Talking Machine Company, becoming the first Black recording artists.

Booker T. Washington publishes his autobiography, *Up from Slavery*.

George H. White, the last Black congressman elected in the nineteenth century, leaves the House of Representatives. Twenty-eight years would pass before another Black congressperson served again.

1895–99

1900s

1903

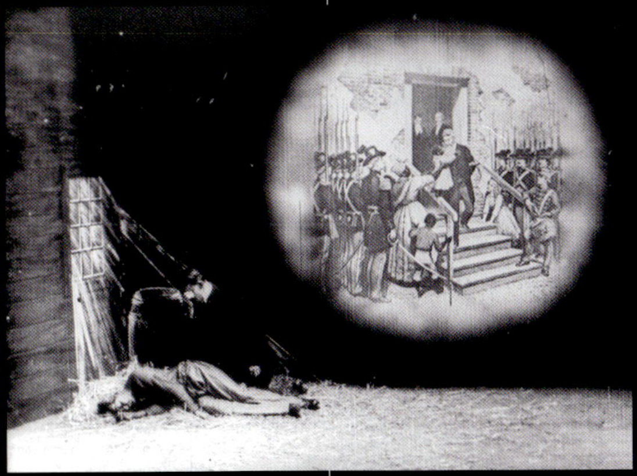

Uncle Tom's Cabin, or, Slavery Days (1903), film still

Edwin S. Porter releases *Uncle Tom's Cabin, or, Slavery Days*, based on Harriet Beecher Stowe's novel, the first of many film adaptations.

W. E. B. Du Bois publishes *The Souls of Black Folk*, in which he writes, "One ever feels his twoness,—an American, a Negro; two souls, two thoughts, two unreconciled strivings; two warring ideals in one dark body."

1905

The *Chicago Defender* begins publication, eventually becoming one of the most important Black newspapers in the country.

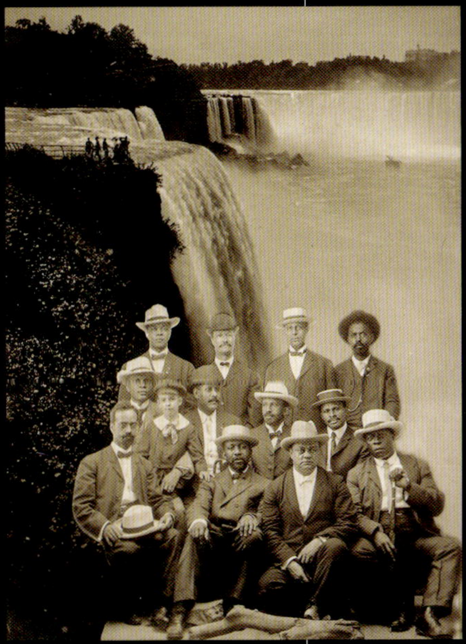

R. P. Slater (photographer), Niagara Movement founding members, including W. E. B. Du Bois (center), 1905

1907

Bertha Regustus stars in the Edison comedy short *Laughing Gas*.

1909

The George W. Broome Exhibition Company releases the actuality film *A Trip to Tuskegee*, which promotes the positive impact of the Tuskegee Institute.

Building on the Niagara Movement, an early civil rights organization, an interracial group of activists establishes the National Association for the Advancement of Colored People (NAACP), pledging "to promote equality of rights and eradicate caste or race prejudice among citizens of the United States."

The *Amsterdam News* is founded in New York; by the 1930s it is one of the leading Black newspapers.

1910s

CINEMATIC HISTORY

1910

The producer William D. Foster establishes the Foster Photoplay Company in Chicago, in part to create new roles for Black actors. Considered the first African American production company, it would release *The Railroad Porter* (1912) and *The Fall Guy* (1913).

Jeffries–Johnson World's Championship Boxing Contest, a film documenting the heavyweight championship bout in which Jack Johnson beat "the Great White Hope," James J. Jeffries, leads to social unrest and racial uprisings nationwide. The film was banned in many cities days after its release. Congress later bans the distribution of prizefight films across state lines.

1911

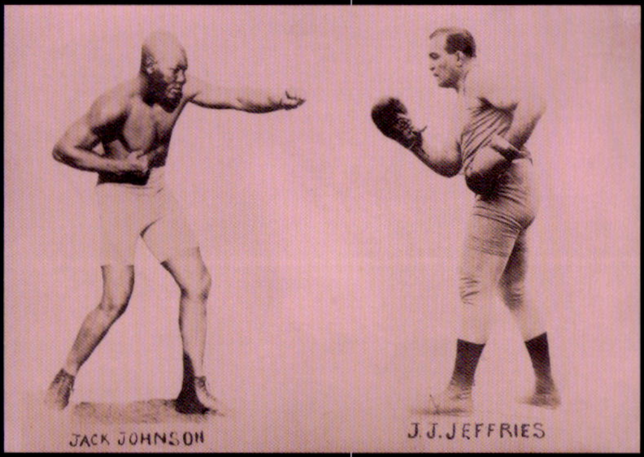

Jack Johnson and James J. Jeffries, 1910, postcard

1912

Alice Guy-Blaché directs the comedy short *A Fool and His Money*, one of the first films to feature an all-Black cast.

1913

The Black-cast feature now known as *Lime Kiln Club Field Day*, featuring Bert Williams and Odessa Warren Grey, begins production at Biograph's Bronx studios. A cache of the unfinished film's camera negatives from Biograph's vaults is acquired by the Museum of Modern Art, New York, in 1938 and is later compiled into an "archival assembly," which premieres at the museum in 2014.

1914

The vaudeville actor Sam Lucas stars in an adaptation of *Uncle Tom's Cabin*, becoming the first Black actor to play the role of Uncle Tom in a film.

Bert Williams stars in *Darktown Jubilee*, his screen debut.

The Hampton Institute releases the industrial film *Making Negro Lives Count*, which documents Black rural life and the training provided by the institute to bring about positive social change.

SOCIAL & POLITICAL HISTORY

1910

The NAACP begins publishing *The Crisis*, edited by W. E. B. Du Bois. Later editions would feature film reviews.

1911

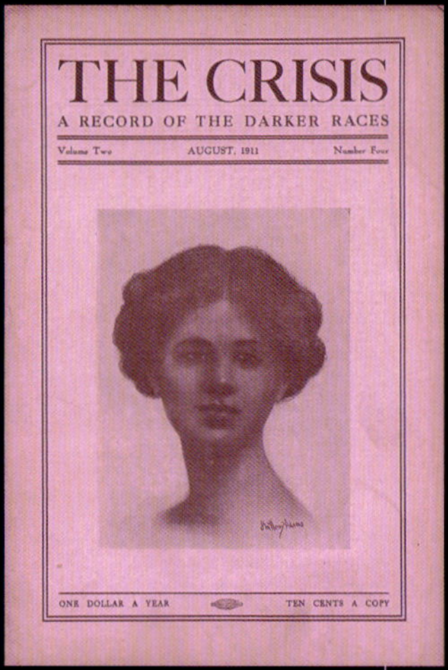

The Crisis 2, no. 4 (August 1911)

1913

The fiftieth anniversary of the Emancipation Proclamation is celebrated nationwide.

President Woodrow Wilson implements racial segregation in federal offices across the nation.

1915

The Lincoln Motion Picture Company is founded in Los Angeles, becoming the city's first Black-owned production company. Its first release is *The Realization of a Negro's Ambition* (1916), starring Clarence Brooks and Bessie Baker.

D. W. Griffith releases *The Birth of a Nation*, adapted from the book *The Clansman*. It screens at the White House and becomes the first American blockbuster. The film leads to the resurgence of the terrorist organization the Ku Klux Klan. Organizations like the NAACP mobilize to prevent the film from screening.

1916

Produced by the Frederick Douglass Film Company, *The Colored American Winning His Suit* is the first five-reel race film. It features a nonprofessional cast, filmed on location at Howard University.

Madame E. Touissant Welcome and Ernest Touissant Welcome establish the Touissant Motion Picture Exchange and later produce the documentary *Doing Their Bit* (1918), highlighting the role of Black soldiers in the war effort.

The first wave of the Great Migration begins: Black Americans leave rural southern communities for urban centers in the North and West.

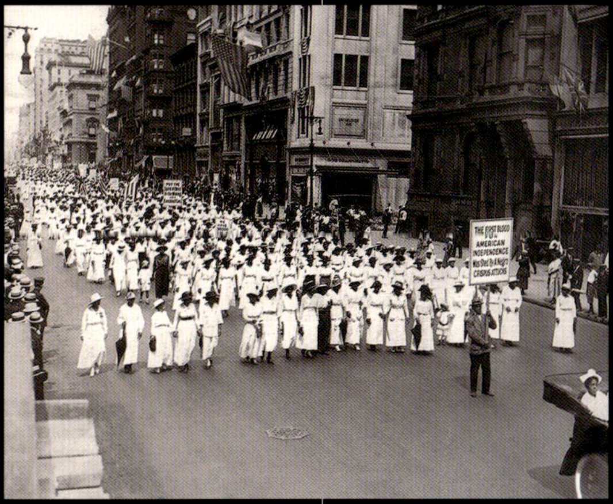

NAACP silent protest, New York, 1917

1917

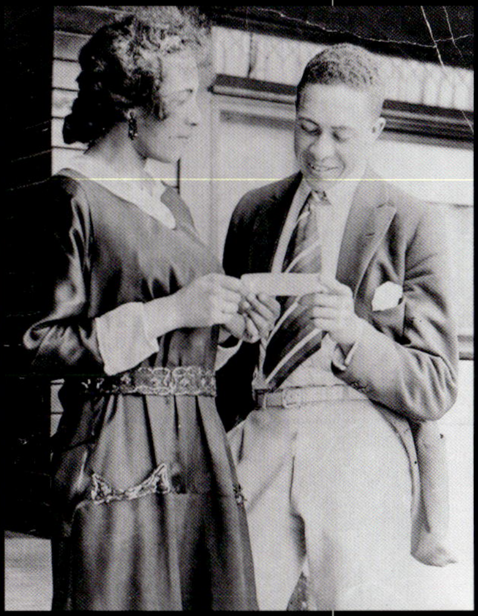

Clarence Brooks (right) in *The Realization of a Negro's Ambition* (1916), production still

On April 6, the United States declares war on Germany and enters World War I.

The NAACP leads a silent march along Fifth Avenue in New York City on July 28 to protest racial violence.

1918

The US government commissions the recruitment film *Our Colored Fighters* to showcase the training and participation of Black troops in World War I.

1919

Oscar Micheaux writes, produces, directs, and distributes the film *The Homesteader*, adapted from his autobiographical novel. Micheaux would go on to direct forty-eight features.

Ernest Morrison, better known by the stage name Sunshine Sammy Morrison, becomes the first Black actor to sign a long-term contract with the producer Hal Roach. Morrison goes on to costar in *Our Gang*, the short film series featuring the Little Rascals.

Richard E. Norman releases *The Green-Eyed Monster*. A year later he establishes the Norman Film Company Studios in Jacksonville, Florida, after purchasing Eagle Film Studios.

The news service Associated Negro Press is founded in Chicago by Claude A. Barnett, a graduate of Tuskegee Institute.

Racial violence erupts in more than thirty cities across the nation in what is termed the Red Summer.

1920s

1920

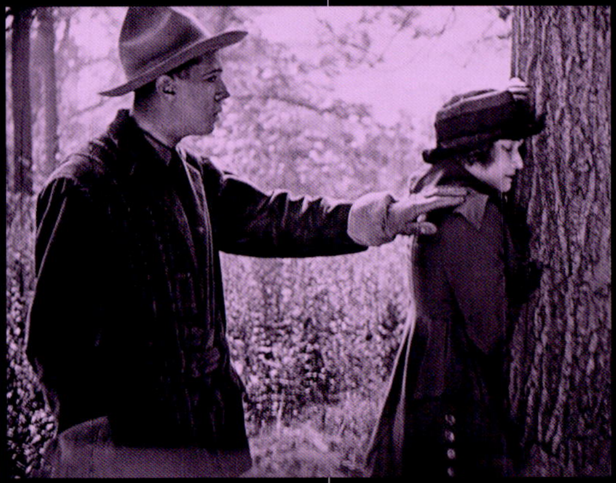

Walker Thompson and Iris Hall, *The Symbol of the Unconquered* (1920), film still

CINEMATIC HISTORY

Sack Amusement Enterprises, a theater chain and production company, is founded in San Antonio, Texas.

Oscar Micheaux releases *The Symbol of the Unconquered* and *Within Our Gates*, considered to be his responses to Griffith's *Birth of a Nation*.

SOCIAL & POLITICAL HISTORY

The passage of the Nineteenth Amendment grants women the right to vote. Black women are denied the right in most southern states.

1921

CINEMATIC HISTORY

REOL Productions, based in New York, releases *The Sport of the Gods*, based on the novel by Paul Laurence Dunbar.

Bessie Coleman becomes the first Black person to earn an international pilot's license. The adventure film *The Flying Ace* (1926) is loosely based on her life.

SOCIAL & POLITICAL HISTORY

On May 31 and June 1, violent white mobs attack Black residents of Tulsa's Greenwood district. Hundreds are murdered, and the prosperous neighborhood known as Black Wall Street is destroyed.

1922

CINEMATIC HISTORY

The vaudeville performer Bert Williams dies.

Tressie Souders writes, produces, and directs *A Woman's Error*. She is believed to be the first Black woman to direct a feature film.

SOCIAL & POLITICAL HISTORY

The Dyer Anti-Lynching Bill, which would make lynching a federal offense, passes the US House of Representatives but fails in the Senate.

1923

CINEMATIC HISTORY

Richard E. Norman releases the South Seas adventure film *Regeneration*.

Maria P. Williams produces and stars in the mystery drama *The Flames of Wrath*.

The musical short *Noble Sissle and Eubie Blake Sing Snappy Tunes*, one of the first sound films developed using the Phonofilm technology, is released.

SOCIAL & POLITICAL HISTORY

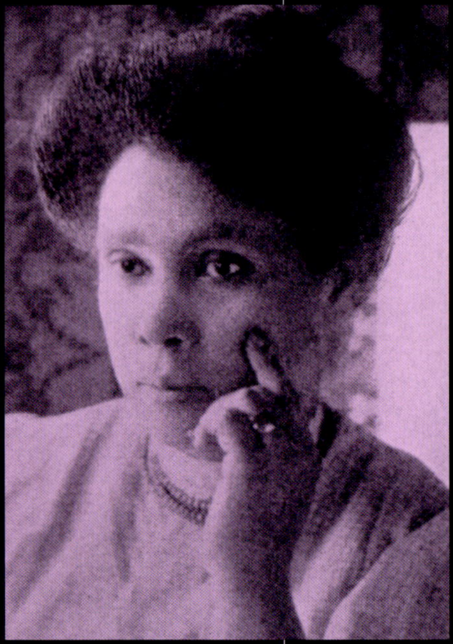

Maria P. Williams, 1916, newspaper clipping

1924

CINEMATIC HISTORY

Paul Robeson stars in Eugene O'Neill's play *The Emperor Jones* in London, which in 1933 would be adapted to a movie, also starring Robeson.

1925

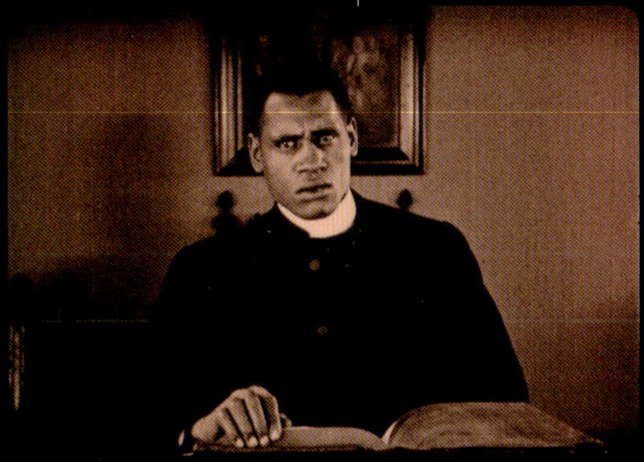

Paul Robeson in *Body and Soul* (1925), film still

Paul Robeson makes his screen debut in Oscar Micheaux's *Body and Soul.*

Josephine Baker makes her Paris debut in the musical spectacle *La revue nègre.*

Alain LeRoy Locke publishes *The New Negro,* the seminal anthology of the Harlem Renaissance, which includes stories, poems, and artworks.

On August 8, the Ku Klux Klan organizes a white supremacist rally that attracts thirty thousand participants, who march down Pennsylvania Avenue in Washington, DC.

1926

Colored Players Film Corporation is established in Philadelphia by Sherman H. Dudley, an African American vaudeville performer and theater entrepreneur, and the Austrian émigré David Starkman. The company would go on to produce *Ten Nights in a Bar Room* and *The Scar of Shame* (1929), among other films.

The poet Langston Hughes publishes the influential essay "The Negro Artist and the Racial Mountain," writing, "We younger Negro artists who create now intend to express our individual dark-skinned selves without fear or shame. If white people are pleased we are glad. If they are not, it doesn't matter. We know we are beautiful. And ugly too."

1927

Lincoln Perry, better known by his stage name, Stepin Fetchit, debuts in the film *In Old Kentucky,* which leads to a five-year contract with the Fox Film Corporation.

Duke Ellington first performs at the Cotton Club in Harlem.

Josephine Baker makes her film debut in the French production *La sirène des tropiques.*

The basketball team the Harlem Globe Trotters plays their first game.

1928

The writer Zora Neale Hurston pioneers ethnographic filmmaking. During her doctoral anthropological research, she uses a 16mm camera to capture life in rural Black communities, producing films such as *Children's Games* (1928), *Logging* (1928), and *Baptism* (1929).

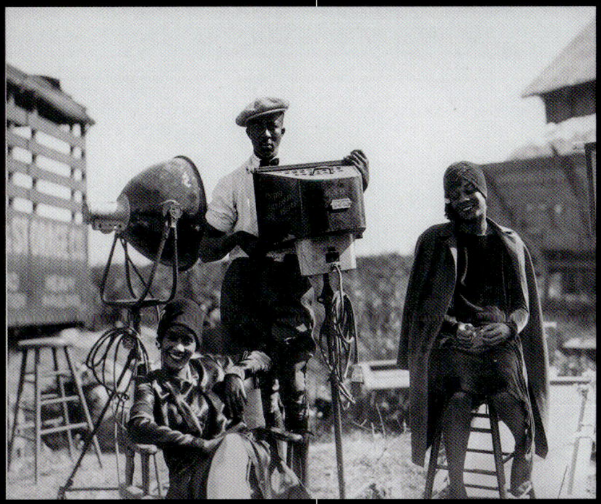

From left: Victoria Spivey, Harold Garrison, and Honey Brown, 1928, on the set of *Hallelujah* (1929), production still

1929

Metro-Goldwyn-Mayer releases its first Black-cast musical feature film, *Hallelujah,* which stars Nina Mae McKinney.

Fox Film Corporation releases its first Black-cast musical, *Hearts in Dixie,* starring Clarence Muse.

Fredi Washington appears with Duke Ellington and his Cotton Club Orchestra in the musical short *Black and Tan,* set during the Harlem Renaissance.

Bessie Smith, known as the Empress of the Blues, appears in the two-reel musical short *St. Louis Blues.*

The stock market crash on Tuesday, October 29, leads to the Great Depression, which disproportionately affects African Americans and temporarily slows the Great Migration.

CINEMATIC HISTORY

1930

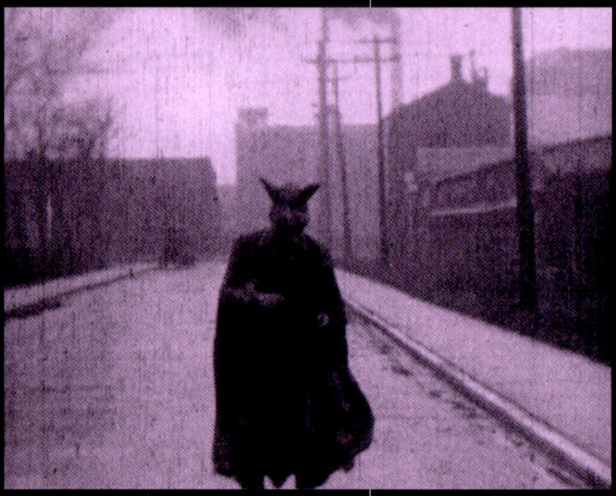

Hell-Bound Train (ca. 1930), film still

Clarence Brooks and Evelyn Preer costar in *Georgia Rose*, one of the first "all-talking" feature-length race films.

The independent filmmakers and evangelists James and Eloyce Gist release *Hell-Bound Train*, which showcased visual allegories about the sins of modern life. The film was screened for their traveling ministry.

1931

1932

Bill "Bojangles" Robinson stars in the semiautobiographical *Harlem Is Heaven*, performing his signature "stair dance" to the music of Eubie Blake's Orchestra.

1933

Ethel Waters stars in *Rufus Jones for President*, a satirical short featuring the screen debut of seven-year-old Sammy Davis Jr., who dreams of becoming president of the United States.

Paul Robeson and Fredi Washington costar in *The Emperor Jones*, based on Eugene O'Neill's play. Robeson re-creates his dramatic stage role of Brutus Jones.

1934

Louise Beavers and Fredi Washington costar in the Academy Award–nominated *Imitation of Life*. The Production Code Administration censors object to the story's treatment of racial passing and a lynching scene in early drafts of the script.

SOCIAL & POLITICAL HISTORY

1930: The Howard University Gallery of Art, one of the earliest venues to show African American art, opens.

1931: Walter White becomes executive secretary of the NAACP. During his tenure he pressured Hollywood studios to expand the roles offered to Black actors.

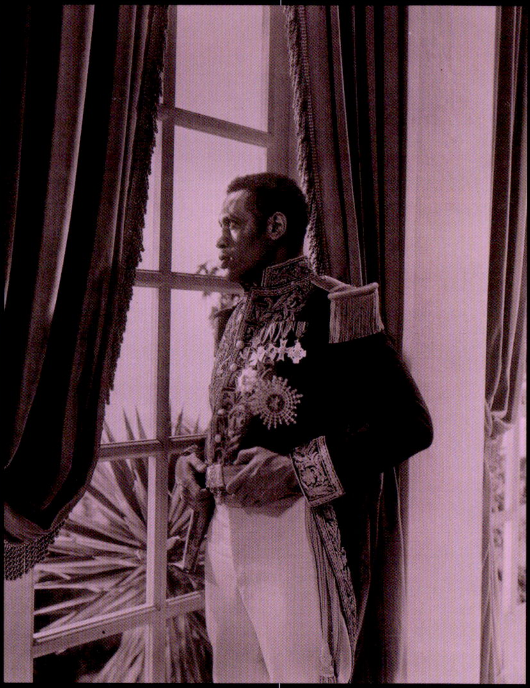

Paul Robeson in *The Emperor Jones* (1933), publicity still

1930s

1935

Josephine Baker stars in *Princesse Tam-Tam*.

The animated film *Little Black Sambo* is released. It is adapted from the children's book *The Story of Little Black Sambo* (1899) by Helen Bannerman.

The Black newspaper the *Detroit Chronicle* is founded.

1936

Warner Bros. releases *The Green Pastures*, a Black-cast musical depicting Bible stories. Starring Rex Ingram, the film is a box-office success, although elements are criticized as stereotypical.

Paul Robeson appears in *Show Boat*; his rendition of "Ol' Man River" would become a standard in his subsequent stage performances.

Fredi Washington, Noble Sissle, Paul Robeson, W. C. Handy, and Ethel Waters cofound the Negro Actors Guild of America, with the goal of increasing opportunities for Black actors and combating racial stereotypes in the entertainment industry.

Jesse Owens wins four gold medals during the Berlin Summer Olympics, held in Nazi-controlled Germany.

1937

The actor and singer Herb Jeffries stars in *Harlem on the Prairie* and goes on to popularize the singing cowboy in other Black-cast westerns, including *The Bronze Buckaroo* (1938), *Two-Gun Man from Harlem* (1938), and *Harlem Rides the Range* (1939).

The actor Ralph Cooper and Harry M. Popkin and Leo C. Popkin establish Million Dollar Productions, producing titles such as *Bargain with Bullets* (1937) and *Gang War* (1940).

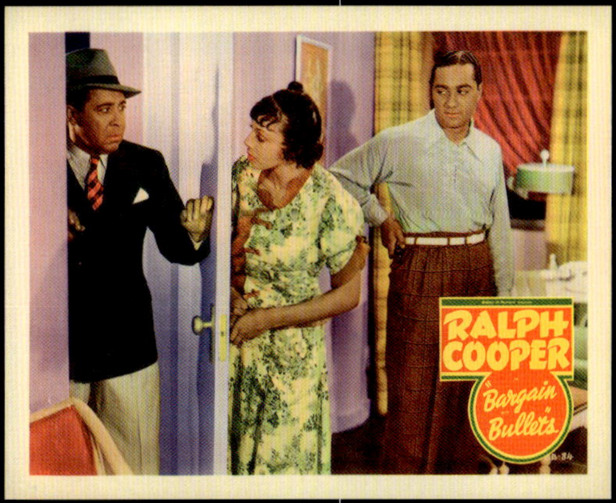

From left: Clarence Brooks, Theresa Harris, and Ralph Cooper in *Bargain with Bullets* (1937), lobby card

1938

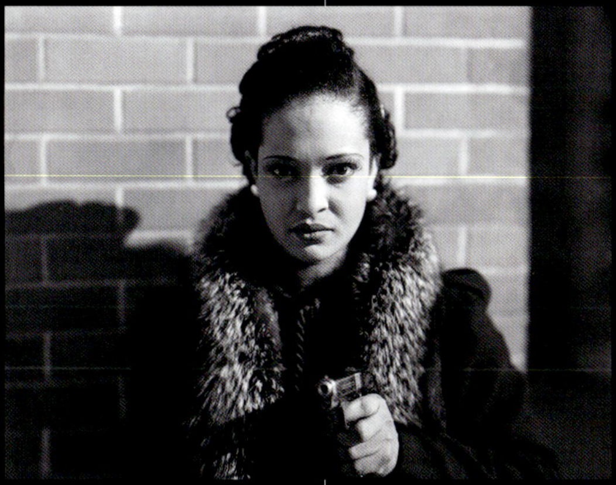

Nina Mae McKinney in *Gang Smashers* (1938), publicity still

The Duke Is Tops, starring Ralph Cooper and Lena Horne, is released. The film is rereleased as *The Bronze Venus* (1943), with the popular Horne receiving top billing.

Gang Smashers, starring Nina Mae McKinney and with a script by Ralph Cooper, is released.

Heavyweight champion Joe Louis beats Max Schmeling in a rematch.

1939

Louise Beavers stars in *Reform School* as the warden of a juvenile prison who implements progressive reforms.

Contralto Marian Anderson performs at the Lincoln Memorial before a crowd of seventy-five thousand after she is prevented from singing at the racially segregated Constitution Hall by the Daughters of the American Revolution.

CINEMATIC HISTORY

1940

Hattie McDaniel wins an Academy Award for her performance as Mammy in *Gone with the Wind* (1939), becoming the first Black actor to receive an Oscar.

The actor Clarence Muse cowrites and stars in *Broken Strings*, in which he plays a concert pianist.

Several production companies start releasing 16mm musical shorts known as Soundies, which were played on musical jukeboxes. Black-cast shorts were usually added at the end of the reel.

1941

Spencer Williams Jr. makes his directorial debut with *The Blood of Jesus*. Made with nonprofessional actors on a budget of $5,000, it showcases various spirituals and hymns. Screening in cinemas and Black churches, the film achieves commercial success.

The NAACP's Walter White calls on Hollywood studios to stop perpetuating racist stereotypes and to create more realistic roles for Black actors.

The distribution and production company Toddy Pictures is founded. It rereleases race films like *Harlem on the Prairie* (1937) and *Reform School* (1939).

Hattie McDaniel becomes chair of the Negro Division of the Hollywood Victory Committee.

1942

The singer, actor, and civil rights activist Lena Horne signs a seven-year contract with Metro-Goldwyn-Mayer.

1943

Ethel Waters, Eddie "Rochester" Anderson, Rex Ingram, and Lena Horne star in the Black-cast musical *Cabin in the Sky*, with musical numbers by Duke Ellington.

Stormy Weather marks the height of Black-cast Hollywood musicals, and featured Lena Horne, Bill "Bojangles" Robinson, Cab Calloway, Katherine Dunham, Fats Waller, the Nicholas Brothers, and others.

1944

Mantan Moreland plays the chauffeur Birmingham Brown in *Charlie Chan in the Secret Service*, reprising the role twelve times in the Charlie Chan series.

The US War Department commissions the propaganda film *The Negro Soldier*, produced by Frank Capra and written by Carlton Moss, who also acted in the film. Initially intended for limited distribution, it is released nationally.

The musical short *Jump Children* stars the iconic all-women swing orchestra International Sweethearts of Rhythm.

The NAACP begins granting awards to actors who advance the image of African Americans. Among the first recipients are Rex Ingram, Lena Horne, and Dooley Wilson, for their roles in *Sahara* (1943), *Thousands Cheer* (1943), and *Casablanca* (1942), respectively.

SOCIAL & POLITICAL HISTORY

1941

After the attack on Pearl Harbor, the United States enters World War II, declaring war on Japan on December 8.

1942

All-American News, produced by William D. Alexander, releases a series of newsreels highlighting the activities of Black men and women in the armed forces. By 1945 it shifts away from newsreels to short musical films.

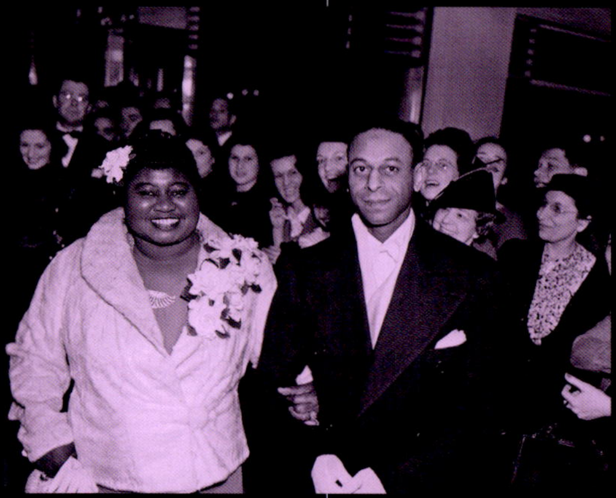

Hattie McDaniel and Ferdinand Yober arriving at the Academy Awards ceremony, 1940

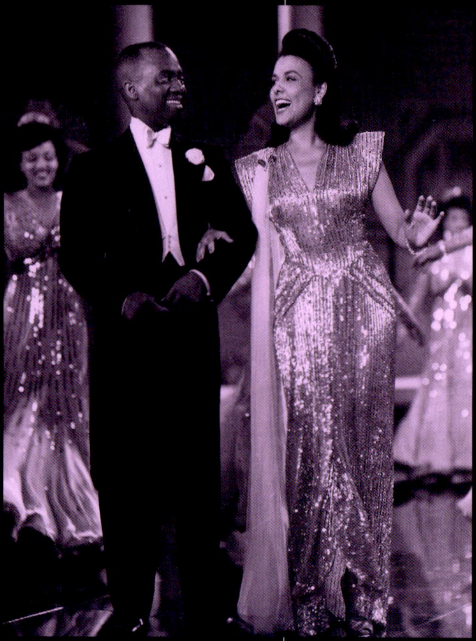

Bill "Bojangles" Robinson and Lena Horne in *Stormy Weather* (1943), production still

1940s

1945

The Negro Sailor, a documentary produced by the US Navy, is released by All-American News.

Toddy Pictures rereleases several titles, including *Am I Guilty?* (1943), under the title *The Racket Doctor*.

John Johnson begins publishing *Ebony* magazine, which highlights entertainment figures.

On September 2, World War II ends.

1946

Spencer Williams Jr. releases *Beale Street Mama* and *Dirty Gertie from Harlem U.S.A.*

Nat King Cole's *King Cole Trio Time* is the first radio program to be sponsored by a Black musician.

1947

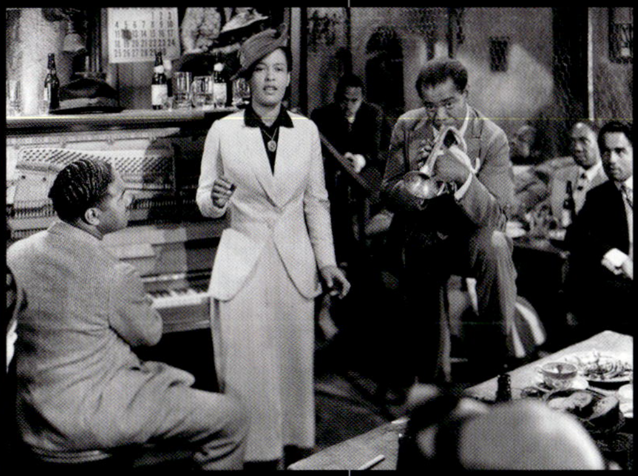

From left: Charlie Beale, Billie Holiday, and Louis Armstrong (on trumpet) in *New Orleans* (1947), production still

Cab Calloway stars in the full-length musical *Hi De Ho*.

Louis Armstrong stars alongside the vocalist Billie Holiday in *New Orleans*.

The NAACP calls attention to the increase in lynchings of Black veterans returning from World War II.

Jackie Robinson is the first Black baseball player to sign with a major league team.

1948

James Baskett receives an Honorary Award from the Academy of Motion Picture Arts and Sciences for his portrayal of Uncle Remus in *Song of the South* (1946). The film, however, was criticized for its depiction of an idyllic master-slave relationship.

Oscar Micheaux releases his last film, *The Betrayal*.

The National Theatre in Washington, DC, is boycotted for its policies of racial discrimination.

President Harry S. Truman signs Executive Order 9981 abolishing discrimination in the armed forces on the basis of race, color, religion, or national origin.

1949

The release of the studio films *Pinky*, *Intruder in the Dust*, *Home of the Brave*, and *Lost Boundaries*—which deal with various racial issues, including passing and discrimination—marks the rise of the social problem film. These films highlight contemporaneous social issues and invite white audiences to empathize with Black characters who face prejudice or injustice.

An outdoor performance by Paul Robeson in Lakeland Acres turns violent when it is disrupted by agitators protesting his affiliation with the Communist Party.

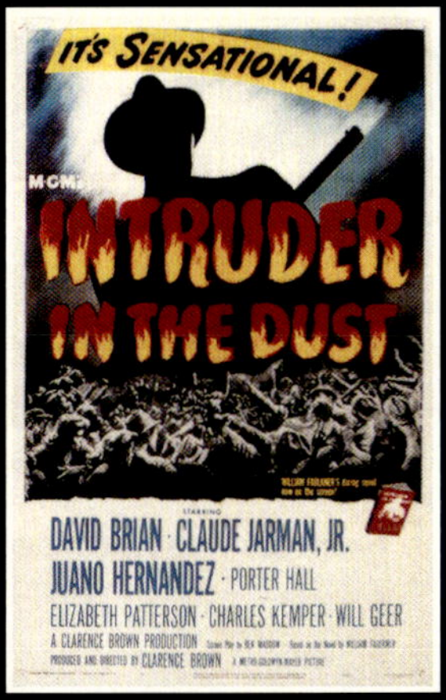

Intruder in the Dust **(1949), theatrical release poster**

1950s

CINEMATIC HISTORY

SOCIAL & POLITICAL HISTORY

1950

Cinematic History

Sidney Poitier makes his screen debut in *No Way Out*, playing a medical doctor confronted with a racist patient. It was noted for its frank treatment of racism.

The jazz singer and musician Nat King Cole stars in the short film *King Cole and His Trio with Benny Carter and His Orchestra*.

Jackie Robinson stars in the biographical drama *The Jackie Robinson Story*, detailing his journey to becoming the first Black baseball player in the major leagues.

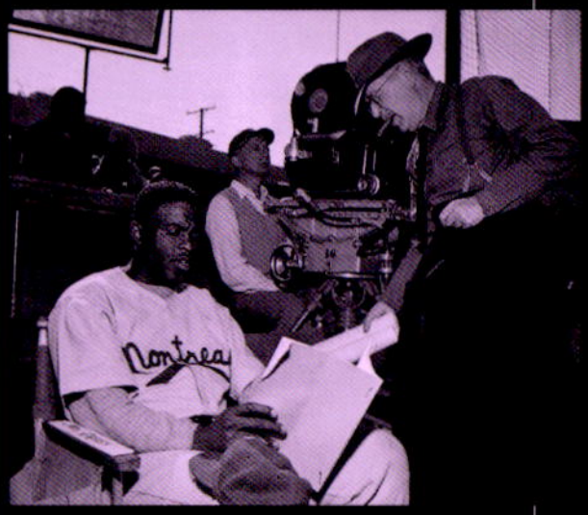

Jackie Robinson in *The Jackie Robinson Story* (1950), production still

1951

Cinematic History

The filmmaker Oscar Micheaux dies on March 25.

Social & Political History

Paul Robeson submits a petition to the United Nations accusing the US government of a policy of genocide against African Americans.

Jet magazine is founded in Chicago. Billed as "The Weekly Negro News Magazine," it gains popularity for its coverage of the civil rights movement as well as the entertainment industry.

1952

Cinematic History

The actor William Walker is elected as a member of the Screen Actors Guild board of directors. He would appear in more than one hundred films over the course of his career.

1953

Cinematic History

The biographical film *The Joe Louis Story* is released, detailing Louis's path to becoming the heavyweight boxing champion of the world.

Social & Political History

The NAACP announces the Fight for Freedom campaign, whose aim is to eradicate racial discrimination by 1963, the hundredth anniversary of the Emancipation Proclamation.

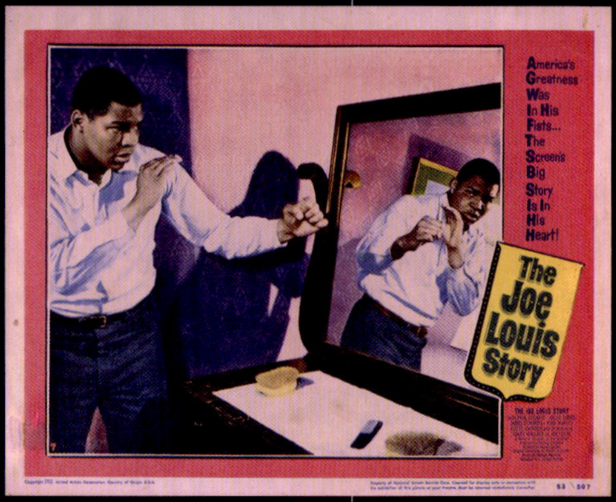

The Joe Louis Story (1953), lobby card

1954

Cinematic History

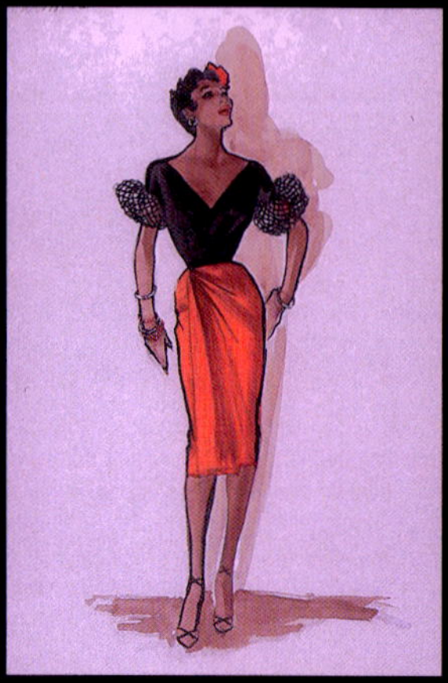

Carmen Jones (1954), costume design drawing by Mary Ann Nyberg

Social & Political History

In *Brown v. Board of Education of Topeka*, the Supreme Court declares, "We conclude that in the field of public education the doctrine of 'separate but equal' has no place. Separate educational facilities are inherently unequal."

1955

Dorothy Dandridge becomes the first Black actor to receive an Academy Award nomination for a performance in a leading role for *Carmen Jones* (1954).

In Montgomery, Alabama, Rosa Parks refuses to give up her bus seat to a white man; a bus boycott is soon organized.

Fourteen-year-old Emmett Till is violently murdered in Money, Mississippi, for allegedly having flirted with a white woman. Photographs published in *Jet* magazine show his brutalized face in the open casket, shocking the country.

1956

Carib Gold, starring Ethel Waters and featuring the screen debuts of Cicely Tyson, Diana Sands, and Geoffrey Holder, is considered to be one of the last race films produced.

Nat King Cole is brutally attacked by members of the Ku Klux Klan during a performance in Birmingham, Alabama.

On June 6, Paul Robeson is called to testify in front of the House Un-American Activities Committee, which questions him about his political activities and communist associations. He is later blacklisted, which severely curtails his career.

1957

Sidney Poitier and John Cassavetes star in *Edge of the City*. The film's depiction of an interracial friendship is groundbreaking, earning praise from the NAACP.

The Civil Rights Act of 1957 is the first federal civil rights legislation passed by the US Congress since Reconstruction. It establishes the Civil Rights Division in the US Justice Department and the US Commission on Civil Rights.

1958

Eartha Kitt and Sammy Davis Jr. star in *Anna Lucasta*. The end credits feature the work of the noted artist Charles White.

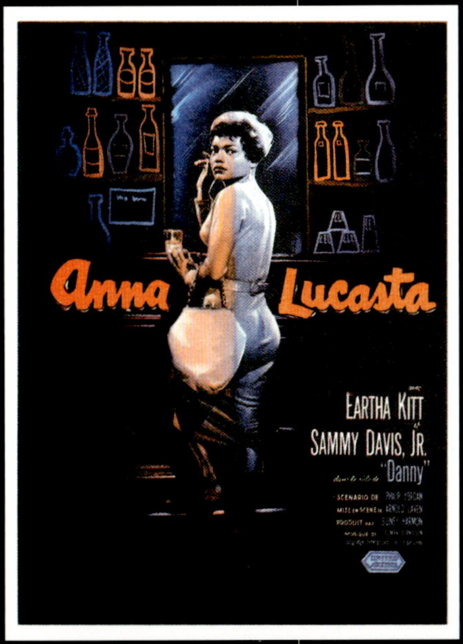

Anna Lucasta (1958), theatrical release poster

1959

Sidney Poitier is nominated for an Academy Award for his performance in *The Defiant Ones* (1958).

Sidney Poitier, Dorothy Dandridge, and Sammy Davis Jr. star in *Porgy and Bess*, adapted from the 1930s Broadway musical written by George Gershwin.

Harry Belafonte stars in the postapocalyptic drama *The World, the Flesh, and the Devil*, which explores an interracial romance after a nuclear catastrophe.

Motown Records, initially named Tamia Records, is founded in Detroit. It would play a crucial role in the integration of popular music.

1960s

CINEMATIC HISTORY

1960

With the broadcast of *Integration Report 1*, Madeline Anderson becomes the first Black woman to direct a televised documentary.

1961

Lorraine Hansberry adapts her Broadway play *A Raisin in the Sun* for the screen. The movie version stars Sidney Poitier, Ruby Dee, Claudia McNeil, and Diana Sands.

1962

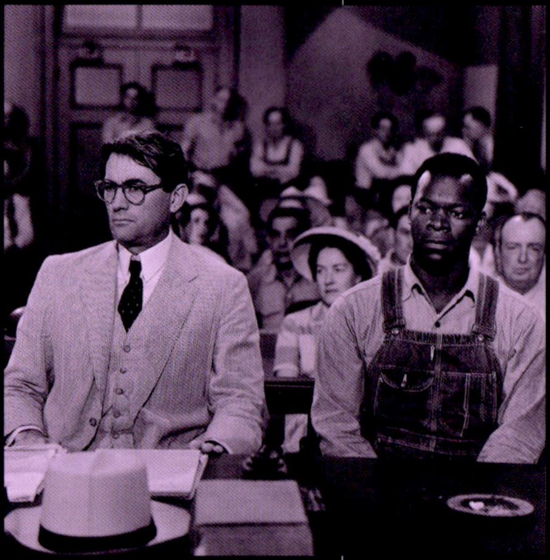

From left: Gregory Peck and Brock Peters in *To Kill a Mockingbird* (1962), production still

Brock Peters plays Tom Robinson in *To Kill a Mockingbird*, adapted from the Pulitzer Prize–winning novel by Harper Lee.

1963

Josephine Baker, Harry Belafonte, Ruby Dee, Ossie Davis, Sidney Poitier, and other Hollywood icons join the March on Washington, advocating equality for African Americans. Martin Luther King Jr. delivers his "I Have a Dream" speech.

1964

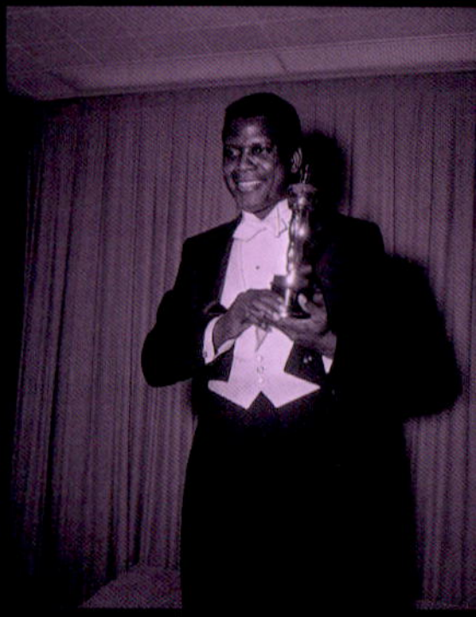

Sidney Poitier after winning the Academy Award for Best Actor, 1964

Nothing but a Man, starring Ivan Dixon and Abbey Lincoln, premieres at the Venice Film Festival to critical acclaim.

Sidney Poitier is named Best Actor for his performance in *Lilies of the Field* (1963), becoming the first Black actor to receive this honor.

SOCIAL & POLITICAL HISTORY

1960

The Student Nonviolent Coordinating Committee (SNCC) adopts a "Jail, No Bail" approach after several students are arrested for protesting racial discrimination and opt to serve jail sentences instead of paying fines.

The passage of the Civil Rights Act of 1960 establishes federal inspection of local voter registration rolls and establishes penalties for obstructing voter registration.

1961

The Congress for Racial Equity (CORE) organizes Freedom Rides throughout the Deep South.

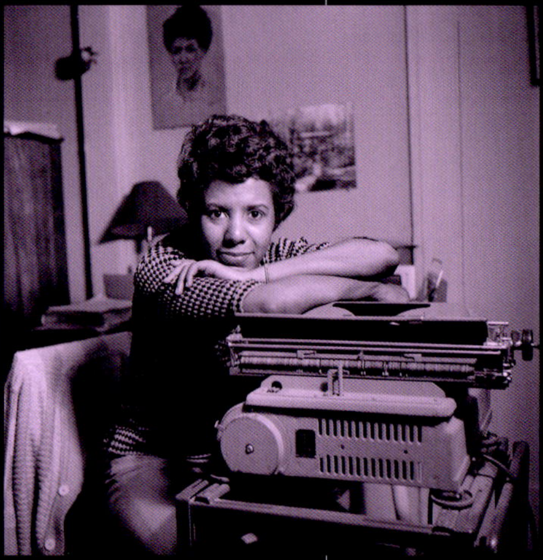

David Attie (photographer), Lorraine Hansberry in her New York City apartment, 1959

1962

Civil rights leaders conduct massive sit-ins and marching campaigns across the South to protest racial segregation.

1963

James Baldwin's book of essays *The Fire Next Time* is published, offering a critical analysis of race relations in America.

Martin Luther King Jr. and peaceful protesters are attacked during demonstrations in Birmingham, Alabama. Assaults on young protesters by police officers using water hoses and police dogs are covered on television and in newspapers, causing international outrage.

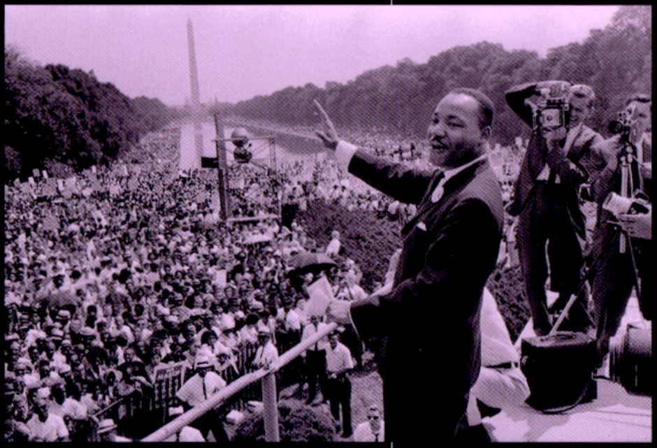

Martin Luther King Jr. speaks at the March on Washington, 1963

1964

Congress passes the Civil Rights Act of 1964, banning discrimination in public spaces, education, and employment.

The Twenty-Fourth Amendment to the Constitution, which abolishes the poll tax, is ratified.

1965

Nine from Little Rock (1964), which chronicles the efforts of nine Black students who are the first to integrate an all-white Arkansas high school, wins an Academy Award for Documentary Short Subject.

The civil rights activist Malcolm X is assassinated at the Audubon Ballroom in New York on February 21.

An uprising occurs on August 11–16 in the predominantly Black neighborhood of Watts in Los Angeles. It is one of the largest race-related rebellions of the civil rights era, leaving thirty dead and more than one thousand injured.

1966

A Man Called Adam is released. Starring Sammy Davis Jr., Ossie Davis, Cicely Tyson, and Louis Armstrong, it tells the story of a famous trumpet player.

The Black Panther Party for Self-Defense, a Black Power political organization, is founded in Oakland, California.

1967

With the release of three films in the same year—*To Sir, with Love*; *In the Heat of the Night*; and *Guess Who's Coming to Dinner*—Sidney Poitier becomes the number one box-office draw.

Ruby Dee, Julian Mayfield, and Jules Dassin cowrite the screenplay for *Uptight*.

Racial violence erupts in cities across the country—including Atlanta, Detroit, and New York—in what is called the "long, hot summer."

The Supreme Court decision *Loving v. Virginia* strikes down laws that prohibit interracial marriage.

1968

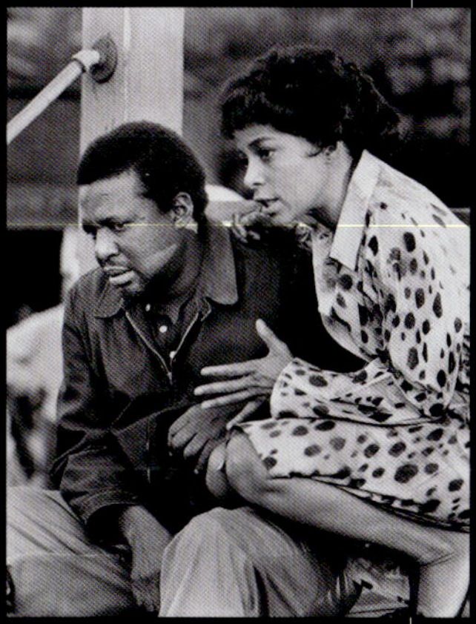

Julian Mayfield and Ruby Dee in *Uptight* (1968), production still

Melvin Van Peebles's *La permission* (*The Story of a Three-Day Pass*) is released in France.

On April 4, Martin Luther King Jr. is assassinated at the Lorraine Hotel in Memphis, Tennessee. Violence erupts across many US cities.

1969

The photographer Gordon Parks directs *The Learning Tree*, the first studio film helmed by a Black director.

Charles Burnett directs his first short, *Several Friends*, while studying film at UCLA. Shot in cinema verité, it features nonprofessional actors.

A documentary following the boxer Muhammad Ali, *Float Like a Butterfly, Sting Like a Bee*, is released.

Following the Watts uprising of 1965 and continued social unrest, a group of students of color at UCLA petition for the creation of an Ethno-Communications initiative. Several students from this program go on to become part of a group now known as the L.A. Rebellion.

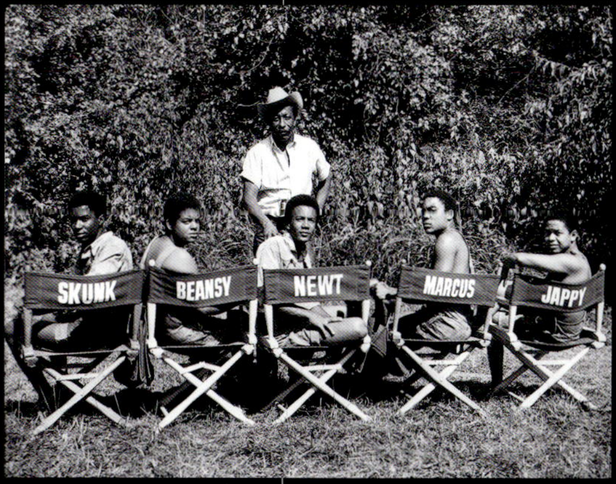

Gordon Parks with the cast of *The Learning Tree* (1969), publicity still

CINEMATIC HISTORY

1970

Robert L. Goodwin begins a crowdfunding campaign to direct *Black Chariot* (1971).

Ossie Davis's *Cotton Comes to Harlem* is released. Shot primarily on location in Harlem, it utilized local actors as extras.

The documentary *King: A Filmed Record... Montgomery to Memphis*, chronicling Martin Luther King Jr.'s nonviolent civil rights campaign, is released.

Melvin Van Peebles's *Watermelon Man* is released, leading Columbia Pictures to offer Van Peebles a three-film contract, which he declines.

1971

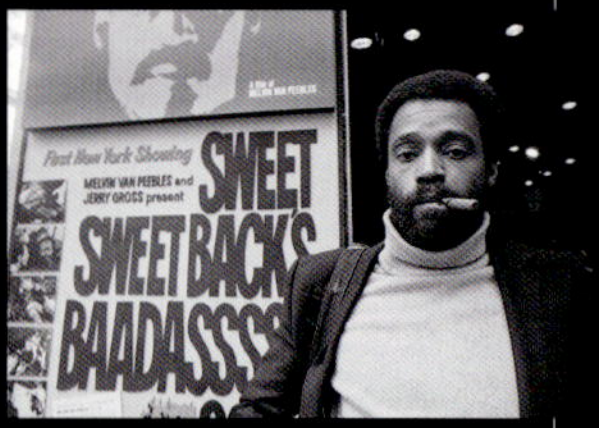

Melvin van Peebles at the New York premiere of *Sweet Sweetback's Baadasssss Song* (1971), publicity still

Melvin Van Peebles's *Sweet Sweetback's Baadasssss Song*, advertised with the tagline "Rated X by an all-white jury," becomes one of the highest-grossing independent films of the era.

Gordon Parks's *Shaft* is released; Isaac Hayes's "Theme from *Shaft*" will win an Oscar for Original Song.

Sounder (1972), featuring Oscar-nominated actors Cicely Tyson and Paul Winfield, begins shooting in Baton Rouge, Louisiana, after racial tensions in Georgia led the producers to change the location.

SOCIAL & POLITICAL HISTORY

The Congressional Black Caucus is formed.

Influential musican Louis Armstrong dies on July 6.

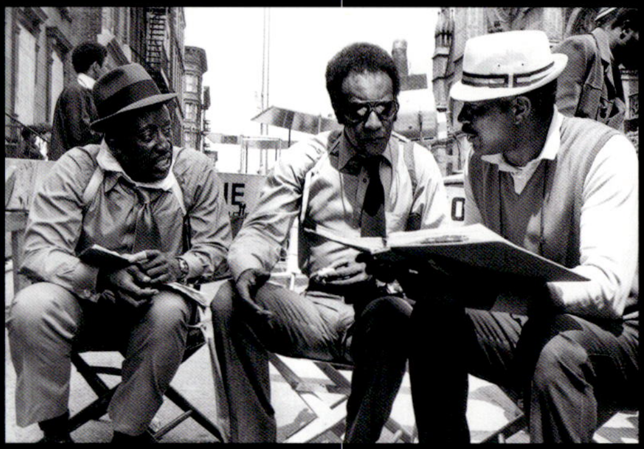

From left: Godfrey Cambridge, Raymond St. Jacques, and director Ossie Davis on set of *Cotton Comes to Harlem* (1970), production still

1970-71

INTERVIEWS

CHARLES

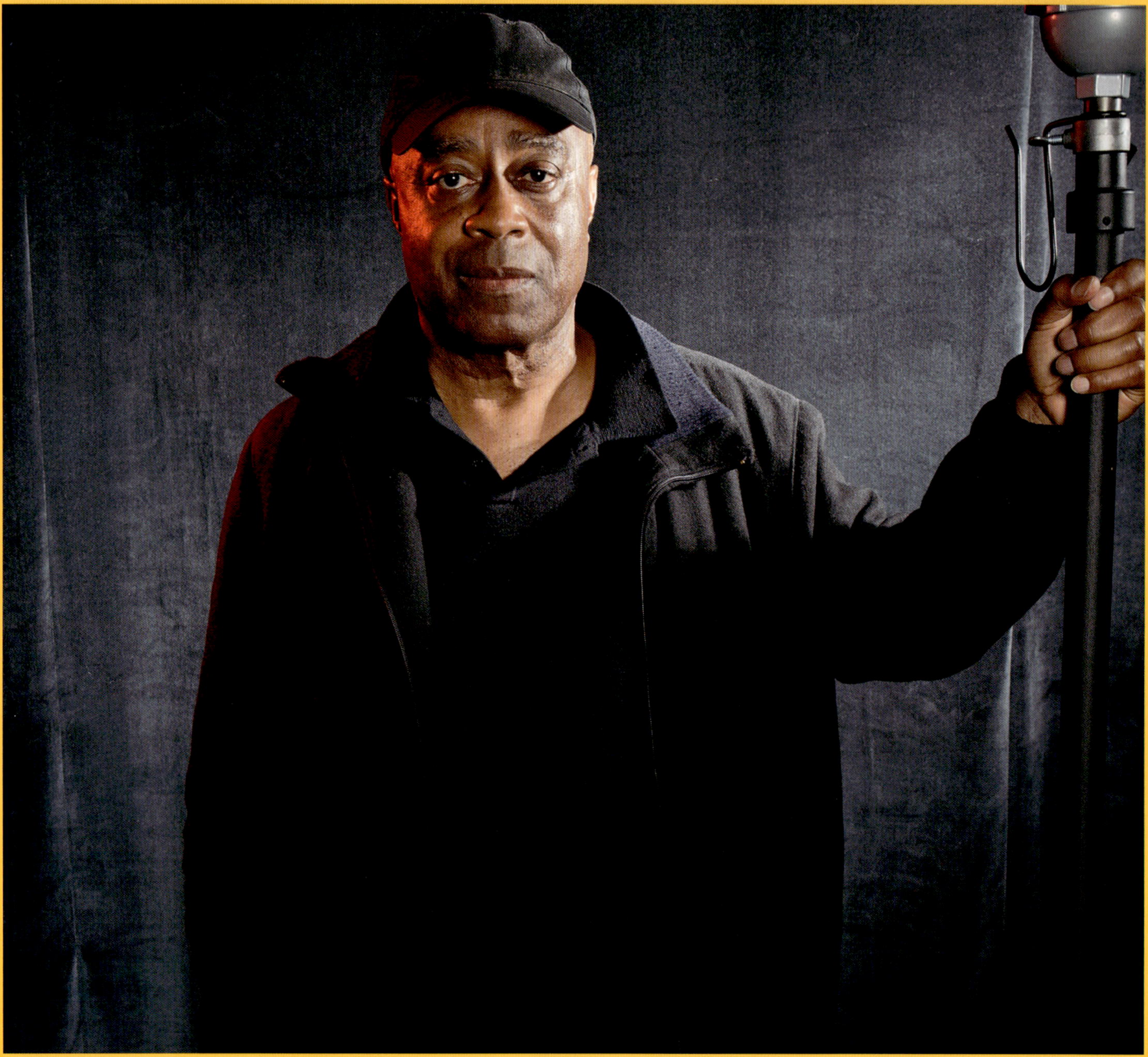

BURNETT

Opposite
Timothy Hiatt (photographer),
Charles Burnett, 2017

Charles Burnett (b. 1944) has the cinematic eye of a poet and an uncanny ability to turn the everyday experiences of working-class Black families into thoughtful stories. His work as a writer, director, and producer is informed by his appreciation for the beauty of the mundane. Burnett's *Killer of Sheep* (1978) presents episodes from the life of a slaughterhouse worker in the Watts neighborhood of Los Angeles in a style that has frequently been compared to Italian neorealism. The *New York Times* called the film "an American masterpiece, independent to the bone," and it was one of the first fifty films selected for the National Film Registry by the Library of Congress.[1] *To Sleep with Anger* (1990), a family drama written and directed by Burnett, received awards for Best Screenplay and Best Director at the Independent Spirit Awards, a Special Jury Prize at the Sundance Film Festival, and a National Society of Film Critics Award for screenwriting. In 2017 the Academy of Motion Picture Arts and Sciences honored Burnett with an Honorary Award.

This interview was conducted at the Academy Museum of Motion Pictures on March 4, 2020. It has been edited and condensed for clarity.

RHEA COMBS

How did growing up in Los Angeles help to shape and craft your stories and storytelling?

CHARLES BURNETT

I was born in Vicksburg, Mississippi. Everyone who lived in my area, South Central [Los Angeles], was from the South: Texas, Arkansas, Louisiana, North Carolina, South Carolina. People had all these stories about their experiences in the South, so in certain ways the South was more this mystery that people talked about that was bigger than life: the things that they experienced, the horror of it. There was a relationship to the South that was real and unreal. The people whom I admired were hardworking, had family. But popular culture said, "Black people don't do this. Black people don't do that." The examples I encountered were just the opposite. Growing up, I was trying to reconcile all this craziness, and because I had a speech impediment, I was always listening and observing, observing more than participating in a lot of things. And I was always looking at compositions and images.

DORIS BERGER

What brought you to film? You went into photography as well, right?

CB

When I was young, I wanted to be a trumpet player but also a photojournalist, because I used to look at old black-and-white photos. I think it was the way journalists expressed themselves, what they would capture, that moved me more than anything. One of the things about still photography, and black-and-white photography in particular, is that it concentrates on an image and a face. You can look at it forever, and it gives you so much information about the character.

RC

I know that you used to play the trumpet growing up. And one of my favorite scenes in *Killer of Sheep* features Earth, Wind & Fire and the little girl singing, and even in *To Sleep with Anger*, music plays an important part. Can you speak a little bit about how your early days as a musician, a trumpeter, influenced your work? How do you see music factoring in to the filmmaking process?

CB

Well, you look for ideas and tones and things like that. Music supplies that. There are certain songs or melodies that help to create images. In fact, I talked to the late playwright August Wilson once about this, and he did the same thing. He used to listen to old records, and he got a lot of his ideas for plays from them. I look at the complexity of music, with the different themes going on and sounds and all these things coming in and out. I like gestures, the times when a gesture can reveal something about the character. One thing I try to think about when I write a character is the contradictions he would face. Is the audience aware of him being aware of something that he's trying to hide? It's not always about verbal things.

RC

You attended film school at UCLA. How did it impact your approach to filmmaking?

CB

Professor Elyseo Taylor was influential in many ways, because he brought in a lot of people of color as part of the Ethno-Communications program. The idea was to tell stories about your people. It wasn't about a Hollywood kind of interpretation or a comic or escapist approach but an attempt to have students delve deeply into their experiences and express them. Elyseo offered examples of "Third World" cinema in which people were making political films about Cuba or Africa and social protests. And it was like the sun started shining all of a sudden. *Beep*. That's what we were supposed to be doing.

In the Ethno-Communications program, we discussed the question "What is a Black film?" And we had almost knock-down, drag-out fights. We didn't come to a conclusion, but it was easier to say what was not a Black film by pointing to things that indicated that the artist's interest was someplace else. In the general film school population, they just made films about anything. They were into exploring their sexuality and stuff like that. We were talking about police brutality and racism. Those were our primary concerns. The films Taylor brought into the department were an eye-opener, a revelation. It was like, "Why weren't these films included in the history of film classes?"

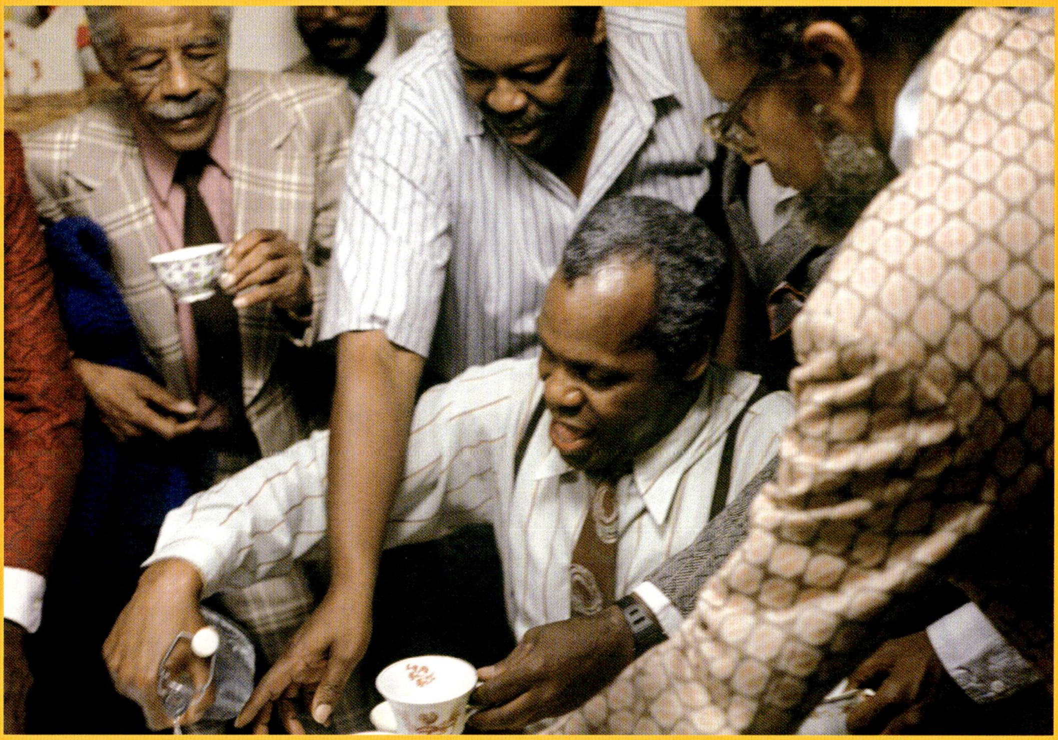

From left: Davis Roberts, Paul Butler, and Danny Glover (seated) in *To Sleep with Anger* (dir. Charles Burnett, 1990), film still

RC

I can see the relationship between your initial interest, after music, in photojournalism and your work in film. Again, it's about documenting these moments that tell us something about life and how people go about their daily existence. Can you expand on this idea?

CB

I remember looking at a picture of the blues musician Mississippi John Hurt, and here was this person who looked like he picked cotton all his life and the sun had just beaten him down and everything. But the man was a poet. That's the thing that really moves me about people, that they have this wealth of information stored. You can't judge a book by its cover when you look at characters like that. And the lyrics that came from this guy are amazing. People like that are not scholars, but they understand feelings and emotions and storytelling and words. And I've always admired those people.

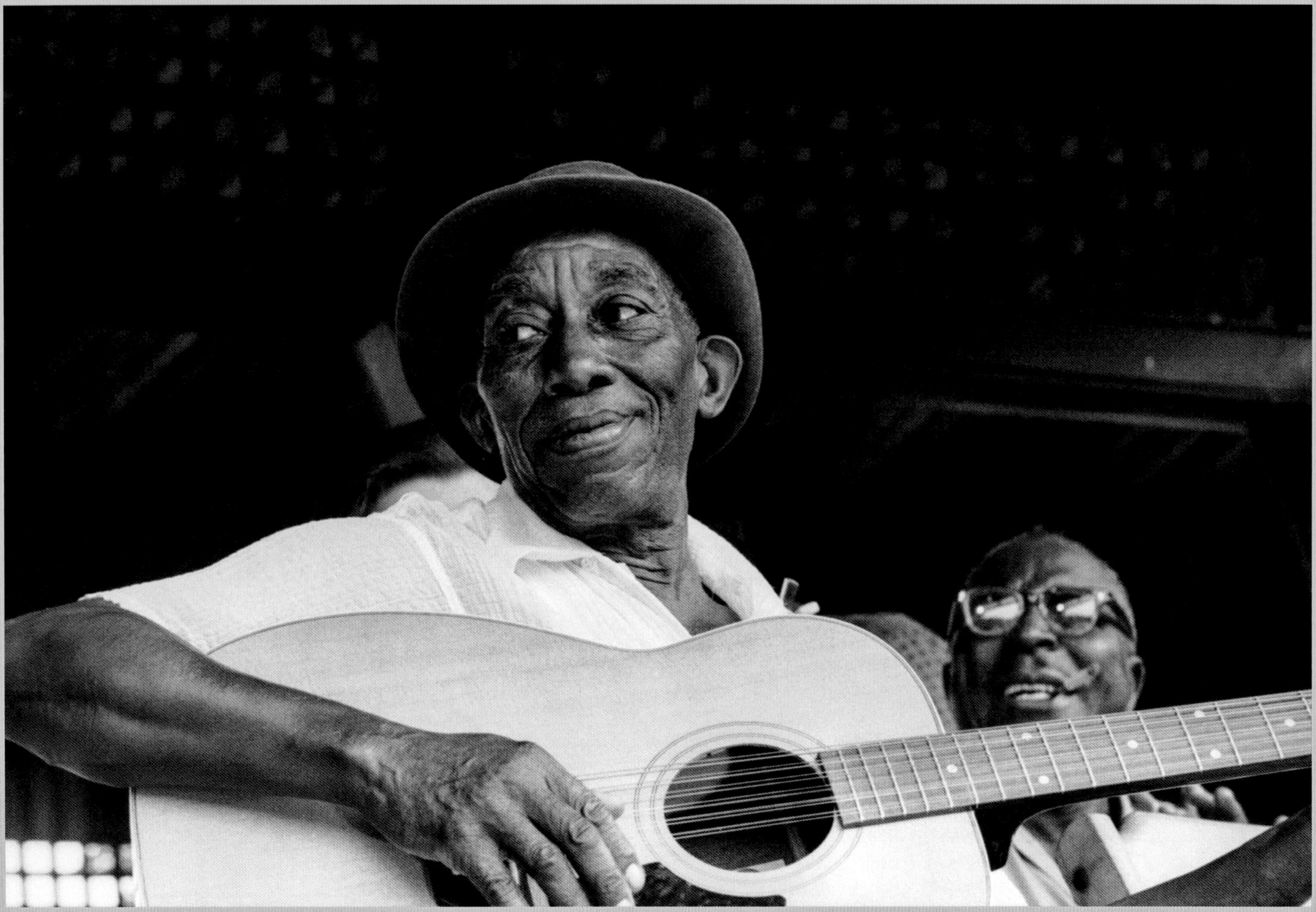

Mississippi John Hurt performing at the Newport Folk Festival, Rhode Island, 1963

These people didn't live in vain. They were appreciated, and they're appreciated by a much larger audience now that you helped to bring that about. Things like that make you hang in there, I suppose.

DB

As a filmmaker, how do you see your role in society?

CB

When we were coming up, there was this silly notion that you spoke for the Black community somehow; you represented. In reality you don't. And that's why I did *Killer of Sheep* the way I did, because I didn't want to impose my values, but I knew that everything in it had happened, that it wasn't anything that I had fabricated. I just put together a whole series of incidents that I had witnessed. I exaggerated them a bit, but they were all there, so I figured that I wouldn't try to make an obvious comment on life as such. But when I did *Killer of Sheep*, I knew that I wanted to have a discussion in the community about social things. I wish more people of color could have seen the film and that I could have made more.

Henry G. Sanders and Kaycee Moore in *Killer of Sheep* (dir. Charles Burnett, 1978), film still

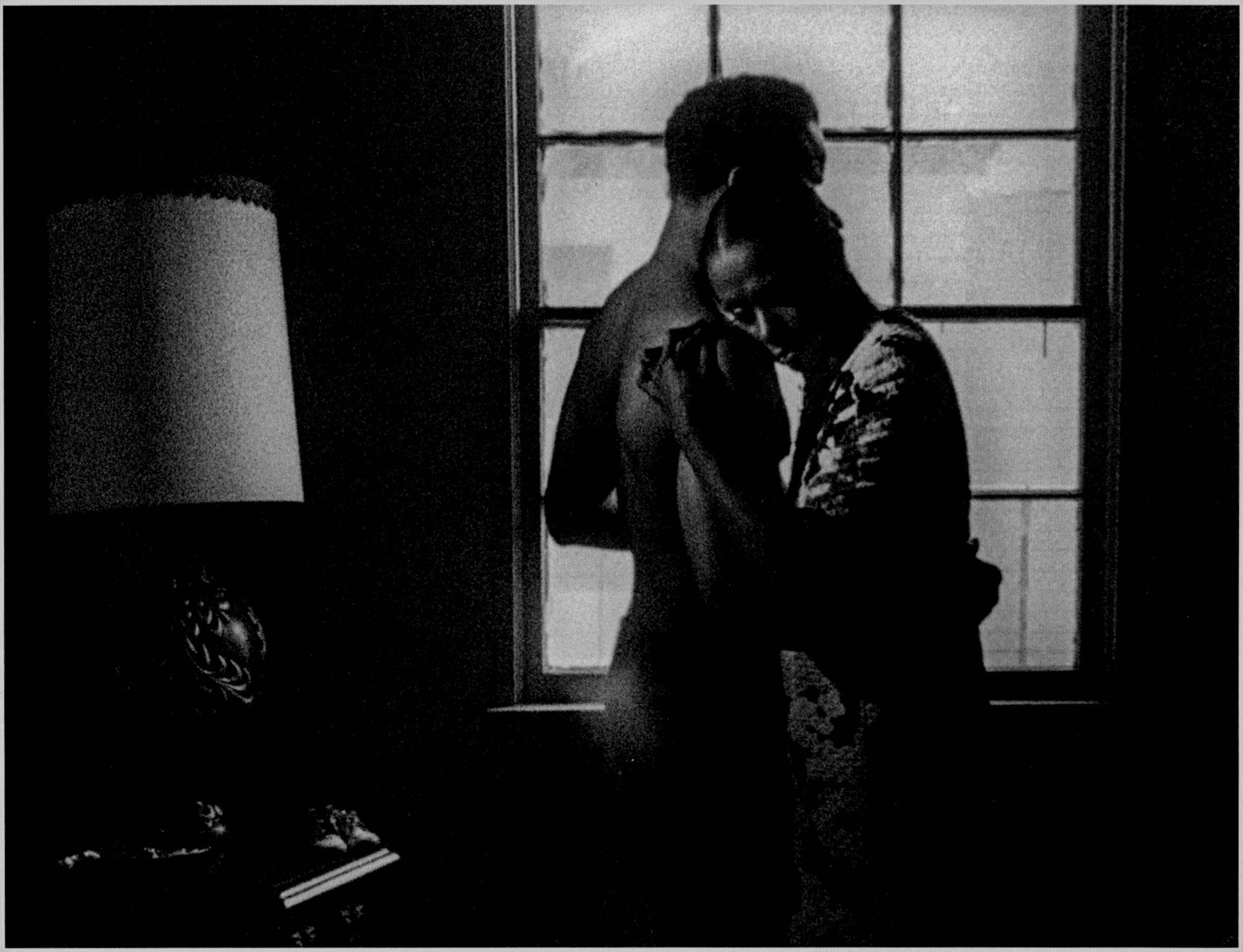

RC

Is there a distinction between the role of the artist, the filmmaker, that is separate from the role of a Black filmmaker, a Black artist? Why do it?

CB

I am a filmmaker primarily because I like it. The kind of films that I make, and that people I know make, try to reveal something about life. I would have enjoyed seeing, as a young person, the stories of my community. People I grew up with, the people I admired, the people who got up in the morning, four o'clock in the morning, to catch a bus to work and then come back. All these elderly ladies you would see on the bus coming home with big shopping bags full of things they bought at Grand Central Market. Where in those days you could get fruit for five cents a pound and lamb chops and all that sort of thing for almost nothing. I guess I romanticized the image in a certain way, but I really admired those folks.

My generation rejected a lot of things that the previous generation had to work through. We didn't want to work as carpenters, didn't want all these things that were given to us. And that's the part I hate; that's the part I'd like to rectify by paying homage to a lot of these folks. In my films I want to show people who, in spite of everything, stick through it and make sure that, if nothing else, the kids go on the right path and just do right.

As a filmmaker, you try and make other people see what you see in these folks, because if you can do that, I think you're doing well. These people didn't live in vain. They were appreciated, and they're appreciated by a much larger audience now that you helped to bring that about. Things like that make you hang in there, I suppose.

Notes

1 Manohla Dargis, "Whereabouts in Watts? Where Poetry Meets Chaos," *New York Times*, March 30, 2007, https://www.nytimes.com/2007/03/30/movies/30kill.html.

JULIE

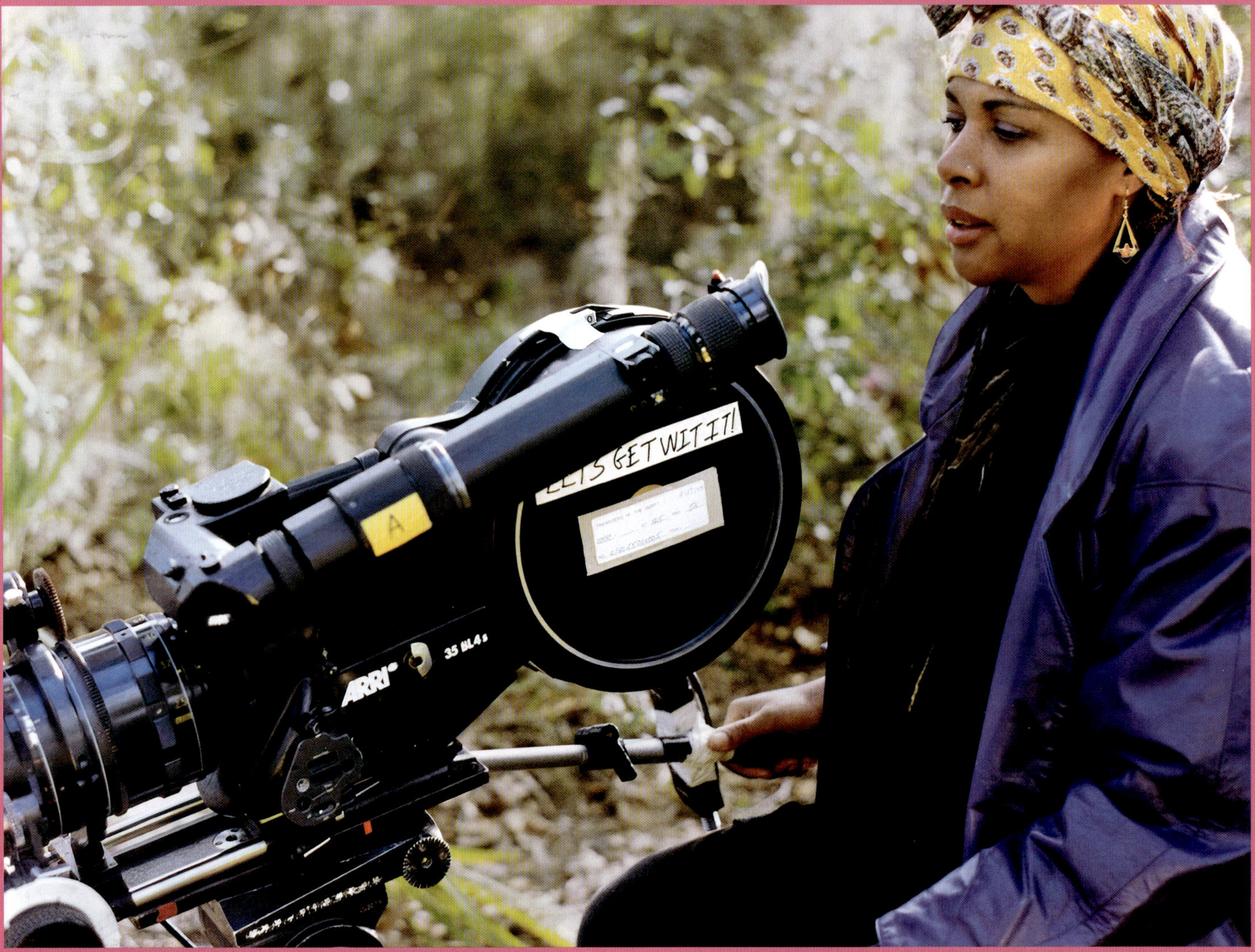

DASH

Opposite
Julie Dash on location for *Daughters of the Dust* (1991), production still

Julie Dash (b. 1952) is a filmmaker, writer, and producer. Dash was a part of a cohort of young Black filmmakers trained at the UCLA, between the late 1960s and the early 1980s who were dubbed the L.A. Rebellion. Her experimental, short, and feature-length film and television works have consistently centered on the Black woman's image and story. *Daughters of the Dust* (1991), her award-winning theatrical feature, revolves around the female members of a Gullah family living on one of the sea islands off the coast of Georgia. Richard Brody of the *New Yorker* wrote, "It's a movie that runs less than two hours and feels like three or four—not in sitting time but in substance, in historical scope and depth of emotion, in the number of characters it brings to life and the novelistic subtlety of the connections between them, in the profusion of its ideas and the cinematic imagination with which they're realized."[1] *Daughters of the Dust* received the Excellence in Cinematography Award at the 1991 Sundance Film Festival, and in 2004 the Library of Congress selected it for the National Film Registry, noting at the time that it was the first feature film by an African American woman to receive general theatrical release.

This interview was conducted via Zoom on January 13, 2021.
It has been edited and condensed for clarity.

RHEA COMBS

When you decided that you wanted to be a filmmaker, were you familiar with people like William Foster or other early Black filmmakers?

JULIE DASH

I became more familiar with the history of African American participation in film once I got to UCLA. Before I was in the MFA program there, I started out in the after-school workshop at the Studio Museum in Harlem, where we watched films by the Russian filmmaker Sergei Eisenstein as well as films by Oscar Micheaux. I also attended City College of New York, where I majored in film as an undergrad. We were looking at films made by Americans at the time. Then I went to the AFI Conservatory, and there was no mention of Black films. I once approached the director of the program, Toni Vellani, and said, "Why can't we see any films made by Black filmmakers?" He used to smoke with a long cigarette holder, and he slowly and dramatically removed his cigarette, looked at me, and said, "There are no Black filmmakers." That was at the American Film Institute in the late seventies. Then I went on to UCLA, where my instructors included Teshome Gabriel, Robert Nakamura, and Jorge Preloran, and I was able to learn more, not only about the Johnson brothers, Foster, Micheaux, and others, but the world of international filmmaking and filmmakers opened up to me, literally.

RC

It's encouraging to know that even though you've had this varied trajectory in film education, you weren't discouraged when someone so brazenly told you, a Black filmmaker, that there are no Black filmmakers. That's a powerful testament to your determination and grit.

JD

Well, I knew it not to be true. I didn't have anyone pointing me in any direction, but I knew from the discussions at the Studio Museum in Harlem that Micheaux was not the one and only, that there were other people making films. And of course years later we learned about Black women filmmakers and were able to see snippets of their work.

DORIS BERGER

What do you see as the role of a Black filmmaker in society, and do you see filmmaking as distinct from other creative professions?

JD

The role of the Black filmmaker in society depends on the generation, because when I started making films, I had no idea that this would be my profession. I started out in high school, and I wasn't thinking in terms of a career. Other than Sarah Maldoror, who made the film *Sambizanga* [1972], and also Sara Gómez in Cuba, and later Kathleen Collins, there were no other Black women filmmakers that I knew about. I could not see their films at the time. I only saw stills from their films.

Film is an interesting thing. You get bitten by the film bug, and you start shooting and editing, and it becomes an obsession. It becomes a passion, a joy. It becomes everything. Well, it did for me, but I came up during a very particular time. It was right after the Black Arts Movement [ca. 1965–75]. And I had things to say, but I was not a photojournalist, I was not a poet. So I kind of melded the two together. Being an undergraduate in New York City and reading Toni Morrison and Toni Cade Bambara, I started thinking, "Why can't I see *Sula*? Why can't I see stories from *Gorilla, My Love*? Why can't I see *Corregidora* by Gayl Jones?" I wanted to see those films. And it was like, "Well, maybe I could make them."

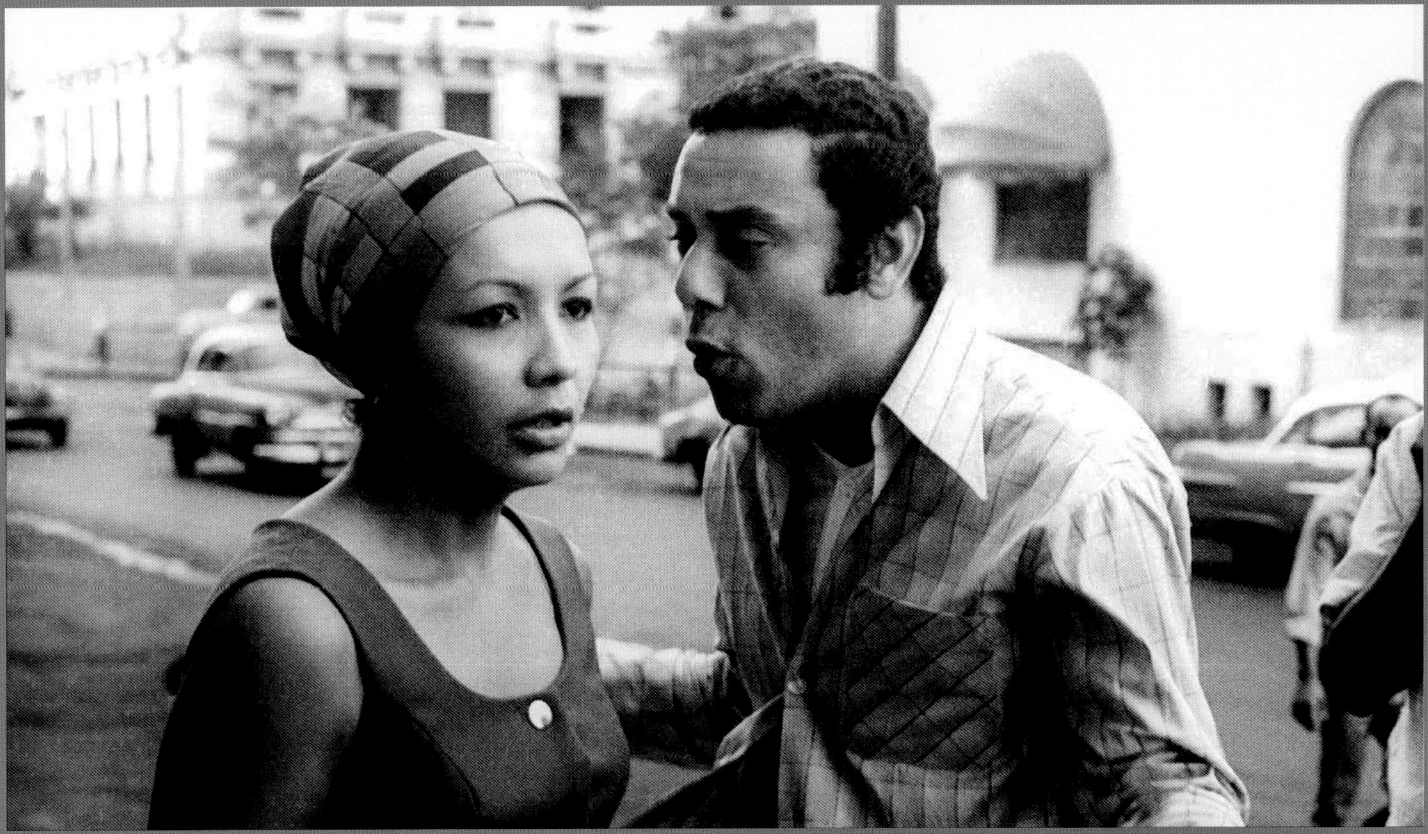

Yolanda Cuellar and Mario Balmaseda in *De cierta manera* (*One Way or Another*, dir. Sara Gómez, Cuba, 1974), film still

RC

How has poetry impacted or influenced your practice?

JD

In the late sixties and early seventies, it was the poetry that caused me to weep. I was reading Jayne Cortez, Nikki Giovanni, all the poets of the time. Sonia Sanchez—I'll just never forget the passage she wrote about the death of Malcolm X:

> do not speak to me of martyrdom,
> of men who die to be remembered
> on some parish day.
> i don't believe in dying
> though i too shall die
> and violets like castanets
> will echo me.[2]

Well, how do you visualize that? That became important to me, a task that I wanted to complete, to create visual poetry, to create a lyricism that was powerful and gentle at the same time. And that was one of the reasons I did the film *Four Women* [1975]. It was a highly experimental film, but when making films that matter, they're all experiments with touching the inner self.

RC

Is there a distinct role for someone who identifies as a Black woman filmmaker?

JD

Yes. I think there is something very distinctive about being a self-identified Black woman filmmaker and a mother. I've always felt that I was on this mission to tell stories that are meaningful, stories that help change the world, in some small way, for the betterment of our children. Black lives do matter, and we have to see that in all kinds of media. I receive a lot of pushback; people keep asking, "What else are you going to do?" That's because my stories are about Black women's issues, agency, identity, and memory—not any kind of addiction story, drugs, sex, money, or alcohol. But my experience as a storyteller is not the case for everyone. It's not just the stories you want to tell; it's the funding sources, the money. Film executives, Black and white, young and old, want me to tell stories that they're curious about, not stories that I'm curious about exploring and bringing to the screen.
So that's the dance that's been going on for forty years. One of the stories I've been working on for over a decade is a limited series about Major Charity Adams and the 6888th Central Postal Directory Battalion, the 855 African American women who served overseas during World War II.

People say, "Well, do you have any other ideas?" It's like, yes. Then I pitch them, and I get the blank stare. That's when I know I've got a great story to tell! It's not a part of their worldview.

RC

Is that specific to being a woman within a predominantly male field? Or is it because you're so clear about your mission as a filmmaker?

JD

It's all of the above. It's gender; it's the fact that I'm almost six feet tall, a big Black woman. That I'm African American and not ashamed to say I'm African American and want to do films about women.

DB

You have been a truly independent filmmaker.

JD

I have done a lot of movies for television too.

DB

Is more agency possible in other production platforms such as television?

JD

Not a whole lot. In *Funny Valentines* [1999], I got to include some imagery that I knew to be real about the Black church and female ushers in the church. And canning fruits and vegetables as a way of preserving the best of each spring, the best years of your life—I got to massage that into *The Rosa Parks Story* [2002]. Thankfully Angela Bassett was an executive producer on that show. We included scenes in it that weren't necessarily in the screenplay. We shot them. But some things that we shot were cut out because they said, "Hey, I don't recognize this from the script." So there was a lot of give-and-take. But why does it have to be like that?

RC

How do you persevere and find the strength within yourself to continue the work that you do?

JD

I wrote a novel, the continuing story of *Daughters of the Dust*. And I worked on a second novel after that. But there was a period of about ten years that went by after that when I did not work. I realized that I did not become a filmmaker for them, for the film industry. I became a filmmaker because I loved telling stories. There were so many stories that I wanted to tell. So what I could do is write and speak and teach young filmmakers. The other day the filmmaker Ava DuVernay posted on social media—I'm paraphrasing here—"Things don't happen to you, they happen for you." And I agree. My life is a good life. I'm a mother, a grandmother, a filmmaker, and a professor at Spelman College.

RC

What draws you to a topic or a story or a person? How do you develop your projects?

JD

I have a stack of screenplays for feature films and limited series that I have been promoting and pitching since *Daughters of the Dust*, and I always get interesting email. People say, "Well, do you have any other ideas?" It's like, yes. Then I pitch them, and I get the blank stare. That's when I know I've got a great story to tell! It's not a part of their worldview.

RC

How do you develop your characters? Do they speak to you?

JD

Yes, and at the risk of sounding schizophrenic, characters will also make you weep. And that's when you really know you're going in the right direction. You're working with dialogue, and all of a sudden you realize that you're weeping while you're typing. It's like, "Oh, my God, this is important. This needs to be said."

DB

Your film *Illusions* still resonates with me today, although you made that in 1982. It's a beautiful short film and a powerful story of a female producer. You made it while you were a student at UCLA, right? You knew so much already about all the problems in Hollywood.

JD

It's all right out there if you read the history of the motion picture industry and the wartime movies that wouldn't be made. There was a whole propaganda machine at work in Hollywood, and we usually associate propaganda with something coming from another country. I thought, "Hmm, that's interesting." And then as I did more research, I found out that even the janitorial staff at the Hollywood studios during the 1940s were all white. So it was like, "How do I get a Black woman in there?" I realized that there were two ways. I knew that the tap dancing by stars like Ginger Rogers and Fred Astaire was embellished by Black dancers. And we all knew that Black women often were the singing voices for Hollywood stars. So I said, "OK, I've got that Black woman. How do I get another Black woman in there?" And it was like, "Oh, my God, she could be passing for white but not like *Pinky* [1949] and not like *Imitation of Life* [1934; remake, 1959]." It's not that she said that she wasn't Black. No one asked her. But *Illusions* offended quite a few people in the eighties because they were so attached to a *Pinky* or *Imitation of Life* story line. So when they saw me doing it, they were like, "Well, she's passing for white, and that's a bad thing." But there are different levels of passing for white.

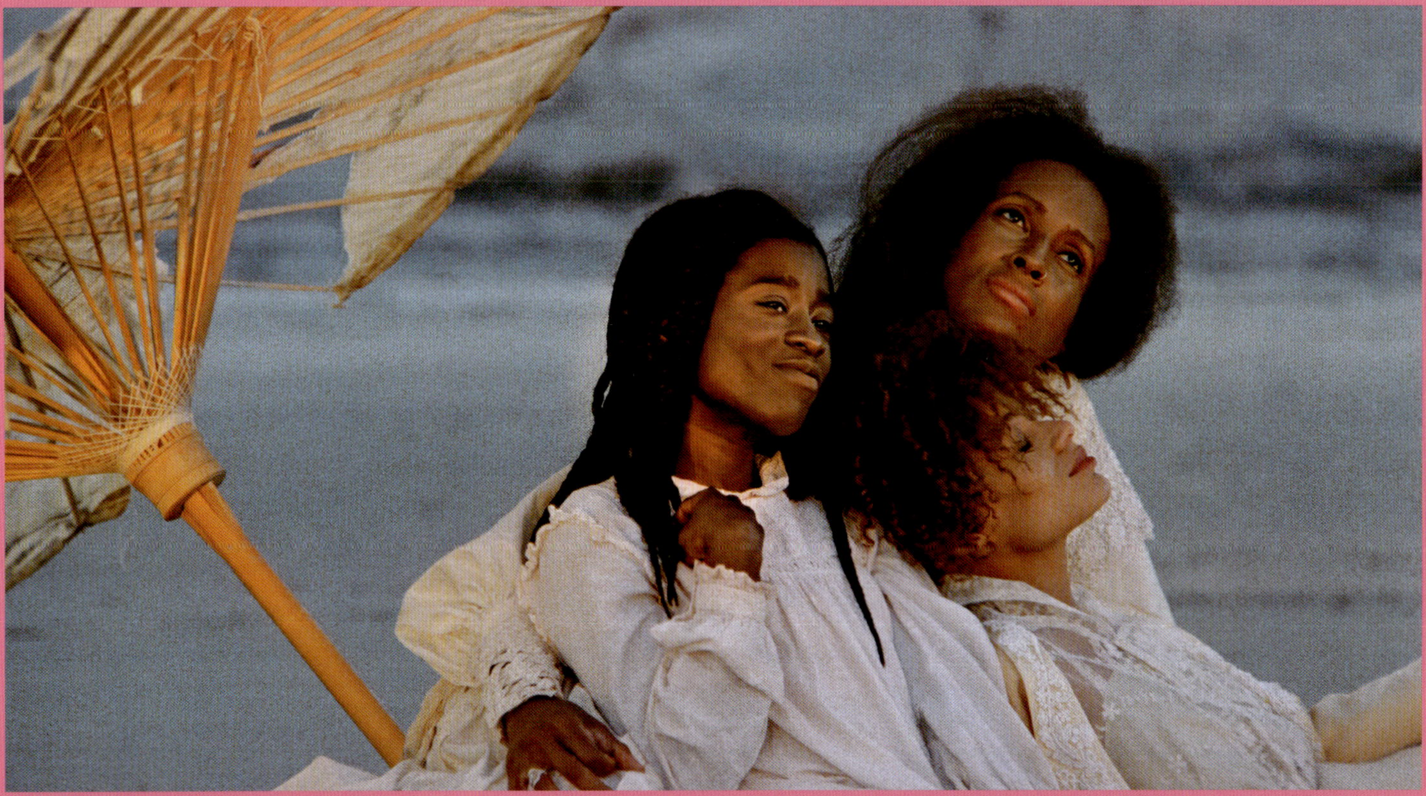

Alva Rogers, Barbara O. Jones, and Trula Hoosier (clockwise from left) in *Daughters of the Dust* (dir. Julie Dash, 1991), film still

Lonette McKee in *Illusions*
(dir. Julie Dash, 1982), film still

RC

How would you define Black film?

JD

Well, that's interesting. And it's something that we've talked about over the years, because back when there were not that many African American filmmakers working, there was a film called *Nothing but a Man* [1964], which was directed by Michael Roemer, who is not a Black filmmaker, but its artistic sensibilities were such that we considered it a Black film. So what is a Black film? It has to do with the authenticity of the subject matter, of the theme, and not trying to exploit the culture or the religion or the traditions. It doesn't necessarily have to be made by a Black filmmaker. And sometimes Black filmmakers just want to make films.

They want to do films that have nothing to do with the culture or the traditions. And so it's difficult to say, but you know it when you see it; it's a feeling. You're watching it, and it's like, "Wow, this really resonates as a product of the Black aesthetic."

DB

The Black aesthetic. There were so many debates when *Lemonade* [2016] came out about Beyoncé referring to *Daughters of the Dust*. But then you also mentioned that you were referring in your film to Bill Gunn's *Ganja & Hess* [1973].

JD

Yes, the cinematic displays and visual rhetoric in *Ganja & Hess*, along with Isaac Julien's *Looking for Langston* [1989]. The visual poetics of *Looking for Langston* and the poetics of *Ganja & Hess*, there's a connection. It's a continuum of postmodernist ideas and visual metaphor as it relates to African diasporic culture.

Notes

1 Richard Brody, "The Return of Julie Dash's Historic 'Daughters of the Dust,'" *New Yorker*, November 18, 2016, https://www.newyorker.com/culture/richard-brody/the-return-of-julie-dashs-historic-daughters-of-the-dust.

2 Sonia Sanchez, "Malcolm," in *Shake Loose My Skin: New and Selected Poems* (Boston: Beacon, 1999), 6.

AVA

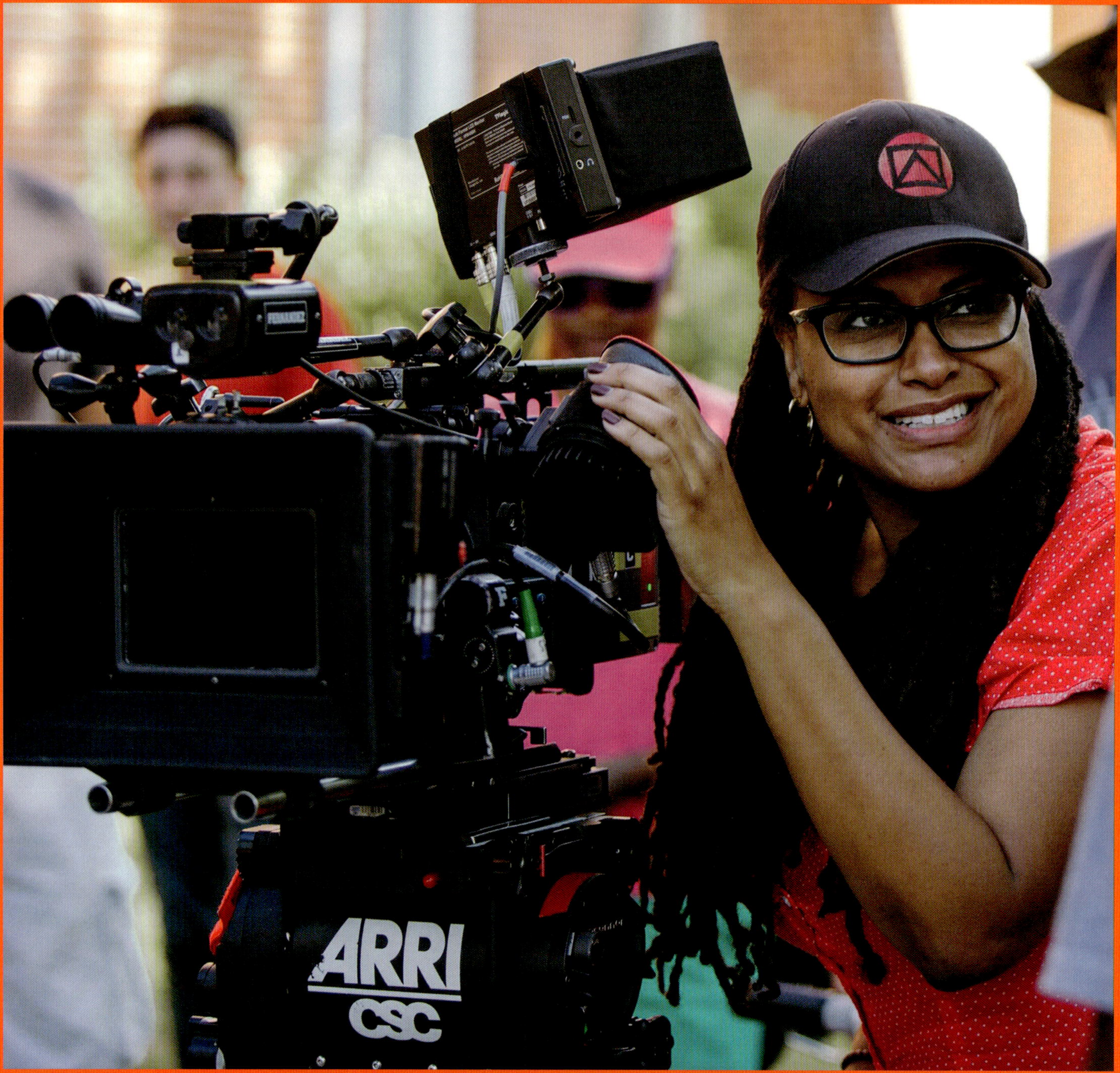

DuVERNAY

Opposite
Ava DuVernay directing *Selma* (2014), production still

Ava DuVernay (b. 1972) is a director, writer, producer and founder of the narrative change collective ARRAY. Her second feature, *Middle of Nowhere* (2012), which chronicles a woman grappling with the incarceration of her husband, won the directing award in the US dramatic category at the Sundance Film Festival. DuVernay was the first Black person to receive this honor. *Selma* (2014), a historical drama about the landmark voting rights marches of 1965, was nominated for an Academy Award for Best Picture, making her the first Black woman director to have a film so honored. Her Oscar-nominated documentary *13th* (2016)—which explores race, justice, and mass incarceration in the United States—received the Primetime Emmy Award for Outstanding Documentary. Beyond her work as a filmmaker, DuVernay seeks through ARRAY to disrupt traditional Hollywood systems in the pursuit of inclusivity and equity for Black people, people of color, and women of all kinds. She was elected to the Board of Governors of the Academy of Motion Picture Arts and Sciences in 2020.

This interview was conducted via Zoom on August 13, 2020. It has been edited and condensed for clarity.

DORIS BERGER

Does filmmaking have a special characteristic, and if so, how would you describe it?

AVA DuVERNAY

There's an absence of singularity in the practice of filmmaking that makes it unique. If I'm in an orchestra, everyone has their own instrument that can stand alone if it has to. There are solos, there are duets, there are smaller configurations. In film, you can't make it by yourself. It is a collaborative, communal process. It is a sculpture, in story form, that everyone places their fingerprints on. And the director's job is to be a watchperson making sure that, with everyone touching it, the sculpture gets as close as possible to what we are all aiming to achieve.

RHEA COMBS

Do you think that the Black filmmaker has a distinct role?

AD

The role of the filmmaker is to bear witness to human behavior: how we were, who we were, and how we felt at a certain time and place. This is true for filmmakers of all kinds. But bearing witness takes on a different meaning for certain kinds of filmmakers—Black filmmakers, filmmakers of color, some women filmmakers—as it relates to conjuring life on film and dealing with issues of representation, normalization, history, distortion, and community building. We're often doing something else with our films that must be done, must be said, must be shared, because we are correcting an absence. The white male filmmaker doesn't have to address the expression of his life on film in the same way. For anyone who's making films and who is not a white man, their films are functioning in a different way within the institutions of film. That's just the truth of it. Images made by people outside the dominant culture are being controlled by people within the dominant culture, and decisions are made as to their monetary worth, cultural value, critical weight, their very meaning; also their prospects for distribution, exhibition, marketing, and promotion within that culture. If a film by a Black filmmaker reaches audiences and keeps some muscularity of Blackness, it is a miracle. And so we have miracles out there, but there should be more. The very structure within which we work is not set up to foster dynamic Black stories, Brown stories, Indigenous stories, Asian stories.

Cinema segregation is something that is very real in this country. Historically there have not been art-house cinemas or even theaters, period, in Black neighborhoods. So how do you see Charles Burnett's *Killer of Sheep* [1978]? How do you know about it? How did we ever know about someone like William Foster? When you talk about education, when you talk about exhibition, distribution, it becomes daunting, and the conversation goes beyond the creative impulses of the Black filmmaker. Barry Jenkins's *Medicine for Melancholy* [2008], Horace Jenkins's *Cane River* [1982], Kathleen Collins's *Losing Ground* [1982]—Black audiences have not seen them widely because of access.

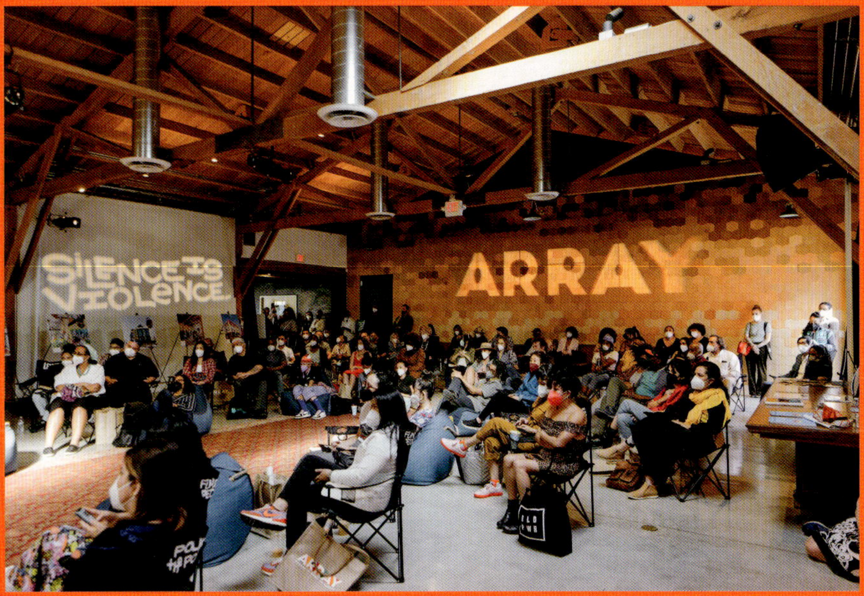

ARRAY Creative Campus in Historic Filipinotown, Los Angeles

RC

Can you describe your film education?

AD

I went to UCLA, home of the L.A. Rebellion filmmakers—Charles Burnett, Haile Gerima, Julie Dash. There was a great deal of pride at UCLA around many aspects of Black student life. The L.A. Rebellion filmmakers are a big part of that. So that's how I was introduced to that work. And I've come to revere them all and, in some cases, to know them personally and to work with them.

DB

Can you explain why and how you established ARRAY as an independent production and distribution company dedicated to images made by women and people of color?

AD

ARRAY focuses on the production, distribution, exhibition, and amplification of cinematic work by Black people, people of color, and women of all kinds. It was first envisioned to be a collective for releasing Black independent films to multiple markets directly, as we did with my first three films. Cut to ten years later, and ARRAY will release our fortieth film this year, distributed by hand. Over the past decade it's become less about survival, which is how it started: if we don't distribute these films, no one's going to do it. It's now more about disrupting the system of distribution and also looking at exhibition, because when I learned how to distribute films, we came up against the horrible system of exhibition. You can be the distributor, and you can bring out a film, but ultimately if you don't have a theater that will open its doors to you or the work, then the distribution has to find alternative ways. That's a big part of the puzzle that people don't understand.

RC

Does activism play a part in how you choose to create work for yourself and select projects?

AD

I approach ARRAY's support of artists and my own work as an artist as two different things. When selecting films or projects by other artists to distribute or offer grants or to amplify, I'm definitely thinking more as an activist. What's missing? Who needs help? Whose voice aren't we hearing? What images aren't we seeing? What system needs to be disrupted? When I'm choosing a project for myself, it's much less about those questions and more about what I'm personally attracted to and want to say and share.

13th (2016), theatrical release poster

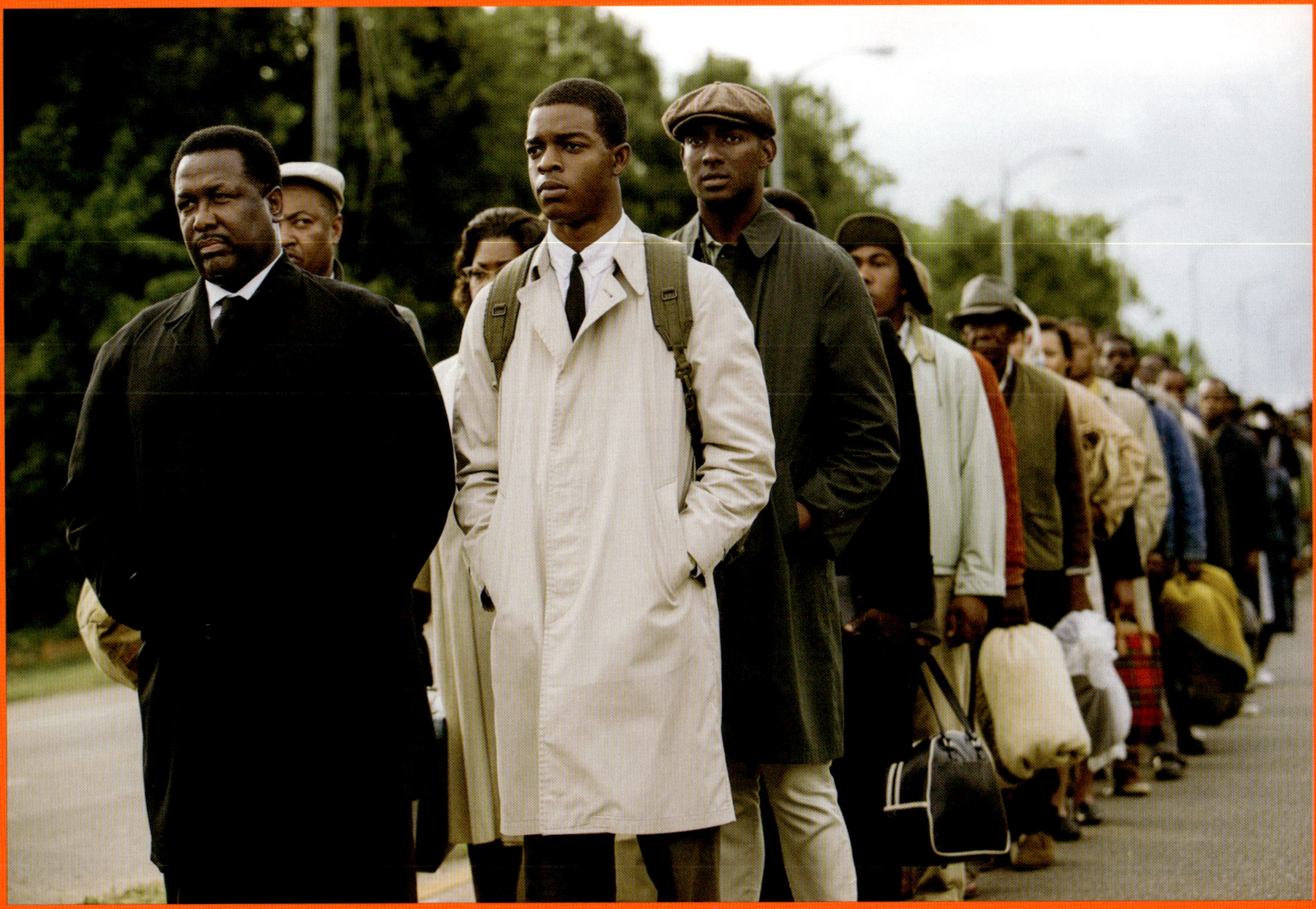

Foreground, left to right: Wendell Pierce and Stephan James in *Selma* (dir. Ava DuVernay, 2014), film still

RC

How do you decide on the stories?

AD

To be honest, as a Black woman filmmaker, a lot of times it's what's in front of you. What will someone finance? What is being offered? That was how it was for me early on; it's not that way for me anymore. This is new to me, to actually be in a space where I have choices. Right now I have an idea for a doc and an idea for a feature. And I'm probably going to do both. I work best when I've got multiple things going; one project feeds another in my mind. So *13th* was running across *Selma* and *Queen Sugar*. What a beautiful thing to be able to think about. I have the privilege to say, "Oh, I'll make a doc, I'll make a film, I'll make a limited series." And to work across genre, across format and category. I feel every day that I'm walking in the footsteps of people who came before. But you realize that at some point their footsteps run out and it's your footsteps. That you are going beyond what they were allowed to do and were supported in doing. It's a bittersweet feeling.

RC

How do you find your path forward while staying true to the core of your work?

AD

These days I'm more interested in making sure that what I'm making satisfies me personally and intimately. Not pursuing accolades that I'm told I should care about or climbing someone else's ladder. A lot of emerging filmmakers tell me that they worry that someone's going to steal their idea. I tell them, "First of all, you've stolen your idea, and you don't even know it. There's no idea that's new. And second, even if they tried to take your idea, they couldn't do it like you'd do it. And you can't do it like they'd do it. So just make your thing." That whole idea of theft, especially with Black filmmakers and women filmmakers—the feeling that "I've got to protect this thing"—is based on real trauma. But ultimately we've got to get past that to a free place, so that the work we're making isn't shackled by these old ways of thinking and these antiquated systems.

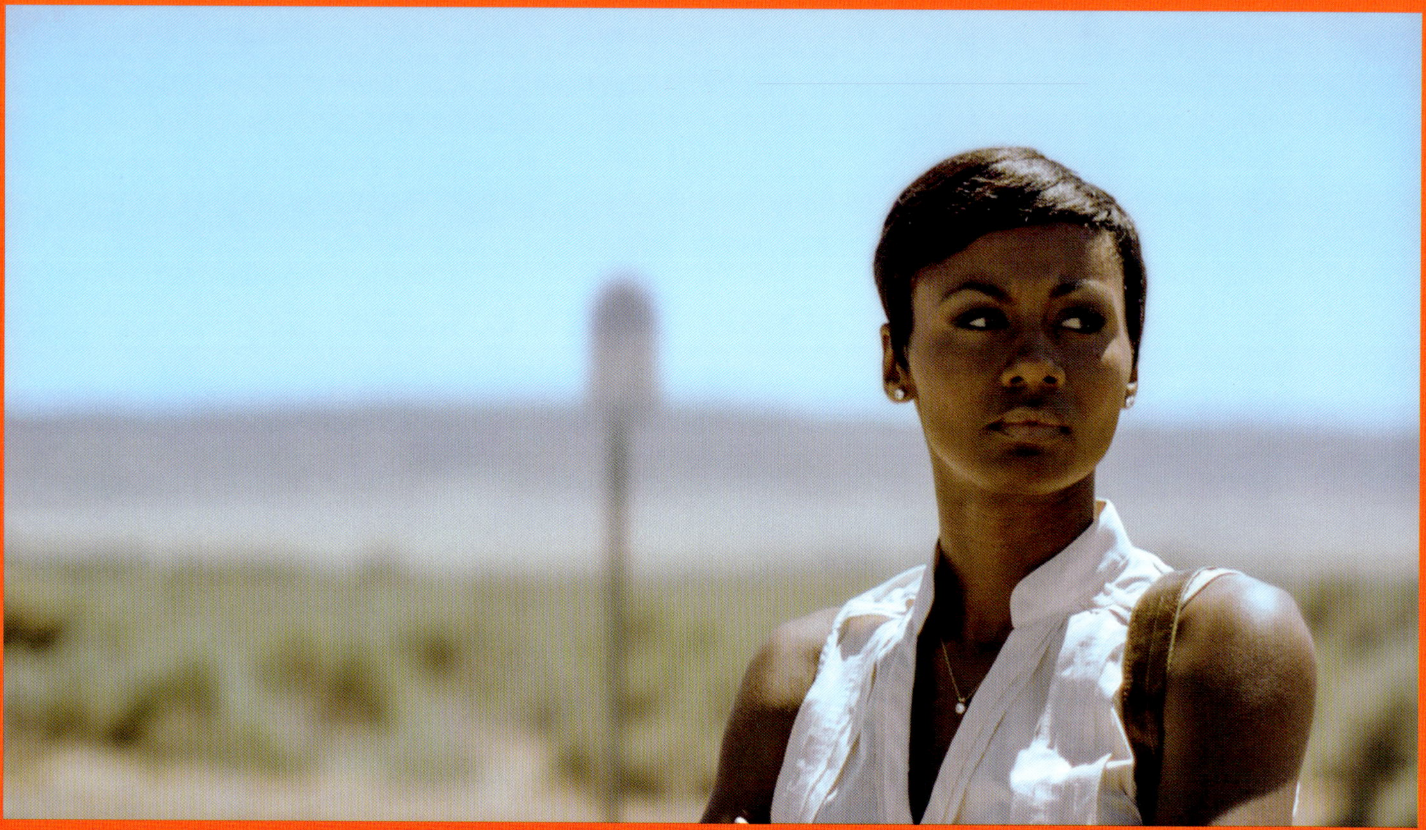

Emayatzy E. Corinealdi in *Middle of Nowhere* (dir. Ava DuVernay, 2012), film still

I feel every day that I'm walking in the footsteps of people who came before. But you realize that at some point their footsteps run out and it's your footsteps. That you are going beyond what they were allowed to do and were supported in doing. It's a bittersweet feeling.

RC

What do you see as the possibilities for contemporary filmmakers?

AD

It's a beautiful time. I think the reason why I've tried to work across a bunch of different categories and platforms and genres is truly to spread my wings and safeguard my creative freedom. If the film work dries up, then I can go to TV. If TV dries up, then I can make docs. I make music videos, commercials, art installations. Back to the sculpture analogy, Elizabeth Catlett worked with bronze, limestone, onyx, cedar, turquoise, mahogany, and marble. That's how I see streaming and theatrical features and limited and ongoing series and docs and shorts and commercials. Wherever the story takes me, I can go. I just started nonscripted, and I love it. We've got animation projects; that's new, directing animation. Completely different. The ability to work in these different spaces, I hope, will allow me to always be able to find a space to tell a story. That's my dream. Not to be bigger or richer or famous. To just be consistent. To always be able to tell my story somewhere, somehow.

BARRY

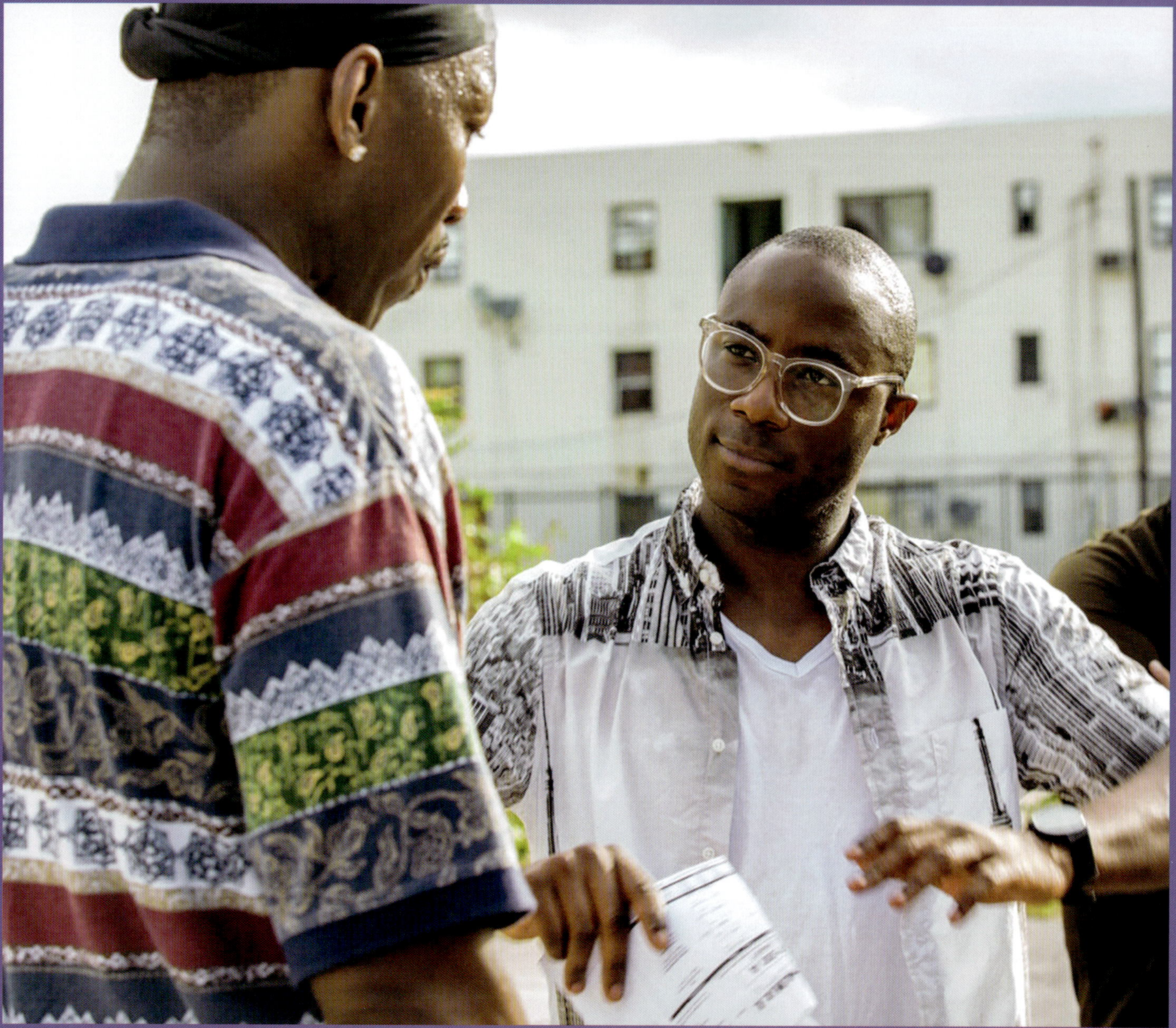

JENKINS

Opposite
Mahershala Ali (left) and Barry Jenkins on location for *Moonlight* (2016), production still

Barry Jenkins (b. 1979) is a screenwriter, director, and producer. *Medicine for Melancholy* (2008), a romantic drama written and directed by Jenkins, was nominated for an Independent Spirit Award for Best First Feature and later credited by the *New York Times* with helping to "unleash a new wave of auteur-driven, idiosyncratic black filmmaking."[1] His second feature, *Moonlight* (2016), was groundbreaking in its visual language and narrative, telling a compassionate and haunting coming-of-age story of a gay Black man from the South. The film received Academy Awards for Best Picture and Adapted Screenplay as well as a Golden Globe for Best Picture—Drama. Other works by Jenkins include his film adaptation of James Baldwin's novel *If Beale Street Could Talk* (2018) and the ten-part streaming series *The Underground Railroad* (2021), based on Colson Whitehead's Pulitzer Prize–winning novel.

This interview was conducted at Jenkins's production office in Los Angeles on April 9, 2019. It has been edited and condensed for clarity.

RHEA COMBS

When I look at your work, it reminds me of photographers who look at this kind of everyday beauty as well. Is this a deliberate choice?

BARRY JENKINS

It is. My first love as an artist was literature—Black letters, Black literature, Black essayists—and the way I absorbed that influence is such an interior process that it has organically affected the way I approach creative imagery. I went to college at Florida State, and in the basement of the main science library, there was just this treasure trove of photography and painting books. There was a lot of Roy DeCarava, a lot of Gordon Parks, and a lot of Chester Higgins there. Also, a lot of Mexican photographers. So that was where I began to pair the literature I was reading—James Baldwin, Richard Wright—with images, not necessarily motion pictures.

I remember reading *The Fire Next Time*. When I picked it up, I thought it was a novel by James Baldwin. I started reading it, and I realized that it was an essay formed as a letter to his nephew. So I was thinking, "Oh, that's interesting," because someone's passing on knowledge, but in this passing, they're speaking to me as well. At the time I was trying to make a short film about a very personal experience I had growing up in Miami and what it felt like the first time someone handed me a gun, which happened when I was twelve years old. There was a photo by Gordon Parks of this kid lying in the grass [*Boy with June Bug, Fort Scott, Kansas* (1963)]. I remember seeing that and going, "This is kind of what this feels like, because I went from being this kid, then this gun was in my hand." It was a loss of innocence in a certain way. I was thinking about how to synthesize it into a single image. I thought, "OK, cool, let me keep leaning into this, because there's something about this that's going to help me."

RC

Has this become part of your process?

BJ

Yes, absolutely, because I do think that art begets art in a certain way. Also, there's no way I'd be a filmmaker without Florida State. Florida State was a public university, so state funds were the foundation of the school. We didn't pay for film cameras. We didn't pay for film stock. They paid for everything. They owned the film, but they paid for everything. It guaranteed that everyone would get the opportunity to make a film. The difference was that the running times were limited. You had a very limited amount of film stock. The films needed to be, I think, eight minutes max.

It was the last window before digital technology came in. We shot everything on film, everything. We even cut on a flatbed in the first semester. I still try to think of it the same way. It's not just arbitrarily pointing the camera this way or that way, arbitrarily saying, "Let's do thirty takes." I remember the time when you literally had to do the math. OK, if I do another take of this, I'm not doing a take of that.

RC

You've long worked with the director of photography James Laxton and the editors Joi McMillon and Nat Sanders. What is gained from establishing this creative nucleus?

BJ

It wasn't a conscious decision until it was. I couldn't get anybody else to work with me when I started. And in film school you gravitate toward people, so that was that. But when I was making my first feature in 2008, *Medicine for Melancholy*, those were the only people I could get to work with me. Nobody else would take a chance. Then, when it came to *Moonlight*, it was like, well, why would I change anything? It's like a filmmaking family.

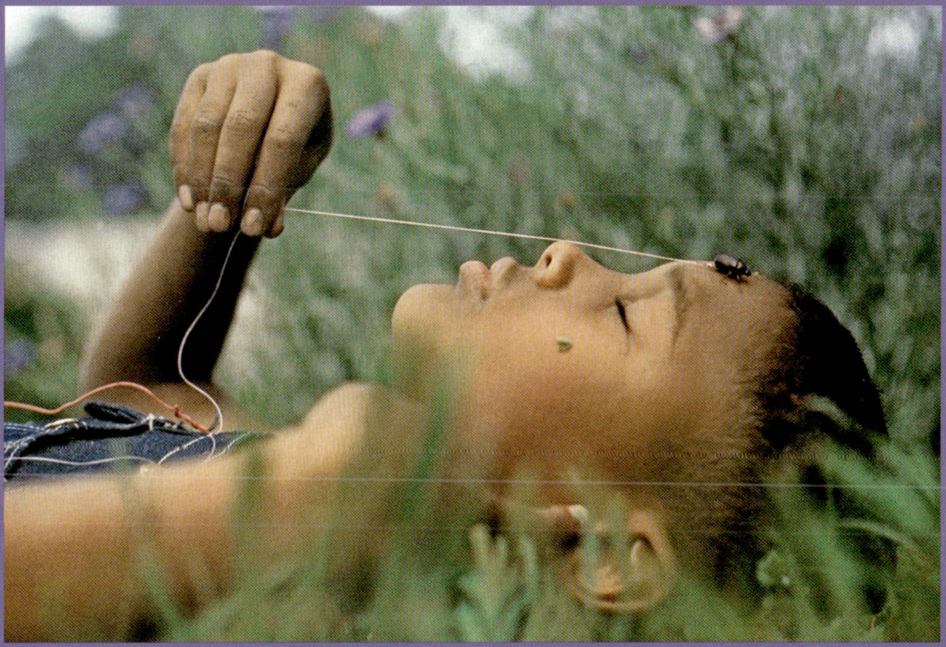

Gordon Parks (American, 1912–2006), *Boy with June Bug, Fort Scott, Kansas*, 1963, archival pigment print, 11 × 14 in. (27.9 × 35.6 cm)

RC

You've mentioned that some of your biggest film influences are foreign. Has travel outside of the United States influenced your work?

BJ

I would say that traveling through cinema outside the States has had a profound effect on me. The French New Wave, Claire Denis, and then what I guess you'd call the Asian New Wave have had the biggest effect on my understanding of what I could do with my voice in cinema. My background was one that had clearly disadvantaged me purely in a nuts-and-bolts sense of how films are made. It wasn't until I saw a different mode than the Hollywood mode of expression that I realized that there was a different way. What I was most impressed by with the French New Wave was understanding right away how bare-bones it was. When I first started studying it, it was so elevated, so heightened. It was just a bunch of random ex–film critics running around with whatever they had, including dear Agnès Varda, and just making things in the most concrete way they possibly could, but I would consider these things to be some of the highest forms of the art.

So I was like, "Maybe I can do this my way. Let me just throw caution to the wind and see how I can open my process." Now the cool part was, after I made *Medicine for Melancholy*, that was the first time I really got to travel, to actually go and see the world. It was so wild to me, because *Medicine* is really personal. It is about three or four blocks in San Francisco, two young Black people, and yet I would be in Argentina. I would be in London. I would be in Poland. I would be in Vienna. People just got it. They felt it.

I was like, "Oh, shit. This is interesting. I can just be myself. I can just tell stories that are personal to me, and there's no limitation on what people can receive."

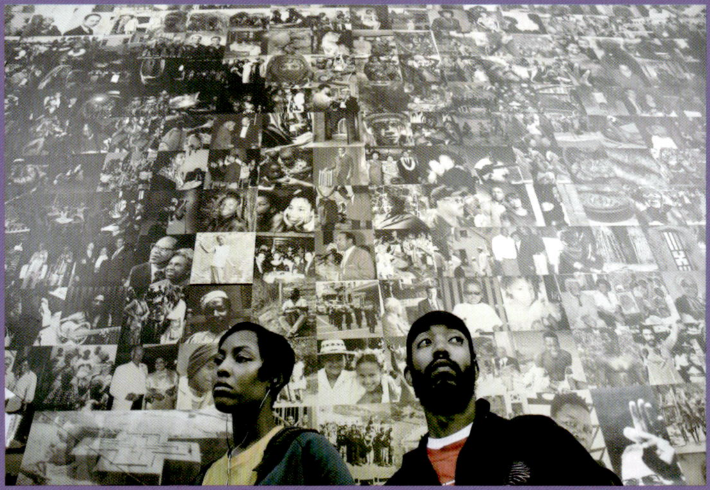

Tracey Heggins and Wyatt Cenac in *Medicine for Melancholy* (dir. Barry Jenkins, 2008), film still

RC

Do you think the role of the Black filmmaker is distinct from that of any other artist or filmmaker?

BJ

I think it is distinct right now, because we're watching much more than we're reading. We're bombarded with moving images, and those images are taking on a great importance.

We think it's not as relevant now, because there's such an overabundance of images, but people are looking to images to function in a way they didn't previously. James Baldwin would be a filmmaker right now. He would not be an essayist. That's what I mean. Right now we are living in a moment when it is very possible to push certain ideas through certain imagery. You can't be ignorant about the fact that these images have

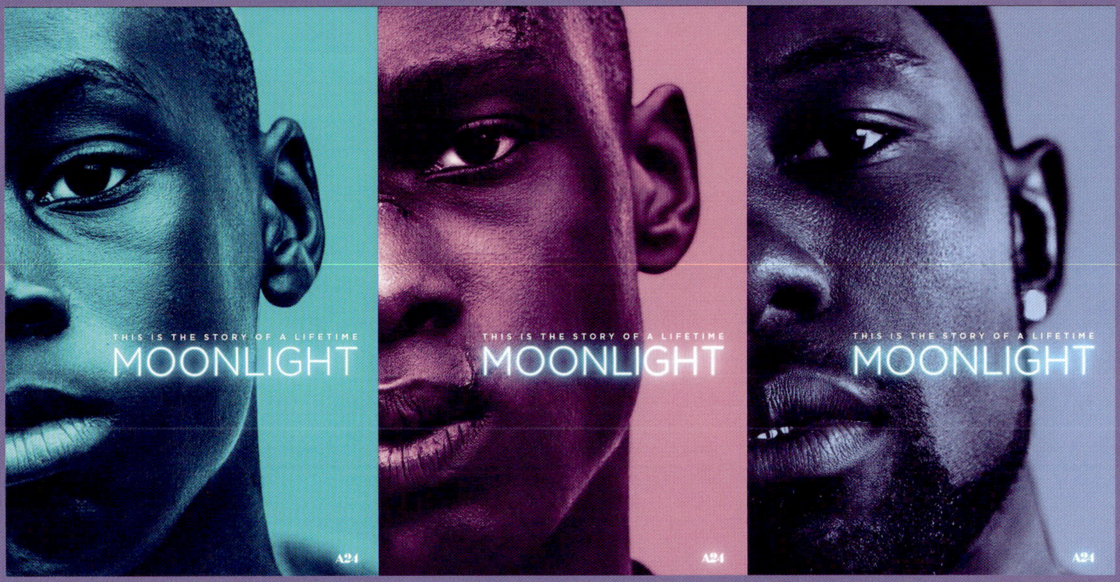

Moonlight (2016), theatrical release poster

the potential to be quite powerful, both for good and for bad. I do think that this idea of consciousness and the importance of imagery is particularly relevant when stories are told by Black people for Black people. It's never been more important. With *Moonlight*, I've had kids say to me, "This movie literally saved my life." Even if only one person says that, that's an incredible thing to hear. I try to divorce myself from that in the making of the thing, but I can't *not* be aware that that is what's at stake in some ways. Not that I can always save someone's life when I make a film, but the potential is there, so we have to be very diligent about the images that we put out in the world.

RC

How do you go about selecting the projects that you work on?

BJ

It starts with a character. If the character has something very truthful and authentic to speak to, then that's worth chasing. Me making *The Underground Railroad* now versus before I made *Medicine* is very different. Now I know someone's going to see this image. I know someone who maybe saw themselves in *Moonlight* is now going to ask, "What am I going to see here?" What am I showing them? There is a responsibility there to tell the truth once again. So I try to find characters I'm obsessed with and who have something productive to say within the framework of my work, my aesthetic, and then I just chase it.

DORIS BERGER

How do you chase it? What space do you create for yourself?

BJ

Going from *If Beale Street Could Talk* to *Underground*, I am taking a greater possession of the narrative and allowing myself not just to listen to what the author has done with the character but to make the character mine. What is the character actually saying?

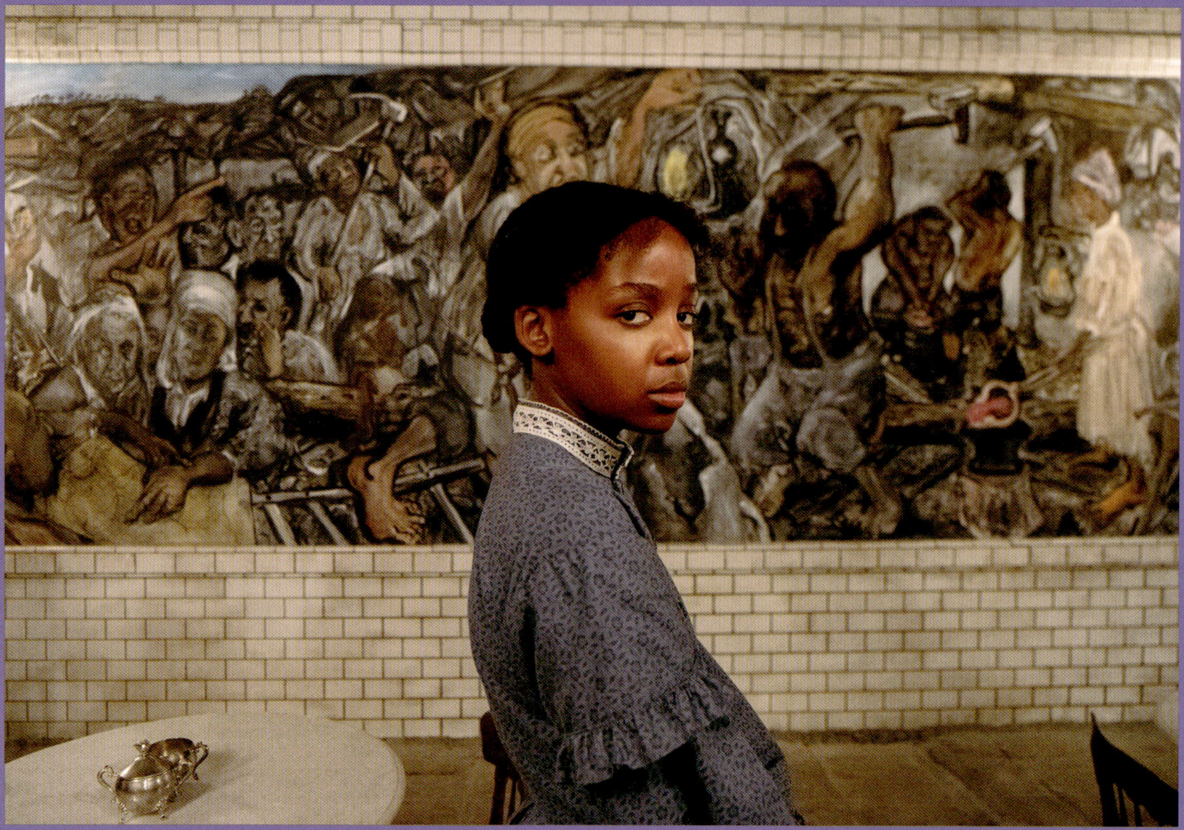

Thuso Mbedu in *The Underground Railroad* (dir. Barry Jenkins, 2021), production still

When it was first announced that I was doing *Underground Railroad*, everybody said, "Oh, not another slave narrative. This dude wins Best Picture, and here he goes, he's got to go to slavery." Do you know how many movies there have been about the Holocaust? There have been like eight thousand movies about the Holocaust. Do you know why it's hard to go to Germany right now and find any overt signs of Nazism? It's because we have very clearly owned up to the history of the Holocaust. There have been five or six, maybe seven narratives that we can openly identify that have been about the American condition of slavery. So there is much more material to be covered.

We often talk about slavery, but we divorce it from the present day. We don't really get the nuts and bolts of how we got from there to here. Not just the emotional trail but also the financial trail. So I'm like, "I'm going to do what I do. I'm going to keep telling these stories."

RC

You mentioned that your last three projects have been adaptations. But what about your creative writing background?

BJ

My first job in the industry was at Harpo Films, which was all adaptations, so that's part of it. And then a good story is a good story. I don't have to originate it. I'm not Stanley Kubrick, but every film Kubrick made was an adaptation, every single one. There's no shame in that. But also, because of the financial limitations of cinema, Black authors have been telling these

No matter who I'm making things with, everybody has always been aware that I'm making things in my voice. I think that's really beautiful.

stories in literature and academia for so long. That muscle has been worked and worked and worked and refined. Now cinema, Black cinema, is catching up. We're refining our muscles as well. As an artist, the more you create, the better you get. With the advent of digital tools, the barrier to entry in cinema has been almost removed. Cinema-making tools are so ubiquitous now. We all have cameras on our phones that are more powerful than the one I made *Medicine* with.

I'm just a dude who tells stories. When people get into my background and then match that with the films I make, there is something strange about being from the place I'm from and making films the way I do. I grew up in a very Black world. I wasn't exposed to people like Claire Denis until I was already more or less a fully formed adult. So I think the person I was raised to be is the bedrock of who I am as an artist, even if the aesthetics aren't speaking directly to that or if the aesthetics on the surface recall these other influences. I'm someone who clearly is obsessed with French and Asian New Wave cinema, and yet the images I create are exclusively Black.

There's something about the medium of cinema that I think is quite profound and provocative. As an optimist, I like to think that this is something that we all share. You know, my DP is white, my producer is white, the film school I went to was not a very diverse place. But making films has always been a shared process. No matter who I'm making things with, everybody has always been aware that I'm making things in my voice. I think that's really beautiful. It speaks as much to the power of cinema as it does to the power of Blackness. It speaks to the combination of those two things. It's vibranium.

Notes

1 Reggie Ugwu, "How a $15,000 Movie Rallied a New Generation of Black Auteurs," *New York Times*, November 21, 2018, https://www.nytimes.com/2018/11/21/movies/medi-cine-for-melancholy-black-auteurs.html.

DAWN

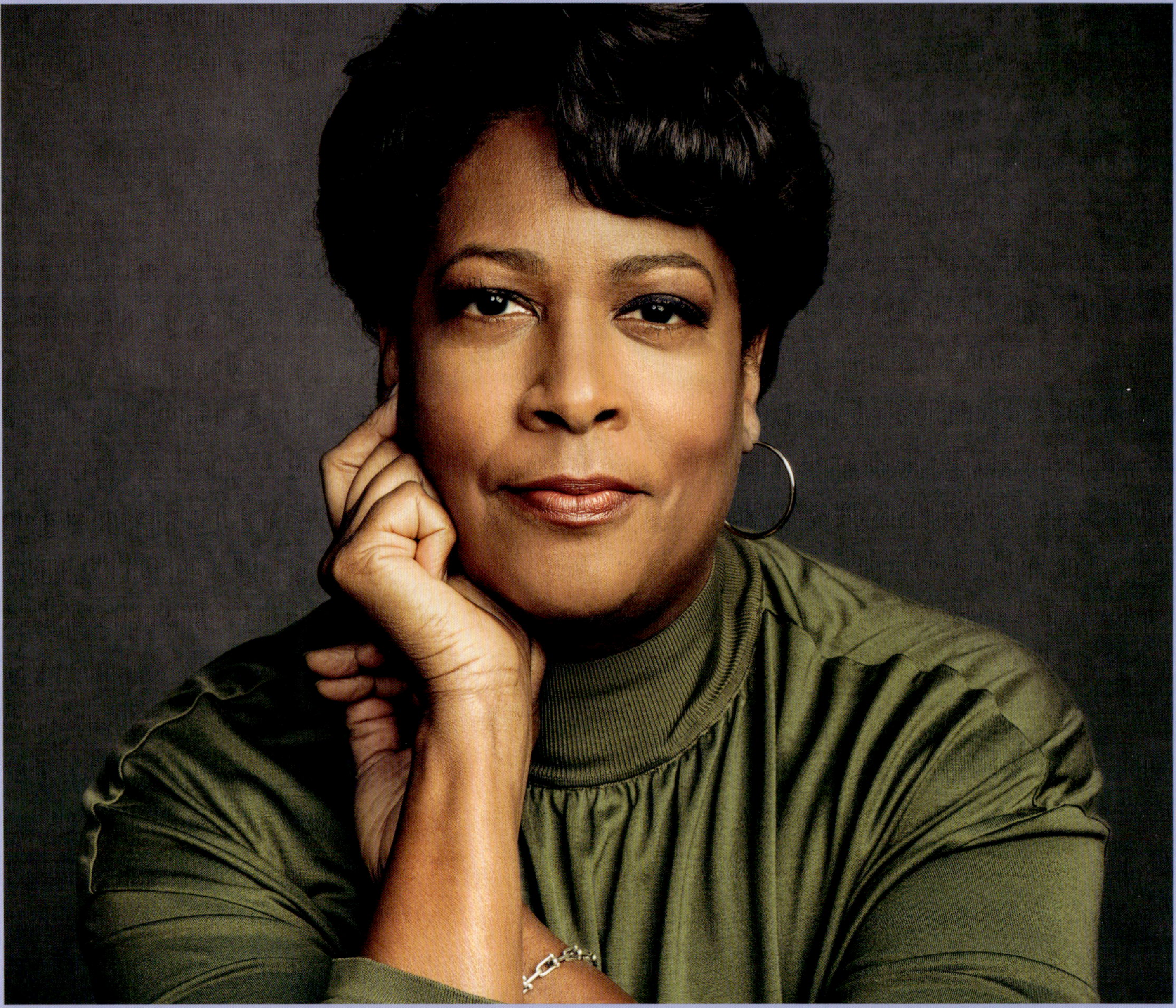

PORTER

Opposite
Kevin Scanlon (photographer),
Dawn Porter, 2021

Dawn Porter is a documentary filmmaker and founder of the production company Trilogy Films. Trained as an attorney, Porter made her directorial debut with *Gideon's Army* (2013), which chronicles the efforts of three Black public defenders working in the Deep South. The film was awarded the Ridenhour Documentary Film Prize in 2014. Porter has pursued her passion for visual storytelling and her interest in social justice in subsequent films such as *Trapped* (2016), which follows abortion providers in their fight against restrictive state laws and the patients, largely poor women of color, who seek their services. *Trapped* received a US Documentary Special Jury Award for Social Impact Filmmaking at the Sundance Film Festival. Porter has also directed biographical series and feature films such as *Bobby Kennedy for President* (2018) and *John Lewis: Good Trouble* (2020).

This interview was conducted via Zoom on December 3, 2020.
It has been edited and condensed for clarity.

RHEA COMBS

Can you speak a little bit about how and why you left a career as a practicing attorney to switch to filmmaking?

DAWN PORTER

I saw a need to portray Black people the way that I was seeing them. Often the story for women, definitely for women of color, is that we want to be überqualified because we're so used to being told that we're not qualified. Who was I to think I could make a film? The audacity of that. The people who helped me see that were people who look like me. It was the grantors at the Ford Foundation, especially Orlando Bagwell and Kirsten Levingston.

In the course of my conversations with them, I started to see that I had something to say. If you can articulate a vision for what you want to show, then it's not so scary to say, "I'm going to be a filmmaker." You're just trying to explain something, and I was trying to explain it with film, with pictures and with interviews. Orlando and Kirsten, probably unknowingly, were able to tap into what I was confident about because of my law career, which is my ability to make a complex story comprehensible, to take complex ideas and make them understandable. I've continued what I think is a creative partnership with Ford Foundation. Darren Walker really admires not just art but the process of making art and supports artists as they are figuring out their process. That's very rare and very important when you are trying to learn and grow.

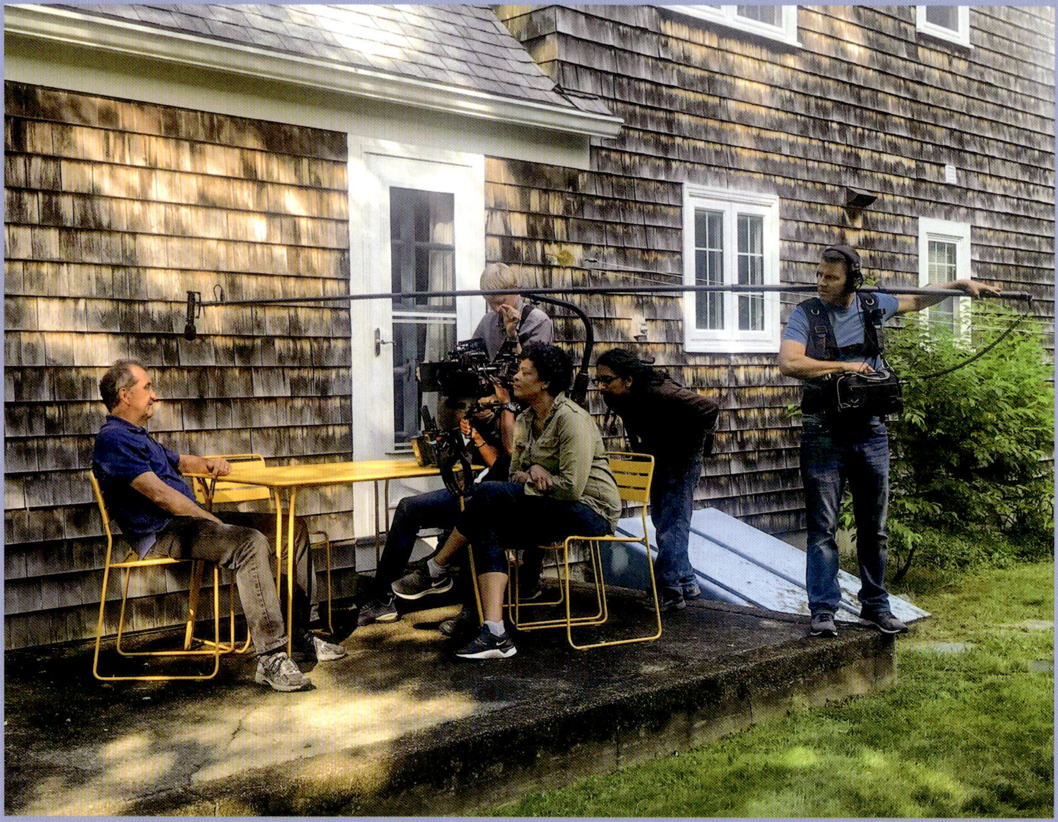

Dawn Porter (center, seated) directing *The Way I See It* (2020), production still

It's important to expose people to as much truth as you can. I don't take to a heavy-handed, didactic style of filmmaking in which I'm making conclusions. I'd rather look for moments when people can explore on their own and come away with their own impressions.

Then the other influence, of course, is my father, who was a photographer. I always had this visual language growing up. I had a still camera in my hand from the time I was fifteen years old. I went to his studio. I watched him compose images. We used to go into the woods and make little Super 8 films; that was our language. He died when I was very young, when I was twelve, but I kept that somehow.

Documentary was perfect for marrying those ideas. I have these pictures and these ideas, and now I can make the pictures talk. I started around 2010, and if you think about that period in media, it was a time when reality television was very popular. What I was seeing was a reality that wasn't real, and I wanted to bring in some of the real. The other piece of this was my children. If I was going to leave the home and my most important job, which is being a mother, I wanted it to be worth something. I had a seven-year-old boy and a nine-year-old boy, and I was very conscious of the example I was setting as a working person but also as a citizen. I was interested in marching in the streets, but also interested in a different kind of participation; filmmaking fulfilled all those things.

DORIS BERGER

Could you speak more about your activist approach to filmmaking?

DP

It's important to expose people to as much truth as you can. I don't take to a heavy-handed, didactic style of filmmaking in which I'm making conclusions. I'd rather look for moments when people can explore on their own and come away with their own impressions. In my filmmaking, I try hard to give people enough information so they can draw their own conclusions. So it's not activism in the sense of "this is what you should think." I'm offering information, and I'm assuming that people are going to take that and add it to whatever experiences they have so they can form their own opinions. I don't expect everyone to agree, and I do try hard not to be manipulative in my filmmaking.

RC

What do you consider when you're deciding which projects you want to work on?

DP

The first is, do I have something to say? Is there something that my voice adds to the story? Anytime you interact with something, you change it. How is my interaction with the subject going to change me or the story? I think about that a lot. I came to John Lewis as a person who respected and loved him already, so how was my interaction with his story going to change that? It's not going to change his story. But I have to be clear with people that I feel love for this man. So I'm coming in with an opinion, but I try and choose things that allow me to grow as an artist. *Bobby Kennedy for President*, for example, that was probably the most strategic film project that I've ever embarked on. It was about a white man of privilege. It was all archival footage. It was not anything the film community expected that I would be attracted to or interested in or maybe that I could do. I'm also attracted to films that have layered stories. It's obvious why you would want to make a film about John Lewis because he's John Lewis, but to me there was a deeper question of what happens to activists over time and how their role in our body politic changes. I was interested in how he changed over time with his differing roles in public life.

For *Trapped*, which is a film about reproductive rights, I was interested in how a former evangelical Black southern doctor became an abortion advocate and what all those complexities of identity meant for his work. He brought a very different face to the abortion conversation, and so did all the women that we showed. People do not focus on the fact that most of the women in the South who are being denied abortion services are Black and brown.

RC

How do you deal with a shifting political or cultural landscape as a production carries on?

DP

That's the best part of it, that it's never what you thought it was. So if you have all the great ingredients, if you have real access, you have to create a relationship that allows your subject to trust you so that whatever you pitch to them at first, they know that it might change based on what's really happening. You also must have that relationship with your funders and your broadcaster, because those are the people who are most married to your original narrative. Going back and saying "You know what, it's

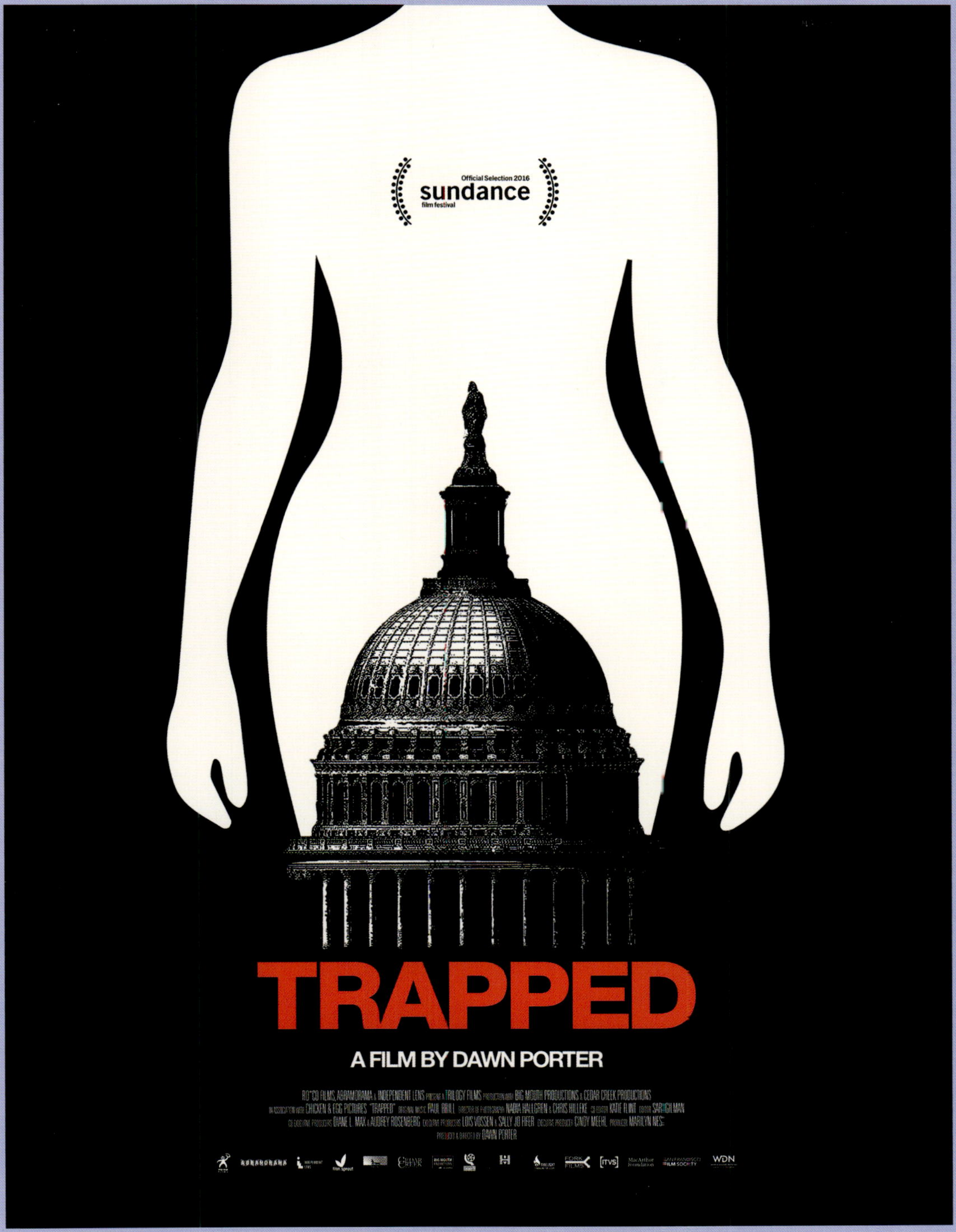

Trapped (2016), theatrical release poster

really not this, it's that" is hard unless you have a relationship. Documentary is very relationship driven. You don't just get a check and then turn in a movie. It's a constant conversation. You pressure-test your ideas constantly, and that is very different from scripted [work], where you can give somebody a script and they basically know what's going to happen. Maybe it doesn't work in the shooting, but it's not like in documentaries, where people are asking, "How's it going to end?" and I'm like, "I don't know." I don't know. I've got a year to see where it goes, and I have to communicate enough to tell you where it's going.

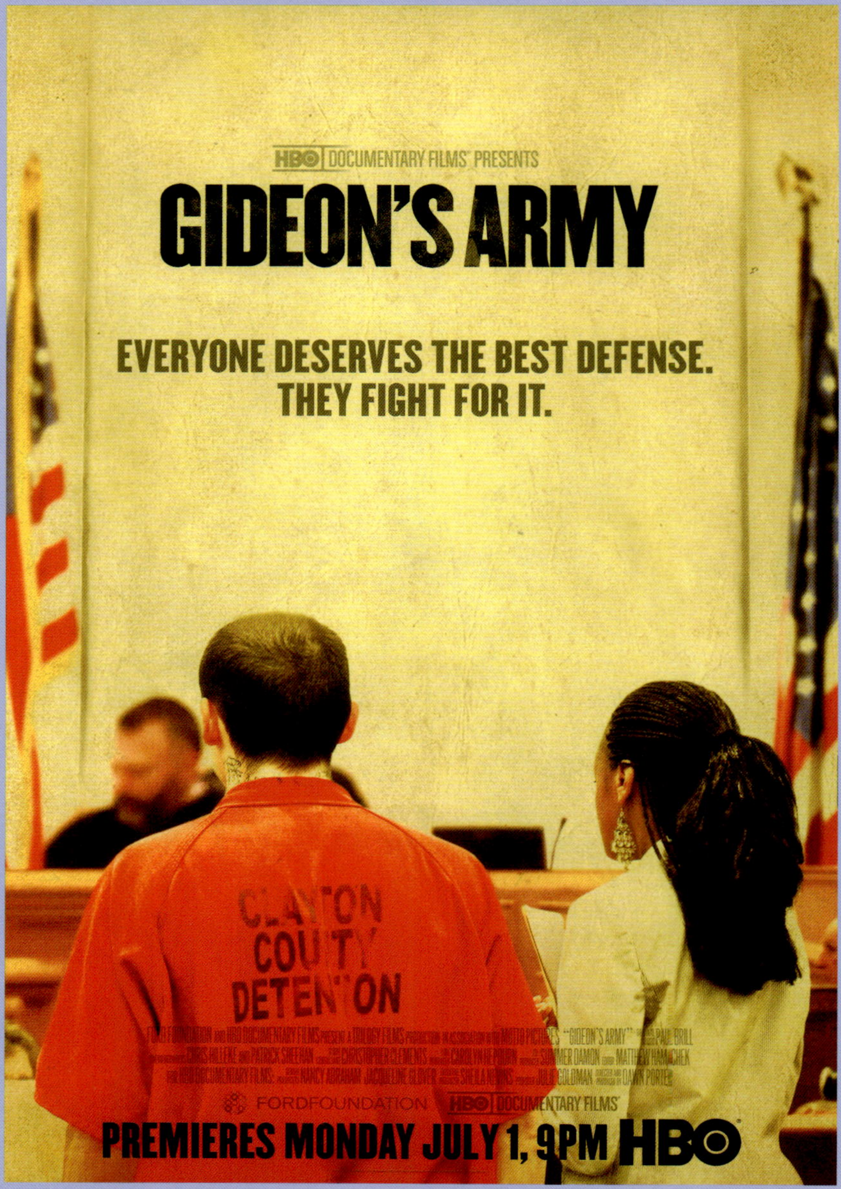

Gideon's Army (2013), theatrical release poster

RC

Have there been examples you can share with us in which you went in with a particular idea and then somehow that shifted over the course of things?

DP

Well, *Gideon's Army*, my first film. I went in with the idea that I was a lawyer. I went in with the idea, believe it or not, that the training that they were going through was going to be this great spine that would elucidate . . . I don't know what I was thinking. I'm a geek, so I was like, "Watching them do these exercises is so interesting in helping us understand the mind of a lawyer." That wasn't the story at all. The story was the emotional story of how these young people deal with questions of identity, financial pressures, and emotional pressures. The movie became much more, and this was where Orlando and Kirsten helped me through that process because they said, "Don't be afraid of that."

They were the first to tell me, "It's not going to be what you think, so lean into whatever it is."

I don't even know if people can understand the importance of what Orlando did, but he would have me come in, and he would watch scenes with me. He would just talk through what he was seeing and would ask, "Is that what you're seeing? Is that what you want to say?" He was the one who kept saying, "What do you want to say?" Can you imagine the gift of that as a first-time filmmaker, having a person who is not just smart but visually smart?

DB

What do you think is the role of a filmmaker in society and, maybe more particularly, the role of a Black filmmaker?

DP

It is not just one thing. There's entertainment. There's activism. There's just pure beauty. When I think of Steve McQueen's movies, I just think of beauty, you know? Films make you feel something, so there's this emotional outlet. They allow our imaginations to have the space to breathe. What it is for me is a creative outlet. It's a political outlet. I really work through a lot of my thinking about what's happening in the world in my films.

It's not an accident that I did the John Lewis movie at this time in history. I needed to believe in government and to believe in leadership and to believe that the president at the time was an aberration and not a trend. Living with John Lewis for a year, I would say to him, "Mr. Lewis, I'm worried about kids in cages. I'm worried about"—insert the ever-longer list of social problems—and he would say, "That's why we have to do this or that." I'm like, "This man has seen so much, and he's not defeated."

RC

Is there something that defines Black films?

DP

I'm always hesitant to box people in, but I do think that, more often than not, there is a subtext to Black film that you should always be looking for. Even in Eddie Murphy's movies, he's kind of clowning, but there's always a little bit of societal commentary in there. He's in on the joke; he's powerful about the comedy. I love that. Ava DuVernay is so much about the visuals. She just loves to create. If you are not paying attention to the way she's pushing herself artistically, you're missing it. I think in some ways one of the freest filmmakers and one that I aspire to be like is Spike Lee. He's really free, I think. I wonder if he would say that.

RC

What do you mean by that?

DP

If you think of his early work—like *She's Gotta Have It* [1986] and then *Malcolm X* [1992]—just that range of work, the small story and then the big, sweeping story, is remarkable. He's not pinned down by anyone. People are like, "It's a Spike Lee Joint," but I see a lot of range in there. That, to me, is freedom. That's what most filmmakers, but particularly filmmakers of color, are looking for. Can I have that freedom to just try whatever I want to try?

DB

Do you consider, for example, Spike Lee or Ava DuVernay as your cine-family, or who would you consider to be your idols and your peers? You've also mentioned Madeline Anderson and D. A. Pennebaker. Who are the filmmakers you look up to?

DP

I look up to all those people. I love Dee Rees's work, the layers and texture and visual style that she brings to her work. She pays attention to every single element. The music in her films is just . . . We used the same composer that she used in *Mudbound* [2017], Tamar-kali, for the John Lewis movie. I would say Dee Rees and Steve McQueen are two of the people I really admire. I watch their films over and over and think about their choices.

RC

Were there certain questions and types of stories that you wanted to see and that you felt you weren't seeing?

DP

I'm just insatiably curious about people. In the last couple of years, I've started to let myself loosen up a little bit and say, "I could explore that in fiction too." I think it comes from being a lawyer. I was like, "I want to know the truth." I'm very wary of trying to create the truth, but I think the more I learn about the fiction process and how much it's drawn from personal experience, the more I'm easing up on my snobbishness around that f-word, *fiction*.

Tom Lankford (photographer), protesters, led by John Lewis (far right) and Hosea Williams, at Edmund Pettus Bridge in Selma, Alabama, March 7, 1965

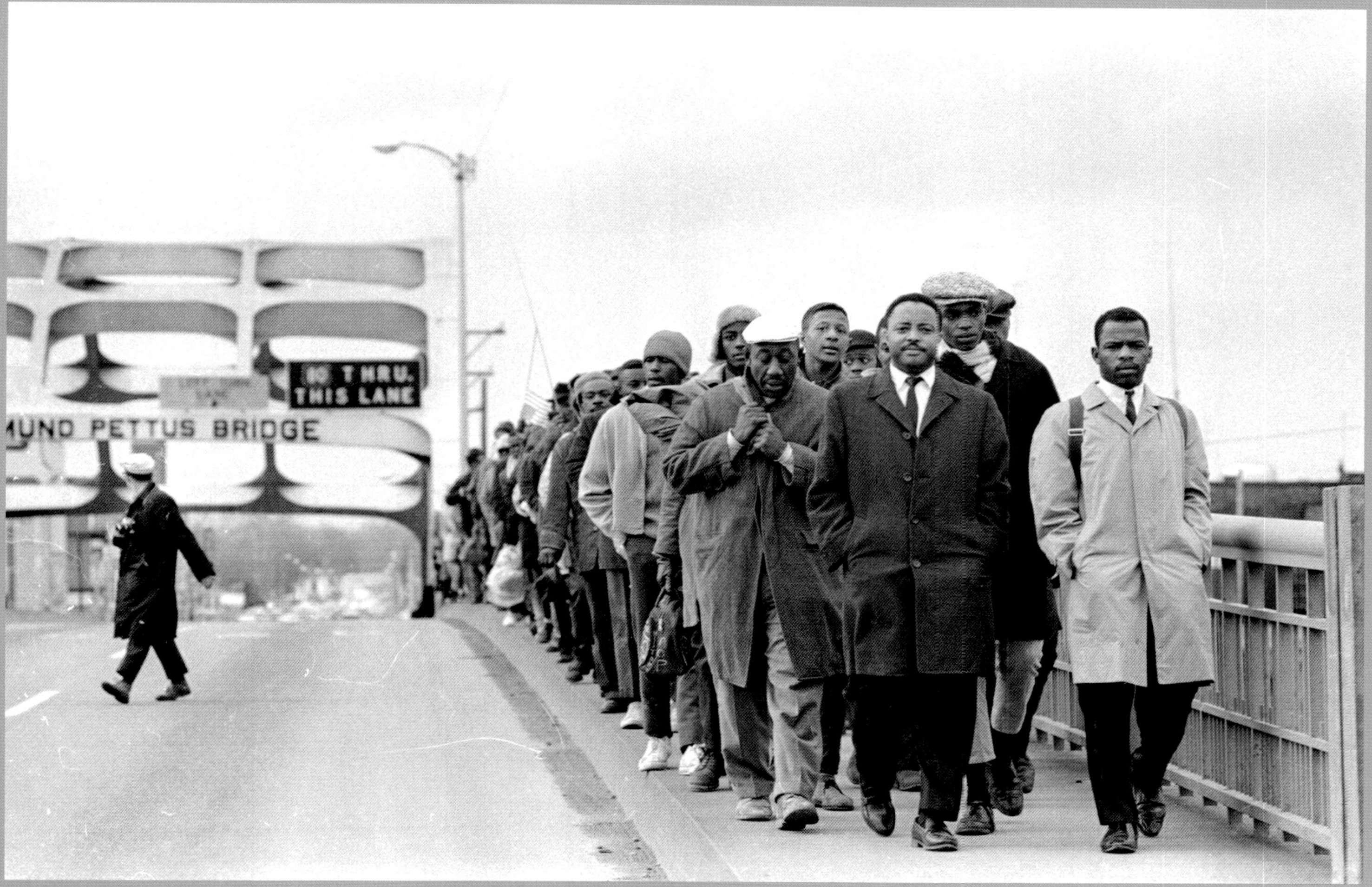

Selected Bibliography

Compiled by
Emily Rauber Rodriguez

Abbott, Lynn, and Doug Seroff. *The Original Blues: The Emergence of the Blues in African American Vaudeville*. Oxford: University Press of Mississippi, 2017.

———. *Out of Sight: The Rise of African American Popular Music, 1889–1895*. Oxford: University Press of Mississippi, 2009.

Abel, Elizabeth. *Signs of the Times: The Visual Politics of Jim Crow*. Berkeley: University of California Press, 2010.

Anderson, Elijah. "The White Space." *Sociology of Race and Ethnicity* 1, no. 1 (2014): 10–21.

Anderson, Lisa M. *Mammies No More: The Changing Image of Black Women on Stage and Screen*. Lanham, MD: Rowman & Littlefield, 1997.

Archer, Ina. "Conspiracies and Caretakers: Making Homes for African American Home Movies." *World Records Journal* 3, no. 1 (2020): 16–24.

Archer, Leonard C. *Black Images in the American Theatre: NAACP Protest Campaigns — Stage, Screen, Radio and Television*. Brooklyn, NY: Pageant-Poseidon, 1973.

Baker, Josephine, and Marcel Sauvage. *Les mémoires de Josephine Baker*. Paris: Kra, 1927.

Baldwin, Davarian L., and Minkah Makalani. *Escape from New York: The New Negro Renaissance beyond Harlem*. Minneapolis: University of Minnesota Press, 2013.

Baldwin, James. "Black English: A Dishonest Argument." In *The Cross of Redemption: Uncollected Writings*, edited by Randall Kenan, 125–30. New York: Vintage, 2010.

———. *The Devil Finds Work: An Essay*. New York: Dial, 1976.

———. *Notes of a Native Son*. Boston: Beacon, 1955.

Baldwin, James, and Raoul Peck. *I Am Not Your Negro: A Major Motion Picture*. New York: Vintage International, 2017.

Berger, Doris. *Projected Art History: Biopics, Celebrity Culture, and the Popularizing of American Art*. New York: Bloomsbury, 2014.

Berger, Maurice. *For All the World to See: Visual Culture and the Struggle for Civil Rights*. New Haven, CT: Yale University Press, 2010.

Bernstein, Matthew H. *Screening a Lynching: The Leo Frank Case on Film and Television*. Athens: University of Georgia Press, 2009.

Bernstein, Matthew H., and Dana F. White. "'Imitation of Life' in a Segregated Atlanta: Its Promotion, Distribution and Reception." *Film History* 19, no. 2 (2007): 152–78.

Berry, Torriano, and Venise T. Berry. *The 50 Most Influential Black Films: A Celebration of African-American Talent, Determination, and Creativity*. New York: Citadel, 2001.

———. *Historical Dictionary of African American Cinema*. Lanham, MD: Rowman & Littlefield, 2015.

Bobo, Jacqueline. *Black Women as Cultural Readers*. New York: Columbia University Press, 1995.

Bogle, Donald. *Bright Boulevards, Bold Dreams: The Story of Black Hollywood*. New York: Penguin Random House, 2006.

———. *Brown Sugar: Over One Hundred Years of America's Black Female Superstars*. New York: Bloomsbury, 2008.

———. *Dorothy Dandridge: A Biography*. New York: Amistad, 1999.

———. *Hollywood Black: The Stars, the Films, the Filmmakers*. Philadelphia: Running Press, 2018.

———. *Toms, Coons, Mulattoes, Mammies, and Bucks: An Interpretive History of Blacks in American Films*. 5th ed. New York: Bloomsbury, 2016.

Bowser, Pearl, Jane Gaines, and Charles Musser. *Oscar Micheaux and His Circle: African-American Filmmaking and Race Cinema of the Silent Era*. Bloomington: Indiana University Press, 2001.

Bowser, Pearl, and Louise Spence. *Writing Himself into History: Oscar Micheaux, His Silent Films, and His Audiences*. New Brunswick, NJ: Rutgers University Press, 2000.

Bryant, Clora. *Central Avenue Sounds: Jazz in Los Angeles*. Berkeley: University of California Press, 1999.

Bryant, Tisa. *Unexplained Presence*. Providence, RI: Leon Works, 2007.

Bunch, Lonnie G. *Through the African American Lens*. Washington, DC: National Museum of African American History and Culture, Smithsonian Institution, 2014.

Bunch, Lonnie G., and Rhea L. Combs. *Through the African American Lens: Double Exposure*. Washington, DC: National Museum of African American History and Culture, Smithsonian Institution, 2015.

Butters, Gerald, Jr. *Black Manhood on the Silent Screen*. Lawrence: University Press of Kansas, 2002.

Caddoo, Cara. "Black Newspapers, Real Property, and Mobility in Memphis after Emancipation." *Journal of African American History* 102 (Fall 2017): 468–91.

———. *Envisioning Freedom: Cinema and the Building of Modern Black Life*. Cambridge, MA: Harvard University Press, 2014.

Cahan, Susan. *Mounting Frustration: The Art Museum in the Age of Black Power*. Durham, NC: Duke University Press, 2016.

Calloway, Cab, and Bryant Rollins. *Of Minnie the Moocher & Me*. New York: Crowell, 1976.

Cantor, Mark. *The Soundies: A History and Catalog of Jukebox Film Shorts of the 1940s*. Jefferson, NC: McFarland, 2022.

Clammer, John. "Performing Ethnicity: Performance, Gender, Body and Belief in the Construction and Signaling of Identity." *Ethnic & Racial Studies* 38, no. 13 (2015): 2159–66.

Cohen, Harvey G. "Duke Ellington on Film in the 1930s." *Musical Quarterly* 96, no. 3/4 (2013): 406–25.

Combs, Rhea. *Through the African American Lens*. London: Giles, 2015.

Cooks, Bridget R. *Exhibiting Blackness: African Americans and the American Art Museum*. Amherst: University of Massachusetts Press, 2011.

Courtney, Susan. *Hollywood Fantasies of Miscegenation: Spectacular Narratives of Gender and Race*. Princeton, NJ: Princeton University Press, 2004.

Cripps, Thomas. *Black Film as Genre*. Bloomington: Indiana University Press, 1979.

———. *Making Movies Black: The Hollywood Message Movie from World War II to the Civil Rights Era*. New York: Oxford University Press, 1993.

———. *Slow Fade to Black: The Negro in American Film, 1900–1942*. New York: Oxford University Press, 1977.

———. "'Walter's Thing': The NAACP's Hollywood Bureau of 1946; A Cautionary Tale." *Journal of Popular Film and Television* 33, no. 2 (2005): 116–25.

Davis, Angela Y., and Joy James. *The Angela Y. Davis Reader*. Malden, MA: Blackwell, 2008.

Davis, Ossie, and Ruby Dee. *With Ossie and Ruby: In This Life Together*. New York: William Morrow, 1998.

Delson, Susan. *Soundies and the Changing Image of Black Americans on Screen: One Dime at a Time*. Bloomington: Indiana University Press, 2021.

Diawara, Manthia, ed. *Black American Cinema*. New York: Routledge, 1993.

Donalson, Melvin Burke. *Black Directors in Hollywood*. Austin: University of Texas Press, 2003.

Dootson, Kirsty Sinclair. "'The Hollywood Powder Puff War': Technicolor Cosmetics in the 1930s." *Film History* 28, no. 1 (2016): 107–31.

Duberman, Martin. *Paul Robeson: A Biography*. New York: Open Road Media, 2014.

Du Bois, W. E. B. *The Souls of Black Folk: Essays and Sketches*. Chicago: McClurg, 1903.

DuCille, Ann. *Technicolored: Reflections on Race in the Time of TV*. Durham, NC: Duke University Press, 2018.

Edwards, Adrienne, ed. *Jason Moran*. Minneapolis: Walker Art Center, 2018.

Everett, Anna. *Returning the Gaze: A Genealogy of Black Film Criticism, 1909–1949*. Durham, NC: Duke University Press, 2001.

Fanon, Frantz. *Black Skin, White Masks*. New York: Grove, 2008.

Farrington, Lisa E. *Creating Their Own Image: The History of African-American Women Artists*. Oxford: Oxford University Press, 2011.

Field, Allyson Nadia. "Archival Rediscovery and the Production of History: Solving the Mystery of *Something Good—Negro Kiss* (1898)." *Film History: An International Journal* 33, no. 2 (2021): 1–33.

———. *Uplift Cinema: The Emergence of African American Film and the Possibility of Black Modernity*. Durham, NC: Duke University Press, 2015.

Field, Allyson Nadia, and Marsha Gordon, eds. *Screening Race in American Nontheatrical Film*. Durham, NC: Duke University Press, 2019.

Field, Allyson Nadia, Jan-Christopher Horak, and Jacqueline Najuma Stewart, eds. *L.A. Rebellion: Creating a New Black Cinema*. Oakland: University of California Press, 2015.

Foster, William. “News of the Moving Picture,” *Indianapolis Freeman*, December 20, 1913.

Francis, Terri Simone. *Josephine Baker's Cinematic Prism*. Bloomington: Indiana University Press, 2021.

Friedman, Lester D. *Unspeakable Images: Ethnicity and the American Cinema*. Urbana: University of Illinois Press, 1991.

Friedman, Ryan Jay. *Hollywood's African American Films: The Transition to Sound*. Piscataway, NJ: Rutgers University Press, 2011.

Gainer, Nichelle. *Vintage Black Glamour*. London: Rocket 88, 2014.

Gaines, Jane. *Fire and Desire: Mixed-Race Movies in the Silent Era*. Chicago: University of Chicago Press, 2001.

Gates, Henry Louis. *“Race,” Writing, and Difference*. Chicago: University of Chicago Press, 1995.

Gates, Philippa. “Always a Partner in Crime: Black Masculinity in the Hollywood Detective Film.” *Journal of Popular Film and Television* 32, no. 1 (2004): 20–29.

Gevinson, Alan, ed. *Within Our Gates: Ethnicity in American Feature Films, 1911–1960*. Berkeley: University of California Press, 1997.

Gillespie, Michael Boyce. *Film Blackness: American Cinema and the Idea of Black Film*. Durham, NC: Duke University Press, 2016.

Godfrey, Mark, and Zoe Whitley, eds. *Soul of a Nation: Art in the Age of Black Power*. New York: D.A.P./Tate, 2017.

Golden, Thelma. *Black Male: Representations of Masculinity in Contemporary American Art*. New York: Whitney Museum of American Art, 1995.

Gomery, Douglas. *Shared Pleasures. A History of Movie Presentation in the United States*. Madison: University of Wisconsin Press, 1992.

Greenspun, Roger. “The Learning Tree.” *New York Times*, August 7, 1969.

Groo, Katherine. “Shadow Lives: Josephine Baker and the Body of Cinema.” *Framework: The Journal of Cinema and Media* 54, no. 1 (2013): 7–39.

Guerrero, Ed. *Framing Blackness: The African American Image in Film*. Philadelphia: Temple University Press, 1993.

Hall, Stuart. “Cultural Identity and Cinematic Representation.” *Framework: The Journal of Cinema and Media*, no. 36 (1989): 68–81.

Hall, Stuart, Jessica Evans, and Sean Nixon. *Representation: Cultural Representations and Signifying Practices*. London: Sage, 2013.

Hall, Stuart, Dorothy Hobson, Andrew Lowe, and Paul E. Willis. *Culture, Media, Language: Working Papers in Cultural Studies, 1972–79*. London: Routledge, 2013.

Haygood, Wil. *Colorization: One Hundred Years of Black Films in a White World*. New York: Knopf, 2021.

hooks, bell. *Black Looks: Race and Representation*. Boston: South End Press, 1992.

———. “Micheaux: Celebrating Blackness.” *Black American Literature Forum* 25, no. 2 (1991): 315–60.

———. *Yearning: Race, Gender, and Cultural Politics*. New York: Routledge, 2015.

Horne, Lena, and Richard Schickel. *Lena*. Garden City, NJ: Doubleday, 1965.

Hyatt, Marshall. *The Afro-American Cinematic Experience: An Annotated Bibliography & Filmography*. Wilmington, DE: Scholarly Resources, 1983.

Jackson, Carlton. *Hattie: The Life of Hattie McDaniel*. Seattle: Madison, 1993.

Johnson, James Weldon. *Black Manhattan*. New York: Knopf, 1930.

Johnson, Michael K. *Hoo-Doo Cowboys and Bronze Buckaroos: Conceptions of the African American West*. Jackson: University Press of Mississippi, 2014.

Jones, G. William. *Black Cinema Treasures: Lost and Found*. Denton: University of North Texas Press, 1997.

Joseph, Peniel E. *Waiting 'til the Midnight Hour: A Narrative History of Black Power in America*. New York: Henry Holt, 2013.

Jules-Rosette, Bennetta. *Josephine Baker in Art and Life: The Icon and the Image*. Champaign: University of Illinois Press, 2007.

Kahana, Jonathan. *The Documentary Film Reader: History, Theory, Criticism*. New York: Oxford University Press, 2016.

Kendi, Ibram X. *Stamped from the Beginning: The Definitive History of Racist Ideas in America*. New York: Bold Type, 2017.

Kisch, John. *Separate Cinema: The First 100 Years of Black Poster Art*. London: Reel Art Press, 2014.

Kisch, John, and Edward Mapp. *A Separate Cinema: Fifty Years of Black-Cast Posters*. New York: Noonday, 1992.

Klotman, Phyllis R. *Frame by Frame: A Black Filmography*. Bloomington: Indiana University Press, 1979.

Klotman, Phyllis R., and Janet K. Cutler, eds. *Struggles for Representation: African American Documentary Film and Video*. Bloomington: Indiana University Press, 1999.

Lee, Felicia R. “Coming Soon, a Century Late: A Black Film Gem.” *New York Times*, September 20, 2014.

Leeming, David. *James Baldwin: A Biography*. New York: Knopf, 1994.

Ligon, Glenn. *Yourself in the World: Selected Writings and Interviews*. New Haven, CT: Yale University Press, 2011.

Lupack, Barbara Tepa, ed. *Early Race Filmmaking in America*. New York: Routledge, 2016.

———. *Richard E. Norman and Race Filmmaking*. Bloomington: Indiana University Press, 2014.

MacDonald, Scott, and Jacqueline Najuma Stewart, eds. *William Greaves: Filmmaking as Mission*. New York: Columbia University Press, 2021.

Mapp, Edward. *Black in American Films: Today and Yesterday*. Metuchen, NJ: Scarecrow, 1972.

Marable, Manning. *Let Nobody Turn Us Around: Voices of Resistance, Reform, and Renewal; An African American Anthology*. Lanham, MD: Rowman & Littlefield, 2003.

Martin, Jacques, et al. *Le modèle noir: De Géricault à Matisse*. Paris: Musées d'Orsay et de l'Orangerie and Flammarion, 2019.

Mask, Mia, ed. *Contemporary Black American Cinema: Race, Gender and Sexuality at the Movies*. New York: Routledge, 2012.

———. *Divas on Screen: Black Women in American Film*. Urbana: University of Illinois Press, 2009.

Massood, Paula J. *Black City Cinema: African American Urban Experiences in Film*. Philadelphia: Temple University Press, 2003.

Matalon, Rebecca. *Garrett Bradley: American Rhapsody*. Houston: Contemporary Arts Museum Houston, 2020.

Maurice, Alice. "'Cinema at Its Source': Synchronizing Race and Sound in the Early Talkies." *Camera Obscura: A Journal of Feminism, Culture, and Media Studies* 49 (2002): 31–72.

McCluskey, Audrey Thomas. *Imaging Blackness: Race and Racial Representation in Film Poster Art*. Bloomington: Indiana University Press, 2007.

Moon, Spencer. *Reel Black Talk: A Sourcebook of 50 American Filmmakers*. Westport, CT: Greenwood, 1997.

Morris, Catherine, and Rujeko Hockley. *We Wanted a Revolution: Black Radical Women, 1965–85: A Sourcebook*. Brooklyn, NY: Brooklyn Museum, 2017.

Muñoz, José Esteban. *Disidentifications: Queers of Color and the Performance of Politics*. Minneapolis: University of Minnesota Press, 1999.

Musser, Charles. "Paul Robeson and the Cinema of Empire." In *Empire and Film*, edited by Lee Grieveson and Colin McCabe, 261–80. London: Palgrave, 2011.

Musser, Charles, and Jacqueline Najuma Stewart, eds. *Pioneers of African-American Cinema*. New York: Kino Lorber, 2016.

Patterson, Lindsay, ed. *Black Films and Film-makers: A Comprehensive Anthology from Stereotype to Superhero*. New York: Dodd, Mead, 1975.

Peterson, Bernard L., Jr. *The African American Theatre Directory, 1816–1960*. Westport, CT: Greenwood, 1997.

Petty, Miriam J. *Stealing the Show: African American Performers and Audiences in 1930s Hollywood*. Oakland: University of California Press, 2016.

Poitier, Sidney. *The Measure of a Man: A Spiritual Autobiography*. San Francisco: Harper San Francisco, 2007.

Powell, Richard J. *The Color Line: African-American Artists and Segregation (1865–2016)*. Paris: Flammarion, 2016.

Powers, Anne. *Blacks in American Movies: A Selected Bibliography*. Metuchen, NJ: Scarecrow, 1974.

Quinn, Eithne. *A Piece of the Action*. New York: Columbia University Press, 2019.

Redmond, Shana. *Anthem: Social Movements and the Sound of Solidarity*. New York: New York University Press, 2013.

———. *Everything Man: The Form and Function of Paul Robeson*. Durham, NC: Duke University Press, 2020.

Regester, Charlene B. *African American Actresses: The Struggle for Visibility, 1900–1960*. Bloomington: Indiana University Press, 2010.

———. "Black Films, White Censors: Oscar Micheaux Confronts Censorship in New York, Virginia, and Chicago." In *Movie Censorship and American Culture*, edited by Francis G. Couvares, 159–86. Washington, DC: Smithsonian Institution Press, 1996.

Reid, Mark A. *African American Cinema through Black Lives Consciousness*. Detroit: Wayne State University Press, 2019.

———. *Black Lenses, Black Voices: African American Film Now*. Lanham, MD: Rowman & Littlefield, 2005.

———. "Early Black Independents." *Black Film Review* 2, no. 4 (1986): 21–22.

———. *Redefining Black Film*. Berkeley: University of California Press, 1993.

Richards, Larry. *African American Films through 1959: A Comprehensive, Illustrated Filmography*. Jefferson, NC: McFarland, 2005.

Robeson, Paul, and Philip S. Foner. *Paul Robeson Speaks: Writings, Speeches, Interviews, 1918–1974*. New York: Brunner/Mazel, 1978.

Robeson, Paul, Jr. *The Undiscovered Paul Robeson: Quest for Freedom, 1939–1976*. Hoboken, NJ: Wiley, 2010.

Rocchio, Vincent Floyd. *Reel Racism: Confronting Hollywood's Construction of Afro-American Culture*. Boulder, CO: Westview, 2000.

Rogin, Michael Paul. *Blackface, White Noise: Jewish Immigrants in the Hollywood Melting Pot.* Berkeley: University of California Press, 2007.

Rome, Dennis. *Black Demons: The Media's Depiction of the African American Male Criminal Stereotype.* Westport, CT: Praeger, 2004.

Russworm, TreaAndrea M. *Blackness Is Burning: Civil Rights, Popular Culture, and the Problem of Recognition.* Detroit: Wayne State University Press, 2016.

Sammond, Nicholas. *Birth of an Industry: Blackface Minstrelsy and the Rise of American Animation.* Durham, NC: Duke University Press, 2015.

Sampson, Henry T. *Blacks in Black and White: A Source Book on Black Films.* Metuchen, NJ: Scarecrow, 1995.

Scott, Ellen C. *Cinema Civil Rights: Regulation, Repression, and Race in the Classical Hollywood Era.* New Brunswick, NJ: Rutgers University Press, 2015.

———. "'We Proudly Present . . . The Picture They Didn't Want You to See!': Black Film Advertisements, 1946–1960." *Black Camera* 5, no. 1 (2013): 5–33.

Sheppard, Samantha N. *Sporting Blackness: Race, Embodiment, and Critical Muscle Memory on Screen.* Berkeley: University of California Press, 2020.

Shohat, Ella, and Robert Stam. *Unthinking Eurocentrism: Multiculturalism and the Media.* London: Routledge, 1996.

Smith, Danez. *Black Movie.* Minneapolis: Button Poetry / Exploding Pinecone, 2015.

Smith, Eric Ledell. *African American Theater Building: An Illustrated Historical Directory, 1900–1955.* Jefferson, NC: McFarland, 2011.

Snead, James. *White Screens / Black Images: Hollywood from the Dark Side.* London: Routledge, 1994.

Stanfield, Peter. *Body and Soul: Jazz and Blues in American Film, 1927–63.* Urbana: University of Illinois Press, 2005.

Stauffer, John, Zoe Trodd, and Celeste-Marie Bernier. *Picturing Frederick Douglass: An Illustrated Biography of the Nineteenth Century's Most Photographed American.* New York: Liveright, 2018.

Stewart, Jacqueline Najuma. "Discovering Black Film History: Tracing the Tyler Texas Black Film Collection." *Film History* 23, no. 2 (2011): 147–73.

———. *Migrating to the Movies: Cinema and Black Urban Modernity.* Berkeley: University of California Press, 2005.

Stewart, Jeffrey C., ed. *Paul Robeson: Artist and Citizen.* New Brunswick, NJ: Rutgers University Press, 1998.

Stovall, Tyler. *Paris Noir: African Americans in the City of Light.* Boston: Houghton Mifflin, 1996.

Sullivan, Patricia. *Days of Hope: Race and Democracy in the New Deal Era.* Chapel Hill: University of North Carolina Press, 1996.

———. *Lift Every Voice: The NAACP and the Making of the Civil Rights Movement.* New York: New Press, 2010.

Svitil, Torene, and Thomas Cripps. *Close Up in Black: African American Film Posters from the Academy of Motion Picture Arts and Sciences.* Beverly Hills, CA: Academy of Motion Picture Arts and Sciences, 2002.

Syms, Martine. *Implications and Distinctions. Format, Content and Context in Contemporary Race Film.* Houston: Future Plan and Program, 2011.

Taylor, Yuval, and Jake Austen. *Darkest America: Black Minstrelsy from Slavery to Hip-Hop.* New York: Norton, 2012.

Wallace, Michele, and Gina Dent. *Black Popular Culture.* Seattle: Bay Press, 1992.

Watts, Jill. *Hattie McDaniel: Black Ambition, White Hollywood.* New York: Amistad, 2005.

Weisenfeld, Judith. *Hollywood Be Thy Name: African American Religion in American Film, 1929–1949.* Berkeley: University of California Press, 2007.

West, Cornel. *Race Matters.* New York: Vintage, 1994.

White, Deborah Gray. *Too Heavy a Load: Black Women in Defense of Themselves, 1894–1994.* New York: Norton, 1999.

Widener, Daniel. *Black Arts West: Culture and Struggle in Postwar Los Angeles.* Durham, NC: Duke University Press, 2010.

Wilderson, Frank B., III. *Red, White & Black: Cinema and the Structure of U.S. Antagonisms.* Durham, NC: Duke University Press, 2010.

Williams, Megan E. "The *Crisis* Cover Girl: Lena Horne, the NAACP, and Representation of African American Femininity, 1941–1945." *American Periodicals* 16, no. 2 (2006): 200–218.

Willis, Deborah. *Picturing Us: African American Identity in Photography.* New York: New Press, 1997.

Willis, Sharon. *The Poitier Effect: Racial Melodrama and Fantasies of Reconciliation.* Minneapolis: University of Minnesota Press, 2015.

Wintz, Cary D. *African American Political Thought, 1890–1930.* New York: Routledge, 1995.

Yearwood, Gladstone L., ed. *Black Cinema Aesthetics: Issues in Independent Black Filmmaking.* Athens: Center for Afro-American Studies, Ohio University, 1982.

Zinn, Howard. *A People's History of the United States, 1492–Present.* New York: HarperCollins, 1980.

Index

Page numbers in *italics* refer to illustrations.

C

N

O

P

Illustration Credits

Most photographs are reproduced courtesy of the creators and lenders of the material depicted. For certain photographs we have been unable to trace copyright holders. The publishers would appreciate notification of additional credits for acknowledgment in future editions.

pp. 2, 212 (right): © 1943 Twentieth Century Fox; photo courtesy of Margaret Herrick Library, Academy of Motion Picture Arts and Sciences

pp. 13, 16 (left and bottom right), 28, 46, 50 (top and bottom) 62 (top and bottom), 65 (top, center, and bottom), 67, 68, 110 (left), 111, 113, 114, 117, 118, 125 (top), 126, 142 (Spivey, Best, S. McDaniel, Sul Te Wan), 143 (Haynes, Horne), 144 (Moreland, J. Moore, Edwards, Perry, O'Neal, E. McDaniel), 145 (Anderson, Whitman), 146 (O. Davis, H. Johnson), 147 (Armstrong, Drake, Wilson, Belafonte, H. and F. Nicholas, McQueen), 148 (Brooks, Poitier, Hernandez, Waters, H. McDaniel), 149 (Robinson), 174, 176–81, 183–87, 190, 195, 207 (top), 208, 209 (bottom), 210 (bottom), 211 (top and bottom), 212 (left), 214 (bottom right), 216 (top right): Courtesy of Margaret Herrick Library, Academy of Motion Picture Arts and Sciences

p. 15, 48 (bottom), 204, 208 (bottom): Schomburg Center for Research in Black Culture, Photographs and Prints Division, The New York Public Library, The New York Public Library Digital Collections, 1850–1995

p. 16 (top right): © R. E. Norman Family Collection; photo: Norman Studios Silent Film Museum, Jacksonville Florida

p. 20: Courtesy of and © Icarus Films

p. 31 (top): Collection of the Smithsonian National Museum of African American History and Culture, 2013.207.1. Photo: Smithsonian Institution Open Access

p. 31 (bottom): Collection of the Smithsonian National Museum of African American History and Culture, 2009.37.1. Photo: Smithsonian Institution Open Access

p. 32: From American Monthly Review of Reviews 22, no. 130 (November 1900): 576. Photo: https://www.loc.gov/pictures/item/2001697152/

p. 34: Library of Congress, Prints and Photographs Division, Daniel Murray collection, LC-DIG-ppmsca-33863. Photo: Library of Congress http://hdl.loc.gov/loc.pnp/ppmsca.33863

p. 35 (top): Collection of the Smithsonian National Museum of African American History and Culture, 2009.37.3. Photo: Smithsonian Institution Open Access

p. 35 (bottom): Collection of the Smithsonian National Museum of African American History and Culture, 2009.37.2. Photo: Smithsonian Institution Open Access

p. 36, back cover: Courtesy of USC HMH Foundation Moving Image Archive

p. 38: © Glenn Ligon; Courtesy of the artist, Hauser & Wirth, New York, Regen Projects, Los Angeles, Thomas Dane Gallery, London and Chantal Crousel, Paris

p. 40 (top): Courtesy of George Eastman Museum

p. 40 (bottom): Theater Posters Collection [V06], Historical Society of Pennsylvania; reproduced by permission of the Historical Society of Pennsylvania

p. 41: © Kara Walker; courtesy of Sikkema Jenkins & Co., New York, and Sprueth Magers, Berlin; photo: Gene Pittman

p. 42: Schomburg Center for Research in Black Culture, Photographs and Prints Division, The New York Public Library, psnypl_scg_355

p. 44 (top and center): Photo: Ngfoster / Wikipedia (CC BY 3.0)

p. 44 (bottom): Smithsonian National Museum of African American History and Culture 1921, 2019.28.27

pp. 45, 142 (N. Johnson), 172, 173: Courtesy of Library Special Collections, Charles E. Young Research Library, UCLA

pp. 48 (top), 132, 209: © Warner Bros. Entertainment, Inc.

p. 52: © Gary Simmons; photo: Brian Forrest; courtesy of the artist and Hauser & Wirth

p. 53: Photo courtesy of Christina Sekaer and Howard Greenberg Gallery

p. 54: © Roger-Viollet

p. 57 (left and right): Cinémathèque Française, 79481 (left) and 79478 (right)

p. 58 (top): Photo: HF Davis / Getty Images

p. 58 (center): Courtesy of Deutsches Bundesarchiv, BArch, R 58/9692

pp. 58 (bottom), 107, 143 (S. Davis Jr., Ellington), 146 (Cole), 147 (Robeson), 149 (Le Gon), 214 (bottom left): Photo: Bettmann / Getty Images

p. 59 (top and bottom): © 1961 Pennebaker Productions and Jason Inc., Monica Corp. Inc. and Monmouth Inc. Photo courtesy of MGM Media Licensing and Margaret Herrick Library, Academy of Motion Picture Arts and Sciences

pp. 60: Smithsonian National Museum of African American History and Culture, Gift of Cabella Calloway Langsam, 2013.237.12. Photo: Smithsonian Institution Open Access

p. 63: Courtesy of Beinecke Rare Book and Manuscript Library, Yale University, BrSides Double Folio 2016 34

p. 64: ©Academy Museum Foundation. Photo: Joshua White / JWPictures

p. 70: © Carrie Mae Weems; courtesy of the artist and Jack Shainman Gallery, New York. Photo courtesy of National Gallery of Art, Washington, DC

p. 72: © Time Inc. Photo: Albert Fenn / The LIFE Picture Collection / Shutterstock

pp. 75 (top), 216 (bottom left): Photo: David Attie / Getty Images

p. 75 (center): © 1961, renewed 1989 Columbia Pictures Industries, Inc. Courtesy of Columbia Pictures. Photo courtesy of Margaret Herrick Library, Academy of Motion Picture Arts and Sciences

p. 75 (bottom): © Bob Adelman

p. 76: Photo: Charles Del Vecchio / The Washington Post via Getty Images

p. 77 (top): Photo: Rowland Scherman / USIA / PhotoQuest / Getty Images

p. 77 (bottom): Photo: PhotoQuest / Getty Images

p. 78 (top): Center for the Study of Political Graphics, ID no. 1768

p. 78 (bottom): Smithsonian National Museum of African American History and Culture, Gift of Arthur J. "Bud" Schmidt, 2017.71.4. Photo: Smithsonian Institution Open Access

p. 79: © Theaster Gates; courtesy of the artist and Regen Projects, Los Angeles

pp. 80 (top), 85 (bottom): Smithsonian National Museum of African American History and Culture, Gift of the family of Robert L. Goodwin Sr., A2021.8

pp. 80 (bottom), 201: Courtesy of and © Janus Films; photo courtesy of Margaret Herrick Library, Academy of Motion Picture Arts and Sciences

pp. 82, 84, 85 (top), 119, 120, 127: Courtesy of Academy Film Archive

pp. 92, 93, 94, 95: Courtesy of The Museum of Modern Art, New York, Department of Film Special Collections

p. 97: From *The Crisis* 10, no. 2 (June 1915): 88

p. 99: From *Indianapolis Freeman* (October 21, 1905): 5

p. 100: From *St. Louis Argus* (September 26, 1919): 4

p. 102: Photo: White Studio. © Photographs and Prints Division, Schomburg Center for Research in Black Culture, The New York Public Library

pp. 103 (top), 112, 115, 116, 193, 197, 200: © Warner Bros. Entertainment, Inc.; photo courtesy of Margaret Herrick Library, Academy of Motion Picture Arts and Sciences

p. 103 (bottom): Schomburg Center for Research in Black Culture, Photographs and Prints Division, The New York Public Library, 3884274

pp. 104, 148 (Lee): Photo: John Kisch Archive / Getty Images

p. 105: Maryland Center for History and Culture Library; Special Collections; Paul S. Henderson Photograph Collection, item ID # HEN.00.A2-156. Photo: Paul S. Henderson

p. 109: Smithsonian National Museum of African American History and Culture and National Portrait Gallery, Gift from Jean-Claude Baker, 2016.135.2. Photo: Smithsonian Institution Open Access

p. 110 (right): Attributed to G. Rader, Josephine Baker, Leon Clement & Co. Lithography, Poster, National Portrait Gallery, Smithsonian Institution, NPG.86.66. Photo: Smithsonian Institution Open Access

p. 122: Courtesy of California African American Museum

p. 123: Library of Congress, Motion Picture, Broadcasting, and Recorded Sound Division, https://www.loc.gov/item/2018600174/

p. 125 (bottom): © 1974 Paramount Pictures. Photo: Bettmann / Getty Images

p. 128: Smithsonian National Museum of African American History and Culture, Gift of Naomi Long Madgett, 2011.79.3.1abc

p. 129: Smithsonian National Museum of African American History and Culture, Gift of Cabella Calloway Langsam, 2015.273.2.2.1c. © Cabella Calloway Langsam, Creative Arts by Calloway, LLC

p. 131: Courtesy of Louise Greaves

p. 133: Courtesy of and © Janus Films

p. 135: Smithsonian National Museum of African American History and Culture, 2011.20.2. Photo © Sedat Pakay | www.sedatpakay.com

p. 136: Cover design Jack Ribik, © Penguin Random House LLC

p. 137: © 1967 Metro-Goldwyn-Mayer Studios Inc. Photo courtesy of MGM Media Licensing

p. 138: © 1958 Metro-Goldwyn-Mayer Studios Inc. Photo courtesy of MGM Media Licensing

p. 142 (Sands): Library of Congress, Prints and Photographs Division, NYWT&S Collection, LC-USZ62-90145, https://www.loc.gov/item/2017659312/

p. 142 (Fitzgerald): Photo: Gilles Petard / Redferns / Getty Images

p. 142 (Carroll, Scott): Photo: Hulton Archive / Getty Images

p. 142 (Beavers): Black Film Center & Archive, Indiana University, Bloomington, PA 22 / GEN

p. 143 (Cooper): Smithsonian National Museum of African American History and Culture, The Laura Cathrell Show-Down Magazine Collection, 2013.46.25.42

p. 143 (P. Moore): Black Film Center & Archive, Indiana University, Bloomington, Phil Moore-Photographs, Col 6 PA 238

p. 143 (Washington): Photo: Maurice Seymour; courtesy of Ronald Seymour and The New York Public Library

p. 143 (Simms): Photo: George Karger / Getty Images

pp. 144 (Marshall), 145 (Dee), 146 (Kitt): Photo: John Springer Collection / CORBIS / Corbis via Getty Images

p. 144 (Dandridge): Photo: GAB Archive / Redferns / Getty Images

p. 144 (McKinney): Courtesy of Collections La Cinémathèque de Toulouse

pp. 144 (Polk), 146 (Norman): Photo: Carl Van Vechten Collection / Getty Images

p. 145 (Baker): Photo: adoc-photos / Corbis via Getty Images

p. 145 (Greaves): Billy Rose Theatre Division, The New York Public Library. The New York Public Library Digital Collections

p. 145 (Dunham): Black Film Center & Archive, Indiana University, Bloomington, PA 116 / GEN

p. 145 (Muse): Photo: Library of Congress / Corbis / VCG via Getty Images

p. 145 (L. Randolph): Photo: CBS via Getty Images

pp. 146 (Jeffries), 149 (Lincoln), 149 (James): Photo: Michael Ochs Archives / Getty Images

p. 146 (Spencer): Photo: Stiftung Deutsche Kinemathek

p. 146 (Peters): Photo: John D. Kisch / Separate Cinema Archive / Getty Images

p. 146 (Harris): © 1940 Paramount Pictures; photo courtesy of Margaret Herrick Library, Academy of Motion Picture Arts and Sciences

p. 146 (Calloway): Photo: Metronome / Getty Images

p. 147 (Williams): Billy Rose Theatre Division, The New York Public Library, The New York Public Library Digital Collections, 1950–1960, TH-62474

p. 148 (Welch): Photo: Sasha / Hulton Archive / Getty Images

p. 148 (Moten Barnett): Photo: Afro American Newspapers / Gado / Getty Images

p. 148 (B. Bailey): Smithsonian National Museum of African American History and Culture, The Laura Cathrell Show-Down Magazine Collection, 2013.46.25.41. Photo: K. Progress / N.Y.

p. 148 (P. Bailey): Smithsonian National Museum of African American History and Culture, 2013.118.182.3. Photo: Marvin Smith

p. 149 (Glenn): © 1954 Twentieth Century Fox; photo: Glasshouse Images / Alamy Stock Photo

p. 149 (Dixon): Black Film Center & Archive, Indiana University, Bloomington, COL 5 / PA 903

p. 149 (A. Randolph): Photo: Historic Collection / Alamy Stock Photo

p. 149 (Ingram): Photo: Universal History Archive / Universal Images Group via Getty Images

p. 175: Photo: Swim Ink 2, LLC / Corbis via Getty Images

p. 182: Black Film Center & Archive, Indiana University, Bloomington

p. 188: © 1950 Jewel Pictures Corp. Photo courtesy of MGM Media Licensing

p. 189: © 1951, renewed 1979 Columbia Pictures Industries, Inc. Courtesy of Columbia Pictures. Photo courtesy of Margaret Herrick Library, Academy of Motion Picture Arts and Sciences

p. 191: © 1954 Twentieth Century Fox; photo courtesy of Margaret Herrick Library, Academy of Motion Picture Arts and Sciences

p. 192: © 1959 Harbel Productions Inc. Photo courtesy of MGM Media Licensing and Margaret Herrick Library, Academy of Motion Picture Arts and Sciences

p. 194: © 1961, renewed 1989 Columbia Pictures Industries, Inc. Courtesy of Columbia Pictures

pp. 196, 217 (top): © 1968 Paramount Pictures; photo courtesy of Margaret Herrick Library, Academy of Motion Picture Arts and Sciences

p. 198: © 1970 Samuel Goldwyn Jr. Photo: Movie Poster Image Art / Getty Images; courtesy of MGM Media Licensing

p. 204 (bottom): Library of Congress Prints and Photographs Division, LC-USZ62-124652

p. 205 (top): Retrieved from https://www.loc.gov/item/88709151/

p. 205 (bottom): Library of Congress Prints and Photographs Division, LC-DIG-ppmsca-37818

p. 206 (top and bottom): Smithsonian National Museum of African American History and Culture, 2015.97.14.1 (top) and 2010.36.1.4 (bottom)

p. 207 (bottom): Photo: Underwood Archives / Getty Images

p. 208 (top): Courtesy of Kino Lorber, Inc.

p. 210 (top): Courtesy of Library of Congress and Kino Lorber, Inc.

p. 213 (top): Photo: George Rinhart / Corbis via Getty Images; courtesy of MGM Media Licensing

p. 213 (bottom): © Warner Bros. Entertainment, Inc. Photo: LMPC via Getty Images; courtesy of MGM Media Licensing

p. 214 (top): Cinémathèque Française, Left; D012 - 33 Cote: TIROIR 131

p. 215: © 1958 Longridge Enterprises, Inc. Photo: LMPC via Getty Images; courtesy of MGM Media Licensing

p. 216 (top left): © 1962 Pakula-Mulligan Productions, Inc. and Brentwood Productions, Inc. Courtesy of Universal Studios Licensing, LLC

p. 216 (bottom right): Photo: AFP via Getty Images

pp. 217 (bottom), 251: Courtesy of and © The Gordon Parks Foundation

p. 218 (top): Photo: Pix / Michael Ochs Archives / Getty Images

p. 218 (bottom): © 1970 Samuel Goldwyn Jr. Courtesy of MGM Media Licensing

p. 222: Photo: Timothy Hiatt / Getty Images for Ebertfest

p. 225: © 1990 TSWA, Inc.; photo courtesy of Margaret Herrick Library, Academy of Motion Picture Arts and Sciences

p. 226: Photo: David Gahr / Getty Images

p. 228: © Milestone Film and Video Inc.; photo courtesy of Margaret Herrick Library, Academy of Motion Picture Arts and Sciences

pp. 230, 237: © 1991 Geechee Girls Productions, Inc. Courtesy of Cohen Film Collection LLC and Geechee LLC

p. 233: © Cinemateca de Cuba Dirección

p. 238: Courtesy of and © Women Make Movies

p. 240: © 2014 Paramount Pictures. Photo: Atsushi Nishijima / Photo 12 / Alamy Stock Photo

p. 243: © 2022 ARRAY

p. 244: © 2016 Netflix. Photo courtesy of Margaret Herrick Library, Academy of Motion Picture Arts and Sciences

p. 245: © 2014 Paramount Pictures. Photo courtesy of Margaret Herrick Library, Academy of Motion Picture Arts and Sciences

p. 246: KANDOO FILMS 20 January 2012, © 2022 ARRAY. Photo: AF archive / Alamy Stock Photo

p. 248: © A24 Films LLC. Photo: Atlaspix / Alamy Stock Photo

p. 252: © Medicine for Melancholy, LLC 2008. Photo: AF archive / Alamy Stock Photo

p. 253: © A24 Films LLC. Photo: © Plan B Entertainment. AF archive / Alamy Stock Photo

p. 254: © 2010–2022 Prime Video / Kyle Kaplan

p. 256: © Kevin Scanlon / CPi Syndication

p. 258: © 2020 Focus Features LLC. Courtesy of Universal Studios Licensing, LLC. Photo: PictureLux / The Hollywood Archive / Alamy Stock Photo

p. 261: Courtesy of and © Trilogy Films

p. 262: Courtesy of and © Trilogy Films. Photo courtesy of Margaret Herrick Library, Academy of Motion Picture Arts and Sciences

p. 265: © Alabama Department of Archives and History. Donated by Alabama Media Group. Photo: Tom Lankford, Birmingham News

Contributors

Doris Berger

Doris Berger is vice president of curatorial affairs at the Academy Museum of Motion Pictures. She was previously a Getty postdoctoral fellow; a curator at the Skirball Cultural Center, Los Angeles; and director of the Kunstverein Wolfsburg, Germany. Berger curated numerous art and film exhibitions, including *Light & Noir: Exiles and Émigrés in Hollywood, 1933–1950* (Skirball, 2014), and *Isaac Julien: Baltimore* (Academy Museum, 2022). She cocurated the Academy Museum's inaugural exhibitions *Stories of Cinema* and *Backdrop: An Invisible Art* (both 2021). She is the author of *Projected Art History: Biopics, Celebrity Culture, and the Popularizing of American Art* (Bloomsbury, 2014). She has published essays in books and journals and has taught courses in art history, film, and gender studies in Austria and Germany.

Donald Bogle

Donald Bogle, one of the foremost authorities on African Americans in film, is the award-winning author of nine books, including the groundbreaking *Toms, Coons, Mulattoes, Mammies, and Bucks: An Interpretive History of Blacks in American Films* (5th ed., Bloomsbury, 2016); the critically acclaimed *Dorothy Dandridge: A Biography* (Amistad, 1997); the evocative social history *Bright Boulevards, Bold Dreams: The Story of Black Hollywood* (Ballantine, 2005); *Heat Wave: The Life and Career of Ethel Waters* (Harper, 2011); *Hollywood Black: The Stars, the Films, the Filmmakers* (Running Press, 2019); and *Brown Sugar: Over One Hundred Years of America's Black Female Superstars* (Continuum, 2007), which was adapted by Bogle into a PBS docuseries. He teaches at the University of Pennsylvania and at New York University's Tisch School of the Arts.

Cara Caddoo

Cara Caddoo is associate professor of history and of cinema and media studies at Indiana University, Bloomington. Her research and teaching focus on American history, race, visual culture, and mass media. She is the author of *Envisioning Freedom: Cinema and the Building of Modern Black Life* (Harvard University Press, 2014), named by *Huffington Post* as one of the best film books of 2015 and a recipient of the 2015 biennial Vincent P. DeSantis Prize for best first book published on the Gilded Age and Progressive Era. She is currently writing a book about the actor, writer, and film producer Noble Johnson and the Lincoln Motion Picture Company.

Rhea L. Combs

Rhea L. Combs is director of curatorial affairs at the Smithsonian's National Portrait Gallery, where she is responsible for the exhibitions and conservation teams. She has curated numerous exhibitions nationally and internationally, including *Now Showing: Posters from African American Movies* (2019–21), *Watching Oprah: The Oprah Winfrey Show and American Culture* (2018–19), and *Everyday Beauty: Photographs and Films from the Permanent Collection* (2016–19) for the National Museum of African American History and Culture, where she previously served as supervisory curator of photography and film and director of the Earl W. and Amanda Stafford Center for African American Media Arts. Her writings on African American cinema, Black women filmmakers, visual aesthetics, photography, and other topics have appeared in anthologies, academic journals, and numerous exhibition catalogues. She has lectured in the United States and abroad and has taught courses on visual culture, film, race, and gender.

Terri Simone Francis

Terri Simone Francis is the author of *Josephine Baker's Cinematic Prism* (Indiana University Press, 2021). Her research has also been published in *Film History*, *Feminist Media Histories*, and *Film Quarterly*, where she is a contributing editor. She delivered the National Gallery of Art's 2021 Rajiv Vaidya Memorial Lecture, "Josephine Baker as a 'Rememory' of Global Black Cinema?" Francis is associate professor of cinematic arts and associate dean for inclusive and critical publics in the School of Communication at the University of Miami in Coral Gables, Florida.

Michael Boyce Gillespie

Michael Boyce Gillespie is associate professor in the Department of Cinema Studies at New York University. His research and writing focus on Black visual and expressive culture, film theory, visual historiography, popular music, and contemporary art. He is the author of *Film Blackness: American Cinema and the Idea of Black Film* (Duke University Press, 2016) and coeditor of *Black One Shot*, an art criticism series on ASAP/J. His recent writing has appeared in *Film Quarterly*, *Criterion Collection*, *Film Comment*, and *Ends of Cinema*.

Whoopi Goldberg

Whoopi Goldberg is one of a very elite group of artists who have won a Grammy, an Academy Award, a Golden Globe, an Emmy, and a Tony. She is also a prolific producer and is well known around the world for her many humanitarian endeavors. Born and raised in New York City, she performed in San Diego and in the Bay Area with the Blake Street Hawkeyes theater troupe. Eventually she would create the characters that formed the basis for her one-woman performance *The Spook Show*, which begat her hit Broadway show, Grammy Award–winning album, and the HBO special that helped launch her career.

J. Raúl Guzmán

J. Raúl Guzmán is assistant curator at the Academy Museum of Motion Pictures, where he has worked on *Hayao Miyazaki* (2021), *Installation: Pedro Almodóvar* (2021), *The Pixar 3D Zoetrope* (2021), and *Isaac Julien: Baltimore* (2022). Before joining the Academy Museum, he served as assistant director of the New York–based Cinema Tropical, where he organized film series in collaboration with the Solomon R. Guggenheim Museum, Museo del Barrio, and the Museum of the Moving Image, among other institutions. In 2015 he was selected as a Smithsonian Institution Latino Museum Studies Fellow. Before that, he was a commercial and TV art director. He received his BA in history from UCLA and studied at the National Autonomous University of Mexico. He holds an MA in Latin American and Caribbean studies from New York University and an MA in museum studies from Johns Hopkins University.

Shola Lynch

Shola Lynch is an award-winning American filmmaker best known for the internationally acclaimed feature documentary *Free Angela and All Political Prisoners* (2013) and the Peabody Award–winning documentary *Chisholm '72: Unbought & Unbossed* (2004). Her independent films and other collaborative projects feed her passion to bring history alive with captivating stories of people, places, and events. Since 2013 she has also served as curator of the Moving Image and Recorded Sound Division of the New York Public Library's Schomburg Center for Research in Black Culture. In 2016 Lynch became a member of the Academy of Motion Picture Arts and Sciences.

Ron Magliozzi

Ron Magliozzi is curator in the Department of Film at the Museum of Modern Art, New York. Since he joined the museum in 1979, Magliozzi has organized gallery and theatrical exhibitions and headed special collections acquisitions. Film restoration projects include *Lime Kiln Club Field Day* (1913) and the Last Poets' *Right On!* (1971). He served as chair of the International Federation of Film Archives Documentation Commission and edited the landmark book *Treasures from the Film Archives: A Catalog of Short Silent Fiction Films Held by FIAF Archives* (Scarecrow, 1988).

Ellen C. Scott

Ellen C. Scott is associate professor of cinema and media studies and associate dean of the School of Theater, Film and Television at UCLA. Her research focuses on the meanings of media in African American communities and the relationship of media to the struggle for racial justice and equality. She is the author of *Cinema Civil Rights: Regulation, Repression, and Race in the Classical Hollywood Era* (Rutgers University Press, 2015). She is currently working on two projects, one exploring Black women film critics and another examining the history of slavery on the American screen, which has received a grant from the Academy of Motion Picture Arts and Sciences' Academy Scholars program.

Jacqueline Stewart

Jacqueline Stewart is chief artistic and programming officer at the Academy Museum of Motion Pictures, where she leads the museum's curatorial, education, public engagement, film programming, and publications teams. She is on the faculty of the Department of Cinema and Media Studies at the University of Chicago, where she founded the South Side Home Movie Project. She is the author of *Migrating to the Movies: Cinema and Black Urban Modernity* (University of California Press, 2005) and coeditor of *L.A. Rebellion: Creating a New Black Cinema* (University of California Press, 2015) and *William Greaves: Filmmaking as Mission* (Columbia University Press, 2021). She is cocurator of the Kino Lorber five-disc set *Pioneers of African American Cinema* and the host of Silent Sunday Nights on Turner Classic Movies.

Lenders to the Exhibition

Academy Film Archive
Los Angeles

Madeline Anderson

Autry Museum of the American West
Los Angeles

Beinecke Rare Book & Manuscript Library, Yale University
New Haven, CT

Black Film Center & Archive, Indiana University, Bloomington

Center for the Study of Political Graphics
Los Angeles

Charles E. Young Research Library, University of California, Los Angeles

La Cinémathèque Française
Paris

Jeffrey Deitch

Deutsche Kinemathek
Berlin

Deutsches Bundesarchiv
Berlin

The George Eastman Museum
Rochester, NY

Louise Greaves

HMH Moving Image Archive, University of Southern California
Los Angeles

Hauser & Wirth
Los Angeles

The Historical Society of Pennsylvania
Philadelphia

Houghton Library, Harvard University
Cambridge, MA

Howard Greenberg Gallery
New York

Library of Congress
Washington, DC

Louis Armstrong House Museum
New York

Lucas Museum of Narrative Art
Los Angeles

Ron Magliozzi

Margaret Herrick Library, Academy of Motion Picture Arts and Sciences
Los Angeles

Minnesota Historical Society
Saint Paul

The Museum of Modern Art
New York

National Gallery of Art
Washington, DC

National Library of Norway
Oslo

National Museum of American History
Washington, DC

National Portrait Gallery, Smithsonian Institution
Washington, DC

New York Public Library

The Nicholas Family

Joanna Poitier

Regen Projects
Los Angeles

Schomburg Center for Research in Black Culture, New York Public Library

Greg Schreiner

Smithsonian National Museum of African American History and Culture
Washington, DC

Special Research Collections, University of California, Santa Barbara, Library

UCLA Film & Television Archive
Los Angeles

University of Chicago

W. E. B. Du Bois Library, University of Massachusetts Amherst

Western Costume Company
North Hollywood, CA

Academy Museum of Motion Pictures Board of Trustees

Designed by
Eddie Opara
Brankica Harvey
Jack Collins
Jun Jung
Dana Reginiano

Edited by
Karen Jacobson

Indexed by
Jane Friedman

Proofread by
Dianne Woo

Color separations
Echelon, Los Angeles

Academy Museum of Motion Pictures

Director of Publications
Stacey Allan

Editor
Martha Polk

Publications Coordinator
Lars Eckstrom

DelMonico Books

Publisher
Mary DelMonico

Director of Production
Karen Farquhar

This publication accompanies the exhibition *Regeneration: Black Cinema 1898–1971*, cocurated by Doris Berger and Rhea L. Combs and presented at the Academy Museum of Motion Pictures, Los Angeles, August 21, 2022–April 9, 2023.

This exhibition will travel to Detroit Institute of Arts, February 4–June 23, 2024.

Regeneration: Black Cinema 1898–1971 is the recipient of the 2018 Sotheby's Prize. The Sotheby's Prize was founded to support and encourage museums to break new ground by recognizing curatorial excellence and facilitating an upcoming exhibition that explores overlooked or underrepresented art history. The Sotheby's Prize was awarded by a jury of museum curators and directors comprising Sir Nicholas Serota, Donna De Salvo, Okwui Enwezor (1963–2019), Connie Butler and Emilie Gordenker, and chaired by Allan Schwartzman.

THE SOTHEBY'S PRIZE
TO BREAK NEW GROUND

This exhibition is made possible in part by major grants from the National Endowment for the Humanities.

NATIONAL ENDOWMENT FOR THE HUMANITIES

Major support provided by Campari.

CAMPARI
Davide Campari
MILANO

Technology solutions generously provided by Christie®.

CHRISTIE®

Regeneration is also supported by grants from the National Endowment for the Arts, the Los Angeles County Board of Supervisors through the Los Angeles County Department of Arts and Culture, and Furthermore: a program of the J. M. Kaplan Fund.

NATIONAL ENDOWMENT for the ARTS arts.gov
Los Angeles County Arts & Culture
Furthermore: a program of the J.M. Kaplan Fund

Generous support provided by Lyndon J. Barrois Sr. and Janine Sherman Barrois, Max and Kahlia Konan, Emma Koss, Mary Parent and Javier Chapa, and Yeardley Smith.

Academy Film Archive restorations are funded in part by grants from the National Endowment for the Arts and the Capital Group Companies Charitable Foundation.

Academy Museum Digital Engagement Platform sponsored by Bloomberg Philanthropies.

Bloomberg Philanthropies

Published in 2022 by the Academy Museum of Motion Pictures and DelMonico Books • D.A.P.

Academy Museum of Motion Pictures
6067 Wilshire Boulevard
Los Angeles, California 90036
academymuseum.org

DelMonico Books available through
ARTBOOK | D.A.P.
75 Broad Street, Suite 630
New York, NY 10004
artbook.com
delmonicobooks.com

Printed and bound in China

ISBN
978-1-63681-051-5

Library of Congress Control Number:
2022936938

Back cover
Gertie Brown and Saint Suttle in *Something Good—Negro Kiss* (1898), film still